Business, Entrepreneurship and Innovation Toward Poverty Reduction

Ways in which poverty can be reduced in both countries and regions through business, entrepreneurship and government has been a hot issue for researchers and policymakers in recent years. Governments can play an important role in helping the poor people by non-profit organizations and others that help to seed business among the poor. Businesses increasingly also see the large number of people in severe poverty not only as an issue for social concern, but also as a potentially large untapped market of consumers for goods and services. Some scholars have called for poverty reduction through entrepreneurship owing to the fact that it can be an efficient path to also change the poor's attitudes and behaviours from a passive mode to a more active mode toward poverty reduction economically and socially. In addition, the sharing economy brings opportunities where everyone is a micro-entrepreneur. There is a recognition that these types of entrepreneurship could offer the greatest single potential means to move individuals out of poverty in nations and regions in the next 5–10 years.

This book provides new and valuable analyses of poverty and business, entrepreneurship and innovation in current nations and regions including developing and developed countries. As business, entrepreneurship and innovation can help to generate greater business activity in settings of severe poverty, they will help to solve poverty, as individuals in severe poverty are able to both generate greater incomes and accumulate greater assets as they participate with large firms in those activities.

The chapters in this book were originally published as a special issue of the *Entrepreneurship & Regional Development.*

Steven Si is Distinguished Professor (entrepreneurship/innovation) at Zhejiang University and research professor at Bloomsburg University of Pennsylvania. Professor Si has published about 100 peer-reviewed articles in journals such as *Journal of Business Venturing, Strategic Entrepreneurship Journal, Journal of Applied Psychology, Academy of Management Perspectives* and others. He has served as guest editor for six Special Issues for the prestigious journals such as *Technovation, Journal of Business Venturing, Journal of Engineering and Technology Management, Entrepreneurship and Regional Development, Strategic Entrepreneurship Journal, International Journal of Conflict Management*, and *Asia Pacific Journal of Management*. Professor Si currently serves as an associate editor for the journal *Technovation* and the editorial board of *Journal of Management Studies* and other prestigious journals.

David Ahlstrom is Professor at The Chinese University of Hong Kong. Professor Ahlstrom has published over 150 peer-reviewed articles in journals such as the *Strategic Management Journal, Academy of Management Review, Journal of International Business Studies, Journal of Management Studies, Organization Science, Journal of Business Venturing* and *Academy of Management Perspectives*. He was recognized as a 'Highly Cited Researcher' in 2017–2019 by Web of Science.

Jiang Wei (PhD) is Changjiang Chair Professor of innovation and strategy management at Zhejiang University, China. He is now serving as the Dean of School of Management at Zhejiang University. Professor Wei has published 17 academic monographs and over 400 papers in Chinese and/or international academic journals such as *Journal of International Business Studies, Management and Organizational Review, Technovation, R&D Management, Asia Pacific Journal of Management* and others.

John Cullen (PhD, Columbia University) is Professor Emeritus of entrepreneurship, organization theory and international business/management at Washington State University. Formerly, Professor Cullen was the Huber Chair of Entrepreneurial Studies and Associate Dean for Graduate Programs. He has published over 150 peer-reviewed articles in journals such as the *Academy of Management Journal, Administration Science Quarterly, American Journal of Sociology, Journal of International Business Studies, Entrepreneurship Theory and Practice* and many other prestigious management/business journals. He is a past president of the Western Academy of Management.

Business, Entrepreneurship and Innovation Toward Poverty Reduction

Edited by
Steven Si, David Ahlstrom, Jiang Wei and John Cullen

Routledge
Taylor & Francis Group
LONDON AND NEW YORK

First published 2022
by Routledge
2 Park Square, Milton Park, Abingdon, Oxon OX14 4RN

and by Routledge
605 Third Avenue, New York, NY 10158

Routledge is an imprint of the Taylor & Francis Group, an informa business

British Library Cataloguing in Publication Data
A catalogue record for this book is available from the British Library

ISBN: 978-1-032-00851-6 (hbk)
ISBN: 978-1-032-00852-3 (pbk)
ISBN: 978-1-003-17610-7 (ebk)

Typeset in Myriad Pro
by Newgen Publishing UK

Publisher's Note
The publisher accepts responsibility for any inconsistencies that may have arisen during the conversion of this book from journal articles to book chapters, namely the inclusion of journal terminology.

Contents

Citation Information

The chapters in this book were originally published in *Entrepreneurship & Regional Development*, volume 32, issue 1–2 (2020). When citing this material, please use the original page numbering for each article, as follows:

Introduction

Business, Entrepreneurship and Innovation Toward Poverty Reduction
Steven Si, David Ahlstrom, Jiang Wei and John Cullen
Entrepreneurship & Regional Development, volume 32, issue 1–2 (2020), pp. 1–20

Chapter 1

An anatomy of entrepreneurial pursuits in relation to poverty
Douglas Cumming, Sofia Johan and Ikenna Uzuegbunam
Entrepreneurship & Regional Development, volume 32, issue 1–2 (2020), pp. 21–40

Chapter 2

Regional determinants of poverty alleviation through entrepreneurship in China
Song Lin, Christoph Winkler, Shanshan Wang and Hui Chen
Entrepreneurship & Regional Development, volume 32, issue 1–2 (2020), pp. 41–62

Chapter 3

Uncovering the scaling of innovations developed by grassroots entrepreneurs in low-income settings
Marleen Wierenga
Entrepreneurship & Regional Development, volume 32, issue 1–2 (2020), pp. 63–90

Chapter 4

Entrepreneurial aspirations and poverty reduction: the role of institutional context
Sanjay Goel and Ranjan Karri
Entrepreneurship & Regional Development, volume 32, issue 1–2 (2020), pp. 91–111

Chapter 5

Untangling the effects of entrepreneurial opportunity on the performance of peasant entrepreneurship: the moderating roles of entrepreneurial effort and regional poverty level
Aiqi Wu, Di Song and Yang Yang
Entrepreneurship & Regional Development, volume 32, issue 1–2 (2020), pp. 112–133

Chapter 6

An exploratory study of entrepreneurs in impoverished communities: when institutional factors and individual characteristics result in non-productive entrepreneurship
Stelvia Matos and Jeremy Hall
Entrepreneurship & Regional Development, volume 32, issue 1–2 (2020), pp. 134–155

Chapter 7

Call the midwife! Business incubators as entrepreneurial enablers in developing economies
Helen Haugh
Entrepreneurship & Regional Development, volume 32, issue 1–2 (2020), pp. 156–175

Chapter 8

Crafting markets and fostering entrepreneurship within underserved communities: social ventures and clean energy provision in Asia
Sanjay Jain and James Koch
Entrepreneurship & Regional Development, volume 32, issue 1–2 (2020), pp. 176–196

Chapter 9

Climbing the poverty ladder: the role of entrepreneurship and gender in alleviating poverty in transition economies
Julia Korosteleva and Paulina Stępień-Baig
Entrepreneurship *& Regional Development*, volume 32, issue 1–2 (2020), pp. 197–220

Chapter 10

Trust, poverty, and subjective wellbeing among Chinese entrepreneurs
Yiyi Su, Shaker A. Zahra, Rui Li and Di Fan
Entrepreneurship & Regional Development, volume 32, issue 1–2 (2020), pp. 221–245

Notes on Contributors

David Ahlstrom, Department of Management, The Chinese University of Hong Kong, Shatin, NT, Hong Kong.

Hui Chen, School of Management, Zhejiang University, Hangzhou, China.

John Cullen, Department of Management, Washington State University, Pullman, WA, USA.

Douglas Cumming, DeSantis Distinguished Professor of Finance and Entrepreneurship, College of Business, Florida Atlantic University, Boca Raton, FL, USA.

Di Fan, Management & Organisations, UWA Business School, The University of Western Australia, Crawley, Australia.

Sanjay Goel, Department of Management Studies, Labovitz School of Business and Economics, University of Minnesota Duluth, Duluth, USA.

Jeremy Hall, Science Policy Research Unit (SPRU), University of Sussex Business School, Falmer, UK.

Helen Haugh, Judge Business School, University of Cambridge, Cambridge, UK.

Sanjay Jain, Department of Management, Nazarian College of Business and Economics, California State University – Northridge, Northridge, CA, USA.

Sofia Johan, Birmingham Business School, University of Birmingham, Birmingham, UK.

Ranjan Karri, Department of Management, College of Business and Management, University of Illinois Springfield, One University Drive, Springfield, USA.

James Koch, Santa Clara University, Santa Clara, CA, USA.

Julia Korosteleva, School of Slavonic and East European Studies, University College London, London, UK.

Rui Li, School of Management and Economics, University of Electronic Science and Technology of China, Chengdu, China.

Song Lin, Business School, Central University of Finance and Economics, Beijing, China.

Stelvia Matos, Surrey Business School, University of Surrey, Guildford, UK.

Steven Si, Department of Entrepreneurship, Innovation and Strategy, Zhejiang University, Hangzhou, Zhejiang, China; Zeigler College of Business, Bloomsburg University of Pennsylvania, Bloomsburg, PA, USA.

Di Song, Department of Innovation, Entrepreneurship and Strategy, School of Management, Zhejiang University, Hangzhou, China.

Paulina Stępień-Baig, School of Slavonic and East European Studies, University College London, London, UK.

Yiyi Su, School of Economics and Management, Tongji University, Shanghai, China.

Ikenna Uzuegbunam, Entrepreneurship & International Business, Center for Entrepreneurship, College of Business, Ohio University, Athens, OH, USA.

Shanshan Wang, Business School, Central University of Finance and Economics, Beijing, China.

Jiang Wei, Department of Entrepreneurship, Innovation and Strategy, Zhejiang University, Hangzhou, Zhejiang, China.

Marleen Wierenga, Department of Management Studies, Aalto University School of Business, Espoo, Finland.

Christoph Winkler, Hynes Institute for Entrepreneurship & Innovation, Iona College, New Rochelle, NY, USA.

Aiqi Wu, Department of Innovation, Entrepreneurship and Strategy, School of Management, Zhejiang University, Hangzhou, China.

Yang Yang, Department of Innovation, Entrepreneurship and Strategy, School of Management, Zhejiang University, Hangzhou, China.

Shaker A. Zahra, Carlson School of Management, University of Minnesota, Minneapolis, MN, USA.

Foreword

The editors introduce us to this great collection of papers around the pressing and important issues surrounding entrepreneurship and poverty. They explain how, despite remarkable improvements and significant reduction of poverty, some 10% of the world's population, 630 million, remain very poor. Yet as Si et al. explain, it is relatively recently that entrepreneurial scholars have turned their attention to how entrepreneurship might alleviate the problem of poverty. Entrepreneurship seems to offer more purchase, more leverage and gets a better grip of the causes and consequences of poverty than simply offering aid.

This volume reflects the sea change in entrepreneurial perspectives on poverty. The prospect, the possibilities and opportunities seem to be shifting from dismissing the informal micro entrepreneuring of the poor as simply necessity; a marginal and unimportant distant cousin of glamorous opportunity enterprise. Instead, we now begin to see recognition of the frugal, clever and remarkably ingenious ways of resourcing, whereby poor entrepreneurs create their own opportunities.

Indeed, Si et al. show us how entrepreneurship in poverty has begun to generate serious scholarship with a presence in the top journals. Nonetheless, there remains much investigative scope in this pressing issue that is not yet well explained, perhaps not always understood and certainly not yet well theorised. Moreover, it may be that entirely new theories based on a profound understanding of what it means to be a poor entrepreneur and how and why those marginalised by poverty operate differently are needed.

I am convinced that our scholarship, our thoughtful engagement with the different and intertwined dimensions of poverty can develop the understanding that will allow us to theorise how things work and what works well. In turn, to use these appropriate contextualised theories to create tools, ideas, describe best practices that we as academics can offer to give that essential leg up, the boost that will help unstick them from the quagmire of the poverty traps that holds them down. This academic responsibility informs this volume. It is towards this end that Si et al. insightfully and critically review different academic perspectives on poverty amelioration.

The remediation perspective recognises that poverty restricts access to resources. Entrepreneurial efforts are impeded by these constraints and will always struggle to realise potential. This economic perspective of resource deficiency signals the solution of providing access. Hence, addressing shortfalls by means such as microfinance hold considerable appeal. Politically too, this helping the poor to help themselves fits a liberal agenda. However, whilst many have benefitted, some groups, for example, women; some places, for example, remote rural places have seen less progress. This suggests that the social and the spatial have some explanatory baring on the problem of poverty and that it is not entirely an economic issue.

Si et al. describe how this is seen as a reform perspective. Reaching beyond resources limitations, this view takes into account the conditions in which micro entrepreneuring works. It notes how formal and informal institutions lay down the rules of the game. In essence, these rules can work against the efforts of the poor and to the detriment of how well their businesses can operate.

Broader still is Si et al.'s novel 'Plight' perspective which looks closely at the nature of poverty itself. Reaching deeper into social, cultural and attitudinal dimensions, this contextualisation of entrepreneurship in poverty seems a very promising avenue. It recognises poverty as a 'wicked' problem with multiple and interlaced dimensions. Most promising of all lies in the possibility of comprehending the versatility of entrepreneuring. We now know that entrepreneuring is much, much more than new venture creation. We recognise it as a change engine that connects, that engages and employs abilities, resources and ingenuity to produce new value. It works through people, by people, for people but the values it uses, as well as those it creates, are often determined by the contexts in which it operates. Accordingly, synthesising, using our insights into contexts and conditions in conjunction with our burgeoning appreciation of entrepreneurial versatility and agency to get things done, should open up an informing appreciation of how best to overcome the wicked problem of poverty.

Historically, entrepreneurship is said to have largely brought about the changes, the technological and social advances that have created our affluent comfortable western world. In this world, poverty still exists but is now much less prevalent. The clues to why entrepreneurship has not been a universal solution may thus lie in the context. We know, for example, how institutions, formal and informal shape what is entrepreneurially possible. This suggests that our theories for explaining entrepreneurship by the poor are likely to have to take full account of how entrepreneurship and indeed poverty itself is socially, culturally and economically embedded.

I believe that each of the papers in this volume share an understanding of the complexity of entrepreneurship in poverty. They take account of the many different contexts and begin to show us nuanced views of interactions. Together, they build a picture of the many dimensions of poverty, but also begin to show us how entrepreneuring can address these dimensions. The picture drawn is one of potential and opportunity. I strongly recommend that using Si et al.'s introduction as a guide you study the accounts, the explanations, insights and theory that each paper offers. This volume is a significant step forward.

Alistair R. Anderson

Introduction

Business, Entrepreneurship and Innovation Toward Poverty Reduction

Steven Si, David Ahlstrom, Jiang Wei and John Cullen

ABSTRACT

Poverty reduction has become a core subject for researchers across the social sciences from economics to finance, management and entrepreneurship. In general, the faster and more widespread economic growth in recent decades has enabled large numbers of people to move out of poverty such that extreme poverty has fallen to less than ten percent of world population. However, it is increasingly clear that while some countries and regions have seen dramatic improvement of poverty, there are other places with large numbers of people still in poverty that can greatly benefit from poverty alleviation efforts. Management scholars and economists increasingly recognize that entrepreneurship may offer a significant part of the solution to poverty around the world. A related focus regarding the ways in which poverty can be reduced in through entrepreneurship and new venture creation, however, how to link the key issues above with the current platform, network/digital and sharing economies, how to find new ways and new solutions to effectively reduce poverty in now political, economic and global contexts still needs to be better understood. This Special Issue has set the goals of publishing work that builds knowledge about thenature of poverty reduction and business, entrepreneurship and innovation activities in both developed and developing economies, as well as their models, antecedents and consequences related with the current platform.

Introduction

Poverty reduction has increasingly become a core subject for researchers across the social sciences from economics and finance, to management and entrepreneurship (Ahlin and Jiang 2008; Chen, Chang and Bruton, 2017; Dollar, and Kraay, 2002; Dollar, Kleineberg, and Kraay 2016; Sutter, Bruton, and Chen 2019). This is in response to the severity of the problem of extreme poverty and the decidedly mixed results of poverty alleviation measures (Easterly 2006). These measures include foreign aid programs, microfinance and property rights promotion, and bottom of the pyramid initiatives (Alvarez, Barney, and Newman 2015), These initiatives have not had much impact on extreme poverty and may have actually created some additional problems (Easterly 2006; Roodman 2012).

Yet in recent years, researchers have started to examine economic growth and its link to poverty reduction through entrepreneurship and the development of new technology and new techniques (Ahlstrom 2014, 2015; Bloom et al. 2013; Bloom, Drăca, and Van Reenen 2016; McCloskey 2017). This has in turn generated new approaches to (and ways of looking at) poverty reduction which challenges existing poverty research theory traditionally more centred on financial aid and other basic poverty alleviation measures (Easterly 2002; Sachs 2003; Whitacre, Meadowcroft, and Gallardo 2019). The fast and increasingly widespread economic growth in recent decades has enabled large numbers of people to move out of poverty (Ahlstrom 2010) such that extreme poverty has fallen to less than 10% of the world's population (Dollar, Kleineberg, and Kraay 2016; Roser and Ortiz-Ospina 2017). However, it is evident that while some countries and regions have seen dramatic improvement of poverty, there are other places with large numbers of people still in poverty that can greatly benefit from poverty alleviation efforts.

Research ranging from trade policy and globalization (Pearce 2005; Bergh, Mirkina, and Nilsson 2016; Bhagwati and Srinivasan 2002; Dollar and Kraay 2004) to legal and institutional reform (Rodrik, Subramanian, and Trebbi 2004) to management (Bloom et al. 2013) are making dramatic progress on understanding many key factors in the alleviation of extreme poverty and the seeding of economic growth (Tomizawa, Zhao, Bassellier, and Ahlstrom, 2019). In particular, management as well as related research in economics have made some strides in identifying its cause and ways in which poverty can be reduced through institutional reform, microfinance, innovation and new venture creation (Ahlstrom 2010; Bloom, Draca, and Van Reenen 2016; Bruton, Ketchen, and Ireland 2013; Chen, Chang, and Bruton 2017; Perkins et al. 2013). Researchers increasingly recognize that entrepreneurship may offer a significant part of the solution to poverty around the world (Alvarez, Barney, and Newman 2015; Bruton, Ketchen, and Ireland 2013). The challenge is to further understand entrepreneurship's link to poverty reduction and how productive entrepreneurship can be encouraged (Baumol et al., 2009b, 2009a; Si et al. 2015). A related focus regarding the ways in which poverty can be reduced through network/digital and sharing economies still needs to be better understood.

This Special Issue in *Entrepreneurship and Regional Development* on Business, Entrepreneurship and Innovation Toward Poverty Reduction has set the goals of first publishing work that builds knowledge about the nature of poverty reduction, business, entrepreneurship and innovation activities in both developed and developing economies, and second developing further a theoretical foundation with different perspectives for future research under the current political, technological, economic and global contexts. In this lead paper of the special issue, we seek to provide an overview of the existing literature with respect to poverty and poverty reduction. We analyze the poverty research of where poverty and entrepreneurship research now stands and, in turn, develop an understanding of where the research needs to move in the future. We then develop and analyze the current hot issues of poverty research in the platform, network/digital and sharing economies. The 10 papers in this special issue, individually and each in their own way, offer key insights into how we might better understand how to reduce poverty through business, innovation and entrepreneurship as we develop an agenda for future poverty reduction research.[1] This special issue intends to mainly address these important but underexplored issues with different perspectives that explain the current research of poverty research, and predict its likely development trajectory and its impact on future research.

Poverty and entrepreneurship's role

The more extreme form of poverty as focused on in this special issue is that where the poor suffer from serious deprivation such that they live at or near subsistence, and their health and well-being can be under serious threat with minor set-backs. According to the biennial 'Poverty and shared prosperity: Putting together the poverty puzzle,' living on less than $3.20 a day represents the poverty line for lower-middle income countries while extreme poverty is defined as living on less than $US 1.90 per day (in 2011 dollars). Extreme poverty fell to less than 10% of the world's population in 2018, or about 630 million people, though the pace of poverty reduction has slowed somewhat (Goalkeepers report, 2018).

As foreign aid and other infrastructure schemes have not been shown to be very effective in terms of poverty reduction (Easterly 2002, 2013), entrepreneurship's role in poverty reduction research has become an increasingly important topic in management (Bruton, Ketchen, and Ireland 2013; Bruton et al. 2015; Sutter, Bruton, and Chen 2019). Entrepreneurship is widely defined in terms of situations in which new goods, services, raw materials, markets and organizing methods can be introduced through the formation of new means, ends, or means-ends relationships (Eckhardt and Shane 2003; Shane and Venkataraman 2000). Indeed, entrepreneurship can be seen as encompassing radical change in terms of innovation and new ventures (Acs and Audretsch 1988; Denning 2016) that may extend to social or institutional spheres or improving on the poor's social standing through improved social entrepreneurship. (Battilana, Leca, and Boxenbaum 2009; Rindova, Barry, and Ketchen 2009). As noted, other entrepreneurship topics held as a solution to poverty, including 'microfinance', 'crowdfunding', 'informal firm', 'informal economy', 'social entrepreneurship', 'base of the pyramid,' and disruptive innovation are discussed within the special issue. This special issue also holds that while poverty is typically measured in economic terms, poverty can be multidimensional. As such, poverty may also involve a variety of other challenges beyond economic ones including plight (Sen 1999), marginalization, and social poverty (Halpern-Meekin, 2019). This may suggest some different business and entrepreneurial solutions as addressed in this special issue.

Poverty reduction through entrepreneurship

Over the past years, scholars have conducted a manifold research on poverty reduction that has been published increasingly in the top journals. In general, the existing research on poverty and business and entrepreneurship cover many topics and perspectives. This paper provides an overview of a list of significant poverty literature that's selected from top-tier journals and some prestigious journals in Table 1

1. Remediation perspective

Remediation is the perspective that entrepreneurship can alleviate poverty when resources and capital are directly addressed (Sutter, Bruton, and Chen 2019). The remediation perspective has several common underlying assumptions, in that it sees poverty as driven by scarce resources such as a lack of seed capital or other physical assets (Alvarez and Barney, 2014; Berge, Bjorvatn, and Tungodden 2014; Chliova and Ringov 2017; Karlan and Valdivia 2011Wu and Si 2018). It assumes that resources and other capital assets are at the centre of entrepreneurial activity (Ahlin and Jiang 2008; Sutter et al., 2014) and thus providing resources through grants, foreign aid, microfinance is a key to poverty reduction (Newman, Schwarz, and Ahlstrom 2017). The remediation perspectives thus holds that entrepreneurial activity can be better funded and that entrepreneurship among the poor will result in a 'win-win' that benefits all participants (e.g., London, 2009; Khavul 2010). Thus, this perspective generally focuses on the resources.

Related to the remediation principle is one whereby poverty is researched and addressed more from a development economic perspective that tends to focus more on capital endowments and returns, particularly improved productivity (Perkins et al. 2013). Typically, the research contends that more endowments in land, labour, education, resources, and infrastructure result in lower poverty (Leff 1979; Lucas 2002; Romer 1986). In addition, some other scholars have examined research on poverty from a transitional or developing economic perspective that has tended to focus on microloan, low technology-based industries, informal debts, and e-commerce. Others in the rural areas such as China and Brazil focused their developmental efforts in these ways, particularly toward the expansion of rural and farmer economics toward poverty reduction

Table 1. Selected significant literature on poverty with business and entrepreneurship.

Author	Journal	Year	Title
Hofstede,Haveman Pearce	Academy of Management Review Administration Science Quarterly Academy of Management Journal	1978 1993 Pearce 2005	The Poverty of Management Control Philosophy Follow the leader: mimetic isomorphism and entry into new markets Organizational Scholarship and the Eradication of Global Poverty
Vaona	Research Policy	2005	Understanding Globalization, Employment and Poverty Reduction
Fairchild	Journal of Business Venturing	2008	The Influence of Residential Segregation and Its Correlates on Ethnic Enterprise in Urban Areas
Mair and Marti	Journal of Business Venturing	2009	Entrepreneurship in and Around Institutional Voids: A Case Study from Bangladesh
Bruton	Academy of Management Perspective	2010	Business and the World's Poorest Billion – The Need for an Expanded Examination by Management Scholars
Ahlstrom	Academy of Management Perspective	2010	Innovation and Growth: How Business Contributes to Society
Kaplinsky	Research Policy	2011	Schumacher Meets Schumpeter: Appropriate Technology below the Radar
Mair, Marti, and Ventresca	Academy of Management Journal	2012	Building Inclusive Markets in Rural Bangladesh: How Intermediaries Work Institutional Voids
Kistruck et al.	Academy of Management Journal	2013	Mitigating Principal-Agent Problems in Base-of-the-Pyramid Markets: An Identity Spillover Perspective
Bruton, Ketchen, and Ireland	Journal of Business Venturing	2013	Entrepreneurship as a Solution to Poverty
Tobias, Mair, and Barbosa-Leiker	Journal of Business Venturing	2013	Toward a Theory of Transformative Entrepreneuring: Poverty Reduction and Conflict Resolution in Rwanda's Entrepreneurial Coffee Sector
Khavul, Chavez, and Bruton	Journal of Business Venturing	2013	When Institutional Change Outruns the Change Agent: The Contested Terrain of Entrepreneurial Microfinance for Those in Poverty
Kent and Dacin	Journal of Business Venturing	2013	Bankers at the Gate: Microfinance and the High Cost of Borrowed Logics
Sutter et al.	Journal of Business Venturing	2013	Entrepreneurs' Responses to Semi-Formal Illegitimate Institutional Arrangements
Allison, McKenny, and Short	Journal of Business Venturing	2013	The Effect of Entrepreneurial Rhetoric on Microlending Investment: An Examination of the Warm-Glow Effect
Ault and Spicer	Strategic Management Journal	2014	The Institutional Context of Poverty: State Fragility as a Predictor of Cross-National Variation in Commercial Microfinance Lending
London et al.	Strategic Entrepreneurship Journal	2014	Connecting Poverty to Purchase in Informal Markets
Gras and Nason	Journal of Business Venturing	2015	Bric by Bric: The Role of the Family Household in Sustaining a Venture in Impoverished Indian Slums
Chliova, Brinckmann, and Rosenbusch	Journal of Business Venturing	2015	Is Microcredit a Blessing for the Poor? A Meta-Analysis Examining Development Outcomes and Contextual Considerations
Rivera-Santos, Holt, and Littlewood	Academy of Management Perspective	2015	Social Entrepreneurship in Sub-Saharan Africa
Cobb, Wry, and Zhao	Academy of Management Journal	2016	Funding Financial Inclusion: Institutional Logics and the Contextual Contingency of Funding for Microfinance Organizations
George et al.	Strategic Management Journal	2016	Social Structure, Reasonable Gain, and Entrepreneurship in Africa
Woodson	Research Policy	2016	Public Private Partnerships and Emerging Technologies: A look at Nanomedicine for Diseases of Poverty

(*Continued*)

Table 1. (Continued).

Author	Journal	Year	Title
Fischer	Research Policy	2016	Why New Crop Technology is not Scale-Neutral – A Critique of the Expectations for a Crop-Based African Green Revolution
Zhao and Lounsbury	Journal of Business Venturing	2016	An Institutional Logics Approach to Social Entrepreneurship: Market Logic, Religious Diversity, and Resource Acquisition by Microfinance Organizations
Shantz, Kistruck, and Zietsma	Journal of Business Venturing	2018	The Opportunity not Taken: The Occupational Identity of Entrepreneurs in Contexts of Poverty
Bhuiyan and Ivlevs	Journal of Business Venturing	2019	Micro-Entrepreneurship and Subjective Well-Being: Evidence from Rural Bangladesh
Sutter, Bruton, and Chen	Journal of Business Venturing	2019	Entrepreneurship as a Solution to Extreme Poverty: A Review and Future Research Directions

(Harding, 1987). Microloans and other economic and financial help led by the government, wealthy charities are largely applied to poverty reduction.

A variety of new solutions centred more on resources such as crowdfunding and other internet platforms largely related with the internet, digital and sharing economies that enable individuals to solicit small investments, donations, or loans over the Internet from a wide variety of funders; they have emerged as a new and potentially important source of funds for entrepreneurial and philanthropic initiatives (Ahlstrom, Cumming, and Vismara 2018). The capital and resources view has some support (e.g., Sachs 2003) but is not without controversy. Foreign aid, in particular, has shown a very limited ability to impact poverty due to the misallocation of resources and other policy problems (Easterly 2013; Easterly, Levine, and Roodman 2004). Microfinance and other capital provision schemes have been likewise limited in their effect on poverty (Bruton et al. 2015; Chen, Chang, and Bruton 2017). Related to this, in terms of the efficacy of capital provision and accumulation to grow economies and alleviate poverty (Lucas 2002; Findlay & O'Rourke, 2009; Piketty, 2014), recent work in economic history has shown that in Britain, an early exemplar of economic growth, investment in physical capital as a share of national income was actually below European norms of the nineteenth century and earlier (McCloskey 2010, 2017). Though capital accumulation and provision have garnered some support in the literature for its seeding of economic growth and new venture creation – though much of it is strictly deductive evidence (Van Zanden 2009) – it has not historically conferred lasting advantages to an economy and its firms and citizens (McCloskey 2010, 2017).

2. Reform perspective

A second perspective to entrepreneurship and poverty reduction centres less on resources and capital investment and more on a reform perspective (Sutter, Bruton, and Chen 2019). This perspective address reform in institutions, both formal and informal (Scott, 2013; Alston, 2018). If formal institutions can be fixed, according to this perspective; entrepreneurship is more likely to be encouraged and nurtured (Acemoglu & Robinson, 2012; Tomizawa, Zhao, Bassellier, & Ahlstrom, 2019). Thus, the reform perspective assumes that poverty is significantly due to institutional voids and other social issues including the exclusion of the poor, such as limiting women's access to the market. In this view, a good institutional regime generally has three broad characteristics. These include the enforcement of property rights for broad segments of society, so that individuals, particularly entrepreneurs, can receive funding and make investments, in terms of both financial and human capital. Also, important in this view are the constraints on the actions of politicians, well-connected elites, and other powerful groups, so that they cannot expropriate the innovations and incomes of others while preventing competition from new ventures and innovations. Generally, a productive institutional regime encourages innovation and entrepreneurship and discourages extractive, zero-sum behaviour (Acemoglu & Robinson, 2012). Such a good institutional regime contrasts with that of many economies lacking property rights and allowing societal elites to run roughshod over firms and entrepreneurs.

There is evidence that institutions matter a great deal in terms of economic growth (Rodrik, Subramanian, and Trebbi 2004). Significant differences in institutional quality between two countries such as South Korea and Bolivia, for example, explain much of the two countries' differences in per capita income. The difference between the quality of institutions (using a standard measure) in Bolivia compared with South Korea is equivalent to one standard deviation in measured institutional quality, which portends a sixfold difference in terms of explained income. In other words, if Bolivia was to successfully improve its institutions to the comparable quality of Korea's, its per capita GDP would be predicted to rise to about $40,000 from its recent level of about $7000, and these hypothesized levels are in line with the actual per capita GDP of the two countries (Rodrik, Subramanian, and Trebbi 2004; CIA World Factbook, 2017). While the remediation perspective would examine how to provide female entrepreneurs, for example, with the financing they need to participate in markets, the reform perspective would examine how to give woman access to markets and what formal institutions need to be present to insure female entrepreneurs can own their properties and businesses. (e.g., Mair, Marti, and Ventresca 2012). Thus, poverty alleviation through entrepreneurship occurs as the institutional or social context is changed (e.g., Ghani et al., 2014; Sutter, Bruton, and Chen 2019).

3. *Social and plight perspectives*

A third perspective is the social poverty and plight perspective. In this context, plight means poverty in that the poor's difficult situation is likely caused by a variety of economic, social and personal reasons in which change is impeded by a variety of difficulties and restrictions. In this view, poverty can be reduced, though stubborn pockets are likely to persist. Based on recent studies of poverty (e.g., Si et al. 2015), some countries and regions, charities and organizations and governments often call for reducing poverty, but they seem to be avoiding the multiple factors leading to the difficult intractability of plight in poor communities. Thus, an emphasis on basic handouts as a solution for solving poverty problems is likely to be ineffective, which recent evidence has shown to be the case (Easterly 2002, 2013; Hwang and Christensen 2008).

We recently tested various solutions to poverty reduction in the different regions in the world and find the plight is a key issue of poverty reduction (e.g., Si et al. 2015). Ways in which the poor can be helped to get out of plight through the solving of specific difficulties and removing burdensome restrictions can prove an effective, individual or community level solution. By this solution, the poor people could consciously or unconsciously change their attitudes and behaviours and tend to be subsistence entrepreneurs (e.g., Lin and Si, 2014; Si et al., 2015). Thus, researchers should do more in-depth research of the plight, as well as the analysis of plight entailing the reform of not only formal, but informal institutions and other factors that may be interacting to cause the stubborn persistence of poverty.

The social and plight perspective also generally assumes that markets are the primary drivers of poverty alleviation, though markets need institutional restructuring in order to be more inclusive (e.g., George, McGahan, and Prabhu 2012; Sutter et al. 2017). Finally, the perspective also pays attention to the socially constructed realities of the poor, and the challenges in making institutional change, particularly of informal institutions (McCloskey 2010). This social and plight perspective suggests ways that can make poverty alleviation through helping improving poverty people's mindset to be out of poverty. This perspective also suggests that social and institutional change can help incorporate the poor into more inclusive markets, while the related revolution perspective questions the very essence of informal institutional structures as they are currently organized (e.g., Sud and VanSandt 2011). The social and plight perspective also pays attention to how power is exercised to reproduce the existing social order and how the empowerment of the poor can be enhanced (e.g., Levy, 2008).

4. *Learning and change perspective*

This perspective focuses on poor's learning mindset and behaviour change. A shift from passive to active attitudes and behaviour towards fighting poverty, particularly toward a growth mindset that permits trial and error learning may be key for effectively reducing poverty in the poor areas (Dweck 2007; Si et al. 2015). The growth mindset boosts learning while encouraging entrepreneurship and not punishing the failure that can yield learning innovation (Dweck 2007; Sims 2013). Investigating many poor people in the different countries and regions, evidence suggests that they are able to actively change their attitudes and behaviours toward entrepreneurship, trial and error and achievement through learning and achievement, even if that mindset was not actively encouraged in the schools (Dweck 2007; McClelland 1967; McCloskey 2010). Encouraging learning, trial and error entrepreneurship, allowing for mistakes, and strengthening the social validation for those activities (McCloskey, 2006, McCloskey 2010) enables poor societies to find ways to create new approaches to help them move out from their plight.

For example, it was long thought that Confucian societies that favour order and harmony, such as that of China or Korea would resist entrepreneurship, and only experience faster economic growth if large, stable organizations were established in those societies (Weber, 1932). But this turned out to be incorrect, Confucian-based societies proved very able to innovate and create new ventures (Ahlstrom and Wang 2010). It turned out that improving how entrepreneurs and business people were accorded liberty and dignity in their societies and encouraged to pursue entrepreneurial ventures likely made a big difference in seeding and sustaining economic growth (McCloskey 2010). China's former Premier Deng Xiaoping made multiple trips to Special Economic Zones and entrepreneurial firms during China's early reforms in the 1980s and 1990s to ensure the legitimacy of those ventures and to provide encouragement and dignity to entrepreneurs trying to make their way in an increasingly competitive and open East Asian commercial environment (Ahlstrom and Bruton 2001). This likely accorded and validated learning and trial and error entrepreneurship in China while further sustaining economic reforms there (Ahlstrom, Bruton, and Yeh 2008; Ahlstrom and Wang 2010).

In the existing literature of poverty reduction, microfinance and other governmental and institutional props (e.g., Baumol et al., 2009b, 2009a; Busenitz, Gomez, and Spencer 2000; Hu et al., 2000; Fu, 2006; Scott, 2013) were seen as main solutions to poverty. These were mostly reliant on external support and intervention to alleviate poverty. Yet the traditional model of governmental country-to-country grants on a very large scale that have often been and advocated are now generally viewed as ineffective on their own (in absence of learning and social validation of entrepreneurship) (Easterly 2002, 2013; Hwang and Christensen 2008). The importance of the poor's learning and attitude-behavior change from passive to active status, as well as the society valuing entrepreneurship further (McCloskey 2010) has been observed in empirical and case-
based studies in the faster growth parts of both Asia and Africa (Hwang and Christensen 2008; McCloskey 2017). An active attitude-behavior in the literature can be defined as personal initiative at the base of a work behaviour defined as self-starting and proactive (Tomizawa et al., 2019). Such a learning-based attitude and the actions which stem from it can overcome barriers to achieve a goal that can enable people to deal with job difficulties more actively and relate to success as entrepreneurs (e.g., Frese and Fay 2001). Impoverished people with proper entrepreneurial attitudes and behaviour can also learn and improve as they receive feedback from their work (Ashford and Tsui 1991; Dweck 2007).

5. *Subsistence and innovation entrepreneurship*

In addition to the learning perspective above, when the poor people acquire an active set of attitudes and behaviour and legitimacy, they may be further empowered to move beyond mere subsistence levels and try to upgrade their status to becoming subsistence entrepreneurs. The subsistence entrepreneurship refers to ventures in settings of poverty in which a new venture offers little in terms of the potential to significantly improve the entrepreneur's life or that of the entrepreneur's family and subsistence entrepreneurs engage in entrepreneurial activities out of necessity. As such, another area of poverty reduction is an emphasis on new venture creation and innovation. This goes beyond delivering resources to the poor and seeding development as in the resources line of research above. It seeks to create a more sustaining development at the individual and household level through the development of local enterprise, microfinance and also the delivery of simple innovations such as in the base of the pyramid (BoP) research (Prahalad and Hammond 2002).

The creation of new business has particularly been examined through the lens of disruptive innovation theory (Christensen and Raynor 2013). For example, major new markets created in recent decades by disruptive microcomputers such as notebook computers other portable information technology devices, which have grown to more than 10 times that of the previously dominant mainframe computer market (Anthony et al. 2008). The disruptive innovation of the microcomputer opened up major new markets for computing not only directly through job creation and improved business opportunities but also by bringing inexpensive and uncomplicated computing products to increasing numbers of new users, which has in turn has seeded numerous turnkey businesses, even in BoP markets (Prahalad 2006; Zeng and Williamson 2007).

Many such possibilities for entrepreneurs and firms exist at the lower end of world markets, where many earn less than $1,500 annually but are starting to demand some of the goods and services previously available only to wealthier people or organizations (Ahlstrom 2010; Friedman, 2000). Consider the circumstances that lead to the success of a disruptive innovation. The product or service must be a weak substitute for an existing product, one that initially is not as good but is more accessible in terms of price, convenience, or simplicity (Anthony et al. 2008). Thus, disruptive innovation can develop well in new or less demanding applications, often among customers and applications outside of the mainstream or in developing economies. (Prahalad 2006).

Previous studies of BoP have not linked to disruptive innovation a lot; however, disruptive innovation helps regional entrepreneurship and economies grow in the poverty regions through the creation of new businesses, subsistence entrepreneurships and the development of new products. Disruptive innovation also helps poor people to find and develop potential markets and customers, while providing users with important products previously out of reach. This is why disruptive innovation has been regarded as an approach moving out of plight (e.g., Si et al. 2015). In addition, some scholars (e.g., Hart and Christensen, 2002; Prahalad 2006) observed that disruptive innovation also facilitates entrepreneurship by giving access of new technologies and products to smaller, lower end firms that they can, in turn, integrate into their existing and new products and services. Low-end retailers have been helped greatly by advanced point of sale and inventory technology that can be bought cheaply or even used in app form on the newer mobile phones and tablets. Inexpensive communications devices have been particularly beneficial to farmers in the poorer rural regions where access to outside information such as current crop prices was limited. With the new, mobile devices, farmers can access the Internet and get better prices for their crops (Prahalad 2006).

Companies may also be able to work with entrepreneurs in developing economies to co-develop disruptive products that can serve lower-income communities (Hart, 2010). A number of years ago, Abbott chose to reorient its strategy toward cost-effective medicine, which seeks to develop lower end alternatives to more expensive medical treatments (Collins 2001). Abbott enabled a new group of providers and patients to enter the market for such products and procedures, often for client and providers in remote clinics or villages (Hwang and Christensen 2008; Prahalad 2006). In addition to facilitating new markets and consumption, these disruptive innovations help to create new ventures, economic growth. They address the poverty problem from the demand side (new venture creation) and supply side (serving the base of the pyramid).

Special issue articles

Entrepreneurship and Regional Development has published a few articles related to the issue of poverty reduction (e.g., Tasavori, Zaefarian, and Ghauri 2015; Sarkar 2018; Yessoufou, Blok, and Omta 2018). The current special issue expands existence understanding of poverty reduction. The papers in this special issue are briefly reviewed below and summarized in Table 2.

The first paper is "An Anatomy of Entrepreneurial Pursuits in Relation to Poverty by Douglas Cumming, Sofia Johan and Ike Uzuegbunam. Their study examines the causal relationships between inequality, poverty, and entrepreneurship. They hypothesize that income inequality influences entrepreneurial activity, and in turn entrepreneurial activity alleviates absolute poverty. Findings drawn from a longitudinal analysis of a dataset from all 50 U.S. states over an 18-year period provide robust support for these hypotheses. Furthermore, the results showed that anti-poverty public policy aimed at encouraging work (i.e. Earned income tax credit, EITC) can be detrimental to entrepreneurial activity. These findings underscore the importance of linking public

Table 2. Summary of papers in this special issue.

Authors	Title	Findings
Cumming, Johan, and Uzuegbunam 2019	An Anatomy of Entrepreneurial Pursuits in Relation to Poverty	An empirical study examines the relationship among income inequality, poverty, and entrepreneurship. The authors find that inequality influences entrepreneurial activity, while entrepreneurial activity in turn can alleviate absolute poverty. In addition, the authors also find antipoverty public policy aimed at encouraging work would hinder entrepreneurial activity, highlighting the importance of associating public policy aimed at poverty alleviation with public policy aimed at encouraging additional entrepreneurship.
Lin, Winkler, Wang and Chen 2019	Regional Determinants of Poverty Alleviation through Entrepreneurship in China	An empirical study employing the economic theory of dual structure, this study examines regional determinants of poverty reduction. While entrepreneurship can facilitate poverty alleviation in general, the effect of entrepreneurship on poverty alleviation is stronger in urban areas than in rural areas, and in developed areas than in underdeveloped areas. Furthermore, it is also observed that financial development at regional level can moderate the influence of entrepreneurship on poverty reduction.
Wierenga 2019	Uncovering the Scaling of Innovations Developed by Grassroots Entrepreneurs in Low-income Settings	A qualitative study examines entrepreneurship in low-income settings through the theoretical lens of entrepreneurial bricolage. Based on the grounded theory approach, the author finds that a unique group of grassroots entrepreneurs from India developed, commercialized, and scaled innovations by utilizing and combining locally available contacts and a broader network as resources in novel ways. The author also contributes to the literature by uncovering the scaling process of innovations developed by these grassroots entrepreneurs.
Goel and Karri 2019	Entrepreneurial Aspirations and Poverty Reduction: The Role of Institutional Context	A conceptual study explores the poverty reduction across different institutional environments by integrating institutional theory and a subjective view of entrepreneurial action. Institutional context is found to affect the subjective value of resources, and thus can moderate the effect of aspirations on entrepreneurial action. Further, the poor can observe unique ways to exploit entrepreneurial opportunities with the change of aspirations among them. In contrast with interventionist approaches, this study sheds light on poverty reduction by providing the 'poor-as-owners' model.
Wu, Song, and Yang 2019	Untangling the Effects of Entrepreneurial Opportunity on the Performance of Peasant Entrepreneurship: The Moderating Roles of Entrepreneurial Effort and Regional Poverty Level	An empirical study investigates the influence of different types of opportunities to the performance of peasant entrepreneurship. The authors find that dependence on self-identified opportunities can positively enhance entrepreneurial performance, whereas dependence on social network-identified opportunities and government-identified opportunities do not contribute to the performance. They further observe that both entrepreneurial effort and regional poverty level play a significant role in moderating the above relationships. The study helps answer the question why some entrepreneurial activities facilitate poverty reduction while others not.

(Continued)

Table 2. (Continued).

Authors	Title	Findings
Haugh 2019	Call the Midwife! Business Incubation, Enterprise Development and Entrepreneurship Enablement in Developing Economies	An empirical study examines the role that business incubation and enterprise development play in poverty reduction in developing economies. With the help of empirical data from four philanthropy-funded business incubators, business incubation and enterprise development are found to alleviate poverty by creating sustainable new ventures and forms multiple capitals. This study offers valuable insights on poverty reduction through enabling domestic entrepreneurship.
Jain and Koch 2019	Crafting Markets and Fostering Entrepreneurship within Underserved Communities: Social Ventures and Clean Energy Provision in Asia	A qualitative examination of four social ventures across India, Bangladesh, and Cambodia that crafts new markets by introducing clean energy solutions for underserved local communities. The authors find these social ventures incorporate their technologies with local institutions in several ways and contribute to local communities by seeding micro-entrepreneurship activity, generating employment, and improving their standards of living. This study underscores the significance of the engagement with local institutions for crafting markets and poverty reduction.
Korosteleva and Stępień-Baig 2019	Climbing the Poverty Ladder: The Role of Entrepreneurship and Gender in Alleviating Poverty in Transition Economies	An empirical study examines the relationship among entrepreneurship, gender and poverty alleviation in the context of transition economies. By distinguishing self-employment and business ownership, this study contributes to our understanding of which entrepreneurial process is possible to contribute to poverty reduction in the region. The authors also provide interesting findings with regard to the important role of women in poverty reduction via entrepreneurship.
Su et al. 2019	Trust, Poverty, and Subjective Wellbeing Among Chinese Entrepreneurs	An empirical examination of the significance of trust, poverty, and formal institutions to subjective wellbeing of entrepreneurs. Drawing on a sample of Chinese entrepreneurs, the authors find that generalized trust is positively associated with entrepreneurs' subjective welling. The relationship is contingent on economic poverty and social poverty, as well as the degree of institutional voids. Compared with economic poverty, the level of trust across the regions is more relevant in social poverty.
Hall and Matos 2019	An exploratory study of entrepreneurs in impoverished communities: When institutional factors and individual characteristics result in non-productive entrepreneurship	A qualitative study with a concentration of institutional factors and individual characteristics of entrepreneurs examines why some entrepreneurial activities in impoverished regions fail. Based on the data collected from an impoverished community in Brazil, the authors find that temporal myopia, misjudgment of the abilities, and counter-productive use of the social network would lead to non-productive entrepreneurship. This study indicates that non-productive entrepreneurship is a result of the interactions between individual characteristics and the institutional environment.

policy efforts aimed at poverty alleviation with those aimed at encouraging additional entrepreneurship.

The second paper in the special issue is "Regional Determinants of Poverty Alleviation through Entrepreneurship in China" by Song Lin, Christoph Winkler and Shanshan Wang. Based on the economic theory of dual structure, the authors of this study conducted an empirical analysis on the relationship between entrepreneurship and poverty alleviation using panel data collected in 31 provinces in China from 2000 to 2017. The study arrived at three conclusions. First, entrepreneurship in urban and rural areas can generally facilitate poverty alleviation. Second, the correlation between entrepreneurship and poverty alleviation in urban areas is significantly stronger than in rural areas. Moreover, the correlation is also significantly stronger in developed areas than in underdeveloped areas. Third, the level of financial development in an area can moderate the effect of entrepreneurship on poverty alleviation. These conclusions suggest that entrepreneurial activities in emerging economies have a stronger effect on alleviating poverty in urban regions instead of helping less developed or rural areas. The authors recommend that government agencies should institute policies aimed at vigorously improving the business environment in rural and underdeveloped areas. Particularly a strengthening of the financial system in these areas could further enhance the positive effect of entrepreneurship on poverty alleviation.

The third paper is 'Uncovering the Scaling of Innovations Developed by Grassroots Entrepreneurs in Low-income Settings' by Marleen Wierenga. Low-income entrepreneurs operating in resource-scarce settings are typically referred to as subsistence entrepreneurs – informal, operating on a small scale and selling products developed and produced by others. This study establishes the notion of a unique category of low-income entrepreneurs who have developed, commercialized and scaled innovations and are self-employed by choice. Further, the paper investigates the scaling process of these innovative grassroots entrepreneurs. The sample consists of four grassroots entrepreneurs from India who founded an enterprise to sell their self-developed innovations. The study follows the grounded theory approach, which is suitable for the exploration of complex questions in unusual settings. The theoretical lens used in this study is entrepreneurial bricolage since the interest of the study lies in understanding action and the usage of existing resources. The contribution of the paper is twofold. First, it contributes to the literature on low-income entrepreneurship by bolstering the theoretical archetype of grassroots entrepreneurs and developing a process model for their scaling process. Second, the study contributes to the literature on bricolage by introducing the notion of grassroots bricolage as a behaviour to utilize and combine both locally available contacts and a broader network as resources in novel ways.

The next paper is "Entrepreneurial aspirations and poverty reduction: The role of institutional context" by Sanjay Goel & Ranjan Karri. Integrating insights from institutional theory and a subjectivist view of entrepreneurial action, they developed a conceptual model of poverty reduction in different institutional environments through the mediating influence of aspirations. Our model portrays institutional context moderating the influence of aspirations on entrepreneurial action by affecting the subjective value of resources. In addition, because our starting premise is the agency by the poor, and because the value of resources is subjective in our exposition, our model suggests conditions and contexts where a change in aspirations among the poor may provide them with unique insights to exploit entrepreneurial opportunities visible only to them. Our 'poor-as-owners' model can be contrasted with interventionist approaches to poverty reduction. Several policy implications can be derived from our paper that may be more effective in achieving regional development and reducing regional disparities that arise from a higher incidence of poverty.

The fifth paper is 'Untangling the Effects of Entrepreneurial Opportunity on the Performance of Peasant Entrepreneurship: The Moderating Roles of Entrepreneurial Effort and Regional Poverty Level' by Wu, Song and Yang. The literature suggests that entrepreneurship is a critical means of poverty alleviation and that entrepreneurial opportunity is at the heart of entrepreneurial activity. Yet, the extant research has devoted little attention to the role of entrepreneurial opportunity in entrepreneurial activity and poverty reduction. This paper explores the relationship between the types of entrepreneurial opportunity and entrepreneurial performance of peasant entrepreneurs. Using a sample of peasant entrepreneurs from Zhejiang, China, the authors find that while dependence on self-identified opportunities is positively associated with entrepreneurial performance, dependence on social network- or government-identified opportunities does not contribute to the performance. Furthermore, we find that both entrepreneurial effort and regional poverty level moderate the relationship between entrepreneurial opportunity and performance. This article theoretically contributes to the study of peasant entrepreneurship and poverty alleviation by demonstrating a more complex and nuanced role of entrepreneurial opportunity in achieving improved entrepreneurial performance.

The sixth paper is 'Call the midwife! Business incubation, enterprise development and entrepreneurship enablement in developing economies' by Helen Haugh. Enabling domestic entrepreneurship is one pathway for alleviating poverty. In developing economies, however, public policies prioritize health and education above entrepreneurship promotion. While international development funding has traditionally supported social and environmental interventions, more recent corporate philanthropic funding has been invested in business incubators to support domestic entrepreneurship. This article examines how business incubation and enterprise development impact on poverty alleviation in developing economies. From the analysis of empirical data gathered from four philanthropy-funded business incubators, their role in how sustainable new venture creation and multiple capital formation contributes to poverty alleviation is explained. The findings contribute to entrepreneurship enablement theory.

The seventh paper is "Crafting markets and fostering entrepreneurship within underserved communities: Social ventures and clean energy provision in Asia" by Sanjay Jain & James Koch. In this paper, the authors conceptualize markets for underserved communities as being constituted by local institutions that reflect the modalities of these individuals's lives. Using data on the activities that four social ventures across India, Bangladesh and Cambodia have undertaken to craft new markets for their clean energy solutions, we highlight how these actors incorporate their technologies within native material understandings, develop transaction systems consistent with resident consumption practices and entrench their organizations into the existing infrastructure. These processes are termed indigenizing, microprovisioning and codeveloping, respectively. In meshing local context as part of their market crafting efforts, these ventures seed micro-entrepreneurship activity, generate employment for locals as well as improve standards of living within the community through the provision of productivity-enhancing products and services. Our findings highlight the significance of engaging with local institutions as part of market crafting efforts in these scenarios. This paper offers insights that contribute to the sociology of markets, and poverty reduction via entrepreneurship literatures as well as have important practical and policy implications.

The eighth paper is Climbing the Poverty Ladder: The Role of Entrepreneurship and Gender in Alleviating Poverty in Transition Economies by Julia Korosteleva & Paulina Stępień-Baig. Poverty reduction remains a critical issue for a vast proportion of the population globally. Substantial body of literature on poverty reduction has focused on the role played by government support and charity institutions, whereas entrepreneurship as a channel for poverty reduction, and the role of gender in shaping this relationship has been under-researched, especially in the context of transition economies.

Using the recent wave of the EBRD Life in Transition Survey III (2016) data, this study explores the relationship between poverty alleviation, entrepreneurship and gender. They extend the understanding of the mechanism via which entrepreneurial process is likely to contribute to poverty reduction in this region, distinguishing between self-employment and business ownership, with the latter regarded as Schumpeterian entrepreneurship (Block, Fisch, and van Praag 2017). The study provides some interesting findings shedding light on the important role women play in shaping the entrepreneurship–poverty relationship.

The ninth paper is 'Trust, Poverty, and Subjective Wellbeing Among Chinese Entrepreneurs' by Yiyi Su and Shaker Zahra. Entrepreneurs' subjective wellbeing has become an important topic in research; entrepreneurs undertake risks and create their companies seeking personal satisfaction and fulfilment. As a result, researchers have given considerable attention to the antecedents and the conditions under which wellbeing materializes especially in emerging economies where poverty may be acute. In this study, the authors propose that generalized trust serves as an informal institution that affects entrepreneurs' subjective wellbeing. Further, we advance that this relationship is subject to boundary conditions of economic and social poverty as well as context-specific formal institutional features. They test the predictions using a multi-sourced sample of 818 Chinese entrepreneurs and found that trust is positively associated with entrepreneurs' subjective wellbeing. This association is moderated by both economic poverty and social poverty. When high or low institutional voids are evident among the different regions of China, the main and moderating effects are further differentiated. The study suggests that as a mechanism to mitigate the negative effect of lacking formal institutions, the level of trust in different regions is more relevant in social poverty rather than in economic poverty.

Finally, 'An exploratory study of entrepreneurs in impoverished communities: When institutional factors and individual characteristics result in non-productive entrepreneurship' by Jeremy Hall and Stelvia Matos. It is widely acknowledged that entrepreneurship can help the poor escape poverty. However, while many people in impoverished regions engage in entrepreneurial activities, many fail to develop successful businesses. This paper examines why impoverished people may choose to engage in entrepreneurship, the characteristics that shape their entrepreneurial behaviour and the struggles they face. The authors draw on the entrepreneurship literature that suggests institutional factors and individual characteristics shape new venture development. Following an inductive methodological approach utilizing a survey, interviews and focus groups collected from an impoverished community in Brazil, they develop an exploratory study of entrepreneurial behaviour focused on perceived alertness, utilization of social networks, formal business registration and participation in training. The paper also found that temporal myopia, misjudgment of their abilities, and counter-productive use of their social network result in non-productive entrepreneurship. As such, the paper thus contributes theoretically by suggesting that, in addition to productive, unproductive and destructive entrepreneurial outcomes shaped by institutions, non-productive entrepreneurship is also a prevalent problem, but is heavily shaped by the interactions between individual characteristics and the institutional environment.

Discussion

1. Poverty reduction status quo

Looking around the world over the years, large numbers of people moved out of poverty through variety of ways. Some historically poor countries like China, India and Africa have made great achievement in reducing poverty. Particularly, China, followed by India has made the most contribution to reducing the world's poverty in the past few decades. The United Nation (UN) Millennium Development Goals Report 2015 pointed out that China has contributed more than 70% of the world's poverty reduction in recent years (Si et al. 2015; Zhejiang Statistics Bureau 2016). Today, poverty is lower than ever. Recent estimates suggest those living in extreme poverty (less than 1.90 US dollars per day) has dropped to under 10% of the world population, perhaps for the first time in recorded history. Growth in China and India and increasingly Africa have been prime movers behind this decline.

2. *Poverty standards*

Dynamically define and understand the poverty standards that should be a prerequisite for poverty research and practice. Actually, it seems pretty clear, but, objectively speaking, that is because people view this issue as a static and constant case. How to understand the poverty standards? We observed that when the governments, relevant organizations and people act for poverty reduction, they often mechanically understand the existent poverty standard and follow it to implement. However, as a matter of fact, the poverty standards are changeable over time and this dynamic characteristic of poverty standard is for the current poverty reduction practice and research. For instance, China has publicly announced that it will eliminate absolute poverty nationwide by 2020 (China's poverty alleviation database 2019). This goal is to eradicate poverty in a specific year may prove quite difficult in that it ignores that the nature of poverty standards is changeable over time, not in a static and constant case.

Although scholars have completed a lot of valuable research with increasingly extensive insights about poverty reduction (e.g., Mair, Marti, and Ventresca 2012; Haveman 1993; George et al. 2016; Sutter, Bruton, and Chen 2019), there are problems of clarity with respect to poverty definitions and not conflating poverty incorrectly with income inequality (or even wealth inequality). Thus, some of the existing research could be technically well done but conceptually flawed and thus generate misunderstandings regarding poverty. In this special issue, we raise this question and argue that poverty standards are changeable case rather than static, and have searched for a standard definition and application regardless of what country or region may be studied.

3. *Social poverty*

Social poverty is a new problem arisen that some poor people escape poverty economically, they do not escape poverty socially. There are still plenty of mental and behavioural mismatches with their economic status that generates a phenomenon that there is a growing population, they are rich economically but poor socially. These people, though no longer poor, often have a negative impact on society and may be included with people who are considered socially poor. Thus, the issue of how to help poverty people move out of both poverty and social poverty which may be a new poverty research issue and research question, especially in developing countries and emerging economy countries.

This problem may be the most intractable in that institutional systems need to be changed (particularly informal ones) with respect to how entrepreneurship is valued and the dignity accorded to entrepreneurs (McCloskey 2010). Weber argued that the Protestant work ethic was important for resolving the social entrepreneurship problem, that is resolving how much people worked as well as how hard they worked. But not only the attitude of the poor that has to be addressed in the social aspect of entrepreneurship, but also the liberty, dignity and legitimacy accorded to entrepreneurs and private enterprise by the society. Societies can do this through legitimacy building activities and other inculcation strategies regarding entrepreneurship, innovation, and earning profit (Ahlstrom, Bruton, and Yeh 2008; McCloskey 2010). That is to provide increased liberty and dignity for entrepreneurs. The liberty comes in terms of property rights and the legal protection from professional and governmental elites (McCloskey 2017; Ogilvie, 2019). The dignity is the stronger social validation that entrepreneurs receive from society so they can get more legitimacy and support (McCloskey 2010; Tomizawa et al., 2019). Liberty for entrepreneurs and dignity accorded to them, along with a tolerance of failure is crucial to improving the social entrepreneurship environment for new venture creation (McCloskey 2016; Wang, Ahlstrom, Nair, and Hang 2008).

4. Technology and poverty

In recent years, the technology development, especially digital technology, has promoted the social and economic development that directly generates new approaches and solutions to poverty reduction and challenges the existing poverty research theory. High technologies were usually used in high-tech firms, but, now they have been largely used in not only technological entrepreneurship but also inclusive entrepreneurship. Inclusive entrepreneurship is a key part of the inclusive development that explores the growing problem of social exclusion and narrow the gap between the rich and the poor (World Bank, 2012). In recent years, as more and more technological elements are incorporated into inclusive entrepreneurship that has been applied as an effective solution to poverty reduction. The companies such as Alibaba that use 'Big data' to help targeted poverty alleviation and make a series of great achievements. So, the relationships between technology and poverty reduction have been attracting more and more attention from both academic circle and policymakers.

Conclusion

This special issue shows that poverty reduction has garnered increased attention in recent years from researchers in business, entrepreneurship and innovation studies (Ahlstrom 2010; Bruton, Ketchen, and Ireland 2013; Sutter, Bruton, and Chen 2019). Research on subjects ranging from regional development, globalization and economic growth has emerged in recent years, and have dynamically defined poverty standards. It should be recognized that poverty standards can be changeable over time (referring to social measures as well as economic) and this dynamic characteristic of poverty standard is important for all for poverty research. And, it is equally important for researchers to not conflate poverty with income or wealth inequality as these are much different concepts and are not substitutable for each other. This special issue has addressed these important but underexplored issues with different perspectives that address and explain the current research of poverty research.

For instance, plight means poverty in that the poor's difficult situation is likely caused by a variety of economic, and personal reasons in which change is impeded by a variety of difficulties and restrictions. Thus, how business and entrepreneurship can find ways to improve the plight in poor communities should be a topic researchers address regarding poverty reduction. The current basic handouts from governments, charities and organizations as a solution for solving poverty problems are likely to be ineffective, especially for the peaceful regions in the world (Easterly 2006; Easterly, Levine, and Roodman 2004). In addition to above, this special issue also addresses the issues of social poverty, inclusive entrepreneurship, crowdfunding and technology-based solutions.

Technology development, especially digital technology, has generated new approaches to (and ways of looking at) poverty reduction which challenges existing poverty research theory traditionally centred on financial aid and alleviation. This special issue in *Entrepreneurship and Regional Development* on business, entrepreneurship and innovation toward poverty reduction has published work that builds new knowledge about the nature of poverty reduction and business, entrepreneurship and innovation activities in both developed and developing economies, as well as addressing institutional factors and network/digital and sharing economies. This special issue has also developed further a theoretical foundation with different perspectives for future research under the current political, economic, network and global contexts (Ahlstrom and Bruton 2006). In addition to the above, this special issue has analyzed the poverty research of where poverty reduction and entrepreneurship research now stands and, in turn, allows us to develop an understanding of where the research needs to move in the future as we develop an agenda for future poverty reduction research.

Note

1. The special issue will place five articles in this issue of *Entrepreneurship and Regional Development* and five in the next issue.

Disclosure statement

No potential conflict of interest was reported by the authors.

References

Acemoglu, D., and J. A. Robinson. 2012. *Why Nations Fail: The Origins Of Power, Prosperity and Poverty.* . New York: Crown Books. doi: 29 168 doi:10.1355/ae29-2j

Acs, Z., and D. Audretsch. 1988. "Innovation in Large and Small Firms: An Empirical Analysis." *The American Economic Review* 78 (4): 678–690.

Ahlin, C., and N. Jiang. 2008. "Can Micro-credit Bring Development?" *Journal of Development Economics* 86 (1): 1–21. doi:10.1016/j.jdeveco.2007.08.002.

Ahlstrom, D., and L. C. Wang. 2010. "Entrepreneurial Capitalism in East Asia: How History Matters." In *Historical Foundations of Entrepreneurship Research*, edited by H. Landstrom and F. Lohrke, 406–428. Cheltenham, UK: Edward Elgar Publishing.

Ahlstrom, D. 2010. "Innovation and Growth: How Business Contributes to Society." *The Academy of Management Perspectives* 24 (3): 10–23.

Ahlstrom, D. 2014. "The Hidden Reason Why the First World War Matters Today: The Development and Spread of Modern Management." *Brown Journal of World Affairs* 21 (1): 201–218.

Ahlstrom, D. 2015. "Innovation and Growth in Emerging Economies." In Austrian Council for Research and Technology Development (ed.). *Designing the Future: Economic, Societal, and Political Dimensions of Innovation*, 353-387. Vienna: Echomedia.

Ahlstrom, D., D. J. Cumming, and S. Vismara. 2018. "New Methods of Entrepreneurial Firm Financing: Fintech, Crowdfunding and Corporate Governance Implications." *Corporate Governance: An International Review* 26 (5): 310–313. doi:10.1111/corg.v26.5.

Ahlstrom, D., and G. D. Bruton. 2001. "Learning from Successful Local Private Firms in China: Establishing Legitimacy." *The Academy of Management Executive* 15 (4): 72–83.

Ahlstrom, D., and G. D. Bruton. 2006. "Venture Capital in Emerging Economies: Networks and Institutional Change." *Entrepreneurship Theory and Practice* 30 (2): 299–320. doi:10.1111/etap.2006.30.issue-2.

Ahlstrom, D., G. D. Bruton, and K. S. Yeh. 2008. "Private Firms in China: Building Legitimacy in an Emerging Economy." *Journal of World Business* 43 (4): 385–399. doi:10.1016/j.jwb.2008.03.001.

Alston, E., L. J. Alston, B. Mueller, and T. Nonnenmacher. 2018. *Institutional and Organizational Analysis: Concepts and Applications*. Cambridge: Cambridge University Press. doi:10.1017/9781316091340.

Alvarez, S. A., and J. B. Barney. 2014. "Entrepreneurial Opportunities and Poverty Alleviation." *Entrepreneurship Theory and Practice* 38 (1): 159–184. doi:10.1111/etap.12078.

Alvarez, S. A., J. B. Barney, and A. M. B. Newman. 2015. "The Poverty Problem and the Industrialization Solution." *Asia Pacific Journal of Management* 32 (1): 23–37. doi:10.1007/s10490-014-9397-5.

Anthony, S. D., M. W. Johnson, E. J. Altman, and J. V. Sinfield. 2008. *The Innovator's Guide to Growth: Putting Disruptive Innovation to Work*. Cambridge, MA: Harvard Business Press.

Ashford, S. J., and A. S. Tsui. 1991. "Self-regulation for Managerial Effectiveness: The Role of Active Feedback Seeking." *Academy of Management Journal* 34 (2): 251–280.

Battilana, J., B. Leca, and E. Boxenbaum. 2009. "How Actors Change Institutions: Towards a Theory of Institutional Entrepreneurship." *The Academy of Management Annals* 3 (1): 65–107. doi:10.1080/19416520903053598.

Baumol, W. J., M. A. Schilling, and E. N. Wolff. 2009b. "The Superstar Inventors and Entrepreneurs: How Were They Educated?." *Journal of Economics & Management Strategy* 18 (3): 711–728. doi:10.1111/j.1530-9134.2009.00227.x.

Baumol, W. J., R. E. Litan, and C. J. Schramm. 2009a. *Good Capitalism, Bad Capitalism, and the Economics of Growth and Prosperity*. New Haven, CT: Yale University Press.

Berge, L. I. O., K. Bjorvatn, and B. Tungodden. 2014. "Human and Financial Capital for Microenterprise Development: Evidence from a Field and Lab Experiment." *Management Science* 61 (4): 707–722. doi:10.1287/mnsc.2014.1933.

Bergh, A., I. Mirkina, and T. Nilsson. 2016. "Do the Poor Benefit from Globalization Regardless of Institutional Quality?" *Applied Economic Letters* 23 (10): 708–712. doi:10.1080/13504851.2015.1102835.

Bhagwati, J., and T. N. Srinivasan. 2002. "Trade and Poverty in the Poor Countries." *American Economic Review* 92 (2): 180–183. doi:10.1257/000282802320189212.

Block, J. H., C. O. Fisch, and M. van Praag. 2017. "The Schumpeterian Entrepreneur: A Review of the Empirical Evidence on the Antecedents, Behaviour and Consequences of Innovative Entrepreneurship." *Industry and Innovation* 24 (1): 61–95. doi:10.1080/13662716.2016.1216397.

Bloom, N., B. Eifert, A. Mahajan, D. McKenzie, and J. Roberts. 2013. "Does Management Matter? Evidence from India." *The Quarterly Journal of Economics* 128 (1): 1–51. doi:10.1093/qje/qjs044.

Bloom, N., M. Draca, and J. Van Reenen. 2016. "Trade Induced Technical Change? the Impact of Chinese Imports on Innovation, IT and Productivity." *The Review of Economic Studies* 83 (1): 87–117. doi:10.1093/restud/rdv039.

Bruton, G. D., D. Ketchen, and D. Ireland. 2013. "Entrepreneurship as a Solution to Poverty." *Journal of Business Venturing* 28 (6): 683–689. doi:10.1016/j.jbusvent.2013.05.002.

Bruton, G. D., S. Khavul, D. Siegel, and M. Wright. 2015. "New Financial Alternatives in Seeding Entrepreneurship: Microfinance, Crowdfunding, and Peer-to-peer Innovations." *Entrepreneurship Theory and Practice* 39 (1): 9–26. doi:10.1111/etap.2015.39.issue-1.

Busenitz, L. W., C. Gomez, and J. W. Spencer. 2000. "Country Institutional Profiles: Unlocking Entrepreneurial Phenomena." *Academy of Management Journal* 43 (5): 994–1003.

Chen, J., A. Y. Chang, and G. D. Bruton. 2017. "Microfinance: Where are We Today and Where Should the Research Go in the Future?" *International Small Business Journal* 35 (7): 793–802. doi:10.1177/0266242617717380.

China's poverty alleviation database. 2019.

Chliova, M., and D. Ringov. 2017. "Scaling Impact: Template Development and Replication at the Base of the Pyramid." *The Academy of Management Perspectives* 31 (1): 44–62. doi:10.5465/amp.2015.0010.

Christensen, C. M., and M. E. Raynor. 2013. *The Innovator's Solution*. Boston: Harvard Business Review Press.

CIA, US. 2017. *World Factbook*. Washington, DC: Government Printing Office.

Collins, J. 2001. *Good to Great: Why Some Companies Make The Leap and Others Don't*. New York: Harper Business.

Cumming, D. J., S. Johan, and I. S. Uzuegbunam 2019."An Anatomy of Entrepreneurial Pursuits in Relation to Poverty." Entrepreneurship and Regional Development, this issue.

Denning, S. 2016. "Christensen Updates Disruption Theory." *Strategy & Leadership* 44 (2): 10–16.

Dollar, D., and A. Kraay. 2002. "Growth Is Good for The Poor." *Journal of Economic Growth* 7 (3): 195-225. doi:10.1023/A:1020139631000.

Dollar, D., and A. Kraay. 2004. "Trade, Growth, and Poverty." *The Economic Journal* 114 (493): F22–F49. doi:10.1111/j.0013-0133.2004.00186.x.

Dollar, D., T. Kleineberg, and A. Kraay. 2016. "Growth Still Is Good for the Poor." *European Economic Review* 81: 68–85. doi:10.1016/j.euroecorev.2015.05.008.

Dweck, C. S. 2007. *Mindset: The New Psychology of Success*. New York: Ballantine Books.

Easterly, W. 2002. "The Elusive Quest for Growth": *Economists' Adventures and Misadventures in the Tropics*. Cambridge, MA: MIT Press.

Easterly, W. 2006. *The White Man's Burden: Why the West's Efforts to Aid the Rest Have Done so Much Ill and so Little Good*. New York: Penguin Press.

Easterly, W. 2013. *The Tyranny of Experts: Economists, Dictators, and the Forgotten Righys of the Poor*. New York: Basic Books.

Easterly, W., R. Levine, and D. Roodman. 2004. "Aid, Policies, and Growth: Comment." *American Economic Review* 94 (3): 774–780. doi:10.1257/0002828041464560.

Eckhardt, J., and S. Shane. 2003. "Opportunities and Entrepreneurship." *Journal of Management* 29 (3): 333–349.

Fu, K. B. 2006. "Sprite of Yiwu: Power of The Development of Yiwu's Economy." *Observation May* 16: 3–16. in Chinese.

Findlay, R. 2009. *Power and Plenty: Trade, War, and The World Economy in The Second Millennium. Princeton*. New Jersey: Princeton University Press.

Frese, M., and D. Fay. 2001. "4. Personal Initiative: An Active Performance Concept for Work in the 21st Century." *Research in Organizational Behavior* 23: 133–187. doi:10.1016/S0191-3085(01)23005-6.

Friedman, T. L. 2000. *The Lexus and The Olive Tree: Understanding Globalization*. New York: Farrar, Straus and Giroux.

World Bank. 2012. An Update to the World Bank's Estimates of Consumption Poverty in the Developing World. Accessed November 15 2018. http://siteresources.worldbank.org/INTPOVCALNET/Resources/Global_Poverty_Update_2012_02-29-12.pdf

George, G., A. M. McGahan, and J. Prabhu. 2012. "Innovation for Inclusive Growth: Towards a Theoretical Framework and Research Agenda." *Journal of Management Studies* 49 (4): 661–683. doi:10.1111/j.1467-6486.2012.01048.x.

George, G., R. Kotha, P. Parikh, T. Alnuaimi, and A. S. Bahaj. 2016. "Social Structure, Reasonable Gain, and Entrepreneurship in Africa." *Strategic Management Journal* 37 (6): 1118–1131. doi:10.1002/smj.2381.

Ghani, E., W. R. Kerr, and S. O'Connell. 2014. "Spatial Determinants of Entrepreneurship in India." *Regional Studies* 48 (6): 1071–1089.

Goalkeepers. 2018. Goalkeepers Data Report 2018. Accessed July 11 2019. https://www.gatesfoundation.org.cn/goalkeepers/report?download=false

Goel, S., and R. Karri. 2019. "Entrepreneurial Aspirations and Poverty Reduction: The Role of Institutional Context". Entrepreneurship and Regional Development, this issue.

Hall, J., and S. Matos. 2019. "An Exploratory Study of Entrepreneurs in Impoverished Communities: When Institutional Factors and Individual Characteristics Result in Non-Productive Entrepreneurship". Entrepreneurship and Regional Development, this issue.

Halpern-Meekin, S. 2019. *Social Poverty Low-income Parents and The Struggle for Family and Community Ties*. New York: NYU Press.

Harding, H. 1987. *China's Second Revolution: Reform after Mao*. Washington, DC: Brookings Institution Press.

Hart, S. L., and C. M. Christensen. 2002. "The Great Leap: Driving Innovation from The Base of The Pyramid." *Sloan Management Review* 44 (1): 51–56.

Haugh, H. 2019. "Call The Midwife! Business Incubation, Enterprise Development and Entrepreneurship Enablement in Developing Economies." Entrepreneurship and Regional Development, this issue

Haveman, H. A. 1993. "Follow the Leader: Mimetic Isomorphism and Entry into New Markets." In *Administrative Science Quarterly*, 593–627.

Hu, Q., S. Yang, G. Fu, G. Xie, Z. Chen, G. Zhou, Z. He, and A. Feng. 2000. "The Phenomenal Rise of The Yiwu Small-commodities MarketIn Zhejiang Province." *Chinese Economic Studies* 33 (5): 3–99.

Hwang, J., and C. M. Christensen. 2008. "Disruptive Innovation in Health Care Delivery: A Framework for Business-model Innovation." *Health Affairs* 27 (5): 1329–1335. doi:10.1377/hlthaff.27.5.1329.

Jain, S., and J. Koch 2019. "Crafting markets and fostering entrepreneurship Within Underserved Communities: Social Ventures and Clean Energy Provision in Asia". Entrepreneurship and Regional Development, this issue.

Karlan, D., and M. Valdivia. 2011. "Teaching Entrepreneurship: Impact of Business Training on Microfinance Clients and Institutions." *Review of Economics and Statistics* 93 (2): 510–527. doi:10.1162/REST_a_00074.

Khavul, S. 2010. "Microfinance: Creating Opportunities for the Poor?" *Academy of Management Perspectives* 24 (3): 58–72. doi:10.5465/amp.24.3.58.

Kistruck, G. M., C. J. Sutter, J. R. B. Lount, and B. R. Smith. 2013. "Mitigating Principal-agent Problems in Base-of-the-pyramid Markets: An Identity Spillover Perspective." *Academy of Management Journal* 56 (3): 659–682. doi:10.5465/amj.2011.0336.

Korosteleva, J., and P. Stępień-Baig. 2019. "Climbing the Poverty Ladder: The Role of Entrepreneurship and Gender in Alleviating Poverty in Transition Economies". Entrepreneurship and Regional Development, this issue.

Leff, N. H. 1979. "Entrepreneurship and Economic Development: The Problem Revisited." *Journal of Economic Literature* 17 (1): 46–64.

Levy, D. L. 2008. "Political Contestation in Global Production Networks." *Academy Of Management Review* 33 (4): 943–963.

Lin, S., C. Winkler, S. S. Wang, and H. Chen 2019. "Regional Determinants of Poverty Alleviation through Entrepreneurship in China." Entrepreneurship and Regional Development, this issue.

Lin, S., and S. Si. 2014. "Factors Affecting Peasant Entrepreneurs'intention in The Chinese Context." *International Entrepreneurship and Management Journal* 10 (4): 803–825.

London, T. 2009. "Making Better Investments at The Base of The Pyramid." *Harvard Business Review* 87 (5): 106-113.

Lucas, R. E. 2002. *Lectures on Economic Growth*. Cambridge, MA: Harvard University Press.

Mair, J., I. Marti, and M. J. Ventresca. 2012. "Building Inclusive Markets in Rural Bangladesh: How Intermediaries Work Institutional Voids." *Academy of Management Journal* 55 (4): 819–850. doi:10.5465/amj.2010.0627.

McClelland, D. C. 1967. *The Achieving Society*. New York: Free Press.

McCloskey, D. N. 2006. *The Bourgeois Virtues: Ethics for an Age of Commerce*. Chicago: University of Chicago Press.

McCloskey, D. N. 2010. *Bourgeois Dignity: Why Economics Can't Explain the Modern World*. Chicago: University of Chicago Press.

McCloskey, D. N. 2016. "The Great Enrichment: A Humanistic and Social Scientific Account." *Social Science History* 40 (Winter): 583–598. doi:10.1017/ssh.2016.23.

McCloskey, D. N. 2017. *Bourgeois Equality: How Ideas, Not Capital or Institutions, Enriched the World*. Chicago: University of Chicago Press.

Newman, A., S. Schwarz, and D. Ahlstrom. 2017. "Microfinance and Entrepreneurship: An Introduction." *International Small Business Journal* 35 (7): 787–792. doi:10.1177/0266242617719314.

Ogilvie, S. 2019. *The European Guilds: an Economic Analysis*. Princeton, New Jersey, NJ: Princeton University Press.

Pearce, J. L. 2005. "Organizational Scholarship and the Eradication of Global Poverty." *Academy of Management Journal* 48 (6): 970–972. doi:10.5465/amj.2005.19573100.

Perkins, D. H., S. Radelet, D. L. Lindauer, and S. A. Block. 2013. *Economics of Development*. 7th ed. New York: W.W. Norton.

Piketty, T. 2014. *Capital in The Twenty First Century*. Cambridge, MA: Harvard University Press. doi:10.4159/9780674369542.

Prahalad, C. 2006. *The Fortune at the Bottom of the Pyramid: Eradicating Poverty through Profits*. Prentice Hall, Upper Saddle River, NJ: Wharton Publishing.

Prahalad, C. K., and A. Hammond. 2002. "Serving the World's Poor, Profitably." *Harvard Business Review* 80 (9): 48–59.

Rindova, V., D. Barry, and J. D. J. Ketchen. 2009. "Entrepreneuring as Emancipation." *Academy of Management Review* 34 (3): 477–491. doi:10.5465/amr.2009.40632647.

Rodrik, D., A. Subramanian, and F. Trebbi. 2004. "Institutions Rule: The Primacy of Institutions over Geography and Integration in Economic Development." *Journal of Economic Growth* 9 (2): 131–165. doi:10.1023/B:JOEG.0000031425.72248.85.

Romer, P. 1986. "Increasing Returns and Long Run Growth." *Journal of Political Economy* 94 (5): 1002–1037. doi:10.1086/261420.

Roodman, D. 2012. *Due Diligence: An Impertinent Inquiry into Microfinance*. Washington, DC: CGD Books.

Roser, M., and E. Ortiz-Ospina. 2017. "Global Extreme Poverty." accessed 15 June 2019. OurWorldInData.org,https://ourworldindata.org/extreme-poverty/

Sachs, J. D. 2003. "Institutions Matter, but Not for Everything." *Finance & Development* 40 (2): 38–41.

Sarkar, S. 2018. "Grassroots Entrepreneurs and Social Change at the Bottom of the Pyramid: The Role of Bricolage." *Entrepreneurship & Regional Development* 30 (3–4): 421–449. doi:10.1080/08985626.2017.1413773.

Scott, W. R. 2013. *Institutions and Organizations: Ideas, Interests, and Identities*. Thousand Oaks, CA: Sage Publications.

Sen, A. 1999. *Development as Freedom. New York:* AlfredA. Knopf.

Shane, S., and S. Venkataraman. 2000. "The Promise of Entrepreneurship as a Field of Research." *Academy of Management Review* 25 (1): 217–226.

Si, S., X. Yu, A. Wu, S. Chen, S. Chen, and Y. Su. 2015. "Entrepreneurship and Poverty Reduction: A Case Study of Yiwu, China." *Asia Pacific Journal of Management* 32 (1): 119–143. doi:10.1007/s10490-014-9395-7.

Sims, P. 2013. *Little Bets: How Breakthrough Ideas Emerge from Small Discoveries*. New York: Simon & Schuster.

Su, Y., S.A. Zahra, R. Li, and D. Fan. 2019. "Trust, Poverty, and Subjective Wellbeing Among Chinese Entrepreneurs". Entrepreneurship and Regional Development, this issue.

Sud, M., and C. V. VanSandt. 2011. "Of Fair Markets and Distributive Justice." *Journal of Business Ethics* 99 (1): 131–142. doi:10.1007/s10551-012-1230-9.

Sutter, C., G. D. Bruton, and J. Chen. 2019. "Entrepreneurship as A Solution to Extreme Poverty: A Review and Future Research Directions." *Journal of Business Venturing* 34 (1): 197–214. doi:10.1016/j.jbusvent.2018.06.003.

Sutter, C., J. Webb, G. Kistruck, J. D. J. Ketchen, and R. D. Ireland. 2017. "Transitioning Entrepreneurs from Informal to Formal Markets." *Journal of Business Venturing* 32 (4): 420–442. doi:10.1016/j.jbusvent.2017.03.002.

Sutter, C.J., G.M. Kistruck, and S. Morris. 2014. "Adaptations to Knowledge Templates in Base-of-the-pyramid Markets: The Role Of Social Interaction." *Strategic Entrepreneurship Journal* 8 (4): 303–320. doi:10.1002/sej.v8.4.

Tasavori, M., R. Zaefarian, and P. N. Ghauri. 2015. "The Creation View of Opportunities at the Base of the Pyramid." *Entrepreneurship & Regional Development* 27 (1–2): 106–126. doi:10.1080/08985626.2014.1002538.

Tomizawa, A., L. Zhao, G. Bassellier, and D. Ahlstrom 2019. "Economic Growth, Innovation, Institutions, and the Great Enrichment." Asia Pacific Journal of Management. doi:10.1007/s10490-019-09648-2.

Van Zanden, J. L. 2009. *The Long Road to the Industrial Revolution*. Boston: Brill.

Vaona, A. 2005. "Understanding Globalization, Employment and Poverty Reduction, Palgrave Macmillan." *Research Policy* 34 (6): 977–978. doi:10.1016/j.respol.2005.05.002.

Wang, L. C., D. Ahlstrom, A. Nair, and R. Z. Hang. 2008. "Creating Globally Competitive and Innovative Products: China's Next Olympic Challenge." *SAM Advanced Management Journal* 73 (3): 4–16.

Weber, M. 1932. *The Protestant Ethic and The Spirit Of Capitalism*. London: Allen and Unwin.

Whitacre, B. E., D. Meadowcroft, and R. Gallardo. 2019. "Firm and Regional Economic Outcomes Associated with a New, Broad Measure of Business Innovation." *Entrepreneurship & Regional Development*. doi:10.1080/08985626.2019.1630486.

Wierenga, M. 2019. "Uncovering the Scaling of Innovations Developed by Grassroots Entrepreneurs in Low-income Settings." Entrepreneurship and Regional Development, this issue. doi:10.1080/08985626.2019.1640478

Wu, A., D. Song, and Y. Yang. 2019."Untangling the Effects of entrepreneurial Opportunity on the Performance of Peasant Entrepreneurship: The Moderating Roles of Entrepreneurial Effort and Regional Poverty Level." Entrepreneurship and Regional Development, this issue.

Wu, J., and S. Si. 2018. "Poverty Reduction through Entrepreneurship: Incentives, Social Networks, and Sustainability." *Asian Business & Management* 17 (4): 243–259. doi:10.1057/s41291-018-0039-5.

Yessoufou, A. W., V. Blok, and S. W. F. Omta. 2018. "The Process of Entrepreneurial Action at the Base of the Pyramid in Developing Countries: A Case of Vegetable Farmers in Benin." *Entrepreneurship & Regional Development* 30 (1–2): 1–28. doi:10.1080/08985626.2017.1364788.

Zeng, M., and P. J. Williamson. 2007. *Dragons at Your Door: How Chinese Cost Innovation Is Disrupting Global Competition*. Boston, MA: Harvard Business School Press.

Zhejiang Statistics Bureau. 2016. *Zhejiang Statistical Yearbook*. Beijing, China: China Statistics Press.

An anatomy of entrepreneurial pursuits in relation to poverty

Douglas Cumming, Sofia Johan and Ikenna Uzuegbunam

ABSTRACT

This study examines the causal relationships between inequality, poverty and entrepreneurship. We hypothesize that income inequality influences entrepreneurial activity, and entrepreneurial activity alleviates absolute poverty. Findings from longitudinal analyses of a dataset from all 50 US states over an 18-year period provide robust support for these hypotheses. Furthermore, the results suggest that antipoverty public policy aimed at encouraging work (i.e. Earned income tax credit, EITC) can be detrimental to entrepreneurial activity. These findings underscore the importance of linking public policy efforts aimed at poverty alleviation with those aimed at encouraging additional entrepreneurship.

Introduction

> If the poor are abundant, wages will be low, which makes it much more tempting to be an entrepreneur who hires labor rather than a small-
> scale producer who works on his own. When the rich are relatively abundant, the opposite it true.
>
> (Banerjee and Newman 1994, 214)

The notion that entrepreneurship is an engine for poverty alleviation in society has recently become more popular among scholars and policymakers (Zhara et al., 2009; Ahlstrom 2010; Al-Dajani et al., 2015; Banerjee and Newman 1994; Baumol 1990; Bruton, Ahlstrom, and Si 2015; Burns, 2012; Fairlie 2012; McMullen 2011; Ribeiro-Soriano 2017; Schumpeter 1934; Si et al. 2015.). Conventional wisdom dictates that entrepreneurial activity creates wealth in society (e.g. through employment and spillovers), which in turn increases the potential for poverty alleviation and economic growth in society (Fairlie 2005), although we would expect differences in these effects across countries depending on institutional considerations (Cullen, Johnson, and Parboteeah 2014; Nam et al. 2014; Tomizawa et al., forthcoming). These widely held views about the importance of entrepreneurial activity have fueled many government initiatives across the world aimed at fostering entrepreneurship (Nikolaev, Boudreaux, and Palich, forthcoming). Some notable examples include the $2 Billion *Startup America* White House initiative in the United States (US), the Chinese Government-backed $6.5 billion venture capital fund in China, and the Youth Enterprise Support (YES) government initiative in Ghana.

Extant research suggests that the broad determinants of entrepreneurial activity include the following factors: market conditions, education, finance, information, spillovers and agglomeration economies (Fairlie and Chatterji 2013; Koryak et al. 2015; Marlow et al. 2018); as well as institutional, legal and political factors such as taxation, intellectual property rights, start-up costs and failure costs (Djankov et al. 2002; Klapper, Laeven, and Rajan 2006; Klein et al. 2010; Nikolaev, Boudreaux, and Palich, forthcoming; Xue and Klein 2010). Nevertheless, research interest on the relationship between poverty and entrepreneurial activity from a management perspective is still at a nascent stage, with very limited empirical insights on the phenomenon (Beal and Astakhova 2017; Halvarsson, Korpi, and Wennberg 2018). Some of these recent efforts have yielded insights related to the functioning of entrepreneurial activities in base-of-the-pyramid (BOP) markets, especially in developing countries (Bradley et al. 2012; Hall et al. 2012; Prahalad 2004). Still, we lack a coherent empirical picture of the causal mechanisms that underlie the relationship between entrepreneurship and poverty. Specifically, it is unclear to what extent inequality may contribute to entrepreneurial activity. Or what mechanisms may enable entrepreneurial activity to impact poverty?

In this study, we focus attention on these related questions with the view to develop a coherent understanding of the complex relationship between entrepreneurial activity and poverty. Entrepreneurship is a complicated and multifaceted concept. We make two principal claims in our work. First, we suggest that income inequality actually has a positive impact on entrepreneurial activity by highlighting the tension between opportunity costs and entrepreneurial action (see first opening quote from Banerjee and Newman 1994). Second, we advance the notion of an *entrepreneurial activity hierarchy* (EAH), which suggests that some forms of entrepreneurial activity have a greater potential to alleviate poverty than other forms. In particular, we highlight the dominance of entrepreneurial activity that is firm-centric or opportunity-centric for alleviating poverty. The idea is that entrepreneurial activity that resembles firms not markets, opportunities not necessity are more efficient for poverty alleviation because of their signalling potential, which can help orchestrate economic opportunities, spillovers and economic growth in society.

We examine these hypotheses using a comprehensive US state-level, panel dataset over an 18-year period (1996–2013). The empirical evidence suggests that the relationship between inequality, entrepreneurship and poverty is rather complex. The findings demonstrate that as a matter of economic and ethical consequences, inequality causes entrepreneurial activity of different forms. However, entrepreneurial activity does not cause inequality. In addition, we did find evidence consistent with the view that there is a hierarchy in entrepreneurial activity relative to absolute poverty alleviation.

Theoretically, our work departs from previous efforts by disentangling two related forms of income distribution problems in modern society, that is, inequality and absolute poverty, and then considering their distinct relationships with entrepreneurial activity. In our view, income inequality is concerned with the distribution of wealth in society, wherein higher wealth concentration in uppermost decile of a given society is indicative of higher levels of income inequality (Halvarsson, Korpi, and Wennberg 2018). On the other hand, absolute poverty is concerned with the proportion of people that are living below the poverty line in a society. By disentangling these two forms of income distribution problems, our research contributes to a better understanding of how, on the one hand, income inequality can cause entrepreneurial activity; and on the other hand, how entrepreneurial activity, in turn, influences absolute poverty.

The second contribution of our research is to reify recent theoretical reasoning that different forms of entrepreneurial activity are not created equal (Baumol, Litan, and Schramm 2007), particularly with respect to their varying influence on poverty alleviation. Specifically, we delineate the influence of firm-centric and opportunity-centric entrepreneurial activity in poverty alleviation. In addition, post-hoc analysis reveals that public policy aimed at alleviating poverty through work-based programs (i.e. the Earned Income Tax Credit, EITC) is actually detrimental to firm-centric and opportunity-centric entrepreneurial activity. Overall, the study demonstrates that future research, discussions, and public policy may need to adopt a more nuanced view when considering the relationships between inequality, poverty and business; and should consider the potential of strategically, linking public policy efforts aimed at poverty alleviation with those aimed at encouraging entrepreneurship.

Background

The primary focus of this study is on the interplay between poverty and entrepreneurial activity at the state level. There are two broad views of poverty in the prior literature. One perspective suggests that poverty is the degree to which people in a given state or political economy experience income shortfalls. This view of poverty is often referred to absolute poverty since it captures the overall income shortfalls based on a chosen poverty line in the given society. The second perspective of poverty is the relative view of poverty, which is more concerned with the degree to which a greater proportion of people in society have very limited wealth. We focus on absolute poverty because it is often a target for policymakers who are interested in alleviating economic deprivation in society.[1] In a related manner, the distribution of income in society has garnered recent attention in the literature and in policymaking. As a topic of economic and ethical concern, inequality embodies the differences in the regular receipt of economic resources over time, in exchange of labour or capital usage (Beal and Astakhova 2017), and the inherent morality of such differences (Simpson 2009). Thus, income inequality accounts for social referencing between members of the same society, which has the potential to stimulate economic activity among disadvantaged members of the society.

In advanced economies such as the US, income is officially used to measure absolute poverty levels. There is growing recognition that poverty measures based on income alone tend to overlook dynamic disparities in consumption patterns that result from inequalities across families in the accumulation of assets or access to credit (Meyer and Sullivan 2003, 2004; Ziliak 2006). In the US, the country's reputation for fostering meritocracy has, historically, been a source of pride; it is striking that income inequality is at its highest levels since the 1920s (Beal and Astakhova 2017), though this excludes transfer payments and other benefits which have risen sharply since that time.

Theory and hypotheses

Inequality and entrepreneurial activity

To examine the theoretical relationship between inequality and entrepreneurial activity, we must consider two potential arguments. First, the level of inequality in society is important due to its potential influence on opportunity costs for the individual considering entrepreneurial activity. Theory suggests that at higher levels of inequality in society, entrepreneurs will find it more tempting to start new businesses because their alternative income/opportunity cost is less attractive than being an entrepreneur (Banerjee and Newman 1994; Evans and Leighton 1989). For example, Fairlie and Chatterji (2013) found that while large opportunity costs (due to a very tight labour market in the 1990s Silicon Valley compared to the rest of the country) suppressed entrepreneurial rates during this period; lower opportunity costs in the post-late 1990s increased entrepreneurial activity relative to the US. Also, Hsu, Roberts, and Eesley (2007), in a study of the entrepreneurial activity of MIT alumni, found that lower opportunity costs due to high unemployment or economic recessions could provide incentives to enter entrepreneurship. Furthermore, historical accounts have shown that entrepreneurial activity rises during periods of high inequality, because '... of a perception by those who innovate that they have an unequal position relative to some key referent group in their society, and who subsequently pin their hopes on undertaking entrepreneurial activities that will reduce this gap' (Brenner 1987, 97).

Second, relatively higher levels of income inequality in society can lead to opportunities for entrepreneurs to act for both self and collective interest. That is, extremely high levels of inequality help reveal systemic inefficiencies/imperfections in the society that would translate to greater, scalable opportunities for entrepreneurial action. The critical assumption here is that entrepreneurs are motivated, not just by self-interest, but by collective (prosocial) interest as well (Van de Ven, Sapienza, and Villanueva 2007; Miller et al. 2012; Simpson 2009). On the one hand, inequality will spur entrepreneurial action because human beings are egotistic, and cannot survive without taking actions to improve their economic condition. Yet, on the other hand, inequality as a moral concern could also lead citizens to take actions toward wealth redistribution (see Simpson 2009).

This suggests that entrepreneurs need not be poor themselves to recognize and take action to address inefficiencies in society. For example, Muhammad Yunus, the notable founder of Grameen Bank, empathized for poor families and recognized they did not have access to regular banking. As Van de Ven, Sapienza, and Villanueva (2007, 358) state, 'Had Dr. Yunus been interested exclusively in his self-interest, he could not have seen or envisioned this opportunity, and Grameen Bank would have probably never existed' (p. 358).

In sum, the arguments described above suggest that higher rates of inequality in a state have the potential to encourage more entrepreneurs, who are motivated by either self-interest or/and collective interest to reduce inequality in society. Therefore,

Hypothesis 1 (H1): States with higher levels of income inequality will subsequently have higher rates of entrepreneurial activity.

Entrepreneurial activity hierarchy for poverty alleviation

In the previous analysis, we argued that inequality, which is a construct of wealth disparity in society, would lead to increased entrepreneurial activity of different forms. Yet, we expect that entrepreneurial activity also has the potential to mitigate absolute poverty, oftentimes due to increases in wealth, productivity, and economic opportunities (Baumol 1967, 1990; World Bank 2004).[2] For example, entrepreneurial activity provides a source of income that enables economic development including access to health care, reduced unemployment, and education. It also improves consumption through the introduction of goods and services previously unavailable to the poorer segments of society (Ahlstrom 2010; Newman, Schwarz, and Ahlstrom 2017).

Not all entrepreneurial activity, however, will lead to poverty alleviation at the same levels. That is, entrepreneurial activities and their wealth creation potential vary. Therefore, we advance the notion of an entrepreneurial activity hierarchy (EAH), which suggests that certain entrepreneurial activities are better inclined to yield economic wealth and spillovers in the form of employment, human capital development (Georgen et al. 2012), institutional development, and economic development. In this hierarchy, we contend that entrepreneurial activities that centre around firm creation, or the pursuit of an identified market opportunity, will have the tendency to elicit configurations that are scalable, thereby attracting the resources that can lead to systemic wealth creation.

First, entrepreneurs who engage in the process of firm creation often implicitly have the intentions to employ others and to scale their ventures. Creating and running a formal firm takes effort and cost, which can be better justified when entrepreneurs intend the scale their ventures. In addition, firms provide the necessary legitimacy and platform for acquiring complementary resources for growing the new venture (e.g. financing, partnerships and gaining tax incentives). This is consistent with the view that the higher the degree to which entrepreneurs appeal to the collective (in addition to self-interest) in developing a new venture, the greater the likelihood that they will be successful in mobilizing resources (Van de Ven, Sapienza, and Villanueva 2007), developing networks, and adapting to changing conditions (Bryson, Wood, and Keeble 1993). In contrast, self-employment activities (in their basic form) are not scalable and are rarely a source of employment for others (Chen et al. 2017). The psychological differences between self-employment and entrepreneurship could exacerbate these effects (Wiklund et al., forthcoming), whereby entrepreneurship feeds into a critical psychological resource in terms of optimism and reliance; while self-employment affords fewer psychological feedback effects through limited wealth creation. Thus, we argue that firm-centric entrepreneurial activity would lead to greater economic wealth in society than mere self-employment.

Second, entrepreneurs who pursue opportunities that leverage their experience in industries and markets often elicit entrepreneurial configurations that are scalable (i.e. opportunity-centric entrepreneurial activity). This is because their prior knowledge will influence the quality of opportunities they choose, thereby providing them with an advantage over competitors (Hayek 1945). Opportunities that are derived from deep knowledge and experience in an industry also help signal the quality of the new venture. Therefore, opportunity-centric entrepreneurs are able to establish a greater legitimacy to access complementary resources, which would increase the performance of their venture (Ahlstrom, Bruton, and Yeh 2008).

Furthermore, entrepreneurs with this sort of prior knowledge have higher aspirations (Chivers 2017) and are more likely to strive for the betterment of self and society. Thus, they are also more likely to establish higher thresholds for their performance, meaning that they are less likely to tolerate lower performance after they establish their ventures (Gimeno et al. 1997). This tendency to establish a higher threshold for entrepreneurial performance at the outset would act as a fulcrum for creating a more effortful and scalable venture. In contrast, an individual who is unemployed before entering into entrepreneurial activity may be more focused on self-interest because they are lacking in options (Nikolaev, Boudreaux, and Palich, forthcoming), and therefore, maybe more willing to accept a lower threshold of performance because of the comparative lack of alternative employment opportunities. Thus, we expect that opportunity-centric entrepreneurs will create higher systemic wealth than ordinary self-employment entrepreneurs, who tend to be driven by the necessity to be in employment. This leads to the following hypotheses,

Hypothesis 2 (H2): There is an entrepreneurial activity hierarchy at the state level in which the:

H2a: Firm-centric entrepreneurial activity will lead to a more significant decline in absolute poverty rates than self-employment.

H2b: Opportunity-centric entrepreneurial activity will lead to a more significant decline in absolute poverty rates than self-employment.

Sample and data

To test our hypotheses, we leverage annual state-level quantitative data from the US The sample frame for this study included all 50 US states over an 18-year time period (1996–2013). This period is especially important to analyze because of the potential impact of the passage of major welfare reform in the US in 1996. A key theme from these reforms was the decentralization of welfare policy choices to the state and local levels (Ziliak 2007). Given the increased local divergence in welfare and poverty-related policies, we would expect to observe variation on poverty outcomes.

The data for this research were assembled from various archival sources. The entrepreneurial activity data were drawn from the Kauffman Index for Entrepreneurial Activity (KIEA), which is based on the Current Population Survey of the United States (c.f. Fairlie 2012; Fairlie and Chatterji 2013). The poverty and state welfare policies data were drawn from US government data sources including the Bureau of Labor Statistics, the Census Bureau, the Social Security Administration, and the Departments of Agriculture, Health and Human Services, Commerce, and Labor. Inequality data is drawn from data assembled by the Economic Policy Institute (Frank et al. 2015).

The food insecurity data come from a nationally representative survey of over 50,000 households per year in the US (Current Population Survey, CPS; Ziliak and Gundersen 2009). The US Census Bureau administers this survey as an annual supplement for the monthly CPS survey. Each household is asked to respond to a number of questions about experiences and behaviours that indicate the household's level of food insecurity. These questions include being unable to afford balanced meals, having to cut the size of meals because of too little money for food, or being hungry because of too little money for food (Coleman-Jensen et al. 2012). Other data in the analysis were drawn from the Council of State Government's database and Stats America.

Measures

Dependent variables – entrepreneurial activity

Three measures of entrepreneurial activity were used in this study (see Morelix et al. 2015). The first measure, *firm-centric entrepreneurial activity* is a measure of startup density, which means the proportion of new businesses in a state to the total population of the state (in thousands) in a state at time, t. The second measure of entrepreneurial activity, *opportunity-centric entrepreneurial activity* is a proportion of entrepreneurs in a state that is focused on exploiting an opportunity (i.e. entrepreneurs that are driven primarily by 'opportunity' as opposed to 'necessity,' Morelix et al. 2015). The third measure, *rate of new entrepreneurs* is the rate of business creation at the individual owner level (i.e. self-employment), aggregated at the state level (c.f. Kauffman index of entrepreneurial activity, Fairlie 2012; Fairlie and Chatterji 2013). This is defined as the percent of individuals (ages 20–64) who do not own a business in the first month that start a business in the following month with 15+ hours (Fairlie 2012). The microdata used to create the entrepreneurial activity index is based on the basic monthly files to the Current Population Surveys (Fairlie and Chatterji 2013). This measure of the rate of new entrepreneurs is particularly advantageous over existing measures which fail to capture the dynamic nature of entrepreneurship in terms of the time the business is created (Fairlie and Chatterji 2013).

Dependent variable – poverty

We developed a measure of absolute poverty using the US state-level measure of poverty, which captures the proportion of families in a state that are living below the US established threshold of poverty, but which tend to exclude in-kind transfers such as food stamps (Ziliak 2006). Thus, this measure of poverty accounts for the percentage of poor in thousands in a given state based on US Census Bureau's definition of poverty thresholds (Osberg 2000).

As an alternative measure to poverty, we use the proportion of households in a state that are classified as *very low food secure*. This measure of *food insecurity* has been used in prior economic research (e.g. Ziliak and Gundersen 2012) and has been shown to be highly correlated with measures of poverty.

Independent variable – inequality

Income inequality can be measured in a variety of ways (Atems and Shand, forthcoming; Beal and Astakhova 2017). Thus, we measure inequality using a composite measure of different measures, a novel approach when compared to prior literature. Using a principal components factor analysis with varimax rotation, we constructed a composite indicator of *inequality* based on six well-established measures of inequality used prior research (i.e. Gini Coefficient, Atkinson Index, Theil Entropy, Relative Mean Deviation, Top 1% Income Share, and Top 10% Income Share). These six measures are highly correlated (as shown in correlation matrix in Table I), and they loaded into a single factor of eigenvalue 5.07, with a very high interitem reliability coefficient (Cronbach alpha, standardized) of 0.96. This single factor, which we used in our regressions, accounted for 0.85 proportion of the total variance in the original six variables. In order to avoid potential problems of generated regressor bias, we use the Bartlett method to generate the factor scores for poverty. This method tends to yield less accurate though unbiased factors compared with factor scores obtained with the regression method (Westphal and Stern 2007). Our results proved robust using either the Bartlett or regression method.

Control variables

We include some control variables to account for alternative explanations in our model. We controlled for state antipoverty policies such as state earned income tax credit (EITC). Antipoverty public policies such as the Earned Income Tax Credit (EITC) are intended to reduce the incidence of poverty among people with low or no incomes by encouraging them to work. We suspect that while the EITC is intended to encourage work, especially among needy families, it could potentially undermine entrepreneurial activity. The EITC maximum credit (which is a measure of the generosity of the EITC for each state) is calculated for a family with two dependents, and it includes both the federal and state credits. Results are consistent when we used EITC maximum credit for a family of one dependent. Consistent with the argument that wage levels also affect entrepreneurial activity (Banerjee and Newman 1994), we controlled for the minimum wage in each state. We use the labour economics definition of minimum wage, which is the higher of the federal or state minimum wage, measured in US dollars (Neumark and Wascher 2000). In our main analysis, we reported models that only included the minimum wage control measures but not the EITC credit, since the two were highly correlated ($r= 0.76$). The results are not sensitive to excluding the EITC from the model. These alternative results are available from the authors.

We control for the influence of political heterogeneity in the state legislature and the political affiliation of the governor. These controls help capture the variance and dynamics of political differences across states. Finally, we controlled for year effects using annual *year dummies*. In some models, we also include *state dummies* to control for state fixed effects, which may not be captured by other control variables. In many cases, we specified models with state fixed effects alongside models without state fixed effects to check for consistency of our estimates.

In the post-hoc analysis of the effects of EITC on entrepreneurial activity, we included public policy and labour market controls, which could have a bearing on specifications including the EITC. First, we control for the effect of welfare policies (i.e. the Aid to Families with Dependent Children benefit or its replacement, the Temporary Aid to Need Families benefit, AFDC-TANF) for a three-person family. Second, we control for the state unemployment rate. Third, we control for college-educated rate in the state, which determines the proportion of state that has a college education. Fourth, we control for the gross state product. In addition, we controlled for year effects and state fixed effects.

Empirical analyses

In selecting a model for our empirical analyses, we considered the need to account for multiple observations for each state in our sample, as well as accounting for a high degree of autocorrelation between one year in our period and the previous year (Marquis and Huang 2009). Our model also needs to account for state-specific factors that we are unable to assess but that can also affect growth in the outcome variables of interest (Khaire 2010). One fixed effects option for this sort of scenario is the Feasible Generalized Least Squares method (FGLS, i.e. xtgls in STATA). Since our dataset has 50 panels (N) and 18 time periods (T), we ruled out using the FGLS (xtgls). Beck and Katz (1995) demonstrate that when $T < N$, FGLS tends to produce extremely overconfident standard errors in finite sample analyses such as this study's.

Guided by prior literature, we selected the Ordinary Least Squares (OLS) regression with panel-corrected standard errors (PCSE, xtpcse in STATA) (Blackwell 2005). This technique employs the Prais-Winston regression with a panel-specific autoregressive disturbance structure (PCSE, xtpcse command in STATA). Specifically, the approach entails a Generalized Least Squares (GLS) estimator corrected for first-order serially correlated residuals that are panel specific (Marquis and Huang 2009). Previous tests of this model show that it performs well, even under conditions of high heteroscedasticity and contemporaneous correlation of error terms (Beck and Katz 1995); which was an issue of concern in our model specifications. We use a one-year lag between our independent and dependent variables because we expect the effects of inequality would take some time to manifest into entrepreneurial activity. Similarly, we expect a similar lag between entrepreneurial activity and poverty alleviation because the time interval between entrepreneurs starting their businesses and generating impact in society is likely to take at least one year. Nevertheless, in robustness checks, we considered two lags between the independent and dependent variables. The results using an additional lag are very consistent with the results using one-year lag.

In addition to our primary empirical specifications, we also conducted some tests to check for reverse causality in our models. Though we theorized that inequality will have a positive impact on entrepreneurial activity, some scholars have argued that entrepreneurial activity can lead to inequality (e.g. Atems and Shand, forthcoming). Therefore, this reverse causality was checked. Similarly, we advanced the hypothesis that entrepreneurial activity will alleviate poverty and that there is a hierarchy in the effects of entrepreneurial activity on poverty alleviation. We need to examine the possibility that absolute poverty could lead to more entrepreneurial activity. Thus, we used the Granger causality method to check for reverse causality.

Results

Main results

Table 1 includes the descriptive statistics and the correlation matrix for all the variables in this study. The average state in a given year in our study had 1.73 *firm-centric entrepreneurs* (1.73 new firms per 1000 people in the state), 0.80 *opportunity-centric entrepreneurs* (80% of entrepreneurial activity that is focused on opportunity) and a 0.003 *rate of new entrepreneurs*. Correlations greater than or equal to the absolute value of 0.07 and 0.1 are statistically significant at ($p < 0.05$) and ($p < 0.01$) levels, respectively. Interestingly, while *firm-centric entrepreneurial activity* is highly correlated with *opportunity-centric entrepreneurial activity* ($r = 0.30$) and *rate of new entrepreneurs* ($r = 0.39$); *opportunity-centric entrepreneurial activity* and *rate of entrepreneurs* are scarcely correlated with each other ($r = 0.00$). As indicated in the previous discussion of the factor analysis (and in the shaded area of Table 1), all measures of inequality used in developing the factor variable are highly correlated with each other, and with the factor variable ($0.60 < r < 0.98$).

The study's primary regressions are presented in Tables 2–4. Table 2 shows the results of how *inequality* influences three measures of entrepreneurial activity. For each measure of entrepreneurial activity, we report a model that does not include state fixed effects and a model that includes state fixed effects to check for the sensitivity of our results to unobservable state-level factors. Hypothesis 1 predicts that states with higher levels of inequality will subsequently have higher rates of entrepreneurial activity. Models 1 and 2 test this hypothesis relative to the *firm-centric entrepreneurial activity*. Models 1 and 2 are identical, with the exception that model 2 includes state fixed effects (in addition to the explanatory variable, prior entrepreneurial activity, control variables, and year fixed effects contained in model 1). Both models support hypothesis 1 and indicate that the coefficient of *inequality* relative to *firm-centric entrepreneurial activity* is positive and statistically significant at the ($p < 0.01$) level. The economic significance is such that a 1-standard deviation increase in inequality gives rise to a 0.5% (Model 1) to 2.7% (Model 2) increase in firm-centric entrepreneurial activity relative to the average level over the sample. Models 3 and 4, shown in Table 2, test hypothesis 1 based on the effect of *inequality* on *opportunity-centric entrepreneurial activity*. Similar to models 1 and 2, models 3 and 4 are identical except for the inclusion of state fixed effects in model 4. The coefficient of *inequality* in model 3 is negative and insignificant (contrary to our predictions). However, the coefficient of *inequality* in model 4, as predicted in positive and statistically significant ($p < 0.01$), and the economic significance is such that a 1-standard deviation increase in *inequality* gives rise to a 1.7% increase in *opportunity-centric entrepreneurial activity* relative to the average level over the sample. Finally, models 5 and 6 report the results of the tests of hypothesis 1 relative to the effect of *inequality* on the *rate of new entrepreneurs* in the state. Whereas the coefficient of *inequality* in model 5 (which does not include

Table 1. Summary statistics and bivariate correlations among the study variables.

	1	2	3	4	5	6	7	8	9	10	11	12	13	14	15	16	17	18	19	20
1. Firm-Centric Entrepreneurs	1.00																			
2. Opportunity-Centric Entre.	0.30	1.00																		
3. Rate of New Entrepreneurs	0.39	0.00	1.00																	
4. Poverty Rate	−0.32	−0.22	0.24	1.00																
5. Food Insecurity	−0.36	−0.29	0.32	0.51	1.00															
6. Inequality	0.15	−0.15	0.04	0.02	0.07	1.00														
7. Gini Coefficient	0.07	−0.14	0.31	0.32	0.36	0.71	1.00													
8. Relative Mean Deviation	0.05	−0.22	0.19	0.16	0.23	0.94	0.81	1.00												
9. Theil Entropy	0.20	−0.10	0.01	−0.05	0.02	0.97	0.62	0.88	1.00											
10. Atkinson Index	0.17	−0.12	0.01	−0.08	−0.03	0.97	0.61	0.90	0.97	1.00										
11. Top 10% Income Share	0.03	−0.23	−0.07	0.11	0.12	0.91	0.63	0.81	0.83	0.83	1.00									
12. Top 1% Income Share	0.21	−0.09	−0.02	−0.04	0.00	0.96	0.64	0.83	0.92	0.91	0.93	1.00								
13. ln (EITC max. credit)	−0.40	−0.33	−0.05	0.05	0.36	0.29	0.28	0.40	0.23	0.31	0.26	0.19	1.00							
14. ln (AFDCTANF benefit)	−0.12	−0.18	0.09	−0.31	0.08	0.18	0.10	0.26	0.17	0.23	0.07	0.10	0.55	1.00						
15. Minimum Wage	−0.43	−0.35	0.05	0.13	0.54	0.30	0.31	0.45	0.24	0.28	0.29	0.19	0.76	0.62	1.00					
16. Governor is Democrat	−0.07	−0.08	−0.07	−0.07	0.03	−0.05	−0.10	−0.07	−0.07	−0.04	0.00	−0.04	0.11	0.09	0.12	1.00				
17. Legislative Diversity	0.00	0.04	0.09	0.02	0.04	0.02	0.05	0.02	−0.02	0.01	0.07	0.03	−0.12	−0.21	−0.10	0.12	1.00			
18. Unemployment Rate	−0.50	−0.48	0.08	0.48	0.58	0.12	0.28	0.30	0.05	0.04	0.21	0.01	0.45	0.26	0.62	0.06	0.02	1.00		
19. Gross State prod./capita	−0.16	−0.15	−0.07	0.07	0.01	0.47	0.26	0.51	0.49	0.54	0.30	0.36	0.53	0.39	0.48	0.12	−0.06	0.26	1.00	
20. College Educated Rate	0.03	−0.18	−0.10	−0.28	−0.17	0.43	0.07	0.42	0.45	0.52	0.33	0.32	0.55	0.51	0.42	0.09	−0.06	0.09	0.70	1.00
Mean	1.73	0.80	0.003	0.12	0.04	0.00	0.59	0.83	0.81	0.28	43.47	17.34	8.44	6.68	6.10	0.44	0.45	5.62	0.04	0.17
S.D.	0.46	0.06	0.0008	0.03	0.01	1.00	0.04	0.05	0.20	0.04	4.88	4.40	0.17	0.22	1.09	0.50	0.07	2.02	0.02	0.04
Min	0.74	0.56	0.00	0.05	0.01	−1.64	0.52	0.74	0.44	0.21	33.40	9.70	8.18	6.07	4.25	0.00	0.16	2.30	0.02	0.09
Max	3.39	0.95	0.01	0.25	0.08	5.81	0.76	1.12	2.58	0.53	62.26	36.04	8.93	7.35	9.19	1.00	0.50	13.80	0.18	0.34

Note: All bivariate correlations greater than or equals to the absolute value of 0.07 and 0.1 are significant at the 5% and 1% levels, respectively. All tests are two-tailed. Shaded area indicates the bivariate correlations between different inequality measures (including their correlations with the composite measure of inequality).

Table 2. Effects of income inequality on entrepreneurial activity.

	Model 1	Model 2	Model 3	Model 4	Model 5	Model 6
	Firm-Centric $_{(t+1)}$		Opportunity-Centric $_{(t+1)}$		Rate of New Entre $_{(t+1)}$	
Inequality	**0.00912****	**0.04634****	−0.00036	**0.01362****	**0.00002+**	0.00005
	[0.00283]	**[0.01531]**	[0.00135]	**[0.00462]**	**[0.00001]**	[0.00004]
Firm-Centric Entrepreneurs$_{(t)}$	0.95991***	0.66192***				
	[0.02435]	[0.07681]				
Opportunity-Centric Entrepreneurs $_{(t)}$			0.71044***	0.60001***		
			[0.05555]	[0.06755]		
Rate of New Entrepreneurs $_{(t)}$					0.89468***	0.64125***
					[0.02846]	[0.06353]
Minimum Wage	−0.00597	**−0.01924***	**−0.00448+**	0.00048	0.00000	0.00004
	[0.00521]	**[0.00751]**	**[0.00238]**	[0.00465]	[0.00002]	[0.00003]
Governor is Democrat	0.00317	0.00818	−0.00019	−0.00396	−0.00001	0.00001
	[0.00536]	[0.00580]	[0.00358]	[0.00460]	[0.00002]	[0.00003]
Legislative Diversity	−0.02865	−0.14625	−0.02400	0.01013	−0.00016	0.00016
	[0.04122]	[0.10437]	[0.03026]	[0.05343]	[0.00019]	[0.00045]
Constant	0.12149**	0.77302***	0.28369***	0.29191***	0.00032+	0.00091*
	[0.04588]	[0.15853]	[0.05248]	[0.07026]	[0.00019]	[0.00039]
Year Dummies	YES	YES	YES	YES	YES	YES
State Dummies	NO	YES	NO	YES	NO	YES
Observations	784	784	735	735	735	735
R-squared	0.985	0.987	0.971	0.974	0.932	0.945
Number of state	49	49	49	49	49	49
Chi-squared	159465***	1.940e+07***	6452***	774207***	2062***	1.707e+06***

Note: The table reports parameter coefficient estimates. Panel-corrected standard errors are in parentheses. *** $p < 0.001$, ** $p < 0.01$, * $p < 0.05$, + $p < 0.1$ indicate significance, using two-tailed tests.

state fixed effects) is positive and marginally significant ($p < 0.1$), it still positive but insignificant in model 6 (a model which includes state fixed effects). The economic significance in model 5 is such that a 1-standard deviation increase in inequality gives rise to a 0.7% increase in the *rate of new entrepreneurs* in the state relative to the average level over the sample.

Tables 3 and 4 show the results of the regressions test of hypothesis 2a and 2b, respectively. Hypothesis 2 suggests a hierarchy wherein *firm-centric entrepreneurial activity* (H2a) and *opportunity-centric entrepreneurial activity* (2b) will have a higher impact than *self-employment rates* on poverty alleviation. To assess this hypothesis, we compare the coefficients of entrepreneurial activity in model 7 and model 11, and between model 8 and model 12, respectively. We find statistical support for hypothesis 2a. The coefficient of *firm-centric entrepreneurs* when regressed on poverty rates is negative and statistically significant in models 7 (p <0.01) and 8 (p <0.05), where the economic significance is such that a 1-standard deviation increase in firm-centric entrepreneurs gives rise to a 1.0% to 4.6% reduction in poverty in models 8 and 9, respectively. The coefficient of *the rate of new entrepreneurs* (a measure of *self-employment*) is not significant in Model 11, but positive and statistically significant in Model 12 (p <0.05), whereby a 1-standard deviation increase in *the rate of new entrepreneurs* gives rise to a 1.86% increase in poverty. Although this confirms our reasoning that *firm-centric entrepreneurial activity* will alleviate poverty at a greater rate than *self-employment rates*, we are surprised that controlling for unobservable factors model 12 shows a positive effect of *rate of new entrepreneurs* on *poverty*. That is, *self-employment rates* in a state could actually contribute to *poverty*. We return to this observation in our robustness tests using *food insecurity* as an alternative measure of poverty.

In the entrepreneurial activity hierarchy we proposed, we also posited that *opportunity-centric entrepreneurial activity* will have a greater impact on poverty alleviation that *self-employment*. We directly assess this hypothesis by considering the direction and statistical significance of *opportunity-centric entrepreneurs* in model 9 and 10. Recall that this measure is a proportional measure which represents the share of entrepreneurial activity in a state at a given time period that is

Table 3. The effects of entrepreneurial activity on poverty alleviation.

	Model 7	Model 8	Model 9	Model 10	Model 11	Model 12
	Poverty $_{(t+1)}$	Poverty $_{(t+1)}$	Poverty $_{(t+1)}$	Poverty $_{(t+1)}$	Poverty $_{(t+1)}$	Poverty $_{(t+1)}$
Firm-Centric Entrepreneurs $_{(t)}$	**−0.00272****	**−0.01191***				
	[0.00102]	**[0.00488]**				
Opportunity-Centric Entrepreneurs $_{(t)}$			−0.00532	**−0.02029***		
			[0.00709]	**[0.00858]**		
Rate of New Entrepreneurs $_{(t)}$					−0.10145	**2.78984***
					[0.49559]	**[1.13626]**
Poverty $_{(t)}$	0.89259***	0.30819***	0.92288***	0.33391***	0.92516***	0.32295***
	[0.02434]	[0.07148]	[0.02253]	[0.07866]	[0.02390]	[0.07987]
Minimum Wage	−0.00240**	−0.00163	−0.00218***	−0.00101	−0.00207**	−0.00122
	[0.00086]	[0.00104]	[0.00063]	[0.00092]	[0.00064]	[0.00094]
Governor is Democrat	−0.00019	−0.00133	−0.00009	−0.00225+	−0.00007	−0.00204
	[0.00102]	[0.00119]	[0.00106]	[0.00124]	[0.00110]	[0.00128]
Legislative Diversity	0.00376	−0.02155	0.00163	−0.04082*	0.00125	−0.04212*
	[0.00902]	[0.01629]	[0.00852]	[0.01702]	[0.00884]	[0.01773]
Constant	0.02646**	0.15278***	0.03041***	0.16254***	0.02573***	0.14159***
	[0.00888]	[0.02035]	[0.00908]	[0.01998]	[0.00747]	[0.01889]
Year Dummies	YES	YES	YES	YES	YES	YES
State Dummies	NO	YES	NO	YES	NO	YES
Observations	784	784	686	686	686	686
R-squared	0.943	0.948	0.954	0.963	0.953	0.961
Number of state	49	49	49	49	49	49
Chi-squared	13077***	2.830e+08***	15093***	2.035e+06***	15507***	7.864e+06***

Note: The table reports parameter coefficient estimates. Panel-corrected standard errors are in parentheses. *** $p < 0.001$, ** $p < 0.01$, * $p < 0.05$, + $p < 0.1$ indicate significance, using two-tailed tests.

Table 4. Effect of entrepreneurial activity on food insecurity.

	Dependent Variable (DV): Food Insecurity $_{(t+1)}$					
	Model 13	Model 14	Model 15	Model 16	Model 17	Model 18
Firm-Centric Entrepreneurs $_{(t)}$	**−0.00095+**	**−0.00226+**				
	[0.00049]	**[0.00128]**				
Opportunity-Centric Entrepreneurs $_{(t)}$			**−0.00625***	**−0.00889***		
			[0.00285]	**[0.00380]**		
Rate of New Entrepreneurs $_{(t)}$					**0.42590+**	0.65933
					[0.25314]	[0.43768]
Food Insecurity $_{(t)}$	0.85203***	0.62682***	0.84570***	0.62371***	0.83798***	0.61987***
	[0.04798]	[0.08540]	[0.04934]	[0.08682]	[0.05307]	[0.08794]
Minimum Wage	0.00049	0.00203**	0.00032	0.00213***	0.00035	0.00209***
	[0.00062]	[0.00063]	[0.00062]	[0.00064]	[0.00063]	[0.00063]
Governor is Democrat	−0.00067+	−0.00019	−0.00062	−0.00033	−0.00046	−0.00017
	[0.00040]	[0.00041]	[0.00039]	[0.00044]	[0.00039]	[0.00042]
Legislative Diversity	0.00431	−0.00061	0.00481	0.00015	0.00382	−0.00134
	[0.00418]	[0.00625]	[0.00425]	[0.00650]	[0.00421]	[0.00643]
Constant	0.00584	0.01396+	0.01072+	0.01716*	0.00522	0.00929
	[0.00522]	[0.00768]	[0.00577]	[0.00782]	[0.00522]	[0.00779]
Year Dummies	YES	YES	YES	YES	YES	YES
State Dummies	NO	YES	NO	YES	NO	YES
Observations	539	539	539	539	539	539
R-squared	0.925	0.939	0.925	0.940	0.923	0.939
Number of state	49	49	49	49	49	49
Chi-squared	60754***	475237***	82867***	1.392e+06***	68335***	1.881e+06***

Note: The table reports parameter coefficient estimates. Panel-corrected standard errors are in parentheses. *** $p < 0.001$, ** $p < 0.01$, * $p < 0.05$, + $p < 0.1$ indicate significance, using two-tailed tests.

focused on the pursuit of opportunity. Although the coefficient of *opportunity-centric entrepreneurs* is negative, as hypothesized, in model 9; it is not statistically significant. However, when controlling for state fixed-effects in model 10, the coefficient was still negative but now significant ($p< 0.05$), whereby a 1-standard deviation increase in *the rate of new entrepreneurs* yielded a 1.0% reduction in poverty. Thus, the data indicate preliminary statistical support for hypothesis 2b regarding poverty reduction. We explore this further in the robustness tests documented in Table 4, where we use food insecurity in the states as an alternative dependent variable for poverty. As shown in Table 1, poverty rates are highly correlated to food insecurity rates (r =0.51).

The results in Table 4 lend more support to hypotheses 2a and 2b. For hypothesis 2a, the coefficient of *firm-centric entrepreneurs* in model 13 is negative, and marginally significant ($p < 0.1$) when compared to the coefficient of *the rate of new entrepreneurs* in model 17, which is positive and marginally significant ($p < 0.1$). Furthermore, after controlling for state fixed effects, the coefficient of the *firm-centric entrepreneurs* (as shown in model 14) is negative and marginally significant ($p< 0.1$) when compared to the coefficient of *self-employment* in model 18, which is positive and not significant. For hypothesis 2b, we find full support since the coefficient of *opportunity-centric entrepreneurs* is negative and statistically significant ($p < 0.5$) in both models 15 and 16 of Table 4.

Granger causality results

The results of the Granger causality tests are reported in Tables 5 and 6 below. As indicated previously, we checked for the possibility that poverty will directly lead to entrepreneurial activity of different forms. Table 5 presents the results of regressions with different forms of entrepreneurial activity as the dependent variable, and lagged values of these forms of entrepreneurial activity, as well as measures of poverty and food insecurity on the right-hand side of the equation. Since the *poverty* was not significant in models 19, 20 and 21, we were able to rule out reverse causality between poverty and different forms of entrepreneurial activity. This finding is consistent with the

Table 5. Granger causality tests of entrepreneurial activity.

	Model 19	Model 20	Model 21	Model 22	Model 23	Model 24
	Firm-Centric $_{(t+1)}$	Opportunity-Centric $_{(t+1)}$	Rate of New Entre $_{(t+1)}$	Firm-Centric $_{(t+1)}$	Opportunity-Centric $_{(t+1)}$	Rate of New Entre $_{(t+1)}$
Firm-Centric Entrepreneurs $_{(t)}$	0.94383***			0.88967***		
	[0.04486]			[0.05987]		
Opportunity-Centric Entrepreneurs $_{(t)}$		0.72305***			0.65754***	
		[0.05880]			[0.06672]	
Rate of New Entrepreneurs $_{(t)}$			0.87574***			0.89168***
			[0.02937]			[0.03577]
Poverty $_{(t)}$	0.04202	−0.05795	0.00038			
	[0.26064]	[0.04653]	[0.00045]			
Food Insecurity $_{(t)}$				−4.32142**	−0.30294	0.00049
				[1.67763]	[0.19133]	[0.00131]
Constant	0.05175	0.22687***	0.00030**	0.33658**	0.27956***	0.00030**
	[0.08010]	[0.04767]	[0.00010]	[0.11063]	[0.05657]	[0.00011]
Observations	800	750	750	550	600	600
R-squared	0.937	0.957	0.928	0.927	0.966	0.934
Number of state	50	50	50	50	50	50
Chi-squared	452.1***	154.4***	903.7***	227.8***	130.0***	621.6***

Note: The table reports parameter coefficient estimates. Panel-corrected standard errors are in parentheses. *** $p < 0.001$, ** $p < 0.01$, * $p < 0.05$, + $p < 0.1$ indicate significance, using two-tailed tests.

view that *relative* rather than absolute poverty is more important is determining entrepreneurial activity in societies (Banerjee and Newman 1994) but contrary to the findings in Atems and Shand (forthcoming). For robustness, we check the *food insecurity* measures as well. The results in models 23–24 indicate that *food insecurity* measures are insignificant in predicting *opportunity-centric entrepreneurial activity* and *rate of new entrepreneurs*. However, we did find a negative and statistically significant predicting relationship between *food insecurity* and *firm-centric entrepreneurs* in a state ($p < 0.01$). In essence, this suggests that extremely high rates of food insecurity (or poverty) may substantially reduce the tendency for people to pursue *firm-centric entrepreneurial activity*, which in turn reinforces food insecurity. This cycle has been identified in prior literature as the poverty trap (Banerjee and Newman 1994) and may have implications for poverty eradication.

Table 6 reports the results of Granger causality tests where inequality is the dependent variable and lagged forms of inequality and different forms of entrepreneurial activity are included as the right-hand side predictor variables. We found no evidence that *firm-centric entrepreneurial activity* reverse causes inequality or that self-employment reverse causes inequality. However, the tests indicate that *opportunity-centric entrepreneurs* has a negative and statistically significant effect on inequality in the next time period ($p < 0.01$), though this effect disappears after two time periods, as shown in model 28 of Table 6. This observation is not an issue with our model because it does not disprove the original thesis that inequality leads to entrepreneurial activity. However, it does shed some light on the earlier weak support for the hypothesis that inequality will lead to *opportunity-centric entrepreneurial activity*.

Post-hoc analysis and robustness checks

In post-hoc checks, we assess the possibility that antipoverty policy will have an impact on entrepreneurial activity, especially *firm-centric* and *opportunity-centric* types of activity. Specifically, we evaluate the potential that EITC discourages entrepreneurial activity. The results reported in Appendix A1 provide initial evidence that EITC discourages entrepreneurial activity, though the statistical significance is greater for the *firm-centric entrepreneurial activity* than for the *opportunity-centric activity*.

Table 6. Granger causality tests with inequality as the dependent variable.

	Model 25	Model 26	Model 27	Model 28	Model 29	Model 30
	Inequality $_{(t+1)}$	Inequality $_{(t+2)}$	Inequality $_{(t+1)}$	Inequality $_{(t+2)}$	Inequality $_{(t+1)}$	Inequality $_{(t+2)}$
Inequality $_{(t+1)}$		1.16523***		1.14091***		1.14583***
		[0.18030]		[0.20048]		[0.20026]
Inequality $_{(t)}$	0.94281***	−0.20851	0.94428***	−0.20789	0.94831***	−0.21180
	[0.05541]	[0.18391]	[0.05218]	[0.20160]	[0.05258]	[0.20168]
Firm-Centric Entrepreneurs $_{(t)}$	0.02156	−0.07816				
	[0.10215]	[0.08417]				
Opportunity-Centric Entrepreneurs $_{(t)}$			**−1.56503****	−0.24968		
			[0.58373]	[0.49006]		
Rate of New Entrepreneurs $_{(t)}$					−9.88966	−15.19449
					[27.87295]	[27.20107]
Constant	0.06303	0.22354	1.35745**	0.27986	0.12060	0.12526
	[0.18399]	[0.15761]	[0.47681]	[0.39935]	[0.13859]	[0.13052]
Observations	800	750	700	650	700	650
R-squared	0.815	0.853	0.824	0.846	0.818	0.845
Number of state	50	50	50	50	50	50
Chi-squared	331.6***	462.2***	348.6***	356.5***	342.9***	385.5***

Note: The table reports parameter coefficient estimates. Panel-corrected standard errors are in parentheses. *** $p < 0.001$, ** $p < 0.01$, * $p < 0.05$, + $p < 0.1$ indicate significance, using two-tailed tests.

In the course of our empirical checks, we considered many alternative models with different right-hand-side variables and different variable definitions. These checks include, but are not limited to, controls for differences in state regulation, subsets of different time periods, among other things. Moreover, we considered different clustering of standard errors and other econometric specifications including a two-year lag of the dependent variables. We did not find other specifications that suggested any insignificance or reversal of the major findings reported above. Alternative specifications are available on request from the authors.

Future research

Our study suggests some important directions for management and organizational research. In particular, we show that scholars should account for differences between the form and focus of entrepreneurial activity when investigating different research questions. In addition, we believe that these initial insights suggest some useful avenues for future research that aims to understand how economic and social structure shape egotistic and ethical incentives to undertake entrepreneurial action. These findings also hold important implications for public policy. For example, the results seem to underscore the need for public policymakers to consider a more targeted and nuanced approach towards encouraging entrepreneurial activity, with a view towards the interplay between inequality and poverty and entrepreneurial activity.

We have introduced a few different types of entrepreneurial activity and a few different types of poverty. Both poverty and entrepreneurship are themselves complicated and multifaceted concepts, and there are other types of breakdowns of these concepts through which links could be explored in other work. Our analyses here are somewhat coarse, partly necessitated by the fact that we introduced a new theoretical look under the surface at the links between different types of entrepreneurship and poverty, and provided a new empirical analysis. We hope further research will uncover other insights both theoretically and empirically that link different elements of entrepreneurship to different elements of poverty.

While our theory and evidence focused on the economic motives linking inequality and entrepreneurship, further research on different types of entrepreneurship and different types of poverty could instead focus on the psychological side of the equation. A recent discussion of the connection between psychology and entrepreneurship (Wiklund et al., forthcoming) offers insights as to how different aspects of fulfilment, reliance, and optimism might be at play in some contexts, there is certainly scope for discouragement to be a dominant factor in other institutional settings. How and when these different psychological forces work is beyond the scope of our paper but could prove to be insightful for understanding the link between poverty and entrepreneurship in different regional settings.

While our evidence is focused on the US, where there is significant inequality across states and over time (Beal and Astakhova 2017), further research could likewise examine other countries, as well as policy initiatives that affect poverty, and the intersection of inequality and poverty and entrepreneurial activity with regard to institutional considerations (Cullen, Johnson, and Parboteeah 2014; Nam et al. 2014; Yu et al. 2014). Countries with numerous policy initiatives toward entrepreneurship such as in China (Ahlstrom and Ding 2014) can be of particular interest with respect to this research domain (Cumming et al. 2015). Finally, our evidence is consistent with the view that public policy efforts directed toward entrepreneurial activity should not be made separately from public policy efforts directed toward poverty, as these initiatives will affect one another in the real economy, even in advanced nations such as the US

Conclusion

This study has provided theory and evidence that income inequality actually has the potential to cause additional entrepreneurial activity in a country in the form of *firm-centric* and *opportunity-centric* actions. In addition, we provided supporting theory and evidence that entrepreneurial activity focused on firms and opportunities are generally more productive and effective in poverty alleviation in society when compared to self-employment, consistent with our entrepreneurial activity hierarchy (EAH) proposition (cf. Chen, Chang, and Bruton 2017). This lends credence to the potential spillover effects of entrepreneurial activity based on high aspirations (Chivers 2017). Furthermore, the evidence provided is consistent with the view that self-employment (at its early stages) may not be a suitable proxy for understanding entrepreneurial activity, especially that with more growth potential (Bruton, Ahlstrom, and Obloj 2008; Haltiwanger, Jarmin, and Miranda 2013).To our knowledge, our study is one of the first studies to take a deeper look at the complex relationship between inequality and entrepreneurial activity, and in conjunction with the relationship between entrepreneurial activity and absolute poverty alleviation. Thus, we overcome key limitations in prior empirical work (e.g. Atems and Shand, forthcoming; Nikolaev, Boudreaux, and Palich, forthcoming) by offering a more granular analysis, which delineates the causal links between the different concepts of entrepreneurship and poverty.

Moreover, beyond establishing the causal links between entrepreneurship and poverty reduction, this paper has further demonstrated the role of anti-poverty policy on entrepreneurship rates. Specifically, the findings indicate that EITC anti-poverty policy actually reduces incentives for entrepreneurial activity, especially the type of entrepreneurial activity that alleviates poverty. Though much previous entrepreneurship research has acknowledged the direct role of public policy efforts aimed at encouraging entrepreneurship and better understanding job growth (e.g. Benzing, Chu, and Kara 2009; Haltiwanger 2015), the current study adds to the literature by providing initial evidence of the indirect role of anti-poverty policy and related measures on entrepreneurial activity and the subsequent effects on entrepreneurship on poverty reduction.

Notes

1. We thank a reviewer for highlighting this important rationale.
2. Though we argue that entrepreneurial activity alleviates absolute poverty, we do not, a priori, assume that entrepreneurial activity can directly influence inequality. Indeed, it may be far-fetched to assume that entrepreneurs are capable of directly redistributing wealth in free-market societies.

Acknowledgments

All authors contributed equally to this research. We owe thanks to the Editors Steven Si, David Ahlstrom, John Cullen, and Jiang Wei, as well as three anonymous reviewers, for very helpful comments and suggestions. Also, we owe thanks to the seminar participants at the Academy of Management, British Academy of Management, Strategic Management Society, and the Law and Entrepreneurship Retreat at the University of Alabama. Douglas Cumming and Sofia Johan owe thanks to the Social Sciences and Humanities Research Council of Canada for Financial Support. The authors also thank the University of Kentucky Poverty Research Center for access to some of the data used in this research.

Disclosure statement

No potential conflict of interest was reported by the authors.

References

Ahlstrom, D. 2010. "Innovation and Growth: How Business Contributes to Society." *Academy of Management Perspectives* 24: 11–24.

Ahlstrom, D., G.D. Bruton, and K.S. Yeh. 2008. "Private Firms in China: Building Legitimacy in an Emerging Economy." *Journal Of World Business* 43 (4): 385-399. doi:10.1016/j.jwb.2008.03.001.

Ahlstrom, D., and Z. Ding. 2014. "Entrepreneurship in China: An Overview." *International Small Business Journal* 32 (6): 610–618. doi:10.1177/0266242613517913.

Al-Dajani, H., S. Carter, E. Shaw, and S. Marlow. 2015. "Entrepreneurship among the Displaced and Dispossessed: Exploring the Limits of Emancipatory Entrepreneuring." *British Journal of Management* 26: 713–730. doi:10.1111/1467-8551.12119.

Atems, B., and G. Shand. Forthcoming. "An Empirical Analysis of the Relationship between Entrepreneurship and Income Inequality." *Small Business Economics*.

Banerjee, A. V., and A. F. Newman. 1994. "Poverty, Incentives, and Development." *American Economic Review: Paper and Proceedings* 842: 211–215.

Baumol, W. J. 1967. "Macroeconomics of Unbalanced Growth: The Anatomy of Urban Crisis." *American Economic Review* 573: 41–426.

Baumol, W. J. 1990. "Entrepreneurship: Productive, Unproductive, and Destructive." *Journal of Political Economy* 98: 893–921. doi:10.1086/261712.

Baumol, W. J., R. E. Litan, and C. J. Schramm. 2007. *Good Capitalism, Bad Capitalism, and the Economics of Growth and Prosperity*. New Haven, CT: Yale University Press.

Beal, B. D., and M. Astakhova. 2017. "Management and Income Inequality: A Review and Conceptual Framework." *Journal of Business Ethics* 142: 1–23. doi:10.1007/s10551-015-2762-6.

Beck, N., and J. N. Katz. 1995. "What to Do and Not to Do with Time-series Cross-section Data." *American Political Science Review* 893: 634–647. doi:10.2307/2082979.

Benzing, C., H. M. Chu, and O. Kara. 2009. "Entrepreneurs in Turkey: A Factor Analysis of Motivations, Success Factors, and Problems." *Journal of Small Business Management* 47 (1): 58–91. doi:10.1111/jsbm.2009.47.issue-1.

Blackwell, J. L. 2005. "Estimation and Testing of Fixed-effect Panel-data Systems." *Stata Journal* 52: 202–207. Accessed 8 February 2013. http://www.stata-journal.com/sjpdf.html?articlenum=st0084

Bradley, S., J. S. McMullen, K. Artz, and E. M. Simiyu. 2012. "Capital Is Not Enough: Innovation in Developing Economies." *Journal of Management Studies* 49: 684–717. doi:10.1111/joms.2012.49.issue-4.

Brenner, R. 1987. "National Policy and Entrepreneurship: The Statesman's Dilemma." *Journal of Business Venturing* 2: 95–101. doi:10.1016/0883-9026(87)90001-2.

Bruton, G. D., D. Ahlstrom, and K. Obloj. 2008. "Entrepreneurship in Emerging Economies: Where are We Today and Where Should the Research Go in the Future." *Entrepreneurship Theory and Practice* 32 (1): 1–14. doi:10.1111/j.1540-6520.2007.00213.x.

Bruton, G. D., D. Ahlstrom, and S. Si. 2015. "Entrepreneurship, Poverty, and Asia: Moving beyond Subsistence Entrepreneurship." *Asia Pacific Journal of Management* 32: 1–22. doi:10.1007/s10490-014-9404-x.

Bryson, J., P. Wood, and D. Keeble. 1993. "Business Networks, Small Firm Flexibility and Regional Development in UK Business Services." *Entrepreneurship & Regional Development* 5: 265–278. doi:10.1080/08985629300000016.

Burns, S. K. 2012. *Was There a Race to the Bottom after Welfare Reform?* University of Kentucky Center for Poverty Research Discussion Paper Series, DP 2012–04. Accessed 27 December 2012. http://www.ukcpr.org/Publications/DP%202012%20-%2004.pdf

Chen, J., Chang, A,Y., Bruton, G. D. 2017. Microfinance: Where are we today and where should the research go in the future? International Small Business Journal: Researching Entrepreneurship, 35(7): 793–802

Chivers, D. 2017. "Success, Survive or Escape? Aspirations and Poverty Traps." *Journal of Economic Behavior & Organization* 143: 116–132. doi:10.1016/j.jebo.2017.09.018.

Coleman-Jensen, A., M. Nord, M. Andrews, and S. Carlson 2012. Household Food Security in The United States in 2011. United States Department of Agriculture Economic Research Report Number 141.

Cullen, J., J. Johnson, and K. Parboteeah. 2014. "National Rates of Opportunity Entrepreneurship Activity: Insights from Institutional Anomie Theory." *Entrepreneurship Theory and Practice* 38: 775–806. doi:10.1111/etap.2014.38.issue-4.

Cumming, D., W. Hou, E. Lee, and M. Firth, Eds. 2015. *Developments in Chinese Entrepreneurship: Key Issues and Challenges*. New York: Palgrave-McMillan.

Djankov, S., R. La Porta, F. Lopez-De-Silanes, and A. Shleifer. 2002. "The Regulation of Entry." *Quarterly Journal of Economics* 117: 1–37. doi:10.1162/003355302753399436.

Evans, D. S., and L. S. Leighton. 1989. "Some Empirical Aspects of Entrepreneurship." *American Economic Review* 793: 519–535.

Fairlie, R. 2005. "Entrepreneurship and Earnings among Young Adults from Disadvantaged Families.„ *Small Business Economics* 25 (3): 223-236. doi:10.1007/s11187-003-6457-5.

Fairlie, R. W. 2012. *Kauffman Index of Entrepreneurial Activity 1996–2011*. Kansas City: Kauffman Foundation.

Fairlie, R. W., and A. K. Chatterji. 2013. "High Tech Entrepreneurship in Silicon Valley: Opportunities and Opportunity Costs." *Journal of Economics and Management Strategy* 22 (2): 365–389. doi:10.1111/jems.12015.

Frank, M., E. Sommeiller, M. Price, and E. Saez. 2015. "Frank-Sommeiller-Price Series for Top Income Shares by US States since 1917." Accessed 14 March 2016. http://www.shsu.edu/eco_mwf/usstatesWTID.pdf

Georgen, M., C. Brewster, G. Wood, and A. Wilkinson. 2012. "Varieties of Capitalism and Investments in Human Capital." *Industrial Relations: A Journal of Economy and Society* 51: 501–527.

Gimeno, J., T. B. Folta, A. C. Cooper, and C. Y. Woo. 1997. "Survival of the Fittest? Entrepreneurial Human Capital and the Persistence of Underperforming Firms." *Administrative Science Quarterly* 42 (4): 750–783. doi:10.2307/2393656.

Hall, J., S. Matos, L. Sheehan, and B. Silvestre. 2012. "Entrepreneurship and Innovation at the Base of the Pyramid: A Recipe for Inclusive Growth or Social Exclusion?" *Journal of Management Studies* 49: 785–812. doi:10.1111/joms.2012.49.issue-4.

Haltiwanger, J. 2015. "Job Creation, Job Destruction, and Productivity Growth: The Role of Young Businesses." *Annual Review of Economics* 7: 341–358. doi:10.1146/annurev-economics-080614-115720.

Haltiwanger, J., R. S. Jarmin, and J. Miranda. 2013. "Who Creates Jobs? Small versus Large versus Young." *Review of Economics and Statistics* 95 (2): 347–361. doi:10.1162/REST_a_00288.

Halvarsson, D., M. Korpi, and K. Wennberg. 2018. "Entrepreneurship and Income Inequality." *Journal of Economic Behavior & Organization* 145: 275–293. doi:10.1016/j.jebo.2017.11.003.

Hayek, F. A. 1945. "The Use of Knowledge in Society." *American Economic Review* 35 (4): 519–530.

Hsu, D. H., E. B. Roberts, and C. E. Eesley. 2007. "Entrepreneurship from Technology-based Universities: Evidence from MIT." *Research Policy* 36: 768–788. doi:10.1016/j.respol.2007.03.001.

Khaire, M. 2010. "Young and No Money? Never Mind: The Material Impact Of Social Resources on New Venture Growth." *Organization Science* 21: 168-185. doi:10.1287/orsc.1090.0438.

Klapper, L., L. Laeven, and R. Rajan. 2006. "Barriers to Entrepreneurship." *Journal of Financial Economics* 82: 591–629. doi:10.1016/j.jfineco.2005.09.006.

Klein, P., J. T. Mahoney, A. M. McGahan, and C. N. Pitelis. 2010. "Toward a Theory of Public Entrepreneurship." *European Management Review* 7: 1–15. doi:10.1057/emr.2010.1.

Koryak, O., K. Mole, A. Lockett, J. C. Hayton, D. Ucbasaran, and G. P. Hodgkinson. 2015. "Entrepreneurial Leadership, Capabilities and Firm Growth." *International Small Business Journal* 33: 89–105. doi:10.1177/0266242614558315.

Marlow, S., F.J. Greene, and A. Coad. 2018. "Advancing Gendered Analyses Of Entrepreneurship: a Critical Exploration Of Entrepreneurial Activity among Gay Men and Lesbian Women." *British Journal Of Management* 29: 118-135. doi:10.1111/bjom.2018.29.issue-1.

Marquis, C., and Z. Huang. 2009. "The Contingent Nature of Public Policy and the Growth of U.S. Commercial Banking." *Academy of Management Journal* 526: 1222–1246. doi:10.5465/amj.2009.47084828.

McMullen, J. S. 2011. "Delineating the Domain of Development Entrepreneurship: A Market-based Approach to Facilitating Inclusive Economic Growth." *Entrepreneurship Theory and Practice* 351: 185–193. doi:10.1111/j.1540-6520.2010.00428.x.

Meyer, B. D., and J. X. Sullivan. 2003. "Measuring the Well-being of the Poor Using Income and Consumption." *Journal of Human Resources* 38: 1180–1220. doi:10.2307/3558985.

Meyer, B. D., and J. X. Sullivan. 2004. "The Effects of Welfare and Tax Reform: The Material Well-being of Single Mothers in the 1980s and 1990s." *Journal of Public Economics* 88: 1387–1420. doi:10.1016/S0047-2727(02)00219-0.

Miller, T. L., M. G. Grimes, J. S. McMullen, and T. J. Vogus. 2012. "Venturing for Others with Heart and Head: How Compassion Encourages Social Entrepreneurship." *Academy of Management Review* 37 (4): 616–640. doi:10.5465/amr.2010.0456.

Morelix, A., J. Russell, R. W. Fairlie, and E. J. Reedy. 2015. "The Kauffman Index: Startup Activity, State Trends." Accessed 14 March 2015. http://www.kauffman.org/~/media/kauffman_org/research%20reports%20and%20covers/2015/05/kauffman_index_startup_activity_state_trends_2015.pdf

Nam, D., K. Parboteeah, J. Cullen, and J. Johnson. 2014. "Cross-national Differences in Firms' Undertaking Innovative Initiatives: An Application of Institutional Anomie Theory." *Journal of International Management* 20: 91–106. doi:10.1016/j.intman.2013.05.001.

Neumark, D., and W. Wascher. 2000. "Using the EITC to Help Poor Families: New Evidence and a Comparison with the Minimum Wage." *NBER Working Paper 7599.*

Newman, A., S. Schwarz, and D Ahlstrom. 2017. "Microfinance and Entrepreneurship: an Introduction." *International Small Business Journal: Researching Entrepreneurship* 35: 787–792. doi:10.1177/0266242617719314.

Nikolaev, B. N., C. J. Boudreaux, and L. Palich. Forthcoming. "Cross-country Determinants of Early-stage Necessity and Opportunity-motivated Entrepreneurship: Accounting for Model Uncertainty." *Journal of Small Business Management.*

Osberg, L. 2000. "Poverty in Canada and the United States: Measurement, Trends, and Implications." *Canadian Journal of Economics* 334: 847–877. doi:10.1111/0008-4085.00045.

Prahalad, C. K. 2004. *The Fortune at the Bottom of the Pyramid: Eradicating Poverty through Profits.* Upper Saddle River, NJ: Wharton School Publishing.

Ribeiro-Soriano, D. 2017. "Small Business and Entrepreneurship: Their Role in Economic and Social Development." *Entrepreneurship & Regional Development* 29: 1–3. doi:10.1080/08985626.2016.1255438.

Schumpeter, J.A., . 1934. *The Theory Of Economic Development: an Inquiry into Profits, Capital, Credits, Interest, and The Business Cycle.* Piscataway: Transaction Publishers.

Si, S., X. Yu, A. Wu, S. Chen, S. Chen, and Y. Su. 2015. "Entrepreneurship and Poverty Reduction: A Case Study of Yiwu, China." *Asia Pacific Journal of Management* 32: 119–143. doi:10.1007/s10490-014-9395-7.

Simpson, B. P. 2009. "Wealth and Income Inequality: An Economic and Ethical Analysis." *Journal of Business Ethics* 89: 525–538. doi:10.1007/s10551-008-0014-8.

Tomizawa, A., L. Zhao, G. Bassellier, and D. Ahlstrom. Forthcoming. "Economic Growth, Innovation, Institutions, and the Great Enrichment." *Asia Pacific Journal of Management*.

Van de Ven, A. H., H. J. Sapienza, and J. Villanueva. 2007. "Entrepreneurial Pursuits of Self- and Collective Interests." *Strategic Entrepreneurship Journal* 1: 353–370. doi:10.1002/(ISSN)1932-443X.

Westphal, J. D., and I. Stern. 2007. "Flattery Will Get You Everywhere Especially if You are Male Caucasian: How Ingratiation, Boardroom Behavior, and Demographic Minority Status Affect Additional Board Appointments at U.S. Companies." *Academy of Management Journal* 502: 267–288. doi:10.5465/amj.2007.24634434.

Wiklund, J., B. Nikolaev, N. Shir, M.-D. Foo, and S. Bradley. Forthcoming. "Entrepreneurship and Well-being: Past, Present, and Future." *Journal of Business Venturing*.

World Bank. 2004. *World Bank Group Support for Small Business*. Washington, DC: World Bank.

Xue, J., and P. G. Klein. 2010. "Regional Determinants of Technology Entrepreneurship." *International Journal of Entrepreneurial Venturing* 1 (3): 291–308. doi:10.1504/IJEV.2010.030978.

Yu, B., S. Hao, D. Ahlstrom, S. Si, and D. Liang. 2014. "Entrepreneurial Firms' Network Competence, Technological Capability, and New Product Development Performance." *Asia Pacific Journal of Management* 31 (3): 687–704. doi:10.1007/s10490-013-9365-5.

Zahra, S. A., E. Gedajlovic, D. O. Neubaum, and J. M. Shulman. 2009. "A Typology of Social Entrepreneurs: Motives, Search Processes and Ethical Challenges." *Journal of Business Venturing* 24: 519–532. doi:10.1016/j.jbusvent.2008.04.007.

Ziliak, J., and C. Gundersen. 2009. "Senior Hunger in the United States: Differences across States and Rural and Urban Areas," *University of Kentucky Center for Poverty Research Special Reports*. Accessed 5 February 2013. http://www.mowaa.org/document.doc?id=193

Ziliak, J., and C. Gundersen. 2012. "Multigenerational Families and Food Insecurity." *University of Kentucky Center for Poverty Research Discussion Papers Series DP2012-13*. Accessed 6 February 2013. http://www.ukcpr.org/Publications/DP%202012%20-%2013.pdf

Ziliak, J. P. 2006. "Understanding Poverty Rates and Gaps: Concepts, Trends, and Challenges." *Foundations and Trends in Microeconomics* 13: 127–197.

Ziliak, J. P. 2007. "Making Work Pay: Changes in Effective Tax Rates and Guarantees in U.S. Transfer Programs, 1983–2002." *Journal of Human Resources* 423: 619–642. doi:10.3368/jhr.XLII.3.619.

Appendix A1. Effects of EITC maximum credit on firm-centric and opportunity-centric entrepreneurs.

	Model A1	Model A2	Model A3	Model A4	Model A5	Model A6
	Firm-Centric$_{(t+1)}$	Firm-Centric$_{(t+2)}$	Firm-Centric$_{(t+3)}$	Opportunity-Centric$_{(t+1)}$	Opportunity-Centric$_{(t+2)}$	Opportunity-Centric$_{(t+3)}$
ln (EITC max. credit)	**−1.051*** **	**−0.888*** **	**−0.540*** **	−0.068	**−0.089***	**−0.107***
	[0.133]	[0.132]	[0.128]	[0.064]	[0.043]	[0.046]
ln (AFDCTANF benefit)	−0.434**	−0.403**	−0.475***	−0.125**	0.022	0.052
	[0.135]	[0.129]	[0.143]	[0.044]	[0.047]	[0.045]
State unemployment rate	−0.035***	−0.022**	−0.020*	−0.013***	−0.012***	−0.009***
	[0.008]	[0.009]	[0.009]	[0.003]	[0.003]	[0.003]
College educated rate	−0.458	0.311	−0.458	0.030	0.247	−0.079
	[0.453]	[0.466]	[0.461]	[0.164]	[0.162]	[0.163]
Gross state product per capita	−3.121	−7.113*	−8.158**	1.241	0.582	1.137
	[3.102]	[2.882]	[3.111]	[0.909]	[0.776]	[0.835]
Constant	13.481***	11.907***	9.516***	2.193***	1.390***	1.380***
	[1.255]	[1.200]	[1.160]	[0.661]	[0.406]	[0.411]
Year fixed effects	Yes	Yes	Yes	Yes	Yes	Yes
State fixed effects	Yes	Yes	Yes	Yes	Yes	Yes
Observations	750	750	700	700	750	750
R-squared	0.973	0.973	0.971	0.964	0.960	0.959
Number of states	50	50	50	50	50	50

Note: The table reports parameter coefficient estimates. Panel-corrected standard errors are in parentheses. *** $p < 0.001$, ** $p < 0.01$, * $p < 0.05$, + $p < 0.1$ indicate significance, using two-tailed tests. The EITC maximum credit (which a measure of the generosity of the EITC for each state) is calculated for a family with two dependents, and it includes both the federal and state credits. Results are consistent when we used EITC maximum credit for a family of one dependent. Sub-sample results are consistent across one or two lags between the dependent variables and the independent variable.

Regional determinants of poverty alleviation through entrepreneurship in China

Song Lin, Christoph Winkler, Shanshan Wang and Hui Chen

ABSTRACT

Based on the economic theory of dual structure, the authors of this study conducted an empirical analysis on the relationship between entrepreneurship and poverty alleviation using panel data collected in 31 provinces in China from 2000 to 2017. The study arrived at three conclusions. First, entrepreneurship in urban and rural areas can generally facilitate poverty alleviation. Second, the correlation between entrepreneurship and poverty alleviation in urban areas is significantly stronger than in rural areas. Moreover, the correlation is also significantly stronger in developed areas than in underdeveloped areas. Third, the level of financial development in an area can moderate the effect of entrepreneurship on poverty alleviation. These conclusions suggest that entrepreneurial activities in emerging economies have a stronger effect on alleviating poverty in urban regions instead of helping less developed or rural areas. The authors recommend that government agencies should institute policies aimed at vigorously improving the business environment in rural and underdeveloped areas. Particularly a strengthening of the financial system in these areas could further enhance the positive effect of entrepreneurship on poverty alleviation.

Introduction

Can entrepreneurship help to reduce regional poverty? Through a variety of measures implemented globally since the 1990s great strides have been made toward eliminating poverty. According to the *United Nations Millennium Development Goals Report 2015*, the number of people living in extreme poverty fell from 1.926 billion to 836 million between 1990 and 2015. While these numbers are encouraging, poverty is still prevalent in developing countries. For instance, the proportion of people living in extreme poverty in developing countries is still as high as 14% (United Nations 2015).

As entrepreneurial activities emerged across the world in recent years, many researchers have found that entrepreneurship may help facilitate poverty alleviation (McMullen 2011; Si et al. 2015; Svendsen and Svendsen 2001). Entrepreneurship can create new markets, set up new industries, and raise a country's productivity (Ali and Ali 2013). Entrepreneurship can create and provide a variety of jobs for the poor, as well as increase their income (AzisMuthalib et al. 2014; Furlough-Morris 2017; McMullen 2011; Thurik et al. 2008). Yet some studies have suggested that entrepreneurship does little to help with poverty alleviation (Yanya 2012; Alvarez and Barney 2014; Wujung and Mbella 2014).

Using provincial panel data of Thailand from 1997 to 2010, Yanya (2012) demonstrated that there is a positive correlation between the amount of newly registered businesses and the number of people living in poverty, as well as the levels of income inequality. Moreover, Alvarez and Barney (2014) found that while self-employed entrepreneurship is the dominant type of entrepreneurship in poor areas, it has little effect on poverty alleviation. Wujung and Mbella (2014) conducted a case study of Cameroon and found that most start-ups established in Cameroon between 1980 and 2013 are non-productive enterprises, thus crowding out domestic investment of productive enterprises and undermining the role of entrepreneurship in spurring actual employment.

The examples of the above research demonstrates that further research is needed to analyse the relationship between entrepreneurship and poverty alleviation (Sutter, Bruton, and Chen 2018).

While China has witnessed rapid development since the Chinese economic reform in 1978, China is still home to a large number of people living below the poverty line. The Chinese government launched a series of entrepreneurship initiatives in recent years, which spurred entrepreneurial activities rapidly. However, the larger effects of these initiatives on poverty alleviation are still unknown and only a few – mostly case-based – studies (Naminse, Zhuang, and Awuni 2016; Naminse and Zhuang 2018; Si et al. 2015) have explored whether entrepreneurship can help China address its poverty problem. In addition, our review of the literature in mainstream management and entrepreneurship journals also did not yield any studies that utilize transregional data to analyse the relationship between entrepreneurship and poverty in China.

In order to explore regional differences of entrepreneurial activity and its relationship to address poverty alleviation, this study uses a panel data model to examine the impact of entrepreneurship on the per capita income across different regions in China. The contributions of this study are in the following three areas. First, relatively few studies have explored the relationship between entrepreneurship and poverty alleviation at the regional or national level. This study uses transregional data from different provinces to probe the relationship between entrepreneurship and poverty alleviation. This may help to further clarify the role of entrepreneurship as a catalyst for poverty alleviation. Second, despite abundant studies of the dual economic structure, studies that focus on entrepreneurship and organizations remain scarce. This study elaborates on the impact of China's dual structure on entrepreneurship and expands the existing literature by also considering the moderating effect of financial development. Third, the practical implications of this study may encourage targeted activities that may spur entrepreneurial activity at the regional level; thus offering specific suggestions for poverty alleviation.

Literature review

To date, numerous scholars have conducted studies on the effect of entrepreneurship on poverty at both macro and micro levels. Findings are inconclusive and studies at the macro level give a particularly disparate picture. For instance, using the World Bank's panel data for 189 countries from 2005 to 2013, Djankov, Georgieva, and Ramalho (2018) found that entrepreneurship has a positive effect on poverty through the creation of more job opportunities. This holds particularly true when complete and sound business regulations are in place. Similarly, Thurik et al. (2008) explore the effect of self-employed entrepreneurship on poverty alleviation based on the panel data of 23 OECD countries. Their study demonstrated that high unemployment may lead to increased entrepreneurial practices (the 'refugee' effect). As start-ups grow, subsequent hiring will contribute to a fall in the unemployment rate (the 'entrepreneurial' effect). For self-employed entrepreneurship, the entrepreneurial effect will outweigh the refugee effect in the long run, which will ultimately help alleviate poverty. Lastly, Furlough-Morris (2017) examined the impact of newly registered businesses on poverty alleviation in nine South African provinces. The results demonstrated that provinces with increased new business registrations are more market oriented, show faster economic growth and have fewer people living in poverty.

Conversely, other macro-level studies showed that entrepreneurship may have a negative impact on poverty alleviation. Yanya (2012) conducted a study based on panel data of 76 provinces in Thailand from 1997 to 2010. The findings showed that entrepreneurship (new business registrations) increases the population living in poverty, exacerbates income inequality, and impedes the effort to eliminate poverty. In a second study, Yanya, Abdul-Hakim, and Abdul-Razak (2013) determined that entrepreneurship cannot effectively cut poverty. In addition, Wujung and Mbella (2014) found most start-ups in Cameroon are largely non-productive enterprises that obtain licenses through lobbying. This phenomenon leads to a reduction of domestic investment by productive enterprises, and subsequently to a decrease in job opportunities. The authors conclude that entrepreneurship is not conducive to poverty alleviation.

While most micro-level studies note that entrepreneurship has a positive impact on poverty alleviation, the overall results do not paint a consistent picture. After examining small and micro-businesses in Somalia, Ali and Ali (2013) found that while entrepreneurship can reduce poverty by creating new markets, setting up new industries, and increasing productivity; the overall impact is not as strong. AzisMuthalib et al. (2014) investigated the relationship between entrepreneurship and poverty in South Indonesia (Sulawesi). The research demonstrated that entrepreneurial attitudes of micro-business entrepreneurs prompted them to start new businesses through new approaches and to take risks. This helps micro-businesses boost income; increase household assets; and expand consumption, education, and medical spending; thereby facilitating poverty alleviation.

Based on survey data from Vietnam in 2004 and 2006, Lensink and Pham (2012) use a fixed effects model to explore the impact of micro-credit programs on household self-employment profits. Their findings showed that micro-finance can help households with self-employment activities and thereby enabling them to shake off poverty. Using data from a household income survey (n = 583) in southern Ethiopia, Kimhi (2010) demonstrated that farmers who start a businesses and brought their agricultural products to the market were able to secure higher incomes than those producing agricultural products for self-consumption, while also contributing to the improvement of the distribution structure. Based on these findings, the author concludes that rural entrepreneurship should be encouraged. While these results are promising, other micro-level studies suggest that entrepreneurship fails to attain the goal of poverty alleviation. For example, Beck, Demirguc-Kunt, and Levine (2005) investigated the impact of small and medium enterprises on the impoverished population in 45 developed and developing countries. Their research showed that these enterprises did not reduce poverty as effectively as expected. Alvarez and Barney (2014) further point out that self-employed entrepreneurship is the most prevalent type of entrepreneurship in rural areas but that its effect on poverty alleviation is not satisfactory. Moreover, Alvarez, Barney, and Newman (2015) note that social entrepreneurship has a slim effect on poverty alleviation and cannot fundamentally eradicate poverty.

There are two reasons for the aforementioned inconsistencies between regional and organizational level studies. First, most of the existing studies have ignored an essential feature of emerging economies or developing countries – their dual structure.[1] For example, in most emerging economies or developing countries, the urban economy is dominated by modernized, massive industrial production, whereas the rural economy is characterized by typical family farming (Lewis 1954; Ranis and Fei 1961). In a dual structure, human capital stock, infrastructure development, intellectual property protection, and financial market maturity in urban and rural areas differ significantly. Rationally it follows that the influence of entrepreneurship on poverty alleviation in urban and rural areas may also differ. Nevertheless, existing studies on entrepreneurship and poverty alleviation have yet to consider the impact of the dual structure, thereby offering a novel research opportunity.

Second, existing econometric models on the regional level are relatively simple and do not control for indicators such as regional difference, economic policies, and labour input. Omitting these indicators may lead to results that are not reliable. The marketization index (Koveos and Zhang 2012); value added in the primary, secondary, and tertiary sectors (Wujung and Mbella 2014); and the capabilities of entrepreneurs (Naminse and Zhuang 2018) have been widely applied in regional econometric models, however they lack the ability to directly demonstrate the developmental level of entrepreneurship.

While there are only a few studies focusing on the relationship between entrepreneurial activities and poverty alleviation in China, most of them are micro-level representations in the form of regional case studies, thus failing to account for regional differences. For instance, Si et al. (2015)'s case study of poverty reduction in the Chinese city of Yiwu revealed that establishing trading markets and starting businesses can reduce poverty. After investigating small and micro businesses in Wenzhou, in the Zhejiang Province, Naminse, Zhuang, and Awuni (2016) concluded that farmer entrepreneurship can help build wealth and expand social networks and serve as an effective way to reduce poverty. Naminse and Zhuang (2018) conducted a study on farmers in China's Guangxi Province and found that entrepreneurship is conducive to poverty alleviation and that the capabilities of entrepreneurs can help expand the positive effect of poverty alleviation through entrepreneurship. The aforementioned studies all concentrated on cases from the eastern coastal regions in China. However, given the typical dual economic structure in China, there remain considerable differences between urban and rural areas, as well as developed and underdeveloped areas. These differences are particularly pronounced in terms of infrastructure, human capital and financial development level. We conclude that the results of these case studies are not applicable to other regions in China. In order to address this gap in the research, we aim to investigate the influence of entrepreneurial activity as a means for poverty alleviation across different regions in an emerging economy with a prevalent dual structure.[2]

Theories and hypotheses

Entrepreneurship and poverty alleviation

This study argues that active entrepreneurial activities in a region will contribute to poverty alleviation in the region.

First, entrepreneurial activities can raise the income of entrepreneurs. Existing studies have revealed that the poor face major obstacles when trying to achieve higher income due to their status or social class. To illustrate this point, farmers with extremely low incomes have limited chances to becoming workers, not to mention becoming entrepreneurs. However, starting an own businesses may have the potential to changing the nature of work and identity of low-income earners, and give most self-employed entrepreneurs a higher earning potential (Quadrini 2000).

Second, entrepreneurial activities can help create a large number of jobs and increase the income of people living in poverty. One important reason why so many people live in poverty in underdeveloped areas is that society does not offer enough jobs, leaving the poor no choice other than to sustain life through agricultural activities, part-time jobs, or social relief. Entrepreneurial activities have the potential to create more job opportunities and thus enable more local people to get employed (AzisMuthalib et al. 2014). With more job opportunities, poorer people can obtain employment more easily, increasing their income and alleviating their conditions (AzisMuthalib et al. 2014; Furlough-Morris 2017; Thurik et al. 2008).

Third, entrepreneurship is beneficial to the economic development of the whole society by potentially increasing the overall income of poor people. Entrepreneurial activities can tap into new markets, increase productivity, enable the production of new products (Ali and Ali 2013), and subsequently promote economic growth and accumulation of social wealth in a society. In addition, the poor may indirectly benefit from rising social welfare due to economic development and related entrepreneurial activities in their society (Weil 2009; Wan et al. 2018). We therefore hypothesize:

Hypothesis 1: *The development of entrepreneurial activities is beneficial to poverty alleviation.*

The relationship between entrepreneurship and poverty alleviation under the dual structure

The dual structure in emerging economies has led to notable differences in entrepreneurial resources and the entrepreneurial environment, resulting in varying degrees of influence on entrepreneurship and household income across different areas.

The dual structure is a common phenomenon in most developing countries (Boeke 1953; Higgins 1968). It is reflected in two dimensions, (1) the dual structure of urban and rural areas, and (2) the dual structure between different regions. In terms of the urban–rural dual structure, Lewis (1954) identified the first dual structure model and found that in developing countries a large amount of surplus labour in the traditional agricultural sector provides conditions for the accumulation of capital in urban modern sectors. Ranis and Fei (1961) improved on Lewis' model and highlighted the importance of a balanced development of the traditional agricultural sector and urban modern sectors. Regarding the regional dual structure, Myrdal (1957) proposed, for the first time, a geological dual structure in underdeveloped countries, denoting the coexistence of developed and underdeveloped areas. The high-quality production factors are mostly concentrated in developed regions, causing an imbalance in the development and growth between developed and underdeveloped regions.

Based on the aforementioned models, the literature shows evidence of the relationship between the dual structure and economic activities in emerging economies. For example, Ayonga and Obiero (2009) examine the impact of Kenya's land use control policy on urban-rural differences under the dual structure. By incorporating the dual structure when constructing a growth model, Temple and Wößmann (2006) found that as the dual structure transforms and disappears, the allocation of labour between urban and rural areas and between different regions will be more efficient. The authors concluded that this can boost productivity and facilitate economic growth. Yang and Zhou (1999)'s study on China concluded that various economic policies (e.g. financial policies) prioritize urban areas and are therefore important causes from the urban-rural dual structure. The authors suggest that in order to narrow the urban-rural gap, institutional measures should be taken to remove existing biased policies.

Rural or underdeveloped areas can hardly enjoy the positive effect of entrepreneurship under the dual structure. First, poor infrastructure in rural or underdeveloped areas is not favourable to the development of entrepreneurial activities. Infrastructure includes hardware facilities, such as highways, railways, and aviation, and software facilities, such as scientific research facilities and network communications. Rationally it follows that entrepreneurs are more commonly present in urban and developed areas (Zhu and Zhao 2005; Audretsch, Heger, and Veith 2015; Roig-Tierno, Alcáza, and Ribeiro-Navarrete 2015). In contrast, it is very difficult for people in rural and underdeveloped areas to start their own businesses given the poor infrastructure(Fernández-Serrano, Martínez-Román, and Romero 2018). As a result, they may not be able to lift themselves out of poverty through entrepreneurship.

Second, rural or underdeveloped areas cannot provide a favourable environment for entrepreneurial activities. A sound legal system and institutional environment is an important factor to ensure the smooth operation of entrepreneurial activities and businesses. For example, if the patent protection system is yet to be improved, the motivation of businesses to innovate will be negatively affected. Urban and developed areas have better legal and institutional conditions (degree of difficulty to acquire a business license, enforcement of business contracts, and punishment for defaults) compared to rural and underdeveloped areas, which can ensure the successful operation of entrepreneurial activities (Álvarez and Urbano 2011; Dugguh 2013; Djankov, Georgieva, and Ramalho 2018). Therefore, the rate of entrepreneurial success in rural or underdeveloped areas is lower, and poverty reduction in these areas can hardly be achieved through entrepreneurship.

Third, the entrepreneurial capabilities of entrepreneurs in rural or underdeveloped areas is fairly poor, resulting in a lower rate of entrepreneurial success in these areas. Capabilities are determined by the educational background of entrepreneurs. Compared to their counterparts in urban and developed areas, entrepreneurs in rural and underdeveloped areas are far less educated or competent in terms of business management (Colomboa, Delmastro, and Grilli 2004; Garba 2010; Ogundele, Akingbade, and Akinlabi 2012). Consequently, entrepreneurs in rural or underdeveloped areas have a lower rate of entrepreneurial success, which makes it difficult to reduce poverty through entrepreneurship. Thus, this study puts forward the following hypotheses:

Hypothesis 2a: *Entrepreneurship has a weaker effect on poverty alleviation in rural areas than in urban areas;*

Hypothesis 2b: *Entrepreneurship has a weaker effect on poverty alleviation in underdeveloped regions than in developed regions.*

To further study how the dual structure affects the relationship between entrepreneurship and poverty alleviation, we analyse the moderating effect of the financial development level. This study argues that in the dual structure of emerging economies, the most relevant factor in the development of entrepreneurial activities is the level of financial development.

First, the adequacy of financial resources directly affects the rate of entrepreneurial success. According to Ghatak and Jiang (2002), the availability of financial resources is key for the operation of entrepreneurial activities. A shortage of financial resources will strangle potential entrepreneurial activities, since potential start-ups inevitably need seed money to satisfy their demand for an inaugural fund (Claessens and Laven 2003). In areas with underdeveloped financial systems, it is usually very difficult for entrepreneurs to raise sufficient initial funds for entrepreneurial activities. People in these areas are therefore significantly less motivated to start their own businesses compared to people in areas with a developed financial system.

For established businesses, the adequacy of financial resources noticeably affects the speed of growth. If established businesses cannot gain access to adequate financial support, they will grow at a slower pace (Claessens and Laven 2003), will not create enough jobs, and thus hinder the improvement of the income potential for their employees.

Financial resources can affect the spread of new technologies, new products, and new models, and affect the spillover effect of entrepreneurship (King and Levine 1993; Banerjee and Newman 1993; Demirgüç-Kunt and Levine 2009). If the level of financial development is too low, the spillover effect of the innovation generated by entrepreneurial activities will be negatively affected. Subsequently, the positive effect of entrepreneurial activities will not spread to those who have not participated in these activities. We therefore hypothesize:

Hypothesis 3: *Entrepreneurship has a weaker effect on poverty alleviation in regions with a lower level of financial development than in regions with a higher level of financial development.*

Sample and measure

Sample and indicators

Despite its rapid economic progress over the past four decades, China still has a high level of poverty, as evidenced by the prevalence of the dual economic structure (Hertel and Fan 2006; Kwan, Zhang, and Zhuo 2018). The empirical study in this paper will focus on developments starting from the year 2000 due to the relatively complete provincial-level data available. The specifications of the indicators are as follows.

Dependent variable – regional poverty

Consistent with the practice of Yanya, Abdul-Hakim, and Abdul-Razak (2013), this study adopts the data of disposable income provided by the National Bureau of Statistics (NBS) as an indicator that measures the level of poverty alleviation. To investigate the impact of the dual structure, this study differentiates the per capita disposable income in urban areas from that in rural areas and takes their logarithms as the indicators used in the regression model, labelled *lnpcdi_u* and *lnpcdi_r* respectively.

Independent variable – entrepreneurial activities

Similar to Yanya (2012), this study adopts the ratio of the number of newly registered legal person enterprises to the number of legal entities as the indicator to measure entrepreneurial activities, labelled *entrepreneurship*. To measure the development of entrepreneurial activities, we utilize the number of newly increased entrepreneurial activities across different provinces over the years. The State Administration of Industry and Commerce (SAIC) has provided annual numbers for newly registered legal person enterprises. Data were collected by a professional corporate data company.

To determine the indicator to measure regional entrepreneurial activities, we had to eliminate the impact of different economic development levels and the sizes of businesses. We did this by taking the ratio of newly registered legal person enterprises to the number of legal entities in different provinces over the years. It should be noted that besides newly registered legal person enterprises, entrepreneurial activities can also be conducted in the form of newly established self-employed businesses. In general, legal person enterprises can create significantly more jobs for society compared to self-employed businesses. According to statistics released by NBS of China, the average number of people employed by each self-employed business stood at only 2.16 in 2017.[3] Since legal person enterprises surpass self-employed businesses in both size and number, it can better achieve scaled production, create more economic and social benefits, and thus contribute to employees' rising income. We therefore conclude that legal person enterprises can help to alleviate poverty more effectively than self-employed businesses. On that basis, this paper uses newly registered legal person enterprises to represent entrepreneurial activities in our benchmark regression analysis. Moreover, this paper uses newly established self-employed businesses to reflect entrepreneurial activities in a subsequent robustness test.

Moderating variable – level of financial development

This study employs a share in the GDP of different provinces as an indicator to measure the level of financial development, labeled *finance*.

Control variables

Economic development conditions and disposable income vary considerably across different regions in China. Therefore, this paper also employs several control variables which can affect the per capita disposable income:

Regional infrastructure development can affect entrepreneurs' decision over whether to start businesses in a certain region as well as their specific entrepreneurial activities. In this paper, infrastructure is represented by the natural logarithm of the railway mileage in each province (Audretsch, Heger, and Veith 2015), labeled *lnrailway*.

Higher fiscal revenues in a region are indicative of the government's financial ability to increase transfer payments to residents and raise residents' disposable incomes. This paper adopts the growth rate of fiscal revenue to measure fiscal revenues in regions (Gemmell, Kneller, and Sanz 2011), labeled *revenue*.

Closely correlated with residents' income and business activities, regional economic development is represented by the GDP growth rate in each province in this paper (Huang, Zhang, and Rozelle 2008), labeled *gdp*.

Technological innovation capability is a reflection of technological prowess of research institutes in a region and has a strong correlation with entrepreneurial activities. This paper employs the growth rate of authorized invention patents to measure a region's technological innovation capability (Prud'homme 2012), labeled *patent*.

Labour force represents participants in entrepreneurial activities as well as an essential role in economic growth. Labour force is represented by the percentage of people aged between 15 and 64 in the total population (Hashimoto and Tabata 2010), labeled *labor*.

The level of openness in a region reflects how much it opens up to foreign countries and can exert significant impact on technological innovation and economic growth. This paper measures openness by using the ratio of the total import and export volume to the total output value in each province (Mendoza 1997), labeled *trade*.

The cost of living can also affect where entrepreneurs would start businesses as well as residents' standard of living. This paper employs the growth rate of average selling prices for commodity housing of property developers in each province to represent cost and standard of living (Garrido-Yserte, Mañas-Alcón, and Gallo-Rivera 2012), labeled *house*.

Additionally, this study takes the year 2000 as the base period and deflates urban and rural household income with the CPI to eliminate the impact of price.

Table 1 shows the results for the descriptive statistics of major variables. The mean values of the per capital disposable income of urban and rural residents are 9.414 and 8.360 RMB, respectively, which suggests that the overall per capita income in urban areas is higher than in rural areas.

Characteristics of entrepreneurship and poverty in china

The figures below show the distribution of entrepreneurial activities and poverty for different provinces in China. Figure 1 shows that the entrepreneurial activities are noticeably different across the regions. Generally speaking, entrepreneurial activities in the eastern region are more active than activities in the central and western regions. According to the statistics, in 2017 the average number of newly registered businesses in the eastern region reached 443,067. In contrast, provincial-level

Table 1. Definition of variables and descriptive statistics.

Category	Name	Symbol	Definition	Unit	Mean value	Standard deviation	Max.	Min.
Dependent variable	Regional poverty	lnpcdi_u	Natural logarithm of urban per capita disposable income	RMB	9.414	0.481	10.725	8.460
		lnpcdi_r	Natural logarithm of rural per capita disposable income	RMB	8.360	0.591	9.870	7.194
Independent variable	Entrepreneurial activities	entrepreneurship	Ratio of the number of newly registered businesses to the number of legal entities	%	0.384	0.178	1.251	0.033
Moderating variable	Level of financial development	finance	Share of the financial industry in the GDP	%	0.047	0.028	0.171	0.006
Control variable	Infrastructure	lnrailway	Natural logarithm of the railway mileage	km	7.717	0.768	9.421	5.366
	Level of openness	trade	Total import and export volume to the total output value	%	0.307	0.383	1.698	0.032
	Economic growth rate	gdp	GDP growth rate	%	0.112	0.027	0.238	−0.025
	Labour force	labor	Percentage of people aged between 15 and 64 in the total population	%	0.728	0.037	0.838	0.634
	Technological innovation	patent	Growth rate of authorized invention patents	%	0 .322	0 .613	8.816	−0.772
	Fiscal revenue	revenue	Growth rate of fiscal revenue	%	0 .159	0 .109	0.810	−0.343
	Housing price	house	Growth rate of housing price	%	0.095	0.102	0.567	−0.381

Table 2. Correlation coefficient matrix.

	lnpcdi_u	lnpcdi_r	entrepreneurship	lnrailway	trade	finance	gdp	patent	labor	revenue	house
Lnpcdi_u	1.0000										
Lnpcdi_r	0.9517*	1.0000									
Entrepreneurship	0.0735	0.0721	1.0000								
Lnrailway	−0.0111	−0.0211	0.0957	1.0000							
Trade	0.4500*	0.5039*	0.0593	−0.4596*	1.0000						
Finance	0.6514*	0.6305*	−0.0183	−0.3594*	0.5554*	1.0000					
gdp	−0.2081*	−0.2352*	0.1602	−0.0979	0.0448	−0.3204*	1.0000				
Labor	0.5164*	0.6041*	0.1066	0.0605	0.4396*	0.4089*	−0.0728	1.0000			
Patent	0.0523	0.0300	−0.0145	−0.0637	0.0483	0.0160	0.1010	−0.0107	1.0000		
Revenue	−0.1841*	−0.1945*	0.0859	−0.1678*	0.0358	−0.1956*	0.5853*	−0.0337	0.0750	1.0000	
House	0.0548	0.0333	0.0031	−0.1003	0.0636	−0.0248	0.2634*	0.0532	0.0043	0.2560*	1.0000

Notes: * stands for a significant correlation at the level of 1%.

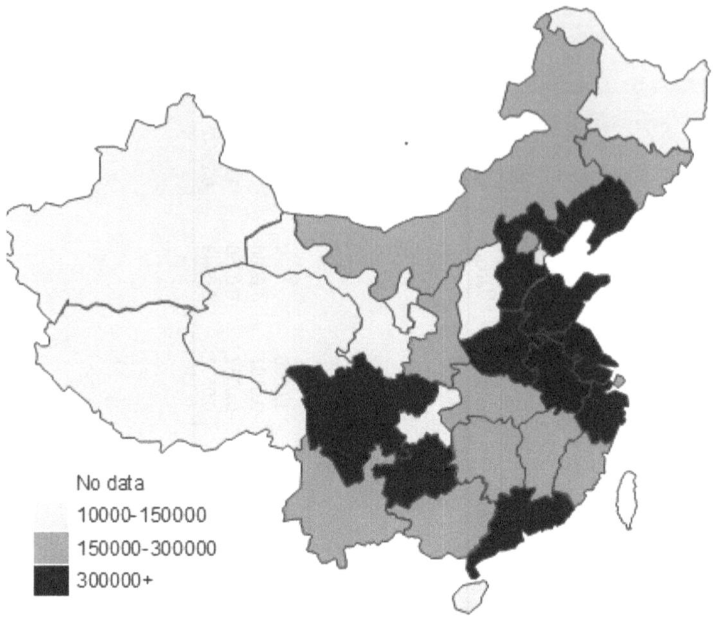

Figure 1. Distribution of the newly registered businesses across China in 2017.

Notes: Due to the availability of data, this paper focuses on 31 provinces in mainland China, excluding Hong Kong, Macao and Taiwan provinces of China. This note also applies to Figure 2.

regions in the western region, including the Xinjiang Uighur Autonomous Region, the Tibet Autonomous Region, Qinghai Province, Ningxia Province, and Gansu Province, saw the fewest growth of newly registered businesses, with an average of only 162,468. This number is equivalent to only 36.7% of the average in the eastern region. Newly registered businesses in the Tibet Autonomous Region ranked last at 17,490, roughly 1.6% of the top-ranking Guangdong Province.

As Figure 2 show (similar to the regional distribution of entrepreneurial activities), the disposable income of urban residents and rural residents differs based on geography. Taking urban areas as an example, in 2017 the per capita income of urban residents in the eastern region (30,051 RMB)

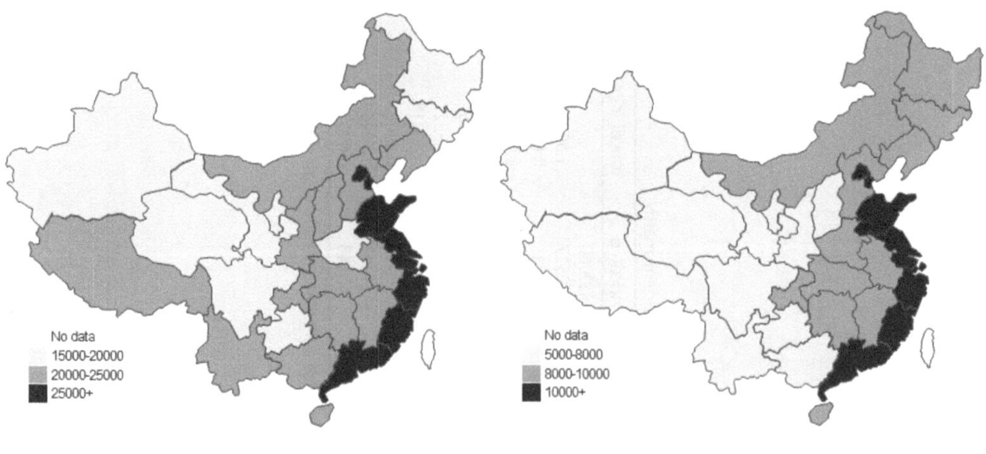

(a) Distribution of the income of urban residents (b) Distribution of the income of rural residents

Figure 2. Distribution of the income of urban and rural residents across China in 2017 (Unit: RMB).

was 1.5 times as high than in the western region (19,957 RMB). Moreover, the per capita income of urban residents in Beijing and Shanghai, the top two regions, were 45,462 RMB and 43,519 RMB, respectively. By contrast, the per capita incomes of residents of the Gansu Province and Qinghai Province, the bottom two regions, were 17,403 RMB and 16,393 RMB, respectively. The disposable incomes in rural areas are about the same.

The above statistical analysis shows that the trend of entrepreneurship and the disposable income of residents correspond closely with each other from both horizontal and vertical perspectives. Meanwhile, the overall trend reflects noticeable urban–rural and regional differences, which can offer preliminary evidence to support the hypotheses in this study.

Empirical results and analysis

The correlation matrix in Table 2 reveals that the correlation between independent variables is low, with all coefficients smaller than 0.6. Meanwhile, the VIF test of the study variables suggests the absence of multicollinearity with an average value ranging between 1 and 3. Therefore a multivariate regression analysis is appropriate for this study.

Notably, previous studies (Yanya 2012; Wujung and Mbella 2014) all argued for a possible two-way causality between entrepreneurship and poverty. This means that entrepreneurship, as the explanatory variable, is endogenous. Thus, the endogeneity of the variable must be eliminated before the regression analysis. Following the approach employed in Acemoglu, Johnson, and Robinson (2001) and other studies, this study chooses the degree of government encouragement for private investment as an instrumental variable since it can affect the dependent variable (regional poverty) through its effect on the endogenous variable (entrepreneurship) (Djankov, Georgieva, and Ramalho 2018). We can assume one-way causality, since we do not observe a change in the dependent variable based on how much the government encourages private investment. Specifically, this study measures government encouragement for private investment by using the proportion of private investment in terms of the total investment of society: The higher the proportion, the more the government encourages private investment. After determining the instrumental variable, this study includes a two-stage least squares regression analysis and uses a Hausman test to identify which method is appropriate for the panel model. The results indicate that the fixed effects model is better suited to this study.

Based on the theoretical model constructed in this study, we employ per capita disposable income in urban and rural areas as dependent variables in the regression analysis to investigate whether entrepreneurship can facilitate poverty alleviation and increase household income. Additionally, the study accounts for the difference between per capita disposable income in urban and rural areas as another dependent variable. In doing so we are able to investigate whether entrepreneurship can better facilitate poverty alleviation in urban areas versus rural areas. Table 3 shows the results are quite similar with one-, two-, and three-period lags, which suggests the results are robust.

To test the study hypotheses, the subsequent analysis was conducted based on the results with models lagged by one period. The regression analysis results show a significant positive correlation between entrepreneurship and regional poverty (per capita urban disposable income and per capita rural disposable income; urban: $b = 3.726$, $p = 0.000$; rural: $b = 3.654$, $p = 0.000$). This indicates that entrepreneurship is conducive to the increase in per capita disposable income in urban and rural areas. We accept Hypothesis 1 because entrepreneurship can facilitate poverty alleviation. A significant positive coefficient exists between entrepreneurship and urban–rural model (urban–rural: $b = 3.666$, $p = 0.000$). Therefore, entrepreneurship has a driving effect on the per capita disposable income in urban areas but not rural areas. We accept Hypothesis 2a because entrepreneurship can better facilitate poverty alleviation in urban areas versus rural areas.

To test Hypothesis 2b, this study conducted a regression analysis on the data collected from the eastern and western regions. In line with the NBS classification, the eastern region includes Beijing,

Table 3. Regression analysis results.

	lagged 1 period			lagged 2 periods			lagged 3 periods		
	Urban	Rural	Urban-rural	Urban	Rural	Urban-rural	Urban	Rural	Urban-rural
Entrepreneurship	3.726***	3.654***	3.666***	4.411***	4.517***	4.248***	4.647***	4.891***	4.427***
	(8.85)	(7.50)	(8.94)	(8.38)	(7.14)	(8.51)	(7.80)	(6.69)	(7.93)
Finance	5.011***	7.456***	3.919***	7.482***	10.283***	6.073***	12.134***	15.791***	10.052***
	(4.34)	(5.58)	(3.48)	(7.02)	(8.03)	(6.01)	(11.23)	(11.90)	(9.93)
Lnrailway	0.508***	0.605***	0.453***	0 .549***	0 .643***	0.494***	0 .461***	0 .567***	0.401***
	(9.86)	(10.16)	(9.03)	(10.19)	(9.92)	(9.66)	(8.41)	(8.44)	(7.82)
Trade	−0.141	−0.018	−0.169*	−0.231**	−0.150	−0.236**	−0.310**	−0.318**	−0.265**
	(−1.50)	(−0.16)	(−1.85)	(-2.14)	(-1.15)	(-2.30)	(-2.56)	(-2.14)	(-2.34)
gdp	−7.089***	−7.382***	−6.659***	−7.438***	−7.874***	−6.942***	−7.513***	−7.856***	−7.104***
	(−7.78)	(−7.00)	(−7.50)	(-7.21)	(-6.35)	(-7.10)	(-6.53)	(-5.56)	(-6.59)
Labor	4.788***	4.871***	4.852***	3.278***	3.742***	3.166***	2.278***	2.690***	2.190***
	(9.16)	(8.05)	(9.53)	(5.34)	(5.08)	(5.44)	(2.96)	(2.85)	(3.03)
Patent	0.007	0.003	0.009	−0.008	−0.007	−0.007	−0.010	−0.007	−0.011
	(0.48)	(0.22)	(0.69)	(-0.56)	(-0.41)	(-0.54)	(-0.77)	(-0.44)	(-0.90)
Revenue	0.192**	0.211*	0.167*	0 .129	0 .175	0 .095	0.285***	0.381***	0.222**
	(1.99)	(1.89)	(1.78)	(1.35)	(1.53)	(1.05)	(2.98)	(3.24)	(2.48)
House	−0.133	−0.211*	−0.080	−0 .028	−0.112	0 .027	−0.058	−0.104	−0.023
	(−1.33)	(−1.83)	(−0.83)	(-0.30)	(-0.98)	(0.30)	(-0.59)	(-0.86)	(-0.25)
C	1.198***	−0.757	1.167***	1.760***	−0.497	1.900***	2.969***	0.578	3.167***
	(2.67)	(−1.51)	(2.76)	(3.91)	(-0.92)	(4.45)	(5.76)	(0.91)	(6.55)
R^2	0.780	0.784	0.756	0.764	0.762	0.742	0.743	0.740	0.720
F	18.84	20.72	20.40	18.27	19.22	20.31	17.11	17.69	19.49

Notes: *, **, and *** stand for a significant correlation at the level of 10%, 5%, and 1%, respectively. Figures in brackets denote the values of *t*-statistic. The term *urban-rural* refers to the natural logarithm of the difference between urban per capita disposable income and rural per capita disposable income.

Tianjin, Hebei Province, Liaoning Province, Shanghai, Jiangsu Province, Zhejiang Province, Fujian Province, Shandong Province, Guangdong Province, and Hainan Province, and the western region includes Sichuan Province, Chongqing, Guizhou Province, Yunnan Province, the Tibet Autonomous Region, Shanxi Province, Gansu Province, Qinghai Province, the Ningxia Hui Autonomous Region, the Xinjiang Uighur Autonomous Region, the Guangxi Zhuang Autonomous Region, and the Inner Mongolia Autonomous Region. Overall, the eastern region is home to coastal cities and is more developed than the western region (Chen and Fleisher 1996). As can be seen in Table 4, entrepreneurship in the eastern region helped reduce poverty and the correlations were all significant at a level of 1%. Conversely, in the western region, models demonstrated lower significant results. In rural areas for one-, two-, and three-period models, entrepreneurship in the eastern region helped reduce poverty, and the correlations were all significant at a level of 1%. In the western region, all three models demonstrated no significant correlation. Hence, we accept Hypothesis 2b.

To test Hypothesis 3, this study conducted a regression analysis of the data collected from regions with a high level of financial development and those with a low level of financial development. We calculated the average value of financial resources across all the provinces. We selected those with financial resources above the mean value plus a standard deviation as *high-level regions*, while those with financial resources below the mean value minus a standard deviation as *low-level regions*. Table 4 shows that in regions with a high level of financial development entrepreneurship increases urban household income. The results are consistent across all three models at the 1% significance level. Consequently, in regions with a low level of financial development, entrepreneurship had a significant negative impact on income in the model lagged by one period. We concluded that entrepreneurship is subject to funding thresholds. If the level of financial development is severely low, some potential entrepreneurs will be hindered from starting their own businesses (Buera 2008).

Even though entrepreneurs have managed to start up a business, their businesses may face financing constraints if the level of financial development in the region is low. This will then impede their production, operations and expansion, and block their prospects for development

Table 4. Grouped regression results.

		lagged 1 period		lagged 2 periods		lagged 3 periods	
		Urban	Rural	Urban	Rural	Urban	Rural
Eastern region	Entrepreneurship	18.481***	17.192***	19.217***	18.347***	23.684***	23.147***
		(9.87)	(9.03)	(10.47)	(9.22)	(10.77)	(9.34)
	R^2	0 .860	0 .874	0.868	0.871	0.869	0.868
	F	19.10	26.95	21.38	26.40	20.25	24.30
Western region	Entrepreneurship	3.615**	2.626	10.783*	8.259	0.068	0.056
		(1.98)	(1.23)	(1.84)	(1.19)	(1.53)	(1.04)
	R^2	0.808	0.830	0.781	0.811	0.763	0.794
	F	16.56	13.90	15.14	13.19	14.55	12.26
Group with a high level of financial development	Entrepreneurship	6.572***	6.270***	3.820***	3.609***	3.624***	3.480***
		(3.86)	(3.80)	(4.21)	(3.91)	(4.36)	(3.94)
	R^2	0.783	0.798	0.832	0.831	0.855	0.842
	F	7.46	10.33	6.67	10.04	6.50	11.15
Group with a low level of financial development	Entrepreneurship	−1.804**	−1.807**	0.313	0.193	0.251	0.210
		(-2.54)	(-2.69)	(1.29)	(0.69)	(0.82)	(0.82)
	R^2	0.545	0.585	0.798	0.755	0.695	0.786
	F	3.00	6.76	7.53	15.37	1.88	8.51

*, **, and *** stand for a significant correlation at the level of 10%, 5%, and 1%, respectively. Figures in brackets denote the values of *t*-statistic. The control variable in the table is the same as that in Table 3. To save space, this study presents only the regression results of major explanatory variables and omits the results of the control variables. The group with a high level of financial development refers to a subsample consisting of individuals whose level of financial development is at least one standard deviation higher than the average level of financial development of all samples; the group with a low level of financial development refers to a subsample consisting of individuals whose level of financial development is at least one standard deviation lower than the average level of financial development of all samples. In addition, hypothesis 2b and hypothesis 3 mainly focus on the regional dual structure, hence we did not consider the *urban-rural* results.

and profitability (Hamilton 2000). Moreover, as some entrepreneurial activities require huge investments (Buera 2008), entrepreneurs will have lower net incomes when they get less return on their investment. We accept Hypothesis 3 and conclude that the influence of entrepreneurship on poverty alleviation is weaker in regions with lower levels of financial development.

Robustness testing

In order to further verify the reliability of research conclusions in our benchmark analysis, we conducted two types of robustness testing to verify the aforementioned hypotheses and transmission mechanisms.

In the first type of robustness testing, businesses are classified into three major sectors in accordance with the classification standard provided by the NBS. The primary industry includes agriculture, forestry, animal husbandry, and fishery (excluding the service industry of agriculture, forestry, animal husbandry, and fishery); the secondary industry involves the mining (excluding auxiliary activities), manufacturing (excluding the metalware, machinery and equipment repair industries), production and supply of electricity, heat, gas, and water, and the construction industries; and the tertiary industry is the service industry, which refers to all industries other than the first and secondary industries. The paper categorizes the newly registered businesses accordingly and conducts the same regression models as above.

First, we studied the impact of entrepreneurship in the primary, secondary, and the service industries on the incomes of urban and rural areas respectively. Subsequently, we compared the differences of its impact to observe the robustness of Hypotheses 1 and 2a. It can be seen from the robustness test results (as shown in Appendix 1) that the regression result, based on the categorization of three industries, is consistent with the original model. Entrepreneurial activities in all of the three industries are conducive to raising the income of urban and rural residents, which shows that Hypothesis 1 is robust. Moreover, entrepreneurship in all of the three industries is significantly and positively correlated to 'urban–rural,' implying that the driving effect of entrepreneurial activities in urban areas is indeed stronger than in rural areas. We conclude that Hypothesis 2a is robust.

Second, we studied the impact of entrepreneurial activities across various industries in the eastern and western regions to test the robustness of Hypothesis 2b. The results of a robustness test (as shown in Appendix 2) are consistent with the original model. It should be noted that while entrepreneurship in the eastern region is more favourable to poverty reduction, the effect of entrepreneurship on poverty reduction is not significant in the lagged models. We conclude that Hypothesis 2b is robust since the poverty reduction effect of entrepreneurial activities in developed areas is more evident than in underdeveloped areas.

Third, this paper studied the impact of entrepreneurial activities on the income of residents in financially developed and financially underdeveloped regions. The results of the robustness test for Hypothesis 3 (as shown in Appendix 3) indicate that entrepreneurial activities in financially developed areas are more conducive to poverty reduction. Specifically, for regions with a higher level of financial development, the poverty reduction effects of the secondary and tertiary industries are all highly significant at a level of 1% for the models lagged by one period, two periods, or three periods. In contrast, for regions with a lower level of financial development, the regression results for the models lagged by two and three periods are completely not significant. We conclude that Hypothesis 3 is robust since financial resources have a significant effect on the relationship between entrepreneurship and poverty reduction.

In a second type of robustness testing, we conducted an empirical analysis using data concerning newly established self-employed businesses in each province to represent entrepreneurial activities. This Data was from the State Administration for Industry and Commerce. Results for all lagged models (Appendix 4) show that self-employed entrepreneurship can help increase residents' income in both urban and rural areas. Regression results are all significantly positive at the level of 1%. We conclude that the results of Hypothesis 1 are robust. Moreover, the regression coefficients of urban-rural are also all significantly positive at the level of 1%. We conclude that self-employed entrepreneurship can better help reduce poverty in urban areas than in rural areas; Hypothesis 2a is robust.

Conclusions and discussion

Built on the economic theory of dual structure, we conducted a quantitative analysis of the correlation between entrepreneurship and poverty alleviation. According to respective economic data of China's 31 provinces during 2000 and 2017, entrepreneurial activities generally help raise the per capita income. However, the data also reveal that while entrepreneurial activities keep progressing in an emerging economy, the existence of a dual economic structure widens the income gap between urban and rural people. The correlation between entrepreneurship and poverty alleviation is particularly stronger in developed regions compared to less developed countries. Furthermore the role of financial development, the most important factor in the dual economic structure analysed here, confirms the influence of this structure. Therefore, this study concludes that, in general, entrepreneurial activities have a positive effect on poverty alleviation (measured as increased income) mainly in urban and developed eastern regions.

This study provides two main contributions. First, analysing the relationship between entrepreneurship and poverty alleviation greatly enhances our understanding of entrepreneurship at the regional and national level while revealing inconclusive evidence and methodological limitations of existing studies on entrepreneurship and poverty alleviation. For example, most macro-level studies on entrepreneurship and poverty alleviation use relatively simple econometric models and employ methods of ordinary least squares, vector autoregression, and Granger causality test (Yanya 2012; Yanya, Abdul-Hakim, and Abdul-Razak 2013; Wujung and Mbella 2014). Meanwhile, micro-level studies usually focus on case studies involving specific regions. As a result, their conclusions have limited applicability to different regions (Naminse, Zhuang, and Awuni 2016; Naminse and Zhuang 2018; Si et al. 2015). In contrast, this paper uses panel data of different provinces in China to explore the relationship between entrepreneurship and poverty alleviation through an econometric modelling that involves control variables like innovation capability, infrastructure and level of openness. In addition our study compares the different effects of entrepreneurship on poverty alleviation between (1) urban and rural areas, (2) developed and underdeveloped areas, and (3) areas with a higher/lower level of financial development. Therefore, our study provides a deeper understanding about the circumstances under which entrepreneurship can more effectively facilitate poverty alleviation (and raise income).

Second, this study further explored China's dual economic structure and the influence of the structure on entrepreneurship. Our results add to the existing body of literature on the economic structure of emerging economies and developing countries. While studies of the dual economic structure are now abundant, they mainly look at the economic growth and differences in regional development (Yang and Zhou 1999; Temple and Wößmann 2006) Studies in the field of entrepreneurship and in organizations are relatively scarce. This study, using China's economic activities as an example, proves the existence of a dual economic structure (between urban and rural areas and between developed and less developed areas) and the influence of such a structure on the regional economic changes. Moreover, this study also applies financial development as a key factor in such a structure to analyse its moderating effect. All of these findings supplement the existing literature on the dual economic structure and contribute to the body of literature for developing economies.

This study has obvious and practical implications. As mentioned above, in rural China and the central and western regions entrepreneurial activities have been less vibrant and failed to reduce poverty effectively. This was primarily due to the lack of various infrastructure facilities and policies; especially the scarcity of financial support. To date, there are still a large number of people living in poverty in particularly rural China, which makes these regions comparable to other developing countries. Therefore, China's dual structure (transformation of the eastern regions and urban areas from poverty to prosperity versus the remaining poverty in the western regions and rural areas) has the potential to provide significant reference points for other developing countries.

Our research shows that, in areas with less developed economies and insufficient infrastructure we need to strengthen the regional systems and infrastructure to bring the role of entrepreneurship into full play (especially with regards to financial support). Specific measures of government departments may include: (1) enhancing infrastructure development in the central and western regions and rural areas; (2) providing more substantial supporting policies for entrepreneurship such as tax cuts and lowering the threshold for entrepreneurship in central and western regions, as well as rural areas; (3) and attracting funds from various channels in underdeveloped regions to offer small start-up funds to entrepreneurial activities.

Limitations and future direction

This study has certain limitations in terms of index measurement and mechanism analyses. Firstly, to measure poverty, the most appropriate index should have been the impoverished population or poverty indices of each region. However, because we were unable to capture the relevant data, we had to rely on the per capita disposable income of residents as a proxy measure. In future studies, a more suitable index is needed to measure entrepreneurship and poverty. Secondly, the conclusion of the paper is also limited by the type of entrepreneurial activities. For example, non-productive enterprises are evidently weaker than productive enterprises regarding the capacity to increase employment and create social value. Therefore, it is necessary to further collect data in the future to focus on certain types of entrepreneurial activities if the effect of entrepreneurship on poverty reduction is to be more accurately assessed. Thirdly, given that China provides a very unique context, future research may further focus on the impact of factors such as: differences in policies, culture and economic development across different regions. The assessment of the relationship between entrepreneurship and poverty alleviation across different regions can also provide references for other emerging countries or regions.

Notes

1. Developing countries were the object of study when the theory of dual economy was first brought forth. With their economic and social development, developing countries have split into different groups: countries like China, India and Brazil have achieved particularly prominent economic development and are thus called 'emerging economies'. Nevertheless, as the dual structure is still prevalent in emerging economies, the theory of dual structure also applies to such countries.
2. It is specified in the report to the 19th National Congress that 'some acute problems caused by unbalanced and inadequate development await solutions', and that 'there are still large disparities in development and income distribution between rural and urban areas'.
3. Source: Calculations based on data in the China Statistical Yearbook 2018.

Disclosure statement

No potential conflict of interest was reported by the authors.

Funding

This work was supported by the National Natural Science Foundation of China (71572208).

References

Acemoglu, D., S. Johnson, and J. A. Robinson. 2001. "The Colonial Origins of Comparative Development: An Empirical Investigation." *American Economic Review* 91 (5): 1369–1401. doi:10.1257/aer.91.5.1369.

Ali, A. Y. S., and A. H. Ali. 2013. "Entrepreneurship Development and Poverty Reduction: Empirical Survey from Somalia." *American International Journal of Social Science* 2 (3): 108–113.

Álvarez, C., and D. Urbano. 2011. "Environmental Factors and Entrepreneurial Activity in Latin America." *Academia Revista Latinoamericana De Administración* 48: 31–45.

Alvarez, S. A., and J. B. Barney. 2014. "Entrepreneurial Opportunities and Poverty Alleviation." *Entrepreneurship Theory and Practice* 38 (1): 159–184. doi:10.1111/etap.12078.

Alvarez, S. A., J. B. Barney, and A. M. B. Newman. 2015. "The Poverty Problem and the Industrialization Solution." *Asia Pacific Journal of Management* 32: 23–37. doi:10.1007/s10490-014-9397-5.

Audretsch, D. B., D. Heger, and T. Veith. 2015. "Infrastructure and Entrepreneurship." *Small Business Economy* 44: 219–230. doi:10.1007/s11187-014-9600-6.

Ayonga, J. N., and S. Obiero. 2009. "Rural-Urban Dualism and Ineffective Land Use Control Instruments at the Rural-Urban Interface." *Africa Habitat Review Journal* 3 (3): 148–158.

AzisMuthalib, A., L. M. Harafah, M. Yani, R. Rostin, and A. S. Mahmudin. 2014. "The Influence of Micro Industry Entrepreneurship in the Process of Poverty Alleviation (studies in the Food Industry Center at Southeast Sulawesi)." *IOSR Journal of Business and Management* 16 (11): 48–53. doi:10.9790/487X-161164853.

Banerjee, A. V., and A. F. Newman. 1993. "Occupational Choice and the Process of Development." *Journal of Political Economy* 101 (2): 274–298. doi:10.1086/261876.

Beck, T., A. Demirguc-Kunt, and R. Levine. 2005. "SMEs, Growth, and Poverty: Cross-Country Evidence." *Journal of Economic Growth* 10 (3): 199–229. doi:10.1007/s10887-005-3533-5.

Boeke, J. H. 1953. *Economics and Economic Policy of Dual Societies*. New York: Institute of Pacific Relations.

Buera, F. J. 2008. "Persistency of Poverty, Financial Frictions, and Entrepreneurship." Working Paper.

Chen, J., and B. M. Fleisher. 1996. "Regional Income Inequality and Economic Growth in China." *Journal of Comparative Economics* 22 (2): 141–164. doi:10.1006/jcec.1996.0015.

Claessens, S., and L. Laven. 2003. "Financial Development, Property Rights, and Growth." *The Journal of Finance* 58 (6): 2401–2436. doi:10.1046/j.1540-6261.2003.00610.x.

Colomboa, M. G., M. Delmastro, and L. Grilli. 2004. "Entrepreneurs' Human Capital and the Start-up Size of New Technology-based Firms." *International Journal of Industrial Organization* 22: 1183–1211. doi:10.1016/j.ijindorg.2004.06.006.

Demirgüç-Kunt, A., and R. Levine. 2009. "Finance and Inequality: Theory and Evidence." *Annual Review of Financial Economics* 1 (1): 287–318. doi:10.1146/annurev.financial.050808.114334.

Djankov, S., D. Georgieva, and R. Ramalho. 2018. "Business Regulations and Poverty." *Economics Letters* 165: 82–87. doi:10.1016/j.econlet.2018.02.002.

Dugguh, S. I. 2013. "Entrepreneurship and Small Business: Strategic Approach to Alleviating Poverty and Corruption in Nigeria." *GSTF Journal on Business Review* 3 (1): 57–66.

Fernández-Serrano, J., J. A. Martínez-Román, and I. Romero. 2018. "The Entrepreneur in the Regional Innovation System: A Comparative Study for High- and Low-income Regions." In *Entrepreneurship &*. Regional Development, forthcoming.

Furlough-Morris, S. 2017. "Examining Poverty, Entrepreneurship, and Multinational Corporation Participation in South Africa." Walden Dissertations and Doctoral Studies.

Garba, A. S. 2010. "Refocusing Education System Towards Entrepreneurship Development in Nigeria: A Tool for Poverty Eradication." *European Journal of Social Sciences* 15 (1): 140–150.

Garrido-Yserte, R., E. Mañas-Alcón, and M. T. Gallo-Rivera. 2012. "Housing and Cost of Living: Application to the Spanish Regions." *Journal of Housing Economics* 21: 246–255. doi:10.1016/j.jhe.2012.07.002.

Gemmell, N., B. Kneller, and I. Sanz. 2011. "The Timing and Persistence of Fiscal Policy Impacts on Growth: Evidence from OECD Countries." *The Economic Journal* 121 (550): 33–58. doi:10.1111/j.1468-0297.2010.02414.x.

Ghatak, M., and N. N. Jiang. 2002. "A Simple Model of Inequality, Occupational Choice, and Development." *Journal of Development Economics* 69: 205–226. doi:10.1016/S0304-3878(02)00059-7.

Hamilton, B. H. 2000. "Does Entrepreneurship Pay? an Empirical Analysis of the Returns to Self-Employment." *Journal of Political Economy* 108 (3): 604–631. doi:10.1086/262131.

Hashimoto, K., and K. Tabata. 2010. "Population Aging, Health Care, and Growth." *Journal of Population Economics* 23: 571–593. doi:10.1007/s00148-008-0216-5.

Hertel, T., and Z. Fan. 2006. "Labour Market Distortions, Rural–Urban Inequality and the Opening of China's Economy." *Economic Modelling* 23 (1): 76–109. doi:10.1016/j.econmod.2005.08.004.

Higgins, B. H. 1968. *Economic Development: Problems, Principles, and Policies*. New York: W. W. Norton.

Huang, J., Q. Zhang, and S. Rozelle. 2008. "Economic Growth, the Nature of Growth and Poverty Reduction in Rural China." *China Economic Journal* 1: 107–122. doi:10.1080/17538960701770547.

Kimhi, A. 2010. "Entrepreneurship and Income Inequality in Southern Ethiopia." *Small Business Economics* 34 (1): 81–91. doi:10.1007/s11187-009-9196-4.

King, R. G., and R. Levine. 1993. "Finance, Entrepreneurship and Growth: Theory and Evidence." *Journal of Monetary Economics* 32 (3): 513–542. doi:10.1016/0304-3932(93)90028-E.

Koveos, P., and Y. Zhang. 2012. "Regional Inequality and Poverty in Pre- and Postreform China: Can Entrepreneurship Make A Difference?" *Thunderbird International Business Review* 54 (1): 59–72. doi:10.1002/tie.v54.1.

Kwan, F., Y. Zhang, and S. Zhuo. 2018. *Labour Reallocation, Productivity Growth and Dualism: The Case of China*. International Review of Economics and Finance, forthcoming.

Lensink, R., and T. T. T. Pham. 2012. "The Impact of Microcredit on Self-employment Profits in Vietnam." *Economics of Transition* 20 (1): 73–111. doi:10.1111/j.1468-0351.2011.00427.x.

Lewis, A. 1954. "Economic Development with Unlimited Supplies of Labour." *The Manchester School of Economic and Social Studies* 22: 139–191. doi:10.1111/j.1467-9957.1954.tb00021.x.

McMullen, J. S. 2011. "Delineating the Domain of Development Entrepreneurship: A Market-based Approach to Facilitating Inclusive Economic Growth." *Entrepreneurship Theory and Practice* 35 (1): 185–215. doi:10.1111/j.1540-6520.2010.00428.x.

Mendoza, E. G. 1997. "Terms-of-trade Uncertainty and Economic Growth." *Journal of Development Economics* 54: 323–356. doi:10.1016/S0304-3878(97)00046-1.

Myrdal, G. 1957. *Economic Theory and Underdeveloped Regions*. London: Harper and Row.

Naminse, E. Y., and J. Zhuang. 2018. "Does Farmer Entrepreneurship Alleviate Rural Poverty in China? Evidence from Guangxi Province." *PLoSONE* 13 (3): 1–18. doi:10.1371/journal.pone.0194912.

Naminse, E. Y., J. Zhuang, and J. A. Awuni. 2016. "Economic Growth, Farmer Entrepreneurship and Rural Poverty Alleviation in China: A Critical Review." *Asian Journal of Agricultural Extension, Economics and Sociology* 11 (4): 1–15. doi:10.9734/AJAEES/2016/26034.

Ogundele, O. G. K., W. A. Akingbade, and H. B. Akinlabi. 2012. "Entrepreneurship Training and Education as Strategic Tools for Poverty Alleviation in Nigeria." *American International Journal of Contemporary Research* 2 (1): 148–156.

Prud'homme, D. 2012. "Dulling the Cutting-edge: How Patent-related Policies and Practices Hamper Innovation in China." European Chamber Research Report. doi:10.1094/PDIS-11-11-0999-PDN.

Quadrini, V. 2000. "Entrepreneurship, Saving and Social Mobility." *Review of Economic Dynamics* 3 (1): 1–40. doi:10.1006/redy.1999.0077.

Ranis, G., and J. C. H. Fei. 1961. "A Theory of Economic Development." *American Economic Review* 51 (4): 533–565.

Roig-Tierno, N., J. Alcáza, and S. Ribeiro-Navarrete. 2015. "Use of Infrastructures to Support Innovative Entrepreneurship and Business Growth." *Journal of Business Research* 68: 2290–2294. doi:10.1016/j.jbusres.2015.06.013.

Si, S., X. Yu, A. Wu, S. Chen, S. Chen, and Y. Su. 2015. "Entrepreneurship and Poverty Reduction: A Case Study of Yiwu, China." *Asia Pacific Journal of Management* 32 (1): 119–143. doi:10.1007/s10490-014-9395-7.

Sutter, C., G. D. Bruton, and J. Chen. 2018. *Entrepreneurship as A Solution to Extreme Poverty: A Review and Future Research Directions*. Journal of Business Venturing, forthcoming.

Svendsen, G. L. H., and G. T. Svendsen. 2001. "Alleviating Poverty: Entrepreneurship and Social Capital in Rural Denmark 1800-1900." *Belgeo* 3: 231–246.

Temple, J., and L. Wößmann. 2006. "Dualism and Cross-country Growth Regressions." *Journal of Economic Growth* 11 (3): 187–228. doi:10.1007/s10887-006-9003-x.

Thurik, A. R., M. A. Carree, A. Stel, and D. B. Audretsch. 2008. "Does Self-employment Reduce Unemployment?" *Journal of Business Venturing* 23: 673–686. doi:10.1016/j.jbusvent.2008.01.007.

United Nations. 2015. *The Millennium Development Goals Report 2015*. New York.

Wan, G., C. Wang, H. Yin, and Y. Zhang. 2018. "From Equality of Deprivation to Disparity of Prosperity: The Poverty–Growth–Inequality Triangle in Post-reform China." *China & World Economy* 26 (2): 50–67. doi:10.1111/cwe.12236.

Weil, D. N. 2009. *Economic Growth*. 3rd ed. New York: Addison Wesley Press.

Wujung, V. A., and M. E. Mbella. 2014. "Entrepreneurship and Poverty Reduction in Cameroon: A Vector Autoregressive Approach." *Archives of Business Research* 2 (5): 1–11. doi:10.14738/abr.

Yang, D. T., and H. Zhou. 1999. "Rural-urban Disparity and Sectoral Labour Allocation in China." *Journal of Development Studies* 35 (3): 105–133. doi:10.1080/00220389908422575.

Yanya, M. 2012. "Causal Relationship between Entrepreneurship Poverty and Income Inequality in Thailand." *International Journal of Trade, Economics and Finance* 3 (6): 436–440.

Yanya, M., R. Abdul-Hakim, and N. A. Abdul-Razak. 2013. "Does Entrepreneurship Bring an Equal Society and Alleviate Poverty? Evidence from Thailand." *Procedia-Social and Behavioral Sciences* 91: 331–340. doi:10.1016/j.sbspro.2013.08.430.

Zhu, M., and H. Zhao. 2005. "Entrepreneurial Growth and the Perceived Quality of Environmental Factors in China." *China and World Economy* 13 (4): 70–82.

Appendix 1. Robustness test results on three industries.

		lagged 1 period			lagged 2 period			lagged 3 period		
		Urban	Rural	Urban-rural	Urban	Rural	Urban-rural	Urban	Rural	Urban-rural
Primary industry	Entrepreneurship	26.062***	25.560***	25.642***	20.828***	21.332***	20.063***	17.095***	17.992***	16.287***
		(8.85)	(7.50)	(8.94)	(8.38)	(7.14)	(8.51)	(7.80)	(6.69)	(7.93)
	R^2	0.780	0.784	0.756	0.764	0.762	0.742	0.743	0.740	0.720
	F	18.74	20.72	20.40	18.27	19.22	20.31	17.11	17.69	19.49
Secondary industry	Entrepreneurship	320.776***	314.600***	315.606***	132.473***	135.679***	127.602***	140.298***	147.663***	133.673***
		(8.85)	(7.50)	(8.94)	(8.38)	(7.14)	(8.51)	(7.80)	(6.69)	(7.93)
	R^2	0.780	0.784	0.756	0.764	0.762	0.742	0.743	0.740	0.720
	F	18.84	20.72	20.40	18.27	19.22	20.31	17.11	17.69	19.49
Tertiary industry	Entrepreneurship	12.504***	12.263***	12.302***	11.211***	11.483***	10.799***	10.985***	11.562***	10.467***
		(8.85)	(7.50)	(8.94)	(8.38)	(7.14)	(8.51)	(7.80)	(6.69)	(7.93)
	R^2	0 .780	0.784	0.756	0.764	0.762	0.742	0.743	0.740	0.720
	F	18.84	20.72	20.40	18.27	19.22	20.31	17.11	17.69	19.49

Notes: *, **, and *** stand for a significant correlation at the level of 10%, 5%, and 1%, respectively. Figures in brackets denote the values of *t*-statistic. The term *urban-rural* refers to the natural logarithm of the difference between urban per capita disposable income and rural per capita disposable income. To save space, this study presents only the regression results of major explanatory variables and omits the results of the control variables.

Appendix 2. Robustness test results on three industries in the eastern and western regions

			lagged 1 period		lagged 2 period		lagged 3 period	
			Urban	Rural	Urban	Rural	Urban	Rural
The Eastern Regions	Primary industry	entrepreneurship	57.633***	53.614***	47.049***	44.920***	51.799***	50.626***
			(9.87)	(9.03)	(10.47)	(9.22)	(10.74)	(9.34)
		R^2	0. 860	0 .874	0 .868	0 .871	0 .869	0 .868
		F	19.10	26.95	21.38	26.40	20.25	24.30
	Secondary industry	entrepreneurship	891.365***	829.212***	1350.289***	1289.212***	−485.700***	−474.693***
			(9.87)	(9.03)	(10.47)	(9.22)	(−10.74)	(-9.34)
		R^2	0. 860	0 .874	0 .868	0 .871	0 .869	0 .868
		F	19.10	26.95	21.38	26.40	20.25	24.30
	Tertiary industry	entrepreneurship	14.242***	13.249***	14.733***	14.067***	14.444***	14.117***
			(9.87)	(9.03)	(10.47)	(9.22)	(10.74)	(9.34)
		R^2	0. 860	0 .874	0 .868	0 .871	0 .869	0 .868
		F	19.10	26.95	21.38	26.40	20.25	24.30
The Western Regions	Primary industry	entrepreneurship	12.523**	9.098	8.966*	6.868	5.912	4.851
			(1.98)	(1.23)	(1.84)	(1.91)	(1.53)	(1.04)
		R^2	0.808	0.830	0.781	0.811	0.763	0.794
		F	16.56	13.90	15.14	13.19	14.55	12.26
	Secondary industry	entrepreneurship	−303.765**	−220.691	51.922*	39.769	47.471	38.954
			(−1.98)	(−1.23)	(1.84)	(1.19)	(1.53)	(1.04)
		R^2	0.808	0.830	0.781	0.811	0.763	0.794
		F	16.56	13.90	15.14	13.19	14.55	12.26
	Tertiary industry	entrepreneurship	21.612**	15.702	13.226*	10.130	19.309	15.845
			(1.98)	(1.23)	(1.84)	(1.19)	(1.53)	(1.04)
		R^2	0.808	0.830	0.781	0.811	0.763	0.794
		F	16.56	13.90	15.14	13.19	14.55	12.26

Notes: *, **, and *** stand for a significant correlation at the level of 10%, 5%, and 1%, respectively. Figures in brackets denote the values of *t*-statistic. To save space, this study presents only the regression results of major explanatory variables and omits the results of the control variables.

Appendix 3. Robustness test results on three industries in financially developed and under-developed groups

			lagged 1 period		lagged 2 period		lagged 3 period	
			Urban	Rural	Urban	Rural	Urban	Rural
Group with a high level of financial development	Primary industry	entrepreneurship	−1336.562***	−1275.241***	105.553***	99.725***	−127.219***	−122.125***
			(-3.86)	(-3.80)	(4.21)	(3.91)	(−4.36)	(−3.94)
		R^2	0 .783	0 .798	0.832	0.831	0.855	0 .842
		F	7.46	10.33	6.67	10.04	6.50	11.15
	Secondary industry	entrepreneurship	107.672***	102.732***	40.703***	38.456***	39.470***	37.890***
			(3.86)	(3.80)	(4.21)	(3.91)	(4.36)	(3.94)
		R^2	0.783	0.798	0.832	0.831	0.855	0 .842
		F	7.46	10.33	6.67	10.04	6.50	11.15
	Tertiary industry	entrepreneurship	8.199***	7.823***	5.216***	4.928***	5.165***	4.959***
			(3.86)	(3.80)	(4.21)	(3.91)	(4.36)	(3.94)
		R^2	0.783	0 .798	0.832	0.831	0.855	0 .842
		F	7.46	10.33	6.67	10.04	6.50	11.15
Group with a low level of financial development	Primary industry	entrepreneurship	19.336**	19.364**	38.542	23.777	35.718	29.931
			(2.54)	(2.69)	(1.29)	(0.69)	(0.82)	(0.82)
		R^2	0.545	0.585	0.798	0.755	0.695	0.786
		F	3.00	6.76	7.53	15.37	1.88	8.51
	Secondary industry	entrepreneurship	−12.158**	−12.176**	3.292	2.031	2.836	2.376
			(−2.54)	(−2.69)	(1.29)	(0.69)	(0.82)	(0.82)
		R^2	0.545	0.585	0.798	0.755	0.695	0.786
		F	3.00	6.76	7.53	15.37	1.88	8.51
	Tertiary industry	entrepreneurship	−4.369**	−4.375**	1.136	0.701	0.907	0.760
			(−2.54)	(−2.69)	(1.29)	(0.69)	(0.82)	(0.82)
		R^2	0.545	0.585	0.798	0.755	0.695	0.786
		F	3.00	6.76	7.53	15.37	1.88	8.51

Notes: *, **, and *** stand for a significant correlation at the level of 10%, 5%, and 1%, respectively. Figures in brackets denote the values of *t*-statistic. To save space, this study presents only the regression results of major explanatory variables and omits the results of the control variables. The group with a high level of financial development refers to a subsample consisting of individuals whose level of financial development is at least one standard deviation higher than the average level of financial development of all samples; the group with a low level of financial development refers to a subsample consisting of individuals whose level of financial development is at least one standard deviation lower than the average level of financial development of all samples.

Appendix 4. Robustness testing result of the assessment of entrepreneurial activities with self-employed businesses

	lagged 1 period			lagged 2 period			lagged 3 period		
	Urban	Rural	Urban-Rural	Urban	Rural	Urban-Rural	Urban	Rural	Urban-Rural
entrepreneurship	0.425***	0.417***	0 .418***	0.411***	0.421***	0.396***	0.414***	0.436***	0 .395***
	(8.85)	(7.50)	(8.94)	(8.38)	(7.14)	(8.51)	(7.80)	(6.69)	(7.93)
C	3.921***	1.914***	3.846***	4.002***	1.799***	4.056***	4.249***	1.925**	4.386***
	(7.20)	(3.04)	(7.25)	(7.01)	(2.62)	(7.49)	(6.89)	(2.54)	(7.59)
R^2	0.780	0.784	0.756	0.764	0.762	0.742	0.743	0.740	0.720
F	18.84	20.72	20.40	18.27	19.22	20.31	17.11	17.69	19.49

Notes: *, **, and *** stand for a significant correlation at the level of 10%, 5%, and 1%, respectively. Figures in brackets denote the values of *t*-statistic. To save space, this study presents only the regression results of major explanatory variables and omits the results of the control variables.

Uncovering the scaling of innovations developed by grassroots entrepreneurs in low-income settings

Marleen Wierenga

ABSTRACT

Low-income entrepreneurs operating in resource-scarce settings are typically referred to as subsistence entrepreneurs – informal, operating on a small scale, and selling products developed and produced by others. This study establishes the notion of a unique category of low-income entrepreneurs who have developed, commercialised, and scaled innovations and are self-employed by choice. Further, the paper investigates the scaling process of these innovative grassroots entrepreneurs. The sample consists of four grassroots entrepreneurs from India who founded an enterprise to sell their self-developed innovations. The study follows the grounded theory approach, which is suitable for the exploration of complex questions in unusual settings. The theoretical lens used in this study is entrepreneurial bricolage since the interest of the study lies in understanding action and the usage of existing resources. The contribution of the paper is twofold. First, it contributes to the literature on low-income entrepreneurship by bolstering the theoretical archetype of grassroots entrepreneurs and developing a process model for their scaling process. Second, the study contributes to the literature on bricolage by introducing the notion of grassroots bricolage as a behaviour to utilise and combine both locally available contacts and a broader network as resources in novel ways.

Introduction

For decades, the world has searched for solutions to eradicate poverty. One of the proposed solutions to overcome this complex grand challenge is entrepreneurship (Bruton, Ketchen, and Ireland 2013; Si et al. 2015; Sutter, Bruton, and Chen 2019). In light of this, considering a broad variety of entrepreneurs, contexts, and activities, entrepreneurship is important as it creates economic and social value (Welter et al. 2017). This study, while shedding light on marginalised entrepreneurs, focuses on how individuals from low-income settings with limited resources engage in entrepreneurship and upscale their businesses.

In the low-income context, entrepreneurship can be understood either as being primarily opportunity-motivated, by choosing to become an entrepreneur, or as being necessity-motivated by the lack of other opportunities and coercion of circumstances (McMullen, Ragby, and Palich 2008). Entrepreneurs in developing countries are predominantly driven by necessity and are often considered micro-entrepreneurs. They are self-employed mostly for subsistence rather than growth (Bruton, Ahlstrom, and Si 2015). Extant literature on entrepreneurship examines entrepreneurs working in a variety of professions such as farmers (Yessoufou, Blok, and Omta 2018; Sutter et al. 2017; Tobias, Mair, and Barbosa-Leiker 2013), selling miscellaneous consumer goods (Webb, Morris, and Pillay 2013) and acting as sales agents for foreign-based companies (Scott et al. 2012; Kistruck et al. 2013b). Low-income entrepreneurs typically make sales by approaching strangers on the street (Scott et al. 2012) and in local marketplaces (Kistruck et al. 2013b).

In contradiction with this perspective of low-income entrepreneurs as a homogeneous group, an emerging stream of literature considers them as innovative and creative problem-solvers (Shepherd, Parida, and Wincent 2017; Prabhu and Jain 2015; Sarkar 2018). Thus, there is a scholarly and practical need to understand the phenomenon of low-income entrepreneurs with the potential for growth beyond the level of subsistence (Bruton, Ahlstrom, and Si 2015; Sutter, Bruton, and Chen 2019). Contributing to this stream of entrepreneurship literature, this study investigates the notion of grassroots entrepreneurs. These entrepreneurs are isolated from the formal business market because they have either no or a low level of education. They live distant from urban centres in unstable financial situations and constantly face extreme levels of resource scarcity. They are familiar with the challenges in the low-income context, the needs of people with limited incomes, and the solutions to overcome their everyday challenges (Sarkar 2018). While acknowledging that innovative entrepreneurs are a small portion of the entire body of entrepreneurs in the market (González-Pernía, Jung, and Peña 2015), this study aims to highlight grassroots entrepreneurs and their activities as a unique subset of low-income entrepreneurs.

In this study, particular emphasis is placed on the process of scaling by these entrepreneurs (Ahlstrom 2010). Scaling, in this context, means first expanding their business to customers outside the entrepreneurs' immediate surroundings and then steadily increasing the number of customers to a point where the entrepreneurs can sustain their livelihood, provide for their family from the enterprise, and even create jobs for others in the community (Bruton, Ahlstrom, and Si 2015).

The upscaling of enterprises has caught the attention of scholars in the past; however, this was either from the perspective of resources and resource-allocation tactics of low-income entrepreneurs (Webb, Morris, and Pillay 2013) or in the context of Western-based organisations operating in the low-income markets of developing countries (Chliova and Ringov 2017). Past studies have not considered a process perspective (Webb, Morris, and Pillay 2013). Scaling makes a business owner feel responsible (Kistruck et al. 2013b) and empowered (Mair and Marti 2009), but it is difficult to realise for entrepreneurs from low-income settings (Shepherd, Parida, and Wincent 2017). Therefore, scaling is an important aspect to investigate (Hart, Sharma, and Halme 2016) in order to better understand how entrepreneurship can contribute to poverty alleviation (Bruton, Ketchen, and Ireland 2013). This study aims to understand how the scaling process of grassroots entrepreneurs takes place in a resource-constrained environment. It focuses on the barriers to scaling and the mechanisms to overcome them. Thus the research question guiding the work is *how do grassroots entrepreneurs scale their enterprises in resource-scarce environments?*

The theoretical lens used in this study is bricolage which increases the understanding of entrepreneurial action, the types of resources at hand, and the different ways of utilising those resources. Entrepreneurial bricolage implies the refusal to be limited by scarce resources, improvisation, and making do with the resources at hand (Baker and Nelson 2005). Bricolage as a theoretical frame can also explain how entrepreneurs overcome resource scarcity in conditions of depravity (George, McGahan, and Prabhu 2012). In addition to entrepreneurial bricolage (Baker and Nelson 2005), various other types of bricolage, such as intrapreneurial bricolage (Halme, Lindeman, and Linna 2012) and social bricolage (DiDomenico, Haugh, and Tracey 2010), have been identified. Previous studies have linked bricolage with the firm growth of Western social enterprises (Tasavori, Kwong, and Pruthi 2018), but studies on bricolage and low-income entrepreneurs (Linna 2013; Sarkar 2018) have thus far ignored the questions related to scaling. Therefore, this study adds to the literature of bricolage by offering an in-depth analysis of how grassroots entrepreneurs overcome resource scarcity for scaling and by developing the notion of grassroots bricolage.

The empirical setting includes four grassroots entrepreneurs from India who have developed innovations and established an enterprise to commercialise and scale it. Since the emphasis is on the lived experiences of the entrepreneur, the analysis is inspired by the grounded theory method proposed by Gioia and his colleagues (2013). The data used in this study are process data (Langley 1999), consisting of interviews and observation data collected from the field. These data are complemented by multiple sources of archival data such as news articles, reports, extensive case studies, and video talks.

This study makes three contributions. Firstly, contributing to the literature on entrepreneurship and poverty alleviation, the study builds a model of scaling up grassroots enterprises. Owing to resource scarcity, the scaling process begins by operating on a small scale in close proximity of the enterprise. Through the utilisation of locally available resources and the expansion of the network, the legitimacy as entrepreneurs grows. Hence, the entrepreneurs gradually begin to operate on a larger scale, eventually becoming entrepreneurs on the state-level. Secondly, the study develops the archetype of grassroots entrepreneurs as a unique category of low-income entrepreneurs who have independently developed, commercialised, and scaled their innovations. In other words, while all grassroots entrepreneurs are low-income entrepreneurs, not all low-income entrepreneurs are grassroots entrepreneurs. This notion contradicts the well-established concept of the low-income entrepreneur as necessity-motivated, operating on a small scale and selling goods developed and produced by third parties (Scott et al. 2012; Webb, Morris, and Pillay 2013), which is typically associated with low-income entrepreneurs. Lastly, the study contributes to the literature on bricolage by establishing the notion of grassroots bricolage. This means the ability to use locally available resources and the expanding network, and to combine these for new purposes in unforeseen ways.

Theoretical background

In the following section, I briefly introduce the literature related to grassroots entrepreneurship. I will then examine bricolage as a way to overcome resource scarcity in various contexts. Bricolage is flexible with regard to what is considered as a resource at hand (Baker, Miner, and Eesley 2003). I also discuss how networks and contacts are used as a resource in the different forms of bricolage. Tables showcasing the prior empirical literature on both low-income entrepreneurship and bricolage can be found in Appendix B.

Grassroots entrepreneurs

Low-income entrepreneurs can be subsumed within the broader definition of entrepreneurship beyond the technology-driven fast growth entrepreneurship (Welter et al. 2017). The low-income entrepreneur is considered as an individual owning an informal and unregistered enterprise, working from home in an informal settlement or working on the street (Webb, Morris, and Pillay 2013). The entrepreneur could be selling cell phone-related accessories or providing services, for instance, such as hairdressing but with no product differentiation and in fierce price competition with other similar low-income entrepreneurs (Webb, Morris, and Pillay 2013).

Innovations that differ from the products already in the market are labelled as differentiation-related innovations, and novelty-related innovations have new sources of demand and supply (Bradley et al. 2012). Low-income entrepreneurs tend to develop differentiation-related innovations (Bradley et al. 2012), sell products developed and produced by third parties (Scott et al. 2012), and execute opportunities created by others (Tobias, Mair, and Barbosa-Leiker 2013). While low-income entrepreneurs typically create imitations of products created by other entrepreneurs and sell them, innovation-driven entrepreneurs create a greater economic impact (González-Pernía, Jung, and Peña 2015).

The group of people living on a low income is diverse, consisting of several sub-groups (Ansari, Munir, and Gregg 2012) similar to the group of low-income entrepreneurs. Innovative low-income entrepreneurs referred to as grassroots entrepreneurs are the primary focus of this study since they differ from the typical low-income entrepreneur described above. Grassroots entrepreneurs develop solutions for the low-income market (Sarkar 2018) and aim to increase their household income, empower the user, reduce production costs, and enhance their own productivity (Pansera and Sarkar 2016). This study acknowledges the local efforts and self-sufficiency of these entrepreneurs (Si et al. 2015). Bottom-up innovations developed by grassroots entrepreneurs carry the potential of benefitting society (Hossain 2016) and being pioneers for the advancement of sustainable development (Pansera and Sarkar 2016). The motivation of grassroots entrepreneurs is not usually profit-oriented (Pansera and Sarkar 2016) and their success lies in the social aim of providing a solution to alleviate poverty, even on a small scale (Hossain 2016). Hence, the solutions are often easy to imitate and, therefore difficult to scale (Shepherd, Parida, and Wincent 2017).

Grassroots entrepreneurs typically operate in environments mainly characterised by resource scarcity and informality. Like any entrepreneur, grassroots entrepreneurs need financial, human, and social capital to develop successful enterprises (Bradley et al. 2012), but they face a capital accumulation struggle (Yessoufou, Blok, and Omta 2018). Finances provide the entrepreneur time to develop products and position these in the appropriate market (Bradley et al. 2012). Human resources, in this context, relate closely to prior entrepreneurial experience and education (Williams and Shepherd 2016) as well as the ability to access resources (Bradley et al. 2012; Engström and McKelvie 2017). Finally, social resources tend to be limited to family and friends living in the same contextual environment as the entrepreneurs (Sarkar 2018). Intermediaries in low-income settings function to increase the capacity of grassroots entrepreneurs and lower the transaction costs to create a more efficient market (Kistruck et al. 2013a). However, the availability of more resources alone is not enough because the business idea needs to be feasible as well (Bradley et al. 2012).

Grassroots entrepreneurs typically reside in an informal environment (Sutter et al. 2017; Bruton, Ahlstrom, and Si 2015) and operate in poor institutional conditions (Mair and Marti 2009). The informal economy is illegal by law but is considered legitimate in terms of social acceptance yet has boundaries beyond which society does not accept the activities of these informal economic actors (Webb et al. 2009). In an informal economy, formal institutions such as banks are substituted with relationship-based saving and lending arrangements (Webb, Morris, and Pillay 2013).

Entrepreneurs are usually part of the informal economy because they want to enhance their self-interest. They either do not see the value of formal institutions or they do not know how to operate as part of the formal economy (Webb et al. 2009). However, not following formal laws and regulations negatively influences the efficiency of an informal economy. The processes are labour-intensive, competing products are present in the market in large numbers, and the quality of their products is poor (Sutter et al. 2017).

In informal contexts, NGOs act as institutional entrepreneurs to build and improve the institutional arrangements for low-income entrepreneurs (Mair and Marti 2009). These organisations operate altruistically, internalising most of the expense and risk (Kistruck et al. 2013a) to help low-income entrepreneurs scale their businesses. This empowers the entrepreneurs (Mair and Marti 2009) and makes social mobility across generations possible despite cultural and infrastructural restrictions (Scott et al. 2012). However, extant literature until now has not provided a detailed explanation about how grassroots entrepreneurs scale up their enterprises in low-income and resource-scarce environments.

Bricolage and network contacts

Bricolage refers to the behaviour exhibited by entrepreneurs working with resource scarcity, for example, in low-income settings (Linna 2013; Sarkar 2018). The key characteristics of entrepreneurial bricolage include utilising the available resources, combining existing resources for new purposes, and making do with the resources at hand (Baker and Nelson 2005). Resources at hand can be both internal, such as organisational practices, assets, and network, and external, such as those borrowed from the institutional context (Mair and Marti 2009). Furthermore, a bricoleur can use resources in ways previously unexplored or to combine resources in novel ways (Baker and Nelson 2005). Bricolage is intuitively associated with innovativeness, and studies have revealed that a higher level of bricolage results in a higher level of innovativeness in resource-constrained young firms in the context of developed countries (Senyard et al. 2014).

Skilful bricoleurs are not particularly creative or mindful. Instead, they are analytical and know when to engage in bricolage and when not to (Senyard et al. 2014). Bricoleurs adopt resourcefulness as a mindset (Halme, Lindeman, and Linna 2012) and do not feel constrained by the pressure of being socially acceptable (Sarkar 2018). They feel comfortable handling atypical resources, and they use both material bricolage and intangible ideational bricolage. Ideational bricolage, for instance, can imply the use of a theatrical play in advocacy work or the use of religion to promote hygienic practices (Mair and Marti 2009). According to a study on social impact reporting, social entrepreneurs did not allow themselves to be restricted by rules and conventions and mixed available resources with their own priorities and interpretations of the rules (Molecke and Pinkse 2017). Other atypical resources include working on the innovations in their free time outside working hours, mobilising professional and private contacts, and building a professional field to support the endeavours (Halme, Lindeman, and Linna 2012).

Network bricolage refers to situations where established contacts constitute the resources at hand. Specifically, in network bricolage, existing professional and private contacts are proactively engaged as a resource (Baker, Miner, and Eesley 2003; Halme, Lindeman, and Linna 2012) instead of being utilised passively and occasionally (Baker 2007). Therefore, it is different from the act of merely networking, which implies seeking resources from strangers (Baker, Miner, and Eesley 2003). In network bricolage, entrepreneurs utilise their existing networks as resources at hand, for instance, in the founding process (Baker, Miner, and Eesley 2003), when seeking funding opportunities (Baker 2007) or when expanding the product and the market scope of a social enterprise (Tasavori, Kwong, and Pruthi 2018).

Social entrepreneurs use stakeholder participation to establish new contacts and links with partners who possess valuable resources (DiDomenico, Haugh, and Tracey 2010), share the best practices and facilities with the network actors (Tasavori, Kwong, and Pruthi 2018), and persuade significant actors to obtain additional resources (DiDomenico, Haugh, and Tracey 2010). For instance, social enterprises using both network bricolage and internal assets are more successful in expanding their product and market scope (Tasavori, Kwong, and Pruthi 2018).

Bricolage creates an environment that encourages a trial and error approach and the development of capabilities such as creativity, improvisation, and network skills. Experimentation and on-the-job learning are frequently used to overcome resource scarcity in the low-income context (Linna 2013). Despite having similar characteristics as improvisation, bricolage is a different construct, since entrepreneurs engage with bricolage in both improvised and pre-planned activities (Baker, Miner, and Eesley 2003; Baker 2007). However, bricoleurs generate improvisational competences that might result in being satisfied with and settling for the second-best solution (Senyard et al. 2014). Bricolage also differs from resource-seeking, which refers to actively acquiring new resources that are not readily available at hand (Baker and Nelson 2005; Baker 2007).

In the low-income context, bricoleurs create social value using both physical and non-material resources, leading to accidental expansion of businesses (Linna 2013). The resources at hand may, for instance, comprise of self-taught skills, utilising own time, and recombining existing structures with new applications (Sarkar 2018). Non-material resources may include existing personal networks, strengthening of social capital, and the knowledge of the local people that can be utilised for the enhancement of the business (Linna 2013). However, the phenomenon of scaling has not been examined in these studies. Instead, scholars have predominantly questioned firm growth (Linna 2013) and the level at which bricolage can hinder innovativeness (Senyard et al. 2014). Therefore, in this study, I aim to explore the question of scaling by studying grassroots entrepreneurs and their scaling process.

Research methodology

This research was prompted by the existence of unique cases of low-income entrepreneurs who have developed, commercialised, and scaled their innovations. I had been following the work of Mansukhbhai Prajapati, one of the entrepreneurs examined in this study, since 2015, and I was fairly familiar with his story before commencing this study. Grassroots entrepreneurs with innovative ideas and emerging enterprises had been identified as the phenomenon of interest at the beginning of the study. While examining the literature on entrepreneurship in low-income settings, I arrived at the research question 'How do grassroots entrepreneurs scale up their enterprises in resource-scarce environments?' Through the analytical process, the theoretical lens of the study shifted from the original idea of network theory to co-creation and to legitimacy, landing finally at bricolage, since it holistically captures the dynamic aspect of utilising different kinds of resources – typical and atypical – in resource-scarce settings.

Sampling criteria

The study aimed to understand better the mechanisms for scaling used by entrepreneurs. Searching for relevant entrepreneurs began from the database of grassroots innovations in India that were awarded by the National Innovation Foundation (NIF). In August 2018, this database contained 560 innovations divided into four categories: general agricultural, agricultural equipment, engineering, and utility (National Innovation Foundation 2018). The listed innovations have been awarded by the NIF and are properly reported. However, a vast majority of the innovations are neither commercialised nor scaled. As the primary focus was on entrepreneurs who had built an enterprise around their innovation and scaled beyond their neighbours and fellow villagers, I employed an initial screening to find these type of innovations. In addition, Sristi, an NGO supporting grassroots entrepreneurs in India, helped in identifying the appropriate cases for the study.

Using the theoretical sampling method (Glaser and Strauss 1967) guided by the literature on bricolage, I sought out information-rich cases about the phenomenon of grassroots entrepreneurship (Patton 1990). I screened for entrepreneurs based on three criteria. First, I looked for reportedly sole entrepreneurs who had predominantly worked alone on developing innovations and had been supported only by their family. Second, the outcome of each innovation process had to be a commercial product sold in the market. Third, I searched for entrepreneurs with similar backgrounds in terms of a low level of education and native origins in rural India. I shortlisted eight cases, six of whom I personally met in their factories in India. Finally, I identified four entrepreneurs suitable for the study. They had engaged in similar bricolage behaviour, developing an innovative and complex product or machine. I was confident I could carve out a detailed analysis of the scaling of entrepreneurs in the low-income context based on four cases. In Table 1, I briefly introduce the final selection of entrepreneurs for the study.

When cases are studied over time, in addition to a rich set of data from various sources, relatively small sample sizes can be justified, since they allow the researchers to delve deep into each case. Contrary to a single case study, four cases allow the necessary depth and width of the analysis (Glaser and Strauss 1967) and exploration of various data sources. This also increases the credibility of the overall study. However, adding more cases would not have enhanced the breadth of the study. Being information-rich cases supported by the intense data collection efforts described in the next section, these cases generated insights which are relevant also for other studies on low-income entrepreneurship (Gioia, Corley, and Hamilton 2013).

Data collection

To understand how processes unfold over time, process data typically combines archival data, interviews, and observations (Langley et al. 2013). For this study, data collection occurred in two phases in order to collect data from multiple sources (Table 2). In the initial phase, I collected

Table 1. Introduction of the entrepreneurs covered in the study.

	Mitticool clay fridge	Bullet Santi	Chetak Cotton Stripper	Groundnut digger
Innovator's name	Mansukhbhai Prajapati	Mansukhbhai Jagani	Mansukhbhai Patel	Sanjay Tilwa
Description of the innovation	Food storage without dependence on electricity supply	Three-wheeled tractor with attachments for different work on the field	Extraction of cotton from the shells	Harvest of groundnuts
Novelty	Materials used and application	Diffusion model	Application	Application
Alternative	No preservation of vegetables and fruits	Use of bullocks on land or a tractor	Labour by women and children	Manual labour on the field
Working on the innovation	Since 2001	Since 1994	Since 1991	Since 2006
First customer	In 2005	In 2004	In 1994	In 2011
Sales channel	Retailers, own shop (physical and online)	Personal sales, online retailers	Personal sales, online retailers	Agricultural dealerships
Geographical spread	Pan-India, Middle East, and UAE	Pan-India, Kenya	Pan-India	Pan-India

archival data since it was readily available online. The sources included various types of documentation such as news articles, websites, documentaries, and short videos. This naturally occurring data helped to explain how the scaling process evolves at different points in time. In the second phase, I conducted thorough field research using the interview method.

Since I was focusing on the depth of the study, I interviewed the users of the innovations and the network contacts as well. This provided a broader perspective and further background information on the cases. Other studies on grassroots entrepreneurship in India (Pansera and Sarkar 2016; Gajendra 2015) used similar approaches but neglected the perspective of the network. Conducting the interviews myself and spending as much time with the entrepreneurs as they were able to contribute to the study, I was also able to make field observations and collect visual data in modes of pictures and videos. This data was valuable in not only understanding the context better but also in directly contributing to the research.

Archival data. In the beginning, the purpose of collecting archival data was to build descriptions of each grassroots entrepreneur in preparation for the field visit. However, while collecting archival data, I noticed the richness of the documented sources. The time-stamped multimedia records were published between 2008 and 2017, and they provided a detailed historical account of the evolvement of innovation and scaling processes. It allowed me to construct a detailed process description, which I used in the data analysis and the construction of the interview questions.

The archival data consists of various sources. First, I studied the websites of three of the four entrepreneurs. They had a professional appearance, built either out of their own expense or by external parties. The websites gave an overview to visitors of the way the grassroots entrepreneurs

Table 2. Data used in the study.

Type of data	Use in analysis	Mitticool	Bullet Santi	Chetak Cotton Stripper	Groundnut Digger	Network Contacts
Archival data	Initial and primary analysis	74 pages	56 pages	104 pages	91 pages	
Interviews	Primary analysis	3 h	1.5 h	1.5 h	2 h	6 h
Field notes from observation	Understanding the context and the life of the entrepreneur	5 pages	3 pages	4 pages	4 pages	2 pages
Visual data from observation	Understanding the context	112 pictures	32 pictures	22 pictures	43 pictures	

wanted to present themselves to the outside world. Second, all four innovations have been widely covered by different kinds of Indian newspapers, such as the Hindustan Times, the Economic Times, India Today, and Outlook India. Similarly, these innovations have also drawn the attention of international media, receiving coverage on for instance BBC and Discovery Channel. Third, the organisations working with the entrepreneurs have written reports and case studies with rich descriptions of the entrepreneurs and their innovations. These were either publicly available or provided by the organisations upon request. Finally, I found videos of Mansukhbhai Prajapati speaking about the Mitticool refrigerators in a TED Talent Search event and demonstrations of the use of Bullet Santi, Chetak, and the groundnut digging machine.

Interviews and observations. In order to interview the grassroots entrepreneurs, I visited their factories and offices. During the field visits, a local research assistant and an interpreter translating the responses from Gujarati, the local language, to Hindi accompanied me. The interpreter was necessary as some of the entrepreneurs and users were more comfortable talking in Gujarati than in Hindi. All the interviews were transcribed from either Hindi or Gujarati directly into English. In the field, we spent as much time with the entrepreneurs as they were willing to give us, which ranged between 3 to 6 hours. My objective behind interviewing the entrepreneurs was twofold: first, to verify the narrative as told by archival sources and, second, to get answers to the questions not covered in the archival sources.

Visiting each entrepreneur in their everyday habitat, we gained their trust, and they shared their story with us. Understanding the context where the grassroots entrepreneurs lived and worked in and the environment the products are used in helped to build a background for the research. My research assistant conducted the interviews in Hindi – occasionally with the help of the Gujarati translator – and translated the responses into English for me in between the questions. We used semi-structured interview questions we had prepared together. We asked the entrepreneurs to tell us about the journey that led them to develop the innovation and what followed the initial recognition and success. This method was chosen to focus on the experiences as lived by the individual and obtain greater depth that the archival sources were unable to provide. Towards the end of each interview, we also asked clarifying questions about the issues that continued to be unclear. These included questions, for instance, related to the awards received, the patent registration, and plans for the future.

It was imperative to interview the entrepreneurs to get a broader understanding of the cases. Additionally, I interviewed six users of the innovations – three of the Bullet Santi tractor, one of the Chetak Cotton Stripper, and two of the groundnut digger machine. At the end of each interview, we asked the entrepreneurs for the contact details of users who had purchased a product from them. Following the interviews with the entrepreneurs, we visited the users who lived in close proximity. Even though they were not informed about the visits in advance, calling to announce our arrival was sufficient, and the people welcomed us with open arms. In those interviews, we mainly asked questions related to the product and the relationship between the user being interviewed and the entrepreneur. We interviewed those living at a distance or those who were unavailable over the phone.

In addition, I interviewed the organisational representatives who work with the grassroots entrepreneurs – the NIF, Sristi, and the Gujarat Grassroots Augmentation Network (GIAN). Within these organisations, the interviewees were selected based on their relevance to the research. I interviewed all the employees who had worked and/or continue to work directly with the entrepreneurs, which was, in total, six informants. These interviews took place in the offices of the support organisations during office hours in English. We used semi-structured interviews and focused only the entrepreneurs who are part of the study instead of attempting to obtain a general picture about grassroots entrepreneurs in India. These interviews provided me with a detailed account of the support given to the entrepreneurs and enhanced my understanding of the journey of the entrepreneurs.

In addition to conducting the interviews, I used field visits to observe how and where the entrepreneurs lived and worked. I made a note of all the interactions outside the recorded interview setting in detail. These instances included the factory visit and the informal discussions between the entrepreneur and the employees. These observations resulted in rich and detailed notes about the presence of computers, award trophies, pictures, and other objects in the office. Another noteworthy observation was the distance between the offices/factories and the nearest town as well as the road conditions. For instance, Jagani's factory was located in a remote area, and the roads leading to it were in poor condition. He travelled on a motorbike, while the other people in his area mostly used either auto rickshaws or tractors. This limits the mobility of the people, possibly impacting Jagani's entrepreneurial activities.

Data analysis

I completed multiple rounds of analysis for this study. I started the analysis with the data retrieved from the archives and compiled case narratives for each case. While doing this, I also wrote reflective research memos about the observations drawn from the data. Following this, I conducted fieldwork by interviewing the entrepreneurs and observing their environment. As is typical for grounded theory, the interview phase and analysis phase blurred into one (Gioia, Corley, and Hamilton 2013). Following the steps of the process research, I constructed a timeline for each case to synthesise the data and identify the steps in the scaling process (Langley 1999). Although the experience of the entrepreneur was the primary focus of the study, the perspective of the network also informed the data analysis and the development of the scaling model. For instance, these practices helped to outline the role of the partners in the process and the evolution of the network of the entrepreneurs from local informal partners to national formal partners.

I used both the archival data and the interviews to develop the data structure (Figure 1), and I used the research memos I had written after each interview to develop the codes. I developed the first order codes based on what the entrepreneurs told me about their scaling process, the challenges they faced, and the mechanisms they used to overcome resource scarcity during the process. While consulting the literature on bricolage and going back and forth between the data and the literature, I used the second order codes to link the first order codes with the extant

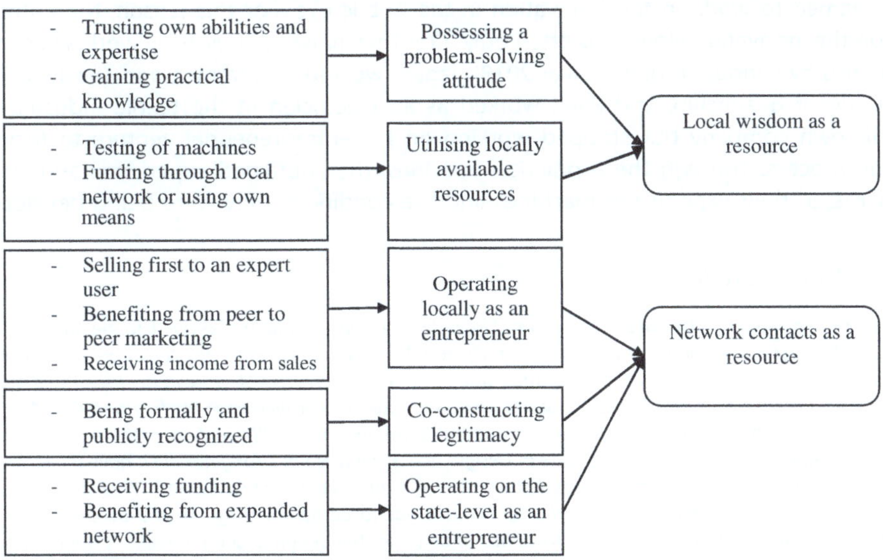

Figure 1. The data structure for scaling of grassroots entrepreneurs.

literature on bricolage and low-income entrepreneurs. Finally, aggregate dimensions emerged from both – the data and the theory – and depicted the answer to the research question.

Scaling process of grassroots entrepreneurs

The data structure (Figure 1) depicts that grassroots entrepreneurs use both their local wisdom and network contacts to overcome constraints of resource scarcity. Local wisdom refers to locally relevant skills, expertise, and the ability to use the same when appropriate. The local network consists of friends, family members, and other individuals in the villages of the entrepreneurs who were perceived as knowledgeable by the entrepreneurs. In a later phase, when their network had grown, the network contacts included representatives from non-governmental and governmental organisations. The findings highlight that the entrepreneurs begin the initiative with solving the problems of people similar to them and with the aspiration to create social value, which confirms the findings in other studies (Linna 2013; Pansera and Sarkar 2016; Sarkar 2018). This study adds to the body of entrepreneurship literature by illuminating the scaling process of grassroots entrepreneurs. It highlights, for instance, the crucial role of the first customer or the benefits of working with formal organisations in the scaling process.

India has a unique ecosystem to support grassroots initiatives. Organisations such as the NIF, Sristi, and GIAN work together with aspiring entrepreneurs to commercialise and scale their innovations, and previous studies have covered the operations of these organisations (Fressoli et al. 2014). Interestingly, the entrepreneurs do not refer to these organisations as organisations but use the names of the individuals working there – Gupta, Professor, Patel – to refer to the organisation. Since the focus of this study is on the perspective of the entrepreneurs, I incorporated these into network contacts. Furthermore, since the organisations work closely together and the boundaries between them are blurred, it is logical to club the organisations together. Other members of the network of the grassroots entrepreneurs are mentioned using their labels, such as family, villagers, and friends.

Local wisdom as a resource

During the product development phase, all the entrepreneurs were ridiculed by their community, feeling ashamed to work on the innovation in the public eye. For this reason, the entrepreneurs worked on the innovation alone and often only after they finished their daily work, which has been observed also by various studies (Sarkar 2018). Jagani worked as a farmer, and Tilwa worked in his brother's tractor dealership, and Patel worked as an electrician in the textile industry. Prajapati owned his own company but stopped working on his entrepreneurial venture to focus on the innovation process. Through these practical activities, they obtained experience and knowledge, which increased their expertise in machines and the conditions they were being developed for.

Problem-solving attitude

> *"I did not have a bike, and the bullet belonged to Mohanbhai [uncle], and he had given it to me and asked me to make this. The first one I made, I gave to him. Initially, it did not have supporters; the tires were not covered, and I put a chain later. In the second one, no one understood that the motorcycle will work in the field. I said that it will work. The villagers were saying that this will not work but I said that it will work. He [my uncle] had made the design, but the reverse gear box was missing. It was made by NIF and the IIM [Indian Institute of Management] people. The design that NID [National Institute of Design] had given was not strong nor did it have the technology – they had just given the design, but it was not useable. – I told Christo sahib; Mahesh Bhai and Gupta sahib [representatives of formal organisations] who said that it has to be designed by the NID people – a designing person doesn't have a technical idea as to what has to be done. The design is good in looks, it does not have the needed strength. I have just left it in the office. There is just one model, and I knew that this [design] will not work." (Mansukhbhai Jagani, personal interview 19.09.2017).*

In the beginning of the scaling process, the grassroots entrepreneurs made do with the resources at hand, which included their experience and the practical knowledge gathered from working on developing the innovation. During the product development process, the entrepreneurs developed the skill of problem-solving (Linna 2013), and this attitude remained throughout the scaling process. Most of the innovations aimed at easing the manual work done by labourers in the agricultural and pottery industry, offering a solution to the problems faced by the entrepreneurs and their community members. Creating social value and spreading it to as many people as possible motivated the entrepreneurs to scale.

Throughout the product development process, the grassroots entrepreneurs developed a habit of experimentation, trusted their own abilities, and became experts on the conditions that the machine was being developed to address. This self-taught expertise, gained through trial and error and improvisation, proved to be a strength in the scaling process. Meanwhile, the members of their community continued making fun of them and their efforts to work on the innovation. At times, it was because the villagers did not understand what the entrepreneurs were working on. In other cases, some sceptical individuals feared that if the machine became popular and used by many people one day, it might push them out of work. For instance, Patel's fellow villagers were worried about their income after the cotton stripper machine would scale in the market.

The grassroots entrepreneurs valued their practical knowledge and experience over external design expertise. The efforts of the network contacts in providing the entrepreneurs with aid to improve the machines they had developed and connecting them with high-quality educational institutions such as NID, IIM, and the Indian Institute of Technology (IIT) were not perceived as helpful by the entrepreneurs. In the experience of the entrepreneurs, the work of these organisations was limited to improving the aesthetics of the design, and they did not help enhance the technical specifications. The entrepreneurs trusted their own practical understanding and knowledge regarding the local conditions more than that of people working or studying in urban institutions away from their villages.

Even though the design support was not perceived as helpful, they valued some of the suggested technological improvements. Following the bricolage logic of using and combining available resources, entrepreneurs used only what they perceived as helpful, while the other parts were left unutilised. For instance, the quality of the Bullet Santi improved when Jagani accepted help to develop a reverse gearbox. The users also confirmed that this led to a significant improvement in the functioning of the machine.

Locally available resources

> *"I had told them in 2009 to test my machine, but they asked me to leave it as it was not giving results. But in 2011, I officially started this business and submitted it for testing. Then they gave me a test performance report. [I wanted to test the machine] to get the subsidy as well as I wanted to know its result of testing. They directly purchased a machine also after getting the result.*
>
> *I have a relative who works in the real estate business. He told me that I should do some good business and he was ready to fund me. He asked how much I need and I asked for around 25 to 30 lakhs [45 000 USD]. [. . .] We have very good relations with him – that is why and he has confidence that we will do something. He supported me at that time. So whenever I needed any money – a lakh or two lakh [1500–3000 USD] – I used to borrow from him."*
> *(Sanjay Tilwa, personal interview, 06.10.2017)*

The grassroots entrepreneurs understood that it was important to test the machines before they could be sold in the market. They then used their network to test their product. For instance, Patel's initial sales failed because the machine broke down during everyday use. All the sold machines were returned to Patel, who had to refund the customers and accumulated a huge financial loss. Had the machine been tested, he would have predicted its weak points and improved it before starting the sales process. He realised that the machine was best tested when used in real-life situations to ensure durability and proper functioning. He used his network and rented the machine to cotton ginners he was familiar with because it allowed him to observe, supervise, and monitor the functioning of the machine. Through this testing and observation, he learned how to further improve the machine.

When an external organization tested and approved the product, the reliability of the innovation and the self-confidence of the entrepreneur increased. For instance, Tilwa approached the Junagadh Agriculture University, a university that he knew of through his work as a tractor salesman and asked them to test his machine. Testing conducted by an outsider was imperative to prove the safety and durability of the product as well. The results of these tests strengthened sales arguments in the market and increased the credibility of the entrepreneur. The testing was also proof for the entrepreneurs themselves that their efforts were coming to fruition.

Throughout the processes of product development and scaling, the grassroots entrepreneurs struggled with funding. When it was time to start large-scale manufacturing of the product and selling it in the market, the entrepreneurs lacked the capital to buy raw materials for manufacturing. Moreover, debt and financial loss during the innovation process added to their financial issues. Therefore, the grassroots entrepreneurs were compelled to make do with the resources at hand. This meant either using their own financial resources earned from their labour – selling clay products or farming – or turning to people in their network for financial support. Since they were not aware of the funding possibilities available within banks, the entrepreneurs did not apply for loans from banks to finance the scaling of their innovation.

Since the grassroots entrepreneurs lacked access to or awareness about organisations that supported entrepreneurs, they relied on their locally available network. The entrepreneurs felt most comfortable approaching people they already knew, and they used private contacts to advance their entrepreneurial endeavours. This worked best when the friend or family member saw private benefits in working with the grassroots entrepreneur. These benefits could include the chance to use the cotton stripper machine for free or fulfilling the duties of being a respectedfamily member, for instance.

The network as a resource

The grassroots entrepreneurs first sold locally and then expanded to the markets beyond their villages. In this process, the entrepreneurs relied mostly on tangible and external resources such as the contacts they created and the networks they built in addition to the awards, patents, and media attention they received. The findings reveal that the entrepreneurs used these resources for purposes other than the ones they were originally intended for. The grassroots entrepreneurs used their creativity to invent new interpretations and modified the existing means at hand for new purposes (Baker and Nelson 2005).

When the grassroots entrepreneurs operated locally, people in their community became aware of them, and they built a reputation of being either creative entrepreneurs or crazy lunatics. Through different mediums, word about them finally reached the representatives of formal organisations. Prajapati met a representative after a journalist wrote an article about him in the local newspaper. A student who participated in the annually organised Summer Scout project approached Patel. In the case of Jagani, the support organisation reached him with the help of the community, since his villagers knew he had developed the Bullet Santi. Tilwa was contacted when a network contact visited the Junagadh Agriculture University and saw the groundnut digging machine that the university had tested. Through these encounters, the network of the entrepreneurs expanded naturally, and they did not engage in an act of active resource-seeking. This is an important detail since it explains how grassroots entrepreneurs encountered formal organisations.

The initial recognition received from the first customer was important to kick start the scaling process. The grassroots entrepreneurs were isolated since they lacked the formal education and skills taught in school besides being located in areas difficult to reach and, in some cases, also hesitant about speaking in Hindi. Living and working in the informal context, the grassroots entrepreneurs were also not aware of the benefits offered by the formal system. Operating with resource constraints, the networks became an important resource for the entrepreneurs – sometimes the only resource at hand. Since they were resourceful and clever, they capitalized on their interaction with formal organisations in various ways. The awards, recognition, and media attention that followed those milestones were important to strengthen the credibility of an entrepreneur despite coming from an informal setting. The received support helped the entrepreneurs see the potential of the innovations they developed as well as themselves as entrepreneurs. Formally, the innovations were also granted a patent and, despite not understanding the rationale of having a patent, they use it as a means to enhance their legitimacy. In conclusion, through these activities, the grassroots entrepreneurs have expanded their network and gained the skills and expertise needed to scale and operate as entrepreneurs beyond their own village.

Operating locally as an entrepreneur

> *"The trust is built when I give it to someone and that someone recommends it to other people. The fridge is good because it uses electricity and when the apple or tomatoes that are put in it taste different, but when it is put in the Mitticool fridge, the taste is still good, and also it does not consume any electricity. Mitticool has given me such a name and has progressed so much because of it." (Mansukhbhai Prajapati, personal interview, 18.09.2017)*

Their first customer was an expert within the field of the innovation as well as someone from within the network of the entrepreneur and was, therefore, a trusted individual who suggested improvements for the innovation. For Mitticool, the first customer was a civil engineer, and for Jagani, it was a farmer from his village. Tilwa's first customer was an individual working with the Junagadh Agriculture University that conducted the testing. In the beginning, a sales agency of a local ginning cooperative supported Patel. Through this organisation, he sold his first machine. Finding a first paying customer who was satisfied with the product was of the utmost importance. It increased the self-confidence of the entrepreneur, displayed the credibility of the innovation, and provided financial gains to the entrepreneur. Customers were important advocates of the products they had purchased, and the grassroots entrepreneurs used peer-to-peer marketing as a mode to spread the word about their product. Receiving appreciation from one fellow villager created a snowball effect that convinced others within the same and surrounding villages to purchase the machine. In conclusion, satisfied customers were an important resource to boost sales, learn about necessary improvements required in the machines, and improve the self-confidence of the entrepreneur.

Interested people who had learned about the innovation from other users or the media called the entrepreneurs and ordered a product for themselves. Patel paid for an advertisement in a newspaper only once and had started advertising on social media recently, but word-of-mouth continues to be important. The entrepreneurs collectively agree that customers keep coming back if their product is good and, thus, the advertisement is not necessary. Moreover, they did not perceive machines that were similar but cheaper or poor-quality imitations as direct competition. Rather, they perceived it as proof of the demand for their products and machines.

The agricultural machines were developed for farmers at the beginning of the value chain while the clay products were developed for families using traditional cooking tools. The clay fridge was particularly beneficial for households living in rural areas with no or unreliable access to electricity. The entrepreneurs wanted to create a positive impact on their communities. Therefore, the products were sold at a price that the user could afford but one that still provided the entrepreneurs with income. Furthermore, users often bought multiple machines from them. For instance, despite being large machines, each user tended to own two, three, or sometimes even five cotton stripper machines.

Developing, commercialising, and scaling innovations became the livelihood that sustained the family of the grassroots entrepreneurs. The entrepreneurs had grown up in poverty and, as a result, were compelled to discontinue their education to work and support their family. This was one reason they were not respected during the product development process. Therefore, the income served multiple purposes. First, it functioned as proof of appreciation for their work. Second, it offered a path to escape poverty. Third, it allowed the entrepreneurs to provide better living conditions to their own family. For instance, Prajapati grew up trading pottery items made by his parents for grains. Thus, becoming a factory owner and providing for his family was important to him. In addition, this income also served as a resource to construct their legitimacy as an entrepreneur.

The users confirmed the use of peer-to-peer marketing. They shared information regarding the innovation with other potential users who asked them about new products in the market. For instance, annual meetings of farmers working in a certain industry provided a forum where farmers met each other and shared news about new machines and technology.

> *"He recommended Sanjaybhai to me, saying that he is a good engineer, and he had made a very good digger machine. [. . .] [It] is 15 kilometres from my village, and there the groundnut machine had come, and I had seen it. After seeing it, I felt it was a good machine and need less labour to be engaged in the field. That's why I thought that I should buy the machine." (Groundnut Digger User, 13.10.2017)*

For prospective customers, it was important to hear about the experiences with the machine directly from a user. Furthermore, knowing someone who had used the machine provided them with an opportunity to scrutinise the machine in use and learn about its usage from the user. After witnessing the machine in use, potential customers trusted the machine better, making it easier to make a purchase decision. Hence, the proactive contact between the grassroots entrepreneurs and their customers proved to be an important resource.

Co-constructing legitimacy

> *"The patent for the fridge, the cooker and the tava [clay pan] is all a show. I am not bothered about the patent – I don't feel it is important. I had taken the patent for my happiness. Everyone can copy a patent – the world is very big, and I am a very small person, so there is no point in my teaching anything. I say that I give training and also for all these things – so what is the point of teaching others to make and not allow them to make them? What is a patent? Nokia also has a patent but doesn't it also get copied? You can get a copy of Samsung in Delhi for Rs. 2000 [30 USD] – keep both [original and duplicate] together, and no one will know the difference. This is only for my name and nothing else. I allow whoever wants to do this. Whatever we make is ultimately used by the common people and that is a thing that makes me happy. I am happy that others copy my work, but no one should make it better than me. I am always striving to make quality products. I am interested to make the products in quantity and reach as many people as I can." (Mansukhbhai Prajapati, personal interview, 18.9.2017)*

The grassroots entrepreneurs who are part of the study received the National Grassroots Innovation award from the NIF. The President of India awards it every two years to individuals from the grassroots level who have developed a technological innovation without the support of external agencies (National Innovation Foundation 2018). The award, as well as the encounter with the president of the country, had a huge impact on the entrepreneurs, serving as a resource for scaling in multiple ways. First, it increased their self-confidence and motivation to continue pursuing the occupational choice of being an entrepreneur. They perceived the award as an appreciation of their hard work, and the award encouraged them to continue working with the endeavour to serve their community. Second, the award gave reputational benefit to the entrepreneur. Each innovation developed by grassroots innovators is well documented and verified before the award is bestowed upon them. Therefore, the award carries credibility, which is also perceived by outsiders. Third, the award had a positive impact on their sales. Thus, the grassroots entrepreneurs utilised the award not only as a form of recognition but also as a resource to advance their business.

Receiving the award also generated media attention, and the grassroots entrepreneurs were covered widely by newspapers and television channels at a local, national, and even international level. In addition to the advertisement value, media attention also helped build the legitimacy of the entrepreneur. There were no questions of authenticity when an international media house aired a story about the innovations. On those occasions, the entrepreneurs were given the opportunity to share their story, the functioning of their innovation, and their vision for the future to a wider audience. Media and publicity functioned, therefore, also as a resource for scaling their enterprises.

The grassroots entrepreneurs accepted various suggestions from their network contacts if they saw value in them, or at least perceived no harm in them. Hence, the entrepreneurs accepted that the network contacts assisted them in applying for the patent. In 2006, the patent was granted to Patel for the Chetak Cotton Stripper machine, and in 2007, it was granted to Jagani for the Bullet Santi. The application for the groundnut digger by Tilwa was submitted in February 2013, and its patent is still pending. Prajapati has applied for design registration on his designs, in 2009 and 2016. Since this is a complicated and costly procedure, the entrepreneurs cannot do it themselves. They provide information about their innovation and sign the application, but all the practicalities are carried out by the network organisations.

Despite appreciating the suggestion to apply for a patent, the entrepreneurs know very little about their network contacts' rational of applying for a patent. Therefore, they attach their own interpretation to it. First, it is a confirmation that their machines and products are really an innovation. Second, having a patent helps grassroots entrepreneurs to be perceived as legitimate in the eyes of third parties and customers. The grassroots entrepreneurs mentioned that the patent was for their own confidence and that it strengthens their products. However, they understood that the patent had limitations. If someone changed the design, it would not be covered by the patent. Therefore, the value of the patent in practice is more instrumental, and it serves the purpose of constructing legitimacy and enhancing self-confidence.

> *"Even these achievements are very much helpful for us. When someone comes to the showroom then seeing the photo, the product quality or standard related questions are answered because 60% of the doubts are getting over there only – if there are so many achievements, then there must be something in these products." (Raja Prajapati, Marketing Manager at Mitticool and son of Mansukhbhai Prajapati, personal interview, 18.09.2017)*

The formal recognition received – whether in terms of awards from the government of India, local banks, or universities – were merits the entrepreneurs shared in the public or private sphere whenever possible years later as well. When visiting the entrepreneurs in their offices, I noticed they all kept pictures hanging in the form of large posters on the wall and displayed the trophies received from different competitions in vitrines for their guests to see. Many of the entrepreneurs also drew my attention to the objects as proof that it really happened and narrated stories related to the events.

In addition to the awards and patents, the publicity also helped in advancing the scaling process of grassroots entrepreneurs. The original function of the award and media attention was to recognise the grassroots actors for their efforts, and the function of the patent was to ensure that the intellectual property rights remained with the inventor of the machines and products. However, the entrepreneurs used these functions as resources at hand for new purposes (Baker and Nelson 2005). These new purposes, for instance, included building the credibility of their innovation, increasing their self-confidence, and spreading the word of the new product available on the market. These also contributed to the scaling process of the enterprises of grassroots entrepreneurs.

Operating at the state-level as an entrepreneur

> *"I have actually 5 to 6 firms – there is Geeta; Uma; Maruti; Chetak; Marshal; Dharti. Around two years back, the turnover was of 30 crores [450 000 USD], and right now also it is around 20 to 25 crore [300 000 – 375 000 USD]. But since demonetization, it has been very slack – everywhere it has slowed down. Slowly we are in the process of consolidating all these companies. We couldn't do business more than Rs. 1 crore [150 000 USD] because of the excise duty, and that is why we had to open so many new companies. Now, because of GST, there is no excise duty, and we can consolidate all the companies under one name." (Mansukhbhai Patel, personal interview, 4.10.2017)*

After receiving the award and gaining immense attention by the media, scaling proceeded faster, and the demand for the innovations increased. However, the entrepreneurs then faced difficulties in trying to respond and meet the increased demand. Even though the grassroots entrepreneurs had developed innovations addressing the needs of the users, they were not aware of aspects such as marketability and usability. They knew they had access to people representing formal organisations whom they could approach anytime with any concern. Working together with these network contacts, grassroots entrepreneurs managed to build partnerships with other organisations. They would not have been able to reach these organisations without help from their network contacts. However, trusting their own expertise and knowledge on the needs of their customers, the grassroots entrepreneurs did not perceive all the suggestions or efforts to help as relevant for them.

The network contacts were valued most for opening doors to formal testing facilities and providing the entrepreneurs access to funding. For instance, the Mitticool fridge was tested in various institutions to verify if its claims of preservation of food held true. With regard to funding, the Micro Venture and Innovation Fund (MVIF) is the funding instrument of the NIF. Being a public institution, it provides risk capital to grassroots entrepreneurs. The MVIF supported Prajapati and Jagani with a capital of INR 500,000 [7,800 USD]. The Technopreneur Promotion Program (TePP) supported Patel with INR 580,000 [9,100 USD]. The trust between the grassroots entrepreneur and the network contacts was an important component in the funding process since reporting of the fund usage was not done formally.

The funding provided by MVIF in the early phases of scaling was a significant financial resource for grassroots entrepreneurs. First, MVIF provided them with the capital to operate as an enterprise and scale their business. Second, for the grassroots entrepreneurs, it was yet another validation and acceptance of their innovative machines and products. Third, since this was collateral-free funding, the entrepreneurs did not have to worry about paying high-interest rates. Additionally, working together with the NIF and GIAN was provided as an in-kind donation, therefore, the entrepreneurs did not have to pay for these services.

Further, also the willingness and motivation of the entrepreneur to scale up the activities affected the scaling process. While others were happy pursuing emerging opportunities, others were more hesitant. For example, Jagani's enterprise has mostly scaled to neighbouring villages but not much beyond. He works on selling the products based on orders, which come in when interested users turn to Jagani after a referral from another user. Jagani continues working on his farming and sees the Bullet Santi as a way to receive additional income. Interestingly, other fabricators are making their own versions of the machine. In contrast, Prajapati, Patel, and Tilwa are selling their machines and products also to customers in other states and actively seeking to find new customers.

Coming from the informal context, the grassroots entrepreneurs were ill-informed about what was feasible and necessary to be done, the sequence of activities in a business, and the skills required, such as marketing. This led to inefficiency in the operation of the grassroots entrepreneurs and frustration when they learned that certain things could have been done better and more efficiently. Tilwa explained that he lacked financial knowledge, did not plan his work in advance, and was unaware about government subsidies. In order to apply for subsidies, he had to write reports and make plans, and for this, he required external help.

Despite trusting their own abilities, being proud of their achievements, and feeling confident about their own work, the entrepreneurs did not feel comfortable working on all issues of the business by themselves. They were aware of their lower status in society, and they often felt like outsiders among formal sector actors. This was especially true when changes in the regulatory system created new situations, making them feel insecure. This predominantly included accounting and taxation-related issues that needed to be completed in accordance with the current legislation. In these situations, the grassroots entrepreneurs utilised their network contacts as a resource and turned to their trusted contacts for formal support.

The close involvement of the network contacts was imperative because it helped the grassroots entrepreneurs on a mental level. Since all the entrepreneurs were seen by their community members as a little bit strange, it was crucial to have a person to turn to – someone both willing and skilled enough to help.

> *"He said that he was trying to manage everything, but it was possible that it was getting stuck at some level because his education was maybe not adequate. Many times he must have felt that because he had a lot of office staff as well as relatives, but he was not getting a good feel about it." (Raja Prajapati, son of Mitticool entrepreneur Mansukhbhai Prajapati, personal interview, 18.9.2017)*

Discussion

This study enriches the discussion around entrepreneurship and poverty alleviation. It makes contributions to the literature on low-income entrepreneurship by (1) building a model of the scaling of grassroots entrepreneurs and (2) defining grassroots entrepreneurs as a unique archetype of low-income entrepreneurs. Furthermore, it contributes to the discussion on bricolage by introducing the concept of grassroots bricolage explaining how grassroots entrepreneurs deal with resource scarcity. Finally, the study involves practical implications, limitations, and avenues for further research.

The scaling process of grassroots entrepreneurs

This study investigated low-income entrepreneurs who have developed, commercialised, and scaled their innovations to different degrees. Previous literature focuses on the lack of resources for scaling (Linna 2013; Webb, Morris, and Pillay 2013) and on subsistence entrepreneurs with little growth potential (Tobias, Mair, and Barbosa-Leiker 2013). Therefore, this study contributes to the discussion by showing that low-income entrepreneurs have the potential and ability to scale their enterprises, and how they do it.

As the scaling model (Figure 2) depicts, the scaling starts from the status quo, where the grassroots entrepreneurs utilise both their own problem-solving skills and locally available contacts. Equipped with these resources, they can operate independently as entrepreneurs in their close locality (Si et al. 2015). At this stage, their network contacts primarily consist of friends, family, and other knowledgeable persons in close proximity with the entrepreneur. Since these people

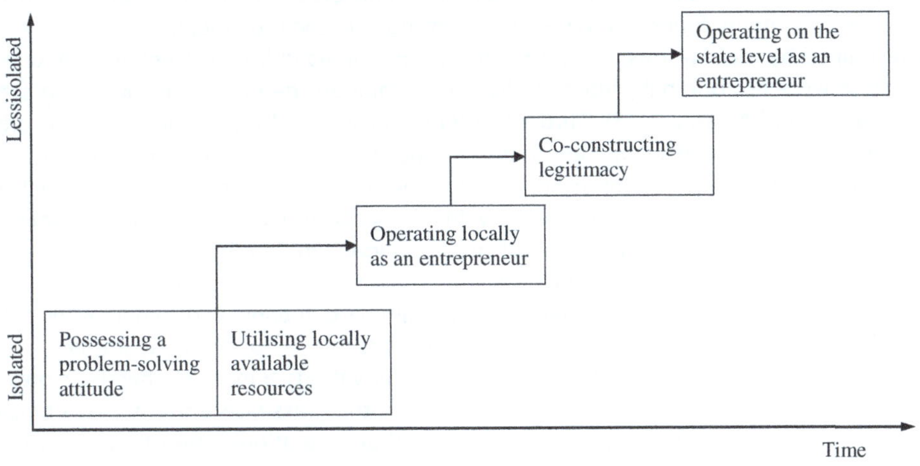

Figure 2. Scaling process of grassroots entrepreneurs.

share a similar knowledge background with the grassroots entrepreneurs, they were unable to provide the entrepreneurs with additional resources necessary for scaling. The local contacts provided the grassroots entrepreneurs with meagre funding and partners for testing and acted as first customers of the machine or product. After the encounter with a formal organisation, the resources available to the entrepreneur increase. Their legitimacy as entrepreneurs, despite coming from a rural setting, gets constructed slowly, together with other actors such as users, the media, and organisations offering formal recognition. Receiving an award, being granted a patent and working with formal organizations contributed to the legitimizing of the grassroots entrepreneurs. Being perceived as legitimate entrepreneurs helps the expansion of the network of the grassroots entrepreneur.

The entrepreneurs face a variety of challenges and difficulties in the scaling process. These relate to a lack of sufficient networks to provide feedback, a lack of funding to advance the entrepreneurial endeavour, and a lack of understanding on how to operate in the system. Though the study reveals the perspective of the entrepreneurs, it does not fully account for the support for product development and business development provided by formal organisations the entrepreneurs worked with. Based on their own interpretation of the situation, the entrepreneurs trust their own experience and gained knowhow, and do not fully acknowledge the support provided by formal organisations in addition to the award, the patent, and the funding. However, it is important to recognise that this was gained by working with the organisations and, hence, requires further investigation.

In addition to the scaling model, this study contributes to literature also by providing further insights related to the scaling process. These relate to (1) the type of innovations, (2) financial resources, (3) the network of the entrepreneur and (4) the degree of informality.

Each entrepreneur has developed an innovative machine or product that cannot be easily imitated since the machines are large, complex, and difficult to produce. Therefore, they differ from the innovations of creative low-income entrepreneurs explored in previous studies (Shepherd, Parida, and Wincent 2017). Moreover, while entrepreneurs from low-income settings typically struggle with scaling due to challenges related to the business idea (Bradley et al. 2012), the entrepreneurs covered in this study had a good sense of business. They responded to the needs of their customers and the market, and their products and machines created a large market demand.

For the scaling process, the grassroots entrepreneurs needed financial resources which came from multiple sources. Initially, the primary source of funding was one's own available means or provided by relatives or a sales agency. Later in the scaling process, publicly funded financial support was accessed through the formal partners of the grassroots entrepreneur. In addition to direct financial support, the formal organisations also offered in-kind support related to product refinement and development, business development, and other trainings. Noteworthy is that the grassroots entrepreneurs found the banking system out of reach for them.

Not restrained by social norms, the grassroots entrepreneurs utilised the networks and resources in ways these were not originally intended for and combined the existing resources to serve new purposes (Baker and Nelson 2005). Through interacting with a broader network, the grassroots entrepreneurs were exposed to operation in the wider society, which included the formal sector. The grassroots entrepreneur stems from an informal environment with informal practices, and available resources are used in an informal way. Instead of contracts and formal agreements, these relationships are based on the foundation of mutual understanding and trust.

At the beginning of the scaling process, the grassroots entrepreneurs were informal and, therefore, illegal actors, yet they worked using legitimate means and activities (Webb et al. 2009). Scaling, they understood, required them to be a formal actor with a legitimate position in the society. The entrepreneurs wanted to sell their innovations and were therefore prepared to formalise their activities. Throughout the scaling process, the grassroots entrepreneurs became less isolated and began to see the benefits of formalising their operations. This observation highlights the uniqueness of these innovative entrepreneurs in resource-scarce settings. It contradicts many previous studies on low-income entrepreneurs who resisted the formalisation of their activities as it would increase competition and expenditure (Webb et al. 2009).

To conclude, this study demonstrates how grassroots entrepreneurs develop their business opportunities (Si et al. 2015) and scale beyond the level of subsistence (Bruton, Ahlstrom, and Si 2015). Had the formal network contacts not provided support, it can be assumed, that the scaling process would have been less successful. The journey would have taken longer, creating additional financial and mental challenges for the entrepreneurs. Therefore, aspiring entrepreneurs hailing from low-income settings who do not entertain the possibility of expanding their network with formal organisations give up easily when disappointments and failures follow and lead to financial and mental setbacks. The entrepreneurs in the study relied on their network throughout the scaling process. Despite the growth of their experience as a result of working as an entrepreneur, the sense of not belonging and isolation remains.

Grassroots entrepreneurs

The second contribution of this study is illustrating the grassroots entrepreneurs with growth potential as a distinctive category of low-income entrepreneurs. In this capacity, they contribute to the welfare of their community through, for instance, job creation. This is noteworthy since the grassroots entrepreneur has more potential for scaling compared to the typical low-income entrepreneurs as described in literature. Low-income entrepreneurs have been understood typically as local sales agents selling consumer goods, which can potentially be sold with low effort also by other individuals in the same locality, and goods which are produced by third-party organisations (Scott et al. 2012; Webb, Morris, and Pillay 2013; Kistruck et al. 2013b).

To advance the literature on low-income entrepreneurship, this study shows that grassroots entrepreneurs develop, commercialise, and scale their products independently for the most part. They continue innovating until they develop the best option and do not settle for the second-best option (Senyard et al. 2014). They also produce and manufacture the products and machines they developed. If the grassroots entrepreneurs had been unwilling to commercialise and scale their innovation, these products would not have reached the market. Therefore, it is justified to claim that these grassroots entrepreneurs are a unique subset among low-income entrepreneurs. The entrepreneurial endeavour of grassroots entrepreneurs is innovation-driven (Yessoufou, Blok, and Omta 2018), although low-income entrepreneurs are typically necessity-driven (McMullen, Ragby, and Palich 2008) and the innovations developed are differentiation-related (Bradley et al. 2012).

It is important to understand this type of entrepreneurship, even though it does not comply with the traditional Silicon Valley model of entrepreneurship (Welter et al. 2017). Firstly, western-based organisations often do not recognise the appropriate local needs or lack awareness of the level of corruption rampant in local institutions and, therefore, fail to embed a solution suitable to the local context (Khavul and Bruton 2013). The innovation-driven locally-embedded grassroots entrepreneurs are aware of local issues. Secondly, venture creation is a tool to create a new identity (Williams and Shepherd 2016), and in the case of grassroots entrepreneurs, it helped them to transition from ridiculed madmen to legitimate entrepreneurs. Thirdly, scaling also leads to the emancipation of the grassroots entrepreneur from resource constraints and changing the power structures in their surrounding society (Rindova, Barry, and Ketchen 2009).

Grassroots bricolage

To advance our understanding of how low-income entrepreneurs operate and to contribute to previous studies on bricolage in low-income contexts (Linna 2013; Sarkar 2018), I developed the concept of grassroots bricolage. Grassroots bricolage is a type of behaviour necessary when developing, commercialising, and scaling of innovations of grassroots entrepreneurs from low-income settings. It means utilizing the locally available resources and network contacts in unforeseen ways. Similar to entrepreneurial bricolage (Baker and Nelson 2005), grassroots entrepreneurs work in a penurious environment with new challenges and limited resources. However, grassroots entrepreneurs do not feel limited by their resource-scarce context and overcome challenges imposed by the context.

The entrepreneurs use the means at hand and prioritise what they believe complements their existing expertise and what they perceive as relevant. Grassroots bricolage involves both local wisdom and networks that the entrepreneurs combine and use in novel ways. Locally available resources include indigenous knowledge, the resourcefulness of the entrepreneur, expertise about the self-developed innovation, and awareness of the conditions for which the innovation has been developed. The network consists of both informal actors from the locality as well as formal actors representing organisations that work with low-income entrepreneurs from resource-scarce settings. The network is utilised as a resource, for instance, to gain access to funding, testing, and marketing strategies. The efforts made by the network contacts are appreciated but utilised only when perceived as useful, since the local wisdom of the bricoleur prevails over outsider expertise. The resources available, such as the skills and experiences of the entrepreneur and the network contacts, also accumulate over time. Since the network expands organically and naturally, this cannot be considered as resource-seeking, where the entrepreneur makes an effort to find new network contacts (Baker 2007).

The network also provides awards, patents, and media attention that the entrepreneurs can skilfully utilise to contribute to their legitimacy as entrepreneurs. Utilizing these intangible resources in new ways is the uniqueness in grassroots bricolage and an important contribution to the literature on bricolage. Hence, instead of seeing the patent as protection against counterfeits, it is a seal of proof that the innovation is real and authentic. Similarly, having others copy the innovation is a sign and further proof of demand. These intangible resources are also key ingredients for co-constructing legitimacy.

To summarize, the study provides contributions to different literature streams. Firstly, the study shows how low-income entrepreneurs scale beyond selling to people living in close proximity to the enterprise. The study further advances the literature on low-income entrepreneurs by highlighting innovation-driven grassroots entrepreneurs as a unique archetype of low-income entrepreneurs, contrasting with the necessity-motivated entrepreneur typically referred to when discussing low-income entrepreneurs. Lastly, grassroots bricolage and the unique way of combining intangible resources in unforeseen new ways is an important contribution to the literature on entrepreneurial bricolage. These main contributions are provided in the table above (Table 3).

Practical implications

This study carries a number of practical implications for policymakers and organisations working with low-income entrepreneurs, minority entrepreneurs, and entrepreneurs isolated from access to resources for other reasons such as a disability. It demonstrates valuing what is already available locally – ideas, experiences, knowledge, or awareness of local issues – when planning entrepreneurship programs. The entrepreneurs have a unique knowledge base that gives them agency. This study also indicates that grassroots entrepreneurs are legitimate stakeholders for companies, whether local or international. Not only are they resourceful and creative problem-solvers, but they are also experts on local needs and locally suitable solutions. Therefore, the grassroots entrepreneur can be a prospective local partner for entrepreneurs, under the condition that they are treated as equals, listened to, and given a real voice.

The entrepreneurs benefit from experts in their network who can provide them with access to other important resources as well as feedback. Nevertheless, it is important to listen to aspiring entrepreneurs and their own assessment of their needs when developing support programs and policies. The study further demonstrates that the aspiring entrepreneurs from resource-scarce environments value relationships based on trust since they come from a context where

Table 3. Summarizing the main contributions of the study.

Contemporary understanding	The findings
Low-income entrepreneurs face difficulty scaling their enterprises due to lacking access to sufficient resources.	Innovative low-income entrepreneurs have the potential to scale. Starting from operating locally as an entrepreneur, the network of the entrepreneur little by little grows and hence also the available resources increase. Through working with formal actors, the legitimacy as an entrepreneurs is established which eventually helps with scaling and reaching state-level markets.
Low-income entrepreneurs tend to be necessity-driven entrepreneurs, selling products created by others and being innovative in mundane activities.	Highlighting the heterogeneity of low-income entrepreneurship, grassroots entrepreneurs are a distinct archetype. These innovation-driven entrepreneurs develop complex products and machines, which are difficult to imitate. The entrepreneurs commercialise and scale these innovations to different degrees. Further, grassroots entrepreneurs are low-income entrepreneurs with growth potential beyond subsistence level.
Entrepreneurial bricolage is applied to entrepreneurs operating in resource-scarce settings, and hence it is also used to describe the conditions of low-income entrepreneurs.	Grassroots bricolage refers to the ability to utilise both locally available resources and network contacts. Further, grassroots bricolage means using intangible resources in new and unforeseen ways to advance entrepreneurial activities in resource-scarce settings.

institutional voids are replaced by social relationships. As an organisation working with these settings, it is important not to be faceless but work with entrepreneurs at a human-to-human level. It is important for entrepreneurs to work with individuals they not only trust but also perceive as knowledgeable. Moreover, this study shows that enhanced capabilities increase the self-confidence of the entrepreneurs. Attention should be paid to ensure that the entrepreneurs feel as comfortable among the formal actors as among their peers.

Limitations of the study and directions for further research

The entrepreneurs selected for this study were all based in the same state in India, the western state of Gujarat. This state was selected as it is known for its entrepreneurial spirit, and the support organisations studied were also located in Gujarat. This can be perceived as a bias, but for this particular research, setting the choice was justified, since the aim was to study grassroots entrepreneurs who have already scaled their innovations. Another potential limitation is related to the translation of the interviews, which were an important source of data for the study. Despite being accurate translations, the translated versions may contain discrepancies or changes in meaning.

During the data collection of this research project, I met one entrepreneur who was unable to expand his network and was still struggling to find his first paying customer. The visit was useful to rule out alternative explanations and investigate counterfactuals. It also helped me better understand the factors involved in scaling beyond one's own village and the role of organisations acting as key network contacts. These include, for instance, the lack of recognition, no mental support from someone who understands the innovation, and minimal financial means. Since this case could not help to answer the research question of how grassroots entrepreneurs scale their enterprises in resource-scarce settings, I decided to exclude the case from the sample. However, as a direction for future research, it is important to study entrepreneurs unsuccessful in their scaling as these can reveal more on the factors related to the scaling process of low-income entrepreneurs.

Actors in a network have multiple perspectives on the same events (Baker 2007), and this study focused on the perspective of the entrepreneur. This appears to differ from the perspective of formal organisations working with grassroots entrepreneurs. In future research, giving a voice to other perspectives of the scaling process can enhance our understanding of the difficulty of scaling. Taking another perspective can also give a more nuanced version than the current study does, for instance, in the degree of support required by grassroots entrepreneurs for product development and scaling. Further, co-constructing legitimacy requires further investigation, particularly on the work done by the network contacts. Furthermore, the low-income context is a potential ground to investigate the negative effects of bricolage and contribute to the ongoing discussion on it (Senyard et al. 2014).

It would also be enlightening to study similar entrepreneurial activities and organisations in geographical locations other than Gujarat, India, including in other Indian states with different institutional environments. Grassroots innovation movements have been identified, for example, in Argentina and Brazil (Smith, Fressoli, and Thomas 2014). Other research could examine entrepreneurial activities in China (Ahlstrom and Ding 2014; Wang et al. 2008) and in much different provinces with respect to entrepreneurial climate (Gong, Chow, and Ahlstrom 2011; Huang 2008). Furthermore, the entrepreneurs covered in the study were Hindu men. It is beyond the scope of this study to assess the role of gender and religion in scaling, but it may be an interesting field for future research (Audretsch, Bönte, and Tamvada 2013).

This study strengthens the case for grassroots entrepreneurs who have developed innovations that scale widely instead of imitations that are diffused locally (González-Pernía, Jung, and Peña 2015). Looking closely at the financial status of grassroots entrepreneurs can help to understand the economic viability of these enterprises in the long run. Further, a closer look at the various financial sources the grassroots entrepreneurs used and the gaps in funding would provide valuable insights, for example, for public policy to support the grassroots entrepreneurs.

It would also be interesting to delve deeper into the challenges faced by the grassroots entrepreneurs on a social and cultural level, following the observations of this study and those of previous studies and examining the influence of social class on occupational choice (Audretsch, Bönte, and Tamvada 2013). This would shed light on prevalent social norms, hierarchies, and the lack of self-confidence limiting the grassroots entrepreneurs. Social acceptability (Webb et al. 2009) or working in the intersection between the formal and the informal, for instance, could also be interesting for further studies.

Conclusion

This study investigated the scaling process of innovative low-income entrepreneurs operating in resource-scarce settings. The entrepreneurs started by establishing a position in the local market, which led to an organic expansion of their network. Through working with the network, the entrepreneurs scaled up to a position wherein they could sustain a livelihood for themselves and their family by selling their self-developed innovation. Further, these grassroots entrepreneurs represent a unique subset of low-income entrepreneurs as they have developed, commercialised, and scaled their innovation. Lastly, the grassroots entrepreneurs manifest the behaviour of grassroots bricolage, which is a combination of the usage of local wisdom and networks as a resource. It refers to utilizing intangible resources provided by the network in new and unforeseen ways. To conclude, if this article could contain only one message, it would be that grassroots entrepreneurs are innovation-driven, resourceful, that they develop, commercialize, scale their innovations, and that they manufacture and sell the products and machines.

Disclosure statement

No potential conflict of interest was reported by the author.

ORCID

Marleen Wierenga http://orcid.org/0000-0002-0457-6897

References

Ahlstrom, D. 2010. "Innovation and Growth: How Business Contributes to Society." *Academy of Management Perspectives* 24 (3): 11–24.

Ahlstrom, D., and Z. Ding. 2014. "Entrepreneurship in China: An Overview." *International Small Business Journal* 32 (6): 610–618. doi:10.1177/0266242613517913.

Ansari, S., K. Munir, and T. Gregg. 2012. "Impact at the 'bottom of the Pyramid: The Role of Social Capital in Capability Development and Community Empowerment." *Journal of Management Studies* 49 (4): 813–842. doi:10.1111/j.1467-6486.2012.01042.x.

Audretsch, D. B., W. Bönte, and J. P. Tamvada. 2013. "Religion, Social Class, and Entrepreneurial Choice." *Journal of Business Venturing* 28 (6): 774–789. doi:10.1016/j.jbusvent.2013.06.002.

Baker, T. 2007. "Resources in Play: Bricolage in the Toy Store(Y)." *Journal of Business Venturing* 22 (5): 694–711. doi:10.1016/j.jbusvent.2006.10.008.

Baker, T., A. S. Miner, and D. T. Eesley. 2003. "Improvising Firms: Bricolage, Account Giving, and Improvisational Competencies in the Founding Process." *Research Policy* 32 (2): 255–276. doi:10.1016/S0048-7333(02)00099-9.

Baker, T., and R. E. Nelson. 2005. "Creating Something from Nothing: Resource Construction through Entrepreneurial Bricolage." *Administrative Science Quarterly* 50 (3): 329–366. doi:10.2189/asqu.2005.50.3.329.

Bradley, S. W., J. S. McMullen, K. Artz, and E. M. Simiyu. 2012. "Capital Is Not Enough: Innovation in Developing Economies." *Journal of Management Studies* 49 (4): 684–717. doi:10.1111/j.1467-6486.2012.01043.x.

Bruton, G. D., D. Ahlstrom, and S. Si. 2015. "Entrepreneurship, Poverty, and Asia: Moving beyond Subsistence Entrepreneurship." *Asia Pacific Journal of Management* 32 (1): 1–22. doi:10.1007/s10490-014-9404-x.

Bruton, G. D., D. J. Ketchen, and R. D. Ireland. 2013. "Entrepreneurship as a Solution to Poverty." *Journal of Business Venturing* 28 (6): 683–689. doi:10.1016/j.jbusvent.2013.05.002.

Chliova, M., and D. Ringov. 2017. "Scaling Impact: Template Development and Replication at the Base of the Pyramid." *The Academy of Management Perspectives* 31 (1): 44–62. doi:10.5465/amp.2015.0010.

DiDomenico, M., H. Haugh, and P. Tracey. 2010. "Social Bricolage: Theorizing Social Value Creation in Social Enterprises." *Entrepreneurship Theory and Practice* 34 (4): 681–703. doi:10.1111/j.1540-6520.2010.00370.x.

Engström, P., and A. McKelvie. 2017. "Financial Literacy, Role Models, and Micro-enterprise Performance in the Informal Economy." *International Small Business Journal* 35 (7): 855–875. doi:10.1177/0266242617717159.

Fressoli, M., E. Around, D. Abrol, A. Smith, A. Ely, and R. Dias. 2014. "When Grassroots Innovation Movements Encounter Mainstream Institutions: Implications for Models of Inclusive Innovation." *Innovation and Development* 4 (2): 277–292. doi:10.1080/2157930X.2014.921354.

Gajendra, R. 2015. "The Essence of Lived Experiences of Grassroots Innovators: A Phenomenological Study." PhD diss., University of Technology, Sydney. https://opus.lib.uts.edu.au/handle/10453/43358

George, G., A. M. McGahan, and J. Prabhu. 2012. "Innovation for Inclusive Growth: Towards a Theoretical Framework and a Research Agenda." *Journal of Management Studies* 49 (4): 661–683. doi:10.1111/j.1467-6486.2012.01048.x.

Gioia, D. A., K. G. Corley, and A. L. Hamilton. 2013. "Seeking Qualitative Rigor in Inductive Research: Notes on the Gioia Methodology." *Organizational Research Methods* 16 (1): 15–31. doi:10.1177/1094428112452151.

Glaser, B. G., and A. L. Strauss. 1967. *The Discovery of Grounded Theory*. New York: Aldine.

Gong, Y., I. H.-S. Chow, and D. Ahlstrom. 2011. "Cultural Diversity in China: Dialect, Job Embeddedness, and Turnover." *Asia Pacific Journal of Management* 28 (2): 221–238. doi:10.1007/s10490-010-9232-6.

González-Pernía, J. L., A. Jung, and I. Peña. 2015. "Innovation-Driven Entrepreneurship in Developing Economies." *Entrepreneurship & Regional Development* 27 (9–10): 555–573. doi:10.1080/08985626.2015.1075602.

Halme, M., S. Lindeman, and P. Linna. 2012. "Innovation for Inclusive Business: Intrapreneurial Bricolage in Multinational Corporations." *Journal of Management Studies* 49 (4): 743–784. doi:10.1111/j.1467-6486.2012.01045.x.

Hart, S., S. Sharma, and M. Halme. 2016. "Poverty, Business Strategy, and Sustainable Development." *Organization & Environment* 29 (4): 401–415. doi:10.1177/0269094211428865.

Hossain, M. 2016. "Grassroots Innovation: A Systematic Review of Two Decades of Research." *Journal of Cleaner Production* 137: 973–981. doi:10.1016/j.jclepro.2016.07.140.

Huang, Y. 2008. *Capitalism with Chinese Characteristics: Entrepreneurship and the State*. New York: Cambridge University Press.

Khavul, S., and G. D. Bruton. 2013. "Harnessing Innovation for Change: Sustainability and Poverty in Developing Countries." *Journal of Management Studies* 50 (2): 285–306. doi:10.1111/j.1467-6486.2012.01067.x.

Kistruck, G. M., P. W. Beamish, I. Qureshi, and C. J. Sutter. 2013a. "Social Intermediation in Base-of-the-Pyramid Markets." *Journal of Management Studies* 50 (1): 31–66. doi:10.1111/j.1467-6486.2012.01076.x.

Kistruck, G. M., C. J. Sutter, R. B. Lount Jr, and B. R. Smith. 2013b. "Mitigating Principal-Agent Problems in Base-of-the-Pyramid Markets: An Identity Spillover Perspective." *Academy of Management Journal* 56 (3): 659–682. doi:10.5465/amj.2011.0336.

Langley, A. 1999. "Strategies for Theorizing from Process Data." *The Academy of Management Review* 24 (4): 691–710. doi:10.5465/AMR.1999.2553248.

Langley, A., C. Smallman, H. Tsoukas, and A. Van de Ven. 2013. "Process Studies of Change in Organization and Management: Unveiling Temporality, Activity and Flow." *Academy of Management Journal* 56 (1): 1–13. doi:10.5465/amj.2013.4001.

Linna, P. 2013. "Bricolage as A Means of Innovating in A Resource-Scarce Environment: A Study of Innovator-Entrepreneurs at the BOP." *Journal of Developmental Entrepreneurship* 18 (3): 1–23. doi:10.1142/S1084946713500155.

Mair, J., and I. Marti. 2009. "Entrepreneurship in and around Institutional Voids: A Case Study from Bangladesh." *Journal of Business Venturing* 24 (5): 419–435. doi:10.1016/j.jbusvent.2008.04.006.

McMullen, J. S., D. R. Ragby, and L. E. Palich. 2008. "Economic Freedom and the Motivation to Engage in Entrepreneurial Action." *Entrepreneurship Theory & Practice* 32 (5): 875–895. doi:10.1111/j.1540-6520.2008.00260.x.

Molecke, G., and J. Pinkse. 2017. "Accountability for Social Impact: A Bricolage Perspective on Impact Measurement in Social Enterprises." *Journal of Business Venturing* 32 (5): 550–568. doi:10.1016/j.jbusvent.2017.05.003.

National Innovation Foundation – India. "National Innovation Foundation", Accessed 5 July 2018. http://nif.org.in/

Pansera, M., and S. Sarkar. 2016. "Crafting Sustainable Development Solutions: Frugal Innovations of Grassroots Entrepreneurs." *Sustainability* 8 (1): 51. doi:10.3390/su8010051.

Patton, M. Q. 1990. *Qualitative Evaluation and Research Methods*. 2nd ed. Newbury Park: Sage Publications.

Prabhu, J., and S. Jain. 2015. "Innovation and Entrepreneurship in India: Understanding Jugaad." *Asia Pacific Journal of Management* 32 (4): 843–868. doi:10.1007/s10490-015-9445-9.

Rindova, V., D. Barry, and D. J. Ketchen. 2009. "Entrepreneuring as Emancipation." *The Academy of Management Review* 34 (3): 477–491. doi:10.5465/amr.2009.40632647.

Sarkar, S. 2018. "Grassroots Entrepreneurs and Social Change at the Bottom of the Pyramid: The Role of Bricolage." *Entrepreneurship & Regional Development* 30 (3–4): 421–449. doi:10.1080/08985626.2017.1413773.

Scott, L., C. Dolan, M. Johnstone–Louis, K. Sugden, and W. Maryalice. 2012. "Enterprise and Inequality: A Study of Avon in South Africa." *Entrepreneurship Theory and Practice* 36 (3): 543–568. doi:10.1111/j.1540-6520.2012.00507.x.

Senyard, J., T. Baker, P. Steffens, and P. Davidsson. 2014. "Bricolage as a Path to Innovativeness for Resource-Constrained New Firms." *Journal of Product Innovation Management* 31 (2): 211–230. doi:10.1111/jpim.12091.

Shepherd, D. A., V. Parida, and J. Wincent. 2017. "The Surprising Duality of Jugaad: Low Firm Growth and High Inclusive Growth." *Journal of Management Studies* (Advance online publication). doi:10.1111/joms.12309.

Si, S., Y. Xuebao, W. Aiqi, S. Chen, S. Chen, and S. Yiyi. 2015. "Entrepreneurship and Poverty Reduction: A Case Study of Yiwu, China." *Asia Pacific Journal of Management* 32 (1): 119–143. doi:10.1007/s10490-014-9395-7.

Smith, A., M. Fressoli, and H. Thomas. 2014. "Grassroots Innovation Movements: Challenges and Contributions." *Journal of Cleaner Production* 63: 114–124. doi:10.1016/j.jclepro.2012.12.025.

Sutter, C., G. D. Bruton, and J. Chen. 2019. "Entrepreneurship as A Solution to Extreme Poverty: A Review and Future Research Directions." *Journal of Business Venturing* 34 (1): 197–214. doi:10.1016/j.jbusvent.2018.06.003.

Sutter, C., J. Webb, G. Kistruck, D. J. Ketchen, and R. D. Ireland. 2017. "Transitioning Entrepreneurs from Informal to Formal Markets." *Journal of Business Venturing* 32 (4): 420–442. doi:10.1016/j.jbusvent.2017.03.002.

Tasavori, M., C. Kwong, and S. Pruthi. 2018. "Resource Bricolage and Growth of Product and Market Scope in Social Enterprises." *Entrepreneurship & Regional Development* 30 (3–4): 336–361. doi:10.1080/08985626.2017.1413775.

Tobias, J. M., J. Mair, and C. Barbosa-Leiker. 2013. "Toward a Theory of Transformative Entrepreneuring: Poverty Reduction and Conflict Resolution in Rwanda's Entrepreneurial Coffee Sector." *Journal of Business Venturing* 28 (6): 728–742. doi:10.1016/j.jbusvent.2013.03.003.

Wang, L. C., D. Ahlstrom, A. Nair, and R. Z. Hang. 2008. "Creating Globally Competitive and Innovative Products: China's Next Olympic Challenge." *SAM Advanced Management Journal* 73 (3): 4–16.

Webb, J. W., R. Laszlo Tihanyi, D. Ireland, and D. G. Simon. 2009. "You Say Illegal, I Say Legitimate: Entrepreneurship in the Informal Economy." *The Academy of Management Review* 34 (3): 492–510. doi:10.5465/AMR.2009.40632826.

Webb, J. W., M. H. Morris, and R. Pillay. 2013. "Microenterprise Growth at the Base of the Pyramid: A Resource-Based Perspective." *Journal of Developmental Entrepreneurship* 18 (4): 1–20. doi:10.1142/S108494671350026X.

Welter, F., T. Baker, D. B. Audretsch, and W. B. Gartner. 2017. "Everyday Entrepreneurship—A Call for Entrepreneurship Research to Embrace Entrepreneurial Diversity." *Entrepreneurship Theory and Practice* 41 (3): 311–321. doi:10.1111/etap.12258.

Williams, T. A., and D. A. Shepherd. 2016. "Victim Entrepreneurs Doing Well by Doing Good: Venture Creation and Well-being in the Aftermath of a Resource Shock." *Journal of Business Venturing* 31 (4): 365–387. doi:10.1016/j.jbusvent.2016.04.002.

Yessoufou, A. W., V. Blok, and S. W. F. Omta. 2018. "The Process of Entrepreneurial Action at the Base of the Pyramid in Developing Countries: A Case of Vegetable Farmers in Benin." *Entrepreneurship & Regional Development* 30 (1–2): 1–28. doi:10.1080/08985626.2017.1364788.

Appendix A. Case descriptions

The four selected cases are the Mitticool clay fridge, the Bullet Santi multi-purpose agricultural machine, the Chetak Cotton Stripper, and the groundnut digger. In the following section, I briefly explain the background of each entrepreneur and the origin of each innovation and Table 4 offers a summary of the cases.

(1) Clay fridge 'Mitticool' and Mansukhbhai Prajapati

Mansukhbhai Prajapati was the only son in a pottery family. He dropped out of school after tenth grade and has been working ever since. He joined a tile manufacturing company, where he learned about machines and automated operations. In 1988, he left the tile manufacturing company to establish his own enterprise that manufactured tava pans made out of clay. He later developed a water cooler made out of clay. During the earthquake in Gujarat in 2001, a local newspaper published a picture of a broken water cooler but wrongly reported that the poor man's fridge was broken. This triggered Prajapati to start developing a fridge made out of clay, because he understood that the need for a fridge to keep food cool may arise in the absence of electricity.

During the product development process, Prajapati faced huge challenges finding the right combination of the clay mixture. He sought the help of his family, who also worked with pottery, and his more educated friends for this

Table 4. Table summarizing data of the cases.

	Possessing a problem-solving attitude	Utilizing locally available resources	Operating locally as an entrepreneur	Co-constructing legitimacy	Operating on the state level as an entrepreneur
Mitticool		(1988)2001–2005		2005–2017	
	Practical experimenting: with clay, soil and design; Chakda for distribution Trusting own abilities	Family: clay expertise Informal money lender: funding Customers: feedback	Operating locally: selling from a chakda Pans break Stopped working with skillet to develop fridge	2007: MVIF 2009: Award 2009: Future group 2011: ISO certificate Trade mark registration	2017: 50 000 fridges sold
Bullet Santi		1994–2000		2001–2017	
	Chakda as example for building Bullet Santi	Uncle: initial idea Customers: feedback Family	1994 – sold 1 1995 – sold 3 1996 – sold 8	Award and cash prize: 2001 MVIF loan: 2001 Exhibition in South Africa: 2002 Gear box developed by IIMA people	Sales to Kenya By 2017 – sold 400 bullets
Chetak		1991–1998		2000–2017	
	Practical knowledge: electrification, machines Trusting own abilities	Ginning cooperative: funds, sales agency Plants for cotton ginning: testing Sons working on the enterprise	Operating locally as entrepreneur Failed sales	2002: Award & cash prize 2004: Patent Word of mouth Funding: TePP Media attention	Diversifying company Exhibitions & fairs Made based on demand
Groundnut digger		2006–2011		2011–2017	
	Develop machines based on perceived problem and own skills	Brother Friend (storage) Relative (funding) Agriculture University (testing)	Machines unsold, or sold but returned Develop ploughing machine to survive	Positive test results Award Patent application First customers	100 machines sold Lacking skills to grow internationally Personal sales

process. He obtained a loan from a moneylender at a high interest rate. When he was unable to repay the loan, he was compelled to sell his parental home, which was the collateral for the loan. After three years of product development, he finished creating the clay fridge, and the first customer he sold it to was a civil engineer in 2004. Prajapati later also developed a non-stick pan and a pressure cooker out of clay.

(2) Multipurpose tractor 'Bullet Santi' and Mansukhbhai Jagani

Mansukhbhai Jagani dropped out of school to help his father with farming activities. He opened his own workshop but continued working on the farm. In the workshop, he carried out reparation and fabrication jobs.

Farmers traditionally use bullocks on their land, as tractors are too expensive. Tractors also require diesel, but only when they are being used. Bullocks require care and fodder all year long, which is difficult to obtain in drought-prone areas. In 1993, Jagani's village faced a drought, and he had to sell the bullocks his family owned. After this, it became impossible to buy new bullocks. Therefore, he started to develop a machine that had the strength of a bullock but at an affordable cost of ownership. Furthermore, farmers lacked the labour force required for their fields, since many labourers moved to the city. Using the engine of an old motorcycle, Jagani built a three-wheeled tractor. The vehicle is smaller than a tractor but stronger than an animal. It turns with ease and applied less pressure on the soil since it is lighter than a tractor. For these reasons, it is very suitable for cotton farming.

His first customer was a farmer from Jagani's own village. Since then, he has not been very eager to structurally expand the business and is happy with the constant flow of customers. There are a total of about 100 fabricators who build machines similar to the Bullet Santi. With the help of Sristi and its local university partner, the Bullet Santi has also been introduced in the Kenyan market.

(3) Cotton Stripper 'Chetak' and Mansukhbhai Patel

As a child, Patel worked as a cotton stripper, extracting cotton fibres out of the shell. He had thought about a machine that would automate the tedious work of cotton stripping. Patel studied until 9th grade, after which he started working as an electrician in the textile industry. While working in the textile industry, he discussed his idea of building a cotton stripper machine with his manager who was also a relative of his. The manager supported Patel, as did the leader of the local ginning mill cooperative, and with this initial capital, he started developing the machine.

Patel had learned about machines while working in textile industry factories. Nevertheless, it took him a lot of time to develop the cotton stripping machine. Since the community made fun of his work, he was forced to work in the evenings. The first prototype was introduced in the market in 1991, and Patel sold 50 machines through an agency owned by the ginners' association. These were soon returned as they broke when being used. Patel had to repay all the initial buyers, and he wanted to improve the machine. In this period, his biggest challenge was the lack of sufficient financial resources. There were days when his family did not have enough to eat. Patel has two sons who dropped out of school to work on the innovation while he worked at his salaried job.

The second prototype reached the market in 1994, and four years later, the third prototype was ready. This version was a success, and even today the machine is still working on the same principle as the third prototype. The customers are ginners, and each customer typically buys 2 to 3 machines from Patel.

(4) Groundnut digging machine and Sanjay Tilwa

Tilwa's father is a teacher, and he himself is educated as well. He moved to Junagadh to complete his B. Com degree while working occasionally to cover the costs. When he graduated in 2003, he moved back to his village and became a farmer. He also worked for his brother's tractor business, taking care of any requirement that came up in the business, but he predominantly worked with sales. A few years later, he wanted to start dealing in agricultural machines, and with the support of a relative, he started his firm Akshar Agro Engineering.

Tilwa was a groundnut farmer. While working on the field, he observed the other workers and realised how difficult it was to dig up groundnuts. Labour costs were high, and due to a lack of labourers, it was difficult to find skilled labour. In 2007, he started developing a machine to aid groundnut harvesting.

The original model was a handheld device. However, this was inefficient and required labour. Next, he developed a tractor-operated plough, but this too did not work properly, as the nut would break or stay in the ground when being dug out. Throughout the developmental process, Tilwa discussed these issues with other farmers. In 2009, Tilwa developed a first working prototype. The support and advice he received from his brother and his friend were very important for the development process.

The groundnut digger was tested at the Junagadh Agricultural University in 2011, and it received positive feedback. The machine digs, cleans, and dries the nuts. It saves time, labour, and money compared to the manual digging of groundnuts. However, the machine was not a commercial success in the beginning. Tilwa also developed a ploughing machine that is currently selling well and using the profit gained from its sales, he was able to develop processes for selling and manufacturing the groundnut-digging machine. He has ambitious targets for the future and is currently looking proactively into the international market.

Appendix B. Tables with prior literature

Below are two tables showing the previous literature, firstly from empirical studies related to low-income entrepreneurship and secondly from studies related to bricolage. (Tables 5 and 6).

Table 5. Prior empirical studies related to low-income entrepreneurship.

Authors	Research context	Key findings related to low-income entrepreneurship
Bradley, McMullen, Artz, and Siiyu 2012	Nairobi, Kenya	Human capital (expertise and family business experience), financial capital (loans) and social capital (networks and weak ties) important for business development. Differentiation-related innovations and novelty-related innovations Indebtedness decreasing likelihood of innovation
González-Pernía, Jung, and Peña 2015	45 developing countries	Focusing on innovative entrepreneurs, the study finds that they contribute to society by developing new technologies, creating jobs, and increasing revitalization in different areas.
Kistruck, Beamish, Qureshi, and Sutter 2013a	11 countries in Africa, Asia and Latin America	Social intermediaries have altruistic intentions, and hence incorporate unprofitable transaction functions and are driven by the motivation of empowering low-income actors.
Mair and Marti 2009	Bangladesh	Departing from institutional voids preventing entrepreneurial activity, the study examines the institutional factors and the work done by an NGO as an institutional entrepreneur to overcome barriers for access to the market.
Pansera and Sarkar 2016	India	Grassroots innovators are driven by improving social conditions in their community and reducing environmental harm. They also have the potential to contribute to achieving sustainable development.
Sarkar 2018	India	For grassroots entrepreneurs, resource-scarce environment is not an impossible limitation as these entrepreneurs reuse tangible and intangible resources through bricolage.
Scott et al. 2012	Townships in South Africa	Exploring women working as sales representatives for Avon showed that entrepreneurship combined with training and other support leads to emancipation, more income, and improved self-confidence.
Shepherd, Parida, and Wincent 2017	India	When bringing the creative poor individuals to the centre of the discussion on inclusive growth, the creative problem-solving leads to both the facilitation of inclusive growth and low firm growth due to the development of imitable products.
Si, Yu, Wu, Chen, Chen, and Su 2015	China	As a case study on entrepreneurial endeavours to alleviate poverty, the findings suggest that peasant entrepreneurs rely on their own efforts to discover business opportunities and they have a deep understanding of the local market.
Sutter, Webb, Kistruck, Ketchen, and Ireland 2017	Nicaragua	Institutional intermediaries helping entrepreneurs to transition from an informal institutional framework to a formal institutional framework use a variety of tactics on individual and network level, but also on a system level. This is called institutional scaffolding.
Tobias, Mair, and Barbosa-Leiker 2013	Rural Rwanda	Rural dwellers exploit entrepreneurial opportunities created by institutional actors for social and economic benefits. More income and better quality of life leads to trust between hostile ethnic groups.
Webb, Morris, and Pillay 2013	Townships in South Africa	Taking a resources-based theory approach, the growth of micro-entrepreneurs depends on the ownership of resources and the formal institutional context, such as access to utilities and efficient access to financial capital.
Williams and Shepherd 2016	Australia	After a natural disaster, venture creation and entrepreneurship functioned as a way to manage a challenging situation and to have naturally occurring social interactions.
Yessoufou, Blok, and Omta 2018	Benin	In a study on vegetable producers, micro-enterprises emerged at the intersection of motivation, uncertainty, and disruptive events.

Table 6. Prior literature related to bricolage.

Authors	Research context	Key findings related to bricolage
Baker and Nelson 2005	United States	Entrepreneurial bricolage means "making do by applying combinations of the resources at hand to new problems and opportunities."
Baker, Miner, and Eesley 2003	United States	Investigating strategic improvisation and introducing the concept of network bricolage referring to contacts as a means at hand.
DiDomenico, Haugh, and Tracey 2010	United Kingdom	Introducing social bricolage as a way social enterprises acquire resources in a resource-scarce environment. Social bricolage includes the processes of entrepreneurial bricolage but also social value creation, stakeholder participation, and persuasion.
Halme, Lindeman, and Linna 2012	Ethiopia and India	Individuals working on projects related to innovations for inclusive business within large organisations facing resource scarcity engage in various practices labeled as intrapreneurial bricolage.
Linna 2013	Kenya	The bricolage activities low-income entrepreneurs engage with are possessing a social mindset, being resourceful, making do with resources at hand and improvising. Further, entrepreneurs need to have the capabilities to use perform these activities.
Mair and Marti 2009	Bangladesh	The process of institutional entrepreneurs working to fill institutional voids can be understood as a form of bricolage. Aspects of bricolage the study highlights are the sense-making of the bricoleur, its political nature and unintended consequences.
Molecke and Pinkse 2017	10 developing countries in Latin America, Asia and Africa	The study on impact measurements conducted by social enterprises shows that material bricolage, referring to the tangible means, and ideational bricolage, meaning the logic, interpretation and intuition of the entrepreneurs, relate to each other and entrepreneurs use these simultaneously.
Sarkar 2018	India	Bricolage behaviour of grassroots entrepreneurs: breaking social norms; utilising old and acquiring new skills; own time
Senyard et al. 2014	Australia	The study shows that the more a new and resource-constrained firm engaged in bricolage, the more innovative it is.
Tasavori, Kwong, and Pruthi 2018	United Kingdom	Social entrepreneurs utilise both internal bricolage with incremental improvisation, and network bricolage when growing their product and market scope.

Entrepreneurial aspirations and poverty reduction: the role of institutional context

Sanjay Goel and Ranjan Karri

ABSTRACT

Integrating insights from institutional theory and a subjectivist view of entrepreneurial action, we developed a conceptual model of poverty reduction in the context of institutional rigidities and institutional contradictions through their influence on aspirations. Based on the 'subjective' stream of entrepreneurship, our model portrays institutional rigidities and contradictions moderating the influence of aspirations on entrepreneurial action by affecting the subjective value that potential entrepreneurs place on their resources. Because the value of resources is subjective in our exposition, our model suggests specific institutional configurations where a change in aspirations among the poor may provide them with unique insights to exploit entrepreneurial opportunities visible only to them. Our 'poor-as-owners' model can be contrasted with interventionist approaches to poverty reduction, which are aimed at creating win-win entrepreneurial models between the poor and the non-poor. Several policy implications can be derived from our paper that may be more effective in achieving regional development and reducing regional disparities that arise from a higher incidence of poverty.

Introduction

Entrepreneurship is an activity that lies at the intersection of two phenomena – the presence of potentially lucrative opportunities and the presence of enterprising individuals (Sarason, Dean, and Dillard 2006; Shane and Venkataraman 2000). Agents author entrepreneurial actions to link perceived opportunities with a future they wish to create and develop (Sarasvathy 2009). Thus, entrepreneurial actions are defined as actions 'intended to not only to create wealth but also to bring about new states in relevant economic, social, institutional, and cultural environments.' (Rindova, Barry, and Ketchen Jr., 2009). Further, Rindova, Barry, and Ketchen (2009) argue that entrepreneurial actions may be 'emancipatory' in that the individuals can take actions to change the status quo by altering their position in the social order in which they are embedded. Following this stream of argument, entrepreneurial actions could lead to sustained poverty reduction, enhancing the quality of life and emancipating the poor across the world.

Poverty is a state of resource scarcity that may be socially exacerbated by high and persistent resource inequality in society (Hagenaar 1988). Persistent poverty indicates a society with little growth or movement along the economic ladder. It has been acknowledged that entrepreneurship as a solution to poverty alleviation is an attractive proposition, but the relationship requires substantial exploration (Bruton, Ahlstrom, and Si 2015). In a comprehensive review of literature on the relationship between entrepreneurship and poverty alleviation, Sutter, Bruton, and Chen (2019), identify three distinct themes – *remediation, reform* and *revolution* perspectives. The *remediation* perspective views the efforts of external actors or institutions directed at the poor or taken *on behalf of the poor*, such as the Base of Pyramid initiatives (Prahalad 2006), foreign aid, training, and providing financial capital (e.g. Chliova, Brinckmann, and Rosenbusch 2015) as solutions to poverty alleviation. Encouraging entrepreneurs to discover and create opportunities in the poverty context (Alvarez and Barney 2014), and alleviating poverty by providing access to resources such as microfinance (e.g. Bruton, Khavul, and Chavez 2011; Bruton, Ketchen and Ireland 2013) also fall under the remediation perspective. The second stream of literature takes the *reform* perspective wherein the main assumption is that the poverty is a result of social exclusion (Mair, Marti, and Ventresca 2012), and can be addressed with institutional reform. Entrepreneurial actions (that may lead people out of poverty) are possible with changes in institutions that facilitate inclusion (Ghani, Kerr, and O'connell 2014) and increase the possibilities of transitioning entrepreneurs from the informal economy to the formal economy (Sutter, Bruton, and Chen 2019). Finally, the *revolution* perspective in the literature addresses poverty alleviation through changes to the economic and institutional order. Instead of viewing poor as passive *recipients* of resources and market for goods and service, the revolution alternative gives agency to the poor to alleviate their poverty via approaches such as community-based entrepreneurship (Peredo and Chrisman 2006).

The poor in this respect are capable individuals undertaking entrepreneurial actions by challenging the existing norms and bringing about new institutional and cultural environment. For example, Brush et al. (2004) provide evidence of entrepreneurial actions undertaken by female entrepreneurs in marginalized social and cultural environments to improve their own economic status. Similarly, Si et al. (2015) present the findings of a case study from China, where the poor relied on their own ability to discover and take advantage of opportunities with changes in attitudes towards entrepreneurship, pursuit of small gains, interactions with more successful entrepreneurs and employing disruptive business models. While relatively sparsely represented compared to other two approaches (Sutter, Bruton, and Chen 2019), this perspective is central to the promise of entrepreneurship as emancipation, and also the perspective we adopt in this paper.

Scholars of both institutional theory (Bruton, Ahlstrom, and Li 2010; Beckert 1999; North 1990, 2005; Scott 2013), as well as entrepreneurship (e.g. Kibler 2013; Liñán, Urbano, and Guerrero 2011) have established that institutional context influences entrepreneurial action. Following this stream, the adequacy or lack of entrepreneurial action is explained due to the presence or absence of appropriate institutions (e.g. Bruton, Fried, and Manigart 2005; McMillan and Woodruff 2002). Entrepreneurial actions are influenced by institutional contexts in which they unfold (see e.g. Kibler 2013). Both opportunities and individuals are embedded in an institutional context (Jack and Anderson 2002; Seo and Creed 2002; Uzzi 1977). Entrepreneurs thus represent actors who create opportunities through innovative manipulation or challenging of institutionalized normative patterns (Barth 1963; Battilana, Leca, and Boxenbaum 2009; Reed 1988; Winkel et al. 2013; Stewart 1991). According to this stream, it is important to understand the larger institutional context and the institutional characteristics that may determine the nature of entrepreneurial actions in terms of both the size and scope of such actions (Zahra and Wright 2011).

We subscribe to the premise that individuals do not simply react to institutional stimuli (Bechky 2011; Hallett and Ventresca 2006). In other words, the institutional environment provides the 'raw material' which entrepreneurs use along with their own cognitive resources to develop their aspirations and pursue subsequent actions. Individuals vary in their capacity to deal with or 'apprehend' the institutional environment they face (Voronov and Yorks 2015). As Voronov and Yorks summarize, '... people are sometimes able to break through the blinders imposed on them by extant institutional arrangements, and some people are more likely to do so than others.' We also deploy the subjective view of entrepreneurship (Alvarez and Barney 2007, 2010; Chiles et al. 2010; Lachmann 1976; Sarasvathy 2001) to develop an individual-centered model of sustained poverty reduction. In particular, we study the effect of entrepreneurial aspiration on poverty reduction at the micro and macro level. We then examine the institutional environments that constrain or enhance entrepreneurial aspirations (Bruton, Ahlstrom, and Obloj 2008)

Linking these central themes of entrepreneurship and institutional theory, we develop a model of poverty reduction that conceptualizes the influence of institutional characteristics (specifically, institutional contradictions and institutional rigidities) on entrepreneurial aspirations among the poor. Following extant literature on the role of aspirations in the pursuit of entrepreneurial opportunities (Lee and Venkatarman 2006; Estrin, Korosteleva, and Mickiewicz 2013), we first argue that entrepreneurial aspirations by the poor could trigger subsequent action that reduces poverty at an individual and population level. Following the developments in incorporating institutional context in entrepreneurship theory (e.g. Ahlstrom and Bruton 2006; Yamakawa, Peng, and Deeds 2008), we then model the influence of institutional contradictions and institutional rigidities on entrepreneurial aspirations of the poor. Our paper contributes to theory by introducing entrepreneurial aspirations (as opposed to entrepreneurial action) as the key consequential construct that institutions affect. When specific institutional characteristics (institutional contradictions and institutional rigidities in our model) suppress entrepreneurial aspirations, it retards entrepreneurial actions by the poor, trapping them in their current state of poverty. A policy implication of our model is that intervention efforts need to be weighed more toward directly attacking specific institutional constraints that suppress entrepreneurial aspirations, rather than providing direct access to resources for sustained poverty reduction at a macro level.

Literature review

Entrepreneurial aspirations

Aspirations are concerned with the goal content of individuals that satisfy an array of individual needs consisting of psychological and physiological needs (Kasser and Ryan 1993, 1996). Aspirations are different from goals in that aspirations are more abstract than goals; goals are more specific in nature and may be considered potential milestones toward the achievement of more general aspirations. This distinction also recognizes that while goals, being more specific and tangible, may be achieved, aspirations, which are more abstract, are never fully achieved. The nature of aspirations, according to the literature in psychology is known to be associated with actions that result in varying levels of satisfaction and the general well-being of individuals (Deci and Ryan 2000; Sheldon et al. 2004).

Consistent with the psychological definition of individual aspirations, entrepreneurship scholars define aspirations as 'a combination of economic, social, and psychological benefits that an individual would like to have or that she believes she has the means and motivations to achieve for herself (Lee and Venkataraman 2006, 114).' Because aspirations are a set of multifaceted benefits (economic, social, psychological and physiological), sought by individuals, such aspirations may be fulfilled by pursuing and achieving a variety of actions. The pursuit of entrepreneurial opportunities is one such line of action. We thus define *entrepreneurial aspirations* as an array of benefits desired by individuals through the pursuit of *entrepreneurial* actions.[1] Our definition includes two aspects – the aspiration to be an entrepreneur or not (a mutually exclusive choice), as well as goals set by those who aspire to be an entrepreneur (a scale and scope decision). Literature on cognition in general, as well as entrepreneurial cognition in particular, makes persuasive conceptual arguments that suggest entrepreneurial intentions (i.e. whether one chooses to be an entrepreneur or not – an aspect of aspirations) as reliable predictors of actual entrepreneurial actions (Ajzen 1991; Krueger 2000, 2007; Krueger, Reilly, and Carsud 2000).

In the extant nomological network, we see entrepreneurial aspirations as positioned between entrepreneurial imagination, which are enactments of the possible futures in the mind of the entrepreneur, and entrepreneurial goals (Sarasvathy 2001; Miller and Le Breton-Miller 2017), which constitute entrepreneur's intermediate goals at a point of time in pursuit of her aspirations (McMullen 2015). Therefore, the entrepreneur's imagination provides the context for her aspirations, which in turn leads to specific goals at a point of time.[2]

A subjectivist view of entrepreneurship

Among several perspectives in entrepreneurship literature describing the entrepreneurial process, one views opportunities as created by individuals and emerging from the subjective cognitions of the entrepreneur (Alvarez and Barney 2007, 2010; Chiles et al. 2010; Lachmann 1976; Sarasvathy 2001, 2009). From this perspective, the entrepreneur actively creates and recreates the social world through actions and interactions, which are necessary and functional because of *uncertainty* in environmental conditions (Lachmann 1976; Shackle 1979). Thus, opportunities do not exist in the environment to be discovered, but are *endogenously* created through mental models of individuals and are based on interpretation of experiences and imagined future expectations leading to a malleable vision of the future (Chiles et al. 2010; Weick 1995); then, these opportunities are acted upon through entrepreneurial activities of experimentation, finally leading to new enterprises (Kerr, Nanda, and Rhodes-Kropf 2014).

Following the subjectivist view, the means or resources, as well as ends, are defined endogenously, suggesting that the ends can change depending on the resources that the entrepreneur conceptualizes (Foss et al. 2008; Sarasvathy 2001, 2009; Mahoney and Michael 2005; Kor, Mahoney, and Michael 2007). Thus the entrepreneurial reasoning process behind the entrepreneurial actions is concerned with how entrepreneurs address their means – i.e. how they increase the value of resources. In other words, entrepreneurial action relies on finding new uses for existing resources, increasing their subsequent 'opportunity costs.' Importantly, a qualitative and subjective feature of 'resources' is the assessment of their relative fungibility and malleability in the mind of the entrepreneur, which makes it valuable for entrepreneurial action. We deploy these features of resources in our model later in this paper. Thus, we hold that poverty refers to both tangible resource scarcity as well as an assignment of current value-in-use to possessions – a diminished cognitive capacity to imagine the value of possessions relative to an envisioned, better future. A model of a relative change in sustainable resource endowment that is initiated by the poor would require the assignment of an entrepreneurial (future) value to their current possessions, which is enabled by entrepreneurial aspiration. Entrepreneurial aspiration is thus a key trigger for actions that lead the poor on a trajectory of change and improvement in their resource endowment.

Institutional characteristics

The influence of institutions on entrepreneurial action and development has been long recognized, in economics (e.g., Beckert 1999; North 1990, 2005; Rodrik, Subramanian, and Trebbi 2004), and entrepreneurship (e.g., Estrin, Korosteleva, and Mickiewicz 2013; Fuentelsaz et al. 2015; Bruton, Ahlstrom, and Li 2010). According to North (1990), institutions are defined as formal and informal constraints devised by humans that structure social, political and economic interaction. Following this definition, our arguments incorporate the understanding of institutions from a micro perspective, where institutions themselves are created by the raw material of human action. For instance, what has been termed as 'new institutionalism' emphasizes the 'unreflective, routine, taken-for-granted nature of most human behavior and views interests and actors themselves constituted by institutions' (Zucker 1983). Institutions, from this perspective, are macro-level abstractions, 'rationalized and impersonal prescriptions' (Meyer and Rowan 1977), shared 'typifications' independent of any particular entity to which moral allegiance may be owed. Institutional environments have a subtle influence on the embedded actors, and 'create the lenses through which actors view the world and the very categories of structure, action, and thought' (DiMaggio and Powell 1991). A key aspect of institutions is the fact that they 'owe their survival to relatively self-activating processes' (Jepperson 1991). Institutions represent a social order or pattern that has attained a certain state or property where this self-activating process is routine and predictable. Institutionalization denotes the process of such attainment. As Jepperson (1991, 145) notes, ' ... routine reproductive procedures support and sustain the pattern, furthering its reproduction – unless collective action blocks or environmental shock disrupts, the reproductive process.'

While institutional theory places emphasis on the *constraints* imposed by institutional arrangements and the institutional embeddedness of agency, extant conversation also addresses the question of how institutions *change* (Greenman 2013). The latter is addressed by dynamic frameworks in which institutions are *both constraints on action* as well as *subject to change through action* (Barley and Tolbert 1997; Giddens 1994; Greenwood and Hinings 1996; Hirsch and Lounsbury 1997). From this perspective, individuals, especially as entrepreneurs, are not powerless actors in an institutional framework but are able to work with and change institutions to their favour (Bechky 2011; Dunbar and Ahlstrom 1995; Hallett and Ventresca 2006). The role of praxis in bringing about change in the existing social and institutional orders is well developed in the dialectical discourse by Seo and Creed (2002). From this perspective, actors' consciousness is considered *partly autonomous* from the contexts in which actors exist, which provides the raw material both for institutional change, as well as individuals' unique aspirations. For example, Friedland and Alford (1991) argue that although institutions constrain both the means and ends of action, human beings are artful in mobilizing different institutional logics to serve their purposes (Friedland and Alford 1991). Whittington (1992) suggests that individuals may actively exploit the tensions and conflicts between divergent structural principles and rules derived from the wider society. Individuals vary in their capacity to improvise and are capable of applying, transposing, and extending a wide range of different and even incompatible cultural schemas to new contexts (Lawrence, Suddaby, and Leca 2011; Sewell 1992; Voronov and Yorks 2015).

Based on the review of institutional theory arguments, two important characteristics of institutions gain significance. First, institutional arrangements emerge in response to the need for orderly maintenance of social patterns. The normative mechanisms govern and condition the actions of individuals. Over time such norms become constraints on agency leading to *rigidities*. Second, there is a degree of loose and somewhat asynchronous interconnectedness of various institutional arrangements that lead to incompatibilities and consequently *contradictions* between various institutional arrangements. This is because institutional arrangements develop through reiterative, self-activating processes operating at different paces and yet are part of a larger system of social patterns emerging simultaneously.

Institutional rigidities

Institutional rigidity refers to the degree to which institutions are resistant to change. Rigidity is a natural output of institutionalized environments. 'Institutional arrangements are reproduced because individuals often cannot even conceive appropriate alternatives' (DiMaggio and Powell 1991, 11). Thus, once institutions are enacted, the forces that sustain institutionalization may become resistant to change, regardless of their usefulness (Bartunek and Moch 1987; Kirby 1992; Seo and Creed 2002). This rigidity to change could occur because 'they threaten individuals' sense of security, increase the cost of information processing, and disrupt routines' (Powell 1991). This resistance itself has been called a fundamental attribute of institutionalization (Jepperson 1991).

Three aspects of institutional rigidity are salient for the purposes of predicting entrepreneurial aspirations. One aspect of institutional rigidity is inertia, which is characterized by a failure to change and adapt to changes in the external environment (Beckert 1999). Inertia may result in the institutions becoming increasingly irrelevant over time, in their functionality and effectiveness. A typical and oft-cited example of inertia as institutional rigidity is Kafkaesque government bureaucracies, where rules have lost all functionality and have been elevated to ends rather than means toward certain agreed-upon ends. The second dimension of institutional rigidity is institutional isolation (Dodgson 2009), where the institutions become specialized for local conditions, without bridging links enabling knowledge exchange from outside their specialized context (Lowik et al. 2012). While these institutions change over time (as opposed to being inertial), the changes are largely due to changes within the institutions, rather than due to meaningful knowledge exchange from outside their context. The lack of bridging links results in ossification of institutional mandates, which may create dilemmas and conflicts with other institutional choices, and offer Faustian bargains and pyrrhic victories to individuals.

Institutional isolation also makes institutional mandates particularly irrelevant, dysfunctional, and seemingly capricious, constraining action. Religious rituals, or ideology, that require acceptance without questions, and whose meaning and rationalities are lost in time fit into this particular category. The final aspect of institutional rigidity is a barrier to entry into the specific institutional context (Welter, Smallbone, and Pobol 2015). This aspect refers to the degree of transparency and explicitness of institutional mandates that enable individuals to earn institutional legitimacy and its attendant resources (Puffer and McCarthy 2011). Overall, these barriers could be constituted of social stratification, socialization opportunities (e.g. membership in educational and cultural institutions), requirements of cultural homophily (Jack, Dodd, and Anderson 2008), and economic thresholds, which constrain actors from accessing specific resources, such as social capital (Ruef, Aldrich, and Carter 2003; Wennberg, Pathak, and Autio 2013).

Institutional rigidity dampens opportunity creation by influencing the degree of embeddedness. In the context of institutional rigidity, entrepreneurs may suffer from network over-embeddedness, as they may face strong institutional pressures to conform to institutional norms and maintain institutionally-sanctioned relationships so as to minimize the cost of illegitimacy[3] (Jack and Anderson 2002; Frederking 2004; Bensemann and Anderson 2018). This over-embeddedness also represents the opportunity cost of missed connections outside the institutional framework.

Institutional rigidity may have an especially pernicious effect on the poor by subjecting them to over-embeddedness and limiting their aspirations to subsistence levels and subsequent entrepreneurial actions within specific sub-institutional boundaries (Gherhes, Vorley, and Williams 2018). The poor may pay a significantly higher opportunity cost of institutional over-embeddedness since it prevents them from leveraging and learning from weak ties outside their institutionally sanctioned networks and placing a higher potential value on their assets.

Institutional contradictions

Institutions are produced by social arrangements that are continually reproduced and preserved by social interactions (Barley and Tolbert 1997. The linkages between social patterns in adjacent areas are loosely coupled, and at different stages of reification. At any point in time, they are neither complete nor coherent, nor do they always replicate identically, leading to divergent and incompatible structures (Benson 1977). The resultant variety of mutually incompatible institutional arrangements, in turn, are a source of tensions and conflicts within and across institutions termed institutional contradiction (Seo and Creed 2002). The coexistence of incompatible institutions gives rise to institutional contradictions. Friedland and Alford (1991) further suggest that contradictions arise between institutions when disparate institutional logics collide. For example, the institutional logic of planned economy could be contradictory to the institutional logic of market-based economy if they co-exist in the same system without any reconciling narratives. Institutional expectations to respect established institutional segregations may collide with cultural expectations to provide a better life for one's family. Other examples include Battilana and Dorado's (2010) and Besharov and Smith's (2014) studies illustrating the challenges people have navigating the contradictions between development and commercial microfinance logics, and commercial and community, respectively. Although each of the institutional logics may have its own benefits, the contradictions become problematic when individual actions involve simultaneously addressing multiple and contradictory, institutional logics. In this context, the costs of earning legitimacy by conforming to the dominant institutional logic may be more attractive, relative to spending resources to challenging these multiple and contradictory logics (Baum and Oliver 1991; Haveman and Rao 1997).

However, institutional contradictions also provide the basis for individuals (entrepreneurs) to develop a resolving narrative for an imagined future, providing a basis for action. As Voronov and Yorks (2015, 3) put it, 'Contradictions ... alert people to the gap between the way things are and the way they might or should be (Sewell 1992; Swidler 1986; Weber and Glynn 2006), which allows alternative understandings, ideas, and ways of being to emerge that have been effaced or obscured by dominant institutional arrangements.' Entrepreneurs can exploit this aspect of contradictions to forge ahead. The poor can, for example, legitimize their actions as supporting the national mission of self-reliance and use it to stand up to contradictory demands from other institutions (such as their religion or cultural norms). Relative to institutional contradictions, institutional rigidities, constitute a stronger curb on entrepreneurial actions since the latter constrain individual action without providing any intrinsic 'chink in the armor' as a way to sidestep the constraints on action. Therefore, we hold while both are negatively associated with entrepreneurial actions, institutional rigidities are more damaging than institutional contradictions in this context. This allows us to predict the level of entrepreneurial aspirations under different institutional environments (institutional contradictions and institutional rigidities) relevant to entrepreneurial action

Model development

It is established in the literature that individual aspirations are antecedents to entrepreneurial actions. Aspirations are conceptualized as the entrepreneurial drive, rooted in the theory of planned behaviour (Ajzen and Fishbein 1977; Florin, Karri, and Rossiter 2007), entrepreneurial mind set (McGrath and MacMillan 2000) as well as entrepreneurial intent (Thompson 2009). Such individual aspirations are partly influenced by the institutional context in which potential entrepreneurs are embedded (Kibler 2013). Thus, we present the role of aspirations as an intervening mechanism (moderator and mediator) between the institutional setting and the levels of poverty at an individual and population level.

As discussed earlier in the context of a subjectivist view of entrepreneurship, it has been long recognized in entrepreneurship that resources and 'services that the resources can render' are subjectively perceived by individuals and thus 'entrepreneurs' can see and take advantage of opportunities that others may not see (Hayek 1945). For instance, according to Penrose (1959), entrepreneurs' perception and imagination are shaped by the tacit (subjective) knowledge of the attributes of their resources. Entrepreneurship is also viewed as a team activity resulting from interactions of heterogeneous knowledge, judgment and mental models and resources of individuals (Foss et al. 2008). Based on this fundamental tenet of entrepreneurship field, we posit that the aspiration to be an entrepreneur changes the perception of the latent value of resources and also increases the likelihood of actions to unlock the latent value of resources (i.e., the individual takes actions to extract the value of resources he/she has to achieve his/her aspiration to be an entrepreneur). The aspiration to be an entrepreneur also changes the perception of the likelihood of success (i.e., modifies the risk-reward perception by suppressing risk perception and enhancing reward perception). Both these trigger entrepreneurial actions among individuals. These actions include inter alia actions that lead to the accumulation of intermediate resources (e.g. actions that lead to expansion or diversification of one's network).

Entrepreneurship has also long recognized the relationship of resources to risk-taking (Stevenson and Jarillo 1990). In the subjective view of entrepreneurship, the value of resources is malleable since it is relative to the entrepreneur's vision for the future. This value of resources is also tied to a capacity for risk-taking such that the greater the perceived value of resources relative to an entrepreneurial vision, the higher the propensity for risk-taking. Because poor have a very low level of resources to start with (with resources close to subsistence level), the resources that they can allocate as 'affordable losses' are limited (Sarasvathy 2001). However, as soon as their aspiration changes to be an entrepreneur, their perception of the value of their extant resources increases, so even the 'low level of resources' in an objective sense becomes irrelevant when the assessment of those resources turns 'entrepreneurial.' It is to be emphasized that there is no change tangibly in the resources of the poor – the only change is in the aspiration to be an entrepreneur. With this change, the poor view whatever they have (e.g. their own lives) with new 'eyes' and assign them a value related to its use in the future. Thus aspirations play a critical role in risk-taking, as well as the perceived capacity for risk tolerance. Therefore, we propose:

Proposition 1

Aspiration to be an entrepreneur would be associated with actions that have a higher expected value for resource accumulation, reducing the state of poverty for the actors and their dependents.

The above exposition traces the aspiration at an individual level. We now trace the effect at the macro level by aggregating the effect of actions by a population of poor that aspire to be entrepreneurs. At the macro level, it would reduce the number of people needing subsistence support since a higher proportion of individuals will achieve positive resource accumulation – due to independent (relatively uncorrelated) risk-taking actions among a whole population, several such actions will meet or exceed their expected values of payoffs, even though some will fall short. These outcomes would be better than the counter-factual – the condition where the population did not aspire to be an entrepreneur, resulting in an absence of entrepreneurial action. Thus:

Proposition 2

When a greater proportion of poor in a population aspire to be entrepreneurs, ceteris paribus, it would lead to a reduction in poverty in that population.

Institutional contradictions (IC), institutional rigidity (IR) and entrepreneurial aspirations

Entrepreneurial visions challenge extant orthodoxies and resources need to be expended to earn legitimacy for the vision. The risk of failure to earn legitimacy is the risk that entrepreneurs take (Vaillant and Lafuente 2007). Institutional contradictions with respect to entrepreneurial vision occur when entrepreneurs face conflicting demands of behaviour to earn legitimacy from the institutions in which entrepreneurial actions need to be embedded (Bensemann, Warren, and Anderson 2018). For instance, the institutional pressures of markets may require entrepreneurs to pursue the most economically lucrative opportunities, whereas, the cultural institutions in which the entrepreneur is embedded may require adherence to non-market values of emphasis on traditions, frugality, and self-development (Fayolle, Basso, and Bouchard 2010). Contradictions can, of course, exist even within a specific category of institutional context. For instance, the regulatory apparatus to promote entrepreneurship may conflict with that of achieving social justice by regulating minimum employment levels over and above perceived economic rationality. In the context of developed economies, Spencer, Murtha., and Lenway (2005) show how national governments' efforts to spur economic activities, including innovation, driven by perceived national interests, may be at odds with perceived economic logic from the point of view of technological entrepreneurs (Spencer, Murtha., and Lenway 2005). Institutional contradictions curb entrepreneurial aspirations by having a paralytic and inertial effect on entrepreneurs' calculus of returns on the action – i.e. in the entrepreneurs' mind, the benefits of entrepreneurial actions (exploiting institutional conditions that are favorable to such actions) are washed out by the costs/obstacles of incurring such action.

Resolving institutional contradictions requires the deployment of three kinds of resources. First, resolving the contradictions may require diverting *fungible entrepreneurial resources* from directly investing in the entrepreneurial vision to constructing the resolving logic to achieve legitimacy for the vision. Second, resolving institutional contradictions may require acquiring and deploying *specialized resources* to develop the logic and bridges that wins over the orthodoxies preserving the contradictions. Finally, resolving institutional contradictions may require *more diverse resources* to provide the rich ore from which solutions to institutional contradictions can be alloyed. More importantly, these aspects of resources relative to institutional contradictions also increase the cognitive challenges faced by individuals to visualize the 'way out,' dampening aspirations and encouraging subscription to extant orthodoxies for survival. These constraints are asymmetric relative to resource endowments – i.e. these constraints loom exponentially larger for the poor, and concurrently dampen their aspirations exponentially. A high degree of institutional contradictions needs more resources to resolve the contradictions. Thus, this state has an especially pernicious effect on the resource-poor, since it further reduces the perceived value of their resources, curbing their aspirations.

On the other hand, institutional rigidity curbs the aspirations of the poor in three different ways. First, it acts as blinders to entrepreneurial imagination, which limits entrepreneurial aspirations. Institutional rigidity implies that institutional arrangements at the cognitive level are imagined as based on mutual recognition of 'peers' resulting in mimetic behavior and making it a normative expectation for acquiring legitimacy. As this normative expectation becomes ingrained, it acts as a real barrier for individuals seeking alternative courses of action (Standifird 2001), since these actions are immediately rejected as illegitimate. Second, it reduces expected returns to individuality, and by doing so, curbs aspirations, reducing the motivation for individual actions.

Rigidity in the existing institutional norms reinforced by expected mimetic behavior requires a collective or a critical number of actors to make a shift from the established patterns of social reproduction of institutional arrangements (Barley and Tolbert 1997). Third, institutional rigidity acts as barriers to access to resources, which in turn lowers aspirations. Any deviation from existing norms is discouraged via punitive mechanisms that harm the legitimacy of actions on part of the individual actor (DiMaggio and Powell 1983). Since legitimacy is important is key to access resources, a lack of legitimacy not only limits access to resources but also bounds aspirations of entrepreneurial pursuits by reducing the perceived value of other resources that an individual possesses. For example, Liao and Welsch (2003) found that the growth aspirations of entrepreneurs were positively related to the measures of the value of social capital, which is a form of entrepreneurial resources.

We now develop conceptual arguments for predicting the level of entrepreneurial aspirations under varying institutional environments – institutional environments that are characterized by combinations of high and low levels of institutional contradictions and institutional rigidity (Figure 1). In addition, we also suggest how entrepreneurial aspirations mediate the effect of institutional environments on entrepreneurial action.

Institutional contradictions	Institutional rigidity: High	Institutional rigidity: Low
High	Cell 1. **Low** entrepreneurial aspirations among the poor **Lowest** proportion of entrepreneurs among the poor	Cell 2. **High – Moderate** entrepreneurial aspirations among the poor Proportion of entrepreneurs among the poor > cell 1 and 3 < cell 4
Low	Cell 3. **Low – Moderate** entrepreneurial aspirations among the poor Proportion of entrepreneurs among the poor < cell 2 and 4 > cell 1	Cell 4. **High** entrepreneurial aspirations among the poor **Highest** proportion of entrepreneurs among the poor

Figure 1. The effect of institutional rigidity and institutional contradictions on entrepreneurial aspirations and entrepreneurial action.

High levels of IC and IR (cell 1)

When the poor are confronted with a high level of institutional contradiction, the problem of legitimacy, building on competencies, and acquisition of resources becomes highly problematic. First, the effect of competing institutional logics will inhibit important stakeholders that are embedded in particular institution logics from making the leap to accept a competing institutional logic due to legitimacy concerns and fear of sanctions that may be handed down by the dominant institutional logic (Obloj, Obloj, and Pratt 2010). For example, in the first half of the 20th century China, entrepreneurial pursuits that relied on market-based competition were undermined by dominant social and political institutions in its communist or social-political economy (Hsu 2006). Second, individual competencies are formed by previous knowledge and experiences (Kogut and Zander 1992). As knowledge and experiences are embedded within specific institutional contexts (domain specific), demands on competencies far outside their institutional context may result in failure (Haveman 1992). Third, resource acquisition strategies vary for individuals embedded in different institutional logics. Because access to resources (for example, financial capital) is an important element in the pursuit of entrepreneurial opportunities, the familiarity of the institutional logics to the individuals that enables such access becomes significant. Differential access to resources may be attributable to differences in familiarity to relevant institutional logics – for example, individuals belonging to a certain social group may be shut out from access to resources available to individuals that are associated with more powerful institutions.

Conditions of high institutional rigidity and high institutional contradictions[4] severely curb entrepreneurial aspirations. High institutional rigidity increases legitimacy costs and diverts resources from the pursuit of opportunity creation to achieving legitimacy. For instance, Tsang (1996) documents how institutional rigidities in China, lead some entrepreneurs to adopt an 'escape' strategy, by lowering their expectations from the venture, limiting the growth of their venture, devoting surplus to personal consumption, planning protect their children from the low status of an entrepreneur and entrepreneurial lifestyle (Tsang 1996). Due to high institutional rigidity, and high institutional contradictions, this context creates obstacles to aspirations in three specific ways. One, it obfuscates the clarity of means-end relationship, requiring only the most tenacious, and visionary, entrepreneur to visualize the achievement of her starting aspirations. Two, it entails a long-linked path to aspirations – the entrepreneur is forced to take a circuitous route to her aspirations. In essence, an entrepreneur has to resort to institutional improvisation in pursuit of her vision – compensate for the absence of functional aspects of institutions (i.e. presence of 'institutional voids'. Mair and Marti 2009; Khanna and Palepu 2000) with personal resources. And third, this context is fraught with deep path dependencies, with actions at each stage resulting in relatively rigid trajectories. These conditions mean that entrepreneurs spend a much higher proportion of their resources on opportunity exploration which is more expensive (Gupta, Smith, and Shalley 2006; Voss, Sirdeshmukh, and Voss 2008), and with a much lower chance of success (i.e. is riskier). These conditions affect the relative poor especially hard, since their tangible resource endowment is low, and much of it is allocated to survival. An overall low net perceived chance of success leads entrepreneurs to scale back their scale and scope aspirations, and at a macro level, more individuals may choose to accept the market value of their skills rather than start entrepreneurial ventures (Lee and Venkataraman 2006). This leads to the following propositions:

Proposition 3a

Under conditions of high institutional contradictions, and high institutional rigidity, the entrepreneurial aspirations of the poor will be the lowest, compared to aspirations in other institutional contexts.

Proposition 3b

Under conditions of high institutional contradictions, and high institutional rigidity, fewer poor would aspire to be entrepreneurs, relative to other institutional contexts.

In this context, the poor undertake subsistence level, necessity or survival entrepreneurship (Chen, Chang, and Bruton 2017). The poor also can become fatalistic, are less optimistic about the future, and rely on external institutional interventions from the government or other actors. It is in this context that incentives for external (i.e. not belonging to or classified as 'the poor') entrepreneurs to establish their ventures to utilize the job skills available among the poor and unilateral actions by the top of the pyramid actors such as multinational enterprises to reach out and offer products and services targeted at the poor may be directly effective.

High levels of IC and low IR (cell 2)

Because institutional contradictions arise from incompatible institutional arrangements and result in tensions and conflicts, high levels of institutional contradictions lead to lowering entrepreneurial aspirations as discussed above. On the other hand, less rigid institutions suggest that there are fewer barriers to entry into specific institutional contexts. institutions are less formal (more amenable to change and improvisation) and are less isolated from other institutions and actors in the larger context. Individuals in this context may be freer to aspire to utilize institutional resources and take entrepreneurial actions. The institutional flexibility (as opposed to rigidity may allow entrepreneurs to address high levels institutional contradictions by resolving conflicts among competing institutional logics – thereby allowing them to pursue opportunities by accessing resources, exploiting competencies, and gaining legitimacy. As the entrepreneurs process this context, it allows them to set a higher level of entrepreneurial aspirations.

We now view these conditions from the perspective of the poor. As we argue above, resolving institutional contradictions require deploying poor's limited *fungible* resources, acquiring and deploying *specialized and more diverse* resources to develop the logic and bridges that wins over the orthodoxies preserving the contradictions. We also emphasized that these aspects of resources relative to institutional contradictions also put increased demands on their cognitive capacities. This, in turn, makes possible solutions more intractable and increases the possibility of production of negative attitudes such as defeatism and fatalism that curb entrepreneurial aspirations and encourage subscription to extant orthodoxies for survival. As a result, poor may be much less likely to be able to take advantage of conditions of low institutional rigidity in this cell. We thus propose:

Proposition 4a

Under conditions of high institutional contradictions and low institutional rigidity, entrepreneurial aspirations of poor will be lower than the context in which both institutional contradictions and institutional rigidity is low but higher than other contexts.

Proposition 4b

Under conditions of high institutional contradictions and low institutional rigidity, a higher proportion of poor will aspire to be entrepreneurs than the context in which both institutional contradictions and institutional rigidity is low but higher than other contexts.

In this context, one may observe an increase in enactments of aspirations by the poor. Instead of merely passive recipients of charity or subsistence aid, one may observe efforts to change their institutional context (e.g. geography, community, and even religion), efforts to collaborate across traditional network boundaries, developing bridging capital, and experimentation and improvisation to resolve institutional contradictions they face. Subsistence aid and top-down interventionist policies and actions may be reformulated as entrepreneurial capital, for example.

Low levels of IC and high IR (cell 3)

As argued earlier, because of low levels of institutional contradictions, entrepreneurs may have clearer perceptions of the institutional arrangements that they will be required to navigate to secure resources and gain legitimacy of their pursuits. In addition, low contradictions between institutional logics will lower the burden on entrepreneurs to develop competencies in multiple domains, and expend capital to create the bridging logic to resolve the contradictions and gain legitimacy, as well as attract more stakeholders to pursue their vision as the entrepreneurial vision is less likely to get entangled in contradictory institutional logics. However, the institutions may also be highly rigid imposing severe restrictions on non-conformist actions of individuals, without any institutional mechanisms to negotiate away these restrictions. This scenario is highly likely in relatively closed economies that have been able to establish a relatively high level of homogenous and mutually compatible institutions that are also resistant to change. As an extreme example, we surmise economies under totalitarian regimes such as dictatorships and under junta rule would fall under such an institutional categorization. Individuals that face such institutional environments are likely to have low entrepreneurial aspirations because of the relatively predictable institutional responses (often punitive) to entrepreneurial actions since these actions may result in creating new contradictions and thus disrupt the broader goals of these institutions. Access to resources may be possible as a result of dutiful adherence to social norms and institutions such as families, friends, and kinships (Kao 1993; Portes and Landolt 2000). However, due to the presence of institutional rigidities, opportunities that arise in such scenarios are available only to those individuals who enjoy power through their relationships to powerful institutions that control resources (e.g. see Redding, 1990 study on Chinese family businesses). Similarly, in India, mercantile groups (part of the traditional caste system) provide differential access to resources and legitimacy for prospective entrepreneurs (Rutten 2003). Restrictions imposed by institutional rigidities in acquiring resources thus may exert downward pressure on aspirations of the poor.

The context of Institutional rigidities also reduces the *subjective* malleability and fungibility of resources in the mind of the poor. The ruts of institutional rigidities may appear deeper and more stolid to the poor, leading to a tunnel vision and inability to visualize resources in alternate uses beyond the space defined by their institutional boundaries. As a result, the poor would face much-reduced visibility and ability to exploit opportunities that may have opened up due to the low institutional contradictions in this cell. Hence we propose:

Proposition 5a

Under conditions of low institutional contradictions and high institutional rigidity, entrepreneurial aspirations of poor will be higher than the context in which both institutional contradictions and institutional rigidity is high but lower than other contexts.

Proposition 5b

Under conditions of low institutional contradictions and high institutional rigidity, a higher proportion of poor will aspire to be entrepreneurs than the context in which both institutional contradictions and institutional rigidity is high but lower than other contexts.

In this context, we expect to see necessity entrepreneurship (e.g. Fuentelsaz et al. 2015) that does not challenge the institutional orthodoxies that the poor face, but allows them to exploit limited opportunities within their context. The reason why entrepreneurial aspirations are lower in the context of low institutional contradictions and high institutional rigidities than vice versa is because, as we argued earlier, institutional rigidity is a more intractable barrier for entrepreneurship than institutional contradictions. Institutional rigidity acts as a relatively insurmountable trap for the poor, and acts as a more tangible barrier to their aspirations. On the other hand, institutional contradictions allow the enterprising poor the possibility to 'see the way out' by designing a resolving logic to the contradictions they face.

Low levels of IC and low IR (cell 4)

In the case of a low level of institutional contradictions, the context of institutional arrangements is relatively clearer for entrepreneurs in their pursuit of resources. In addition, the path to gain legitimacy is also easier to comprehend for entrepreneurs. When this is combined with low levels of institutional rigidity, entrepreneurs are in a position to perceive the relatively clear means-end relationship with respect to their unique entrepreneurial vision. Perceptually, entrepreneurs visualize a short-linked (lower number of intermediate milestones or diversions) and a more direct path to their aspirations. In addition, these contexts provide perceptually shallower path dependencies, with a larger number of equifinal options. Under these conditions, entrepreneurs may feel empowered and set their aspirations *higher*, leading to more entrepreneurial action. Higher entrepreneurial aspirations may lead to an increase in entrepreneurial scale (Wiklund and Shepherd 2003), as well as search for and creation of more entrepreneurial resources at the micro level via increased entrepreneurial bricolage (Baker and Nelson 2005). In turn, increase in entrepreneurial activity may lead to a positive spiral of increase in aspirations (Bygrave and Minniti 2000) – at a micro level (i.e. increase in scale and/or geographic scope), leading to higher entrepreneurial goals, and at a macro level (i.e. aspiring to become an entrepreneur rather than not), leading to new entrepreneurs. While an increase in the number of entrepreneurs may result in greater competition for resources, it does not suppress entrepreneurial aspirations because, by definition, entrepreneurial ideas are unique, and hence earn economic rents. The greater competition also forces entrepreneurs to sharpen the uniqueness of their vision.

In line with their high entrepreneurial aspirations, low institutional contradictions and low rigidity allow individuals easier access to resources embedded in ties across multiple institutional contexts and deepen their relationships to access resources within their institutional contexts. Low levels of institutional rigidity imply low barriers to enter alternative institutional contexts (for example, reach outside their communities) and a readiness to adapt to changing circumstances that entrepreneurial opportunities may engender. The support to pursue opportunities from within the social institutions encourages stronger bonds, resulting in access to resources, thus encouraging entrepreneurial actions.

The conditions of low institutional contradictions and low institutional rigidity have an especially exacerbated effects on the aspiration levels of the poor, as well as the number of poor with entrepreneurial aspirations, leading to entrepreneurial actions and creating a 'culture of entrepreneurship' within the institutional context. Due to low institutional contradictions, the poor can directly visualize the path of deploying their resources to achieving their aspirations – in effect, magnifying the future value of their resources. Further, due to low institutional rigidity, the imagined fungibility and malleability of sparse resources of the poor increases exponentially.

Proposition 6a

Under conditions of low institutional contradictions and low institutional rigidity, entrepreneurial aspirations of poor will be the highest, compared to aspirations in other institutional contexts.

Proposition 6b

Under conditions of low institutional contradictions and low institutional rigidity, a higher proportion of poor will aspire to be entrepreneurs, relative to other institutional contexts.

In such contexts, one would expect to see more opportunity-based entrepreneurs (Cullen, Johnson, and Parboteeah 2014), even among the poor – resources directed at the poor (e.g. transfer payments, subsidies by the government, or charitable donations) may also be used as entrepreneurial resources. Due to increased entrepreneurial aspirations, there may be more risk tolerance, and one would expect more economic and social mobility among the poor.

Discussion

We developed a conceptual model of poverty reduction based on entrepreneurial aspirations, and how these aspirations are influenced by specific characteristics of institutional environments – institutional rigidities and institutional contradictions. The model contributes to the relatively sparsely covered 'revolution' perspective in the context of poverty reduction, that gives agency to the poor to alleviate their poverty themselves (Sutter, Bruton, and Chen 2019). The model argues that aspirations are the trigger of agency for actions among the poor.

Our arguments suggest that while institutions (specific categories) per se may have a direct impact on entrepreneurial action, it would be an incomplete account of explaining differences in poverty reduction via entrepreneurial action by the poor. One theoretical contribution of our paper is that entrepreneurial aspiration is a crucial variable in providing a powerful argument in explaining the impact of institutional context on entrepreneurial action. In contrast to a less abstracted conceptualization of institutions (such as a descriptive list of institutions such as legal infrastructure, culture, religion, etc.), we conceptualized institutions in an abstract sense based on their characteristics (contradictions and rigidities) following neo-institutionalism (DiMaggio and Powell 1991). The conceptual arguments advanced in this paper demonstrate the conditions under which entrepreneurial aspirations are heightened and under which conditions such aspirations are dampened.

Our study contributes to theory on institutional constraints and entrepreneurial action by arguing for the mediating role of entrepreneurial aspirations. It explains why entrepreneurship is often suppressed under institutional constraints, precisely when one would expect more entrepreneurial actions to break the constraints – for example, by sidestepping these constraints by choosing alternate institutional environments – this 'entrepreneurial paralysis' in the context where we would expect entrepreneurial action is a paradox. For example, Lee and Venkataraman's (2006) study implies that when institutional constraints are high, the reward for conforming to the institutional context (or being identified as the in-group relative to institutions) are higher than the risk-adjusted rewards of being an entrepreneur. However, in their model, it is not clear why this happens.

In the context of higher institutional constraints, the rewards to break the constraints should also be higher, which should increase the rewards to entrepreneurship, per the extant understanding of entrepreneurship. Using aspirations contributes to bridging the paradox of lack of entrepreneurship even when opportunities and incentives exist to break institutional constraints that shackle entrepreneurs and innovators (Wang et al. 2008). Our model resolves the paradox by offering the insight that institutional contradictions and rigidities lower the *value of entrepreneurship* by lowering the level of *aspirations* and increasing the opportunity cost (and perceived risk) of pursuing entrepreneurship.

Our research also leads to certain policy directions that may better serve the cause of sustainable poverty reduction. Policy initiatives that directly tackle institutional rigidities and contradictions (be it from specific religious mandates, customs, and institutional routines) that the poor face are likely to be far more fruitful than policies aimed at resource transfers. The latter would seem expedient and superficial, while sometimes serving the needs of the poor as well as allowing intervening agencies to 'justify their budget' – however, these transfers do not create a basis for entrepreneurial actions, since they are less likely to change aspirations of most of the recipients. Policy initiatives that work on improving the competencies and 'widening the world' of the poor may be more cost-effective in the long run and may be better able to leverage community-based and volunteer resources. For instance, even attending a single talk by someone who was able to lift herself from poverty via entrepreneurial action may sow the seeds of changes in aspirations that may lead to sustainable poverty reduction via subsequent actions.

Future research

Based on the line of reasoning advanced in this paper, several areas of future research can be suggested. At a macro level, an interesting research stream to pursue would be to study the antecedents to changes in aspirations. For instance, how does the geography of poor affect their aspirations? Do integrated communities help in raising aspirations, or suppressing them? Do segregated communities create a sustaining culture of 'poverty of aspirations'? Is segregation the cause or the consequence of income inequality in countries or contexts with higher income inequality? For instance, in the US, the segregation of the poor increased by 9% between 1970 and 1990 Abramson, Tobin, and VanderGoot 1995. How does this segregation affect the macro level measures of entrepreneurship and entrepreneurs? Segregation of the poor may lead to the flight of people with higher aspirations, depriving the poor of the crucial resources and comparative metrics to influence their own aspirations. The greater linkage between literature in geography and entrepreneurship at the micro and macro levels may yield more effective policy prescriptions regarding appropriate interventions for regional development and poverty reduction (Acs 2006).

More broadly, one of the key questions to pursue would be, 'how do entrepreneurial aspirations of the poor change over time?' Work by Peng and his colleagues (Peng 2003; Peng and Luo 2000; Yamakawa, Peng, and Deeds 2008) traces the changes in ventures in emerging economies in response to institutional transitions. In a similar vein, a fruitful area for research could be changes in entrepreneurial aspirations of the poor as mediating variable during transitions in emerging economies and their institutions. Changes in aspirations, may, for example, explain, why first generation entrepreneurs from emerging economies such as India, even in the presence of substantial institutional contradictions and rigidities, are shaping global ventures. Based on both institutional theory and entrepreneurship theory, it can be defended that institutions lag aspirations, or do not perfectly support aspirations. It can also be argued that aspirations rise faster than institutions change (Ahlstrom et al. 2018). This begs a key follow on question, 'what are the qualitative changes that accompany the widening gap between aspirations and institutional changes?' Along the same vein, future research can differentiate between the aspirations of entrepreneurs with different levels and variety of social capital, as well as other personal resources.

The availability of powerful, alternative, entrepreneurship-friendly institutions across institutional settings can be particularly important for less powerful institutional challengers, such as the poor who could also be the first-generation entrepreneurs with rising aspirations stuck in contradictory and rigid institutional regimes closer to home (Acemoglu and Robinson 2012). Various networks of professionals, professional institutions, and social movement organizations can provide entrepreneurs with various types of resources and support, such as sponsorship, legitimated authority, models of organizing, performance standards and political pressures that can be enacted in diverse settings (e.g. Brint and Karabel 1991; DiMaggio and Powell 1991; Lounsbury 2001; Seo and Creed 2002). Of course, at a minimum, this assumes that the national governments of these entrepreneurs do not hinder their efforts to sidestep country-level institutions, for example by enacting excessive protectionist legislation or restricting capital flows and investment (Spencer, Murtha and Lenway 2005; Witt and Lewin 2007). The key questions that emerge from this line of reasoning are how institutional logics are perceived by home and foreign entrepreneurs, and whether there are degrees of foreignness, affecting their perception of institutional contexts, and thereby opportunities that entrepreneurs visualize. Research that studies differences in individual enactments of institutions could be a particularly rich avenue to explore since differences in enactments offer arbitrage opportunities. The value of this arbitrage should vary depending on the divergence of such enactments from each other, as enactments that are more favourable for entrepreneurial action would be able to negotiate resources at much lower prices from actors whose enactments are much more pessimistic about entrepreneurial actions.

Conclusion

In summary, institutions do not completely determine entrepreneurial action, nor do they completely constrain the poor, other things also matter (cf. Tomizawa et al. 2019). In this paper, we presented a model based on entrepreneurial agency of the poor, embedded in the specific and unique institutional rigidities and contradictions they face. A key contribution of our paper is the insight that sustained poverty reduction via entrepreneurship needs to incorporate *aspirations* of the poor in the context of institutional rigidities and contradictions. Public policies that focus on removing or eroding institutional barriers that *suppress aspirations*, and building or supporting institutions that encourage formation of aspirations, are more likely to succeed in agency driven sustainable poverty alleviation. Broadly, a continued focus on studying institutional influences in formation of entrepreneurial aspirations, especially of the poor, and entrepreneurial action in response to such aspirations in leading to gradual changes in absolute and relative position of the poor, as well as the process of eroding irrelevant institutional mandates, would help develop theory and practice by raising the understanding and stature of entrepreneurial agency.

Notes

1. Entrepreneurial actions constitute a distinct domain compared to other actions because the actions are aimed at creating resources and finding new application for existing resources that are not fully visible on account of dispersed knowledge about means-ends relationship (Hayek 1945). Entrepreneurial actions are in pursuit of opportunities that are characterized by relative uncertainty (see Lee and Venkataraman 2006 for a detailed account of the differences between entrepreneurial and non-entrepreneurial opportunities).
2. The time dimension is critical in the definition of goals since over time, there is transitivity in the goals and means.
3. While entrepreneurial action is likely to be illegitimate relative to some institutional norms because of its very nature, successful entrepreneurial action is likely to be rather 'efficient' in challenging institutional legitimacy, so that the cost of challenging the legitimacy is more than compensated by the expected benefits. In aspects of entrepreneurial action where there is no benefit of illegitimacy, successful entrepreneurial action would hew close to institutional norms.
4. While, poor and underdeveloped economies may typically face high institutional rigidities and high institutional contradictions with respect to entrepreneurial action, these problems could be characteristic of the institutional environments of developed economies as well. However, the magnitude of such problems is on an average likely to be higher in the context of poor/under developed economies and transitioning economies.

Disclosure statement

No potential conflict of interest was reported by the authors.

References

Abramson, A. J., M. S. Tobin, and M. R. VanderGoot. 1995. "The Changing Geography of Metropolitan Opportunity: The Segregation of the Poor in US Metropolitan Areas, 1970 to 1990." *Housing Policy Debate* 6 (1): 45–72. doi:10.1080/10511482.1995.9521181.

Acemoglu, D., and J. A. Robinson. 2012. *Why Nations Fail: The Origins of Power, Prosperity, and Poverty*. New York: Crown Books.

Acs, Z. 2006. "How Is Entrepreneurship Good for Economic Growth?" *Innovations: Technology, Governance, Globalization* 1 (1): 97–107. doi:10.1162/itgg.2006.1.1.97.

Ahlstrom, D., and G. D. Bruton. 2006. "Venture Capital in Emerging Economies: Networks and Institutional Change." *Entrepreneurship Theory and Practice* 30 (2): 299–320. doi:10.1111/etap.2006.30.issue-2.

Ahlstrom, D., X. Yang, L. Wang, and C. Wu. 2018. "A Global Perspective of Entrepreneurship and Innovation in China." *Multinational Business Review* 26 (4): 302–318. doi:10.1108/MBR-08-2018-0058.

Ajzen, I. 1991. "Theory of Planned Behavior." *Organizational Behavior and Human Decision Processes* 50 (2): 179–211. doi:10.1016/0749-5978(91)90020-T.

Ajzen, I., and M. Fishbein. 1977. "Attitude-behavior Relations: A Theoretical Analysis and Review of Empirical Research." *Psychological Bulletin* 84 (5): 888. doi:10.1037/0033-2909.84.5.888.

Alvarez, S. A., and J. B. Barney. 2007. "Discovery and Creation: Alternative Theories of Entrepreneurial Action." *Strategic Entrepreneurship Journal* 1 (1–2): 11–26. doi:10.1002/(ISSN)1932-443X.

Alvarez, S. A., and J. B. Barney. 2010. "Entrepreneurship and Epistemology: The Philosophical Underpinnings of the Study of Entrepreneurial Opportunities." *Academy of Management Annals* 4 (1): 557–583. doi:10.1080/19416520.2010.495521.

Alvarez, S. A., and J. B. Barney. 2014. "Entrepreneurial Opportunities and Poverty Alleviation." *Entrepreneurship Theory and Practice* 38 (1): 159–184. doi:10.1111/etap.12078.

Baker, T., and R. E. Nelson. 2005. "Creating Something from Nothing: Resource Construction through Entrepreneurial Bricolage." *Administrative Science Quarterly* 50 (3): 329–366. doi:10.2189/asqu.2005.50.3.329.

Barley, S. R., and P. S. Tolbert. 1997. "Institutionalization and Structuration: Studying the Links between Action and Institution." *Organization Studies* 18: 93–117. doi:10.1177/017084069701800106.

Barth, F., Ed.. 1963. *Introduction*. Oslo: Universitetsforlaget.

Bartunek, J. M., and M. K. Moch. 1987. "First-order, Second-order, and Third-order Change and Organizational Development Intervention: A Cognitive Approach." *Journal of Applied Behavioral Psychology* 23: 483–500.

Battilana, J., B. Leca, and E. Boxenbaum. 2009. "How Actors Change Institutions: Towards a Theory of Institutional Entrepreneurship." *The Academy of Management Annals* 3 (1): 65–107. doi:10.1080/19416520903053598.

Battilana, J., and S. Dorado. 2010. "Building Sustainable Hybrid Organizations: The Case of Commercial Microfinance Organizations." *Academy of Management Journal* 53 (6): 1419–1440. doi:10.5465/amj.2010.57318391.

Baum, J. A. C., and C. Oliver. 1991. "Institutional Linkages and Organization Mortality." *Administrative Science Quarterly* 36: 187–218. doi:10.2307/2393353.

Bechky, B. A. 2011. "Making Organizational Theory Work: Institutions, Occupations, and Negotiated Orders." *Organization Science* 22 (5): 1157–1167. doi:10.1287/orsc.1100.0603.

Beckert, J. 1999. "Agency, Entrepreneurs, and Institutional Change: The Role of Strategic Choice and Institutional Practices in Organizations." *Organization Studies* 20 (5): 777–799. doi:10.1177/0170840699205004.

Bensemann, J., L. Warren, and A. Anderson. 2018. "Entrepreneurial Engagement in a Depleted Small Town: Legitimacy and Embeddedness." *Journal of Management and Organization* 1–17. doi:10.1017/jmo.2018.63.

Benson, J. K. 1977. "Organizations: A Dialectical View." *Administrative Science Quarterly* 22: 1–21. doi:10.2307/2391741.

Besharov, M. L., and W. K. Smith. 2014. "Multiple Institutional Logics in Organizations: Explaining Their Varied Nature and Implications." *Academy of Management Review* 39 (3): 364–381. doi:10.5465/amr.2011.0431.

Brint, S., and J. Karabel. 1991. "Institutional Origins and Transformations: The Case of American Community Colleges." In *The New Institutionalism in Organizational Analysis*, edited by W. W. Powell and P. J. DiMaggio, 337–360. Chicago: University of Chicago Press.

Brush, C., N. Carter, E. P. Greene, and M. Hart. 2004. *Clearing the Hurdles: Women Building High-growth Businesses*. New Jersey: FT Prentice Hall.

Bruton, G. D., D. Ahlstrom, and H. L. Li. 2010. "Institutional Theory and Entrepreneurship: Where are We Now and Where Do We Need to Move in the Future?" *Entrepreneurship Theory and Practice* 34 (3): 421–440. doi:10.1111/j.1540-6520.2010.00390.x.

Bruton, G. D., D. Ahlstrom, and K. Obloj. 2008. "Entrepreneurship in Emerging Economies: Where are We Today and Where Should the Research Go in the Future." *Entrepreneurship Theory and Practice* 32 (1): 1–14. doi:10.1111/j.1540-6520.2007.00213.x.

Bruton, G. D., D. Ahlstrom, and S. Si. 2015. "Entrepreneurship, Poverty, and Asia: Moving beyond Subsistence Entrepreneurship." *Asia Pacific Journal of Management* 32 (1): 1–22. doi:10.1007/s10490-014-9404-x.

Bruton, G. D., D. J. Ketchen Jr, and R. Duane Ireland. 2013. "Entrepreneurship as a Solution to Poverty." *Journal of Business Venturing* 28 (6): 683–689. doi:10.1016/j.jbusvent.2013.05.002.

Bruton, G. D., S. Khavul, and H. Chavez. 2011. "Microlending in Emerging Economies: Building a New Line of Inquiry from the Ground Up." *Journal of International Business Studies* 42 (5): 718–739. doi:10.1057/jibs.2010.58.

Bruton, G. D., V. H. Fried, and S. Manigart. 2005. "Institutional Influences on the Worldwide Expansion of Venture Capital." *Entrepreneurship Theory and Practice* 29: 737–760. doi:10.1111/(ISSN)1540-6520.

Bygrave, W., and M. Minniti. 2000. "The Social Dynamics of Entrepreneurship." In *Entrepreneurship Theory and Practice* \ 24(3): 25–36.

Chen, J., A. Y. Chang, and G. D. Bruton. 2017. "Microfinance: Where are We Today and Where Should the Research Go in the Future?" *International Small Business Journal* 35 (7): 793–802. doi:10.1177/0266242617717380.

Chiles, T. H., D. M. Vultee, V. K. Gupta, W. D. Greening, and C. S. Tuggle. 2010. "The Philosophical Foundations of a Radical Austrian Approach to Entrepreneurship." *Journal of Management Inquiry* 19 (2): 138–164. doi:10.1177/1056492609337833.

Chliova, M., J. Brinckmann, and N. Rosenbusch. 2015. "Is Microcredit A Blessing for the Poor? A Meta-analysis Examining Development Outcomes and Contextual Considerations." *Journal of Business Venturing* 30 (3): 467–487.l. doi:10.1016/j.jbusvent.2014.10.003.

Cullen, J. B., J. L. Johnson, and K. P. Parboteeah. 2014. "National Rates of Opportunity Entrepreneurship Activity: Insights from Institutional Anomie Theory." *Entrepreneurship Theory and Practice* 38 (4): 775–806. doi:10.1111/etap.2014.38.issue-4.

Deci, E. L., and M. R. Ryan. 2000. "The 'what' and 'why' of Goal Pursuits: Human Needs and the Self-determination of Behavior." *Psychological Inquiry* 11: 227–268. doi:10.1207/S15327965PLI1104_01.

DiMaggio, P. J., and W. W. Powell. 1991. "Introduction." In *The New Institutionalism in Organizational Analysis*, edited by W. W. Powell and P. J. DiMaggio, 1–38. Chicago: University of Chicago Press.

DiMaggio, P. J., and W. W. Powell. 1983. "The Iron Cage Revisited: Institutional Isomorphism and Collective Rationality in Organizational Fields." *American Sociological Review* 48: 147–160. doi:10.2307/2095101.

Dodgson, M. 2009. "Asia's National Innovation Systems: Institutional Adaptability and Rigidity in the Face of Global Innovation Challenges." *Asia Pacific Journal of Management* 26 (3): 589–609. doi:10.1007/s10490-008-9105-4.

Dunbar, R. L. M., and D. Ahlstrom. 1995. "Seeking the Institutional Balance of Power: Avoiding the Power of a Balanced View." *Academy of Management Review* 20 (1): 171–192. doi:10.5465/amr.1995.9503272001.

Estrin, S., J. Korosteleva, and T. Mickiewicz. 2013. "Which Institutions Encourage Entrepreneurial Growth Aspirations?" *Journal of Business Venturing* 28 (4): 564–580. doi:10.1016/j.jbusvent.2012.05.001.

Fayolle, A., O. Basso, and V. Bouchard. 2010. "Three Levels of Culture and Firms' Entrepreneurial Orientation: A Research Agenda." *Entrepreneurship and Regional Development* 22 (7–8): 707–730. doi:10.1080/08985620903233952.

Florin, J., R. Karri, and N. Rossiter. 2007. "Fostering Entrepreneurial Drive in Business Education: An Attitudinal Approach." *Journal of Management Education* 31 (1): 17–42. doi:10.1177/1052562905282023.

Foss, N. J., P. G. Klein, Y. Y. Kor, and J. T. Mahoney. 2008. "Entrepreneurship, Subjectivism, and the Resource-based View: Toward a New Synthesis." *Strategic Entrepreneurship Journal* 2 (1): 73–94. doi:10.1002/(ISSN)1932-443X.

Frederking, L. C. 2004. "A Cross-national Study of Culture, Organization and Entrepreneurship in Three Neighbourhoods." *Entrepreneurship & Regional Development* 16 (3): 197–215. doi:10.1080/0898562042000197126.

Friedland, R., and R. R. Alford. 1991. "Bringing Society Back In: Symbols, Practices, and Institutional Contradictions." In *The New Institutionalism in Organizational Analysis*, edited by W. W. Powell and P. J. DiMaggio, 232–266. Chicago: University of Chicago.

Fuentelsaz, L., C. González, J. P. Maícas, and J. Montero. 2015. "How Different Formal Institutions Affect Opportunity and Necessity Entrepreneurship." *BRQ Business Research Quarterly* 18 (4): 246–258. doi:10.1016/j.brq.2015.02.001.

Ghani, E., W. R. Kerr, and S. O'connell. 2014. "Spatial Determinants of Entrepreneurship in India." *Regional Studies* 48 (6): 1071–1089. doi:10.1080/00343404.2013.839869.

Gherhes, C., T. Vorley, and N. Williams. 2018. "Entrepreneurship and Local Economic Resilience: The Impact of Institutional Hysteresis in Peripheral Places." *Small Business Economics* 51 (3): 577–590. doi:10.1007/s11187-017-9946-7.

Giddens, A. 1994. *The Constitution of Society*. Berkeley, CA: University of California Press.

Greenman, A. 2013. "Everyday Entrepreneurial Action and Cultural Embeddedness: An Institutional Logics Perspective." *Entrepreneurship and Regional Development* 25 (7–8): 631–653. doi:10.1080/08985626.2013.829873.

Greenwood, R., and C. R. Hinings. 1996. "Understanding Radical Organizational Change: Bringing Together the Old and New Institutionalism." *Academy of Management Review* 21 (4): 1022–1054. doi:10.5465/amr.1996.9704071862.

Gupta, A. K., K. G. Smith, and C. E. Shalley. 2006. "The Interplay between Exploration and Exploitation." *Academy of Management Journal* 49 (4): 693–706. doi:10.5465/amj.2006.22083026.

Hagenaars, A. 1988. "The Definition and Measurement Of Poverty." *Journal Of Human Resources* 23 (2): 211–221.

Hallett, T., and M. J. Ventresca. 2006. "Inhabited Institutions: Social Interactions and Organizational Forms in Gouldner's Patterns of Industrial Bureaucracy." *Theory and Society* 35 (2): 213–236. doi:10.1007/s11186-006-9003-z.

Haveman, H. 1992. "Between a Rock and a Hard Place: Organizational Change and Performance under Conditions of Fundamental Environmental Transformation." *Administrative Science Quarterly* 37 (1): 48–75. doi:10.2307/2393533.

Haveman, H., and H. Rao. 1997. "Structuring a Theory of Moral Sentiments: Institutional and Organizational Coevolution in Th Eearly Thrift Industry." *American Journal of Sociology* 102 (6): 1606–1651. doi:10.1086/231128.

Hayek, F. A. 1945. "The Use of Knowledge in Society." *American Economic Review* 35 (4): 519–530.

Hirsch, P. M., and M. Lounsbury. 1997. "Ending the Family Quarrel: Toward Reconcilation of 'old' and 'new' Institutionalisms." *American Behavioral Scientist* 40: 406–418. doi:10.1177/0002764297040004004.

Hsu, C. L. 2006. "Market Ventures, Moral Logics, and Ambiguity: Crafting a New Organizational Form in Post-Socialist China." *The Sociological Quarterly* 47 (1): 69–92. doi:10.1111/j.1533-8525.2006.00038.x.

Jack, S., S. D. Dodd, and A. R. Anderson. 2008. "Change and the Development of Entrepreneurial Networks over Time: A Processual Perspective." *Entrepreneurship and Regional Development* 20 (2): 125–159. doi:10.1080/08985620701645027.

Jack, S. L., and A. R. Anderson. 2002. "The Effects of Embeddedness on the Entrepreneurial Process." *Journal of Business Venturing* 17 (5): 467–487. doi:10.1016/S0883-9026(01)00076-3.

Jepperson, R. L. 1991. "Institutions, Institutional Effects, and Institutionalism." In *The New Institutionalism in Organizational Analysis*, edited by W. W. Powell and P. J. DiMaggio, 143–163. Chicago: University of Chicago Press.

Kao, J. 1993. "The Worldwide Web of Chinese Business." In *Harvard Business Review* Z1(2): 24-33.

Kasser, T., and M. R. Ryan. 1993. "A Dark Side of the American Dream: Correlates of Financial Success as A Central Life Aspiration." *Journal of Personality and Social Psychology* 65 (2): 410–422.

Kasser, T., and M. R. Ryan. 1996. "Further Examining the American Dream; Differential Correlates of Intrinsic and Extrinsic Goals." *Personality and Social Psychology Bulletin* 22 (3): 80–87. doi:10.1177/0146167296223006.

Kerr, W. R., R. Nanda, and M. Rhodes-Kropf. 2014. "Entrepreneurship as Experimentation." *Journal of Economic Perspectives* 28 (3): 25–48. doi:10.1257/jep.28.3.25.

Khanna, T., and K. Palepu. 2000. "The Future of Business Groups in Emerging Markets: Long-Run Evidence from Chile." *Academy of Management Journal* 43 (3): 268–285.

Kibler, E. 2013. "Formation of Entrepreneurial Intentions in a Regional Context." *Entrepreneurship and Regional Development* 25 (3–4): 293–323. doi:10.1080/08985626.2012.721008.

Kirby, M. W. 1992. "Institutional Rigidities and Economic Decline: Reflections on the British Experience." *Economic History Review* 45: 637–660. doi:10.2307/2597412.

Kogut, B., and U. Zander. 1992. "Knowledge of the Firm, Integration Capabilities, and the Replication of Technology." *Organization Science* 3: 383–397. doi:10.1287/orsc.3.3.383.

Kor, Y. Y., J. T. Mahoney, and S. C. Michael. 2007. "Resources, Capabilities and Entrepreneurial Perceptions." *Journal of Management Studies* 44 (7): 1187–1212. doi:10.1111/joms.2007.44.issue-7.

Krueger, N. 2000. "The Cognitive Infrastructure of Opportunity Emergence." *Entrepreneurship Theory and Practice* 24 (3): 5–23. doi:10.1177/104225870002400301.

Krueger, N. 2007. "What Lies Beneath? the Experiential Essence of Entrepreneurial Thinking." *Entrepreneurship Theory and Practice* 31 (1): 123–138. doi:10.1111/etap.2007.31.issue-1.

Krueger, N., M. Reilly, and A. Carsud. 2000. "Competing Models of Entrepreneurial Intentions." *Journal of Business Venturing* 15 (5/6): 411–532. doi:10.1016/S0883-9026(98)00033-0.

Lachmann, L. M. 1976. "From Mises to Shackle: An Essay on Austrian Economics and the Kaleidic Society." *Journal of Economic Literature* 14 (1): 54–62.

Lawrence, T., R. Suddaby, and B. Leca. 2011. "Institutional Work: Refocusing Institutional Studies of Organization." *Journal of Management Inquiry* 20: 52–58. doi:10.1177/1056492610387222.

Lee, J., and S. Venkataraman. 2006. "Aspirations, Market Offerings, and the Pursuit of Entrepreneurial Opportunities." *Journal of Business Venturing* 21: 107–123. doi:10.1016/j.jbusvent.2005.01.002.

Liao, J., and H. Welsch. 2003. "Social Capital and Entrepreneurial Growth Aspirations: A Comparison of Technology- and Non-Technology-Based Nascent Entrepreneurs." *Journal of High Technology Management Research* 14: 149–170. doi:10.1016/S1047-8310(03)00009-9.

Liñán, F., D. Urbano, and M. Guerrero. 2011. "Regional Variations in Entrepreneurial Cognitions: Start-up Intentions of University Students in Spain." *Entrepreneurship and Regional Development* 23 (3–4): 187–215. doi:10.1080/08985620903233929.

Lounsbury, M. 2001. "Institutional Sources of Practice Variation: Staffing College and University Recycling Programs." *Administrative Science Quarterly* 46: 29–56. doi:10.2307/2667124.

Lowik, S., D. van Rossum, J. Kraaijenbrink, and A. Groen. 2012. "Strong Ties as Sources of New Knowledge: How Small Firms Innovate through Bridging Capabilities." *Journal of Small Business Management* 50 (2): 239–256. doi:10.1111/jsbm.2012.50.issue-2.

Mahoney, J. T., and S. C. Michael. 2005. "A Subjectivist Theory of Entrepreneurship." In *Handbook of Entrepreneurship Research*, edited by S. Alvarez, A. Agarwal, and O. Sorenson, 33–54. Boston, MA: Springer.

Mair, J., and I. Marti. 2009. "Entrepreneurship in and around Institutional Voids: A Case Study from Bangladesh." *Journal of Business Venturing* 24 (5): 419–435. doi:10.1016/j.jbusvent.2008.04.006.

Mair, J., I. Marti, and M. J. Ventresca. 2012. "Building Inclusive Markets in Rural Bangladesh: How Intermediaries Work Institutional Voids." *Academy of Management Journal* 55 (4): 819–850. doi:10.5465/amj.2010.0627.

McGrath, R. G., and I. C. MacMillan. 2000. *The Entrepreneurial Mindset: Strategies for Continuously Creating Opportunity in an Age of Uncertainty*. Boston, MA: Harvard Business Press.

McMillan, J., and C. Woodruff. 2002. "The Central Role of Entrepreneurs in Transition Economies." *Journal of Economic Perspectives* 16: 153–170. doi:10.1257/089533002760278767.

McMullen, J. S. 2015. "Entrepreneurial Judgment as Empathic Accuracy: A Sequential Decision-Making Approach to Entrepreneurial Action." *Journal of Institutional Economics* 11 (3): 651–681. doi:10.1017/S1744137413000386.

Meyer, J. W., and B. Rowan. 1977. "Institutional Organizations: Formal Structure as Myth and Ceremony." *American Journal of Sociology* 83: 340–363. doi:10.1086/226550.

Miller, D., and I. Le Breton-Miller. 2017. "Sources of Entrepreneurial Courage and Imagination: Three Perspectives, Three Contexts." *Entrepreneurship Theory and Practice* 41 (5): 667–675. doi:10.1111/etap.12281.

North, D. C. 1990. *Institutions, Institutional Change and Economic Performance*. Cambridge: Cambridge University Press.

North, D. C. 2005. *Understanding the Process of Economic Change*. Princeton, NJ: Princeton University Press.

Obloj, T., K. Obloj, and M. G. Pratt. 2010. "Dominant Logic and Entrepreneurial Firms 'performance in a Transition Economy." *Entrepreneurship Theory and Practice* 34 (1): 151–170. doi:10.1111/etap.2010.34.issue-1.

Peng, M. W. 2003. "Institutional Transitions and Strategic Choices." *Academy of Management Review* 28 (2): 275–296. doi:10.5465/amr.2003.9416341.

Peng, M. W., and Y. Luo. 2000. "Managerial Ties and Firm Performance in a Transition Economy: The Nature of a Micro-Macro Link." *Academy of Management Journal* 43 (3): 486–501.

Penrose, E. T. 1959. *The Theory of the Growth of the Firm*. Oxford: Basil Blackwell.

Peredo, A. M., and J. J. Chrisman. 2006. "Toward a Theory of Community-Based Enterprise." *Academy of Management Review* 31 (2): 309–328. doi:10.5465/amr.2006.20208683.

Portes, A., and P. Landolt. 2000. "Social Capital: Promise and Pitfalls of Its Role in Development." *Journal of Latin American Studies* 32 (2): 529–547. doi:10.1017/S0022216X00005836.

Powell, W. W. 1991. "Expanding the Scope of Institutional Analysis." In *The New Institutionalism in Organizational Analysis*, edited by W. W. Powell and P. J. DiMaggio, 183–203. Chicago: University of Chicago Press.
Prahalad, C. K. 2006. *The Fortune at the Bottom of the Pyramid*. Upper Saddle, New Jersey: Prentice Hall.
Puffer, S. M., and D. J. McCarthy. 2011. "Two Decades of Russian Business and Management Research: An Institutional Theory Perspective." *Academy of Management Perspectives* 25 (2): 21–36.
Redding, S. G. 1990. *The Spirit of Chinese Capitalism*. New York: Walter de Gruyer.
Reed, M. I. 1988. "The Problem of Human Agency in Organization Analysis." *Organization Studies* 9: 33–46. doi:10.1177/017084068800900109.
Rindova, V., D. Barry, and D. J. Ketchen Jr. 2009. "Entrepreneuring as Emancipation." *Academy of Management Review* 34 (3): 477–491. doi:10.5465/amr.2009.40632647.
Rodrik, D., A. Subramanian, and F. Trebbi. 2004. "Institutions Rule: The Primacy of Institutions over Geography and Integration in Economic Development." *Journal of Economic Growth* 9 (2): 131–165. doi:10.1023/B:JOEG.0000031425.72248.85.
Ruef, M., H. E. Aldrich, and N. M. Carter. 2003. "The Structure of Founding Teams: Homophily, Strong Ties, and Isolation among US Entrepreneurs." *American Sociological Review* 68 (2): 195–222. doi:10.2307/1519766.
Rutten, M. 2003. *Rural Capitalists in Asia*. New York: Routledge-Curzon.
Sarason, Y., T. Dean, and J. F. Dillard. 2006. "Entrepreneurship as the Nexus of Individual and Opportunity: A Structuration View." *Journal of Business Venturing* 21: 286–305. doi:10.1016/j.jbusvent.2005.02.007.
Sarasvathy, S. D. 2001. "Causation and Effectuation: Toward a Theoretical Shift from Economic Inevitability to Entrepreneurial Contingency." *The Academy of Management Review* 26 (2): 243–263. doi:10.5465/amr.2001.4378020.
Sarasvathy, S. D. 2009. *Effectuation: Elements of Entrepreneurial Expertise*. Cheltenham, UK: Edward Elgar Publishing.
Scott, W. R. 2013. *Institutions and Organizations: Ideas, Interests, and Identities*. Thousand Oaks, CA: Sage Publications.
Seo, M., and W. E. D. Creed. 2002. "Institutional Contradictions, Praxis, and Institutional Change: A Dialectical Perspective." *Academy of Management Review* 27 (2): 222–247. doi:10.5465/amr.2002.6588004.
Sewell, W. H. 1992. "A Theory of Structure: Duality, Agency, and Transformation." *American Journal of Sociology* 98 (1): 1–29. doi:10.1086/229967.
Shackle, G. L. S. 1979. *Imagination and the Nature of Choice*. New York: Columbia University Press.
Shane, S., and S. Venkataraman. 2000. "The Promise of Entrepreneurship as a Field of Research." *Academy of Management Review* 25 (1): 217–226.
Sheldon, K. M., M. R. Ryan, E. L. Deci, and T. Kasser. 2004. "The Independent Effects of Goal Contents and Motives on Well-being: It's Both What You Pursue and Why You Pursue It." *Personality and Social Psychology Bulletin* 30: 475–486. doi:10.1177/0146167203261883.
Si, S., X. Yu, A. Wu, S. Chen., S. Chen, and Y. Su. 2015. "Entrepreneurship and Poverty Reduction: A Case Study of Yiwu, China." *Asia Pacific Journal of Management* 32 (1): 119–143. doi:10.1007/s10490-014-9395-7.
Spencer, J. W., T. P. Murtha., and S. A. Lenway. 2005. "How Do Governments Matter to New Industry Creation." *Academy of Management Review* 30 (2): 321–337. doi:10.5465/amr.2005.16387889.
Standifird, S. S. 2001. "Conceptual Bonds: Network Analysis as A Way of Understanding Institutional Rigidity." *Emergence* 3 (3): 7–21. doi:10.1207/S15327000EM0303_2.
Stevenson, H., and J. C. Jarillo. 1990. "A Paradigm of Entrepreneurship: Entrepreneurial Management." *Strategic Management Journal* 11: 17–27.
Stewart, J. M. 1991. "Capitalizing on New Opportunities: Entrepreneurship in Biotechnology." In *The Business of Biotechnology: from the Bench to the Street*, edited by R. Ono, 23: 36. Stoneham, MA: Butterworth-Henemann.
Sutter, C., G. D. Bruton, and J. Chen. 2019. "Entrepreneurship as A Solution to Extreme Poverty: A Review and Future Research Directions." *Journal of Business Venturing* 34 (1): 197–214. doi:10.1016/j.jbusvent.2018.06.003.
Swidler, A. 1986. "Culture in Action: Symbols and Strategies." *American Sociological Review* 51: 273–286. doi:10.2307/2095521.
Thompson, E. R. 2009. "Individual Entrepreneurial Intent: Construct Clarification and Development of an Internationally Reliable Metric." *Entrepreneurship Theory and Practice* 33 (3): 669–694. doi:10.1111/etap.2009.33.issue-3.
Tomizawa, A., L. Zhao, G. Bassellier, and D. Ahlstrom. 2019. "Economic Growth, Innovation, Institutions, and the Great Enrichment." *Asia Pacific Journal of Management* 36. doi:10.1007/s10490-019-09648-2.
Tsang, E. W. K. 1996. "In Search of Legitimacy: The Private Entrepreneur in China." *Entrepreneurship Theory and Practice* 21 (1): 21–30. doi:10.1177/104225879602100102.
Uzzi, B. 1977. "Social Structure and Competition in Interfirm Networks: The Paradox of Embeddedness." *Administrative Science Quarterly* 42: 35–67. doi:10.2307/2393808.
Vaillant, Y., and E. Lafuente. 2007. "Do Different Institutional Frameworks Condition the Influence of Local Fear of Failure and Entrepreneurial Examples over Entrepreneurial Activity?" *Entrepreneurship and Regional Development* 19 (4): 313–337. doi:10.1080/08985620701440007.
Voronov, M., and L. Yorks. 2015. "Did You Notice That? Theorizing Differences in the Capacity to Apprehend Institutional Contradictions." *Academy of Management Review* 40 (4): 563–586. doi:10.5465/amr.2013.0152.
Voss, G. B., D. Sirdeshmukh, and Z. G. Voss. 2008. "The Effects of Slack Resources and Environmental Threat on Product Exploration and Exploitation." *Academy of Management Journal* 21: 147–164. doi:10.5465/amj.2008.30767373.

Wang, L. C., D. Ahlstrom, A. Nair, and R. Z. Hang. 2008. "Creating Globally Competitive and Innovative Products: China's Next Olympic Challenge." *SAM Advanced Management Journal* 73 (3): 4–16.

Weber, K., and M. A. Glynn. 2006. "Making Sense with Institutions: Context, Thought and Action in Karl Weick's Theory." *Organization Studies* 27: 1639–1660. doi:10.1177/0170840606068343.

Weick, K. E. 1995. *Sensemaking in Organizations*. Thousand Oaks, CA: Sage Publications.

Welter, F., D. Smallbone, and A. Pobol. 2015. "Entrepreneurial Activity in the Informal Economy: A Missing Piece of the Entrepreneurship Jigsaw Puzzle." *Entrepreneurship & Regional Development* 27 (5–6): 292–306. doi:10.1080/08985626.2015.1041259.

Wennberg, K., S. Pathak, and E. Autio. 2013. "How Culture Molds the Effects of Self-Efficacy and Fear of Failure on Entrepreneurship." *Entrepreneurship and Regional Development* 25 (9–10): 756–780. doi:10.1080/08985626.2013.862975.

Whittington, R. 1992. "Putting Giddens into Action: Social Systems and Managerial Agency." *Journal of Management Studies* 29 (6): 693–712. doi:10.1111/joms.1992.29.issue-6.

Wiklund, J., and D. Shepherd. 2003. "Aspiring For, and Achieving Growth: The Moderating Role of Resources and Opportunities." *Journal of Management Studies* 40: 1919–1940. doi:10.1046/j.1467-6486.2003.00406.x.

Winkel, D., J. Vanevenhoven, A. Yu, and J. Bronson. 2013. "The Invisible Hand in Entrepreneurial Process: Bricolage in Emerging Economies." *International Journal of Entrepreneurship and Innovation* 17 (4): 214–223. doi:10.1504/IJEIM.2013.059885.

Witt, M. A., and A. Y. Lewin. 2007. "Outward Foreign Direct Investment as Escape Response to Home Country Institutional Constraints." *Journal of International Business Studies* 38 (4): 579–594. doi:10.1057/palgrave.jibs.8400285.

World Bank. 2004. *World Bank Group Support for Small Business*. Washington, DC: World Bank.

Yamakawa, Y., M. W. Peng, and D. L. Deeds. 2008. "What Drives New Ventures to Internationalize from Emerging to Developed Economies?" *Entrepreneurship Theory and Practice* 32 (1): 59–82. doi:10.1111/j.1540-6520.2007.00216.x.

Zahra, S. A., and M. Wright. 2011. "Entrepreneurship's Next Act." *Academy of Management Perspectives* 25 (4): 67–83. doi:10.5465/amp.2010.0149.

Zucker, L. G. 1983. "Organizations as Institutions." In *Research in the Sociology of Organizations*, edited by S. B. Bacharach, 1–47. Vol. 2. Greenwich, CT: JAI Press.

Untangling the effects of entrepreneurial opportunity on the performance of peasant entrepreneurship: the moderating roles of entrepreneurial effort and regional poverty level

Aiqi Wu, Di Song and Yang Yang

ABSTRACT

The literature suggests both that entrepreneurship is a critical means of poverty alleviation, and that entrepreneurial opportunity is at the heart of entrepreneurial activity. Yet the extant research has devoted little attention to the role of entrepreneurial opportunity in entrepreneurial activity and poverty reduction. This paper explores the relationship between the types of entrepreneurial opportunity and the entrepreneurial performance of peasant entrepreneurs. Using a sample of peasant entrepreneurs from Zhejiang, China, we find that while dependence on self-identified opportunities is positively associated with entrepreneurial performance, dependence on social network- or government-identified opportunities does not positively contribute to the performance. Furthermore, we find that both entrepreneurial effort and the regional poverty level moderate the relationship between entrepreneurial opportunity and performance. This article contributes to the study of peasant entrepreneurship and poverty alleviation by demonstrating that the role of entrepreneurial opportunity is more complex and nuanced when it comes to achieving improved entrepreneurial performance.

Introduction

Peasant entrepreneurship is a significant driver of poverty reduction across the globe (Si et al. 2015; Bruton, Ahlstrom, and Si 2015; Ahlstrom 2010). However, not every practice of peasant entrepreneurship seems successful (Sutter, Bruton, and Chen 2019; Alvarez and Barney 2014). This encourages us to ask: What determines the performance of peasant entrepreneurship? As entrepreneurship is characterized as a process of opportunity pursuit (Shane and Venkataraman 2000), we explore the answer by studying entrepreneurial opportunity.

Past studies have identified many characteristics unique to peasant entrepreneurship. For instance, peasant entrepreneurs usually lack sophisticated technical knowledge (Lin and Si 2014; Fan, Chen, and Kirby 1996), and their entrepreneurial activities are heavily dependent on local knowledge (Anderson and Obeng 2017). This suggests that the entrepreneurial activities of peasant entrepreneurs are uniquely associated with knowledge that they can access and possess. By effectively creating value, peasant entrepreneurship can largely contribute to poverty reduction through increased income and employment (Si et al. 2015). Nevertheless, although some scholars have already observed that peasant entrepreneurship is not necessarily successful (Alvarez and

Barney 2014; Sutter, Bruton, and Chen 2019), what remains unclear is why and how some peasant entrepreneurship activities succeed while others fail.

As Alvarez and Barney (2014) have indicated, one approach to study entrepreneurship and poverty reduction is concentrating on the influence of entrepreneurial opportunities, which are theorized as heterogeneous (Shane and Venkataraman 2000; Schumpeter 1934). To date, the existing entrepreneurship literature has investigated why and how different types of opportunity arise (Young, Welter, and Conger 2018; Hmieleski and Baron 2008). However, little work has been done to understand the relationship between opportunity types and performance outcomes.

To address these gaps, the current study focuses on the three types of entrepreneurial opportunity – self-identified opportunity, social network-identified opportunity, and government-identified opportunity – that are predominantly available for peasant entrepreneurs, and associates them with the performance of peasant entrepreneurship. Opportunity pursuit heavily depends on knowledge (Shane 2000). Thus, by considering the unique features of peasant entrepreneurship, we follow traditional (Shane 2000; Hayek 1945) and recent (Foss, Lyngsie, and Zahra 2013) emphases on a knowledge-based understanding of entrepreneurial opportunity. We examine the entrepreneurial opportunity–performance relationship of peasant entrepreneurship based on knowledge-based view (KBV) arguments (e.g., Grant 1996; Cohen and Levinthal 1990). From the knowledge perspective of entrepreneurial opportunity, we depict the role of knowledge in the different types of opportunities during the process of opportunity identification and exploitation, which in turn, explains the varied performance outcomes when exploiting different types of opportunity.

We have conducted our study using survey data obtained from peasant entrepreneurs living in Zhejiang Province, China. Zhejiang Province offers a suitable research setting for our research for the following reasons. First, peasant entrepreneurship has been flourishing in Zhejiang over the past decades, and such activities have largely contributed to poverty reduction and Zhejiang's exponential economic growth (Si et al. 2015; Lin, Li, and Yang 2011). Second, the variation of poverty level across different regions of Zhejiang allows further exploration of the contextual factor.

By examining entrepreneurial opportunities from different sources, our study shows that while self-identified opportunity can positively contribute to entrepreneurial performance, the influence of social network-identified opportunity is not significant. At the same time, government-identified opportunity has a negative impact on performance outcome. Furthermore, more intensive entrepreneurial effort and a higher regional poverty level will facilitate the transformation of entrepreneurial opportunity to produce a better performance.

Our study enriches the understanding of how different types of opportunity can lead to varied performance outcomes of peasant entrepreneurship, and contributes to entrepreneurship and poverty reduction studies by providing a plausible explanation as to why some entrepreneurial activities reduce poverty successfully while others do not (Sutter, Bruton, and Chen 2019). Additionally, by integrating KBV arguments (Grant 1996; Cohen and Levinthal 1990), our study extends the entrepreneurial opportunity literature by investigating how knowledge matters for opportunity identification and exploitation, thus untangling the complicated relationship between entrepreneurial opportunity and performance outcome (Alvarez and Barney 2014).

Theory and hypothesis

Economic performance is a key indicator in measuring whether or not poverty eradication efforts are successful (Alvarez and Barney 2014). A superior entrepreneurial performance can not only allow the peasant entrepreneur to be wealthier, but also facilitate the process of fighting poverty by creating jobs and improving enthusiasm for working (Sutter, Bruton, and Chen 2019; Leong et al. 2016; Si et al. 2015). While past studies have explained how entrepreneurial orientation (Lumpkin and Dess 1996), organizational legitimacy (Wang, Thornhill, and De Castro 2017), and an entrepreneur's experience (Spanjer and van Witteloostuijn 2017) influence entrepreneurial performance, little is known with regard to the impact of entrepreneurial opportunity. While opportunity identification and exploitation have been shown to be central to entrepreneurship (Davidsson 2015; Shane and Venkataraman 2000), we investigate how entrepreneurial opportunity affects performance of peasant entrepreneurship.

The literature has suggested that entrepreneurial opportunities may vary in several aspects (Alvarez and Barney 2014; Shane and Venkataraman 2000). In line with this argument, we argue that looking at heterogeneous types of opportunity can facilitate a better interpretation of the mixed and complicated relationship between entrepreneurial opportunity and performance outcome (Hmieleski and Baron 2008; Alvarez and Barney 2014). On the one hand, ignoring opportunity heterogeneity may lead to a failure to reveal the nature of entrepreneurial activities. Entrepreneurial opportunities are generated from many sources (Alvarez and Barney 2007; Suddaby, Bruton, and Si 2015), including innovative efforts (Hargadon and Douglas 2001), perception of technology-market combination (Grégoire and Shepherd 2012), or even pure luck (Chandra 2017). On the other hand, entrepreneurs may have different attitudes towards each of the heterogeneous types of opportunity. One critical element of understanding opportunity is associated with one's perception of the environment (Hmieleski and Baron 2008; Young, Welter, and Conger 2018). For instance, Young, Welter, and Conger (2018) have illustrated that whether an entrepreneur chooses to take advantage of innovative or imitative opportunities is dependent on their perceptions of regulatory institutions.

Following the aforementioned arguments, we highlight the theoretical importance of advancing our understanding of entrepreneurial opportunity, and its complicated impact on entrepreneurial outcomes, by considering the heterogeneity of entrepreneurial opportunities.

Knowledge perspective of entrepreneurial opportunity pursuit

The entrepreneurship literature (e.g., Shane and Venkataraman 2000; Eckhardt and Shane 2003; Choi, Lévesque, and Shepherd 2008; Shane 2012; Williams and Wood 2015) has indicated that entrepreneurial opportunity pursuit can be decomposed into several steps, including opportunity identification and exploitation. However, identification of entrepreneurial opportunity does not necessarily mean that entrepreneurs are able to exploit the opportunity properly (Foss, Lyngsie, and Zahra 2013; Shane and Venkataraman 2000). Thus, this effort cannot be automatically translated into favorable entrepreneurial performance (Shane 2012; Choi, Lévesque, and Shepherd 2008). This argument suggests that, while opportunity identification has been widely accepted to be crucial for entrepreneurship, the role of opportunity exploitation in transforming entrepreneurial opportunities into superior performance outcome still remains unclear.

Following the emphasis on the importance of knowledge in entrepreneurship literature (Foss, Lyngsie, and Zahra 2013; Shane 2000; Hayek 1945), we draw on KBV arguments (e.g., Grant 1996; Cohen and Levinthal 1990) to address the gap. KBV demonstrates that knowledge – a group of intangible but critical resources – determines firm's performance outcomes (Grant 1996). This perspective views firms as knowledge coordinators, and maintains that the overall knowledge base varies across firms. Moreover, it has been argued that knowledge can be generated by the firm from the external environment (Grant and Baden-Fuller 2004; Foss, Lyngsie, and Zahra 2013). The ability to acquire and apply the external knowledge is dependent on a firm's absorptive capacity (Pollitte, Miller, and Yaprak 2015; Zahra and George 2002).

Knowledge can influence both opportunity identification and opportunity exploitation. On the one hand, the knowledge base has an impact on the novelty of the identified opportunities. The degree of opportunity novelty for the entrepreneur is a result of different knowledge bases among entrepreneurs (Subramanian, Wang, and Chai 2018; Zahra, Ireland, and Hitt 2000). Opportunity identification is highly dependent on an entrepreneur's idiosyncratic prior knowledge that creates a 'knowledge corridor' (Shane 2000, 452). In general, opportunities generated by entrepreneurs are less novel as they are easier to interpret compared with those introduced by other individuals. Moreover, the degree of opportunity novelty for the entrepreneur is associated with the opportunity explorer's broadness of knowledge. Innovative opportunities are related to significant novelty (Samuelsson and Davidsson 2009). Compared with others, certain subjects are more likely to identify more innovative opportunities owing to their broader knowledge base of the market (Shearmur and Doloreux 2016) and technology (Yayavaram and Chen 2015; Schumpeter 1934). A broad knowledge base allows entrepreneurs to come up with more novel means–ends combinations; ones that differ from dominant trajectories (Pérez-Luño, Wiklund, and Cabrera 2011). When the identified opportunities are too novel, however, entrepreneurs deviate from the original organizational routine to an extent (Sapienza et al. 2006). Consequently, they may have difficulties in deploying existing resources and expert actions on the opportunity.

On the other hand, once an opportunity is ready for exploitation, entrepreneurs ought to search for external complementary knowledge to exploit such an opportunity (Foss, Lyngsie, and Zahra 2013; Matthews 2009; Hmieleski and Baron 2008; Choi, Lévesque, and Shepherd 2008; March 1991). Specifically, in order to capture opportunity, firms should be prepared for the need for necessary complementary assets (Teece 1986) and become familiar with market demand (Foss, Lyngsie, and Zahra 2013). We argue that peasant entrepreneurs are more motivated to search, capable to acquire, and able to effectively assimilate external knowledge for opportunities than others. First, people have a greater tendency 'to continue an endeavor once an investment in money, effort, or time has been made' (Arkes and Blumer 1985, 124). Following this logic, when peasant entrepreneurs have invested much time and resources in identifying an opportunity, they are more motivated to make a continuous investment on a complementary knowledge search. Second, as knowledge acquisition is maximized when the existing knowledge domain is close to complementary knowledge (Autio, Sapienza, and Almeida 2000), the possession of a similar knowledge base allows peasant entrepreneurs to know where and how to search for complementary knowledge (Foss, Lyngsie, and Zahra 2013). Third, after acquiring knowledge from the environment, peasant entrepreneurs can assimilate and apply the acquired new knowledge to pursue the opportunity (Grant 1996). In this case, assimilation is facilitated by a more nuanced comprehensibility, resulting from the possession of complementary knowledge within the firm (Zahra and George 2002; Teece 1986).

Entrepreneurial opportunity type and peasant entrepreneurship

In recent years, scholars have increasingly paid attention to peasant entrepreneurship (e.g., Si et al. 2015; Petit, Kuper, and Ameur 2018). Although entrepreneurship researchers have already achieved tremendous progress in terms of understanding how entrepreneurship alleviates poverty (Bruton, Ahlstrom, and Si 2015; Si et al. 2015; Sutter, Bruton, and Chen 2019), there is still a lack of clarity on the issue when it comes to peasant entrepreneurship. Peasants are rural residents who are relatively resource-constrained and short of advanced knowledge (Seelos and Mair 2007; Hart and Christensen 2002). For these people, taking advantage of identified opportunities might not be easy, given that exploitation requires certain levels of knowledge broadness and resource endowment. Therefore, deciding on which opportunity to pursue at the very first stage might influence the opportunity exploitation process and performance outcome.

Entrepreneurial opportunities can be generated from diverse sources (George et al. 2016; Shane and Venkataraman 2000). First, entrepreneurial opportunity can be identified by peasant entrepreneurs themselves (Chandra 2017; Shane 2000). Entrepreneurial opportunities are developed by entrepreneurs in business activities. Doing business in a specific domain, and participating in self-improvement training and learning projects help entrepreneurs to broaden their knowledge base. Knowledge is dispersed in society and differently interpreted by entrepreneurs (Hayek 1945), and the possibility of identifying opportunities in a specific domain may be enhanced with the accumulation of related knowledge (Shane 2000). Consequently, new opportunities can emerge through the everyday business activities of entrepreneurs. Second, entrepreneurial opportunity can be introduced by individual social networks (Granovetter 1973). Past entrepreneurship studies agree that critical information derived from a social network brings opportunities to entrepreneurs (e.g., Shantz, Kistruck, and Zietsma 2018; Shu, Ren, and Zheng 2018). Third, the government may also introduce entrepreneurial opportunities. Studies have suggested that the government plays an important role in stimulating entrepreneurship (Ribeiro-Soriano and Galindo-Martín 2012; Williams and Nadin 2012). For example, the Chinese government is usually characterized as a proactive player in many economic activities (Gaur, Ma, and Ding 2018), including alleviating poverty by encouraging rural peasants to engage in entrepreneurship (Lin and Si 2014). To sum up, entrepreneurial opportunities can be rooted from any of the three sources mentioned above.

Although these three types of entrepreneurial opportunity can be developed by any entrepreneur, two unique features of peasant entrepreneurship should be addressed. First of all, peasant entrepreneurs have relatively low levels of knowledge about state-of-the-art technologies (Hall et al. 2012; Lin and Si 2014; Fan, Chen, and Kirby 1996), and their entrepreneurial activities are heavily associated with the motivation to meet market demands (Si et al. 2015). Consequently, peasant entrepreneurs are not likely to identify opportunities that deviate from their daily operations or to exploit successfully an opportunity related to breakthrough technologies. Second, unlike other entrepreneurs, peasant entrepreneurs usually live in comparatively isolated rural areas. This geographic characteristic heightens the heavy reliance of peasant entrepreneurship on local knowledge (Anderson and Obeng 2017). These two distinctive features motivate us to investigate how different types of opportunity uniquely influence the entrepreneurial performance of peasant entrepreneurship.

Entrepreneurial opportunity type and performance

Different types of opportunity can have varied performance implications when it comes to peasant entrepreneurship. We outline the first of our hypotheses by examining the effects of self-identified opportunities. We propose that opportunities mainly derived from peasant entrepreneurs themselves exert a positive influence upon entrepreneurial performance. Primarily, self-identified opportunities are scarcely novel. As entrepreneurs from rural areas do not usually receive a great deal of education (Si et al. 2015; Anderson and Obeng 2017; Rao and Ye 2016), they are discouraged from exploring innovative opportunities that require sufficient technical knowledge background. Instead, peasant entrepreneurs tend to develop entrepreneurial opportunities during daily operations. For instance, the way to serve their markets is easily recognized given their familiarity with the process of creating new products by simply recombining existing resources at hand (Shane 2000; Si et al. 2015). As a result, self-identified opportunities are highly related to established industrial routines and processes, which in turn allow the firm to pursue the opportunity better by deploying existing resources and expertise. Moreover, peasant entrepreneurs are motivated and capable of gathering the complementary necessary knowledge and expertise to exploit an identified opportunity. The identification of entrepreneurial opportunity (Choi, Lévesque, and Shepherd 2008; Shane and Venkataraman 2000) incurs costs, including the investment for information accumulation. Once initial investments are made, profit-seeking peasant entrepreneurs tend to rack their brains searching for external knowledge to exploit for further opportunities. And, as self-identified opportunities are developed from corporate operations, peasant entrepreneurs are likely to know how to assimilate complementary knowledge. As a result, peasant entrepreneurs are considered proficient in the opportunity exploitation stage. Therefore, we propose that:

Hypothesis 1a (H1a): *Self-identified opportunity is positively associated with the entrepreneurial performance of peasant entrepreneurs.*

We also predict a positive relationship between social network-identified opportunity and the performance of peasant entrepreneurship. The first reason for this is that social network-identified opportunities are comparatively less novel. In rural areas, people become acquainted with each other (Turgo 2016) and peasants in the same place share similar knowledge domains (Owoo and Naudé 2017; Cruz and Teixeira 2010). After repeated everyday interactions, opportunity providers become familiar with the focal peasant entrepreneurs and their businesses. Thus, social network-identified opportunities are not very likely to deviate much from the already established organizational routines and processes of the firm, which will incur fewer extra costs for the entrepreneurs. The second reason is that peasant entrepreneurs are relatively effective in searching for complementary knowledge to realize social network-identified opportunities. Although peasant entrepreneurs do not directly invest financial resources and exert huge efforts in the opportunity identification stage, social network-identified opportunities nonetheless incur indirect costs. Based on the reciprocity principle (Emerson 1976), peasant entrepreneurs tend to feel obliged to pay back all the kindness of network players. As a result, they have strong incentives to seek and accumulate complementary knowledge. Furthermore, the acquaintance society facilitates the gathering of effective knowledge. As tacit knowledge is commonly shared by the community in rural areas (Anderson and Obeng 2017; Dodd, Jack, and Anderson 2013), peasant entrepreneurs can effectively find useful and necessary complementary knowledge. Therefore, we propose that:

Hypothesis 1b (H1b): *Social network-identified opportunity is positively associated with the entrepreneurial performance of peasant entrepreneurs.*

In contrast to self- and social network-identified opportunities, we conjecture that government-identified opportunities are negatively associated with the performance of peasant entrepreneurship. Governments play a vital role in entrepreneurship initiation and poverty reduction through several means, such as initiating entrepreneurial training and education (Lin and Si 2014; Williams and Nadin 2012), formulating policies and guidelines (Ahlstrom, Bruton, and Lui 2000; Ribeiro-Soriano and Galindo-Martín 2012), promoting entrepreneurial models (Lin and Si 2014), and providing financial resources (Shakya and Rankin 2008; Anguloruiz 2014). However, when governments directly introduce opportunities to peasant entrepreneurs, the latter do not achieve superior entrepreneurial performance as the opportunities are too novel for them and complementary knowledge is less likely accumulated.

In comparison with self- and social network-identified opportunities, government-identified opportunities are generally more novel. The critical reason is that government-identified opportunities are policy-oriented (O'Connor 2013; Michael and Pearce 2009). Typical examples are the Five-Year Plans proposed by China's central and local governments. These policies provide guidelines for the priorities of subsequent industrial development (Lei et al. 2017), and intentionally aim to develop industrial clusters (Yu and Gibbs 2018). Government-identified opportunities are largely dependent on these guidelines and tend to disregard peasant entrepreneurs' actual knowledge domain. As a result, governments' initiatives might deviate from established organizational routines and processes. Moreover, governments have a broader knowledge base than peasant entrepreneurs (Rogers 2014). This information advantage allows policy makers and officials to engender innovative ways to fulfill market demand that may not be appropriate for peasant entrepreneurs.

In addition to the novelty issue, government-identified opportunities are difficult to pursue given that peasant entrepreneurs are usually less motivated and unable to search for complementary knowledge (Hughes et al. 2014). As the policy-oriented nature of government-identified opportunities means they are seldom directed at one firm (O'Connor 2013), scarce costs are incurred for opportunity identification. In this sense, peasant entrepreneurs are not highly motivated to search for complementary knowledge. As the existing knowledge of the firm and the knowledge required by government-identified opportunities do not match well, peasants would find difficulties in acquiring and assimilating useful complementary knowledge (Hughes et al.

2014). To sum up, peasant entrepreneurs are unlikely to be easily able to pursue the opportunity within their current organizational processes as well as accumulate sufficient and useful complementary knowledge for opportunity exploitation, and as a consequence, alternative profitable opportunities are less likely to be captured and a wealth of resources can be wasted (Shane and Venkataraman 2000). Therefore, we propose that:

Hypothesis 1c (H1c): *Government-identified opportunity is negatively associated with the entrepreneurial performance of peasant entrepreneurs.*

Contingent effects of entrepreneurial effort and regional poverty level

Although we have proposed that different opportunity types have distinct impacts on entrepreneurial performance, those relationships are moderated by internal and external contingencies. Here, we demonstrate how entrepreneurial efforts (as an internal enabler) and regional poverty levels (as an external enabler) moderate the relationship between opportunity types and the entrepreneurial performance of peasant entrepreneurs.

As aforementioned, opportunity exploitation is critical in transforming opportunities into performance outcomes. During this process, entrepreneurs are required to have enough relevant knowledge and skills to exploit the opportunities at hand and successfully capitalize on potential gains inherent in opportunities (Cohen and Levinthal 1990; Shane and Venkataraman 2000). Entrepreneurial effort has a critical role in the growth of entrepreneurial organizations (Carson et al. 1995). In this section, we argue that entrepreneurial effort can expedite the opportunity exploitation process and facilitate the operability of the opportunity. In line with previous literature, 'entrepreneurial effort' here refers to the intensity of work performed on entrepreneurial tasks (Foo, Uy, and Baron 2009; Uy, Foo, and Ilies 2015). Entrepreneurs need to put efforts into several entrepreneurial activities, including generating business ideas, developing plans, strategizing to obtain critical resources and expand into new markets, applying for licenses, investing in R&D fields, and running daily operations. This needs to take place throughout the whole process of entrepreneurship, in order to broaden the organizational search for opportunities and further exploit opportunities (Zahra 2008). Strong entrepreneurial effort implies high levels of energy, zeal, commitment, determination, persistence, and focus exhibited by the entrepreneur (Carson et al. 1995).

When peasant entrepreneurs exert high levels of effort and commitment, they have a better understanding of possible opportunities owing to 'learning-by-doing effect' (Parker 2013; Autio, Sapienza, and Almeida 2000). Such effort optimizes their external knowledge searching strategy and the acquisition of more useful complementary knowledge about logistics, production, and market demands. Furthermore, acquired knowledge is more likely to be assimilated and transformed into opportunity exploitation by peasant entrepreneurs, as entrepreneurial efforts facilitate their knowledge integration (Hughes et al. 2014). By contrast, when entrepreneurial effort is low, even if opportunities are already identified, it is still challenging to transform it into superior performance (Uy, Foo, and Ilies 2015; Drnovsek, Cardon, and Patel 2016). To sum up, we predict that increased entrepreneurial effort enables peasant entrepreneurs better to capture the identified opportunity. Therefore, we propose that:

Hypothesis 2a (H2a): *Entrepreneurial effort will strengthen the positive relationship between self-identified opportunity and the entrepreneurial performance of peasant entrepreneurs.*

Hypothesis 2b (H2b): *Entrepreneurial effort will strengthen the positive relationship between social network-identified opportunity and the entrepreneurial performance of peasant entrepreneurs.*

Hypothesis 2c (H2c): *Entrepreneurial effort will weaken the negative relationship between government-identified opportunity and the entrepreneurial performance of peasant entrepreneurs.*

The environmental context has long been considered in the entrepreneurship literature as an important factor in assessing outcomes (Chliova, Brinckmann, and Rosenbusch 2015; Davidsson 2015; Hmieleski and Baron 2008). As documented in previous literature (Bruton, Ahlstrom, and Si 2015), some regions in China are far less developed than others. For example, in Zhejiang Province, the GDP per capita of Northern Zhejiang cities (e.g., Hangzhou and Ningbo) is approximately twice as much as that of some Southern Zhejiang cities (e.g., Quzhou and Lishui) (Zhejiang Statistical Yearbook 2017). Thus, investigating the moderating effect of the regional poverty level is meaningful and empirically important. When the regional poverty level is low, indicating that the region is comparatively more developed, customers become pickier with their increased disposable income (Auer, Chaney, and Sauré 2018). Owing to their comparatively low technical knowledge (Si et al. 2015; Anderson and Obeng 2017), peasant entrepreneurs normally have a limited capacity to meet such demands. Meanwhile, in areas where regional poverty is lower still, the markets become more attractive, leading to fiercer competition between firms (Khandelwal et al. 2013; Meyer et al. 2009). Thus, the transformation from entrepreneurial opportunities to performance is inhibited by the relatively low competitiveness of the firm owned by peasant entrepreneurs. By contrast, when the regional poverty level is high, peasant entrepreneurs are under greater pressure to get rid of the unfavorable living conditions, increasing their motivation to search for the complementary knowledge that is essential for effective opportunity exploitation. Therefore, we propose that:

Hypothesis 3a (H3a): *Higher regional poverty level will strengthen the positive relationship between self-identified opportunity and the entrepreneurial performance of peasant entrepreneurs.*

Hypothesis 3b (H3b): *Higher regional poverty level will strengthen the positive relationship between social network-identified opportunity and the entrepreneurial performance of peasant entrepreneurs.*

Hypothesis 3c (H3c): *Higher regional poverty level will weaken the negative relationship between government-identified opportunity and the entrepreneurial performance of peasant entrepreneurs.*

Methods

Sample and data

Peasant entrepreneurship is a proven way out of poverty (Bruton, Ketchen, and Ireland 2013; Wu and Si 2018; Si et al. 2015; Sutter, Bruton, and Chen 2019). We tested our hypotheses using a sample of peasant entrepreneurial firms from Zhejiang Province, China. We believe this is a suitable setting to study our research questions. Although China has achieved great economic development in the past decades (Ahlstrom, Bruton, and Lui 2000), it still currently faces issues of poverty reduction, having the largest rural economy in the world. Nevertheless, China has seen a rapid rise in peasant entrepreneurship since the 1980s, and more peasant entrepreneurs have come into existence in the past few years (Ma 2018). Among these entrepreneurs, peasant entrepreneurs from Zhejiang have spearheaded the miraculous rise of rural entrepreneurship and poverty reduction in China. Many of the largest businesses in China today, such as Wanxiang, Wahaha, and Geely, were founded by Zhejiang's peasant entrepreneurs. Therefore, Zhejiang's peasant entrepreneurship is a successful model for China, as the region has made tremendous progress in the eradication of poverty through the rise of peasant entrepreneurship during these last decades. To be precise, the GDP per capital in the province dramatically increased, from 212.57 US dollars in 1978 to 12,288.86 US dollars in 2016, with an annual growth rate of 11% (Zhejiang Statistical Yearbook 2017).

One representative example is the poverty reduction practices of Yiwu, a town located in the central part of Zhejiang province, which is now termed as the world's largest commodity center. Peasant entrepreneurs enormously contributed to regional poverty reduction and economic development in Yiwu (Si et al. 2015). Under such circumstances, it has been demonstrated that peasant entrepreneurs can find entrepreneurial opportunity either independently through the local industrial value chain (Cruz and Teixeira 2010), or introduced by social networks (Wang 2016; Batjargal and Liu 2004) or provided by the government (Peng and Luo 2000). Therefore, we believe the context of peasant entrepreneurship in Zhejiang provides a suitable setting to solve our research question and proffer us abundant information and insights.

The data for our study was obtained through a survey. With the assistance of Economy and Information Commission of Zhejiang Province, we randomly selected a sample of 5000 entrepreneurial enterprises that had already established their own firms and started their business, based on the Directory of Small and Medium Enterprises in Zhejiang. The data were collected in January, 2017. The questionnaire was first developed in English, then translated into Chinese and translated back into English twice to avoid cultural bias and ensure construct validity. The questionnaire validation process was strengthened by analysis from other researchers: following their feedback, we modified questions which were too ambiguous, vague, or unclear. Subsequently, we also tried to minimize consistency artifacts by reducing the length of questions and keeping the questionnaire relatively short (two pages) following the example of previous research (e.g., Ambos, Andersson, and Birkinshaw 2010; Valentino, Caroli, and Mayrhofer 2018). And last, we placed the dependent variables after the independent variables in the survey to diminish the effects of consistency artifacts (Salancik and Pfeffer 1977).

Measures were taken to limit potential common method variance. First, the ambiguities in the questionnaire items were kept to a minimum and respondents' anonymity was considered before and during the data collection process (Podsakoff et al. 2003). Second, dependent and independent variables for constructs were placed at different positions in the survey, and scale anchors were changed. Third, during the data collection, we used different sets of questions to measure different constructs, and the order of the questions varied between participants, which was designed to reduce participants' perceptions of a direct connection between the constructs (Podsakoff et al. 2003). Fourth, both self-reported (e.g., opportunity type, entrepreneurial performance) and objective indicators (e.g., regional poverty level, firm age) were adopted in our model. Further, in the subsequent analysis, the potential influence of common method variance was tested using Harman's one-factor test (Podsakoff and Organ 1986). Principal factor analysis was performed to determine whether a single factor explained a majority of the variance. The statistics indicate that common method variance was unlikely to present a potential bias for model estimates.

The survey contains a series of questions about regional-level characteristics, entrepreneur-level characteristics, firm-level characteristics, and performance. It also contains detailed information on entrepreneurial opportunity identification. The questionnaire was answered by the founders and entrepreneurs of the sampled firms, so the bulk of our data are based on the perceptions of the entrepreneurs. We finally got 2465 questionnaires returned, with a response rate of 49.3%. To assess the non-response bias, we compared the responding firms with the non-responding firms and found no significant differences in firm size and age. Since this paper focuses on peasant entrepreneurship, we constrained our informants to those entrepreneurs who have their roots in rural areas, and are now founders of an entrepreneurial firm (Fan, Chen, and Kirby 1996). Specifically, we constrained our observations to entrepreneurs who are reported to be registered at rural residences and who lived in the rural areas or worked on the land before their entrepreneurial activities. This reduced our sample to 931 observations.

The sample composition showed significant variance. Table 1 provides an overview of the sample profile, highlighting the sample characteristics and the baseline information. The respondent firms were engaged in various industrial sectors such as metal products, textile, and rubber and plastic products. Most of the respondent firms (96.9%) were small and micro enterprises, only 3.1% of them were enterprises with 300 or more employees. In addition, the majority of our

Table 1. Sample profiles.

Sample Characteristics	Frequency	Percentage (%)
Industry type		
Metal products	136	14.6
Textile	130	14.0
Rubber & plastic products	82	8.8
Clothing & clothing accessories	61	6.6
General equipment manufacturing	49	5.3
Special Equipment Manufacturing	26	2.8
Chemical materials & products	23	2.5
Electrical machinery & equipment manufacturing	21	2.3
Others	403	43.3
Firm size (number of full-time employees)		
Less than 20	147	15.8
20–300	755	81.1
More than or equal to 300	29	3.1
Firm age		
Less than 8 years	199	21.4
8–20 years	622	66.8
More than 20 years	110	11.8
Geographic location		
Jinhua	199	21.4
Ningbo	152	16.3
Taizhou	144	15.5
Hangzhou	103	11.1
Huzhou	102	11.0
Quzhou	70	7.5
Others	161	17.3
Market scope		
Local market	165	17.7
Domestic market	567	60.9
Global market	199	21.4

sampled firms (66.8%) were mid-aged firms (aged between 8 and 20 years). The majority of the sampled firms (more than 51%) were also located in non-coastal areas. And finally, with regard to the firms' market scope, a large proportion of these firms targeted a relatively narrow market, i.e., local markets (17.7%) and domestic markets (60.9%).

Variables and measures

Three variables in our model were operationalized as multi-item constructs. They were all rated based on the five-point Likert Scale (1 = very poor, 5 = very good), and we averaged the items to create the scores for these constructs.

Dependent variable

Entrepreneurial performance

Following the suggestion by Wiklund (1999) and Keh, Nguyen, and Ng (2007), we used three items to measure the entrepreneurial performance of the firm. In order to provide an anchor for the respondents to answer the questions, we asked them to rate the extent to which their firms were successful relative to their major competitors in terms of (1) sales growth, (2) profit growth, and (3) market share growth. The 5-point Likert scale was used. Reliability tests and factor analysis indicate that the standardized scores of the three items can be aggregated to create one factor (Cronbach's alpha = 0.930). We averaged the items to create the scores for this construct.

Independent variables

Entrepreneurial opportunity type

This variable measures the nature and sources of various opportunities captured and exploited by peasant entrepreneurs. In this study, we focus on three types of opportunities: self-identified opportunity, social network-identified opportunity, and government-identified opportunity. The phrasing of the question (single choice) was 'How do you mainly identify new opportunities?' The possible answers are: 'based on own knowledge, observation or inspiration', 'recommended by relatives, friends or partners' and 'recommended by governments' policy or guidance'. We operationalized these three items as dichotomous variables that take the value 1 for a certain type of opportunity, and value 0 for others.

Moderating variables

Entrepreneurial effort

Previous literature measured entrepreneurial effort by focusing on the amount of entrepreneurial effort an entrepreneur commits to the entrepreneurial engagement process (Foo, Uy, and Baron 2009; Zhu et al. 2016). Some papers directly capture the effort through examining the working hours invested in the company (e.g., Jia and Zhang 2018), while others pay attention to the content of the entrepreneurial effort by taking into consideration various kinds of entrepreneurial activities (Uy, Foo, and Ilies 2015; Edelman and Yli-Renko 2010). In this study, we counted the number of activities with which a peasant entrepreneur had engaged, in line with Edelman and Yli-Renko (2010), and used this to measure entrepreneurial efforts. These entrepreneurial activities include expanding business into a new market, establishing a new subsidiary or business unit, introducing new products, overseas investment, establishing employee venturing fund, establishing venturing investment department, cross-sectional investment, incubate a new project, merger & acquisition, and renewing firm strategies.

Regional poverty level

We used regional GDP to reverse code regional poverty level. A higher level of regional GDP indicates a lower level of poverty. Following previous research (e.g., Fagerberg and Srholec 2008), we measured regional GDP using a three-year (year 2014–2016) average GDP per capita in the prefecture-level city (e.g., Hangzhou) where the firm was located.

Controls

Several control variables were included in the study. Firm-level characteristics were controlled. Namely, (1) firm age, which is measured by the number of years since incorporation; (2) firm size, as measured by natural logarithm of sales; (3) ownership types, using two dichotomous variables, i.e., joint venture and privately-owned; (4) enterprise type, using a dichotomous variable, micro-enterprise or not; and (5) market scope. In respect of the market scope variable, we designed a single choice question, asking the respondents to answer the question: 'The products/service of your enterprise are mostly serviced for: (1) local market, (2) domestic market, (3) global market'. Based on the answers, we manipulated this variable as follows: 1 = local market; 2 = domestic market; 3 = global market. We also controlled the regional level contingencies. As well as this, we controlled factor market development in terms of financing, infrastructure and intermediary service, because an endowed factor market helps firms capture profitable economic opportunities and might thereby might have an impact on entrepreneurial performance (Hoskisson et al. 2013). We asked respondents to rate the level of regional factor market development in terms of: (1) easiness for financing; (2) industry infrastructure; (3) intermediary service of law, technology and management etc. Factor analysis shows that the three items were consistently loaded on a single factor (Cronbach's alpha = 0.765, factor loadings were 0.706, 0.854, and 0.824 respectively), and an average score of these items was used in the subsequent analyses. Moreover, to rule out the potential influence of regional policy support on the entrepreneurial performance of local enterprises, we controlled for policy support. A multi-item scale was used, which assessed regional policy support in terms of: (1) preferential policies in tax or land price, (2) entrepreneurship projects initiated by local government, and (3) talent policy for entrepreneurs. This scale was also rated on the five-point Likert Scale. Reliability tests and factor analysis indicated that scores of the three items can be aggregated to create one factor (Cronbach's alpha = 0.804). Finally, we also controlled the effect of incubator existence as this could proffer information and professional advice for start-ups and help them survive and grow. We measured it using a single dimension question, framed as follows: 'Please indicate the development of regional incubator or maker space for entrepreneurship.'

Results

Table 2 presents the means, standard deviations, and correlations among the variables examined in the study. Ordinary least squares (OLS) was used to analyze the differences in entrepreneurial performance due to the different types of entrepreneurial opportunity for peasant entrepreneurship. The variance inflation factors (VIF) for the regression models did not exceed 10 (VIF< 2.05), indicating that there were no serious problems with multicollinearity in our study (Neter, Wasserman, and Kutner 1990). To test the moderating effects of international legitimacy and strategic flexibility, we produced six interaction terms; to reduce any potential problem of multicollinearity, independent and moderating variables were standardized prior to the creation of the interaction terms (Aiken, West, and Reno 1991).

Table 3 presents the results of the main effects of different opportunity types on entrepreneurial performance, as well as showing the moderating effects of entrepreneurial efforts and regional poverty level. The results are largely consistent with our hypotheses.

The results for main effects are reported in Model 2. Hypothesis 1a predicts that a peasant entrepreneur who mainly takes advantage of self-identified opportunity is positively associated with good entrepreneurial performance. As shown in Model 2, the coefficient for self-identified opportunity in a regression function with entrepreneurial performance is positive and significant ($b = 0.1163$, $p < 0.05$), which suggests that self-identified opportunity positively contributes to entrepreneurial performance. Thus, Hypothesis 1a is supported.

Hypothesis 1b predicts that social network-identified opportunity has a positive impact on entrepreneurial performance. Unlike our expectation, the coefficient for social identified opportunity in Model 2 is positive but not statistically significant ($b = 0.0522$, n.s.). This indicates that social network-identified opportunities have only a limited effect on entrepreneurial performance. Hence, Hypothesis 1b is not supported. One possible reason for the surprising result is that opportunities introduced by social networks are comparatively less profitable and cannot be translated smoothly into firm growth. After all, if entrepreneurs could identify a profitable opportunity, introducing the discovery to another entrepreneur would not be not 'rational'.

Hypothesis 1c predicts that the dependence of a peasant entrepreneur on government-identified opportunity negatively contributes to entrepreneurial performance. According to Model 2, the coefficient for government-identified opportunity is significantly negative ($b = -0.1725$, $p < 0.1$), which indicates government-identified opportunities have negative implications for entrepreneurial opportunity. Therefore, Hypothesis 1c is supported.

We report the effect of entrepreneurial effort in Model 4. Hypothesis 2a predicts that entrepreneurial effort strengthens the positive relationship between self-identified opportunity and entrepreneurial performance. As shown in Model 4, the interaction term between self-identified opportunity and entrepreneurial efforts is positive but not significant ($b = 0.0233$, n.s.), suggesting that we do not find evidence to support for the moderating role of entrepreneurial effort on the

Table 2. Descriptive statistics and correlation matrix.

Variables	1	2	3	4	5	6	7	8
1.Entrepreneurial performance	1							
2.Government-identified opportunity	−0.042	1						
3.Social network-identified opportunity	−0.049	−0.159***	1					
4.Self-identified opportunity	0.140***	−0.147***	−0.535***	1				
5.Entrepreneurial efforts	0.189***	0.019	−0.058*	0.148***	1			
6.Regional poverty level (reverse coded)	0.059*	0.011	0.077**	−0.087***	0.003	1		
7.Microenterprises	−0.161***	−0.015	0.110***	−0.153***	−0.091***	−0.02	1	
8.Firm age	−0.027	−0.041	−0.039	0.044	0.002	−0.058*	−0.085***	1
9.Firm size	0.180***	−0.025	−0.104***	0.181***	0.115***	−0.116***	−0.352***	0.052
10.Joint venture	0.015	0.139***	0.037	−0.038	−0.019	0.056*	−0.057*	0.044
11.Private-owned firm	−0.015	0.006	0.023	0.045	0.032	−0.169***	−0.007	0.025
12.Market scope	0.033	−0.021	−0.173***	0.145***	0.017	−0.028	−0.188***	−0.03
13.Factor market development	0.280***	0.071**	−0.057*	0.086***	0.091***	0.093***	0.004	0.021
14.Policy support	0.262***	0.131***	−0.114***	0.082**	0.094***	0.026	−0.05	0.071**
15.Incubator	0.286***	0.084***	−0.061*	0.043	0.039	0.079**	0.012	0.014
Mean	2.94	0.04	0.37	0.33	1.43	8.41	0.18	12.88
S.D.	0.6	0.2	0.48	0.47	0.67	2.98	0.39	7.5

Variables	9	10	11	12	13	14	15
1.Entrepreneurial performance							
2.Government-identified opportunity							
3.Social network-identified opportunity							
4.Self-identified opportunity							
5.Entrepreneurial efforts							
6.Regional poverty level							
7.Microenterprises							
8.Firm age							
9.Firm size	1						
10.Joint venture	0.013	1					
11.Private-owned firm	0.063*	−0.246***	1				
12.Market scope	0.063*	0.102***	−0.004	1			
13.Factor market development	0.026	0.04	0	−0.006	1		
14.Policy support	0.090***	0.024	0.03	−0.041	0.482***	1	
15.Incubator	0.014	0.022	−0.022	−0.066**	0.534***	0.669***	1
Mean	7.25	0.02	0.7	2.04	3.14	3.31	3.25
S.D.	1.36	0.16	0.46	0.62	0.59	0.66	0.72

Note: * $p < 0.1$, ** $p < 0.05$, *** $p < 0.01$(two-tailed test).

Table 3. OLS estimation of entrepreneurial performance.

DV: Entrepreneurial performance	1	2	3	4	5	6
Controls						
Firm age	−0.0042	−0.0046*	−0.0043	−0.0044	−0.0044	−0.0045
	(0.0028)	(0.0028)	(0.0027)	(0.0027)	(0.0027)	(0.0027)
Firm size	0.0570***	0.0515***	0.0496***	0.0485***	0.0511***	0.0499***
	(0.0145)	(0.0145)	(0.0145)	(0.0145)	(0.0145)	(0.0146)
Microenterprises	−0.1799***	−0.1742***	−0.1588***	−0.1580***	−0.1576***	−0.1571***
	(0.0517)	(0.0516)	(0.0513)	(0.0512)	(0.0512)	(0.0512)
Joint venture	−0.0385	0.0036	0.014	0.0318	0.0249	0.0409
	(0.1225)	(0.1239)	(0.1227)	(0.1229)	(0.1228)	(0.1230)
Private-owned firm	−0.0323	−0.0343	−0.0274	−0.0241	−0.0246	−0.0216
	(0.0415)	(0.0415)	(0.0416)	(0.0416)	(0.0416)	(0.0417)
Market scope	0.0161	0.0096	0.0115	0.0088	0.0097	0.0072
	(0.0301)	(0.0304)	(0.0301)	(0.0302)	(0.0302)	(0.0302)
Factor market development	0.1670***	0.1611***	0.1477***	0.1465***	0.1484***	0.1469***
	(0.0374)	(0.0373)	(0.0371)	(0.0371)	(0.0371)	(0.0371)
Policy support	0.0631	0.0708*	0.0622	0.0621	0.0612	0.0611
	(0.0387)	(0.0388)	(0.0385)	(0.0385)	(0.0385)	(0.0385)
Incubator	0.1281***	0.1284***	0.1331***	0.1327***	0.1337***	0.1337***
	(0.0364)	(0.0362)	(0.0359)	(0.0359)	(0.0359)	(0.0359)
Main effects						
Government-identified opportunity		−0.1725*	−0.1889*	−0.0352*	−0.0390**	−0.0362*
		(0.0982)	(0.0973)	(0.0196)	(0.0195)	(0.0196)
Self-identified opportunity		0.1163**	0.0931*	0.0462**	0.0405*	0.0430*
		(0.0486)	(0.0485)	(0.0229)	(0.0229)	(0.023)
Social network-identified opportunity		0.0522	0.0412	0.0245	0.0188	0.0234
		(0.0474)	(0.0470)	(0.0228)	(0.0227)	(0.0228)
Entrepreneurial efforts (EE)			0.1190***	0.0875***	0.1206***	0.0882***
			(0.0274)	(0.0189)	(0.0274)	(0.0189)
Regional poverty level (POV)			0.0000	0.0000	0.0247	0.0227
			(0.0000)	(0.0000)	(0.0186)	(0.0186)
Interacting effects						
Government-identified opportunity*EE				−0.0121		−0.0091
				(0.0198)		(0.0205)
Self-identified opportunity*EE				0.0233		0.0239
				(0.0208)		(0.0208)
Social network-identified opportunity*EE				0.0429*		0.0424*
				(0.0226)		(0.0226)
Government-identified opportunity*POV					0.0077	0.0035
					(0.0183)	(0.0189)
Self-identified opportunity*POV					−0.0373*	−0.0373*
					(0.0224)	(0.0224)
Social network-identified opportunity*POV					−0.0082	−0.009
					(0.0224)	(0.0224)
Constant	1.4574***	1.4567***	1.2805***	1.5116***	1.3763***	1.5649***
	(0.1706)	(0.1752)	(0.1852)	(0.1834)	(0.1741)	(0.1731)
F value	18.25***	14.84***	14.48***	12.23***	12.17***	10.58***
R^2	0.1514	0.1625	0.1812	0.1855	0.1848	0.1887
Adjusted R^2	0.1431	0.1515	0.1687	0.1704	0.1696	0.1709
Change of R^2	–	0.0081*	0.0298***	0.0341***	0.0334***	0.0373***

Note: * $p < 0.1$, ** $p < 0.05$, *** $p < 0.01$(two-tailed test).
Standard errors are in parentheses.

self-identified opportunity–entrepreneurial performance relationship. The insignificant interaction of entrepreneurial effort and self-identified opportunity may be a result of being trapped in 'suboptimal stable equilibria' (March 1991, 71). When too many efforts are taken to pursue opportunities in an extremely familiar domain, entrepreneurial performance may not be superior given that interactions could impede additional knowledge exploration. In other words, an entrepreneur is less likely to gain new knowledge in a domain they already know well.

Hypothesis 2b predicts that entrepreneurial efforts can positively moderate the relationship between social network-identified opportunity and entrepreneurial performance. The interaction term between social network-identified opportunity and entrepreneurial efforts is positive and significant ($b = 0.0429$, $p < 0.1$). This suggests that entrepreneurial effort has a significantly positive moderating effect on the relationship between social network-identified opportunity and entrepreneurial performance. As a result, we find support for Hypothesis 2b.

Hypothesis 2c proposes that the negative relationship between government-identified opportunity and entrepreneurial performance can be weakened by entrepreneurial efforts. The results in Table 3 show that the interaction term between government-identified opportunity and entrepreneurial efforts is negative but not significant ($b = -0.0121$, n.s.). This indicates the moderating role of entrepreneurial efforts among the relationship is small. Therefore, we do not find evidence to support Hypothesis 2c. Perhaps the explanation for this unanticipated finding is that the gap of the knowledge base between the government and the peasant entrepreneurs is too wide, and even the investment of great entrepreneurial effort is not sufficient to bridge this.

Hypothesis 3a to 3c were tested in Model 5. Hypothesis 3a predicts that a higher regional poverty level strengthens the effects of self-identified opportunity on entrepreneurial performance. As shown in Model 5, the coefficient of the interaction term between regional poverty level (reverse coded) and self-identified opportunity is significantly negative ($b = -0.0373$, $p < 0.1$), indicating that the positive relationship between self-identified opportunity and entrepreneurial performance is strengthened when the level of regional poverty is high. Therefore, Hypothesis 3a is supported.

Hypothesis 3b proposes that a higher regional poverty level strengthens the effect of social network-identified opportunity on entrepreneurial performance. The coefficient of the interaction term between regional poverty level and social network-identified opportunity is negative and not significant ($b = -0.0082$, n.s.). Thus, hypothesis 3b is not supported. One possible reason is that, in more developed areas, firms of peasant entrepreneurs are able to imitate domestic or foreign firms, which may offset part of the positive influence exerted by the high regional poverty level.

Hypothesis 3c proposes that a high regional poverty level can weaken the negative impact of government-identified opportunity on entrepreneurial performance. As indicated, the coefficient of the interaction term between regional poverty and government-identified opportunity is positive but not significant ($b = 0.0077$, n.s.), which suggests that a high regional poverty level does not have a significantly positive moderating effect on the relationship between government-identified opportunity and entrepreneurial performance. Similar to the explanation for hypothesis 3b, the better chance of learning in comparatively developed areas might also allow for more effective opportunity capture.

We report the full model in Model 6 of Table 3, which simultaneously tests all hypotheses. Model 6 shows that all relationships that are statistically significant remain significant when combined.

To facilitate interpretation, we plot the effect of social network-identified opportunity on entrepreneurial performance for high and low levels of entrepreneurial efforts (Figure 1) and the effect of self-identified opportunity on entrepreneurial performance for high and low levels of regional poverty (Figure 2). As shown in Figure 1, social network-identified opportunity has a positive relationship with entrepreneurial performance when entrepreneurs engage more efforts in the established enterprise (high entrepreneurial efforts), but this positive relationship disappear when the intensity of entrepreneurial efforts is low. The points plotted in Figure 2 suggest that the positive impact of self-identified opportunity on entrepreneurial performance attenuates when the entrepreneurial enterprise is located in a city with a low level of regional poverty.

Discussion and conclusion

Contributions

By untangling the effects of entrepreneurial opportunity on the performance outcome of peasant entrepreneurship, this study makes theoretical, empirical and practical contributions to the

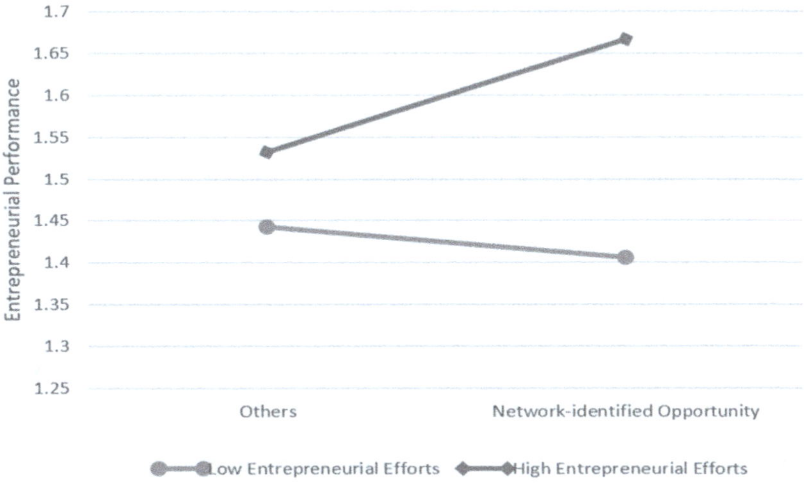

Figure 1. The moderating effect of entrepreneurial efforts on social network-identified opportunity–entrepreneurial performance relationship.

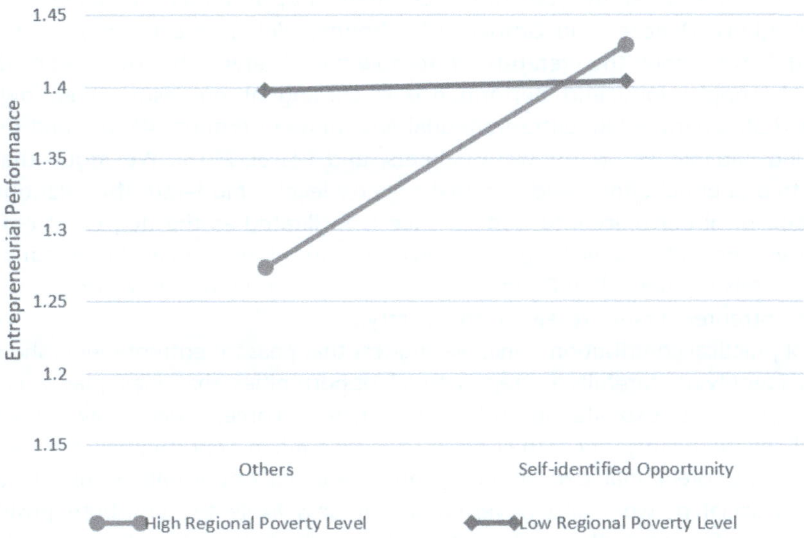

Figure 2. The moderating effect of regional poverty level on self-identified opportunity–entrepreneurial performance relationship.

literature. In terms of theory, our study contributes to entrepreneurship and poverty reduction studies, and entrepreneurial opportunity literature. On one hand, we enrich entrepreneurship and poverty reduction studies by providing a plausible answer to a central question of why certain entrepreneurial activities may be effective as a solution to poverty while others are not (Sutter, Bruton, and Chen 2019; Alvarez and Barney 2014). As peasant entrepreneurship drives global poverty reduction, our research indicates that self-identified opportunities are generally more likely to generate sound outcomes for peasant entrepreneurship than social network- and government-identified opportunities. Our findings also indicate that more intensive entrepreneurial efforts and a higher regional poverty level are key factors feeding successful peasant entrepreneurship.

On the other hand, our study deepens the understanding of entrepreneurial opportunity by theoretically examining the impacts of different types of opportunity on the entrepreneurial performance based on KBV. Previous literature has realized the heterogeneous nature of entrepreneurial opportunities (Alvarez and Barney 2014; Hmieleski and Baron 2008; Shane and Venkataraman 2000), but has not explicitly investigated the impact of different types of opportunity on performance. Following a recent suggestion to incorporate a knowledge perspective into entrepreneurial opportunity studies (Foss, Lyngsie, and Zahra 2013), we demonstrate how knowledge plays a significant role in opportunity identification and exploitation, by explicating how the degree of novelty and complementary knowledge of an entrepreneur matter in order to effectively pursue opportunities. This view illustrates why self-identified opportunity can positively contribute to entrepreneurial performance, while the influence of government-identified opportunity is negative. Consequently, we underscore the significance of opportunity heterogeneity and, more importantly, explain that different types of opportunity have different performance implications on entrepreneurship.

In terms of empirical contribution, through a rigorous survey of peasant entrepreneurship conducted in Zhejiang, China (Ahlstrom 2015, 2017), we find that relying on self-identified opportunities can generate superior entrepreneurial performance of peasant entrepreneurship; however, heavy reliance on social network- and government-identified opportunities does not contribute to sound performance outcomes. The results provide significant empirical evidence for the argument that different types of entrepreneurial opportunity may have different performance implications (Dencker and Gruber 2015; Young, Welter, and Conger 2018; Alvarez and Barney 2014). Furthermore, the literature up to now has observed that the relationship between entrepreneurial opportunity and performance is contingent on resource endowment (Choi, Lévesque, and Shepherd 2008), entrepreneurial environment (Young, Welter, and Conger 2018), and marketing capabilities (Matthews, Chalmers, and Fraser 2018). We argue that two other factors – entrepreneurial efforts and regional poverty level – moderate the relationship as well. The translation of opportunity into performance is facilitated as the degree of entrepreneurial effort increases, and as the regional poverty level becomes higher. In addition, our current study serves as a response to the call of Bruton, Ketchen, and Ireland (2013, 687) for quantitative-based insights into entrepreneurship research on poverty.

In terms of practical contributions, first, we suggest that peasant entrepreneurs should pay more attention to identifying carefully entrepreneurial opportunities that may play a critical role in subsequent opportunity exploitation and performance outcomes. Specifically, peasant entrepreneurs should devote the majority of their effort to self-identified opportunities that can significantly improve their entrepreneurial performance. Entrepreneurial opportunities introduced via other ways, such as social network and government, are less likely to contribute positively to the entrepreneurial performance of peasant entrepreneurs, given that the latter might be unfamiliar with these entrepreneurial opportunities, which are often too new and risky for them and may involve knowledge that they do not possess. Moreover, although entrepreneurial opportunity is important for successful peasant entrepreneurship, peasant entrepreneurs should also exert effort into engaging in various entrepreneurial activities to achieve better entrepreneurial performance. Hence, great effort should be exerted if they choose to exploit the entrepreneurial opportunities introduced by social networks.

Second, our findings suggest governments should not interfere too extensively with peasant entrepreneurship. While certain work should be done by governments, such as improving sound business environments and providing technical training for peasants, they must think twice before directly introducing entrepreneurial opportunities to peasant entrepreneurs. These government-identified opportunities do not easily lead to superior performance in peasant entrepreneurship and may even be harmful for poverty reduction. Meanwhile, as a high regional poverty level negatively moderates the relationship between entrepreneurial opportunity and performance, peasant entrepreneurship seems less effective in areas where the regional economies are more developed. Consequently, peasant entrepreneurs should be encouraged to become involved in more innovative entrepreneurial activities as the region is becoming affluent.

Limitations and future research

While our study proffers some important insights, it is also subject to limitations, which open avenues for future research. The first limitation concerns the issue of the generalizability of our empirical results. Given that Zhejiang province has many unique features, we admit that entrepreneurship in Zhejiang may vary from other regions worldwide due to different business environment, policy support or historical issues. Thus, the generalizability of our research findings remains subject to additional reexamination in different settings, and future research could investigate a similar topic in other regions or countries.

Second, our study restricts entrepreneurial opportunity to three types, which may not fully exhaust the origins of a wide variety of opportunities. For example, researchers have documented the role of non-governmental organizations (NGOs) in entrepreneurship and poverty alleviation (Banerjee and Jackson 2017; Chliova, Brinckmann, and Rosenbusch 2015). In this article, we do not consider the opportunities provided by NGOs because NGOs in China are too weak to offer help (Spires 2011; Hsu 2008). However, these NGOs do serve as crucial opportunity providers in many other areas across the globe. This suggests that future studies could identify other kinds of opportunities while addressing a similar topic.

The third limitation is associated with cross-sectional data. Although we have minimized potential problems, including repeated validation of the questionnaire and minimization of potential common variance, we cannot establish causality based on cross-sectional data. While organizing our hypotheses by KBV seems logical, more rigorous empirical examinations may be conducted in the future using panel data.

Conclusion

This study directly answers the questions of how and when opportunity contributes to peasant entrepreneurs' success and poverty reduction. We propose that different types of opportunities imply different sources of knowledge, and correspondingly may or may not fit with peasant entrepreneurs' distinct absorptive capability and knowledge broadness during exploration and exploitation, thereby contributing to varied performance outcome. Based on our unique survey data set sampled in Zhejiang, we find evidence to support this proposition while underscoring the vital role of the exploitation process. Specifically, we find that the effect of opportunity on entrepreneurial performance is heterogeneous with respect to opportunity types and such an effect is moderated by internal entrepreneurial effort and regional poverty level.

Acknowledgments

We are sincerely grateful to Steven Si, David Ahlstrom, John Cullen and Jiang Wei for their valuable comments, and to Alistair Anderson and other participants in the *Entrepreneurship & Regional Development* special issue workshop for instrumental feedback on the early draft of this paper.

Disclosure statement

No potential conflict of interest was reported by the authors.

Funding

This study is supported by research grants (National Natural Science Foundation of China: 71572174, 71732008).

References

Ahlstrom, D. 2010. "Innovation and Growth: How Business Contributes to Society." *Academy of Management Perspectives* 24 (3): 10–23. doi:10.5465/amp.24.3.11.

Ahlstrom, D. 2015. "From the Editors: Publishing in the Journal of World Business." *Journal of World Business* 50 (2): 251–255. doi:10.1016/j.jwb.2014.12.003.

Ahlstrom, D. 2017. "How to Publish in Academic Journals: Writing a Strong and Organized Introduction Section." *Journal of Eastern European and Central Asian Research* 4 (2): 1–9. doi:10.15549/jeecar.v4i2.180.

Ahlstrom, D., G. D. Bruton, and S. S. Lui. 2000. "Navigating China's Changing Economy: Strategies for Private Firms." *Business Horizons* 43 (1): 5–15. doi:10.1016/S0007-6813(00)87382-6.

Aiken, L. S., S. G. West, and R. R. Reno. 1991. *Multiple Regression: Testing and Interpreting Interactions*. Newbury Park: Sage.

Alvarez, S. A., and J. B. Barney. 2007. "Discovery and Creation: Alternative Theories of Entrepreneurial Action." *Strategic Entrepreneurship Journal* 1 (1–2): 11–26. doi:10.1002/sej.4.

Alvarez, S. A., and J. B. Barney. 2014. "Entrepreneurial Opportunities and Poverty Alleviation." *Entrepreneurship Theory and Practice* 38 (1): 159–184. doi:10.1111/etap.12078.

Ambos, T. C., U. Andersson, and J. Birkinshaw. 2010. "What are the Consequences of Initiative-Taking in Multinational Subsidiaries?" *Journal of International Business Studies* 41 (7): 1099–1118. doi:10.1057/jibs.2010.19.

Anderson, A. R., and B. A. Obeng. 2017. "Enterprise as Socially Situated in a Rural Poor Fishing Community." *Journal of Rural Studies* 49: 23–31. doi:10.1016/j.jrurstud.2016.11.015.

Anguloruiz, F. 2014. "The Impact of Government Financial Support on the Performance of New Firms: The Role of Competitive Advantage as an Intermediate Outcome." *Entrepreneurship & Regional Development* 26 (9–10): 663–705. doi:10.1080/08985626.2014.980757.

Arkes, H. R., and C. Blumer. 1985. "The Psychology of Sunk Cost." *Organizational Behavior and Human Decision Processes* 35 (1): 124–140. doi:10.1016/0749-5978(85)90049-4.

Auer, R. A., T. Chaney, and P. Sauré. 2018. "Quality Pricing-to-Market." *Journal of International Economics* 110: 87–102. doi:10.1016/j.jinteco.2017.11.003.

Autio, E., H. J. Sapienza, and J. G. Almeida. 2000. "Effects of Age at Entry, Knowledge Intensity, and Imitability on International Growth." *Academy of Management Journal* 43 (5): 909–924. doi:10.2307/1556419.

Banerjee, S. B., and L. Jackson. 2017. "Microfinance and the Business of Poverty Reduction: Critical Perspectives from Rural Bangladesh." *Human Relations* 70 (1): 63–91. doi:10.1177/0018726716640865.

Batjargal, B., and M. Liu. 2004. "Entrepreneurs' Access to Private Equity in China: The Role of Social Capital." *Organization Science* 15 (2): 159–172. doi:10.1287/orsc.1030.0044.

Bruton, G. D., D. Ahlstrom, and S. Si. 2015. "Entrepreneurship, Poverty, and Asia: Moving beyond Subsistence Entrepreneurship." *Asia Pacific Journal of Management* 32 (1): 1–22. doi:10.1007/s10490-014-9404-x.

Bruton, G. D., D. J. Ketchen, and R. D. Ireland. 2013. "Entrepreneurship as a Solution to Poverty." *Journal of Business Venturing* 28 (6): 683–689. doi:10.1016/j.jbusvent.2013.05.002.

Carson, D., S. Cromie, P. McGowan, and J. Hill. 1995. *Marketing and Entrepreneurship in SMEs: An Innovative Approach*. Englewood Cliffs, NJ: Prentice-Hall.

Chandra, Y. 2017. "A Time-Based Process Model of International Entrepreneurial Opportunity Evaluation." *Journal of International Business Studies* 48 (4): 423–451. doi:10.1057/s41267-017-0068-x.

Chliova, M., J. Brinckmann, and N. Rosenbusch. 2015. "Is Microcredit A Blessing for the Poor? A Meta-Analysis Examining Development Outcomes and Contextual Considerations." *Journal of Business Venturing* 30 (3): 467–487. doi:10.1016/j.jbusvent.2014.10.003.

Choi, Y. R., M. Lévesque, and D. A. Shepherd. 2008. "When Should Entrepreneurs Expedite or Delay Opportunity Exploitation." *Journal of Business Venturing* 23 (3): 333–355. doi:10.1016/j.jbusvent.2006.11.001.

Cohen, W. M., and D. A. Levinthal. 1990. "Absorptive Capacity: A New Perspective on Learning and Innovation." *Administrative Science Quarterly* 35 (1): 128–152. doi:10.2307/2393553.

Cruz, S. C. S., and A. A. C. Teixeira. 2010. "The Evolution of the Cluster Literature: Shedding Light on the Regional Studies-Regional Science Debate." *Regional Studies* 44 (9): 1263–1288. doi:10.1080/00343400903234670.

Davidsson, P. 2015. "Entrepreneurial Opportunities and the Entrepreneurship Nexus: A Re-Conceptualization." *Journal of Business Venturing* 30 (5): 674–695. doi:10.1016/j.jbusvent.2015.01.002.

Dencker, J. C., and M. Gruber. 2015. "The Effects of Opportunities and Founder Experience on New Firm Performance." *Strategic Management Journal* 36 (7): 1035–1052. doi:10.1002/smj.2269.

Dodd, S. D., S. S. Jack, and A. R. Anderson. 2013. "From Admiration to Abhorrence: The Contentious Appeal of Entrepreneurship across Europe." *Entrepreneurship & Regional Development* 25 (1–2): 69–89. doi:10.1080/08985626.2012.746878.

Drnovsek, M., M. S. Cardon, and P. C. Patel. 2016. "Direct and Indirect Effects of Passion on Growing Technology Ventures." *Strategic Entrepreneurship Journal* 10 (2): 194–213. doi:10.1002/sej.1213.

Eckhardt, J. T., and S. A. Shane. 2003. "Opportunities and Entrepreneurship." *Journal of Management* 29 (3): 333–349. doi:10.1016/S0149-2063(02)00225-8.

Edelman, L., and H. Yli-Renko. 2010. "The Impact of Environment and Entrepreneurial Perceptions on Venture-Creation Efforts: Bridging the Discovery and Creation Views of Entrepreneurship." *Entrepreneurship Theory & Practice* 34 (5): 833–856. doi:10.1111/j.1540-6520.2010.00395.x.

Emerson, R. M. 1976. "Social Exchange Theory." *Annual Review of Sociology* 2 (7): 335–362. doi:10.1146/annurev.so.02.080176.002003.

Fagerberg, J., and M. Srholec. 2008. "National Innovation Systems, Capabilities and Economic Development." *Research Policy* 37 (9): 1417–1435. doi:10.1016/j.respol.2008.06.003.

Fan, Y., N. Chen, and D. A. Kirby. 1996. "Chinese Peasant Entrepreneurs: An Examination of Township and Village Enterprises in Rural China." *Journal of Small Business Management* 34 (4): 72–76.

Foo, M. D., M. A. Uy, and B. A. Baron. 2009. "How Do Feelings Influence Effort? an Empirical Study of Entrepreneurs' Affect and Venture Effort." *Journal of Applied Psychology* 94 (4): 1086–1094. doi:10.1037/a0015599.

Foss, N. J., J. Lyngsie, and S. A. Zahra. 2013. "The Role of External Knowledge Sources and Organizational Design in the Process of Opportunity Exploitation." *Strategic Management Journal* 34 (12): 1453–1471. doi:10.1002/smj.2135.

George, N. M., V. Parida, T. Lahti, and J. Wincent. 2016. "A Systematic Literature Review of Entrepreneurial Opportunity Recognition: Insights on Influencing Factors." *International Entrepreneurship and Management Review* 12 (2): 309–350. doi:10.1007/s11365-014-0347-y.

Granovetter, M. S. 1973. "The Strength of Weak Ties." *American Journal of Sociology* 78 (6): 1360–1380. doi:10.1086/225469.

Grant, R. M. 1996. "Toward a Knowledge-based Theory Of The Firm." *Strategic Management Journal* 17 (S2): 109-122. doi: 10.1002/smj.4250171110.

Grant, R. M., and C. Baden-Fuller. 2004. "A Knowledge Accessing Theory of Strategic Alliances." *Journal of Management Studies* 41 (1): 61–84. doi:10.1111/j.1467-6486.2004.00421.x.

Grégoire, D. A., and D. A. Shepherd. 2012. "Technology-Market Combinations and the Identification of Entrepreneurial Opportunities: An Investigation of the Opportunity-Individual Nexus." *Academy of Management Journal* 55 (4): 753–785. doi:10.5465/amj.2011.0126.

Hall, J., S. Matos, L. Sheehan, and B. Silvestre. 2012. "Entrepreneurship and Innovation at the Base of the Pyramid: A Recipe for Inclusive Growth or Social Exclusion?" *Journal of Management Studies* 49 (4): 785–812. doi:10.1111/j.1467-6486.2012.01044.x.

Hargadon, A. B., and Y. Douglas. 2001. "When Innovations Meet Institutions: Edison and the Design of the Electric Light." *Administrative Science Quarterly* 46 (3): 476–501. doi:10.2307/3094872.

Hart, S., and C. M. Christensen. 2002. "The Great Leap: Driving Innovation from the Base of the Pyramid." *Sloan Management Review* 44 (1): 51–56. doi:10.1201/b14335-10.

Hayek, F. A. 1945. "The Use of Knowledge in Society." *American Economic Review* 35 (4): 519–530.

Hmieleski, K. M., and R. A. Baron. 2008. "Regulatory Focus and New Venture Performance: A Study of Entrepreneurial Opportunity Exploitation under Conditions of Risk versus Uncertainty." *Strategic Entrepreneurship Journal* 2 (4): 285–299. doi:10.1002/sej.56.

Hoskisson, R. E., M. Wright, I. Filatotchev, and M. W. Peng. 2013. "Emerging Multinationals from Mid-Range Economies: The Influence of Institutions and Factor Markets." *Journal of Management Studies* 50 (7): 1295–1321. doi:10.1111/j.1467-6486.2012.01085.x.

Hsu, C. L. 2008. "'rehabilitating Charity' in China: The Case of Project Hope and the Rise of Non-profit Organizations." *Journal of Civil Society* 4 (2): 81–96. doi:10.1080/17448680802335144.

Hughes, M., R. E. Morgan, R. D. Ireland, and P. Hughes. 2014. "Social Capital and Learning Advantages: A Problem of Absorptive Capacity." *Strategic Entrepreneurship Journal* 8 (3): 214–233. doi:10.1002/sej.1162.

Jia, F., and Y. Zhang. 2018. "The Impact Of Positive Affect on Entrepreneurial Motivational Outcomes–a Self-regulatory Perspective." *International Review Of Entrepreneurship* 16 (4): 627-656.

Keh, H. T., T. T. M. Nguyen, and H. P. Ng. 2007. "The Effects of Entrepreneurial Orientation and Marketing Information on the Performance of SMEs." *Journal of Business Venturing* 22 (4): 592–611. doi:10.1016/j.jbusvent.2006.05.003.

Lei, L., H. Voss, L. J. Clegg, and X. Wu. 2017. "Climate Change Strategies of Multinational Enterprises in China." *Journal of Cleaner Production* 160: 98–108. doi:10.1016/j.jclepro.2017.03.150.

Leong, C. M. L., S. L. Pan, S. Newell, and L. Cui. 2016. "The Emergence of Self-Organizing E-Commerce Ecosystems in Remote Villages of China: A Tale of Digital Empowerment for Rural Development." *MIS Quarterly* 40 (2): 475–484. doi:10.25300/MISQ/2016/40.2.11.

Lin, H., H. Li, and C. Yang. 2011. "Agglomeration and Productivity: Firm-Level Evidence from China's Textile Industry." *China Economic Review* 22 (3): 313–329. doi:10.1016/j.chieco.2011.03.003.

Lin, S., and S. Si. 2014. "Factors Affecting Peasant Entrepreneurs' Intention in the Chinese Context." *International Entrepreneurship and Management Journal* 10 (4): 803–825. doi:10.1007/s11365-014-0325-4.

Lumpkin, G. T., and G. G. Dess. 1996. "Clarifying the Entrepreneurial Orientation Construct and Linking It to Performance." *Academy of Management Review* 21 (1): 135–172. doi:10.5465/amr.1996.9602161568.

Ma, C. 2018. "Nation Sees More Rural Entrepreneurs." *China Daily*, July 26. http://www.chinadaily.com.cn/a/201807/26/WS5b596439a31031a351e90554.html

March, J. G. 1991. "Exploration and Exploitation in Organizational Learning." *Organization Science* 2 (1): 71–87. doi:10.1287/orsc.2.1.71.

Matthews, C. H. 2009. "Making Rational Use of 'irrationality'? Exploring the Role of Need for Cognitive Closure in Nascent Entrepreneurial Activity." *Entrepreneurship & Regional Development* 21 (1): 51–76. doi:10.1080/08985620801912467.

Matthews, R. S., D. M. Chalmers, and S. S. Fraser. 2018. "The Intersection of Entrepreneurship and Selling: An Interdisciplinary Review, Framework, and Future Research Agenda." *Journal of Business Venturing* 33 (6): 691–719. doi:10.1016/j.jbusvent.2018.04.008.

Meyer, K. E., S. Estrin, S. K. Bhaumik, and M. W. Peng. 2009. "Institutions, Resources, and Entry Strategies in Emerging Economies." *Strategic Management Journal* 30 (1): 61–80. doi:10.1002/smj.720.

Michael, S. C., and J. A. Pearce II. 2009. "The Need for Innovation as a Rationale for Government Involvement in Entrepreneurship." *Entrepreneurship & Regional Development* 21 (3): 285–302. doi:10.1080/08985620802279999.

Neter, J., W. Wasserman, and M. H. Kutner. 1990. *Applied Statistical Models*. Burr Ridge, IL: Richard D. Irwin.

O'Connor, A. 2013. "A Conceptual Framework for Entrepreneurship Education Policy: Meeting Government and Economic Purposes." *Journal of Business Venturing* 28 (4): 546–563. doi:10.1016/j.jbusvent.2012.07.003.

Owoo, N. S., and W. Naudé. 2017. "Spatial Proximity and Firm Performance: Evidence from Non-Farm Rural Enterprises in Ethiopia and Nigeria." *Regional Studies* 51 (5): 688–700. doi:10.1080/00343404.2015.1131896.

Parker, S. C. 2013. "Do Serial Entrepreneurs Run Successively Better-Performing Businesses?" *Journal of Business Venturing* 28 (5): 652–666. doi:10.1016/j.jbusvent.2012.08.001.

Peng, M., and Y. Luo. 2000. "Managerial Ties and Firm Performance in a Transition Economy: The Nature of a Micro-Macro Link." *Academy of Management Journal* 43 (3): 486–501. doi:10.2307/1556406.

Pérez-Luño, A., J. Wiklund, and R. V. Cabrera. 2011. "The Dual Nature of Innovative Activity: How Entrepreneurial Orientation Influences Innovation Generation and Adoption." *Journal of Business Venturing* 26 (5): 555–571. doi:10.1016/j.jbusvent.2010.03.001.

Petit, O., M. Kuper, and F. Ameur. 2018. "From Worker to Peasant and Then to Entrepreneur? Land Reform and Agrarian Change in the Saïss (morocco)." *World Development* 105: 119–131. doi:10.1016/j.worlddev.2017.12.031.

Podsakoff, P. M., and D. W. Organ. 1986. "Self-Reports in Organizational Research: Problems and Prospects." *Journal of Management* 12 (4): 531–544. doi:10.1177/014920638601200408.

Podsakoff, P. M., S. B. MacKenzie, J. Y. Lee, and N. P. Podsakoff. 2003. "Common Method Biases in Behavioral Research: A Critical Review of the Literature and Recommended Remedies." *Journal of Applied Psychology* 88 (5): 879–903. doi:10.1037/0021-9010.88.5.879.

Pollitte, W. A., J. C. Miller, and A. Yaprak. 2015. "Returns to US Firms from Strategic Alliances in China: A Knowledge-Based View." *Journal of World Business* 50 (1): 144–148. doi:10.1016/j.jwb.2014.04.002.

Rao, J., and J. Ye. 2016. "From a Virtuous Cycle of Rural-Urban Education to Urban-Oriented Rural Basic Education in China: An Explanation of the Failure of China's Rural School Mapping Adjustment Policy." *Journal of Rural Studies* 47: 601–611. doi:10.1016/j.jrurstud.2016.07.005.

Ribeiro-Soriano, D., and M. Galindo-Martín. 2012. "Government Policies to Support Entrepreneurship." *Entrepreneurship & Regional Development* 24 (9–10): 861–864. doi:10.1080/08985626.2012.742322.

Rogers, S. 2014. "Betting on the Strong: Local Government Resource Allocation in China's Poverty Counties." *Journal of Rural Studies* 36: 197–206. doi:10.1016/j.jrurstud.2014.08.001.

Salancik, G. R., and J. Pfeffer. 1977. "An Examination of Need-Satisfaction Models of Job Attitudes." *Administrative Science Quarterly* 22 (3): 427–456. doi:10.2307/2392182.

Samuelsson, M., and P. Davidsson. 2009. "Does Venture Opportunity Variation Matter? Investigating Systematic Process Differences between Innovative and Imitative New Ventures." *Small Business Economics* 33 (2): 229–255. doi:10.1007/s11187-007-9093-7.

Sapienza, H. J., E. Autio, G. George, and S. A. Zahra. 2006. "A Capabilities Perspective on the Effects of Early Internationalization on Firm Survival and Growth." *Academy of Management Review* 31 (4): 914–933. doi:10.5465/amr.2006.22527465.

Schumpeter, J. A. 1934. *The Theory of Economic Development*. Cambridge, MA: Harvard University Press.

Seelos, C., and J. Mair. 2007. "Profitable Business Models and Market Creation in the Context of Deep Poverty: A Strategic View." *Academy of Management Perspectives* 21 (4): 49–63. doi:10.5465/amp.2007.27895339.

Shakya, Y. B., and K. N. Rankin. 2008. "The Politics of Subversion in Development Practice: An Exploration of Microfinance in Nepal and Vietnam." *Journal of Development Studies* 44 (8): 1214–1235. doi:10.1080/00220380802242461.

Shane, S. 2000. "Prior Knowledge and the Discovery of Entrepreneurial Opportunities." *Organization Science* 11 (4): 448–469. doi:10.1287/orsc.11.4.448.14602.

Shane, S. 2012. "Reflections on the 2010 AMR Decade Award: Delivering on the Promise of Entrepreneurship as a Field of Research." *Academy of Management Review* 37 (1): 10–20. doi:10.5465/amr.2011.0078.

Shane, S., and S. Venkataraman. 2000. "The Promise of Entrepreneurship as a Field of Research." *Academy of Management Review* 25 (1): 217–226. doi:10.5465/amr.2000.2791611.

Shantz, A. S., G. Kistruck, and C. Zietsma. 2018. "The Opportunity Not Taken: The Occupational Identity of Entrepreneurs in Contexts of Poverty." *Journal of Business Venturing* 33 (4): 416–437. doi:10.1016/j.jbusvent.2018.02.003.

Shearmur, R., and D. Doloreux. 2016. "How Open Innovation Processes Vary between Urban and Remote Environments: Slow Innovators, Market-Sourced Information and Frequency of Interaction." *Entrepreneurship & Regional Development* 28 (5–6): 337–357. doi:10.1080/08985626.2016.1154984.

Shu, R., S. Ren, and Y. Zheng. 2018. "Building Networks into Discovery: The Link between Entrepreneur Network Capability and Entrepreneurial Opportunity Discovery." *Journal of Business Research* 85: 197–208. doi:10.1016/j.jbusres.2017.12.048.

Si, S., X. Yu, A. Wu, S. Chen, S. Chen, and Y. Su. 2015. "Entrepreneurship and Poverty Reduction: A Case Study of Yiwu, China." *Asia Pacific Journal of Management* 32 (1): 119–143. doi:10.1007/s10490-014-9395-7.

Spanjer, A., and A. van Witteloostuijn. 2017. "The Entrepreneur's Experiential Diversity and Entrepreneurial Performance." *Small Business Economics* 49 (1): 141–161. doi:10.1007/s11187-016-9811-0.

Spires, A. J. 2011. "Contingent Symbiosis and Civil Society in an Authoritarian State: Understanding the Survival of China's Grassroots NGOs." *American Journal of Sociology* 117 (1): 1–45. doi:10.1086/660741.

Subramanian, A. M., B. Wang, and K.-H. Chai. 2018. "The Role of Knowledge Base Homogeneity in Learning from Strategic Alliances." *Research Policy* 47 (1): 158–168. doi:10.1016/j.respol.2017.10.005.

Suddaby, R., G. D. Bruton, and S. Si. 2015. "Entrepreneurship through a Qualitative Lens: Insights on the Construction And/or Discovery of Entrepreneurial Opportunity." *Journal of Business Venturing* 30 (1): 1–10. doi:10.1016/j.jbusvent.2014.09.003.

Sutter, C., G. D. Bruton, and J. Chen. 2019. "Entrepreneurship as A Solution to Extreme Poverty: A Review and Future Research Directions." *Journal of Business Venturing* 34 (1): 197–214. doi:10.1016/j.jbusvent.2018.06.003.

Teece, D. J. 1986. "Profiting from Technological Innovation: Implications for Integration, Collaboration, Licensing and Public Policy." *Research Policy* 15 (6): 285–305. doi:10.1016/0048-7333(86)90027-2.

Turgo, N. 2016. "'Iaway Lang Ang Kapital' (saliva as Capital): Social Embeddedness of Market Practices in Brokerage Houses in the Philippines." *Journal of Rural Studies* 43: 83–93. doi:10.1016/j.jrurstud.2015.11.001.

Uy, M. A., M. D. Foo, and R. Ilies. 2015. "Perceived Progress Variability and Entrepreneurial Effort Intensity: The Moderating Role of Venture Goal Commitment." *Journal of Business Venturing* 30 (3): 375–389. doi:10.1016/j.jbusvent.2014.02.001.

Valentino, A., M. Caroli, and U. Mayrhofer. 2018. "Establishment Modes and Network Relationships of Foreign Subsidiaries." *International Business Review* 27 (6): 1250–1258. doi:10.1016/j.ibusrev.2018.05.006.

Wang, T., S. Thornhill, and J. O. De Castro. 2017. "Entrepreneurial Orientation, Legitimation, and New Venture Performance." *Strategic Entrepreneurship Journal* 11 (4): 373–392. doi:10.1002/sej.1246.

Wang, Y. 2016. "Bringing the Stages Back In: Social Network Ties and Start-Up Firms' Access to Venture Capital in China." *Strategic Entrepreneurship Journal* 10 (3): 300–317. doi:10.1002/sej.1229.

Wiklund, J. 1999. "The Sustainability of the Entrepreneurial Orientation-Performance Relationship." *Entrepreneurship Theory & Practice* 24 (1): 37–48. doi:10.1177/104225879902400103.

Williams, C. C., and S. Nadin. 2012. "Tackling the Hidden Enterprise Culture: Government Policies to Support the Formalization of Informal Entrepreneurship." *Entrepreneurship & Regional Development* 24 (9–10): 895–915. doi:10.1080/08985626.2012.742325.

Williams, D. W., and M. S. Wood. 2015. "Rule-Based Reasoning for Understanding Opportunity Evaluation." *Academy of Management Perspectives* 29 (2): 218–236. doi:10.5465/amp.2013.0017.

Wu, J., and S. Si. 2018. "Poverty Reduction through Entrepreneurship: Incentives, Social Networks, and Sustainability." *Asian Business & Management* 17 (4): 243–259. doi:10.1057/s41291-018-0039-5.

Yayavaram, S., and W. Chen. 2015. "Changes in Firm Knowledge Couplings and Firm Innovation Performance: The Moderating Role of Technological Complexity." *Strategic Management Journal* 36 (3): 377–396. doi:10.1002/smj.2218.

Young, S. L., C. Welter, and M. Conger. 2018. "Stability Vs. Flexibility: The Effect of Regulatory Institutions on Opportunity Type." *Journal of International Business Studies* 49 (4): 407–441. doi:10.1057/s41267-017-0095-7.

Yu, Z., and D. Gibbs. 2018. "Sustainability Transitions and Leapfrogging in Latecomer Cities: The Development of Solar Thermal Energy in Dezhou, China." *Regional Studies* 52 (1): 68–79. doi:10.1080/00343404.2016.1260706.

Zahra, S. A. 2008. "The Virtuous Cycle of Discovery and Creation of Entrepreneurial Opportunities." *Strategic Entrepreneurship Journal* 2 (3): 243–257. doi:10.1002/sej.47.

Zahra, S. A., and G. George. 2002. "Absorptive Capacity: A Review, Reconceptualization, and Extension." *Academy of Management Review* 27 (2): 185–203. doi:10.5465/amr.2002.6587995.

Zahra, S. A., R. D. Ireland, and M. A. Hitt. 2000. "International Expansion by New Venture Firms: International Diversity, Mode of Market Entry, Technological Learning, and Performance." *Academy of Management Journal* 43 (5): 925–950. doi:10.5465/1556420.

Zhejiang Statistical Yearbook. 2017. *Zhejiang Statistical Yearbook*. Beijing: China Statistics Press.

Zhu, J., N. Tripathi, G. H. Jacob, and N. Wang. 2016. "The Dynamic Construction of Entrepreneurial Identity: A Dual-process Model." *Academy of Management Proceedings* 2016 (1): 12106. doi:10.5465/ambpp.2016.239.

An exploratory study of entrepreneurs in impoverished communities: when institutional factors and individual characteristics result in non-productive entrepreneurship

Stelvia Matos and Jeremy Hall

ABSTRACT

It is widely acknowledged that entrepreneurship can help the poor escape poverty. However, while many people in impoverished regions engage in entrepreneurial activities, many fail to develop successful businesses. This paper examines why impoverished people may choose to engage in entrepreneurship, the characteristics that shape their entrepreneurial behaviour and the struggles they face. We draw on the entrepreneurship literature that suggests institutional factors and individual characteristics shape new venture development. Following an inductive methodological approach utilizing a survey, interviews and focus groups collected from an impoverished community in Brazil, we explore entrepreneurial behaviour focused on perceived alertness, utilization of social networks, formal business registration and participation in training. We found that temporal myopia, misjudgement of their abilities, and counter-productive use of their social networks result in non-productive entrepreneurship. We contribute theoretically by suggesting that, in addition to productive, unproductive and destructive entrepreneurial outcomes shaped by institutions, non-productive entrepreneurship is also a prevalent problem, but is heavily shaped by the interactions between individual characteristics and the institutional environment.

Introduction

It has been widely acknowledged that entrepreneurship and innovation can bring socio-economic development and transform impoverished regions (Hall et al. 2012; Peredo and Chrisman 2006; Ribeiro-Soriano 2017; Si et al. 2015; Sutter, Bruton, and Chen 2019). However, while many impoverished entrepreneurs engage in business activities to survive, most are unable to generate adequate returns and often fail. According to Bruton et al. (2013a), entrepreneurial success is heavily influenced by both the institutional environment and individual characteristics of the entrepreneur. They emphasize that interactions between individual and institutional factors is crucial for shaping the outcome of a new venture. This paper thus addresses the following research questions: Why do impoverished entrepreneurs struggle to succeed, and how do both institutional and individual factors influence such outcomes?

According to Baumol (1990), changes in the structure of institutional factors, or 'rules of the game', such as external support, alliances and access to credit, can modify and influence the nature of entrepreneurs' activities. He argues that policies can be designed to stimulate innovation, which he correlates to productive entrepreneurship (e.g. a net societal gain), and discourage unproductive (e.g. rent seeking) or destructive (e.g. criminal) entrepreneurship. In impoverished regions, the absence of economic and institutional mechanisms hinder innovation and implicitly encourage subsistence business activities, where many entrepreneurs have no alternative for meeting basic survival needs (Webb et al. 2013; Bruton, Ahlstrom, and Si 2015; Viswanathan et al. 2014).

Individual characteristics, such as entrepreneurs' cognitions, prior knowledge, education, self-efficacy, experience and opportunity identification abilities, are also important to entrepreneurship (Bruton et al. 2013; Reynolds et al. 2005). For example, Kirzner (1999) suggests alertness *'the entrepreneur's perception of the way in which creative and imaginative action may vitally shape the kind of transactions that will be entered into in future market periods'* is also crucial. Venture success is usually attributed to individual characteristics such as creativity and self-efficacy, and plays a particularly important role in impoverished regions, where resource constraints, market adversity and low education levels hinder productive entrepreneurship (Kiss, Danis, and Cavusgil 2012; Nichter and Goldmark 2009).

Several studies have examined the interactions between institutional and individual factors, for example correlating entrepreneurs' cognitions to prior experiences, environmental conditions and attitudes towards risk aversion (Batinge and Jenkins 2018; Bruton, Ahlstrom, and Si 2015; Bruton et al. 2013; Ganguly 2018; Zahra, Korri, and Yu 2005). Despite the above contributions, this area remains underexplored. Our motivation for this research thus stems from the following. First, in contrast to studies focused on developed regions, there seems to be a greater emphasis on institutional weaknesses as the cause of entrepreneurial failure in impoverished regions. According to Bruton, Ketchen Jr, and Ireland (2013b), Bruton, Ahlstrom, and Si (2015) and Si et al. (2015), studies in emerging economies have made considerable contributions in identifying how entrepreneurship can reduce poverty. However, they, along with Kiss, Danis, and Cavusgil (2012) and Sutter, Bruton, and Chen (2019), also note that more research is needed to understand the individual characteristics of the impoverished entrepreneur, the decisions they take and how these internal processes can help them channel their behaviour towards more productive forms of entrepreneurship. The interactions between institutional factors and individual characteristics are thus necessary for understanding impoverished entrepreneurship, i.e. one needs to understand both sides of the entrepreneurship 'coin'.

Our second motivation stems from the relative lack of research that takes a 'bottom up' approach to understanding impoverished entrepreneurship, i.e. a focus on why the impoverished may start a new venture, the institutional support and barriers they face, and the individual characteristics that shape their outlook towards entrepreneurship. To address this gap, we conducted an exploratory, inductive study that began with a survey conducted in an impoverished Brazilian community. From here, we identified those that claimed to possess alertness, the right skills, and had started, or plan to start, a new venture. We then conducted face-to-face interviews and focus groups to analyse how these entrepreneurs identify opportunities, develop networks and decide whether to utilize government support mechanisms. Our study thus complements much of the entrepreneurship literature by focusing on the gritty realities that impoverished entrepreneurs face – and sometimes create – in their attempts to improve their lives.

We extend knowledge on entrepreneurship and poverty in the following ways. First, by taking a bottom up approach, our findings differ from many previous studies by including counter-productive behaviour resulting from the interplay between institutional weaknesses and individual entrepreneurial characteristics. By looking primarily at only institutional factors, it is easy to see subsistence entrepreneurs as victims of institutional failure; when looking only at individual characteristics it is equally easy to recognize their deficiencies and willingness to engage in counterproductive practices. By looking at the interactions between these factors, it is possible to identify mechanisms that shape impoverished entrepreneurship.

Venugopal and Viswanathan (2017) suggest that impoverished entrepreneurs' daily struggles to meet basic needs results in a 'here and now' mind-set, which drives them to utilize institutional resources and social networks for immediate, and sometimes non-essential needs at the expense of long-term venture investment. The inability to consider the long-term outcomes of a given decision, what Gaglio and Katz (2001) call 'temporal myopia' thus helps explain why some entrepreneurs struggle. We thus contribute to theory by extending Baumol's (1990) typology by suggesting that within impoverished regions, *non-productive* entrepreneurship, i.e. new ventures that lack successful value propositions (Anderson and Markides, 2007; Hart and Christensen 2002; Henderson 2006), is a common hindrance to regional development. However, in contrast to unproductive or destructive entrepreneurship, non-productive entrepreneurship also requires an understanding of individual characteristics rather than solely the institutional environment. We thus contribute to the development of effective policies for poverty alleviation by enhancing awareness of how institutional factors and individual characteristics result in non-productive entrepreneurship.

We start with an overview of the entrepreneurship literature focused on institutional mechanisms and individual characteristics, particularly in impoverished communities. We then discuss the importance of understanding the interactions between institutional and individual factors. Our methodology is then described, followed by our findings, a discussion of our results and conclusions.

The effect of institutional factors on impoverished entrepreneurship

Policy makers have long emphasized the importance of entrepreneurship in underdeveloped regions as a mechanism for social improvement, which in turn is shaped by institutions. North (1990) for example suggests that economic growth is driven by the incentive structures that encourage individual effort and investment, which is determined by institutions, i.e. society's 'rules of the game'. According to Bygrave and Minniti (2000), establishing such rules is crucial in shaping future productive structures.

Many studies have investigated how entrepreneurs in emerging economies are influenced by institutional factors (Danis, De Clercq, and Petricevic 2011; Lee and Tsang 2001; Kiss and Danis 2008). Under weak institutions, a lack of employment opportunities, low productivity and investment lead to necessity entrepreneurship, most of which are informal, lifestyle or survivalist (Naudé 2010).

According to Williams and Shahid (2016), institutional theorists distinguish between institutions that are formal (e.g. codified laws and regulations) and informal (norms, values and codes of conduct), where informal sector entrepreneurs are typically seen as operating outside of formal institutional boundaries but dependent on informal institutions such as their social networks. In developing regions, Webb et al. (2013) propose that when society fails to help individuals subsist through legitimate means, entrepreneurs are more likely to operate in the informal economy. Furthermore, it is common for legal but informal businesses (i.e. ones that do not register with the government) to suffer from limited growth (Bruton, Ketchen Jr, and Ireland 2013b). Implicit to these propositions is that there are incentives to avoid formally registering their business (such as avoiding taxes, paperwork and dealing with bureaucracy), but disadvantages in the long-term survival of the venture.

Institutional effectiveness is often hindered by corruption and a lack of adequate resources (Valente and Crane 2010), which can result in detrimental outcomes (Hall et al. 2012). As such, entrepreneurship can lead to destructive outcomes (Bowen and De Clercq 2008; Smallbone and Welter 2001) or force entrepreneurs to rely on other mechanisms. For example, Danis, De Clercq, and Petricevic (2011) found that in countries where inefficiency and corruption are pervasive, entrepreneurs rely on social and organizational networks to overcome barriers such as capability deficiencies and a weak institutional environment.

Baumol's (1990) typology of entrepreneurial outcomes addresses this paradox of entrepreneurship as a panacea for economic growth as well as a source of detrimental outcomes. He defines productive entrepreneurship is socially beneficial activities derived from new or improved technologies or ways of doing business. It is thus analogous to Schumpeter's (1934) 'innovative entrepreneurs', i.e. those that find new combinations of resources to create products that did not previously exist. Destructive entrepreneurship is where for example illegal entrepreneurial activities result in a net social loss, i.e. a few benefit at the expense of many. Unproductive entrepreneurship involves rent-seeking activities that for example exploit legal loopholes.

Note that Baumol (1990) assumes that the supply of entrepreneurial talent is roughly constant, so growth is primarily determined by institutions that encourage productive entrepreneurship. In his analysis, individual entrepreneurial characteristics are mostly ignored. We suggest that impoverished entrepreneurs may not necessarily engage in rent-seeking or destructive entrepreneurship, but rather non-productive activities. This includes new ventures that lack attributes of a successful value proposition, such as better prices, simpler and/or more convenient products (Hart and Christensen 2002; Anderson and Markides, 2007; Henderson 2006). We thus suggest that in addition to productive, unproductive and destructive outcomes, non-productive entrepreneurship may also emerge, although such outcomes are likely influenced by the interplay between individual characteristics and institutional failures, rather than solely by the latter.

The effects of individual characteristics on impoverished entrepreneurship

In addition to institutional factors, the mainstream entrepreneurship literature has also identified individual characteristics as crucial for explaining new venture creation. This includes the entrepreneur's alertness to opportunities and ability to see connections that others may not see; self-efficacy; and prior experience, education, training and willingness to learn (Chrisman, McMullan, and Hall 2005; Kirzner 1973; Kiss, Danis, and Cavusgil 2012; Schumpeter 1934). We next discuss these characteristics, including specific discussion about their importance to impoverished entrepreneurship.

Alertness to opportunities

As discussed above, Kirzner's (1973) concept of alertness has been widely used to understand the nature of the entrepreneur and how entrepreneurial opportunities are identified. Alert entrepreneurs are creative, imaginative and explorative, take broad intuitive perspectives that incorporate multiple inputs, and tend to be more effective in recognizing and acting on business opportunities (Kirzner 1973, 1999; Ardichvili, Cardozo, and Ray 2003; Kaish and Gilad 1991). They are also able to transform information advantages into business opportunities (Minniti 2004).

Amorós and Cristi (2010) suggest that there are different perceptions of what constitute an opportunity, depending on the context. For example, they explain that a Sub-Saharan entrepreneur may see selling an extra kilo of wool as a great opportunity, whereas a Silicon Valley engineer would see it as necessity entrepreneurship. Thus, the context and interpretation of 'opportunity' or 'necessity' must be considered when investigating entrepreneurial behaviour. Such limitations have been recognized by the Global Entrepreneurship Monitor (GEM), a multinational initiative created to investigate entrepreneurship within and between countries (Reynolds et al. 2005; Wong, Ho, and Autio 2005). Indeed, Bosma and Levie (2010) suggest that research methods such as surveys often underestimate necessity and overestimate opportunity entrepreneurship. As a result, in-depth interviews for example may be necessary to understand individual perceptions of opportunity identification and other idiosyncrasies of the entrepreneurial process

Self-efficacy

According to Bandura (1997) and Compeau and Higgins (1995), self-efficacy is an individual's perception of their ability to succeed in specific situations. They found that individuals with high levels of self-efficacy invested greater efforts in pursuing goals, were more effective in problem solving, continued to have an interest in the task, persisted when faced with setbacks, and were willing to take on challenges. According to Reynolds et al. (2005), entrepreneurs' assessment of their skills, knowledge, ability to start a business and fear of failing also affects their attitudes towards entrepreneurship.

Learning and training

In addition to alertness and self-efficacy, another related internal characteristic is training and willingness to put in effort to learn. Gielnik et al. (2015) found that training had positive effects on individuals' entrepreneurial goals, action planning, action knowledge, and self-efficacy. For example, Chrisman, McMullan, and Hall (2005) longitudinal study of US-based entrepreneurs found that those that consulted with government-sponsored business support agencies were more likely to succeed after five years than those that did not. However, this only occurred if entrepreneurs were willing to internalize the advice by doing 'homework' on their new venture independently. They found that the more hours they worked independently, the greater their chances of succeeding. However, Glaub and Frese (2011) suggest that many studies do not explore the underlining processes by which training programmes succeed or fail. They noted that lessons learned from those that are unsuccessful remain largely under-examined in the literature.

Individual characteristics and impoverished entrepreneurship

While the importance of individual characteristics in developing countries have been widely recognized, it is still not clear how such factors play a role in the entrepreneurship-poverty alleviation dynamic (Sutter, Bruton, and Chen 2019). This is perhaps disconcerting, as some studies suggest that due to greater resource constraints in impoverished regions such as sub-Saharan Africa, Viet Nam and the Philippines, individual characteristics are even more important when compared to developed regions (Amorós and Cristi 2010; Baughn et al. 2006).

According to Berner, Gomez, and Knorringa (2012), impoverished entrepreneurs are mostly women, many of which would prefer the stability of employment over an entrepreneurial venture, and often share income generated with others within their network. Nichter and Goldmark (2009) found that previous work experience has a positive impact on venture success, while low education levels have a mixed influence. For example, they found that it may encourage survival entrepreneurship in response to no other alternatives, but may also hinder new venture success. Thus, a lack of education may stimulate the start of a business in an effort to survive, but not thrive.

In Brazil, Matos et al. (2018) found that impoverished entrepreneurs are mostly older, more likely to be female, less educated, have less confidence in their skills and know fewer entrepreneurs when compared to non-impoverished entrepreneurs. They also found that while alertness did not differ between low and high-income entrepreneurs, a lack of preparedness and barriers to institutional support may contribute towards their failure. In China, Si et al. (2015) found that individual features such as change in attitude and behaviour, have been crucial for entrepreneurs to break out of extreme poverty. They found that peasant entrepreneurs were able to become successful without external support, by changing their passive attitudes and static business models. They further found that their willingness to delay immediate rewards until profits were sufficiently accumulated played an important role in new venture success.

Interactions between institutional weaknesses and individual characteristics

Levie and Autio (2008) found that the relationship between new business activities and the institutional environment is mediated by opportunity and the individual's perception of their skills and ability to learn. Hayton, George, and Zahra (2002) suggest that individual characteristics such as reasons for starting a business, are heavily influenced by the cultural setting, such as regard for individualism, masculinity and power-distance. Although coming from different directions, these authors are consistent in suggesting that understanding the relationships between institutional factors and individual characteristics is necessary for entrepreneurship research. However, while such relationships have been addressed in the entrepreneurship literature, it remains unclear how interactions among institutional factors and individual characteristics influence entrepreneurial outcomes, especially in developing countries (Bruton et al. 2013a).

As discussed above, much has been written about institutional failure, and progress has been made in identifying individual factors that are linked to entrepreneurial behaviour and venture success (e.g. Brush and Cooper 2012; Lepoutre et al. 2013; Minniti 2004; Naudé 2010; Reynolds et al. 2005; Si et al. 2015; Wong, Ho, and Autio 2005). However, few studies have explored the interaction between ineffective institutional factors and adverse individual characteristics to understand why entrepreneurs in impoverished regions struggle. Indeed, Zahra, Korri, and Yu (2005) note that the literature often assumes entrepreneurs are rational, informed and understand effective governance structures, but in reality, their cognitions are bounded and influenced by prior experiences and environmental conditions. In impoverished regions, such conditions are likely to be worse, further undermining such rationality assumptions.

Empirical studies by for example Batinge and Jenkins (2018) in rural Ghana found that the benefits of micro-lending designed to rectify institutional weaknesses was hindered by female entrepreneurs' lack of understanding regarding their rights to borrow. Other studies suggest that individual characteristics such as entrepreneurs' risk averse attitudes reduces the venture's ability to generate capital and job opportunities, thus also limiting the potential benefit of micro-lending (Bruton, Ahlstrom, and Si 2015; ; Ganguly 2018).

In addition to institutional factors, Zahra, Korri, and Yu (2005) suggest that cognitive biases influence entrepreneurs' decisions. This may include 'temporal myopia', the inability to consider the long-term outcomes of a given decision (Levinthal and March 1993). Gaglio and Katz (2001) use temporal myopia in the context of entrepreneurship to argue that those that fail to recognize entrepreneurial opportunities often misjudge the context and type of behaviour required in a given situation. This includes' *... their market environment and the kind of behaviour demanded by the moment.*' (p 98).

A complementary perspective of temporal myopia is Scott's (1977)'s observation that the constant struggle and fear of deprivation among the very poor foster a mind-set of focusing on the 'here and now'. Venugopal and Viswanathan (2017) combine entrepreneurship and subsistence marketing literatures to examine how poor individuals use their venture to meet their immediate needs, which includes one's basic life necessities for survival. They argue that the poor often move resources between their business and household to address immediate needs. The quest for life necessities therefore has significant influence on economic behaviour of impoverished individuals (Scott 1977), and consequently on entrepreneurial behaviour. Thus, while this hear and now mind-set focused on a daily quest for immediate needs may provide the means for survival, it helps to explain why it hinders venture growth. Note that this contrasts to Si et al. (2015), who found that the long-term view approach of Chinese peasant entrepreneurs played an important role in venture success. Here we suggest that temporal myopia plays a role in whether impoverished entrepreneurs are able to succeed.

Figure 1 summarizes our theoretical approach to understanding entrepreneurial outcomes by combining the institutional environment with individual characteristics. For the purpose of this discussion, we categorize the institutional environment as being either:

Institutional environment	Individual characteristics	Entrepreneurial outcomes
Strong	Alert	Productive
Strong but misguided	Myopic/not considered	Unproductive
Weak	Alert	Destructive
Informal	Myopic	Non-productive

Figure 1. The institutional environment, individual characteristics and entrepreneurial outcomes.

(1) ***Strong,*** where the rules of the game are understood (Baumol 1990; Bygrave and Minniti 2000).
(2) ***Weak***, where there is pervasive corruption (Danis, De Clercq, and Petricevic 2011) and a lack of adequate resources (Valente and Crane 2010) that results in detrimental outcomes (Hall et al. 2012).
(3) ***Informal***, situations where individuals cannot subsist through legitimate but not necessarily illegal means (Webb et al. 2013), and as a result must rely on informal institutions such as their social networks (Williams and Shahid 2016).

For individual characteristics, we contrast Kirzner's (1973) alertness with myopic behaviour, such as a 'here and now' mind-set (Scott 1977), temporal myopia and more generally the inability to judge the context and type of behaviour required for a given situation (Gaglio and Katz 2001).

According to Baumol (1990), strong institutions set the right environment for productive entrepreneurship. However, the emergence of 'innovative entrepreneurs' (Schumpeter 1934), is also shaped by alertness to opportunities, self-efficacy; prior experience, education, training and willingness to learn (Chrisman, McMullan, and Hall 2005; Kirzner 1973; Kiss, Danis, and Cavusgil 2012). Baumol (1990) conceptualizes unproductive entrepreneurship as rent seeking in response to relatively strong, albeit perhaps misguided institutions. For the purpose of this study, we suggest that rent seeking is a rational response to the institutional environment (c.f. Zahra, Korri, and Yu 2005) rather than due to individual characteristics such as a high degree of alertness. For example, the initial growth of new Chinese ventures could be attributed to permitting entrepreneurship that was illegal under previous Communist Party regimes. However, the success of such ventures (productive entrepreneurship) was due to their willingness to change their passive attitudes and static business models (i.e. alertness), and their willingness to delay immediate rewards (Si et al. 2015) rather than focusing on the here and now. The result was productive entrepreneurship, where strong but re-aligned institutions combined with alert individual characteristics helped bring millions out of poverty.

According to Hall et al. (2012), destructive entrepreneurship may be the result of alert entrepreneurs engaged in criminal behaviour. For example, they found that alert entrepreneurs were able to exploit Brazilian government efforts encouraging tourism in the impoverished North Eastern city of Recife, which resulted in a sophisticated and highly exploitative sex tourism industry rife with violence. Other examples summarized by Box, Gratzer, and Lin (2018) include organized crime engaged in the illegal drug trade, racketeering, illegal gambling, human trafficking, blackmail, weapons-related activities and piracy. Although such activities may emerge from impoverished communities by entrepreneurs with limited resources, they typically require high levels of alertness (Kirzner 1973), self-efficacy (Bandura 1997; Compeau and Higgins 1995) and an understanding of governance structures (Zahra, Korri, and Yu 2005). Thus, alert entrepreneurs can be both productive and destructive, depending on the institutional environment.

In addition to encouraging destructive outcomes, weak institutions may force entrepreneurs into legal but informal activities (Webb et al. 2013), where a lack of formal institutional support is replaced with informal institutions (Williams and Shahid 2016). We suggest that this results in non-productive entrepreneurship, which differs from Baumol's (1990) other forms of entrepreneurship. For example, in addition to an absence of institutional support, the entrepreneurs often suffer from myopia, where they may lack training and prior experience, are unwilling to learn, overestimate their self-efficacy and generally fail to exploit opportunities and see connections that others may not see. As we show below, such problems are particularly common for entrepreneurs in impoverished regions, but cannot be rectified without understanding how both institutional and individual characteristic interact.

Methodology

Data used in this study was part of a broader research program aiming to explore poverty alleviation programs in Brazil, and specifically the role of entrepreneurship in impoverished regions. Brazil is a useful country to study impoverished entrepreneurial behaviour for the following reasons. First, it has been identified, along with China, India and Russia (i.e. the BRIC countries), as a major driver of economic growth in the coming decades (Wilson and Purushothaman 2003). The World Economic Forum (2010) classified Brazil, together with Malaysia, Panama, Mexico, Thailand and China, at stage 2 out of 3 stages of development, based on its GDP per capita in the range of US$3000 to US$9000. It however has persistent problems with social inequality (Griesse 2006; Hall et al. 2012; Neri 2009; Matos et al. 2018) and suffers from major institutional weaknesses (Hall et al. 2012), as illustrated by recent corporate and political corruption scandals, economic insecurity and soaring crime rates (World Atlas 2017). Brazil's income distribution has traditionally been heavily skewed towards the wealthy, where for example the top 10% possess almost half of the national income (IBGE, 2016). Finally, Brazilian policy makers recognize entrepreneurship as a potential solution to social improvement (Hall et al. 2011).

Our study was conducted in an impoverished community in Joao Pessoa, the capital of Paraiba, one of the poorest States in Brazil (IBGE, 2016). At the time of the research, Joao Pessoa had a population of about 600,000 and a GDP per capita of approximately US$5000 (IBGE, 2016). About 43% of the inhabitants were living under vulnerable conditions, a quality of living status using indicators based on household income, level of education, number of young children and elderly living in the household, and sanitation conditions (Sposati et al. 2010). The region's socio-economic difficulties are mostly driven by development policies focused on agriculture, as opposed to industrialization that led to economic growth in the more prosperous southern regions of the country (Sposati et al. 2010). Over the years, increasing agricultural concentration resulted in rural migration of former subsistence farmers to urban areas, many of which ended up destitute and living in poverty and crime-stricken shantytowns (Hall and Matos 2010).

Inductive data collection and analysis

We applied inductive methods that included a survey, interviews and focus groups with entrepreneurs to embark on an exploratory approach to understand impoverished entrepreneurship. The majority of studies discussed above typically take a 'top down' approach, where relatively successful entrepreneurs are identified and then analysed. Such studies provide insights about poverty alleviation through entrepreneurship by exploring characteristics that result in success. However, we suggest that insights can also be derived from a 'bottom-up approach', i.e. one that begins by exploring why impoverished people are motivated to start a business, the formal and informal institutional mechanisms that may support or hinder their efforts, and whether such mechanisms interact with individual characteristics. Although many studies have explored each of these phases independently, few have explored them as a process that shapes entrepreneurial outcomes.

We started with desk research, gathering publications and governmental reports from the Brazilian National Institute for Applied Economic Studies. In addition, we consulted with two representatives of the Brazilian Service for Entrepreneurship (*Serviço Brasileiro de Apoio às Micro e Pequenas Empresas*, SEBRAE), the main national government agency that supports small businesses, one representative of the Brazilian GEM office, and two representatives of the Banco do Nordeste, the largest micro-lending bank in the region. These consultations allowed us to gather information about local impoverished entrepreneurs, their behaviour and key institutional issues in the country.

Information drawn from these preliminary interviews plus the GEM Brazil studies were then used to develop a survey questionnaire. In addition to demographic questions (gender, age, income, work status, educational attainment, etc.), the questionnaire included questions related to their entrepreneurial environment (network, competitors, etc.) and their perception about self-efficacy, skills and abilities to identify new business opportunities. We also included questions on their motivation to start a business, whether by necessity or by opportunity identification. Following Bosma and Levie (2010) suggestion that surveys often have limitations in entrepreneurship research, we asked whether they would agree to be contacted for a face-to-face interview. The survey was conducted from May to July, 2012 (see Appendix 1).

In contrast with the more commonly used approach of deductive methods in which researchers start with hypotheses that are later tested with data, we used the survey to develop theoretical insights (Eisenhardt, Graebner, and Sonenshein 2016). We started with a large sample of subjects living in poor neighbourhoods of Joao Pessoa, identified by Sposati et al. (2010) as having high and very high levels of vulnerability, as shown in Figure 2.

In total, 30 neighbourhoods were selected for a stratified sample of 800 subjects, of which 773 agreed to participate in the survey. Of these respondents, 78 indicated that they were involved in starting a venture, and 108 indicated they were already involved in a new business, which in total represent 23% of all subjects. The closest benchmark data available was conducted by GEM Brazil (2016), which combined these two groups into early-stage entrepreneurs. In their data, 28.8% earn less than US$163 a month (the monthly minimum wage mandated by government at that time). The majority of our early entrepreneurs were women (69.3%), which is consistent with GEM Brazil (2012) data that found that the majority of early entrepreneurs in the Northeast region are women and often involved in informal businesses. We found that 61% of our early-stage entrepreneurs earned less than US$163/month and 39% earned between US$163 and US$262/month. A summary

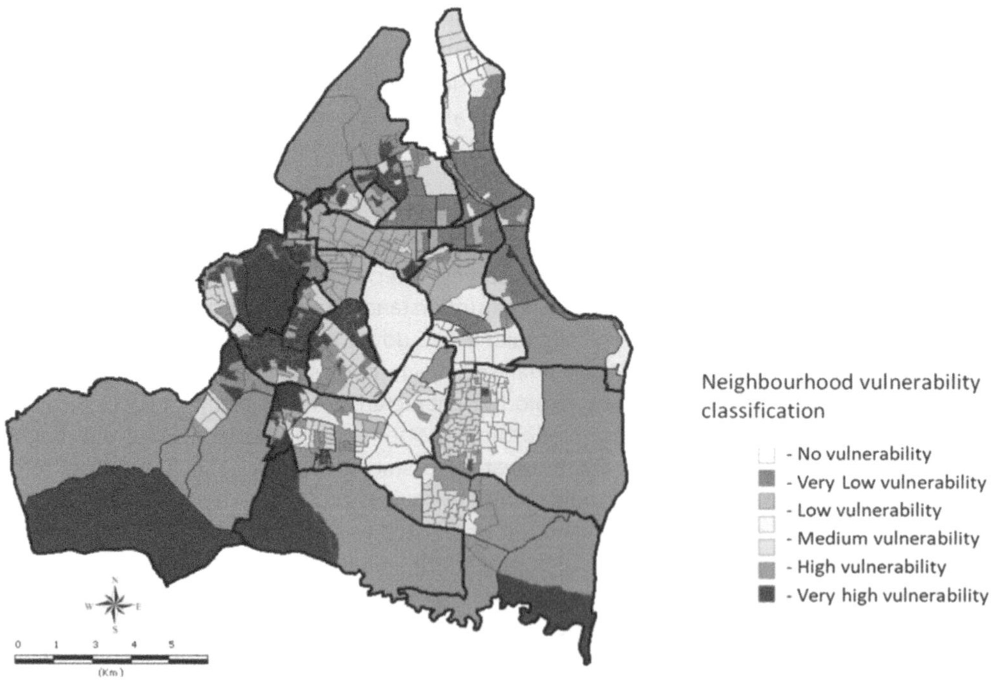

Figure 2. Socio-economic map of Joao Pessoa (Translated from Sposati et al. 2010) .

of the survey results are presented in Table 1. Observations about the representativeness of the sample is discussed in Appendix 2.

We then selected individuals for face-to-face interviews that agreed to be contacted during the survey, reported to be involved in a start-up or in a new business, had identified a business opportunity, and indicated that they possessed key individual characteristics of a potentially successful entrepreneur, i.e. self-reported high levels of efficacy and alertness. Of the 23 selected individuals, five refused to participate after being contacted and five could not be reached, for a total of 13 subjects. We supplemented these individual interviews with three focus groups composed of entrepreneurs identified by a micro-lending agency that they deemed to be successful entrepreneurs. Each focus group lasted about an hour and a half, with 19 participants in total.

Table 1. Survey results (descriptive statistics).

Individual factors	Results	
Gender	Female	69.3%
	Male	30.7%
Income level	Up to US$163/month:	61.0%
	Between US$163–262/month:	39.0%
Age	18–32:	35.6%
	33–44:	35.0%
	45–55:	16.0%
	55+	11.7%
	No response	1.8%
Training/Learning	No training or attendance in learning institution:	83.4%
	Reason for not attending:	
	Lack of time	61.8%
	Other reasons	22.1%
	No support for dependent family members	5.9%
	Did not think it was important	4.4%
	Difficulties accessing locations	2.2%
	Lack of funds for transportation	2.2%
	No response	1.5%
Self-efficacy	Reported having adequate skills and knowledge about business	90.2%
	No	8.0%
	Don't know	1.8%
	Alert to existing opportunities	80.4%
	No	14.7%
	Don't know	4.9%
Reasons to become an entrepreneur	Inability to find employment	25.2%
	Desire to be independent	25.2%
	Identified a business opportunity	25.2%
	Other reasons self-identified as:	
	Family tradition	11.2%
	Flexible hours	1.9%
	Previous work experience	0.9%
	Found it advantageous	0.9%
	'Other'	4.7%
Number of competitors	Many	63.0%
	Few	29.6%
	No competitors	5.6%
	Don't know	1.9%
Inspiration to choose a business	Identified an opportunity	56.5%
	Copied from another person/business	11.1%
	Business Fair	3.7%
	Refused to respond	6.5%
	Other	22.2%
Business sector of early entrepreneurial venture	Retail services	54.8%
	Hospitality and food services	22.6%
	Agriculture, forestry, fishing, and mining	1.2%
	Construction	1.2%
	Personal hygiene services (e.g. hair care, manicure, etc.)	1.2%
	Other activities	19.0%

Note: Individual characteristics of impoverished entrepreneurs (N = 186).

During the interviews and focus groups, we asked individuals to describe their business, explain their motivation, why they chose that type of business and how they gathered resources. We also asked them to talk about their competitors, training and future plans. The interviews were open-ended, giving the interviewees the opportunity to raise any relevant issues. They were conducted in Portuguese and within their community (either their homes or business), usually located in a *favela*, a low-income historically informal urban area. *Favelas* typically have poor infrastructure such as telecommunications and electrical utility access, congested roads and poor signage, making it difficult to find addresses. They are also notoriously dangerous, with high levels of drug and alcohol abuse. According to the World Atlas (2017), Joao Pessoa ranked 30th as the world's most dangerous city in 2017, based on murder cases per capita. Interviews were therefore conducted no later than 2:00 pm, after which it would become too dangerous.

Interviews were recorded, transcribed and coded. From here, we identified four main categories within the data: alertness and opportunity identification; training; formal status of the venture; and social networks. We then used these categories to conduct our analysis, looking for consistencies, differences and complementarities between the survey and interview data, always relating back to the entrepreneurship literature and the expert consultations. This allowed us to develop a better understanding of impoverished entrepreneurship by exploring the interactions between individual characteristics and the institutional environment.

Analysis

Similar to other surveys in emerging economies (Berner, Gomez, and Knorringa 2012; Matos et al. 2018), most entrepreneurs in our sample are young, female and have low levels of education. The perception of self-efficacy was high – over 90% of the 186 early entrepreneur respondents believed they possessed adequate skills and knowledge about business, even though their level of formal education was low. The face-to-face interviews indicated that such skills and knowledge were accumulated through their previous working experience, which in turn influenced where and what type of business they decided to develop.

Alertness and opportunity identification

A large percentage of the survey respondents (80.4%) believed they were alert to potential business opportunities. However, during the face-to-face interviews, we did not find clear indications of alertness such as creativity and imaginative actions as described by Kirzner (1999), or the ability to transform information advantages into business opportunities, as suggested by Minniti (2004). Prior experience and personal interests were the main drivers of opportunity identification. For example, one female interview subject planning to open a sandwich stand stated *'I wanted to open a business, small, bring what I've learned there* [working in a previous restaurant] *and open a business here.'*

Others identified opportunities from when they worked in other cities. *'I used to work in party venues, restaurants, but not here, in Rio ... I always worked with food, something that I love doing. I do it with a lot of love and I like hearing complements.'* (Female entrepreneur that opened a restaurant with her nephew). *'I want to open a car wash, ..., it's been 10 years that I work on this, was in Sao Paulo ...* [There] *I learned more things, how to use the product, the good product, the bad product, I learned more things, more agility to do the work faster.'* (Male entrepreneur). The majority of the survey respondents (54.8%) were engaged in retail activities for cosmetics and garments, followed by the food industry (22.6%), such as opening small restaurants. Consistent with Gaglio and Katz (2001), the interviews suggested that some entrepreneurs misjudged their abilities to understand their market environment. For example, when asked why customers would choose their business over others, they typically provided generic responses:

> *"Quality. I believe always offering the best, hygiene, make the client to come more ... I don't know, I believe that offering the best, spreads around, giving the best of ourselves."* (Female entrepreneur planning to open a sandwich stand).

> *"... we do a careful job, do it better than the others, use better products, it's expensive, it's good. The client likes it because it is guaranteed service and good products."* (Male entrepreneur planning to open a car wash service).

Others seemed oblivious to the market environment, where their immediate needs and pressures took priority, and were unable to tap into institutional support. For example, a restaurant owner stated: *'Here is the thing, my problem is this, me and my wife work here, the others, I don't know'*. This couple stated that the restaurant operated informally on government land that could be expropriated at any time, and that local thieves were a constant threat. When asked if they had accessed government welfare or educational support schemes, they stated they tried several times but were unable to receive support.

We followed up this issue with policy-makers in SEBRAE, asking why such support may not be granted. They indicated that a common problem was the inability for the recipient to obtain the necessary documentation, a problem that is exacerbated if they are illiterate. Another problem is their lack of organizational capabilities. For example, one female entrepreneur that started a small restaurant stated:

> *"My former boss, I worked there for 5 years, business was doing well but she did not know how to manage. I think she is taking steps bigger than her legs. She gets a loan and doesn't know how to use it. She writes too many checks, gets in financial trouble, asks for another loan. She started not paying me, so I couldn't do it, I left."*

In contrast to Berner, Gomez, and Knorringa (2012), our survey data did not indicate that most would prefer to have a steady job. Rather, we found an even spread of responses regarding reasons why they wanted to become an entrepreneur, with the three most common being an inability to find employment, a desire to be independent and because they identified a business opportunity. Our interviews confirmed such a spread of responses. For example, one interviewee stated that having a business is the only option for those that do not have money to invest in their own education and skills to find meaningful employment. In contrast, others valued independence over steady but unfulfilling employment: '...*we spend our whole lives working at somebody's house* [e.g. as a maid, groundskeeper, etc.], *or for some company, but nothing flows, nothing grows, nothing has a future.*' (Female entrepreneur planning to open a luncheonette). Most interviewees see entrepreneurship as an opportunity for a brighter future, *'a dream'*, and made optimistic remarks about their own future, even though they were pessimistic about the future of their community and the country in general.

Training

The majority reported that they have never participated in any training or educational institutions. According to one male entrepreneur that wanted to open a carwash, *'Everything I've learned was with a colleague ....'* Another female entrepreneur that recently opened a bar stated: *'We never had any training, everything was done with God's help. My older sister [business partner], works for an office, she deals with money, but she had no training. She learned by doing. It's been 20 years that she works in that office.'* A third interviewee that wanted to open a clothing business stated: '[Courses] *are about things that I don't want to do and it was taking too much of my time, I wash clothes for a living, work as a maid, it was taking my time.'* Some were unclear about what they should study, or do not have adequate information about the available options. For example, one female entrepreneur stated: *'We take courses but have no experience on what we want to do.'* Another interviewee planning to open a luncheonette stated: *'I'm taking an IT course because my ex-husband took it and work with sales ... To be honest, I have no idea about IT, computers, I'm just waiting to finish this course to take a different one later'*.

Others noted that some courses are only available to those that have a good credit history, '*They [the micro-landing bank] offer credit but you need to have a clean name. You take the course, then after taken the course, they give you the money.*' During the interviews and focus groups, we found that access to capital though micro-lending was emerging as an influential mechanism that linked impoverished entrepreneurs with institutional support, which is discussed in more detail below.

Formal registration

As expected, the majority of survey respondents had never attempted to formally register their business activities. Of the 108 respondents that answered the question 'have you tried to register your business', only 18.5% said yes, 19.5% indicated that they had difficulties, and 62% indicated that they did not try. This low rate of formal registration was in spite of governmental programs available at that time that were developed to simplify and motivate business owners to formalize their activities (Rocha 2012). Bruton, Ahlstrom, and Si (2015) and Webb et al. (2013) have suggested that remaining informal may appear attractive at the early phases of new venture creation, but would likely severely limit their growth. Here, we suggest that such temporal myopia (Gaglio and Katz 2001; Zahra, Korri, and Yu 2005) could be a major reason why none of our entrepreneurs from our dataset could be considered successful.

Social networks

We found from our interviews that social networks such as family and friends could be used productively as a source of customers, marketing, capital and other resources. For example, one female entrepreneur that created a luncheonette states: '*The best place for me to open my business is here. I have this nephew, he is quite known. He knows people here and spread the word. He said, "I opened this place with my aunt, she cooks well, just arrived from Rio".*'

However, some counter-productive activities also arose from their social networks. For example, similar to other impoverished regions, Brazilian banks had recently started offering microcredit loans with low monthly payments and relatively low interest rates to groups of entrepreneurs with similar needs and income. Such microcredit programs had been encouraged and supported by the Brazilian government as part of a social policy to reduce dependence on social assistance (Rocha 2012). Thus, like the conditional cash transfer program *Bolsa Familia* (Family Fund) and *Fome Zero* (Zero Hunger), national poverty alleviation schemes implemented in the early 2000s (Hall et al. 2012), microcredit policy was an attempt to address institutional weaknesses affecting impoverished communities.

A representative from one bank informed us that the default rate of participants was usually low because they offered basic business training and have a good monitoring system. During the three focus groups, we found that the entrepreneurs were able to supplement their household income and pay for basic expenses. Consistent with Chrisman, McMullan, and Hall (2005), we found those that were able to honour their monthly payments were well-organized and closely followed the lessons learned during the training sections. Although not innovative or highly profitable, these entrepreneurs were relatively successful when compared to those selected from the survey. However, counter-productive impacts of their social networks also emerged as a response to easily available credit. Consistent with Webb et al. (2013), many impoverished entrepreneurs are dependent upon friends and family to generate start-up capital, and it is common for them to share credit. According to one female store owner: '*Parents and friends lend their supermarket credit cards, then I buy supplies [at the supermarket] and I have 40 days to pay, and I get the money from my restaurant, money comes in, I pay.*' Sharing credit however often resulted in non-productive results. For example, we found that in some groups, microcredit participants would spend the money on immediate needs rather than their business, an illustration of poor organizational skills and disregard for long-term commitment, i.e. temporal myopia or more specifically, a hear and now mind-set (Scott 1977; Venugopal and Viswanathan 2017). For example:

> *"we borrowed money as a group, we were three, me and those two sisters. I got R$300* [US$72], *it was my first time, and they got R$400* [US$95]... *We ended up in debt, not because of me, but they didn't pay their instalments... now my name is dirty because of them, and I'm waiting for us to make an agreement"... "They spent the money, made debt on top of debt, and it got out of control".*

Others would lend the money they borrowed from a micro-lending institution or credit card issued by a retailer to relatives and other members of their social network, only to have it result in ruined credit.

> *"I want to deal with clothes, but I don't try to get a loan because I made a purchase for my aunt and she let my name* [get] *dirty so I can't get a loan. I bought a complete bedroom set for her and she left and didn't pay. Now my name is on the SPC* [the national credit rating register]."

Other credit schemes are provided by for example motorcycle dealerships, which offer opportunities to purchase vehicles at low monthly payments over long periods of time (on average 6 years) but with high interest rates. Such schemes are attractive to the poor because it requires proof of only a very low income and provides the opportunity to possess a means of transportation that can be used for both work and social purposes. As one interviewee stated:

> *" everybody can have a car or motorcycle, you have a clean name and a driver's license, you can have a motorcycle. It is easy and the owners of the dealerships even help you. Let's assume, you work, you don't have a fixed income, the owner, he arranges things with the bank and sells it to you. You need to have a clean name". "I got a motorcycle while I was working for [a particular company] ..., but the company closed and everybody was laid-off, then I couldn't afford the monthly payments... So I had to give the motorcycle to the bank. But I got a brand new one and used it, so the value went down, so I still owe money to the bank". New motorcycles are easier to buy, second hand ones have higher interest rates".*

As a result, some of these entrepreneurs were unable to pay their debts and had their names 'blacklisted' in the national credit rating register, preventing them from accessing future credit and training programs offered by the microcredit lending agencies. Once blacklisted, it was common for them to try to use their social network to find family or friends whose names are still 'clean'. Numerous interview subjects stated that they lent funds from their loans (either from the micro-lending agencies or from retailer credit cards) to such people, only to have their credit ruined.

Discussion and implications

Consistent with Gaglio and Katz (2001), the data suggests that our entrepreneurs misjudged their abilities to develop a new venture. In addition to overestimating their self-efficacy and market knowledge, they often failed to utilize training programs or manage micro-credit capital, a relatively new phenomenon that was supported by government in an attempt to rectify previous institutional weaknesses. Exacerbating this problem are their social networks, which on the one hand have been recognized as a support mechanism that compensates for institutional weakness (Williams and Shahid 2016), but on the other hand were abused by other network members. The result was widespread non-productive entrepreneurship due to bad credit spreading throughout the network, leading to stagnation. At issue was their temporal myopia (Levinthal and March 1993), i.e. a willingness to gratify immediate needs and wants rather than appreciate the demands of the moment (Gaglio and Katz 2001; Scott 1977). Temporal myopia is further supported by their apparent lack of awareness regarding the benefits of formal registration, which although may be attractive at early phases of new venture creation, hinders its long-term survival (Bruton, Ahlstrom, and Si 2015).

Our study complements others that have explored successful entrepreneurship within impoverished communities. Unlike Si et al. (2015), we did not find entrepreneurs that were able to break out of extreme poverty or become successful without external support. In contrast to their Chinese entrepreneurs, our sample of Brazilian entrepreneurs were not willing to delay receiving immediate rewards until profits were sufficiently accumulated, but rather utilized capital from microloans for more immediate use. Further research could explore why such national and cultural differences result in different degrees of temporal myopia. For example, we speculate that Brazil's history of inflation (i.e. an institutional weakness) may have created an environment where savings are ineffective, whereas a lack of experience dealing with credit (an individual characteristic) hindered successful entrepreneurship. Another reason could be the lack of incentives to engage in, for example, training, careful credit management and formalization when they know such efforts could be negated by the needs and wants of their social networks.

As discussed above, Williams and Shahid (2016), Webb et al. (2013) and Bruton, Ahlstrom, and Si (2015) suggest that impoverished entrepreneurs typically operate outside formal institutional boundaries and are dependent on informal institutions such as their social networks. Our research found that attempts to rectify institutional weaknesses, in this case by microcredit policies, may actually be hindered by impoverished entrepreneurs' dependence on their social networks. Our point is that when attempting to rectify institutional weaknesses, policy makers need to be particularly cognizant of the entrepreneur's individual characteristics and the behavioural dynamics of their networks.

Our research departs somewhat from Baumol's (1990) observation that growth is primarily determined by institutions that encourage productive entrepreneurship. Rather, we found that the key issue is *how* impoverished entrepreneurs respond to institutional changes, which in turn helps explain *why* so many engage in non-productive activities. We thus suggest that in addition to productive, unproductive and destructive outcomes that are shaped by institutions, further research is needed to understand *non-productive* entrepreneurship, which we argue is influenced by both individual characteristics and institutional failures. This is particularly pertinent for impoverished regions, where it appears as if non-productive entrepreneurship is far more prevalent than in developed regions. Indeed, one could test the proposition that non-productive entrepreneurship is more prevalent that other forms of entrepreneurship in impoverished regions.

Figure 3 illustrates our theoretical contribution, specifically the inclusion of non-productive entrepreneurship as a common phenomenon that hinders societally beneficial entrepreneurship in impoverished regions. The vertical axis represents the institutional environment, which for the purpose of this discussion is either weak or strong. The horizontal axis contrasts myopic behaviour such as temporal myopia (Gaglio and Katz 2001) or a mind-set of focusing on the 'here and now' (Scott 1977), with Kirzner's (1973) alertness, which can be enhanced by prior experience, education, training and willingness to learn (Chrisman, McMullan, and Hall 2005; Kiss, Danis, and Cavusgil 2012). In contrast to productive or destructive entrepreneurship, we suggest that a major feature of non-productive entrepreneurship is myopic behaviour by the individual entrepreneurs, which influences their outlook towards training, access to capital and formalization that in the long term improve their ventures.

Institutional Environment	*Myopic*	*Alert*
Strong	**Q3** **Unproductive** • Strong but misguided institutions that encourage rent seeking • Myopically focused on rent seeking or individual entrepreneurial characteristics not considered (i.e. rationality assumption)	**Q4** **Productive** • Strong institutional environment, where rules are fair and understood • Alertness entrepreneurs are able to utilize strong institutions to support innovative endeavours
Weak	**Q1** **Non-productive** • Weak formal institutions result in reliance on informal institutions • Myopic (e.g. overestimated self-efficacy, lack of training/ prior experience, unwilling to learn, here and now mind-set, etc.)	**Q2** **Destructive** • Weak institutions (e.g. pervasive corruption, resource scarcity) • Alert entrepreneurs exploit weak institutional environment for their own gain at expense of wider society

Individual Characteristics

Figure 3. Productive unproductive, destructive and non-productive entrepreneurship in impoverished regions.

As discussed above, while strong institutions set the right environment for productive entrepreneurship (Baumol 1990), truly innovative entrepreneurs must possess alertness. Somewhat paradoxically, alert entrepreneurs may also exploit weak institutions at the expense of society (Hall et al. 2012). Our concern is that increasing alertness of entrepreneurs from impoverished communities (e.g. in Quadrant 1) may very well result in destructive entrepreneurship (Quadrant 2) if the institutional environment remains weak. Indeed, we speculate it is easy for alert entrepreneurs to move from the non-productive quadrant to the destructive one, which perhaps helps explain the high crime rates in for example Brazil.

As outlined in Figure 1 in the theory section, unproductive entrepreneurship includes rent seeking in response to strong, albeit perhaps misguided institutions. For the purpose of this discussion, we suggest that rent seeking can be regarded as myopic behaviour, in that the rational, well informed entrepreneur that understands effective governance structures (Zahra, Korri, and Yu 2005) will focus their efforts on rent seeking to take advantage of the institutional environment rather than innovate. It thus differs from non-productive entrepreneurship, where such rationality assumptions are clearly not the case, as illustrated by our findings with impoverished entrepreneurs. Policy makers may implicitly be tempted to move from Quadrant 1 (non-productive) to Quadrant 3 (unproductive) in an attempt to stimulate regional economic development. Indeed, Brazil has a long history of utilizing import duties to protect local industry, as does many other developing regions. However, in addition to hindering innovation by restricting competition, subsistence entrepreneurs are unlikely to take advantage of such policies, given that they typically suffer from a range of myopic behaviour, such as an overestimated degree of self-efficacy, a lack of training and prior experience, an unwillingness to learn, and a here and now mind-set.

Moving from Quadrant 1 (non-productive) to Quadrant 4 (productive) should thus be the main goal of entrepreneurship policy. In order to do so, policy makers must however go beyond the purely institutional perspective advocated by for example Baumol (1990) and North (1990) to include how individual entrepreneurial characteristics affect attempts at rectifying institutional weaknesses. In addition to identifying the characteristics and behaviour of the alert entrepreneur, it is also crucial to understand the mechanisms by which counter-productive characteristics may negate strengthened institutional policies. For example, social networks that have previously acted as informal institutions (Williams and Shahid 2016) appear to be a barrier towards formulization, such as registering companies and judiciously managing micro-credit. The challenge is thus not only creating more effective institutions, but also managing the transition from informal to formal mechanisms.

Individual entrepreneurs can also play a larger role in improving their lives by, for example, attempting to break away from a here and now mind-set to one that takes a longer-term view. This in turn may provide incentives for formalization and the institutional support that it provides. A greater awareness of how their social networks affect their business, whether positive or negative, would also enhance their chances for success. While we realize the daily pressures of survival are a reality in impoverished communities, the literature provides evidence – and hope – that poverty alleviation is possible through entrepreneurship.

Limitations

As an exploratory study, our intention was to shed light on why impoverished entrepreneurs struggle. We therefore used an inductive approach that utilized a survey as a means to identify key individual characteristics, while the interviews and focus groups provided the opportunity to shed light on the interface between such characteristics and their institutional environment. Further research could develop models that correlates influence, degree of interactions of such characteristics with institutional factors and how these affect the outcome of the venture.

Another limitation is that we conducted the study in one community in one country, and as a result, caution should be used when generalizing to other jurisdictions. Future research could explore how impoverished communities respond to institutional changes (both strengthening and weakening) in different regions and cultural settings. Another related limitation relates to the time in which the survey was conducted. Since the data was collected, Brazil has undergone major political crises, which in turn has likely resulted in greater scepticism towards entrepreneurial opportunities. Follow-up studies could explore how such changes, which unfortunately are all too common in developing regions, affect impoverished entrepreneurs.

Although we believe that we met data saturation, it is perhaps worth noting that conducting research in impoverished communities involves considerable challenges, such as poor traffic conditions and violence that prevented us from interviewing all of the candidates that we selected from the survey. Furthermore, we speculate that many entrepreneurs engaged in illegal activities refused to participate in the research, which in turn may have underestimated the percentage of entrepreneurs that were actually engaged in entrepreneurial (albeit dubious) activities. There are also important challenges regarding respondents' over or underestimation of some of the individual characteristics measured in the survey. As we discussed above, GEM data already recognizes limitations related to how opportunity and necessity are interpreted in surveys (Bosma and Levie 2010). We add that poor entrepreneurs may also overestimate their own skills and underestimate the barriers of their business environment. Thus, when conducting research with impoverished individuals, researchers need to recognize the limitations of survey results and how they are interpreted. We suggest that such limitations can be addressed by supplementing these surveys with qualitative data collection and analysis. We discussed in our methodology how we controlled for some of these issues, but it would be worthwhile for future researchers to share their challenges and advice in how to conduct research within impoverished communities.

Conclusions

In this paper, we focused on why impoverished entrepreneurs struggle to succeed, and specifically looked at the interactions among their individual characteristics and institutional weaknesses they faced. By starting with a large sample of impoverished people, we were able to first explore why some see entrepreneurship as a way out of poverty, and then identify some of the individual characteristics of impoverished entrepreneurs. The individual interviews and focus groups allowed us to explore in greater depth various themes that emerged, such as temporal myopia, counter-productive use of social networks and whether they chose to utilize institutional support such as education programs and formal registration that some have suggested allow for new venture growth.

As noted by Sutter, Bruton, and Chen (2019), individual characteristics appear to have drawn less attention by researchers focused on impoverished entrepreneurship. This is perhaps logical, given that institutional weaknesses in impoverished regions are often obvious and paramount to hindering entrepreneurial efforts. As a result, entrepreneurs may be conceptualized as victims of a hostile institutional environment, regardless of their individual characteristics. While this may indeed be true, we found that a failure to consider individual characteristics may hinder attempts at rectifying institutional weaknesses and the resulting non-productive entrepreneurship.

In addition to considering why some entrepreneurs succeed, we suggest that policies also need to consider the characteristics of those that fail or struggle. More specifically, a key policy implication from this research is that rectifying institutional weaknesses without understanding the context of impoverished entrepreneurs would likely result in non-productive entrepreneurship.

Acknowledgments

We would like to thank those that agreed to participate in our research. We are also grateful for the very insightful advice from the guest editors of this special issue, Steven Si, John Cullen, David Ahlstrom and Jiang Wei, as well as two anonymous reviewers

Disclosure statement

No potential conflict of interest was reported by the authors.

Funding

This work was supported by the Social Sciences and Humanities Research Council of Canada.

References

Amorós, J., and O. Cristi. 2010. "Poverty, Human Development and Entrepreneurship. The Dynamics of Entrepreneurship: Theory and Evidence." Assessed 5 February 2019. https://pdfs.semanticscholar.org/b607/da79558c601adcf36d005c5570a524a7c84f.pdf

Anderson, J., and C. Markides. 2007. "Strategic Innovation at the Base of the Pyramid." *MIT Sloan Management Review* 49 (1): 83.

Ardichvili, A., R. Cardozo, and S. Ray. 2003. "A Theory of Entrepreneurial Opportunity Identification and Development." *Journal of Business Venturing* 18 (1): 105–123. doi:10.1016/S0883-9026(01)00068-4.

Bandura, A. 1997. *Self-efficacy: The Exercise of Control*. New York: WH Freeman.

Batinge, B. K., and H. Jenkins. 2018. "Assessing the Factors Militating against Microfinance in Alleviating Chronic Poverty and Food Insecurity in Rural Northern Ghana." In *Emerging Trends in Banking and Finance*, 181–198. Springer

Baughn, C. C., J. S. Cao, L. T. M. Le, V. A. Lim, and K. E. Neupert. 2006. "Normative, Social and Cognitive Predictors of Entrepreneurial Interest in China, Vietnam and the Philippines." *Journal of Developmental Entrepreneurship* 11 (01): 57–77. doi:10.1142/S108494670600026X.

Baumol, W. J. 1990. "Entrepreneurship: Productive, Unproductive, and Destructive." *Journal of Political Economy* 98 (5) Part 1: 893–921. doi:10.1086/261712.

Berner, E., G. Gomez, and P. Knorringa. 2012. "Helping A Large Number of People Become A Little Less Poor: The Logic of Survival Entrepreneurs." *The European Journal of Development Research* 24 (3): 382–396. doi:10.1057/ejdr.2011.61.

Bosma, N. S., and J. Levie. 2010. "Global Entrepreneurship Monitor 2009 Executive Report." Accessed 2 November 2018. https://dspace.library.uu.nl/bitstream/handle/1874/209570/GEM%202009%20Global%20Report%20Rev%20140410.pdf?sequence=1

Bowen, H. P., and D. De Clercq. 2008. "Institutional Context and the Allocation of Entrepreneurial Effort." *Journal of International Business Studies* 39 (4): 747–767. doi:10.1057/palgrave.jibs.8400343.

Box, M., K. Gratzer, and X. Lin. 2018. "Destructive Entrepreneurship in the Small Business Sector: Bankruptcy Fraud in Sweden, 1830–2010." *Small Business Economics* 1–21. doi:10.1007/s11187-018-0043-3

Brush, C. G., and S. Y. Cooper. 2012. "Female Entrepreneurship and Economic Development: An International Perspective." *Entrepreneurship & Regional Development* 24 (1–2): 1–6. doi:10.1080/08985626.2012.637340.

Bruton, G. D., D. Ahlstrom, and S. Si. 2015. "Entrepreneurship, Poverty and Asia: Moving beyond Subsistence Entrepreneurship." *Asia Pacific Journal of Management* 32 (1): 1–22. doi:10.1007/s10490-014-9404-x.

Bruton, G. D., D. J. Ketchen Jr, and R. D. Ireland. 2013b. "Entrepreneurship as A Solution to Poverty." *Journal of Business Venturing* 28 (6): 683–689. doi:10.1016/j.jbusvent.2013.05.002.

Bruton, G. D., I. Filatotchev, S. Si, and M. Wright. 2013a. "Entrepreneurship and Strategy in Emerging Economies." *Strategic Entrepreneurship Journal* 7 (3): 169–180. doi:10.1002/sej.v7.3.

Bruton, G. D., S. Khavul, D. Siegel, and M. Wright. 2013c. "New Financial Alternatives in Seeding Entrepreneurship: Microfinance, Crowdfunding, and Peer-to-Peer Innovations." *Entrepreneurship Theory and Practice* 39 (1): 9–26. doi:10.1111/etap.12143.

Bygrave, W., and M. Minniti. 2000. "The Social Dynamics of Entrepreneurship." *Entrepreneurship Theory and Practice* 24 (3): 25–36. doi:10.1177/104225870002400302.

Chrisman, J. J., E. McMullan, and J. Hall. 2005. "The Influence of Guided Preparation on the Long-Term Performance of New Ventures." *Journal of Business Venturing* 20 (6): 769–791. doi:10.1016/j.jbusvent.2004.10.001.

Compeau, D. R., and C. A. Higgins. 1995. "Computer Self-Efficacy: Development of A Measure and Initial Test." *MIS Quarterly* 19: 189–211. doi:10.2307/249688.

Danis, W. M., D. De Clercq, and O. Petricevic. 2011. "Are Social Networks More Important for New Business Activity in Emerging than Developed Economies? an Empirical Extension." *International Business Review* 20 (4): 394–408. doi:10.1016/j.ibusrev.2010.08.005.

Eisenhardt, K. M., M. E. Graebner, and S. Sonenshein. 2016. "Grand Challenges and Inductive Methods: Rigor without Rigor Mortis." *Academy of Management Journal* 59 (4): 1113–1123. doi:10.5465/amj.2016.4004.

Gaglio, C. M., and J. A. Katz. 2001. "The Psychological Basis of Opportunity Identification: Entrepreneurial Alertness." *Small Business Economics* 16 (2): 95–111. doi:10.1023/A:1011132102464.

Ganguly, S. 2018. "Micro-Finance and Poverty in India: A State-Level Analysis of Impact Assessment." In *Financial Entrepreneurship for Economic Growth in Emerging Nations*, edited by Atsede Woldie and Brychan Thomas, 194–216. IGI Global, Hershey, Pensylvannia.

GEM Brazil. 2012. "Global Entrepreneurship Monitor Empreendedorismo No Brasil: 2012 Coord." Simara Maria de Souza Silveira Greco. Curitiba, Brazil. doi:10.1094/PDIS-11-11-0999-PDN.

GEM Brazil. 2016. "Global Entrepreneurship Monitor Empreendedorismo No Brasil: 2016 Coord." Simara Maria de Souza Silveira Greco. Curitiba, Brazil.

Gielnik, M. M., M. Frese, A. Kahara-Kawuki, I. Wasswa Katono, S. Kyejjusa, M. Ngoma, J. Munene, et al. 2015. "Action and Action-regulation in Entrepreneurship: Evaluating A Student Training for Promoting Entrepreneurship." *Academy of Management Learning & Education* 14 (1): 69–94. Doi:10.5465/amle.2012.0107.

Glaub, M., and M. Frese. 2011. "A Critical Review of the Effects of Entrepreneurship Training in Developing Countries." *Enterprise Development and Microfinance* 22 (4): 335–353. Doi:10.3362/1755-1986.2011.035.

Griesse, M. 2006. "The Geographic, Political, and Economic Context for Corporate Social Responsibility in Brazil." *Journal of Business Ethics* 73: 21–37. Doi:10.1007/s10551-006-9194-2.

Hall, J., and S. Matos. 2010. "Incorporating Impoverished Communities in Sustainable Supply Chains." *International Journal of Physical Distribution & Logistics Management* 40 (1/2): 124–147. Doi:10.1108/09600031011020368.

Hall, J., S. Matos, B. Silvestre, and M. Martin. 2011. "Managing Technological and Social Uncertainties of Innovation: The Evolution of Brazilian Energy and Agriculture." *Technological Forecasting and Social Change* 78 (7): 1147–1157. Doi:10.1016/j.techfore.2011.02.005.

Hall, J., S. Matos, L. Sheehan, and B. Silvestre. 2012. "Entrepreneurship and Innovation at the Base of the Pyramid: A Recipe for Inclusive Growth or Social Exclusion?" *Journal of Management Studies* 49 (4): 785–812. Doi:10.1111/joms.2012.49.issue-4.

Hart, S. L., and C. M. Christensen. 2002. "The Great Leap: Driving Innovation from the Base of the Pyramid." *MIT Sloan Management Review* 44 (1): 51.

Hayton, J. C., G. George, and S. A. Zahra. 2002. "National Culture and Entrepreneurship: A Review of Behavioural Research." *Entrepreneurship Theory and Practice* 26 (4): 33–52. Doi:10.1177/104225870202600403.

Henderson, R. 2006. "The Innovator's Dilemma as A Problem of Organizational Competence." *Journal of Product Innovation Management* 23 (1): 5–11. Doi:10.1111/jpim.2006.23.issue-1.

IBGE. Instituto Brasileiro de Geografia e Estatística [Brazilian Institute of Geopgraphy and Statistics]. 2016. *Sintese De Indicadores Sociais*. Governo do Brasil: Rio de Janeiro.

Ipardes. Instituto Paranaense de Desenvolvimento Econômico e Social. 2019. "Salario Minimo Nacional." Accessed 15 February 2019. http://www.ipardes.gov.br/pdf/indices/salario_minimo.pdf

Kaish, S., and B. Gilad. 1991. "Characteristics of Opportunities Search of Entrepreneurs versus Executives: Sources, Interests, General Alertness." *Journal of Business Venturing* 6 (1): 45–61. Doi:10.1016/0883-9026(91)90005-X.

Kirzner, I. M. 1973. *Competition and Entrepreneurship*. Chicago, IL: University of Chicago Press.

Kirzner, I. M. 1999. "Creativity And/or Alertness: A Reconsideration of the Schumpeterian Entrepreneur." *The Review of Austrian Economics* 11 (1–2): 5–17. Doi:10.1023/A:1007719905868.

Kiss, A. N., and W. M. Danis. 2008. "Country Institutional Context, Social Networks, and New Venture Internationalization Speed." *European Management Journal* 26 (6): 388–399. Doi:10.1016/j.emj.2008.09.001.

Kiss, A. N., W. M. Danis, and S. T. Cavusgil. 2012. "International Entrepreneurship Research in Emerging Economies: A Critical Review and Research Agenda." *Journal of Business Venturing* 27 (2): 266–290. Doi:10.1016/j.jbusvent.2011.09.004.

Lee, D. Y., and E. W. Tsang. 2001. "The Effects of Entrepreneurial Personality, Background and Network Activities on Venture Growth." *Journal of Management Studies* 38 (4): 583–602. Doi:10.1111/1467-6486.00250.

Lepoutre, J., R. Justo, S. Terjesen, and N. Bosma. 2013. "Designing A Global Standardized Methodology for Measuring Social Entrepreneurship Activity: The Global Entrepreneurship Monitor Social Entrepreneurship Study." *Small Business Economics* 40 (3): 693–714. Doi:10.1007/s11187-011-9398-4.

Levie, J., and E. Autio. 2008. "A Theoretical Grounding and Test of the GEM Model." *Small Business Economics* 31 (3): 235–263. Doi:10.1007/s11187-008-9136-8.

Levinthal and March. 1993. "The Myopia of Learning." *Strategic Management Journal* 14 (1993): 95–112. Doi:10.1002/smj.4250141009.

Matos, S., J. Hall, V. Bachor, and B. S. Silvestre. 2018. "Low Vs. High Income Entrepreneurial Households: Heterogeneous Response to Common Institution Environment in Developing Countries." In *Geopolitics and Strategic Management in the Global Economy*, edited by Angelo Presenza and Lorn R. Sheehan, 242–260. IGI Global, Hershey, Pensylvannia.

Minniti, M. 2004. "Entrepreneurial Alertness and Asymmetric Information in A Spin-Glass Model." *Journal of Business Venturing* 19 (5): 637–658. Doi:10.1016/j.jbusvent.2003.09.003.

Naudé, W. 2010. "Entrepreneurship, Developing Countries, and Development Economics: New Approaches and Insights." *Small Business Economics* 34 (1): 1. Doi:10.1007/s11187-009-9198-2.

Neri, M. 2009. "Income Policies, Income Distribution, and the Distribution of Opportunities in Brazil." In *Brazil as an Economic Superpower? Understanding Brazil's Changing Role in the Global Economy*, edited by L. Brainard and L. Martinez-Diaz, 221-269, Washington, DC: Brookings Institution Press.

Nichter, S., and L. Goldmark. 2009. "Small Firm Growth in Developing Countries." *World Development* 37 (9): 1453–1464. Doi:10.1016/j.worlddev.2009.01.013.

North, D. C. 1990. "A Transaction Cost Theory of Politics." *Journal of Theoretical Politics* 2 (4): 355–367. Doi:10.1177/0951692890002004001.

Peredo, A. M., and J. J. Chrisman. 2006. "Toward A Theory of Community-Based Enterprise." *Academy of Management Review* 31 (2): 309–328. Doi:10.5465/amr.2006.20208683.

Reynolds, P., N. Bosma, E. Autio, S. Hunt, N. De Bono, I. Servais, P. Lopez-Garcia, and N. Chin. 2005. "Global Entrepreneurship Monitor: Data Collection Design and Implementation 1998–2003." *Small Business Economics* 24 (3): 205–231. Doi:10.1007/s11187-005-1980-1.

Ribeiro-Soriano, D. 2017. "Small Business and Entrepreneurship: Their Role in Economic and Social Development." *Entrepreneurship and Regional Development* 29: 1–3. Doi:10.1080/08985626.2016.1255438.

Rocha, G. F. 2012. "Avaliação Do Impacto Do Programa Crediamigo Do Banco Do Nordeste Do Brasil Atraves Do Indice De Progressao Da Pobreza (IPP) – Caso Da Regiao Metropolitana De Joao Pessoa – PB." MSc thesis, Faculdade de Boa Viagem, Pernambuco. doi:10.1094/PDIS-11-11-0999-PDN.

Schumpeter, J. 1934. *The Theory of Economic Development*. Cambridge, MA: Harvard University Press.

Scott, J. C. 1977. *The Moral Economy of the Peasant: Rebellion and Subsistence in Southeast Asia*. New Haven and London, Yale University Press.

Si, S., X. Yu, A. Wu, S. Chen, S. Chen, and Y. Su. 2015. "Entrepreneurship and Poverty Reduction: A Case Study of Yiwu, China." *Asia Pacific Journal of Management* 32 (1): 119–143. doi:10.1007/s10490-014-9395-7.

Smallbone, D., and F. Welter. 2001. "The Distinctiveness of Entrepreneurship in Transition Economies." *Small Business Economics* 16 (4): 249–262. doi:10.1023/A:1011159216578.

Sposati, A., F. Ramos, D. Koga, M. Conserva, J. C. Silveira Jr., and A. Gambardella. 2010. *Topografia Social Da Cidade De João Pessoa*. Editora Universitária da UFPB. João Pessoa, Paraiba.

Sutter, C., G. D. Bruton, and J. Chen. 2019. "Entrepreneurship as A Solution to Extreme Poverty: A Review and Future Research Directions." *Journal of Business Venturing* 34 (1): 197–214. doi:10.1016/j.jbusvent.2018.06.003.

Valente, M., and A. Crane. 2010. "Public Responsibility and Private Enterprise in Developing Countries." *California Management Review* 52 (3): 52–78. doi:10.1525/cmr.2010.52.3.52.

Venugopal, S., and M. Viswanathan. 2017. "The Subsistence Marketplaces Approach to Poverty: Implications for Marketing Theory." *Marketing Theory* 17 (3): 341–356. doi:10.1177/1470593117704282.

Viswanathan, M., R. Echambadi, S. Venugopal, and S. Sridharan. 2014. "Subsistence Entrepreneurship, Value Creation, and Community Exchange Systems: A Social Capital Explanation." *Journal of Macromarketing* 34 (2): 213–226. doi:10.1177/0276146714521635.

Webb, J. W., G. D. Bruton, L. Tihanyi, and R. D. Ireland. 2013. "Research on Entrepreneurship in the Informal Economy: Framing A Research Agenda." *Journal of Business Venturing* 28 (5): 598–614. doi:10.1016/j.jbusvent.2012.05.003.

Williams, C. C., and M. S. Shahid. 2016. "Informal Entrepreneurship and Institutional Theory: Explaining the Varying Degrees of (In) Formalization of Entrepreneurs in Pakistan." *Entrepreneurship & Regional Development* 28 (1–2): 1–25. doi:10.1080/08985626.2014.963889.

Wilson, D., and R. Purushothaman. 2003. "Dreaming with BRICs: The Path to 2050." *Global Economics Paper 99*, Goldman Sachs.

Wong, P. K., Y. P. Ho, and E. Autio. 2005. "Entrepreneurship, Innovation and Economic Growth: Evidence from GEM Data." *Small Business Economics* 24 (3): 335–350. doi:10.1007/s11187-005-2000-1.

World Atlas. 2017. "The Most Dangerous Cities In The World." Accessed 15 September 2018. https://www.worldatlas.com/articles/most-dangerous-cities-in-the-world.html

Zahra, S. A., J. S. Korri, and J. Yu. 2005. "Cognition and International Entrepreneurship: Implications for Research on International Opportunity Recognition and Exploitation." *International Business Review* 14 (2): 129–146. doi:10.1016/j.ibusrev.2004.04.005.

Appendix 1. Sample of survey questionnaire (Translated from Portuguese)

Gender	(1) Male (2) Female
Household income	(1) R$0–622.00 (less than 1 minimum wages) (2) R$622.00 – R$1866.00 (between 1 and 3 minimum wages) (3) More than R$1866.00 (more than 3 minimum wages)
Education	(1) No formal education (2) Some primary school (3) Completed primary school (4) Some secondary school (5) Post-secondary degree (6) Refused
Do you believe that, in the 6 months following the survey, good business opportunities will exist in the area where you live?	Yes; (2) No; (3) Don't know; (3) Refused
Do you believe to have the knowledge, skill and experience required to start a new business? (give examples of skills: creativity, ability to solve problems, leadership and communication)	Yes; (2) No; (3) Don't know; (3) Refused
Are you, alone or with others, currently trying to start a new business, including any self-employment or selling any goods or services to others?	Yes; (2) No; (3) Don't know; (3) Refused
Reasons for being involved in this start-up	(1) Could not find a job elsewhere (2) Identification of an opportunity (3) Flexible hours of work (4) Being independent (5) Family tradition (6) Increase family income (7) Secondary work that became main source of income (8) Other
Are there currently any competitors for your product or service?	(1) Many; (2) Few; (3) None; (4) Don't know
Business sector of early entrepreneurial venture	(1) Agriculture, forestry, fishing, and mining (2) Construction, manufacturing, transportation, communication, utilities, and wholesale (3) Finance, insurance, real estate, other business services (4) Hospitality and food services (5) Personal hygiene services (e.g. hair care, manicure, etc.), health, education and social services, recreational services (6) Other
Are you (alone or with others) currently the owner of a business you help to manage, including self-employment or selling any goods or services to others?	(1) Yes; (2) No; (3) Refused
Where/how did you get the idea for this product or service?	(1) (Open question) (2) Refuse to answer
For how long have you owned this business?	(1) (Months or years)
When you started your business, did you have difficulties registering it?	(1) Yes; (2) No; (3) Never tried
What difficulties did you have?	(1) High cost of registration (2) Too complicated to register (3) Lack of information/guidance (4) Did not want to pay taxes (5) Other

Appendix 2. Sample representativeness

We were able to conduct a t-test to compare the mean sample and the expected population mean for household income. The latter was based on Sposati et al. (2010), which provides average income estimates on the neighbourhoods where we conducted the survey. As shown in the table below, regarding average household income, the sample-estimated mean and the expected population mean is not significantly different ($\rho > 0.05$).

One-Sample Test (average income)						
					95% Confidence Interval of the Difference	
	t	df	Sig. (2-tailed)	Mean Difference	Lower	Upper
Income	–.484	772	.628	–3.991	–20.16	12.18

Looking at gender data, the majority of our 773 survey respondents were women (73.7%) and so were our 186 early entrepreneurs (69.3%). Although this may indicate overrepresentation of individual characteristics of women, according to GEM Brazil (2012), women represent the majority of early entrepreneurs in the Northeast region of Brazil, and are often involved in informal activities seeking to diversify ways of survival, so our data has validity.

Looking at our age data, most of our early entrepreneurs (35.6%) are 18–32 years old, followed by of those between 33–44 years old (35%). This aligns with GEM Brazil (2012) survey.

Call the midwife! Business incubators as entrepreneurial enablers in developing economies

Helen Haugh

ABSTRACT

Enabling domestic entrepreneurship is one pathway for alleviating poverty. In developing economies, however, public policies prioritize health and education above entrepreneurship promotion. While international development funding has traditionally supported social and environmental interventions, more recent corporate philanthropic funding has been invested in business incubators to support domestic entrepreneurship. This article examines how business incubation and enterprise development impact on poverty alleviation in developing economies. From the analysis of empirical data gathered from four philanthropy-funded business incubators, their role in how sustainable new venture creation and multiple capital formation contributes to poverty alleviation is explained. The findings contribute to entrepreneurship enablement theory.

Introduction

Poverty alleviation is an urgent challenge for many developing economies and has attracted the attention of international organizations, such as The World Bank and United Nations, and international development agencies, such as the United States Agency for International Development (USAID), and the Department for International Development (DFID) United Kingdom (UK). For decades these institutions have attempted to alleviate poverty, usually by transferring funds and encouraging domestic governments to advance new policies to support domestic economic growth (Boetkke 2007). The impact of efforts to help the poor out of poverty has, however, been disappointing (Easterly 2006; Collier 2007). The low success rate of poverty alleviation programmes has been attributed to lack of resources, weak institutions (Stiglitz 2002; Valente and Crane 2010), culturally insensitive interventions, and poor community engagement (Bird and Smucker 2007). Poverty alleviation initiatives that overcome these constraints by working closely with local actors are more likely to generate positive impacts and outcomes.

Traditional development aid, either grants or concessional loans, precondition a paternal attitude towards givers and reciprocal dependency, or victim syndrome, in recipients (SIDA 1996; Fowler 2000). Supporting domestic entrepreneurship, however, has been proposed as the foundation of a new development model that is based on market exchange rather than philanthropy (Bertaux and Crable 2007; Boetkke 2007). Enterprise creation considers individuals as producers, not just consumers (Prahalad 2004; Karnani 2007). Enabling sustainable domestic enterprise creation provides one pathway for countries to alleviate poverty and work towards securing economic and fiscal advancement. Supporting the creation of new domestic enterprises has several human development advantages as well, such as creating wealth and employment. The outcomes, especially for young people, are individual empowerment and increased agency and life chances. In rural areas, enabling sustainable enterprise creation increases the likelihood that young people will remain in rural communities rather than migrate to over-populated towns and cities. Enabling sustainable female entrepreneurship, especially, generates benefits in terms of improving economic and social status, enhancing the well-being of families and communities, and contributing more broadly to societal advancement (Mayoux 1996; Servon 1997; Servon and Doshna 2000; Ardrey, Pecotich, and Shultz 2006).

Although the debate concerning whether the role of business is to serve the interests of shareholders (Friedman 1962, 1988; Jensen 2002) or wider stakeholder groups (Freeman 1984; Ahlstrom 2010) shows no sign of abating, multinational corporation (MNC) engagement with host country development is widespread (Margolis and Walsh 2003). Most scholarly work on MNC and host country development has addressed social responsibilities as these have been traditionally prioritised by international development agencies (Visser 2008). More recently attention has turned to examining how MNCs influence the domestic economies of the countries in which they do business and they have been much criticized for stifling domestic industry development, ignoring human rights, disregarding social and environmental issues, and political intrusion (Kolk and Van Tulder 2006; Bhagwati 2007; Frynas 2008; Idemudia 2008). New directions in enacting corporate social responsibility (CSR), however, have seen the investment of philanthropic funds into enabling sustainable domestic entrepreneurship (Ahlstrom, Bruton, and Yeh 2008; Tasavori and Sinkovics 2011). When such investments support MNC supply and distribution chains, the benefit to an MNC is easy to see, and while there may be some impact on income-based poverty measures, enterprise sustainability remains dependent on the fortunes of the MNC (UNDP 2004a; WBCSD 2004). Economic independence and social empowerment are more likely to be associated with exploiting market opportunities independent of the MNC. The research investigates the question of *how does philanthropic investment in enabling entrepreneurship impact poverty alleviation in developing economies?*

From the analysis of four philanthropically funded business incubation programmes, their role in connecting sustainable new venture creation and multiple capital formation to poverty alleviation is explained. The research makes two contributions towards a theory of entrepreneurship enablement. First, theorization of the role of business incubators in sustainable new venture creation, multiple capital formation and poverty alleviation. Second, categorization of business incubators as key actors in entrepreneurship enablement in developing economies. The findings also contribute to the policy by suggesting how policymakers in developing economies can leverage MNC competencies for societal benefit.

Conceptual framework

Poverty alleviation

When compared to developed countries, developing economies perform less well on a range of economic and social indicators and international development initiatives focus on such issues to help people enjoy long, healthy and creative lives (UNDP 2008). The meaning of development is, however, contested. A narrow view of development is based on the fulfilment of basic survival needs, namely access to water, food, health services and education; such basic needs have been defined in the Sustainable Development Goals (SDGs) (UN 2015). A broader view of development describes a change in individual capacity or capabilities (Herrick and Kindleberger 1983; Bebbington 1999) that goes beyond the SDGs to include the increased agency of individuals, especially women (Sen 1999). Common to both narrow and broad development perspectives are *'efforts to bring people out of poverty'* (Frynas 2008, 274).

Most definitions of poverty are based on either an income or consumption indicator. The poverty line measures the minimum income level required to supply basic requirements of everyday goods and services. The SDGs established the poverty line as the equivalent of $1.90 a day (2011 US purchasing power parity). Poverty, however, is a combination of lack of income, opportunity and meaningful choices (Kabeer 1999; Newell and Frynas 2007). Multiple forms of deprivation and exclusion, in turn, mean that poverty alleviation requires multi-stranded solutions to address economic, social and citizenship deficits.

Entrepreneurship in developing economies

Entrepreneurship in developing economies is distinctive in that most entrepreneurs are forced into entrepreneurship for survival. Often because of the lack of alternatives (UNDP 2004b), entrepreneurs in developing economies tend to come from lower socio-economic groups, have little education, and are driven by economic motives (Azmat and Samaratunga 2009). These characteristics mean that their ventures are small, subsistence-oriented, serve local markets (Azmat and Samaratunga 2009), and have little impact on poverty alleviation. Yet, by creating employment, boosting economic growth, and alleviating poverty (Azmat and Samaratunga 2009), entrepreneurship has a central role in development (Naudé 2010). The development and poverty alleviation challenge, therefore, concerns how best to help entrepreneurs identify market opportunities that will enable them to establish sustainable, rather than subsistence, new ventures.

Business incubators typically deliver training and development to aspiring entrepreneurs to strengthen their motivations and skills and provide support and mentorship to help new and young ventures grow (Campbell and Allen 1987; Allen and McCluskey 1990; Laxmana and Ishwara 2008). From a wealth creation perspective (Hitt et al. 2001), the impacts of business incubators comprise both tangible and intangible aspects of capital accumulation and new ventures are known to benefit from higher levels of financial (Coleman 2007), human (Bates 1990; Coleman 2007; Davidsson and Honig 2003); and social capital (Davidsson and Honig 2003; Nahapiet and Ghoshal 1998). For example, Coleman (2007) found a positive effect between education and experience and firm profitability, the ability to secure financial capital only impacted profitability positively on male-owned firms; and Davidsson and Honig (2003) found that both strong and weak ties robustly predicted nascent entrepreneurship and early stage venturing. Delivering formal business incubation and entrepreneurship development training suggests that business incubators enhance multiple capital formation, and thus contribute to poverty alleviation.

Philanthropic investment in enabling entrepreneurship

In many developing economies, the role of MNCs goes beyond their economic functions and includes activities that are traditionally the responsibility of governments (Meyer 2004). Although MNCs may have contributed to development by providing access to health services and building human capital through education and training (Marsden 2000; Margolis and Walsh 2003; Hirwa and Mahadevia 2004; Matten and Crane 2005), the responsibility of public and private sector organizations for ensuring that MNCs contribute to advancing development is rarely made explicit. (An exception is the black economic empowerment transaction, an affirmative action programme introduced in South Africa (1994) to resolve economic disparities resulting from former Apartheid policies). As well as investment in infrastructure (Blowfield and Frynas 2005; Utting 2005), corporate philanthropy has been invested in education, community health and safety, and human capital development (Blowfield 2005), and activities to empower local communities to advance economic development (Eweje 2006).

Corporate philanthropic investment in business incubators contributes to poverty alleviation by empowering individual and community actors to realise their entrepreneurial potential and establish ventures that generate income and create employment opportunities. This can be achieved by stimulating entrepreneurship in activities related to the business of the MNC, such as local supply chains and distribution networks (UNDP 2004b; WBCSD 2004). In addition, incubating new and young ventures that are largely unrelated to the business of the MNC but are deemed to be of value in enhancing the domestic social, economic and political environment (Valente and Crane 2010). This might be in response to government failure to provide services to encourage economic and social development that in some way has led communities to look to MNCs to provide such services (Ite 2004, 2005), or as part of development-oriented corporate philanthropy.

Entrepreneurship enablement in developing economies is, however, not without criticism as there are concerns about the lack of robust data to support a positive relationship between entrepreneurship and poverty alleviation, for example, and the risks associated with patronage, corruption and rent-seeking in developing economies (Naudé 2010bb). In addition, supporting necessity entrepreneurship and prolonging the life of inefficient and low productivity ventures typical of livelihood-based initiatives also detracts from viewing entrepreneurship as a mechanism for alleviating poverty. Although there have been some positive developing country benefits from corporate philanthropy, post-colonial theorists have also criticized MNC philanthropy as the manifestation of imperialistic global capitalism and the persistence of hegemonic economic power (Khan, Westwood, and Boje 2010). The extent to which philanthropic investment in enabling entrepreneurship impacts on poverty alleviation is thus unclear. We investigate this puzzle guided by the question of *how does philanthropic investment in enabling entrepreneurship impact poverty alleviation in developing economies?* The conceptual framework is presented in Figure 1.

Methodology

The research employs an inductive, multiple case study (Eisenhardt 1989) research design. The inductive method is appropriate when little is known about a phenomenon or subject under investigation. Multiple case studies are particularly effective for generating robust and generalizable constructs as associations in newly discovered patterns can be corroborated through cross-case comparison (Eisenhardt 1991). Newly identified constructs can also be examined for their propensity for replication and extension to other contexts (Yin 2014). While prior research has investigated business incubators in developed countries (See Sentana et al. 2017 for review), less is known about their role in enabling entrepreneurship in developing economies.

Case selection

In phenomenon-led research, the selection of case studies is guided by access to data on the context, processes, relationships and constructs associated with the phenomenon under investigation. After

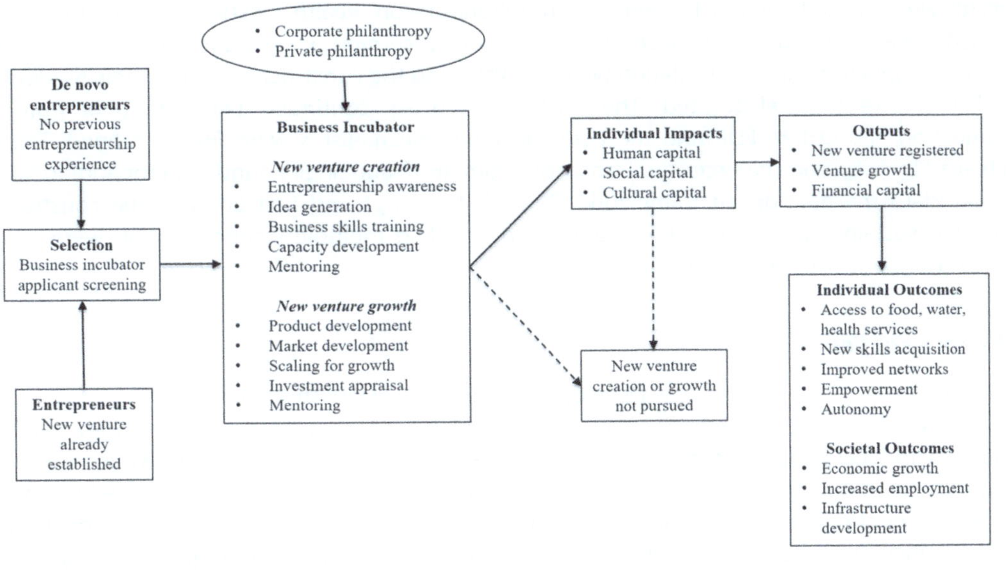

Figure 1. Conceptual framework.

field visits to observe community entrepreneurship projects in rural India, the internet and financial press were searched for examples of corporate philanthropy-funded business incubators and enterprise development programs in developing economies. From this method of purposive sampling (Patton 2002), four business incubation programmes were recruited to the study: Rural Enterprise Development Programme (REDP) established by Tata Chemicals; Shell Foundation; SAB Foundation (Tholoana); and Oxfam enterprise development programme (Oxfam EDP). Oxfam EDP provides a contrasting perspective, or deviant case (Yin 2014; Graebner and Eisenhardt 2004), as it is independent of corporate philanthropy. Business incubation comprises the delivery of enterprise development training and support designed to lead to the founding and growth of sustainable new business ventures (Grimaldi and Grandi 2005; Phan, Siegel, and Wright 2005). Three criteria are common to the case studies: a focus on encouraging and supporting sustainable entrepreneurship; located in communities in which the MNC has a connection, such as production base or product markets; and the aspiring entrepreneurs are local to and embedded in their communities. Finally, microfinance initiatives were excluded as they are already known to be less effective at impacting on poverty than increasing employment opportunities (Karnani 2007). Table 1 summarizes the participants.

Data sources and analysis

Multiple data sources were employed to gather information and develop holistic descriptions of each participating business incubator. In case of study research, multiple data sources are essential to enable data triangulation and thereby strengthen confidence in the emergent concepts and constructs (Flick 2009). The data comprise elite interviews with business incubator executives; an extended field visit to one of the business incubators, and secondary data from each business incubator.

The data were analysed using the principles of grounded theory (Charmaz 2014; Glaser and Strauss 1967) and abduction (Tavory and Timmermans 2014; Timmermans and Tavory 2012) to theorize how philanthropic investment in enabling entrepreneurship impacts on poverty alleviation in developing economies. To begin the author analysed the interview transcripts, secondary data and observation fieldwork notes for REDP. The texts were parsed into keywords and phrases relating to enterprise development processes and impacts. By constant comparison between the data (Charmaz 2014; Glaser and Strauss 1967), and cycling between the data and established theories, the principal mechanisms through which REDP supported entrepreneurship and created wealth were elicited. During this process, the literature on wealth creation and multiple capitals guided the abstraction of the conceptual categories concerning poverty alleviation. Next, the texts and transcripts from Shell Foundation were analysed and the constructs and mechanisms identified in REDP were then elaborated. The analytical process continued with the data from SAB Foundation and Oxfam EDP and the constructs and mechanisms were further refined. This was achieved by revisiting the texts and transcripts from REDP and Shell Foundation for additional data to elucidate the data-driven framework. Through transcript and text analysis, the constructs of enabling sustainable new venture creation and enabling multiple wealth creation were consolidated. The data structure is presented in Figure 2.

The case studies

Tata Chemicals Society for Rural Development (TCSRD) established the REDP in 2004 to raise awareness about the income generation and employment opportunities of entrepreneurship, and to help local people secure finance to establish sustainable new ventures. Aspiring entrepreneurs are recruited from contract workers, women, and young people with less education and access to fewer opportunities than other people living in nearby urban areas. REDP provides three business incubation services: training to stimulate and motivate future entrepreneurs, e.g., marketing, computer skills and network building; access to resources, including introductions to and

Table 1. Case study profiles.

	TCSRD REDP (2006) India	Shell Foundation Enterprise Solutions to Poverty (2005) Africa, Asia, Middle East	SAB Foundation Tholoana (2010) South Africa	Oxfam EDP (2008) Africa, Asia, Middle East
Aim and recruitment focus	To develop entrepreneurial skills in rural youth and to provide technical and financial support from banks to establish new small enterprises	Creates and scales business solutions in low income economies to advance SDGs	To support female and youth entrepreneurship in disadvantaged provinces	To promote a businesslike approach to economic development, more ambitious than conventional livelihoods initiatives whilst underpinned by robust commercial disciplines
Governance	TCSRD, registered charity, established 1980. Managed in association with a Centre for Entrepreneurship and Career Development	Shell Foundation, registered charity, established 2000. Board (8 members)	SAB Foundation, independent trust, established 2009 Board (5 members)	Oxfam, registered charity, established 1942. Board (8 members) Investment Committee (6 members, 3 advisers)
Ventures established/ supported	866 new enterprises (2018) 2662 REDP graduates (2018)	24 enterprises	295 enterprises (2019) 2 375 pre-entrepreneurship training graduates (2018)	Enterprises in EDP portfolio: 11 (2010), 16 (2012), 19 (2013), 14 (2016), 20 (2019)
Incubator funding	Grants from Tata Chemicals and philanthropy	Endowment shareholding in Shell	Endowment shareholding in Anheuser-Busch InBev	Private philanthropy \$3.9 million fund (2009) \$7.9 million fund (2013)
Economic impact	Increased individual income (2019) Increased average investment \$215 000 per annum (2018)	\$7 billion leveraged (2019) 210 000 jobs supported (2019)	Increased average business revenue \$1400 – \$18 000 (2018) Increased average turnover 18% (2018)	Increased individual income 30% (2018) Increased average turnover 15% per annum
Social impact	Increased empowerment Greater food security Improved housing	Increased access to energy Improved health	Increased empowerment Improved access to housing and health services	Increased empowerment Greater food security Improved nutrition

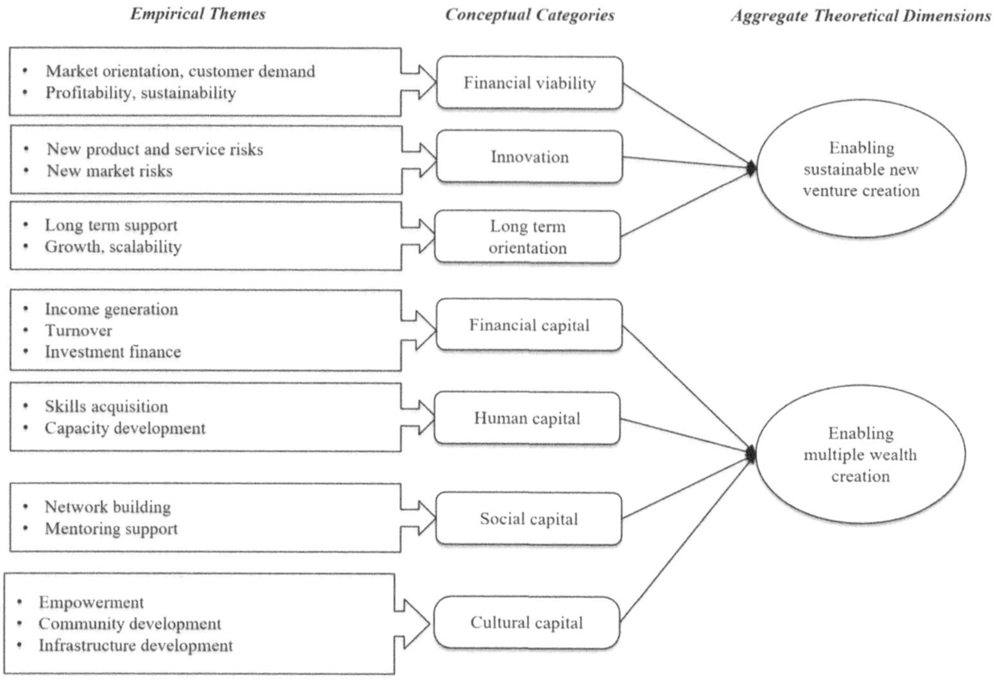

Figure 2. Data structure.

accompanied appointments with banks and investors; and follow-up entrepreneur support and mentoring. The REDP training is offered to individuals and groups and in 2015–2016 TCSRD aligned all its development initiatives with the SDGs (TCSRD 2016). Between 2004 and 2008, 491 participants completed the REDP and were directly linked to 127 new ventures in the community, 57 participants had been connected to banks to secure finance and the equivalent of $198 000 had been approved for lending to entrepreneurs. The impact on income for a sample of 43 REDP graduates (20:23 female: male) found income increased (72%), income unchanged (21%), and income decreased (7%). After completing the REDP, 85% (female) and 83% (male) participants reported that their confidence had increased (Fitton-Kane 2008). By 2018, 2 662 participants had completed the REDP training, 866 sustainable new ventures created and leveraged investment of $280 000 per annum.

> *'In an enterprise development program, what we basically look at is the fact that the participants himself or herself should be one who already has a need and is trying to set up an enterprise but is not able to scale-up or do better or has tried and failed. And for that kind of a person, we could step in and help them structure their enterprise so that not only he or she gets employment, self-employment for themselves, but can also employ other people.' (TA1.3)*

Shell Foundation, funded by the oil MNC Shell, was established in 2005 with the explicit aim to support enterprise solutions to development, especially entrepreneurs in developing economies unable to access finance. Entrepreneurs accepted onto the Shell Foundation business incubation programme receive pre-investment business development assistance and mezzanine finance for new ventures with growth prospects (loans and cash-flow based performance incentives of between $100,000 and $1 million). The Shell Foundation business incubation programme thus fills a gap in service and resource provision and the underpinning philosophy is embedded the strategic commitment to promoting sustainable development. During the financing term, mentoring support is provided to help the ventures achieve growth. Shell Foundation focuses on supporting ventures that aim to impact on development, particularly access to energy, mobility and transportation. The impact is measured in terms of lives impacted, jobs created, emissions reduction and capital leveraged. For example, in 2004 Shell Foundation supported GroFin, a private sector development finance institution, established by a private sector entrepreneur in Africa. By 2017 GroFin had scaled up to operating in 15 countries, extended pre-finance support to 8 840 entrepreneurs and invested in 675 ventures, (113 female owned). GroFin supports entrepreneurs in sectors that directly work towards the SDGs and have the capacity to impact on poverty alleviation (GroFin Impact Report 2017).

> *'Human capital is the biggest challenge the developing countries face, now, because of the quality of education, because they are highly populous, the demographic growth rates, very little job creation, and very little private sector activity.' (SF1.5)*

> *'We invest in ideas we think can address global development ... we would not generally look at health care or education because that is not where our expertise lies. And because of our operating model whereby we work with them closely on a day to day basis, providing expertise, we just couldn't support those the way we do, and we believe it's got to be more than money.' (SF1.10)*

The SAB Foundation, established in 2010 by the drink corporation South African Breweries, aims to advance the economic and social empowerment of historically disadvantaged people. This is achieved through several business incubation programmes, e.g., to encourage potential entrepreneurs, and support enterprises between 6 months and 5 years old (Tholoana) and social entrepreneurs. The programmes recruit women, youth, and people with disabilities and those living in under-served provinces (SAB 2018). Tholoana offers skills development, training, networking, mentorship and access to finance and markets. By 2018, 295entrepreneurs had graduated from Tholoana and all the businesses remain in operation (2019). The impact is measured on multiple poverty indicators, for example, 50% (2015 cohort) and 41% (2016 cohort) reported increased regular and reliable income, average annual turnover increased by 18% and employment opportunities increased from 1 174 to 1 336 (SAB 2017).

> *The Foundation was set up, but with a very clear mandate on entrepreneurship. And it has a clear mandate to support women, people in rural areas, and people with disabilities. And we have to reach out those particular groups. And it's mostly non-white South Africans. (SA1.5)*

> *For the enterprise development programme, we have recruits with slightly higher, a person with slightly better education, because they have to apply online. We get up to 2,000 applications, so we can only take 60, it's an expensive programme, but we have an intensive screening process. (SA1.9)*

The Oxfam EDP was established in 2008 to help people living in poverty in developing countries establish businesses that exploit sustainable market opportunities and financially and socially empower women (King, Sintes, and Alemu 2012). Supporting business incubation represented a new strategic direction for Oxfam as it employed a business-oriented approach to development and aimed to go beyond the traditional small-scale livelihoods initiatives typically associated with NGOs. From the first round of funding ($3.9 million, 2008), private equity and bank guarantees for capital equipment and working capital were provided by country level Oxfam EDPs to 11 domestic enterprises in Africa, Asia and the Caribbean. All investees are allocated a business mentor to provide day-to-day advice and access to networks. Funds are distributed in grants, for example, to support enterprise management and development, promotion opportunities for women and impact measurement. The second round of funding ($7.9 million, 2013) increased the portfolio of entrepreneurs supported to 16. The portfolio is no longer restricted to female entrepreneurs and the number of ventures supported varies from year to year as enterprises join and graduate the programme (Oxfam 2016). Economic and social impacts are measured across of range of poverty alleviation and development indicators, including, access to water, food resilience and female empowerment.

> *Although known for humanitarian aid, Oxfam also has enterprise development role. Looking for long term sustainable development and to help people help themselves ... To be sustainable, our entrepreneurs need to engage with the private sector. (OX1.1)*

> *Oxfam undertakes a market system, a blend of market systems, approach to poverty reduction with a livelihoods approach, a rights-*
> *based livelihoods approach. The livelihoods approach is well known, it looks at assets and systemic change through different systems. And we're doing well, dealing with markets and market systems, about how you change the enabling environment, and the services you create, and impact from both change and enterprises. (OX2.2)*

Oxfam EDP supports new ventures in 11 countries, for example, women dairy farmers (Sri Lanka), vegetable oil producers (Ethiopia), and sisal farmers (Tanzania). The businesses supported are dominated by selling agricultural products to domestic markets (processed food, 24%); dairy products, 22%; fruit and vegetables, 18%; and grains, 6%); domestic and export markets (fibres, 10%; honey, 9%); and exports (spices, 5%). In Ethiopia, for example, the profit margins of 4 500 coffee farmers doubled, and beekeepers' profits and income increased between 30% and 40%. In 2016, Oxfam EDP supported 11 enterprises of which 7 reported profits and created 294 jobs.

Findings

The analysis finds that philanthropic investment in enabling entrepreneurship impacts on poverty alleviation in two ways, first, by teaching entrepreneurs how to establish new ventures that are market-oriented, innovative and sustainable; and second, by helping entrepreneurs to increase their own financial, human, social and cultural wealth. These two mechanisms are explained below, and supplementary empirical data is presented in Table 2.

Enabling sustainable new venture creation

Enabling sustainable new venture creation is abstracted from three conceptual constructs: financial viability, innovation and long-term orientation. The constructs are abstracted from data relating to developing market orientation, sustainable business planning, risk-taking and sustainable growth.

Financial viability

The business incubation training programmes help domestic entrepreneurs to identify markets that are sustainable and have profit potential. The enterprise development training helps entrepreneurs to specify the opportunity they will pursue. Prior to business incubation training, the vision of most participants tends to focus on products, not opportunities. The business incubation training involves helping entrepreneurs to visualize opportunities beyond their own needs and those of the local community and move away from the idea of creating a venture to serve local needs. For example, at REDP, the entrepreneurial opportunities range across a wide variety of goods and services, such as carpentry and joinery, mobile phone repair, bicycle repair, beauty treatments, traditional craft products, retailing, hospitality and transport. At Tholoana, a market gap for a pharmacy and health services was the motivation for establishing a new venture in a township:

> *The premise that REDP comes from is the creation of jobs, if you want livelihood, opportunities cannot all happen through employment with the government, especially in our country where there are so many people and there has to be some amount of enterprise development happening where people set up their own businesses and try and feed into the need of the community you know ... The entrepreneurs ask themselves what can I do? And what can the market expect? What are the products and skills that the market wants? (TA1.3)*

> *We have actually helped a woman who has set up a pharmacy in the township. There are no pharmacies in our townships, which is crazy. And so, she set up one up there ... She's now turning over a lot of money in her pharmacy, and she has medical services attached to that. So, she helps people with ... things like high blood pressure, diabetes, gastric problems, HIV. She does all of that through her pharmacy. (SA1.13)*

Table 2. Supplementary empirical data.

Enabling sustainable new venture creation
Financial viability
Market opportunity orientation
'We do not want to support entrepreneurs who are pushing products that are not needed … if the market isn't there or isn't ready, then it will not respond.' (SF3.3)
'One of our communities in the EDP is the seed cooperative in Nepal. And they were producing seeds and were in competition with other seed producers. And they recognised that there was a gap in the market for coloured seeds because, imported seeds are usually coloured. That's only because the seed producers colour their seeds. So, the gap in the domestic market was for coloured seeds. And so, they did that.' (OX3. 15)
Profitability, sustainability
'The main concern is that the new businesses should be sustainable, and we only ask about impact after they have been running for more than a year.' (TA3.2)
'If we walk away after five or ten years, is there still something there? That's what always worries me when people are doing small scale stuff at the community level. If you look at microfinance, many cases where women can access microfinance for five or ten years very successfully, build a bit of a business but it never really gets them out of poverty. It's just giving them short term cash flow access.' (SF1.11)
Innovation
New product and service risks
'When we have followed the process of identifying people who are willing to put in their effort, to take the risk as I mentioned and wherever we are willing to do the base research and studying and feeling out the market.' (TA1.4)
'The products they're selling can then lead to huge advances in sustainable livelihoods, getting appropriate finance can help reduce risks for people in poverty and can grow businesses, we will do it, and our licensees, passing of information, running financial services etc., etc. over huge distances, very appropriate, those companies come into it, but that's not from an enterprise approach; that is from creating new products that are appropriate, that end up in enterprise development.' (OX2.9)
New market risks
'We want to support pioneers to start new markets. We can support them with more than money, by offering business skills and strategic advice, to help them achieve that.' (SF2.2)
'The pioneers with new technologies and new business models need grants to get them started. We stay with them for 3 to 4 years and are very actively involved, giving them advice, business planning, technical support, networks and help with hiring.' (SF3.4)
'When you're looking at a value chain and the dynamics around value chain and negotiating whatever, by having an enterprise; it's a complete lie to say that you then re-equate those power dynamics. You don't, but what you do is you give those producers the ability to go and find other markets or other buyers, it reduces their, so they become powerful by reducing their risk of getting interlocked into one usurious or unfair relationship, there's an aspect of power around that.' (OX2.5)
Long term orientation
Long term support
'The impact is not that dramatic right now to be very honest because they just started making a bit of a prominence on its own after the last two years. So, the women who are working with Okhai are definitely are glad that they are working here but it's not been that dramatic over the last two years.' (TA2.9)
'People think that in two years you can achieve something. You can't. And we've proven that with our enterprises. The ones that are up and running, it takes a long time.' (SF1.7)
Growth and scalability
'The product is good, the quality, the handicraft itself is very good, then there is a demand, market demand for the products and however, the challenge is of … skills. Only if you have a bigger scale of things happening, would it become a viable business?' (TA1.6)
'When people are doing small scale stuff at the community level, it never really gets them out of poverty. It is just giving them short term cash flow.' (SF1.11)
'Enterprises that develop these kind of for poverty reduction is, in a rural context, is absolutely fundamental, because you're in remote, fractured markets with very, very little power; small villages with very little power and they've got to aggregate and get to somewhere else, it's self evident that you need stable enterprise growth to get those remote, very poor, very vulnerable producers into the market systems. You need an enterprise to link them to that market.' (OX2.4)
Enabling multiple wealth creation
Financial capital
Income generation and turnover
For information about impact on income generation and turnover after business incubation refer to websites:
https://shellfoundation.org/impact/
http://www.tcsrd.org/media-room/annual-report.html
http://sabfoundation.co.za/tholoana-enterprise-programme/
http://edp.oxfam.org.uk
For example, the Chetona Fish Hatchery, Bangladesh, plans to 'increase income and resilience through modern fish farming. This will be achieved by providing training, supporting subsistence farmers to grow into commercial fish farmers, and supporting women's groups to establish 10 new women-led nurseries by 2019'. (Oxfam Enterprise Development Programme, Annual Report 2016, 6)
Investment finance
'We call this 'the pioneer doubt', where you need a lot of capital where you get a company up to the point where they are 'investable' but you have very few folks willing to provide the capital necessary to get there and in our view, particularly where you have pioneers that are looking at new technologies, new business models, the hardest markets to reach, the hardest customer segments to reach … there is a strong case for grants … to get companies up to that stage.' (SF4.5)
'Oxfam has provided investment into the enterprises, but now is more focussed on offering loan guarantees so that they can borrow from lenders.' (OX3.8)

(*Continued*)

Table 2. (Continued).

Enabling sustainable new venture creation
Human capital
Skills acquisition
'Husk Power, it was set up by 3 technology entrepreneurs and uses rice husk to generate power. And developed a business model based on pay per use. We provided help in designing a new meter to monitor household usage, training in technical installation skills and monetizing the waste product into incense sticks.' (SF2.6)
'On the poverty alleviation side. This one programme which is … it's where we actually … we take unemployed people and put them on a five-day acceleration programme, using on-line technology. This is the business model camp.' (SA.7)
Capacity development
'We came up with a thought process of looking at what are the ways that we can help them, and enterprise development was one way where we could look at developing the capabilities of the communities themselves, the people in the communities so that they can set up an enterprise of their own.' (TA1.2)
'The EDP supports them with training and expertise to increase their capacity and skills to manage their businesses successfully. The training is provided in leadership and managerial aspects of the business.' (OX3.5)
Social capital
Network building
'Because in the Enterprise Development Program we are not actually … putting in funds, we are not giving any funding, what we are doing is linking them up with the banks and the financial institutions and trying to see that their project itself is good and robust and that they can get the fund.' (TA1.4)
'And they are able to support the enterprises directly in some areas. When we can't, we find ways and partners who can. So, for example, one of our enterprises in India required a lot of technical support around developing efficiencies around that power plant and we were able to draw on some support from, our parent, to provide that advice.' (SF4.15)
'The cooperative helps us to build social relationships and to expand our worlds. We want to prove as women that we have control over our destinies.' Quote from entrepreneur (Oxfam, 2011, p.13)
Mentoring support
'Maybe there's something wrong with the product, the marketing strategy, or the distribution network, or the governance structure isn't right, or the financing structure is wrong. We will work with them to overcome that.' (SF1.14)
'Also, we try very much … to attract very good entrepreneurs in areas like Johannesburg and Capetown. And also outside of those areas, because in rural areas they get no kind of support and help. We especially prioritise outside metropolitan areas. And yes, they're all disadvantaged.' (SA1.9)
'What we have to do on EDP, we get them a local mentor, a local business mentor who advises that business. That's the bit we pay for. That's one of the bits we pay for out of our business grant … They look at an enterprise and go, this is a good enterprise, it's sustainable with a good business model or not.' OX2.7
Cultural capital
Empowerment
'There are issues then around the women earning income and what they do with it and because if … if all they're doing is handing the money over to the men then that's not really empowerment for them is it?' (TA2.6)
'What we do find is women … we have no problem giving support to the most fantastic entrepreneurs, but we've got a lot of single mothers in this country, and a lot of them get derailed by these issues. Actually, women … normally and because we are finding, they drop out, businesses stall due to, abusive husbands, divorce, and those sorts of things. So we are especially supporting women.' (SA1.9)
'Where we can get innovation around services we can have effective outcomes and where we can have increase in assets around market. The sweet spot we have at the centre is women in economic leadership and smallholder development and enterprise creation. That's systems change.' (OX2.3)
Community development
'Our enterprises are all companies in the developing world that need to generate financial viability and sustainability by selling a product or a service to poor people. They have social impact and we are measuring social impact.' (SF1.9)
'South Africa has conservatively, 27% unemployment. Everybody … everyone who creates a job or, is supporting other family members gets a really good deal … and over and above that, we find some guys will put a vegetable garden and help the community, there's a lot of community activity that happens outside of this, because they are entrepreneurs doing well, and they want to help their community.' (SA1.12)
Infrastructure development
'We are trying to help create a smarter funding eco-system for investment capital; And shift away from foreign capital and foreign ideas into local ideas and local markets.' (SF3.5)
'There are the drastic the gaps that we see in the market that are preventing under-served consumers from receiving access to modern, affordable energy products and services.' (SF4.2)
'There is a missing middle in finance for entrepreneurs. There are small microloans for entrepreneurs and then large loans for bigger businesses. What we are trying to do is to help create access to middle range finance.' (OX1.3)
'The livelihoods approach is well known, it looks at assets and systemic change through different systems. We're doing well. We deal with markets and market systems, and about how you change the enabling environment, and the services you create change through both change and enterprises.' (OX2.2)

Opportunity identification is fundamental to entrepreneurship; however, to impact on poverty alleviation, new ventures need to be rooted in sustainable markets in which goods and services are sold outside the extended family. The focus on market demand, not subsistence, means that new ventures will be shaped by forces beyond the control of the entrepreneur. In addition, business incubation training teaches entrepreneurs business planning and financial management skills. In developing countries, social obligations impose familial obligations, responsibilities and entitlements that overrule commercial considerations (Anderson and Obeng 2016). Such cultural norms impact negatively on new venture sustainability.

Despite the centrality of opportunity recognition and exploitation in new venture creation, the high failure rate of new businesses attests to just how difficult it is for entrepreneurs to recognise and create viable opportunities (Shane and Venkataraman 2000). The rural poor in developing economies primarily depend on agricultural livelihoods and the limited success of livelihood approaches to poverty alleviation has been explained by their inward-looking focus on the needs of households, rather than market-oriented opportunities (Naudé 2101b). Business incubation training thus aims to shift entrepreneurs from establishing new ventures that address personal needs, to market opportunities, commercial business models and long-term sustainability. Creating a sustainable enterprise may require significant business model experimentation and several years of support:

> *Many of the enterprises we support really have to restructure themselves, because they do have a kind of mixed role, and if they want to go into commercial enterprise; that's a huge challenge, for example the dairy producer, it's half a trading enterprise, it's half an NGO ... They really haven't started their organisation to do that well, and that's been a very long, painful process for them to get that restructured. (OX2.7)*

> *We do not give GroFin money anymore. It's sustaining on its own. It's getting revenue from its products and services and it's now operating in different countries in Africa, impacting on hundreds and thousands of lives. It's creating small enterprises that create jobs that are still around in three, four, five years' time. (SF1.11)*

Innovation

Business incubator training teaches entrepreneurs that risk is part of entrepreneurship, how to examine the risks associated with designing new products and services for new markets, and how to sell products in non-local markets. For example, to prepare entrepreneurs for coping with the risks associated with innovation and the possibility of failure, REDP teaches entrepreneurs how to analyse local businesses that have failed, and Oxfam EDP supports entrepreneurs to grow non-traditional crops for export markets. The opportunities draw on the agricultural skills of farmers but at the same increases risk through experimenting with novel crops for new markets. Ultimately though the risks are borne by the entrepreneur where, in developing countries, the consequences of new venture failure can be devastating:

> *In the rural communities, the women themselves, especially the ones who have the skills, and are nomadic in nature and have never done or haven't been out too much, so their approaches are that, "We can do the work, but we don't know how to take the risk and go out and do the program." That's where the risk bit comes in. Women who understand this and are willing to take that extra step and take the risk of new products and new kind of designs and learning, and employing their skills and taking it further, that's where the risk part comes in. (TA1.4)*

> *So, we've invested in ... these innovative service providers who unlock market systems for the people to go and work with. So, in Ethiopia, women cannot work in the honey sector as the hive is put up a tree, culturally they can't climb trees, and two they weigh a tonne ... the new beehives do not need to be in the trees. (OX2.3)*

Two further examples from Oxfam EDP portfolio illustrate the impact of business incubation training on product and market innovations. First, the founder of Shekina, a cassava leaf processor in Rwanda, launched an instant cassava product that is sold in domestic and export markets. Second, local farmers in Latin America evaluated the risks of growing crops that would appeal to non-local markets. Working collectively to share the risk, the farmers established a cooperative and now export cashew nuts to the United States and Germany (Oxfam 2016).

Long-term orientation

The new ventures need to be commercially viable beyond business incubator support and to achieve this goal, domestic entrepreneurs are taught how to protect their business ideas and pursue opportunities for growth. The combination of opportunity identification, market assessment and rigorous financial evaluation ensures that entrepreneurs create ventures that will be financially sustainable. Poverty alleviation is a slow process and of equal concern is the long-term prospects of the new ventures created by participants. To achieve growth by creating employment and generating income, the business incubation training teaches entrepreneurs how to assess the future size and scale of the market. By growing the scale of the new ventures, the opportunity to increase their impact on poverty alleviation is enhanced:

> *You have to have an open-ended goal. It takes five to ten years to create something sustainable. If it's good and we're working with it very closely and we watch it grow and we incubate and support them, then maybe we can scale right up into something really powerful. And if we can we'll continue to put money until that entity can source its own capital from elsewhere. (SF1.7)*

> *I think one extreme of our programme is how much we care for every single person we support, we really . . . we do look, in our process, for somebody who shows the right attitude and who genuinely wants to grow their business. (SA1.10)*

Enabling multiple wealth creation

The second aggregate theoretical construct is abstracted from the connections between business incubator-supported enterprise creation and dimensions of wealth creation. Multiple capital formation builds on prior entrepreneurship research (Hitt et al. 2001) and the broad definition of poverty (Herrick and Kindleberger 1983; Sen 1999).

Financial capital

Interventions to alleviate poverty that only considers income overlook the multidimensionality of poverty. To be sustainable business incubation training helps entrepreneurs to become more economically independent and not to rely on philanthropy. Increased economic independence is derived from income generation, increased turnover and securing investment capital. For example, Tholoana entrepreneurs reported an 18% average annual increase in turnover after completing the programme (SAB 2017). Business incubation also trains entrepreneurs in financial management and raising investment income. Entrepreneurs in developing economies often lack the collateral needed to acquire loans, and banks and lending facilities also may have unrealistic expectations for the new entrepreneurs. For example, an executive from REDP explained that prior to enrolling on REDP a local entrepreneur had worked as a day labourer. After graduating from the REDP in 2007, he established two new ventures, a fabrication unit and a hardware shop. The REDP programme includes introductions to banks from which the founder secured a bank loan to start up the businesses that now employ six people. In an example of a community enterprise raising finance, after graduating from REDP, Bandhani, a bag making business that provides income generation for 150 women, secured a bank loan for $3 161 to invest in product development. REDP matches entrepreneurs with other sources of finance whereas Shell Foundation, Tholoana and Oxfam EDP invest their own funds:

> *It's better to link up with an existing financial institution whose job is basically to finance. To get the buy-in of the financial institution and get adequate funding for small enterprises is a challenge and wherever we have managed to get that link well, the programs have done well, the participations have done really well and have taken that forward. Wherever it has taken longer, it is because of whatever the compulsions of the financial institutions and or their risk-taking ability in terms of giving the funds. (TA1.5)*

> *We'd have a discussion: 'What's your idea? What's your product? What's your service? What are you selling? And we would incubate that. We put maybe, $250 000 into the process of incubating, into testing the idea. (SF1.8)*

Human capital

Economic development is typically measured in terms of growth, per capita income, productivity and increases in employment. Such tangible measures, however, do not capture how income is translated into other important ends for development to occur (Kabeer 1999; Sen 1999). The broader definition of development includes advancing human development and enlarging people's options. The business incubators employ two processes to increase the human capital of participants: skills acquisition and capacity development. The business incubation training is structured into sessions in which entrepreneurs learn business management and technical skills from instructors. The low literacy in developing countries, especially female literacy, means that entrepreneurship training may also involve teaching basic literacy and numeracy skills. The training also includes capacity and confidence building:

> *Like any business they will overstate their income they're going to get threefold, and they're going to underestimate their costs involved. The actual process of working with the lead managers or entrepreneurs in that business is an enormous task to get them to be rational and realistic, and they tend to all come out of the development state, so when you're saying, "you're never going to sell that much, be more realistic", they're thinking right, I'm going to reach half the producers I'm trying to work with, and it's very emotional stuff. (OX2.8)*

> *The REDP Program, besides helping people setup an enterprise, actually helps build the personality or you know that kind of a capacity building has happened where a person was more timid, or he is not able to articulate well or not able to analyse, all those skills are something that they have got out of the program. Everybody has gained to a certain extent, some have gained more, and some have gained less. (TA1.5)*

Social capital

Poverty alleviation initiatives aim to generate social impacts as well as income enhancement. The business incubation programmes develop two aspects of social impact: extending network density by connecting entrepreneurs to other entrepreneurs, and support organizations; and mentoring support arrangements to help entrepreneurs increase the quality of their network links. Increasing the density and quality of network links is particularly important for young entrepreneurs who have had less time to build connections than older entrepreneurs. Further, women's networks in patriarchal and rural communities tend to be limited to family members (Mayoux 1996) and business incubators play an important role increasing opportunities for women to meet other women from outside the family. The network links include bridging connections to financial institutions, social investors, business contacts, markets and clients:

> *Some enterprises are really, really, you know very, very nice, where they have taken one business idea and then they realised that I still have time and I can do another business idea along with this business idea and have built on the contacts that they have created and done well. And there are some who took the training and tried a bit and then decided like that's not for them and would prefer to go and take a job somewhere else.(TA1.5)*

> *The mentor team works closely with each other, often collaborating amongst themselves for advice and clarity on an issue ... the business milestones are tracked in the mentor team feedback, as well as in the finance and grant portfolio. These are seen as 'growth unlockers' or 'growth unblockers', which need to be resolved readily in order to see real and tangible results in the business. (SAB, Quarterly Report, March 2018)*

Cultural capital

The impacts of business incubation training on cultural wealth creation comprise increasing empowerment and infrastructure development. Specific examples of building individual-level cultural capital are empowering women and local communities. For example, Okhai (REDP) supports female empowerment in rural communities and Deaf Empowerment Firm Pty Ltd. (Tholoana) empowers deaf individuals by providing training and access to employment via work placements and internships. At the community level, the outcomes include supporting healthier lifestyles, for example, Little Mermaids Swim School (Tholoana) provides swimming instruction and exercise classes and Envirofit (Shell Foundation) designs, produces and sells energy-efficient cooking stoves that reduce CO2 and smoke emissions, fuel costs, cooking time when compared to traditional open fire food preparation. Impacts are also noted at the community level, for example, access better housing (Tholoana), and infrastructure, such as Husk (Shell Foundation) provides reliable energy distribution to rural homes, and Oxfam EDP supports business development infrastructure:

> *Where I see the strongest connection between these enterprise development programmes, and actually improving the quality of life. Not just about more money coming into communities, but poverty alleviation in the broader context, how that is taking place in these communities. (SA1.14)*

> *We have many outcomes we try and achieve through this work, but one of the primary outcomes is changing the power of the target producers, workers, beneficiaries we're aiming at in the market systems they're in ... where we can get government to do good regulation and pre-commercial investment, where we can get private sector to do investment, and create new business models so they can give solutions to small scale solutions or open up their supply chains too. (OX2.3)*

Discussion

The four business incubators investigated deliver free enterprise development training, support and mentoring however, their individual business models vary in relation to funding, coverage, scale and impact. REDP is funded by grants from Tata Chemicals and NGOs, Shell and SAB Foundations derive income from share endowments held in their respective MNCs, and Oxfam EDP is funded from private philanthropic donations. In contrast to the other business incubators, REDP does not offer entrepreneurs grants or investment funding. As Oxfam EDP relies on private philanthropy, such expenditure can only be sustained by further cycles of fundraising. In relation to coverage, Shell Foundation and Oxfam EDP operate internationally whereas REDP and Tholoana support domestic entrepreneurs. The smallest portfolio of ventures supported (14, Oxfam EDP) contrasts with 866 (REDP) and, in contrast to the other three, Shell does not incubate community enterprises. All the business incubators impact on poverty alleviation and the greatest reported environmental and job creation impacts are achieved by the Shell Foundation business incubation model. The diversity of business models present in the sample suggests that the design of business incubation and enterprise development programmes is influenced by governance, context and resource availability.

In the business incubator programmes analyzed, the business incubation funding gap was filled by corporate and private philanthropy, working either independently or in partnership with other NGOs. Poverty alleviation is a persistent problem that has defied resolution and there are no simple prescriptions for helping developing economies to address poverty and inequality. Integrated strategies that involve public, private and non-profit organizations could, however, provide a mechanism for development that is sensitive to the social, economic and political realities of developing economies. Yet, in developing economies the public sector may be either unwilling or unable to provide services beyond meeting survival needs. Moreover, unwelcoming institutional constraints, such as insecure property rights and corruption, may thwart entrepreneurship (Bruton, Ketchen, and Ireland 2013); and public investment in business incubators is not always economically profitable (Sentana et al. 2017).

The analysis found that sustainable new venture creation is anchored in the combination of financial viability, innovation and long-term orientation. Poverty alleviation requires more than increasing real income, innovation is also important to develop new products and services and find customers in new markets (Boetkke 2007). By supporting entrepreneurs to create new ventures, tackling extreme poverty is approached from the bottom up in which local knowledge and motivation are combined with business training to develop new ventures that are sustainable in the long term.

Multinational corporations have been criticized as symptomatic of neo-Imperialism and the imposition of top-down solutions. Part of this discourse advocates modernization through industrialization.

Such post-colonial criticisms of MNCs may be countered by interventions that involve close engagement with communities. The adoption of participatory approaches to development (TCSRD), pro-poor enterprise development (Shell and SAB Foundations), rigorous understanding of local needs (REDP) and inclusive growth strategies (Oxfam EDP) situates business incubation and enterprise development as community-based social initiatives that are led by the needs of communities and not driven by corporate self-interest, cash transfers and neo-liberal policies. Moreover, MNCs encounter a limitless array of opportunities for CSR, many of which are unrelated to their core competencies. Policy initiatives to encourage MNC philanthropy investment in supporting business incubation training and enterprise development provide a route for harnessing MNC managerial and financial capabilities for societal benefit.

Towards a theory of entrepreneurship enablement

Business incubators are an important mechanism for stimulating entrepreneurship and economic growth in developed economies (Phan, Siegel, and Wright 2005) where their roles are to create a culture to encourage entrepreneurship, provide practical and technical training, and support aspiring entrepreneurs. Prior entrepreneurship enablement research has examined how external considerations, such as regulatory, technological, demographic and societal changes, impact on new venture creation (Davidsson, Recker, and von Briel forthcoming). By teaching entrepreneurs how to identify sustainable market opportunities, providing direct or supported access to financial and social resources, and developing entrepreneur knowledge and skills, business incubators also enable entrepreneurship and positively impact on sustainable new venture creation and growth.

Through supporting sustainable new venture creation, business incubators also lead to the creation of multiple forms of wealth for individuals, communities and society. Individual poverty is alleviated by generating income, creating employment expanding networks and increasing empowerment. Collectively these outcomes increase individual agency and control – the defining characteristics of the broad definition of poverty (Herrick and Kindleberger 1983; Bebbington 1999; Sen 1999). Community-level poverty is also impacted upon by increasing the flow and circulation of money in the community, providing incentives for people, especially youth, to not migrate to urban centres, and generating positive community spirit. Society also gains from entrepreneurship enablement by increasing economic, social and cultural empowerment and infrastructure improvements.

Business incubator training thus enables entrepreneurship by providing access to knowledge, skills and resources and, in developing economies, impact on poverty alleviation by creating multiple forms of wealth. Prior research on entrepreneurship has focused on the creation and discovery of opportunities in which contextual influences are downplayed (such as Shane and Venkatamaran 2000). More recently scholars have highlighted the importance of institutional conditions on entrepreneurship, especially in resource-poor contexts (such as Boetkke 2007; Bruton, Ketchen, and Ireland 2013). Entrepreneurship enablers elaborate opportunity explanations of entrepreneurship by providing support services to help entrepreneurs create and discover opportunities, and to institutional explanations by adumbrating the supportive context in which entrepreneurship can flourish.

Conclusion

The research investigated how four philanthropy-funded business incubation and enterprise development programmes impact on poverty alleviation. While case study research enables the researcher to develop deep knowledge and understanding of phenomena and processes (Yin 2014), case studies lack the generalizability and validity associated with more quantitative business incubator research (e.g., Dutt et al. 2016). Such criticism, however, is misplaced as the value of case study research lies in the contributions to elaborating existing theory (Tavory and Timmermans 2014; Timmermans and Tavory 2012) or generating new theoretical frameworks (Charmaz 2014; Glaser and Strauss 1967). It was only from the deep knowledge acquired about the processes and impacts of each business incubator that the relationships were surfaced between entrepreneurship enablement and multiple wealth creation.

Fundamental to poverty alleviation is that new ventures are sustainable and generate income from sales. The investigation of how these outcomes are achieved rests on teaching aspiring entrepreneurs how to direct their thinking towards new products and markets that have the capacity to create multiple forms of wealth. Three suggestions for future research follow from the research.

First, economies are composed of a variety of organizational forms and the emergence of new ventures generates structural change. The economic impact data (Table 1) suggest that business incubators broaden access to, and increase participation, in the formal economy. When MNCs fund business incubation and entrepreneurship development an obvious market opportunity is for aspiring entrepreneurs to develop goods and services for MNC supply chains (UNDP 2010). Further research that examined the economic, social and environmental spillover effects of new domestic ventures in MNC supply and distribution chains would deepen our understanding of entrepreneurship enablement in developing economies.

Second, the social impacts of new ventures increase community power, autonomy and independence and thus contribute to development (Hamann 2006). Business incubator support of female entrepreneurship in developing countries also impacts on the social and cultural status of women. Although research on female entrepreneurship in developing countries has identified the constraining impact of cultural institutions (Mair and Marti 2009), we know little about the processes through which female entrepreneurship impacts on societal change, especially in patriarchal societies. Research that investigated the emancipatory impacts of business incubators on women and minorities would be both theoretically and practically significant.

The final suggestion concerns institutional boundary work. MNCs have been criticized for adopting an instrumental approach to developing economies that overlooks the real needs of communities. Philanthropy-funded business incubators provide a mechanism for MNCs and NGOs to enable entrepreneurship and impact on poverty alleviation. Yet, investing corporate philanthropy in business incubators risks broadening corporate responsibilities into those of governments and the public sector, and in some cases to replacing some governmental responsibilities. The creation, maintenance and disruption of boundaries is central to institutional theory (Lawrence, Suddaby, and Leca 2009) and research that investigated the processes through which the governance responsibilities of MNCs and NGOs are expanded beyond compliance with legal requirements and humanitarian aid would deepen our knowledge of institutional boundary work and change.

The business incubators and enterprise development training programmes investigated share their sensitivity to contextual influences and the development of close and supporting relationships with aspiring entrepreneurs. Using the midwife metaphor, the role of business incubators is not to create new business ventures but to provide training and resources to support entrepreneurs as they conceive of and develop new business ventures. While new ventures may initially be small, sustainable new venture creation and multiple wealth creation provide a pathway for poverty alleviation in developing economies

Disclosure statement

No potential conflict of interest was reported by the author.

References

Ahlstrom, A., G. D. Bruton, and K. S. Yeh. 2008. "Private Firms in China: Building Legitimacy in an Emerging Economy." *Journal of World Business* 43: 385–399. doi:10.1016/j.jwb.2008.03.001.

Ahlstrom, D. 2010. "Innovation and Growth: How Business Contributes to Society." *Academy of Management Perspectives* 24: 11–24.

Allen, D. N., and R. McCluskey. 1990. "Structure, Policy, Services and Performance in the Business Incubator Industry." *Entrepreneurship Theory and Practice* 15: 61–77. doi:10.1177/104225879101500207.

Anderson, A. R., and B. A. Obeng. 2016. "Enterprise as Socially Situated in a Poor Fishing Community." *Journal of Rural Studies* 49: 23–31. doi:10.1016/j.jrurstud.2016.11.015.

Ardrey, W. J., A. Pecotich, and C. J. Shultz. 2006. "Entrepreneurial Women as Catalysts for Socioeconomic Development in Transitioning Cambodia, Laos and Vietnam." *Consumption, Markets and Culture* 9: 277–300. doi:10.1080/10253860600921811.

Azmat, F., and R. Samaratunga. 2009. "Responsible Entrepreneurship in Developing Countries." *Journal of Business Ethics* 90: 437–452. doi:10.1007/s10551-009-0054-8.

Bates, T. 1990. "Entrepreneur Human Capital Inputs and Small Business Longevity." *The Review of Economics and Statistics* 72: 551–559. doi:10.2307/2109594.

Bebbington, A. 1999. "Capitals and Capabilities: A Framework for Analyzing Peasant Viability, Rural Livelihoods and Poverty." *World Development* 27: 2010–2044. doi:10.1016/S0305-750X(99)00104-7.

Bertaux, N., and E. Crable. 2007. "Learning about Women. Economic Development, Entrepreneurship and the Environment in India: A Case Study." *Journal of Developmental Entrepreneurship* 12: 467–478. doi:10.1142/S1084946707000757.

Bhagwati, J. 2007. "Why Multinationals Help Reduce Poverty." *The World Economy* 211–228. doi:10.1111/j.1467-9701.2007.00879.x.

Bird, F., and J. Smucker. 2007. "The Social Responsibilities of International Business Firms in Developing Areas." *Journal of Business Ethics* 73: 1–9. doi:10.1007/s10551-006-9192-4.

Blowfield, M. 2005. "Corporate Social Responsibility: Reinventing the Meaning of Development?" *International Affairs* 81: 515–524. doi:10.1111/j.1468-2346.2005.00466.x.

Blowfield, M., and J. G. Frynas. 2005. "Setting New Agendas: Critical Perspectives on Corporate Social Responsibility in the Developing World." *International Affairs* 81: 499–513. doi:10.1111/j.1468-2346.2005.00465.x.

Boetkke, P. J. 2007. "Entrepreneurial Responses to Poverty and Social Conflict." *Economic Affairs* 2–5. doi:10.1111/j.1468-0270.2007.00723.x.

Bruton, G. D., D. J. Ketchen, and R. D. Ireland. 2013. "Entrepreneurship as a Solution to Poverty." *Journal of Business Venturing* 28 (6): 683–689. doi:10.1016/j.jbusvent.2013.05.002.

Campbell, C., and D. N. Allen. 1987. "The Small Business Incubator Industry: Micro-Level Economic Development." *Economic Development Quarterly* 1: 178–191. doi:10.1177/089124248700100209.

Charmaz, K. 2014. *Constructing Grounded Theory*. London: Sage.

Coleman, S. 2007. "The Role of Human and Financial Capital in the Profitability of Women-Owned Small Firms." *Journal of Small Business Management* 45 (3): 303–319. doi:10.1111/j.1540-627X.2007.00214.x.

Collier, P. 2007. *The Bottom Billion. Why the Poorest Countries are Failing and What Can Be Done about It*. New York: Oxford University Press.

Davidsson, P., and B. Honig. 2003. "The Role of Human and Social Capital among Nascent Entrepreneurs." *Journal of Business Venturing* 24: 419–435.

Davidsson, P., J. Recker, and F. von Briel. "External Enablement of New Venture Creation: A Framework." *Academy of Management Perspectives*. forthcoming.

Dutt, N., O. Hawn, E. Vidal, A. Chatterji, A. McGahan, and W. Mitchell. 2016. "How Open System Intermediaries Address Institutional Failures: The Case of Business Incubators in Emerging-Market Countries." *Academy of Management Journal* 59 (3): 818–840. doi:10.5465/amj.2012.0463.

Easterly, W. 2006. *The White Man's Burden: Why the West's Efforts to Aid the Rest Have Done so Much Ill and so Little Good*. New York: Oxford University Press.

Eisenhardt, K. M. 1989. "Building Theories from Case Study Research." *Academy of Management Review* 14: 532–550. doi:10.5465/amr.1989.4308385.

Eisenhardt, K. M. 1991. "Better Stories and Better Constructs: The Case for Rigor and Comparative Logic." *Academy of Management Review* 16: 620–627. doi:10.5465/amr.1991.4279496.

Eweje, G. 2006. "The Role of MNEs in Community Development Initiatives in Developing Countries." *Business and Society* 45 (2): 93–129. doi:10.1177/0007650305285394.

Fitton-Kane, V. 2008. "*Measuring Outcomes of REDP*." Unpublished MBA dissertation. Judge Business School, University of Cambridge.

Flick, U. 2009. *An Introduction to Qualitative Research*. London: Sage.

Fowler, A. 2000. "NGO Futures: Beyond Aid: NGDO Values and the Fourth Position." *Third World Quarterly* 21 (4): 589–603. doi:10.1080/713701065.

Freeman, R. E. 1984. *Strategic Management: A Stakeholder Approach*. Boston: Pitman/Ballinger.

Friedman, M. 1962. *Capitalism and Freedom*. Chicago, Il: University of Chicago Press.

Friedman, M. 1988. "The Social Responsibility of Business Is to Increase Its Profits." In *Ethical Issues in Business: A Philosophical Approach*, edited by T. Donaldson and P. H. Werhane, 218–219. Englewood Cliffs, NJ: Prentice Hall.

Frynas, J. G. 2008. "Corporate Social Responsibility and International Development: Critical Assessment." *Corporate Governance* 16 (4): 274–281. doi:10.1111/j.1467-8683.2008.00691.x.

Glaser, B., and A. Strauss. 1967. *The Discovery of Grounded Theory*. New York, NY: Aldine.
Graebner, M. E., and K. M. Eisenhardt. 2004. "The Seller's Side of the Story: Acquisition as Courtship and Governance as Syndicate in Entrepreneurial Firms." *Administrative Science Quarterly* 49: 366–403.
Grimaldi, R., and A. Grandi. 2005. "Business Incubators and New Venture Creation: An Assessment of Incubating Models." *Technovation* 25 (2): 111–121. doi:10.1016/S0166-4972(03)00076-2.
GroFin Impact Report. 2017. Available at http://www.grofin.com/wp-content/uploads/2018/05/GroFin-Impact-Report-2017.pdf
Hamann, R. 2006. "Can Business Make Decisive Contributions to Development? Towards a Research Agenda on Corporate Citizenship and Beyond." *Development Southern Africa* 23 (2): 175–195. doi:10.1080/03768350600707587.
Herrick, B., and C. P. Kindleberger. 1983. *Economic Development*. New York: McGraw-Hill.
Hirwa, I., and D. Mahadevia. 2004. *Gujarat Human Development Report*. Ahmedabad: Mahatma Gandhi Labour Institute.
Hitt, M. A., R. D. Ireland, S. M. Camp, and L. Sexton. 2001. "Strategic Entrepreneurship: Entrepreneurial Strategies for Wealth Creation." *Strategic Management Journal* 22 (6–7): 479–491. doi:10.1002/(ISSN)1097-0266.
Idemudia, U. 2008. "Conceptualising the CSR and Development Debate. Bridging Existing Analytical Gaps." *Journal of Corporate Citizenship* 29 (1): 91–110. doi:10.9774/GLEAF.4700.2008.sp.00011.
Ite, U. E. 2004. "Multinationals and Corporate Social Responsibility in Developing Countries: A Case Study of Nigeria." *Corporate Social Responsibility and Environmental Management* 11: 1–11. doi:10.1002/(ISSN)1535-3966.
Ite, U. E. 2005. "Poverty Reduction in Resource-Rich Developing Countries: What Have Multinational Corporations Got to Do with It?" *Journal of International Development* 17: 913–929. doi:10.1002/(ISSN)1099-1328.
Jensen, M. 2002. "Value Maximization, Stakeholder Theory and the Corporate Objective Function." *Business Ethics Quarterly* 12: 235–256. doi:10.2307/3857812.
Kabeer, N. 1999. "Resources, Agency and Achievements: Reflections on the Measurement of Women's Empowerment." *Development and Change* 30: 435–464. doi:10.1111/dech.1999.30.issue-3.
Karnani, A. G. 2007. "Employment, Not Microcredit, Is the Solution." *Journal of Corporate Citizenship* 32: 23–28.
Khan, F., R. I. Westwood, and D. M. Boje. 2010. "'I Feel like A Foreign Agent': NGOs and Corporate Social Responsibility Interventions into Third World Child Labor." *Human Relations* 63: 1417–1438. doi:10.1177/0018726709359330.
King, S., H. Sintes, and M. Alemu. 2012. "Beyond Participation: Making Enterprise Development Really Work for Women." *Gender & Development* 20 (1): 129–144. doi:10.1080/13552074.2012.663638.
Kolk, A., and R. Van Tulder. 2006. "Poverty Alleviation as Business Strategy? Evaluating Commitments of Frontrunner Multinational Corporations." *World Development* 34: 789–901. doi:10.1016/j.worlddev.2005.10.005.
Lawrence, T. B., R. Suddaby, and B. Leca, Eds. 2009. *Institutional Work: Actors and Agency in Institutional Studies of Organizations*. Cambridge: Cambridge University Press.
Laxmana, P., and P. Ishwara. 2008. "Entrepreneurial Promotion through EDP." *The ICFAI Journal of Entrepreneurship Development* 5: 61–68.
Mair, J., and I. Marti. 2009. "Entrepreneurship in and around Institutional Voids." *Journal of Business Venturing* 24: 419–435. doi:10.1016/j.jbusvent.2008.04.006.
Margolis, J. D., and J. P. Walsh. 2003. "Misery Loves Companies: Rethinking Social Initiatives by Business." *Administrative Science Quarterly* 48: 268–305. doi:10.2307/3556659.
Marsden, C. 2000. "The New Corporate Citizenship of Big Business: Part of the Solution to Sustainability." *Business and Society Review* 105: 9–25. doi:10.1111/0045-3609.00062.
Matten, D., and A. Crane. 2005. "Corporate Citizenship: Towards an Extended Theoretical Conceptualisation." *Academy of Management Review* 30: 166–179. doi:10.5465/amr.2005.15281448.
Mayoux, L. 1996. "Alternative Vision or Utopian Fantasy: Cooperation, Empowerment and Women's Cooperative Development in India." *International Journal of Development* 8: 211–228.
Meyer, K. E. 2004. "Perspectives on Multinational Enterprises in Developing Countries." *Journal of International Business Studies* 35: 259–276. doi:10.1057/palgrave.jibs.8400084.
Nahapiet, J., and S. Ghoshal. 1998. "Social Capital, Intellectual Capital and the Organizational Advantage." *Academy of Management Review* 23 (2): 242–266. doi:10.5465/amr.1998.533225.
Naudé, W. 2010. "Entrepreneurship, Developing Countries and Development Economics: Approaches and Insights." *Small Business Economics* 34: 1–12. doi:10.1007/s11187-009-9198-2.
Naudé, W. 2010b. *Promoting Entrepreneurship in Developing Countries: Policy Changes*. Policy Brief 4. Helsinki: United Nations University World Institute for Development Economics Research.
Newell, P., and J. G. Frynas. 2007. "Beyond CSR? Business, Poverty and Social Justice; an Introduction." *Third World Quarterly* 28: 669–681. doi:10.1080/01436590701336507.
Oxfam. 2011. *The Enterprise Development Programme*. Oxford: Oxfam.
Oxfam, 2016. "The Oxfam Enterprise Development Programme." Annual Report. Available at http://edp.oxfam.org.uk/wp-content/uploads/2017/04/EDP-Annual-Report-2016.pdf
Patton, M. 2002. *Qualitative Research and Evaluation*. Thousand Oaks, CA: Sage.
Phan, P. H., D. Siegel, and M. Wright. 2005. "Science Parks and Incubators: Observations, Synthesis and Future Research." *Journal of Business Venturing* 20: 165–182. doi:10.1016/j.jbusvent.2003.12.001.
Prahalad, C. K. 2004. *The Fortune at the Bottom of the Pyramid*. Upper Saddle River, NJ: Wharton School Press.

SAB. 2017. "Tholoana Enterprise Programme." Available at http://sabfoundation.co.za/wp-content/uploads/2018/10/Tholoana-Enterprise-Programme-Impact-Report-2018-1.pdf

SAB. 2018. SAB Foundation Annual Report. Available at http://sabfoundation.co.za/wp-content/uploads/2018/10/SAB-Foundation-Annual-Report-2018.pdf

Sen, A. 1999. *Development as Freedom*. Oxford: Oxford University Press.

Sentana, E., R. Gonzàlez, J. Gascó, and J. Llopis. 2017. "The Social Profitability of Business Incubators: A Measurement Proposal." *Entrepreneurship and Regional Development* 29 (1–2): 116–136. doi:10.1080/08985626.2016.1255436.

Servon, L. J. 1997. "Microenterprise Programs in U. S. Inner Cities: Economic Development or Social Welfare." *Economic Development Quarterly* 11: 166–180. doi:10.1177/089124249701100205.

Servon, L. J., and J. P. Doshna. 2000. "Microenterprise and the Economic Development Toolkit: A Small Part of the Big Picture." *Journal of Developmental Entrepreneurship* 5: 183–208.

Shane, S., and S. Venkataraman. 2000. "The Promise of Entrepreneurship as a Field of Research." *Academy of Management Review* 25: 217–226.

SIDA. 1996. *Aid Dependency: Causes, Symptoms and Remedies*. Stockholm: Swedish International Development Agency.

Stiglitz, J. 2002. *Globalisation and Its Discontents*. New York: W. W. Norton.

Tasavori, M., and R. R. Sinkovics. 2011. "Socially Entrepreneurial Behaviour of Multinational Corporations: Are MNCs 'social Entrepreneurs'?" In *Firm-Level Internationalization, Regionalism and Globalization*, edited by E. Huston, R. R. Sinkovics, and J. Berill, 397–411. London: Palgrave Macmillan.

Tavory, I., and S. Timmermans. 2014. *Abductive Analysis: Theorizing from Qualitative Research*. Chicago, IL: Chicago University Press.

TCSRD. 2016. "Tata Chemicals Society for Rural Development." Annual Report 2015–2016. Available at http://www.tcsrd.org/upload/pdf/tcsrd-annual-report-2015-16.pdf

UNDP. 2010. The MDGs. Everyone's Business. New York: UNDP.

Timmermans, S., and I. Tavory. 2012. "Theory Construction in Qualitative Research: From Grounded Theory to Abductive Analysis." *Sociological Theory* 30 (3): 167–186. doi:10.1177/0735275112457914.

UN. 2015. "Transforming Our World: The 2030 Agenda for Sustainable Development." United Nations General Assembly http://www.un.org/ga/search/view_doc.asp?symbol=A/RES/70/1andLang=E Accessed 29 August 2018

UNDP. 2004a. *Partnerships for Small ED*. New York: United Nations Development Programme.

UNDP. 2004b. *Unleashing Entrepreneurship. Making Business Work for the Poor*. New York: United Nations Development Programme.

UNDP. 2008. *Creating Value for All: Strategies for Doing Business with the Poor*. New York: United Nations Development Programme.

Utting, P. 2005. "Corporate Responsibility and the Movement of Business." *Development in Practice* 15: 375–388. doi:10.1080/09614520500075797.

Valente, M., and A. Crane. 2010. "Public Responsibility and Private Enterprise in Developing Countries." *California Management Review* 52 (3): 52–77. doi:10.1525/cmr.2010.52.3.52.

Visser, W. 2008. "Corporate Social Responsibility in Developing Countries." In *The Oxford Handbook of Corporate Social Responsibility*, edited by A. Crane, A. McWilliams, D. Matten, J. Moon, and D. S. Siegal, 473–502. Oxford: Oxford University Press.

WBCSD. 2004. *Doing Business with the Poor. A Field Guide*. Switzerland: World Business Council for Sustainable Development.

Yin, R. K. 2014. *Case Study Research and Applications: Design and Methods*. Newbury Park, CA: Sage.

Crafting markets and fostering entrepreneurship within underserved communities: social ventures and clean energy provision in Asia

Sanjay Jain and James Koch

ABSTRACT

In this paper, we conceptualize markets for underserved communities as being constituted by local institutions that reflect the modalities of these individual's lives. Using data on the activities that four social ventures across India, Bangladesh and Cambodia have undertaken to craft new markets for their clean energy solutions, we highlight how these actors incorporate their technologies within native material understandings, develop transaction systems consistent with resident consumption practices and entrench their organizations into the existing infrastructure. We term these processes *indigenizing, microprovisioning* and *codeveloping*, respectively. In meshing local context as part of their market crafting efforts, these ventures seed micro-entrepreneurship activity, generate employment for locals as well as improve standards of living within the community through the provision of productivity enhancing products and services. Our findings highlight the significance of engaging with local institutions as part of market crafting efforts in these scenarios. This paper offers insights that contribute to the sociology of markets, and poverty reduction via entrepreneurship literatures as well as have important practical and policy implications.

Introduction

Over the past two decades, there has been increased recognition in the policy, practitioner and academic communities of the need to further develop markets for the 4 billion people on this planet, fully 65% of the world's population, that live on an annual per capita income less than $3000 in purchasing power parity terms (Hammond et al. 2007). Development actors from the World Bank to many international and local NGO's, have emphasized the integral role that markets can play in attaining sustained increases in living standards across the world (Mair and Marti 2009; Si et al. 2015). Multinational firms, confronting limited growth opportunities in the more advanced economies, are also devoting increased attention to this large pool of 'consumers' as a potentially lucrative opportunity (London and Hart 2010). And a growing number of scholars, spanning the domains of strategy (Prahalad 2004; Karnani 2007; Ansari, Munir, and Gregg 2012), marketing (Viswanathan 2007), entrepreneurship (Mair and Marti 2009; Webb et al. 2009; Bruton, Ahlstrom, and Si 2015; George et al. 2015; Janssen, Fayolle, and Wuilaume 2018), development (Anderson and Ronteau 2017) and economics (Banerjee and Duflo 2011), have initiated a vibrant intellectual discourse focused on building markets in these contexts. More generally, devising mechanisms to provide products and services for this segment of humanity – referred to here as underserved communities – is not only a matter of practical necessity (Mahajan and Banga 2006) but also is a source of fresh theoretical insight related to processes of market development (McCloskey 2010; Christensen, Ojomo, and Dillon 2019).

In this paper, we ask: *How do social ventures craft markets for underserved communities?* To answer this, we examine the activities that four such ventures, across India, Bangladesh and Cambodia, have undertaken to build markets for their clean energy solutions directed at their communities. Theoretically, we rely on the literature in economic sociology and institutional economics, which suggests that markets are complex bundles of institutions that define 'terms of action' within an organizational field (North 1990; Rodrick, Subramanian, and Trebbi 2004; Greif 2006; Acemoglu and Robinson 2013). This includes such elements of social organization as property rights, governance structures (i.e. laws and norms), rules of exchange and conceptions of control that, taken together, enable transactions between buyers and sellers (Fligstein 2001). Much of the prior work in this domain has emphasized the construction and improvement of formal institutions and top down initiatives in the development of markets (Aghion et al. 2016; Fligstein and Mara-Drita 1996; Grief 2006). More recently, researchers have drawn attention to informal institutions and local context in encouraging entrepreneurship and development (Ahlstrom, Bruton, and Yeh 2008; Anderson and Ronteau 2017; Bruton, Ahlstrom, and Li 2010; McCloskey 2006, 2016). However, we submit that our understanding of how markets are crafted in these contexts remains limited. It is this theoretical gap that we address in this paper.

We begin with the premise that a more sociologically informed, process-based account of market development within underserved communities requires an appreciation of the local understandings, practices and infrastructure that suffuse the economic lives of individuals living in these contexts (Banerjee and Duflo 2011; Mair, Martí, and Ventresca 2012). We refer to these cognitive, cultural, material and socio-political arrangements that are encoded in people's stock of practical knowledge as *local institutions*. In order to explicate the relationship between these actors and the local institutions that they encounter, we devise an empirical design that involves examining the histories and activities of four for-profit social ventures in India, Bangladesh and Cambodia that were explicitly initiated to provide clean energy to these poorer segments of society. These ventures are a particularly noteworthy given their attempts to address a significant need – energy provision – in an environmentally sound and operationally viable manner. Over time, each of these ventures has gained traction (some more than others) though all of them faced, and continue to face, considerable challenges in navigating and building these market spaces.

Our study explicates three key processes that these actors have engaged in as part of crafting these markets. They endeavor to incorporate their technologies within native material understandings, develop transaction systems that resonate with resident consumption practices and entrench their organizations into the existing infrastructure; processes that we term *indigenizing, microprovisioning* and *codeveloping*, respectively. Moreover, in meshing local context as part of their market crafting efforts, these ventures seed micro-entrepreneurship activity, generate employment for locals as well as improve standards of living within the community through the provision of productivity enhancing products and services (Ahlstrom 2010). In providing a culturally informed account of market development for underserved communities and highlighting the nuanced relationship between actors and the institutions with which they engage, we contribute to theory in the sociology of markets and poverty reduction via entrepreneurship literatures. We also contribute to practice and policy by providing fresh insights to the discourse on underserved markets and how to serve these better, thereby improving the standards of living of poorer communities.

Theory development

In recent years, both economic sociologists and institutional theorists have contributed significantly to our understanding of markets by conceptualizing them as complex arrays of rules and arrangements that configure fields and set the 'rules of the game' (Fligstein 2001; North 1990). Markets are typically constituted by formal structures such as legal systems, property rights and rules of exchange. Together these arrangements serve to provide common understandings, delineate forms of competition and stabilize laws and patterns of interaction that enable and constrain economic exchange among actors involved in the production, sale and consumption of goods or services. In highlighting the embeddedness of economic exchange (Granovetter 1985), one that is rooted in shared cognitions and concrete social relations (Zukin and DiMaggio 1990), this 'markets as institutions' perspective contrasts somewhat with the neo-classical economic depictions of markets as transactions between atomized actors. Viewing markets as assemblages of institutions that are socially constructed, agreed upon conjective facts and rules enables the tracking of their emergence, acceptance, and transformation over time (Garud, Jain, and Kumaraswamy 2002). However, given that much of the prior work in this domain has employed advanced economy examples as research sites, more attention has been given to formal institutions and the interactions unfolding among producers (and intermediaries) as they attempt to perpetuate their power and status via control of these arrangements (Fligstein and McAdam 2012; McCloskey 2010; Mokyr 1992; Podolny 1993; White 1981).

Even as scholars have turned their attention to examining the nature of markets in transition and emerging economies, a key theme that has emerged from the work of institutional economists is the absence or non-functioning nature of formal institutions and specialized intermediaries – - the existence of institutional 'voids' (Khanna and Palepu 2000; McMullen 2011). These voids manifest themselves as lack of information, scarcity of well-trained people, unbanked populations, weak rule of law, and an absence of effective mechanisms to enforce contracts, among others issues. They raise transaction costs (Coase 1960) and as a consequence significantly hinder market-type activity in these economies (De Soto 2000). This stream of research emphasizes the considerable challenges that actors confront when operating in spaces 'devoid' of institutions (Mair and Marti 2009). In addition, it examines alternate structures such as business groups that fill voids 'left by the missing institutions that normally underpin the efficient functioning of product, capital and labor markets' (Khanna and Rivkin 2001, 46–47). This view of institutions in emerging economies is consistent with the thinking of development economists who advocate the need to transpose formal institutional arrangements in these scenarios, that is, they largely advocate a top-down approach to market development (Sachs 2006). In summary, this line of thinking derives from earlier modernization theory (Rostow 1960), which characterizes these markets as being beset by institutional voids that need to be 'filled,' often with institutions imported whole cloth from developed economies, in order for them to function effectively.

More recently, an alternate reading of these markets has emerged which indicates that a useful starting point for understanding their institutional foundations requires adopting a micro-analytic orientation rooted in the daily realities of this segment of society. According to this perspective, these communities are suspended in webs of values, norms, rules and meanings, or local (often informal) institutions that both form the basis for social action and are partially of their own making (Geertz 1973). Local institutions, then, can be conceptualized as the modalities (Giddens 1984) or the grammar of the speech (Barley and Tolbert 1997; McCloskey 2016) that comprises these individuals' lives. This view highlights the significance of appreciating pre-existing indigenous arrangements, practices and typifications that delineate economic exchange in these communities (Stark 1996; Jain and Koch 2017). Indeed, these domains that have been construed as being beset by voids, are in fact animated by plural local arrangements that specify their own internal order (Biggart and Guillén 1999; Friedland and Alford 1991; Mair, Martí, and Ventresca 2012). In other words, these local institutions that have largely been rendered opaque by the institutional voids perspective, are in fact crucial to understanding market development activity in these contexts.

In articulating this viewpoint, we build on scholarship that has adopted a more grounded and proximate view of institutions and institutionalization processes (Barley and Tolbert 1997; Hallett and Ventresca 2006). This perspective draws its roots from symbolic interactionism (Goffman 1983) and structuration (Giddens 1984) and highlights the significance of bringing people and agency back into institutional analysis. It indicates that the local institutions within which a community is embedded manifest themselves as understandings, practices and infrastructure (DiMaggio 1997; Schatzki, Knorr-Cetina, and Von Savigny 2001; Jack and Anderson 2002; Viswanathan, Sridharan, and Ritchie 2010) that emerge through processes of actor interaction and historical accretion. They provide the raw materials and guidelines for the social interaction that underpin the functioning of markets; in turn these local institutions themselves are reimagined and constructed through social interaction (Hallett and Ventresca 2006). In drawing attention to the lived experiences of actors, this perspective contrasts with the predominant focus in the 'markets as institutions' literature on the macro-dynamics unfolding in organizational fields.

Recent research in development economics and subsistence markets mirrors the use of such a 'micro' orientation. Banerjee and Duflo's (2011) pioneering research significantly details – through the use of household surveys – the lives of the extremely poor, in terms of the choices they face, the constraints they grapple with and the challenges they meet. Many interesting and counter-intuitive insights emerge from this work: for example, the poor spend surprising large proportions of their income on entertainment (i.e. weddings and festivals) and not on food. Moreover these individuals place a high value on remaining close to their social network, so much so that they forgo opportunities to augment their income via temporary migration to other regions (Munshi and Rosenzweig 2006). In a similar vein, Viswanathan's (2007) perceptive scholarship on subsistence markets highlights how resource-poor poverty contexts are typically network rich in face-to-face interactions. Functioning in these conditions requires cultivating trusting relationships that have a medium-to-long term perspective. Employing an explicitly institutional lens, Mair, Martí, and Ventresca (2012) highlight how local political, cultural and religious forces intersect with one another to create market spaces that exclude or marginalize the participation of women. Their insightful work goes on to detail the on-the-ground activity that BRAC, a prominent NGO in Bangladesh, has engaged in over the past few decades to reconfigure these spaces as part of building inclusive markets. This growing body of research accentuates the importance of viewing these communities as being embedded in a pre-existing set of local institutions that need to be accounted for while engaging with them (see also McKague, Zietsma, and Oliver 2015; Anderson and Obeng 2017).

We build upon and extend this perspective in our paper to examine scenarios in which social ventures attempt to introduce goods and services for this segment of society. Our study empirically examines the activities that four such ventures have performed as part of crafting markets for their clean energy solutions. We identify three processes integral to this effort. *Indigenizing* refers to how social ventures attend to native material understandings in designing their technological offerings to be acceptable and relevant to these communities. *Microprovisioning* involves gaining a deep appreciation of resident consumption practices to develop transaction systems that deliver goods in miniscule quantities while charging extremely low prices and providing high levels of service. Finally, *codeveloping* entails both leveraging and upgrading the local infrastructure as part of crafting organizational forms that comprehend and respond to the needs of the native clientele. In engaging in these processes, actors often demonstrate considerable ingenuity in crafting not just material artifacts but also exchange systems and organizational structures that are appropriate for and acceptable to these communities (Prabhu and Jain 2015).

Furthermore, we demonstrate how these social ventures, while engaging in market crafting, provide employment and generate entrepreneurial activity within these communities (see also Ahlstrom 2010). Such entrepreneurship comes in many different forms – upstream via the provision of supplies as well as downstream in terms of sales and service related to the clean energy solution. In essence, these ventures seed an entrepreneurial ecosystem around the products and services that they offer to these people. Moreover, the provision of energy inherently improves productivity within these communities via the extension of working hours that enable additional income and consumption, contributing to an improved standard of living among these people (Vernet et al. 2019). Overall, these dynamics point to another path by which entrepreneurship – and the reduction of poverty – can be fostered within these communities. We further expand on these insights below.

Methodology

The focus of our research study – understanding the crafting of markets for underserved communities – suggested that the use of qualitative methods would be particularly pertinent for illuminating underlying processes and building theory around this understudied phenomenon (Yin 1994). In particular, our analytic strategy involved writing detailed organizational histories for a carefully selected set of ventures in order to trace the ground-level activities that they have engaged in as part of crafting markets for their chosen constituencies. This phenomenon has received relatively little attention until now, and thus represents a fallow opportunity for novel theory development (Bamberger and Pratt 2010).

Specifically, we engaged in theoretical sampling (Glaser and Strauss 1967) and developed case histories for four social ventures – SELCO and Husk Power Systems in India, Grameen Shakti in Bangladesh and Kamworks in Cambodia – each started as a for-profit firm with an explicit mandate to simultaneously balance social mission, environmental sustainability and financial viability even while pioneering the provision of clean energy to people in off-grid communities (Schillebeeckx et al. 2012; Koch and Hammond 2013). This assemblage of operating attributes made these social ventures 'strategic research sites' (Bijker, Hughes, and Pinch 1987) whose activities captured integral aspects of the phenomena being studied (see Table 1 for more details on these ventures). Moreover, differences in technology, geography and years of operating experience across the ventures, provides us with a basis for generalizing our emerging theoretical insights (Eisenhardt and Graebner 2007).

Our focus on these four ventures is rooted in the deep and ongoing history of interaction that the authors had with each of them over the past decade, which enabled us to assemble an unusually rich dataset anchored around three different sources of information: *interviews* with the founders as well as other principals and stakeholders of these ventures (e.g. mentors, funders, and senior team members). In particular, we had strong access to the founders of three of these ventures (Selco, Husk Power & Kamworks), and as a consequence were able to conduct multiple semi-structured interviews with each of them as well as collect clarifying insights through subsequent personal communications. Our dataset included a total of 12 founder interviews of varying

Table 1. Profiles of the social ventures studied.

	Huskpower Systems	SELCO	Grameen Shakti	Kamworks
Country/Region of operation	India(Bihar)	India(Karnataka)	Bangladesh	Cambodia
Year started	2007	1995	1996	2006
Energy source	Small scale power plants that convert rice husk to electricity	Solar	Solar	Solar lamps
Number of installations completed	80 biomass plants that serve over 250 villages (30,000 households)	More than 135,000 solar home lighting systems; $1.75 m revenue in 2009	Over 1 million solar lighting systems installed as of 2013	Provided energy services to over 15,000 people
Early funding sources	Founders savings + money won at various business plan competitions; several impact investors, Shell Foundation	$1 m loan from IFC + Grants from World Bank; subsequently secured equity investments	Grants from IFC and Global Environment Fund	Grants($175K seed from World Bank)
Key awards/ Recognition	International Ashden Award for Sustainable Energy (2011)	Harish Hande won Ramon Magsaysay Award (Asian Nobel Prize) in 2011	Solar World Einstein Award (2010)	The Moonlight received two design awards, the Toon van Tuijl Designprijs, at the Dutch Design Awards (2008) and the Feel the Planet Earth, CIFIAL Design Award (2008).

Table 2. Interview data.

	Huskpower Systems	SELCO	Kamworks	Total
Founders	4	5	3	12
Employees	1	2		3
Stakeholders	2	1	1	4
Time Frame	2009–14	2008–14	2011–13	19

length, with the average lasting approximately 1.5 hours. These conversations took place at different points in time, covering a seven-year period 2008–2014 (see Table 2). This enabled us to track the progress of these ventures, from an insider perspective, in significant depth. In addition we conducted seven additional interviews with other key individuals associated with these organizations that served to provide a more rounded perspective of the activities that these ventures were engaged in. While a majority of our interviews (11) were recorded and transcribed, for the balance, the interviewers took detailed notes that were then incorporated into our dataset.[1]

In addition, two of the ventures (Kamworks and Husk Power Systems) participated in an intensive two-week university-based entrepreneurship incubator program at which the authors were facilitators In this instance, a variety of pedagogical interactions that included business planning exercises, workshops, poster-sessions, and presentations, allowed us to obtain an in-depth understanding of the challenges faced by these ventures and ways in which these were being addressed. The other two ventures (Selco and Grameen Shakti) were winners of a prestigious award in the social venture space, and through our contacts, the authors were able to access detailed information on the functioning of these firms that included rich descriptions of their technology solutions, organizational capabilities, funding sources, milestones achieved, market penetration (units sold), impact, and financial viability. More generally, these interactions provided us with a trove of internal company documents pertaining to their ground operations, business models and value chain activities that were subsequently integrated into the emergent data stream.

In addition, we collected an extensive amount of secondary data that included published interviews with the principals in various outlets, reports from development agencies, academic articles and cases about the ventures, scientific journals that detailed the technologies deployed by them and related media coverage. These materials enabled us to gain a more comprehensive understanding of these social ventures, besides serving as a useful validity check. Equally importantly, they provided us with valuable details about the institutional context in which these ventures were situated, information that we supplemented with a broader reading about the socio-cultural-political context of these regions.

In terms of data analysis, the first step was to organize the rich streams of data that we had generated into chronological histories for each of the four ventures. In particular, we included all of their interactions with the community that could broadly be construed as being associated with crafting markets. Next, we engaged in a process of creating first order codes (Van Mannen, 1979) as a means of systematically classifying these activities. Figure 1 provides a schematic overview of this analytic process. Here, we followed procedures suggested by Miles and Huberman (1984), to develop codes that provide descriptive labels for the different market crafting activities that we observed in our data. We employed a pooled logic approach to theory building that treats each case as being part of a larger sample from which patterns are discerned (Yin 1994). In other words, data from all four cases was used to create our first order codes. As codes were labeled and developed, we returned to the data to assess their categorical fidelity. This iterative process resulted in the first order codes identified in Figure 1.

After assigning first order codes to all of the activities in our dataset, we performed axial coding (Strauss and Corbin 1990) in which we aggregated related first order codes to specify higher-level domains of market crafting activity that these ventures engaged in. In our particular case, the open codes cohered around three salient dimensions: Technology design, business model configuration and organization/ ecosystem assembly. After identifying these dimensions, we reorganized our chronological histories to

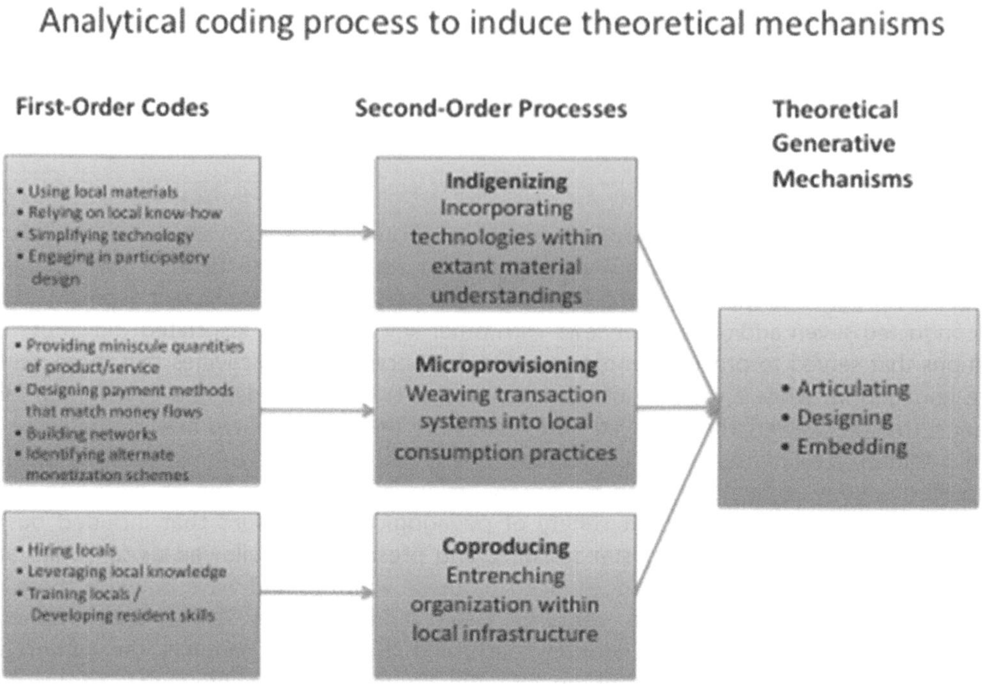

Figure 1. Analytical coding process to induce theoretical mechanisms.

reflect these emergent categories. The reworked case narrative for each social venture was over 50 pages in length (single-spaced). We then used these to discern both the context as well as underlying patterns of activity that would enable us to more carefully characterize the nature of the processes unfolding in each of these categorical domains. We grappled with the terminology that would accurately describe the context and the processes, generating and discarding many options along the way before settling on the following options. In terms of context, the local institutions that we identified were: *material understandings*, by which we mean the local's extant knowledge of tools and techniques that they deployed to craft solutions to meet their daily needs; *consumption practices* that refer to the manner in which the exchange and use of products and services takes place among these individuals; and, *local infrastructure* which alludes to the physical arrangements, social networks and capabilities that reside within these communities. Taken together, these represented key cognitive, normative and structural elements that constitute the economic lives of these communities. Associated with each of these local institutions was a market crafting process that we labeled *indigenizing, microprovisioning* and *co-developing* respectively. These labels capture what we believe were the most relevant and distinctive facets of the processes unfolding within each of these domains. Overall, this form of inductive theorizing is akin to climbing the 'ladder of analytical abstraction' (Carney 1990). Figure 1 provides a schematic of this progression from raw data to first-order codes to aggregate categories and finally, to overarching processes – incorporating and generating relevant theory along the way.

Findings

Indigenizing: incorporating technologies within native material understandings

An important undertaking for actors operating in these contexts involved locating their technologies within native material understandings. From the social ventures perspective, crafting a fit between the possibilities offered by the material artifact and the knowledge structures of these individuals, was key to gaining acceptance for their proposed solution (Hargadon and Douglas 2001). Along these lines, the social ventures we studied spent considerable amounts of effort understanding extant energy consumption in these communities and then figuring out how their proposed offerings could gain approval within these contexts. In most cases, the option currently being employed – ranging from firewood to kerosene – was costly, primitive, inefficient, environmentally unsustainable and represented a health hazard. Yet these technologies were deeply ingrained as a result of the community's long history of use of these alternatives. By contrast, the clean energy solution being crafted by the social venture was by definition novel and as a consequence, faced steep comprehension barriers (Douglas 1986). So even though these solutions represented a marked improvement, across multiple dimensions, over the options being used, there also remained significant barriers to overcome in order for them to gain acceptance. Given this, how did these ventures address this challenge?

The solution that these ventures employed involved *indigenizing* their technologies. By this we imply that these actors focused on matching their product/service offering with knowledge structures already existent in the community, thereby increasing its comprehensibility and acceptability (Hargadon and Douglas 2001). One mechanism they employed for doing this involved devising technologies whose production or use relied on materials and knowledge available within the native context (such as the use of locally available feedstock, or the employment of locals in assembling and servicing the solution). Doing so ensured that these individuals had prior awareness of the underlying elements constituting the product/service offering that made them comfortable using it. Moreover, such indigenization increased the long-term prospects of the technology given that the community was less dependent on outsiders for its ongoing provision and maintenance. Overall, these ventures deployed their deep understanding of local patterns of energy consumption to design technological solutions that invoked a sense of familiarity among community members, that is, they were (relatively) seamlessly weaved into their lived experiences.

A particularly vivid example of indigenizing comes from Huskpower Systems. When Gyanesh Pandey and Ratnesh Yadav, two of the cofounders of this venture, started examining energy solutions for rural Bihar, they initially invested about four months of research in examining Jatropha-based biodiesel, a plant indigenous to the Indian countryside and very much in vogue at the time. However, the underlying economics and supply chain issues led them to conclude finally that this option would not work. They looked at wind and solar as well and reached similar conclusions. Pandey recalled:

> *"Biomass was the only option left. If you know anything about Indian villages, no form of biomass was left unutilized, except for rice husk. And so we decided to focus on that."*

In zeroing in on rice husk (the outer kernel of the rice plant) they identified an input that was grown abundantly in the villages that they came from, but was inedible. Moreover, the high silica content made rice husk unfit for use as animal fodder or household fuel. As a consequence, it was typically discarded. While the duo heard that others had tried to use rice husk to generate electricity, using a technology called biomass gasification that had existed since the Second World War, these efforts had not met with success. Rather, the prevalent gasifier systems operated in a dual-fuel mode, where the gas produced was used in conjunction with 35–50 percent diesel to generate power.[2] The team wondered whether they could get the gasifier system to work in single-fuel mode without any diesel. Acknowledging that the dirty gas produced by rice husk could clog the engine, they designed a process whereby the engine would be manually cleaned on a regular basis to prevent such clogs, thereby enabling the single-fuel mode to work. In order to test their solution, they had a gasifier constructed at a local workshop and then procured a cheap compressed natural gas engine from a small supplier, which they modified to suit their purpose. What had previously been an unyielding goal took the venture less than five months to realize, once the founders figured out their path to indigenization.

The rice-husk based biomass miniplants that Huskpower crafted provided power using a fuel source that was abundantly available in these communities and with which the locals were familiar. Moreover, the production of the plants as well as their ongoing operation relied on indigenously available knowhow. In particular, by designing the plants to be manually operated and monitored, thus eschewing the use of complex feedback loops ubiquitous to such systems, Huskpower was able to simplify their electricity delivery model so that they could employ locals who did not need training beyond that provided at the local facility. As Manoj Sinha, a co-founder, put it:

> *"A good way to test your technology is to ask if it can be operated by a local hire, with minimal training of say 3 to 6 months. That's how we approach technology: it is about making it as simple as possible."*

The above description also draws attention to the manner in which Huskpower created an ecosystem around each plant by providing income generation opportunities to local farmers who supplied them with rice husk and small manufacturers who provided them with equipment for their gasifiers. Additionally, rather than try to dispose of the char that was left over from the gasification process at each plant, they devised a way to roll it into unscented incense sticks. Local village women were trained for this task by a non-governmental organization (NGO) set up by the venture. Huskpower then sold the incense sticks to companies who added various fragrances and sold the incense in the local market under their own brands.

This vignette vividly highlights how successful social ventures attend to native material understandings in designing their technological offerings so as to be acceptable and relevant to the local people. These initiatives are reminiscent of efforts to craft 'appropriate' technologies as chronicled within an earlier discourse in development studies (Schumacher 1973; Dunn 1979). They can involve deploying older technologies that address the current needs of these communities. In a similar vein, these ventures expend considerable effort in 'simplifying' their offerings both in terms of product and process, so that they match with resident knowledge levels. At a broader level, this requires these actors to adopt a mindset that emphasizes 'fitting in' rather than 'pushing the envelope' that is typically associated with technology development in advanced economies. Having said that, it is important to note that even as ventures insert their artifacts into preexisting material understandings, the incorporation of these offerings within these communities is likely to precipitate change – especially in the long term – in local understandings, often in unanticipated ways (Hargadon and Douglas 2001).

Microprovisioning: weaving transaction systems into local consumption practices

A second key task for actors involves devising transaction systems for their product or service that are compatible with consumption practices prevalent in these communities. Here, we employ the term consumption to denote two key dimensions, purchase and use, thereby highlighting both its exchange and utilitarian facets (Warde 2005). These consumption practices are typically poorly understood by outsiders, partly due to ignorance but also because they often differ dramatically from patterns of consumption observed in more developed economies. For the social venture, however, gaining an understanding of these practices and then weaving their proposed transaction systems into this existing fabric is an important step towards gaining traction for their initiatives.

On this front, an integral factor limiting usage in these contexts is the acute resource constraints that members of the community experienced (Mair and Marti 2009). Moreover, there is often a high degree of 'lumpiness' in their income flows that further impacted their ability to pay. Within these rather significant constraints, the willingness to spend on energy appeared to be quite high, ranking second only to food in terms of a category of expenditure (Legros et al. 2009). However, the up-front cost for the clean energy solutions proffered by these ventures was typically prohibitively expensive. It was by no means clear if these individuals had the ability to make a large investment upfront or that they would commit to making payments for the service over time.

Given this set of considerations, what kinds of transaction systems did these actors craft and deploy within these communities?

A key step for the social ventures we studied involved their designing systems that provided members within the community with quantities of the service that they could pay for and were simultaneously economically viable for the venture. Given the miniscule quantities of product/service consumed in each transaction, we refer to such practices as *microprovisioning*. In crafting such systems, these ventures expended considerable effort understanding patterns of energy consumption among local households that provided them with insights into their basic minimum needs. They also attempted to uncover practices associated with the flows of money in these communities. These anthropological incursions provided ventures with a notion of the micro-scale at which their business operations needed to function. Armed with a microprovisioning mindset, these actors then designed transaction systems that aligned with the consumption patterns as well as spending practices of these households. Finally, these ventures enrolled other local actors into their systems, building new networks within these communities as a consequence. In creating transaction systems that were synchronized with the lived experiences of these individuals, these actors enhanced acceptability of their systems within these contexts. We illustrate the process of microprovisioning through an example below.

In the case of SELCO, a key challenge that founder Harish Hande encountered early on involved arranging a source of financing for potential consumers to purchase solar panels. Through ongoing conversations with village locals, Harish came up with an insight that proved crucial to his market crafting efforts. As he put it:

> *"One of the best financial lessons that I learnt was from a street vendor who told me that she can afford to pay INR 10 (20 cents) a day, but would find it difficult to pay INR 300 (US$ 6) every month! This was when I realized that to sell solar lights; the poor need to be provided with financing such that payback patterns were synchronized with their income patterns."*

Based on this insight, SELCO designed financial packages for end users to purchase solar products based on their cash flows, income cycles and spending and living habits. For example if the borrower was a farmer, payment was done in relation to the harvest schedule (this could be quarterly, half yearly or yearly, depending on the type of crop cycle the farmer had), street vendors paid on a daily basis, and women working from home paid according to their product sales. In some cases, loan repayment was deducted from the proceeds of crop sales, with no cash transaction involved between user and lender.

Moreover, SELCO needed to go further to get this transaction system to work – it needed to find a loan provider. However, organizing financing from the banking network in rural India for the purchase of solar panels was difficult given that their mandate was to provide loans for income-generating activities. After two and a half years of effort that included the SELCO staff organizing field trips for the bank officials to demonstrate how solar lights made a difference to the livelihood of the rural poor, the venture was finally able to convince the Malaprabha Grameen Bank to sanction $30,000 for financing 100 solar lights. In building linkages between local actors and residents, SELCO reconfigured the native institutional landscape to enable the crafting of a market for solar energy within these communities.

In addition SELCO also created a network of entrepreneurs within these communities. These individuals ran a micro enterprise that comprised of charging and renting out solar lanterns – which ran on batteries charged by the solar panels – to village vendors and households on a daily basis. The lanterns were fully charged during the day, delivered to consumers in the evening so that they could enjoy clean and efficient lighting – and generate revenues – at night and then returned/collected for recharge in the morning. As Harish recounted the experience of one particularly enterprising entrepreneur:

> *"This guy the entrepreneur (in Hassan) started with 30 lamps and put the solar charging station on the roof of his house that would charge the batteries used in these lamps. He would charge the batteries daily and rent the lamps to the vendors at 5.30 p.m. Then around 9.30 p.m. to 10.00 p.m., he would collect the lamps back and a rent of INR*

12 per lamp. The vendors would thus save INR 2-3 per day since they were earlier spending INR 15 on kerosene. Soon he purchased another 30 and then another lot of 30. Now, he felt the need to purchase a tempo to carry the batteries around and convey them to the vendors and eventually employed two people to transport the batteries. Then one day he came back to us saying that his technicians were getting exhausted lifting so many batteries daily – it would be of help if we could make the batteries lighter. We went back to the drawing board and designed lighter batteries – it's amazing how he made us realize a fundamental problem and led us to solve it."

This pay–per–use model, where entrepreneurs bought the technology and charged customers a tiny cut of their daily cash flow to use it, represented a truly innovative way of bringing affordable lighting services to members within this community. Over the years SELCO helped to generate a number of entrepreneurs who provided solar lighting to street vendors, home based workers and small businesses.

This example illustrate how a profound understanding of local consumption practices is critical for these ventures to design transaction systems that have a high probability of acceptance within these communities, that is, ones that can form the underpinnings of an enduring market. This typically requires these actors to develop a deep appreciation of microprovisioning, which is the delivering of goods in miniscule quantities while charging extremely low prices and providing high levels of service, in order to engender acceptance and trust among these people. In doing so, these ventures literally bring the good to the community member's doorstep, that is, they weave it as seamlessly as possible into their existing consumption fabric. Added to this, these transaction systems are often designed with the explicit intent that they not be exploitative of the communities in which they are engaged (Ansari, Munir, and Gregg 2012). In other words, making significant profits through such transaction systems is perceived as being problematic. Ideally, these transaction mechanisms interact with local practices and norms in a manner that initiates a mutually reinforcing cycle – one that augments the income and purchasing capacity of residents that, in turn, enables expansion of the micro-provisioning system.

Codeveloping: entrenching the organization within the local infrastructure

A third key task that ventures engage in involves integrating their organizational forms with the extant infrastructure of the communities in which they operate. By infrastructure, we refer to the institutional arrangements, socio-political configurations as well as traditions and informal ties that collectively constitute resident 'terms of action' (Fligstein 2001; Van de Ven and Garud 1989) and reflect a community's capabilities and accepted rule sets (Garud and Ahlstrom 1997; Sen 1999). As such, this infrastructure defines power hierarchies, opportunity structures and interaction rules, that is, it establishes key facets of the context within which the transaction of goods takes place (Jain and Sharma 2013).

The social ventures that we tracked typically found significant elements of the infrastructure, and in particular, formal rules and arrangements, existed in various states of dysfunction (De Soto 2000; Sainath 1996) that were often precipitated by the acute resource shortages prevalent in these areas. As examples, most of these communities were characterized by sparse distribution and retailing networks, severely restricting modalities to transact. In a similar vein, formal technical and managerial capabilities were typically scarce in these communities, limiting possibilities to organize. However, in their place, numerous ground rules, customs, power relationships and influence structures peppered the landscape. So while at a surface level, the key actors within this landscape included regional governments, educational institutes and developmental organizations, their influence was often supplanted by such actors as resident governance assemblages, kinship networks and respected individuals as well as women decision makers in households who, due to local customs, were often invisible or inaccessible to outsiders (cf. Ahlstrom and Ding 2014). This posed a two-fold challenge for the ventures. Not only did they have to decode the composition and nature of the intricately intertwined local infrastructure in order to build relationships and trust with these actors, they also needed to get involved in infrastructure building activities in order to ensure smooth ongoing functioning of their operations. How did these actors address this set of issues?

Our study indicates that these ventures engaged in a process we term *codeveloping* as part of their interaction with the extant local infrastructure. This comprised two related subprocesses. On the one hand, these actors designed their organizations to be 'home-grown', i.e. they tapped into the resources and networks available in these communities. Leveraging the local environment enabled these venture to mesh (relatively) unobtrusively with the extant infrastructure and be viewed as trustworthy actors within these communities. In addition, these ventures typically also got involved in efforts to upgrade community capabilities (Sen 1999). This manifested itself in the organizing of training programs (and other educational initiatives) as well as the seeding of local entrepreneurial opportunities. More generally, these actors engaged in activities that enabled the venture to operate more effectively within this environment in the short run as well as became part of the community's infrastructure over the long term. These activities highlight the development orientation that ventures need to adopt while operating in these environments (Desa and Koch 2014; Porter and Kramer 2011). While such efforts can be resource consumptive, they contributed to the venture's standing in the community. These ventures, then, both leverage and contribute to the local infrastructure as part of establishing their operations. Below, we illustrate how a venture in our sample engaged in codeveloping activity.

Grameen Shakti, based in Bangladesh, began setting up rural technology centers in 2005 in order to move production from the capital to the villages and address problems of cost and logistics that had come to characterize the centralized company. In establishing these centers, the venture made a deliberate effort to involve women in both the adoption of renewable energy, and the installation and servicing of these systems. An understanding that much of its business took place in a women's world and the belief that women engineers were ideal role models for the young village women prompted this initiative. As Dipal Barua, co-founder of the organization remarked:

> *"Women are the main victims of the energy crisis. They are the ones who suffer most from indoor air pollution, drudgery, and a lack of time because of the onerous tasks of wood-gathering and cooking. We believe that women should be transformed from passive victims into active forces of good to bring changes in their lives and the communities in which they live."*

To facilitate this transformation, Grameen Shakti ensured that the technology centers – 45 of which existed in 2012 – were all managed by women engineers who lived, worked and trained in these communities. At these centers, unemployed village women who were typically between the age of 18–30 with at least 8 years of schooling and widowed or divorced, were recruited and then put through an initial 15-day course to learn how to assemble mobile phone chargers and to install and maintain solar home systems. With further education, they were able to repair these systems. Over 1,000 women technicians were trained through this program, and they were instrumental in the rapid take-up of the solar power systems in these communities. These technology centers, then, functioned as incubators for the village energy entrepreneur who produced and/or repaired solar accessories. In describing the social transformation wrought by this program, Barua noted:

> *"When we started this program, we were not sure whether we would be able to attract enough rural women or whether they would be able to operate independently. But we trained more than 1,000 women who have developed their self-confidence and now have the opportunity to earn an income of around US$150 a month. These young women from this most conservative of societies can leave home and operate independently as technicians – this was unimaginable only a few years ago."*

Codeveloping, then, is based on the belief that over the long run, operational viability of these ventures is influenced by their ongoing engagement in building underlying community infrastructure. This requires ventures to craft localized organizational forms that are in tune with the norms and customs associated with consumption in these areas and that signal commitment to these communities, thereby increasing their credibility and acceptability. Moreover, it involves making investments in the local infrastructure that are aimed at upgrading the community's capabilities (Porter and Kramer 2011; Sen 1999) as well as enabling the conduct of the venture's operations. This two-way involvement with the resident institutional infrastructure is key to the formation of robust markets within these communities. This suggests a potentially more foundational role that these actors can play in influencing the development of these markets, one that is well illustrated in the Grameen Shakti motto: 'Shakti does well if the community does well' (Wimmer 2012).

Discussion

In this paper, we characterize markets for underserved communities as being constituted by local institutions, that is, modalities (Giddens 1984) or grammars (Barley 1986) that define the underpinnings of social and economic order in these contexts. They manifest as understandings, routines, norms, traditions and local infrastructure that collectively configure exchange arrangements in these communities and represent the resident 'terms of action' (Fligstein and McAdam 2012). The composition and mode of functioning of these local institutions is often very different from the formal institutions that constitute daily reality in more advanced economies. This characterization of the institutional landscape provides us with a useful window from which to view the dynamics that unfold as actors engage in initiatives to craft markets in these contexts.

Our analysis of the four social ventures reveals that they incorporate their technologies into extant material understandings, intertwine their transaction systems with local consumption practices and interleave their organizational forms into the resident infrastructure. That is, they engage in what we refer to as *indigenizing, microprovisioning* and *codeveloping* respectively (see Table 3 for specific examples of these processes across the four ventures). These ground-level incursions by the ventures enable them to navigate these institutional landscapes and collectively contribute to the crafting of markets within these communities. Each of these processes reflects these actors' efforts at discerning the local institutions that constitute these contexts and then designing solutions and offerings that resonate with these surroundings. Put differently, they represent initiatives intended to mesh with the unique elements and rhythms of the institutional environment that characterize these domains (Ahlstrom et al. 2003; Reinecke and Ansari 2015).

In crafting markets in this manner we find that these social ventures contribute to these communities in other significant ways. For instance, they provide employment to locals, seed entrepreneurship related to their ventures and improve standards of living via consumption of their products and services (see Table 4). As part of weaving the solutions into these communities, these ventures hired and train locals to facilitate their business operations – ranging from production to distribution to sales and service – within these settings. Moreover, the presence of these ventures in these towns and villages typically fostered micro-entrepreneurship activity associated with these products and services, in a truly bottom-up fashion. This form of entrepreneurship typically addressed needs that were idiosyncratic to these communities and in many cases had not been anticipated by the ventures. Finally, the consumption of energy as an infrastructural good by households and individuals within these communities enabled them to be more productive and hence raise their incomes and living standards, besides providing them with a cheaper, safer and healthier alternative to traditional solutions such as kerosene and firewood. In summary, the generation of economic activity in myriad ways via the supply of electricity highlights the seeding of an entrepreneurial ecosystem within these communities that, over time, could contribute to an improvement in standards of living for these people even as it likely fosters social change in unanticipated ways.

It should be noted, however, that the emergence and sustenance of such an entrepreneurial ecosystem is by no means straightforward or inevitable (Lerner 2009; Wang et al. 2008). Indeed, our cases reveal attempts by these social ventures to seed entrepreneurship that did not gain traction. As an illustration, Huskpower was interested in pioneering a franchising model where it would build plants that would be financed by local partners who would then operate them – a plan that was crucial in the ventures attempt to scale as an organization. However, it was unable to generate much interest for its proposal among the locals. Retaining employees also proved a challenge for these ventures as these intrepid individuals often left to pursue more lucrative opportunities. More

Table 3. Evidence supporting market crafting processes of indigenizing, microprovisioning and codeveloping.

	Indigenizing	Microprovisioning	Codeveloping
SELCO	* Customized solutions for different groups of users * Innovation lab established to engage in performance testing and consumer research while devising customized solutions * All components of the solar-based system sourced locally	* Developed financial packages that are based on individual's cash flows * Organized loans through rural banking network by conceptualizing service as a revenue generator for households	* Rural service centers that employed local staff who engage in pre-sales and post-sales activity
HUSKPOWER	* Use of native materials – discarded rice husk * Deployment of antiquated technology – biomass gasification * Constructed plants using proximally available machinery * Designed plants to be manually operated and monitored	* Prepaid subscriptions of $2 that enable consumers to light up two lamps and one mobile charger for 6–8 hrs in the evening * Economized on capital/ operational/ distribution costs * Identified multiple monetization mechanisms to bolster revenues	* Established Husk Power University to impart training in large engine repair and maintenance * Established a franchise model for supplying electricity through local entrepreneurs
GRAMEEN SHAKTI	* Customized solar lighting systems to user needs * Invested in R&D programs to reduce system costs and improve quality/reliability	* 50 W panels account for most of their sales (power 4 lamps and 1 TV) * Financing provided through IDCOL; microcredit scheme that involves 15–25% down payment and 2–3 year repayment period subject to a low interest rate	* Technology centers trained local women to assemble mobile phone chargers and to install/ maintain/repair solar home systems
KAMWORKS	* Design team spent 3 months with rural Cambodian community to understand latent needs of prospective users * Technological system designed at home university and field tested with ten households at two locations – design finalized * Local production methods deployed	* Light output of 30 lumens (full power) for 4 hours * Partnered with rural banks to provide low interest loans	* Training center called the Solar Campus founded to provide village micro-entrepreneurs with commercial/technical training

generally, 'management-on-the-ground' was an ongoing task that the leadership of these ventures had to devote significant attention to, given the inherent novelty of the business systems that were being introduced within these communities. This was reflected in the slow (but steady) growth in these enterprises and the ecosystems associated with them. These dynamics reflect the considerable challenges involved in crafting markets and generating entrepreneurship within these communities, with progress likely to come in slow, circuitous steps rather than via a quick fix.

Contributions

Our study adds to a growing body of scholarship on the nature of markets within underserved communities that stands in contrast from the dominant institutional voids perspective. Rather than emphasize market failures due to absence of formal institutions in these contexts, this work highlights the need to understand the economic lives of these people on their own terms (Banerjee and Duflo 2011; Mair, Martí, and Ventresca 2012; Viswanathan, Sridharan, and Ritchie 2010). This, we suggest, requires gaining a deep understanding of the modalities, grammars and routines that collectively govern economic interaction in these contexts. Put differently, these local institutions – that have been glossed over by the institutional voids perspective – are in fact integral to (re)configuring markets. Furthermore, adopting such a microanalytic orientation enables us to appreciate the considerable ground-level processes that ventures engage in as part of crafting exchange spaces for their goods within these communities. In this paper, we have

Table 4. Generating entrepreneurship/economic activity via market crafting initiatives: Evidence from field data.

	Providing employment	Seeding micro-entrepreneurship	Improving standards of living
Grameen Shakti	* Hired women engineers to run their technology centers	* Created a micro-entrepreneurship model in which shopkeepers bought solar systems and rented extra capacity to neighbors.	* Enabled households and businesses in these communities to work at night(and generate extra income)
Huskpower	* Hired locals to operate their biogas plants	* Provide local village women with income generation opportunities through its incense stick manufacturing program	* Facilitated children studying in the evenings * Provided a safer and healthier energy alternative
Kamworks	* Employed sales and service team to sell/fix larger capacity solar installations	* Initiated a 'rent-to-own' model that operated through village entrepreneurs	* Allowed locals to learn new technical and business skills (applies to all four ventures)
Selco	* Employed locals to run its service centers which handled all facets of business operations	* Facilitated micro-entrepreneurship activity in which individuals rented solar power charged lanterns to street vendors every evening	

employed the terms *indigenizing, microprovisioning* and *codeveloping* to describe these efforts. In highlighting these processes, we offer a novel perspective for conceptualizing market crafting within these communities – one that accords significance to energizing ground-level dynamics rather than relying on top-down intervention.

Our insights contribute to ongoing conversations within the sociology of markets literature. While this research has made significant headway in conceiving markets as institutions, much of the empirical work in this domain has focused on examining dynamics within advanced economy contexts – scenarios in which formal institutions are well established and collectively understood by the players attempting to reconfigure (or defend) the existing market order.

In contrast, our account of markets in underserved communities highlights the significance of local institutions, that is, the webs of meaning, practice and structure that define terms of action in these scenarios. These arrangements are typically opaque to outsiders and are shaped by the resource-paucity rampant in these environments. This characterization of the institutional landscape suggests that a qualitatively different sequence of activities need to be performed to craft markets in these contexts. Our empirical account identifies some of the key processes – they involve surfacing resident modalities and practices, crafting product and services that account for these arrangements and then weaving these back into the extant institutional fabric (see also Jain 2012). These ground-level activities involve 'tailoring fits' and highlight empathetic engagement with the local institutions as a crucial first step to market development (Mair, Martí, and Ventresca 2012). More generally, market crafting in these contexts involves bridging the institutional distance between local realities and market awareness conditioned by an advanced economy mindset (Reinecke and Ansari 2015).

Our paper also contributes to the nascent literature on entrepreneurship as a solution to extreme poverty (Bruton, Ahlstom & Si, 2015; Sutter, Bruton, and Chen 2019). The focus in this literature to date has been on actors within these communities that engage in entrepreneurship – as evidenced in the use of concepts and terms such as subsistence entrepreneurship (Khanna 2008) and grassroots entrepreneurs (Sarkar 2018), and in the description of activities such as microfinancing. To these, we add a new actor – social ventures – that have been expressly founded to provide products and services to households with minimal incomes and have been set up to be self-sustaining from a business operations viewpoint. While these actors are outsiders to these communities, our observations from this study have highlighted how they embed their activities within the local institutions that animate activity in these societies. In doing so, they provide employment, generate entrepreneurship and improve standards of living for these people – i.e. they seed an entrepreneurial ecosystem around the products and services that they offer to these people (see also Porter and Kramer 2011 for their description of local cluster development in the case of MNC's). Studying the nature of these actors, the formation of such ecosystems and the challenges involved in supporting/ maintaining them represents an important research opportunity going forward.

From a policy standpoint, conceptualizing and measuring the social and economic impact of the entrepreneurial ecosystems that these social ventures generate would represent an important first step towards allocating resources and support towards such initiatives as a means of facilitating poverty reduction in underserved regions. In many cases, enabling these new, clean alternative forms of energy to co-exist on a level playing field with incumbent options remains an important order of business. Even as it does this, it is vital for governments to retain the 'bottom-up' character of such entrepreneurial activity and operate more as a 'remover of obstacles' rather than a 'trajectory setter' in such instances. This will enable the flowering of many diverse experiments with crafting markets in these scenarios that we believe is critical to devising a multi-pronged approach to reducing poverty within these communities and regions.

In delineating the processes associated with market crafting within these communities our work contributes to the discourse unfolding within the practitioner domain that, till recently, has been largely mired in the debate on whether significant profits exist for actors operating within this segment (Karnani 2007; Prahalad 2004). Our study delineates the specific activities social ventures engage in to make underserved markets an operationally viable, environmentally sustainable and socially relevant space. Along these lines, we suggest that the mission of these firms and the vision of their founders make this organizational form uniquely suited (vis-à-vis MNC's) to build markets and generate entrepreneurship in underserved communities. Having said that, the opaque and fragile nature of these contexts implies that significant attention is required to identify and work with the local institutions that are integral to these communities. Our findings highlight the slow and arduous nature of this process, one that requires considerable immersion in the field to understand the local institutions that constitute exchange spaces in these contexts. Moreover, our study suggests that to the extent that an offering is customized and localized, and thus has the potential to make a meaningful impact, its relevance as a generalized solution that can transcend geographies is likely to be limited. In highlighting these characteristics, we indicate that crafting these markets, while highly gratifying and impactful for the individuals and organizations involved, is likely to be a demanding process. Our findings resonate with and extend more recent practitioner and policy discourses that have highlighted the fragility and precariousness of operating in these domains, one that requires actors to actively engage with these communities to co-create markets (Christensen, Ojomo, and Dillon 2019; London, Sheth, and Hart 2014).

Future research

These findings represent only the tip of the iceberg with respect to this important topic. Future research in this domain can gainfully explore the crafting of markets within other underserved contexts (varying both countries and goods/services provided) to further deepen our understanding of the process of market crafting that we have identified here. Gaining a deeper understanding of the relationship between local institutions and the agency that ventures operating in this space exercise represents another fertile domain for additional work. Comparative studies that examine ventures possessing different identities (multinationals vs. domestic vs. social ventures, for example) and the activities they engage in to craft exchange spaces in this context would be useful for identifying differences in the composition and character of the markets that they construct. And finally, longitudinal studies that track the long-term impact of the introduction of products and services on the local institutions (i.e. observing changes to local understandings, practices and infrastructure) and the growth of new ventures and industries in these contexts would be extremely useful, particularly in emerging economies (Peng et al. 2018). Clearly much more needs to be done as we go about understanding how markets for underserved communities are crafted.

Conclusion

In this paper, we have employed an institutional perspective to understanding the crafting of markets for underserved communities. Specifically, we conceptualize these transaction spaces as being constituted by local institutions – that is, native understandings, practices and norms – that define the economic 'rules of the game' for these individuals. Based on our observations of four social ventures across three different countries, and their efforts to craft markets for their clean energy solutions, we highlight how these actors were able to weave their goods as well as the activities related to their production and distribution, into spaces afforded by the extant institutional fabric of these communities. This underscores the significance that these actors accord to understanding and articulating local context in the crafting and building of these markets. In addition, this research demonstrates how these ventures further generated employment and entrepreneurship and improved standards of living within these communities. In emphasizing the significance of local institutions, and characterizing how actors work with (and within) them, we build on and extend a nascent perspective on market building and entrepreneurship generation within these communities (Mair, Martí, and Ventresca 2012; McKague, Zietsma, and Oliver 2015). In doing so, we highlight how the enabling of bottom-up, distributed micro-initiatives can serve as a valuable complement to the top-down approaches to poverty that have often dominated policy discourse (Aghion et al. 2016; Chen, Chang, and Bruton 2017). Additional studies that further track the engaging with local institutions as part of market crafting efforts in a variety of emerging and developing economy settings can contribute greatly to our understanding of poverty alleviation and the successful introduction of useful and productive entrepreneurship in poorer regions.

Notes

1. For the fourth venture (Grameen Shakti), we relied significantly on our interactions with Nancy Wimmer, who has done 19 years of ongoing fieldwork with the organization (since its inception in 1996) and has written a book (Wimmer 2012) based on this. We conducted three interviews with her in which she recounted her field experiences and the key insights that emerged from it.
2. Rice husk is an amorphous and low-density fuel that produces a gas with high tar content, that experts had deemed unfit for a single-fuel mode of operation.

Acknowledgments

The authors wish to thank Marc Ventresca, Geoff Desa, the editors of this special issue and the participants of the 2014 SEE Conference, the 2015 AOM Conference and the 2018 ERD-SI Workshop in Hangzhou, China for their valuable feedback on earlier versions of this paper.

Disclosure statement

No potential conflict of interest was reported by the authors.

References

Acemoglu, D., and J. A. Robinson. 2013. *Why Nations Fail: The Origins of Power, Prosperity, and Poverty*. New York, NY: Crown Books.

Aghion, P., U. Akcigit, J. Cagé, and W. R. Kerr. 2016. "Taxation, Corruption, and Growth." *European Economic Review* 86: 24–51. doi:10.1016/j.euroecorev.2016.01.012.

Ahlstrom, D. 2010. "Innovation and Growth: How Business Contributes to Society." *The Academy of Management Perspectives* 24 (3): 11–24.

Ahlstrom, D., G. D. Bruton, and K. S. Yeh. 2008. "Private Firms in China: Building Legitimacy in an Emerging Economy." *Journal of World Business* 43 (4): 385–399. doi:10.1016/j.jwb.2008.03.001.

Ahlstrom, D., and Z. Ding. 2014. "Entrepreneurship in China: An Overview." *International Small Business Journal* 32 (6): 610–618. doi:10.1177/0266242613517913.

Ahlstrom, D., M. N. Young, A. Nair, and P. Law. 2003. "Managing the Institutional Environment: Challenges for Foreign Firms in Post WTO China." *SAM Advanced Management Journal* 68 (2): 41–49.

Anderson, A. R., and S. Ronteau. 2017. "Towards an Entrepreneurial Theory of Practice: Emerging Ideas for Emerging Economies." *Journal of Entrepreneurship in Emerging Economies* 9 (2): 110–120. doi:10.1108/JEEE-12-2016-0054.

Anderson, A. R., and B. A. Obeng. 2017. "Enterprise as Socially Situated in A Rural Poor Fishing Community." *Journal of Rural Studies* 49: 23–31. doi:10.1016/j.jrurstud.2016.11.015.

Ansari, S., K. Munir, and T. Gregg. 2012. "Impact at the 'bottom of the Pyramid': The Role of Social Capital in Capability Development and Community Empowerment." *Journal of Management Studies* 49 (4): 813–842. doi:10.1111/joms.2012.49.issue-4.

Bamberger, P. A., and M. G. Pratt. 2010. "Moving Forward by Looking Back: Reclaiming Unconventional Research Contexts and Samples in Organizational Scholarship." *Academy of Management Journal* 53 (4): 665–671. doi:10.5465/amj.2010.52814357.

Banerjee, A. V., and E. Duflo. 2011. *Poor Economics: A Radical Rethinking of the Way to Fight Global Poverty*. New York, NY: Public Affairs.

Barley, S. R. 1986. "Technology as an Occasion for Structuring: Evidence from Observations of CT Scanners and the Social Order of Radiology Departments." *Administrative Science Quarterly* 31 (1): 78–108.

Barley, S. R., and P. S. Tolbert. 1997. "Institutionalization and Structuration: Studying the Links between Action and Institution." *Organization Studies* 18 (1): 93–117. doi:10.1177/017084069701800106.

Biggart, N. W., and M. F. Guillén. 1999. "Developing Difference: Social Organization and the Rise of the Auto Industries of South Korea, Taiwan, Spain, and Argentina." *American Sociological Review* 64 (5): 722–747. doi:10.2307/2657373.

Bijker, W. E., T. P. Hughes, and T. J. Pinch. 1987. *The Social Construction of Technological Systems: New Directions in the Sociology and History of Technology*. Cambridge, MA: MIT Press.

Bruton, G. D., D. Ahlstrom, and H. L. Li. 2010. "Institutional Theory and Entrepreneurship: Where are We Now and Where Do We Need to Move in the Future?" *Entrepreneurship Theory and Practice* 34 (3): 421–440. doi:10.1111/j.1540-6520.2010.00390.x.

Bruton, G. D., D. Ahlstrom, and S. Si. 2015. "Entrepreneurship, Poverty and Asia: Moving beyond Subsistence Entrepreneurship." *Asia Pacific Journal of Management* 32 (1): 1–22. doi:10.1007/s10490-014-9404-x.

Carney, T. F. 1990. *Collaborative Inquiry Methodology*. Windsor, Ontario: University of Windsor Division for Instructional Development.

Chen, J., A. Y. Chang, and G. D. Bruton. 2017. "Microfinance: Where are We Today and Where Should the Research Go in the Future?" *International Small Business Journal* 35 (7): 793–802. doi:10.1177/0266242617717380.

Christensen, C. M., E. Ojomo, and K. Dillon. 2019. *The Prosperity Paradox: How Innovation Can Lift Nations Out of Poverty*. New York: Harper Business.

Coase, R. H. 1960. "The Problem of Social Cost." *Journal of Law and Economics* 3: 1–44. doi:10.1086/466560.

De Soto, H. 2000. *The Mystery of Capital: Why Capitalism Triumphs in the West and Fails Everywhere Else*. New York, NY: Basic Books.

Desa, G., and J. Koch. 2014. "Scaling Social Impact: Building Sustainable Social Ventures at the Base-of-The-Pyramid." *Journal of Social Entrepreneurship* 2 (5): 146–174. doi:10.1080/19420676.2013.871325.

DiMaggio, P. 1997. "Culture and Cognition." *Annual Review of Sociology* 23 (1): 263–287. doi:10.1146/annurev.soc.23.1.263.

Douglas, M. 1986. *How Institutions Think*. Syracuse, NY: Syracuse University Press.

Dunn, P. D. 1979. *Appropriate Technology: Technology with A Human Face*. New York, NY: Schocken Books.

Eisenhardt, K. M., and M. E. Graebner. 2007. "Theory Building from Cases: Opportunities and Challenges." *Academy of Management Journal* 50 (1): 25–32. doi:10.5465/amj.2007.24160888.

Fligstein, N., and I. Mara-Drita. 1996. "How to Make A Market: Reflections on the Attempt to Create A Single Market in the European Union." *American Journal of Sociology* 102 (1): 1–33. doi:10.1086/230907.

Fligstein, N. 2001. *The Architecture of Markets: An Economic Sociology of Twenty-First-Century Capitalist Societies*. Princeton, NJ: Princeton University Press.

Fligstein, N., and D. McAdam. 2012. *A Theory of Fields*. Oxford, UK: Oxford University Press.

Friedland, R., and R. R. Alford. 1991. "Bringing Society Back In: Symbols, Practices and Institutional Contradictions." In *The New Institutionalism in Organizational Analysis:*, edited by P. Dimaggio and W. W. Powell, 232–263. Chicago, IL: University of Chicago Press.

Garud, R., and D. Ahlstrom. 1997. "Technology Assessment: A Socio-cognitive Perspective." *Journal of Engineering and Technology Management* 14 (1): 25–48. doi:10.1016/S0923-4748(97)00005-2.

Garud, R., S. Jain, and A. Kumaraswamy. 2002. "Institutional Entrepreneurship in the Sponsorship of Common Technological Standards: The Case of Sun Microsystems and Java." *Academy of Management Journal* 45 (1): 196–214.

Geertz, C. 1973. *The Interpretation of Cultures: Selected Essays*. New York, NY: Basic Books.

George, G., R. Rao-Nicholson, C. Corbishley, and R. Bansal. 2015. "Institutional Entrepreneurship, Governance & Poverty: Insights from Emergency Medical Response Services in India." *Asia Pacific Journal of Management* 32 (1): 39–65. doi:10.1007/s10490-014-9377-9.

Giddens, A. 1984. *The Constitution of Society: Outline of the Theory of Structuration*. Berkeley, CA: University of California Press.

Glaser, B., and A. Strauss. 1967. *The Discovery of Grounded Theory: Strategies of Qualitative Research*. London, U.K.: Wiedenfeld & Nicholson.

Goffman, E. 1983. "The Interaction Order: American Sociological Association, 1982 Presidential Address." *American Sociological Review* 48 (1): 1–17. doi:10.2307/2095141.

Granovetter, M. 1985. "Economic Action and Social Structure: The Problem of Embeddedness." *American Journal of Sociology* 91 (3): 481–510. doi:10.1086/228311.

Greif, A. 2006. *Institutions and the Path to the Modern Economy: Lessons from Medieval Trade*. Cambridge, UK: Cambridge University Press.

Hallett, T., and M. J. Ventresca. 2006. "Inhabited Institutions: Social Interactions and Organizational Forms in Gouldner's Patterns of Industrial Bureaucracy." *Theory and Society* 35 (2): 213–236. doi:10.1007/s11186-006-9003-z.

Hammond, A. L., W. J. Kramer, R. S. Katz, J. T. Tran, and C. Walker. 2007. *The Next 4 Billion: Market Size and Business Strategy at the Base of the Pyramid*. Washington, DC: World Resources Institute International Finance Corporation.

Hargadon, A. B., and Y. Douglas. 2001. "When Innovations Meet Institutions: Edison and the Fesign of the Electric Light." *Administrative Science Quarterly* 46 (3): 476–501. doi:10.2307/3094872.

Jack, S. L., and A. R. Anderson. 2002. "The Effects of Embeddedness on the Entrepreneurial Process." *Journal of Business Venturing* 17 (5): 467–487. doi:10.1016/S0883-9026(01)00076-3.

Jain, S. 2012. "Pragmatic Agency in Technology Standard Setting: The Case of Ethernet." *Research Policy* 41 (9): 1643–1654. doi:10.1016/j.respol.2012.03.025.

Jain, S., and J. Koch. 2017. "Conceptualizing Markets for Underserved Communities: Trajectories Taken and the Road Ahead." In *The World Scientific Reference on Entrepreneurship (vol. 3): Sustainability, Ethics, and Entrepreneurship*, edited by A. Guerber, G. Markman, and S. Su, 71–91. Singapore: World Scientific.

Jain, S., and D. Sharma. 2013. "Institutional Logic Migration and Industry Evolution in Emerging Economies: The Case of Telephony in India." *Strategic Entrepreneurship Journal* 7 (3): 252–271. doi:10.1002/sej.v7.3.

Janssen, F., A. Fayolle, and A. Wuilaume. 2018. "Researching Bricolage in Social Entrepreneurship." *Entrepreneurship and Regional Development* 30 (3–4): 450–470. doi:10.1080/08985626.2017.1413769.

Karnani, A. 2007. "The Mirage of Marketing to the Bottom of the Pyramid." *California Management Review* 49 (4): 90–111. doi:10.2307/41166407.

Khanna, T. 2008. *Billions of Entrepreneurs: How China and India are Reshaping Their Futures and Yours*. Boston, MA: Harvard Business School Press.

Khanna, T., and K. Palepu. 2000. "Is Group Affiliation Profitable in Emerging Markets? an Analysis of Diversified Indian Business Groups." *Journal of Finance* 55 (2): 867–891. doi:10.1111/0022-1082.00229.

Khanna, T., and J. W. Rivkin. 2001. "Estimating the Performance Effects of Business Groups in Emerging Markets." *Strategic Management Journal* 22 (1): 45–74. doi:10.1002/(ISSN)1097-0266.

Koch, J., and A. Hammond. 2013. "Innovation Dynamics, Best Practices and Trends in the Off-Grid Clean Energy Market." *Journal of Management for Global Sustainability* 2: 121–139. doi:10.13185/JM2013.01207.

Legros, G., I. Havet, N. Bruce, and S. Bonjour. 2009. *The Energy Access Situation in Developing Countries*. New York, NY: United Nation Development Program and the World Health Organization.

Lerner, J. 2009. *Boulevard of Broken Dreams: Why Public Efforts to Boost Entrepreneurship and Venture Capital Have Failed–And What to Do about It*. Princeton, NJ: Princeton University Press.

London, T., and S. L. Hart. 2010. *Next Generation Business Strategies for the Base of the Pyramid: New Approaches for Building Mutual Value*. Upper Saddle River, NJ: FT Press.

London, T., S. Sheth, and S. Hart. 2014. *A Roadmap for the Base of the Pyramid Domain: Re-energizing for the Next Decade*. Ann Arbor, MI: William Davidson Institute. Accessed 25 May 2015. http://wdi.umich.edu/bop-roadmap/BoP-Roadmap.pdf

Mahajan, V., and K. Banga. 2006. *The 86 Percent Solution: How to Succeed in the Biggest Market Opportunity of the Next 50 Years*. Upper Saddle River, NJ: Pearson Education.

Mair, J., and I. Marti. 2009. "Entrepreneurship in and around Institutional Voids: A Case Study from Bangladesh." *Journal of Business Venturing* 24 (5): 419–435. doi:10.1016/j.jbusvent.2008.04.006.

Mair, J., I. Martí, and M. J. Ventresca. 2012. "Building Inclusive Markets in Rural Bangladesh: How Intermediaries Work Institutional Voids." *Academy of Management Journal* 55 (4): 819–850. doi:10.5465/amj.2010.0627.

McCloskey, D. N. 2006. *The Bourgeois Virtues: Ethics for an Age of Commerce*. Chicago, IL: University of Chicago Press.

McCloskey, D. N. 2010. *Bourgeois Dignity: Why Economics Can't Explain the Modern World*. Chicago, IL: University of Chicago Press.

McCloskey, D. N. 2016. *Bourgeois Equality: How Ideas, Not Capital or Institutions, Enriched the World*. Chicago, IL: University of Chicago Press.

McKague, K., C. Zietsma, and C. Oliver. 2015. "Building the Social Structure of A Market." *Organization Studies* 36 (8): 1063–1093. doi:10.1177/0170840615580011.

McMullen, J. S. 2011. "Delineating the Domain of Development Entrepreneurship: A Market-Based Approach to Facilitating Inclusive Economic Growth." *Entrepreneurship Theory and Practice* 35 (1): 185–193. doi:10.1111/etap.2011.35.issue-1.

Miles, M. B., and A. M. Huberman. 1984. *Qualitative Data Analysis*. Beverly Hills, CA: Sage.

Mokyr, J. 1992. *The Lever of Riches: Technological Creativity and Economic Progress*. Oxford: Oxford University Press.

Munshi, K., and M. Rosenzweig. 2006. "Traditional Institutions Meet the Modern World: Caste, Gender, and Schooling Choice in A Globalizing Economy." *American Economic Review* 96 (4): 1225–1252. doi:10.1257/000282806779468607.

North, D. C. 1990. *Institutions, Institutional Change and Economic Performance*. New York: Cambridge University Press.

Peng, M. W., S. Lebedev, C. O. Vlas, J. C. Wang, and J. S. Shay. 2018. "The Growth of the Firm in (and Out Of) Emerging Economies." *Asia Pacific Journal of Management* 35 (4): 829–857. doi:10.1007/s10490-018-9599-3.

Podolny, J. M. 1993. "A Status-Based Model of Market Competition." *American Journal of Sociology* 98 (4): 829–872. doi:10.1086/230091.

Porter, M. E., and M. R. Kramer. 2011. "Creating Shared Value." *Harvard Business Review* 89 (Jan/Feb): 62–77.

Prabhu, J., and S. Jain. 2015. "Innovation and Entrepreneurship in India: Understanding Jugaad." *Asia Pacific Journal of Management* 32 (4): 843–868. doi:10.1007/s10490-015-9445-9.

Prahalad, C. K. 2004. *The Fortune at the Bottom of the Pyramid: Eradicating Poverty through Profits*. Upper Saddle River, NJ: FT Press.

Reinecke, J., and S. Ansari. 2015. "When Times Collide: Temporal Brokerage at the Intersection of Markets and Fevelopments." *Academy of Management Journal* 58 (2): 618–648. doi:10.5465/amj.2012.1004.

Rodrick, D., A. Subramanian, and F. Trebbi. 2004. "Institutions Rule: The Primacy of Institutions over Geography and Integration in Economic Development." *Journal of Economic Growth* 9 (2): 131–165. doi:10.1023/B:JOEG.0000031425.72248.85.

Rostow, W. W. 1960. *The Stages of Economic Growth: A Non-Communist Manifesto*. Cambridge, UK: Cambridge University Press.

Sachs, J. 2006. *The End of Poverty: Economic Possibilities for Our Time*. New York, NY: Penguin.

Sainath, P. 1996. *Everybody Loves a Good Drought: Stories from India's Poorest Districts*. New Delhi, India: Penguin Books.

Sarkar, S. 2018. "Grassroots Entrepreneurs and Social Change at the Bottom of the Pyramid: The Role of Bricolage." *Entrepreneurship & Regional Development* 30 (3–4): 421–449. doi:10.1080/08985626.2017.1413773.

Schatzki, T. R., K. Knorr-Cetina, and E. Von Savigny, Eds. 2001. *The Practice Turn in Contemporary Theory*. London, UK: Routledge.

Schillebeeckx, S., P. Parikh, R. Bansal, and G. George. 2012. "An Integrated Framework for Rural Electrification: Adopting a User-Centric Approach to Business Model Development." *Energy Policy* 48: 687–697. doi:10.1016/j.enpol.2012.05.078.

Schumacher, E. F. 1973. *Small Is Beautiful: Economics as if People Really Mattered*. London, UK: Abacus.

Sen, A. 1999. *Development as Freedom*. Oxford, UK: Oxford University Press.

Si, S., X. Yu, A. Wu, S. Chen, S. Chen, and Y. Su. 2015. "Entrepreneurship and Poverty Reduction: A Case Study of Yiwu, China." *Asia Pacific Journal of Management* 32 (1): 119–143. doi:10.1007/s10490-014-9395-7.

Stark, D. 1996. "Recombinant Property in East European Capitalism." *American Journal of Sociology* 101 (4): 993–1027. doi:10.1086/230786.

Strauss, A. L., and J. Corbin. 1990. *Basics of Qualitative Research*. Newbury Park, CA: Sage.

Sutter, C., G. D. Bruton, and J. Chen. 2019. "Entrepreneurship as A Solution to Extreme Poverty: A Review and Future Research Directions." *Journal of Business Venturing* 34 (1): 197–214. doi:10.1016/j.jbusvent.2018.06.003.

Tomizawa, A., L. Zhao, G. Bassellier, and D. Ahlstrom. 2019. "Economic Growth, Innovation, Institutions, and the Great Enrichment." *Asia Pacific Journal of Management* 36. doi:10.1007/s10490-019-09648-2.

Van de Ven, A. H., and R. Garud. 1989. "A Framework for Understanding the Emergence of the Industries." *Research on Technological Innovation, Management and Policy* 4: 195–225.

Van Maanen, J. 1979. "The Fact of Fiction in Organizational Ethnography." *Administrative Science Quarterly* 24: 539–550. doi:10.2307/2392360.

Vernet, A., J. Khayesi, V. George, G. George, and A. S. Bahaj. 2019. "How Does Energy Matter? Rural Electrification, Entrepreneurship and Community Development in Kenya." *Energy Policy* 126: 88–98. doi:10.1016/j.enpol.2018.11.012.

Viswanathan, M. 2007. "Understanding Product and Market Interactions in Subsistence Marketplaces: A Study in South India." *Advances in International Management* 20: 21–57.

Viswanathan, M., S. Sridharan, and R. Ritchie. 2010. "Understanding Consumption and Entrepreneurship in Subsistence Marketplaces." *Journal of Business Research* 63 (6): 570–581. doi:10.1016/j.jbusres.2009.02.023.

Wang, L. C., D. Ahlstrom, A. Nair, and R. Z. Hang. 2008. "Creating Globally Competitive and Innovative Products: China's Next Olympic Challenge." *SAM Advanced Management Journal* 73 (3): 4–15.

Warde, A. 2005. "Consumption and Theories of Practice." *Journal of Consumer Culture* 5 (2): 131–153. doi:10.1177/1469540505053090.

Webb, J. W., L. Tihanyi, R. D. Ireland, and D. G. Sirmon. 2009. "You Say Illegal, I Say Legitimate: Entrepreneurship in the Informal Economy." *Academy of Management Review* 34 (3): 492–510. doi:10.5465/amr.2009.40632826.

White, H. C. 1981. "Where Do Markets Come From?" *American Journal of Sociology* 87 (3): 517–547. doi:10.1086/227495.

Wimmer, N. 2012. *Green Energy for a Billion Poor*. Germany: MCRE Verlag.

Yin, R. K. 1994. *Case Study Research: Design and Methods*. Thousand Oaks, CA: Sage.

Zukin, S., and P. DiMaggio, Eds. 1990. *Structures of Capital: The Social Organization of the Economy*. Cambridge, UK: Cambridge University Press.

Climbing the poverty ladder: the role of entrepreneurship and gender in alleviating poverty in transition economies

Julia Korosteleva and Paulina Stępień-Baig

ABSTRACT

Poverty reduction remains a critical issue for a vast proportion of the population globally. Substantial body of literature on poverty reduction has focused on the role played by government support and charity institutions, whereas entrepreneurship as a channel for poverty reduction, and the role of gender in shaping this relationship have been under-researched, especially in the context of transition economies. Using the recent wave of the EBRD Life in Transition Survey III (2016) data, this study explores the relationship between poverty alleviation, entrepreneurship and gender. We extend the understanding of the mechanism via which entrepreneurial process is likely to contribute to poverty reduction in this region, distinguishing between self-employment and business ownership, with the latter regarded as Schumpeterian entrepreneurship. The study provides some interesting findings shedding light on the important role women play in shaping the entrepreneurship-poverty relationship.

Introduction

Poverty is a complex phenomenon spanning multiple economic and social issues (Misturelli and Heffernan, 2008). Poverty reduction remains a critical issue for a vast proportion of the world's population with more than two billion individuals in developing countries along surviving on under US $3.10 per day (World Bank 2017). However, the last decade has seen some positive achievements in fighting poverty (Bruton, Ahlstrom, and Si 2015; Wu and Si 2018; Tomizawa et al. 2019). Such success has led many academic scholars and policy-makers to continue exploring the instruments which provide efficient solutions for fighting poverty in the context of specific countries, regions and worldwide. Among others, entrepreneurship has been increasingly recognized as one of the efficient means for achieving economic prosperity and poverty reduction.

One of the widely acclaimed channels via which entrepreneurship promotes economic prosperity and reduces poverty has been job creation, leading to the reduction of unemployment via (a) individuals getting engaged in entrepreneurial activity themselves; (b) creating new jobs via establishing high-growth potential businesses (Estrin, Korosteleva, and Mickiewicz 2013; Phelps 2013). Entrepreneurship also increases economy's productivity via the process of creative destruction (Schumpeter [1934] 2008), disrupting markets with introduction of new products and technologies, and challenging the power of incumbent inefficient firms (Phelps 2013). The overall economic growth benefits resulting from productivity growth accrue not only to the rich but also to the poor given that on average growth is distribution neutral, i.e. it benefits the poor proportionately as much as the rest of the population (Dollar and Kraay 2013).

A substantial body of literature on poverty reduction has focused on the role played by government support and charity institutions, whereas entrepreneurship as a channel for poverty reduction has been under-researched so far (Bruton, Ketchen, and Ireland 2013; Si et al. 2015). In particular, there is still a lack of quantitative evidence to shed some light on the extent to what entrepreneurship is efficient in fighting poverty in the context of emerging economies of Central and Eastern Europe, and Central Asia, known as transition economies.

Furthermore, the debates on poverty have been surrounded by the issue of gender inequality, raising concern that poverty has predominantly a woman's face (Sanchez 2018). Some evidence suggest that worldwide, women are poorer and more disadvantaged than men due to their limited access to education, lack of ability to exercise property, economic and political rights (Duflo 2012; Munoz-Boudet et al. 2018). Economic empowerment of women to widen the opportunities available to them in the labour market is increasingly acclaimed as one of the effective instruments to reduce gender poverty gap (Duflo 2012). Engaging in entrepreneurial activity may offer women such opportunity to break the circle of poverty.

This paper addresses these issues empirically, exploring the linkages between entrepreneurship, gender and poverty alleviation in the setting of transition economies. Our main contributions can be summarized as follows. First, there is still lack of empirical evidence offering insights on the relationship between entrepreneurship, gender and poverty alleviation, in particular in the setting of emerging economies of Central and Eastern Europe, and Central Asia. To investigate our research questions, we utilize the 2016 EBRD Life in Transition Survey (LiTs) data that cover the countries of interest and therefore also enable a comparative perspective to study cross-country group differences.

Second, we extend the understanding of the mechanism via which entrepreneurial process is likely to contribute to poverty reduction, distinguishing between self-employment and business ownership, with the latter viewed here as the Schumpeterian entrepreneurship (Henrekson and Sanandaji 2014). We also provide some interesting findings shedding light on the important role females play in shaping the entrepreneurship–poverty relationship, revisiting the conventional views on this.

Third, we employ a sophisticated methodology, utilizing a multilevel modelling technique. It allows to distinguish between individual and multi-level environmental effects. The data contains information on cities where respondents reside, allowing us to construct a regional district-level variable. We build a three-level model to study the determinants of poverty alleviation via looking at individuals, regional districts and country factors in a multilevel framework, the advantage of which is allowing micro-, meso- and macro-levels to be modelled simultaneously, addressing the clustering effect of individuals within districts and countries, failure of doing which may lead to biased results.

The paper proceeds as follows. Section 2 reviews the existing academic literature exploring the determinants of poverty alleviation, focusing specifically on the issues of entrepreneurship and gender primarily in the setting of transition. Section 3 discusses data and methodology employed in this study. Sections 4 and 5 discuss the empirical results contextualizing them within the literature, whereas Section 6 concludes, summarizing key findings and providing some policy recommendations and agenda for future research.

Determinants of poverty alleviation: theoretical literature overview and hypotheses development

The literature on poverty determinants has been growing fast, spanning different fields of studies, primarily dominated by development economics, but remaining fairly scarce in the field of management (Bruton, Ketchen, and Ireland 2013; Si et al. 2015). Among others, prior studies on poverty reduction emphasize the importance of microcredit schemes (Prahalad 2005; Bruton, Khavul, and Chavez 2011);

literacy (Banerjee et al., 2007); education and skill training (Duflo 2012); institutional change and entrepreneurship (McMullen 2010; Khavul, Chavez, and Bruton 2013).

Entrepreneurship and its role in poverty alleviation

A number of scholars attest to the importance of entrepreneurship in alleviating poverty (McCloskey 2010; Bruton, Ketchen, and Ireland 2013; Si et al. 2015).

Entrepreneurship is seen as a route out of deprivation; business owners in the most deprived areas are more likely to move than comparable non-business owners to more prosperous areas, and therefore more likely to achieve an improvement in their standard of living (Frankish et al. 2014). Whereas the deprived areas are likely to be populated by low-value adding businesses with little scope to grow due to resource constrains, and respectively lower potential to reduce poverty (Blackburn and Ram 2006; Greene, Mole, and Storey 2008).

Prahalad (2005) emphasized the role entrepreneurs may play in serving the needs of the poor, and how serving the bottom of the pyramid may make them prosper in turn. However, it is not only the exploitation of market opportunities with the focus on poor that helps alleviating poverty; entrepreneurs coming from impoverished backgrounds can also help to inspire the poor to engage in entrepreneurship seeing it as a route of poverty (Si et al. 2015).

Entrepreneurial dynamism has been argued to be particularly vital for transition economies (Jackson et al., 1999). With the collapse of communism, which was characterized by the suppression of private initiative, since early 1990s transition economies have undergone a colossal change involving comprehensive institutional reforms as they moved towards a market economy with entrepreneurship assuming one of the core roles in affecting all aspects of economic development in the region (Korosteleva and Belitski 2017).

Despite a number of hardships, including economic instability, institutional deficiencies, lack of public support and hostile social attitudes towards entrepreneurship, *de novo* firms experienced exponential growth in the early 1990s, driven by abundant market opportunities, which were suppressed under the communist system, and emerging institutional opportunities (Smallbone and Welter 2001).

A surge in new venture creation in transition economies throughout the 1990s rendered its outcomes positively affecting economic growth and income distribution across the region. In their study of the relationship between entrepreneurship and the evolution of income distributions in Poland and Russia, Berkowitz and Jackson (2006) show that a one-standard-deviation increase in the share of the workforce in new or small enterprises increases the share of income earned by the lowest 40% of the population by 1.4 and by 1.25 percentage points in Polish and Russian regions, respectively. Poland's greater success in *de novo* firm entry contributes to its more equitable income distribution during the transition. Poland also stands out illustrating the success of self-employment in tackling poverty. Self-employment was introduced in Poland as a new occupational choice category (outside agriculture) in 1992. In his study of income, inequality and poverty during the transition, Milanovic (1998) shows that being a self-employed reduces the probability of poverty by 11 percent, when controlling for other factors such as education, type and size of household, location and so on. Interestingly, this effect is not uniform across all transition economies with lower than average poverty rates observed for self-employed in Hungary and Poland; about average – in Belarus and Slovak Republic, and higher than average in Estonia and Romania. Such divergences across transition countries are likely to reflect lack of homogeneity in defining self-employment, where a category seems to be too broad spanning both small-scale subsistence farmers and rich private entrepreneurs in some transition economies.

The Chinese economy which has also undergone a significant institutional change towards developing a market economy in the last decades, has witnessed significant poverty reduction, largely attributed to entrepreneurial developments taken place in China (Ahlstrom and Ding 2014; Si et al. 2015). Based on the case study of the Eastern Chinese city of Yiwu, Si et al. (2015) showed how individual and collective entrepreneurship helped to reduce poverty in the region via not only disrupting the market with products that are affordable to the bottom of the pyramid, but also setting the positive role model examples, motivating the others to follow suit.

In considering the relationship between entrepreneurship and poverty further, the scholars have also continuously debated about the role of different types of entrepreneurship and its effect on prosperity and poverty reduction, distinguishing between necessity- and opportunity-driven entrepreneurship (Valliere and Peterson 2009), or lower-value adding and high-impact (Schumpeterian) entrepreneurship (Estrin, Korosteleva, and Mickiewicz 2013; Henrekson and Sanandaji 2014). Following Henrekson and Sanandaji (2014), the term 'entrepreneur' conflates two broad categories of individuals: (1) individuals who are effectively self-employed, generating jobs primarily for themselves; (2) Schumpeterian entrepreneurs who aspire to create large-scale businesses that could impact the growth path of their local region or even the national economy. We expect the latter to have disproportionally stronger effect on poverty reduction, given its higher growth-impact potential, whereas a self-employment, viewed as less productive activity and driven often by necessity motive in the setting of transition, to have a less pronounced effect on poverty reduction.

Based on this discussion, we postulate our first set of hypotheses.

Hypothesis 1: *The engagement of individuals in (a) self-employment (H1a) and (b) business ownership with employment creation (H1b) is likely to have respectively positive effect on poverty reduction. The effect of business ownership is expected to be stronger on poverty reduction as opposed to self-employment (H1c).*

Is poverty gender neutral?

It has long been established that poverty disproportionately affects women (Sanchez 2018). All major international organizations such as the UN, the World Bank and European Union in the recent years have undertaken projects aimed at better understanding of poverty among men and women. In most cases, within poor households women are engaged in household and childbearing duties while men work for income. This means that women are often poorer and more vulnerable than men.

A recent initiative between United Nations (UN) Women and the World Bank reassessed survey data for 89 countries focusing specifically on poverty gender gap (Munoz-Boudet et al. 2018). Children account for 44 per cent of the world's extremely poor with girls being disproportionally affected. As the children grow up, the gender gap widens – for every 100 poor men aged 25–34 there are 122 poor women of the same age group. European Institute for Gender Equality (2016) highlighted in their report on the poverty in the EU that women continue being at higher risk of poverty due to inequalities in public and private lives, which weaken women's opportunities in the labour market and devalue their work.

Turning to the transition economies, most of the literature on poverty focuses on the early transition period and the effect of the collapse of communism and economic transformation on poverty and inequality (Rosser, Rosser, and Ahmed 2000; Simai 2006).

The economic and social transformation of post-communist countries was claimed to affect men and women in different ways, creating both challenges and opportunities (Falkingham and Baschieri 2010; Sattar 2011). On the one hand side, with the launch of the economic reforms in early 1990s, it was predicted that impoverishment would predominately take a female face with expected fall in female labour participation, increase of unemployment among women, and a rising gender wage gap (Ashwin 2010). Some evidence suggest that women indeed were affected by the transition experience disproportionately more than men, with many women being forced into unemployment and poverty (Mickiewicz 2010). Gender equality promoted during communism, and argued to contribute to sustaining female labour participation during the early start of transition, has also quickly been eroded particularly in countries of Central Asia and the Caucasus (Falkingham and Baschieri 2010; Sattar 2011). For many women in Central Asia the gains in leadership positions and political representation achieved during the Soviet times, have been reversed with re-emergence of the traditional gender roles in taking primary care of household chores (Harris 2004).

However, other studies suggest only marginal gender differences in poverty observed between men and women (Ashwin 2010). Marginal gender gap could be partly explained via the perseverance of female labour participation rates due to the emergence of new economic opportunities as a result of structural transformation: the contraction of the manufacturing sector with a disproportionate adverse effect on men, and the expansion of the service sector that opened relatively more opportunities for women (Sattar 2011). However, women's gains in the service sector may be only short term with little scope for growth (Sabarwal and Terrell 2008) as discussed further below.

Nevertheless, the World Bank poverty assessments in the region in the first decade of transition even revealed some evidence that female-headed households fared sometimes better than those headed by males; in Kyrgystan in 2003 only 36% of female-headed households were defined as poor, living below USD2.15 PPP a day, as compared to 67% of male-headed households (Alam et al. 2005, 238–41). In her study of Russia's experience of the shock therapy economic reform in the 1990s, Ashwin (2010) reveals continuities in women's attachment to the labour force primarily as a result of economic need and women's responsibility for domestic childcare. Paradoxically, women have proved more resilient than men in facing economic deprivation during the economic reform. If men experience labour market problems with their position as main household 'breadwinners' being challenged, they turn to marginalize themselves even further from their household, immersing into 'binge drinking' which further exacerbate their economic hardships (Jukkala et al. 2008). Women, however, are found less likely to binge drink when experiencing economic problems, and their continuing labour market engagement to support the household at the times of economic hardships helps them to sustain a sense of 'efficacy, competence and meaning' (Jukkala et al. 2008; Ashwin 2010).

Based on the above two-fold argument, we postulate our second hypothesis.

Hypothesis 2: *Poverty is expected to be higher among females as opposed to males in the context of transition economies, although a poverty gap is not substantial.*

Now we turn to considering to what extent gender plays any critical role in explaining the entrepreneurship-poverty relationship. Female entrepreneurship has increasingly become the global phenomenon with businesses owned by women representing between 25 and 33% of formal sector business around the world (Estrin and Mickiewicz, 2011a).

Referring to Global Entrepreneurship Monitor data on entrepreneurship (GEM 2015/2016), we observe some cross-country and cross-regional differences in the role of gender in entrepreneurship. Overall, males dominate entrepreneurial entry and they are more growth ambitious (ibid). In transition economies in 2015, we observe 50% lower entrepreneurial entry for women as compared to men, though women show nearly equal to men opportunity-driven entrepreneurship rates.[1] Macedonia and Slovenia exhibit the lowest female-to-male entrepreneurial entry, equal to 0.4, whereas in Hungary women show lower opportunity-driven motivation as compared to men (0.7). Overall, after more than 25 years since the beginning of transition, observing a higher rate of women entering entrepreneurship out of opportunity motive is a positive trend towards poverty elimination, given that such process was largely dominated by a necessity motive during the early stage of transition (Falkingham and Baschieri 2010).

As highlighted above, women not only exhibit the overall lower entrepreneurial entry rate as compared to men, but also they show some differences in business performance. While the evidence on gender and its effect on firm performance is mixed (for good overview of this literature see Parker 2018), in their majority academic scholars come to consensus that growth and survival rates among female-run businesses are generally smaller compared to males (Sabarwal and Terrell 2008; Parker 2018). Using firm-level data from 26 transition economies of Central and Eastern Europe, and Central Asia, Sabarwal and Terrell (2008) find that female entrepreneurs own and manage smaller and less efficient (in terms of total factor productivity) enterprises, although the difference is small. However, female entrepreneurs' returns to scale are much larger suggesting they would benefit most from increasing their scale of operations (ibid). Sabarwal and Terrell (2008) conclude that the main reasons of females operating suboptimal-size businesses are that they are both financially more constrained and tend to concentrate in industries with predominately small firms such as retail sales and services; they are also less likely to operate high-tech businesses. This is also in line with other studies (e.g. Muravyev et al. 2007; Ashwin 2010). In conclusion, all this may have implications for a type of business women are likely to launch, and its further implications for their welfare. If self-employment is likely to reflect more replicative, small-scale business, we expect women to perform less well than man with also having less opportunities compared to men to climb the poverty ladder. On opposite, business ownership with employment creation shows an effort for creating more sizable growth-ambitious firms. If women launch such enterprises, they are more likely to succeed as compared to men. Based on this, we formulate our next set of the hypotheses.

Hypothesis 3: *Females engaged in (a) self-employment and (b) business ownership are likely to be respectively lower down (H3a) and higher up (H3b) the poverty ladder compared to their male counterparts.*

Regional differences

In this study, we do not only focus on the sample of transition economies as a whole, but also distinguish between different country groups within transition economies. In this, we follow the EBRD classification: Central Europe and Baltic States (CCB); South East Europe (SEE); Eastern Europe (EEC); and Central Asia (CA).[2]

In their study of female entrepreneurship in Lithuania and Ukraine, Aidis et al. (2007) claim that females have less access to finance both formal and informal, less access to informal networks and different attitude to risk. However, they stress that there exist significant differences between the two countries, which affect female entrepreneurs and suggest that the transition region should not be viewed as uniform and regional approach considered when studying it.

The differences across these country groups in determining entrepreneurship–gender–poverty relationships are likely to be driven by the institutional environment (McMullen 2010) that may be more conducive to entrepreneurship in Central and Eastern Europe following their accession to the EU, but provide some constraints for new venture creation in Eastern Europe and Central Asia both spanning the countries of the Former Soviet Union (FSU) (Aidis, Estrin, and Mickiewicz 2008; Manolova, Eunni, and Gyoshev 2008; Estrin and Mickieiwicz, 2011b). Estrin and Mickiewicz (2011b) show that lower rates of entrepreneurial activity in the FSU region as compared to Central European transition economies is attributed to the negative effect of the legacy of communist planning, including the negative attitude of the society to entrepreneurship (Estrin and Mickiewicz, 2011b).

Furthermore, the institutional constraints that entrepreneurs face, do not only determine the rate of entrepreneurial activity but also its type (Baumol 1990; Estrin, Korosteleva, and Mickiewicz 2013). In a more deficient institutional environment, we may expect lower level of high-impact entrepreneurship as opposed to self-employment. We expect to observe more incidences of subsistence entrepreneurship among females in Central Asia, given the scarcity of alternative labour market opportunities. On the other hand, in CCB states the entrepreneurship is likely to be opportunity-driven. Females are more critical of themselves in their entrepreneurial endeavours. This is likely to lead to the emergence of more successful and therefore wealthier female entrepreneurs (Simai 2006; Scott et al. 2012).

Finally, another reason for observing regional differences is rooted into cultural differences in the role females play in business in Central Asia as opposed to Central and East European countries (Welter et al. 2003). Since the launch of transition, the Soviet culture on promoting gender quality was diminished with traditional cultural and social values emphasizing a strong gender hierarchy of power relationship with men playing a dominant role in the household and women playing submissive role within the family, taking care of household chores, having revived in the region (Harris 2004). Furthermore, it is also worth noting that the unitary household assumption with household income being equally shared between men and women, commonly used in assessing poverty (e.g. Alam et al. 2005), is less likely to hold in Asian countries, and therefore actual gender differentials in welfare in this region are likely to be underestimated (Falkingham and Baschieri 2010).

Overall, the lower rates of entrepreneurial activity in EEC and CA as compared to the CCB region; the prevalence of its different types (self-employment as opposed to business ownership with employment); the cultural differences underlying the different role women play in business in Central Asia leads to postulating our last set of hypotheses.

Hypothesis 4: *Regional differences determine the relationship between entrepreneurship, gender and poverty: a poverty reduction effect of female engaging in any form of entrepreneurship is likely to be observed in the context of CEB countries (H4a); in Central Asia we are likely to observe a significant gender gap in the effect of different types of entrepreneurship on poverty to a disadvantage of women (H4b).*

Data and methodology

To test our hypotheses, we utilize the most recent wave of the EBRD Life in Transition Survey (LiTS) III conducted in 2016.[3] It surveys 51,000 households across 34 countries, with the primary focus on transition economies (28 countries).

Measuring poverty

Poverty is a multifaceted concept underlined by different approaches in measuring it, and spanning different economic and social issues, as well as the levels of analysis. At a micro-level, poverty is commonly measured at the household level, utilizing income-based approach, which remains the core concept at present (Munoz-Boudet et al. 2018). More recently developed measures of poverty stress the multi-dimensional aspect of poverty, implying experience of personal deprivation in terms of economic, social, political and psychological traits (Misturelly and Heffernan, 2008). The most well-known example of such measures is the Multidimensional Poverty Index developed by Alkire and Santos (2014) which comprises three equally weighted poverty dimensions – health, education and living standard captured by a number of indicators.

In our study, we employ both subjective and objective measures of poverty using EBRD LiTS Survey data for 2016. Household income in the survey provides an indication of what sort of goods and services families are able to afford. For subjective measure of poverty, we use a 10-step poverty ladder variable, which reflects subjective ranking of a household's social standing.[4] Respondents in LiTS III were asked to *'imagine a 10-step ladder where on the bottom, the first step, stand the poorest 10 per cent of people in [your country] and on the highest step, the tenth, stand the richest 10 per cent of people in [your country].'* They were then asked to state on which step of the 10-step ladder they believe their household currently rests. We contrast this measure of subjective poverty perception with objective one, based on using data on individual net incomes. To enable compatibility between the two measures, we transform net income to generate an objective poverty ladder reflecting 10 deciles of net income distribution of respondents.

Additionally, as part of our robustness checks, we generate a threshold measure of poverty reflecting 20 centile of income distribution of both subjective and objective measures of poverty. It is defined as a binary variable denoting probability of respondents to fall within the bottom 20% of income distribution.

Measuring entrepreneurial activity

The majority of studies available at a macro-level utilize either the rate of self-employment or new registered businesses from World Bank, or the Total Entrepreneurial Activity (TEA) data from Global Entrepreneurship Monitor (GEM) as a measure for entrepreneurial activity (Parker 2018). The advantage of using the latter is to be able to distinguish between opportunity and necessity-driven entrepreneurship. Similarly, following Henrekson and Sanandaji (2014) we distinguish between self-employment (low-value adding activity often triggered by entry due to a necessity motive), and business ownership with employment coined here as the 'Schumpetarian' entrepreneurship), utilizing the data on employment status of respondents. Respectively, based on EBRD LiTs data we distinguish between (a) unemployed; (b) self-employed and (c) business owners with employment, where the latter two categories serve as our measures of low-value adding (self-employment) and high-value adding entrepreneurship (business ownership with employment) respectively. We set the 'employed for wages' as our reference category.

Other variables and controls

Among other variables of interest for testing our key set of hypotheses, we focus on gender, which is measured by using a dummy variable equal one if a respondent is a female, and zero – being a male. At individual level we additionally control for the age of respondents; marital status; location (urban vs. rural); and education attainment.

In this study, we also introduce various controls to capture the effect of different dimensions of local infrastructure development on combating poverty. We distinguish between hard infrastructure (i.e. physical infrastructure) and soft infrastructure, exemplified by various institutional structures and social frameworks. We control for their effect at an individual, regional (district-country) and country levels.

As regards the impact of institutional structures, the last decade saw significant transformations taking place in regions worldwide with the changes in governance structures and infrastructure reshaping the distribution of power, resources and welfare in cities and regions, making some of them thrive while others to decline. This is particularly emblematic for the post-socialist countries, with some of them riddled by economic hardships and poverty, deficient institutions, ethnic conflicts, – manifesting all the core factors that cause mass migration, further impoverishment, and cultural decay. Improvement in the quality of institutions should be associated with poverty reduction. However, this is not always the case as institutional reforms are costly to implement, and it is often the poor who bear higher transactions associated with the implementation of institutional reforms (Chong and Calderon 2000).

In countries with weak formal institutions, there is a wider meso-level variation in social relations (Efendic, Mickiewicz, and Rebmann, 2015) where actions and beliefs of people are shaped not only by the network structure of an individual's social relations, but also normative structures that enable people to act collectively with their relations being governed by intergroup contracts (Pettigrew, 1998). In exploring the social roots of regional development our paper investigates the relationship of the two types of social capital, namely bonding and bridging, on individual's subjective and objective poverty measures. While bonding (i.e. ties with family and community) is shown to render short-term gains in addressing various institutional deficiencies, weak ties, measured here via institutional trust act as bridges across different communities, fostering knowledge sharing and the diffusion of trust, therefore benefiting the process of development in a long run via improving social quality through mitigation of labour precariousness (Sabatini 2008).

We measure the development of the physical infrastructure by looking at the level of satisfaction with tap water provision; electricity; telephone; central heating and gas. At an individual level, we construct a scale variable of all these dimensions of physical infrastructure development with the alpha reliability test statistic equal to 0.82 We also aggregate the individual-level dimensions of satisfaction with physical infrastructure to a NUTS3-country level to capture the meso-level effect of the hard infrastructure development. To capture the effect of the soft infrastructure development we capture the 'bonding' social capital via family trust (Q4.05a LiTS2016) and neighbourhood trust (Q 4.05b LiTS2016), using dichotomous variables with one denoting trust in close family members and neighbourhood respectively, and zero otherwise. The bridging social capital (i.e. institutional trust) is constructed as a scale variable based on the following dimensions: the presidency; the government/cabinet of ministers; the regional and local government; the parliament; court; political parties; army and the police. Such scale construction is validated by the alpha reliability test statistics being equal to 0.93.

At a district-country level, we also control for the extent of informality of the economy, which is likely to be associated with the deprived environment and the higher presence of low-value adding business with the constrained access to formal resources (Greene, Mole, and Storey 2008). All together, in locations where prevalence of informal contracts is high, we are less likely to observe poverty reduction.

At a country level, we control for the quality of institutions, measured here by a composite index of World Wide Governance Indicators (WWGI, World Bank), reflecting various dimensions of the institutional environment of an individual country, including (a) Control for corruption; (b) Government effectiveness; (c) Political stability; (d) Regulatory quality; (e) Rule of law; (f) Voice & Accountability. All these dimensions are highly collinear, so we construct their scale with alpha reliability test statistic being equal to 0.97.

Finally, we also control for macroeconomic indicators such as the level of economic development and GDP growth rate. We lag country-level institutional and macroeconomic variables by one year to allow for some time to elapse prior to realisation of their effect on poverty alleviation. Our constructed index of institutional quality is highly correlated with GDP per capita (0.81) which is well above a common cut-off point of 0.7. We therefore run our models using an alternative control for the level of development – a set of GDP pc dummies denoting the five quintiles of its distribution, which individually are not highly correlated with an index of institutional quality.

For further definition of these variables and descriptive statistics, see Table 1. The correlation matrix of all variables used in estimation is reported in Table 2.

Methodology

To obtain our results we employ an ordered probit model, using a 10-point ladder measures of poverty. Following Ahlstrom, Bruton, and Zhao (2013) we additionally undertake some robustness checks, using a probit model with focus on narrower measures of poverty based on the 20th centile-threshold of poverty ladder distribution. Since our data have hierarchical structure given that individuals are not randomly distributed across and within geographical districts and countries, they are more likely to exhibit similar characteristics or patterns of behaviour within their areas of local (Estrin, Korosteleva, and Mickiewicz 2013; Chasco and Gallo, 2013).

Table 1. Definitions of the variables and descriptive statistics.

Variable	LiTS Questions	Obs.	Mean	Std. Dev.	Min	Max
	Dependent variables					
Subjective poverty ladder	Q3.15: imagine a 10-step ladder where on the bottom, the first step, stand the poorest 10% of people in [your country] and on the highest step, the tenth, stand the richest 10% of people in [your country]	41,342	4.5	1.7	1	10
Objective poverty ladder	Q2.23: What is the total net monthly income of your household at present? Note: This is calculated as the total sum of income of all household members received from wages, pensions, social and family benefits, regular transfers from persons outside the household and from other sources. The variable was transformed by taking 10 centile of income distribution by country.	33,057	5.32	2.85	1	10
	Independent variables					
Unemployed	Q5.15 Occupation type Employment status is equal to 1 if the respondent is unemployed	20,113	0.09	0.29	0	1
Self-employed	Employment status is equal to 2 if the respondent is self-employed (Q5.15 = 5)	20,113	0.06	0.23	0	1
Business owner	Employment status is equal to 3 if the respondent is an employer (Q5.15 = 4)	20,113	0.024	0.15	0	1
Gender	Gender status (female = 1 and male = 0) (Q 1.03)	42,178	0.57	0.49	0	1
	Controls					
	Individual-level characteristics					
Urban	Urbanity status (urban = 1 and rural = 0)	42,178	0.55	0.49	0	1
Age	Q1.04: What is your age?	42,178	49	17	18	95
Married	Q7.01 Marital status (married = 1 and otherwise = 0)	42,178	.58	.49	0	1
Education	Q1.09: What is your education? The variable takes values from 1 = 'no education' to 7 = 'MA/PhD level'	42,178	4.4	1.5	1	7
Internet access	Q2.04: Do you have access to internet at home, inclusively on a smartphone?	42,178	0.63	0.48	0	1
Family trust	Q4.05a: To what extent do you trust family?	38,328	0.96	0.2	0	1
Neighbourhood Trust	Q4.05b: To what extent do you trust neighbourhood?	41,754	0.71	0.45	0	1
Institutional trust	Q4.04: To what extent do you trust the following institutions … (a) The Presidency; (b) The Government/Cabinet Ministers; (c) Regional Government; (d) Local Government; (e) The Parliament; (f) Courts; (g) Political Parties; (h) Armed Forces; (i) The Police A scale of all these questions is constructed	41,651	0.019	0.82	−1.93	1.78
	Regional (NUTS3)-level controls					
Family trust (NUTS3-country)	Aggregated to NUTS3-country level	42,178	0.96	0.04	0.25	1
Neighbourhood trust (NUTS3-country)	Aggregated to NUTS3-country level	42,178	0.71	0.12	0	1
Institutional trust (NUTS3-country)	Averaged at NUTS3-country level	42,178	0.001	0.96	−2.57	3.58
Informal contract arrangements (NUTS3-country)	Q 5.16 What type of contractual arrangement do you have with your employer? A response 'informal' has been coded as equal to 1. The responses are averaged at NUTS3-country level	42,138	0.13	0.155	0	1
	Country-level controls					
Institutional quality	World Bank World Wide Governance Indicators (percentile rankings): (a) Control for corruption; (b) Government effectiveness; (c) Political stability; (d) Regulatory quality; (e) Rule of law; (f) Voice & Accountability. A scale of all 6 variables is constructed.	42,177	−.11	.93	−1.76	1.35
GDP per capita constant 2010 US dollars	World Bank World Development Indicators, 2018. It is split further into five quintile groups (iq1-iq5, where iq1 is set as reference category)	42,177	9039.881	6357.5	932.9	23,781.3
GDP growth (annual %)	World Bank World Development Indicators, 2018.	42,177	2.1	3.2	−9.9	8

Table 2. Correlation matrix.

Variables	(1)	(2)	(3)	(4)	(5)	(6)	(7)	(8)	(9)	(10)	(11)	(12)	(13)
Subjective poverty ladder(1)	1												
Objective poverty ladder (2)	.36	1											
	(.00)												
Unemployed (3)	-.17	-.23	1										
	(.00)	(.00)											
Self-employed (4)	.01	.00	-.08	1									
	(.18)	(.96)	(.00)										
Business owner (5)	.09	.094	-.05	-.04	1								
	(.00)	(.00)	(.00)	(.00)									
Gender (Female=1) (6)	-.04	-.09	-.01	-.05	-.06	1							
	(.00)	(.00)	(.25)	(.00)	(.00)								
Urban (7)	.03	.13	-.05	-.04	.04	.04	1						
	(.00)	(.00)	(.00)	(.00)	(.00)	(.00)							
Age (8)	-.17	-.29	.00	.04	.02	.05	-.00	1					
	(.00)	(.00)	(.54)	(.00)	(.00)	(.00)	(.54)						
Education (9)	.18	.32	-.12	-.05	.02	-.00	.17	-.21	1				
	(.00)	(.00)	(.00)	(.00)	(.00)	(.40)	(.00)	(.00)					
Married (10)	.08	.26	-.00	.03	.03	-.13	-.09	-.03	.02	1			
	(.00)	(.00)	(.60)	(.00)	(.00)	(.00)	(.00)	(.00)	(.00)				
Internet access (11)	.26	.44	-.14	-.02	.03	-.04	.14	-.36	.27	.05	1		
	(.00)	(.00)	(.00)	(.00)	(.00)	(.00)	(.00)	(.00)	(.00)	(.00)			
Physical infrastructure (12)	.11	.07	-.08	-.03	.01	.01	.09	.06	.05	-.06	.07	1	
	(.00)	(.00)	(.00)	(.00)	(.26)	(.02)	(.00)	(.00)	(.00)	(.00)	(.00)		
Physical infrastructure (NUTS3-country) (13)	.05	.06	-.10	-.02	-.01	.03	.15	.11	.03	-.13	.12	.39	1
	(.00)	(.00)	(.00)	(.00)	(.17)	(.00)	(.00)	(.00)	(.00)	(.00)	(.00)	(.00)	
Family trust (14)	.03	.07	.00	-.01	.01	.01	-.00	-.02	.02	.04	.03	.04	-.01
	(.00)	(.00)	(.96)	(.31)	(.24)	(.01)	(.82)	(.00)	(.00)	(.00)	(.00)	(.00)	(.17)
Neighborhood Trust (15)	.04	.00	-.01	.01	.01	-.01	-.08	.08	-.01	.04	-.04	.04	-.02
	(.00)	(.80)	(.15)	(.14)	(.06)	(.26)	(.00)	(.00)	(.06)	(.00)	(.00)	(.00)	(.00)
Institutional trust (16)	.12	.01	-.05	-.01	0.01	.02	.15	-.03	.03	.05	-.12	.08	-.07
	(.00)	(.13)	(.00)	(.08)	(.19)	(.00)	(.00)	(.00)	(.00)	(.00)	(.00)	(.00)	(.00)
Family trust (NUTS3-country) (17)	-.01	.01	.03	-.00	.01	.00	-.02	-.02	-.05	.03	-.04	-.01	-.07
	(.14)	(.09)	(.00)	(.66)	(.24)	(.40)	(.00)	(.00)	(.00)	(.00)	(.00)	(.02)	(.00)
Neighbourhood trust (NUTS3-country) (18)	-.02	.00	.07	.03	.01	-.01	-.19	-.00	-.06	.08	-.12	-.07	-.17
	(.00)	(.81)	(.00)	(.00)	(.07)	(.02)	(.00)	(.32)	(.00)	(.00)	(.00)	(.00)	(.00)
Institutional trust (NUTS3-country) (19)	.05	-.02	-.01	.02	.01	.01	-.10	-.10	.04	.09	-.17	-.04	-.13
	(.00)	(.00)	(.32)	(.03)	(.14)	(.09)	(.00)	(.00)	(.00)	(.00)	(.00)	(.00)	(.00)
Informal contract arrangements (NUTS3-country) (20)	-.05	-.04	.04	.04	-.02	-.02	-.09	-.13	.04	.12	-.06	-.17	-.31
	(.00)	(.00)	(.00)	(.00)	(.03)	(.00)	(.00)	(.00)	(.00)	(.00)	(.00)	(.00)	(.00)
Institutional quality (21)	.01	.02	-.01	-.01	.02	.01	.04	.21	-.11	-.17	.13	.21	.44
	(.13)	(.00)	(.05)	(.42)	(.01)	(.09)	(.00)	(.00)	(.00)	(.00)	(.00)	(.00)	(.00)
GDP growth (annual %) (22)	.06	-.01	.07	.04	.03	-.03	-.12	-.02	-.18	.06	-.09	-.05	-.16
	(.00)	(.76)	(.00)	(.00)	(.00)	(.00)	(.00)	(.00)	(.00)	(.00)	(.00)	(.00)	(.00)
GDP per capita constant 2010 US dollars (iq1) (23)	-.04	-.01	.08	.03	.00	-.01	-.13	-.10	.06	.13	-.12	-.22	-.46
	(.00)	(.14)	(.00)	(.00)	(.99)	(.26)	(.00)	(.00)	(.00)	(.00)	(.00)	(.00)	(.00)
GDP per capita constant 2010 US dollars (iq2) (24)	-.003	-.01	.05	.05	-.00	-.02	.03	-.06	-.09	.10	-.02	-.07	-.1
	(.58)	(.06)	(.00)	(.00)	(.98)	(.00)	(.00)	(.00)	(.00)	(.00)	(.00)	(.00)	(.00)
GDP per capita constant 2010 US dollars (iq3) (25)	.002	.00	-.06	-.05	-.02	.01	.11	-.02	.11	-.06	.05	.07	.09
	(.66)	(.81)	(.00)	(.00)	(.00)	(.00)	(.00)	(.00)	(.00)	(.00)	(.00)	(.00)	(.00)
GDP per capita constant 2010 US dollars (iq4) (26)	.03	.01	-.04	-.03	.03	.02	.05	.14	-.00	-.13	.06	.15	.36
	(.00)	(.01)	(.00)	(.00)	(.00)	(.00)	(.00)	(.00)	(.54)	(.00)	(.00)	(.00)	(.00)
GDP per capita constant 2010 US dollars (iq5) (27)	.01	.01	-.04	.03	-.01	-.02	-.07	.06	-.12	-.07	.05	.11	.17
	(.00)	(.30)	(.00)	(.00)	(.10)	(.00)	(.00)	(.00)	(.00)	(.00)	(.00)	(.00)	(.00)

Variables	(14)	(15)	(16)	(17)	(18)	(19)	(20)	(21)	(22)	(23)	(24)	(25)	(26)	(27)
Family trust (14)	1													
Neighborhood Trust (15)	.22	1												
	(.00)													
Institutional trust (16)	.06	.19	1											
	(.00)	(.00)												
Family trust (NUTS3-country) (17)	.05	.09	.11	1										
	(.00)	(.00)	(.00)											
Neighbourhood trust (NUTS3-country) (18)	.07	.07	.19	0.32	1									
	(.00)	(.00)	(.00)	(.00)										
Institutional trust (NUTS3-country) (19)	.05	.10	.56	.18	.37	1								
	(.00)	(.00)	(.00)	(.00)	(.00)									
Informal contract arrangements (NUTS3-country) (20)	-.02	-.02	.03	.01	.03	.09	1							
	(.00)	(0.00)	(.00)	(.01)	(.00)	(.00)								
Institutional quality (21)	-.00	-.00	-.16	-.14	-.16	-.29	-.48	1						
	(.39)	(.39)	(.00)	(.00)	(.00)	(.00)	(.00)							
GDP growth (annual %) (22)	.07	.07	.22	.16	.26	.36	-.18	.20	1					
	(.00)	(.00)	(.00)	(.00)	(.00)	(.00)	(.00)	(.00)						
GDP per capita constant 2010 US dollars (iq1) (23)	.03	.03	.03	.15	.30	.10	.36	-.64	-.02	1				
	(.00)	(.00)	(.00)	(.00)	(.00)	(.00)	(.00)	(.00)	(.00)					
GDP per capita constant 2010 US dollars (iq2) (24)	-.04	-.04	-.01	-.11	-.09	-.05	.17	-.08	.04	-.30	1			
	(.00)	(.00)	(.29)	(.00)	(.00)	(.00)	(.00)	(.00)	(.00)	(.00)				
GDP per capita constant 2010 US dollars (iq3) (25)	-.01	-.01	-.01	.03	-.13	-.01	-.06	-.16	-.20	-.30	-.27	1		
	(.11)	(.11)	(.22)	(.00)	(.00)	(.04)	(.00)	(.00)	(.00)	(.00)	(.00)			
GDP per capita constant 2010 US dollars (iq4) (26)	.03	.03	.02	-.04	-.05	.01	-.33	.64	.10	-.33	-.30	-.30	1	
	(.00)	(.00)	(.00)	(.00)	(.00)	(.12)	(.00)	(.00)	(.00)	(.00)	(.00)	(.00)		
GDP per capita constant 2010 US dollars (iq5) (27)	-.01	-.01	-.06	-.06	-.06	-.09	-.22	.37	.16	-.16	-.14	-.14	-.16	1
	(.03)	(.03)	(.00)	(.00)	(.00)	(.00)	(.00)	(.00)	(.00)	(.00)	(.00)	(.00)	(.00)	

Thus, our baseline selection equation can be written as follows:

$$\begin{aligned}
Poverty_{ijk} = {} & \alpha_0 \\
& + \alpha_1 l4.poverty_{ijk} + \alpha_1 urban_{ijk} + \alpha_2 age_{ijk} \\
& + \alpha_3 age_sq_{ijk} + \alpha_4 marital\ status_{ijk} + \alpha_5 gender_{ijk} + \alpha_6 unemployed_{ijk} \\
& + \alpha_7 self_employed_{ijk} + \alpha_8 business_owner_{ijk} + \alpha_9 internet_access_{ijk} \\
& + +\alpha_{10} education_{ijk} + \alpha_{11} family_trust_{ijk} + \alpha_{12} NUTS3_family_trust_{jk} \\
& + \alpha_{15} instit_trust_{ijk} + \alpha_{16} NUTS3_instit_trust_{jk} \\
& + \alpha_{17} NUTS3_informal_contract_{jk} + \alpha_{18} l.instit_quality_k + \alpha_{19} l.iq2_k \\
& + \alpha_{20} l.iq3_k + \alpha_{21} l.iq4_k + \alpha_{22} l.iq5_k + \alpha_{23} l.GDPpc\ growth_k + e_{ijk} + g_{jk} + v_k
\end{aligned} \tag{1}$$

Where $Poverty_{ijk}$ is a respective measure of poverty. We control for the initial level of poverty reported by respondents as of four years ago ($l4.poverty_{ijk}$; the operator l4. indicates that this variable is lagged by 4 years). Variables with sub-scripts *ijk* denote individual-level variables, whereas variables with subscripts *jk* and *k* denote respectively NUTS3 and country-level variables. The operator *l.* is added to country-level variables to denote that a variable is lagged by one year. The combination of $e_{ijk} + g_{jk} + v_k$ is the random part of the equation, where v_k are the country level residuals, g_{jk} are the NUTS3 (district-level) residuals, and e_{ijk} represents individual-level residuals.

Also we interact gender with each of employment status variables to test the linkages between entrepreneurship-gender and poverty.

Empirical results

Table 3 below contains the results from using subjective (Models 1 & 3) and objective (models 2 & 4) measures of poverty based on a 10-step ladder of income distribution. These models are used to test Hypotheses 1–2 (Models 1–2), and 3 (Models 3–4). Table 4 reports marginal effects related to our key variables of interest, which come across as significant determinants of poverty alleviation.

First of all, across various specifications reported in Table 3, we find strong and largely consistent support for hypothesis H1b, showing positive and significant effect of business ownership on poverty reduction. The marginal effect results reported in Table 4 suggest that entrepreneurial business owners are 0.5 percentage points more likely than paid employees to self-perceive themselves at the top 10% of income distribution, and about 1 percentage points less likely to be at the bottom of subjective income ladder distribution (see Model 1 reported within the *Business Ownership* column in Table 4). In terms of the economic magnitude of this effect, the results are much stronger when we employ the objective measure of poverty based on a net income reported by respondents, where business owners' probability to be at the top level of distribution surges to 13 percentage points.

At the same time, consistently across all specifications we do not find any significant association between self-employment and poverty reduction (hypothesis H1a). When interpreted jointly with the business ownership results, this sheds some light on the importance of different types of entrepreneurial activity for economic growth and poverty with emphasizing the importance of high-value adding activity as opposed to low-value adding entrepreneurship, confirming hypothesis H1c. Finally, as expected we find unemployment associated with the bottom of the poverty ladder distribution.

The gender results based on different measures of poverty, used in this study, reveal some controversy. Thus, using a subjective measure of poverty we do not observe gender gap in income distribution, implying similarity in perception of income distribution between men and women. However, using objective measure of poverty based on net income reported by respondents, being a female is strongly associated with a lower position on poverty ladder of income distribution. For more in-depth understanding of these results we turn again to the marginal effects results reported in Table 4, contrasting predicted margins of the effects for females versus males. Being female

Table 3. Subjective & objective poverty ladder.

	Model 1	Model 2	Model 3	Model 4
	Subjective	Objective	Subjective	Objective
Subjective poverty ladder (t-4)	0.557***	0.0825***	0.557***	0.0824***
	(0.006)	(0.005)	(0.00588)	(0.00551)
Urban	−0.0475*	0.0777***	−0.0484*	0.0776***
	(0.0196)	(0.0220)	(0.0196)	(0.0220)
Age	−0.0275***	−0.0223***	−0.0278***	−0.0223***
	(0.00507)	(0.00559)	(0.00507)	(0.00559)
Age squared	0.0002***	0.0002**	0.0002***	0.0002**
	(0.000)	(0.000)	(0.000)	(0.000)
Married	0.106***	0.537***	0.104***	0.536***
	(0.0182)	(0.0207)	(0.0182)	(0.0207)
Gender	−0.0197	**−0.0595****	**−0.0444***	**−0.0710*****
(Female = 1)	(0.0163)	**(0.0183)**	**(0.0178)**	**(0.0199)**
Higher education	0.0847***	0.170***	0.0848***	0.170***
	(0.00638)	(0.00720)	(0.00638)	(0.00720)
Internet access	0.292***	0.622***	0.290***	0.622***
	(0.0238)	(0.0262)	(0.0238)	(0.0262)
Empl_status1	−0.415***	−0.707***	−0.511***	−0.731***
(unemployed)	(0.0297)	(0.0327)	(0.0406)	(0.0450)
Empl_status1#Female	-	-	**0.196*****	0.0485
	-	-	**(0.0566)**	(0.0622)
Empl_status3	0.0154	0.0105	−0.0271	−0.00996
(self_employed)	(0.0354)	(0.0409)	(0.0451)	(0.0519)
Empl_status3#Female	-	-	0.102	0.0490
	-	-	(0.0707)	(0.0815)
Empl_status4	**0.350*****	**0.611*****	**0.320*****	**0.528*****
(business owner)	**(0.0523)**	**(0.0653)**	**(0.0632)**	**(0.0775)**
Empl_status4#Female	-	-	0.0814	**0.277^{+}**
	-	-	(0.111)	**(0.142)**
Phys_infrast_satisf	0.104***	0.0533***	0.104***	0.0535***
	(0.0110)	(0.0122)	(0.0110)	(0.0122)
Phys_infrast_satisf (NUTS3-country)	0.00762	0.0306	0.00726	0.0306
	(0.0236)	(0.0262)	(0.0236)	(0.0262)
Inst_Trust	0.185***	0.0437**	0.186***	0.0438**
	(0.0128)	(0.0143)	(0.0128)	(0.0143)
Inst_Trust	−0.0237	−0.0746*	−0.0240	−0.0746*
(NUTS3-country)	(0.0305)	(0.0298)	(0.0305)	(0.0298)
Family_Trust	0.0252	0.268***	0.0251	0.266***
	(0.0443)	(0.0508)	(0.0443)	(0.0508)
Neighbourhood_Trust	0.0505**	0.0253	0.0514**	0.0263
	(0.0187)	(0.0211)	(0.0187)	(0.0211)
Family_Trust	−0.150	0.0759	−0.150	0.0859
(NUTS3-country)	(0.342)	(0.381)	(0.342)	(0.381)
Neighbourhood_Trust	−0.185	−0.0669	−0.189	−0.0687
(NUTS3-country)	(0.152)	(0.176)	(0.153)	(0.176)
Informal_contract	−0.502***	−0.401**	−0.504***	−0.401**
(NUTS3-country)	(0.124)	(0.135)	(0.124)	(0.135)
Institutional_quality	−0.116	0.128*	−0.115	0.128*
(country-level) (t-1)	(0.0733)	(0.0648)	(0.0733)	(0.0647)
GDP growth (t-1)	0.0588***	0.0145^{+}	0.0587***	0.0145^{+}
(country-level)	(0.00944)	(0.00812)	(0.00942)	(0.00811)
GDPpc (iq2)	−0.0789	−0.245*	−0.0810	−0.245*
	(0.109)	(0.0953)	(0.108)	(0.0952)
GDPpc (iq3)	−0.189^{+}	−0.283***	−0.190^{+}	−0.283***
	(0.0978)	(0.0817)	(0.0976)	(0.0816)
GDPpc (iq4)	0.00375	−0.273^{+}	0.000171	−0.274^{+}
	(0.169)	(0.147)	(0.169)	(0.147)
GDPpc (iq5)	−0.0258	−0.0965	−0.0298	−0.0958
	(0.201)	(0.175)	(0.200)	(0.175)
var(countryTE_num)	0.0103^{+}	0.00140	0.0102	0.00136
	(0.00623)	(0.00318)	(0.00620)	(0.00317)
var(NUTS3_CountryTE)	0.129***	0.165***	0.130***	0.165***
	(0.0121)	(0.0147)	(0.0121)	(0.0147)
N	17,983	14,103	17,983	14,103

Standard errors in parentheses; $^{+}p < 0.10$, $^{*}p < 0.05$, $^{**}p < 0.01$, $^{***}p < 0.001$

Table 4. Summary of key marginal effects based on the results reported in Table 3: Contrasts of predictive margins.

Variables	Gender (female==1 vs. male=0)				Business ownership (BO) (BO=1 vs. Paid Employment=0)				Gender_X_Business Ownership (Gender and BO interaction 1 vs. 0)	
Ordinal outcomes/model	Model 1	Model 2	Model 3	Model 4	Model 1	Model 2	Model 3	Model 4	Model 3	Model 4
1 (10th bottom centile)	0.0007	0.005**	-0.0002	0.005**	-0.010***	-0.033***	-0.010***	-0.035***	-0.002	-0.012**
	(0.0006)	(0.001)	(0.0006)	(0.002)	(0.001)	(0.003)	(0.0013)	(0.003)	(0.002)	(0.004)
2 (20th centile)	0.001	0.003**	0.0008	0.003***	-0.017***	-0.027***	-0.0172***	-0.028***	-0.004	-0.010*
	(0.001)	(0.001)	(0.001)	(0.001)	(0.0022)	(0.002)	(0.0023)	(0.002)	(0.005)	(0.004)
3 (30th centile)	0.002	0.004**	0.002	0.004***	-0.033***	-0.037***	-0.034***	-0.04***	-0.008	-0.015*
	(0.002)	(0.001)	(0.002)	(0.001)	(0.005)	(0.003)	(0.005)	(0.004)	(0.01)	(0.007)
4 (40th centile)	0.001	0.003**	0.0024*	0.003***	-0.027***	-0.032***	-0.0278***	-0.034***	-0.007	-0.014*
	(0.001)	(0.001)	(0.001)	(0.001)	(0.004)	(0.003)	(0.0047)	(0.003)	(0.009)	(0.007)
5 (50th centile)	-0.001	0.003**	0.0003	0.0028**	0.003***	-0.033***	0.0024***	-0.036***	-0.00003	-0.015+
	(0.001)	(0.001)	(0.001)	(0.001)	(0.002)	(0.004)	(0.0017)	(0.0042)	(0.0023)	(0.008)
6 (60th centile)	-0.002	0.001**	-0.0019	0.001*	0.027***	-0.025***	0.027***	-0.028***	0.0062	-0.014+
	(0.001)	(0.0004)	(0.0013)	(0.001)	(0.004)	(0.004)	(0.004)	(0.004)	(0.008)	(0.008)
7 (70th centile)	-0.001	-0.0005**	-0.002	-0.001+	0.028***	-0.008***	0.029***	-0.0102***	0.0068	-0.007
	(0.001)	(0.0002)	(0.0012)	(0.0004)	(0.0045)	(0.002)	(0.005)	(0.003)	(0.009)	(0.0055)
8 (80th centile)	-0.001	-0.003**	-0.0012	-0.003***	0.019***	0.013***	0.019***	0.012***	0.0046	0.0005
	(0.001)	0.001	(0.0008)	(0.001)	(0.003)	(0.001)	(0.0035)	(0.002)	(0.007)	(0.003)
9 (90th centile)	-0.0003	-0.006**	-0.0003	-0.006***	0.005***	0.052***	0.006***	0.054***	0.0014	0.018*
	(0.0002)	(0.002)	(0.0002)	(0.0018)	(0.001)	(0.004)	(0.001)	(0.004)	(0.002)	(0.007)
10 (10th top centile)	-0.0002	-0.01**	-0.0003	-0.009**	0.005***	.131***	0.005***	.145***	0.001	0.068+
	(0.0002)	(0.003)	(0.0002)	(0.003)	(0.001)	(0.017)	(0.001)	(0.019)	(0.002)	(0.039)

Note: Ordinal outcomes correspond to the respective centile of the poverty ladder distribution. For example, outcome 1 corresponds to the 10th bottom centile of poverty ladder distribution (i.e. the 10th centile of the poorest respondents in the sample). We report contrasts of predictive margins (the difference in probabilities) for the respective variables of interest, based on the results of the models reported in Table 3. Standard errors in parentheses; $^{+}p < 0.10$, $^{*}p < 0.05$, $^{**}p < 0.01$, $^{***}p < 0.001$

instead of male increases respondent's probability of being at the bottom of income distribution by 0.5 percentage points, and respectively reduces probability of being at the top of income distribution by 1 percentage points (see Model 2 within the *Gender* column in Table 4). This provides partial (using objective measure of poverty) support for Hypothesis 2, although in terms of the economic magnitude of this effect, these results reveal only marginal differences between females in males.

When we turn to examining the interaction term results (Models 3 and 4 in Table 3), we find that female business-owners are likely to be richer than their male counterparts (Model 4, based on the objective measure of poverty). Being female business-owner increases probability to be at the top of income distribution by 6.8 percentage points (see Table 4 last column, outcome 10). Therefore, we also partly (using the objective measure of poverty and focusing on business ownership with employment creation) support Hypothesis 3.

We turn now to exploring cross country-group differences (Table 5). First, the results using a 10-step poverty ladder of income distribution reveal the following. Consistently across all specifications, we find a positive effect of business ownership on poverty reduction. Second, being female retains its significance and positive association with lower position on poverty ladder of income distribution in the case of Central Europe and Baltic States, but not elsewhere. The positive association of unemployed status of females with subjective poverty is found in all country groups except for South Eastern Europe, implying that unemployed females on average are better off than their male counterparts.

Finally, we turn to Table 6, which provides some robustness checks for our results using a narrower definition of poverty. Table 6 reports the results based on the probit model looking at the probability of respondents falling within the bottom quintile of income distribution. First of all, the results on business ownership lose their significance, implying that we do not have many cases where the 20% of poorest individuals happen to be business owners. Second, we find that the gender differences are almost erased retaining their marginal significance in the CEB region in the case of objective measure of poverty only. This further strengthens the evidence in support of Hypothesis H2. However, we get some contrasting results illustrating the regional differences: in the CEB region, self-employed females are likely to be more associated with the bottom 20% of income distribution, using subjective measure of poverty, whereas in the CA region, based on a net income measure of poverty (objective poverty), they are richer than their male counterparts, although the results are only marginally significant at 10% level of significance. We do not find any significant regional gender differences in business ownership affecting poverty alleviation. Overall, these findings partly reject our Hypotheses H4a and H4b.

In addition to this main set of the results, we also obtain some other interesting results on other determinants of poverty.

First, we find that individuals higher up the poverty ladder tend to be better educated; having access to internet; married, being about middle-age.

Satisfaction with the physical infrastructure development at an individual level is positively related to poverty reduction. However, as regards the aggregated-NUTs3 effect this result holds only in the case of CEB countries, using subjective measure of poverty. We also find strong support for the importance of institutional trust at individual-level, but negative effect at a NUTS3 level, in particular in the context of the CA region, showing, perhaps, that at the district-aggregated level the costs of institutional reforms are likely to disproportionally negatively affect the poorest in the CA region. Finally, we find some positive linking between inbound trust (bonding social capital), proxied by trusting family and neighbourhood at an individual level, but primarily insignificant at a district level of aggregation. The prevalence rate of individuals with informal contractual arrangements in a district is strongly associated with a higher state of impoverishment.

Finally, at a country-level we find positive effect of the overall institutional quality on poverty reduction, using objective measure of poverty. As regards to cross-region-country differences, we

Table 5. Subjective and objective poverty ladder: Regional differences & entrepreneurship–gender interaction effects.

	CEB		SEE		EEC		CA	
Variables/Model specification	Model 5 Subjective	Model 6 Objective	Model 7 Subjective	Model 8 Objective	Model 9 Subjective	Model 10 Objective	Model 11 Subjective	Model 12 Objective
Subjective poverty ladder (t-4)	0.601***	0.0784***	0.670***	0.0882***	0.451***	0.0795***	0.509***	0.0870***
	(0.0105)	(0.00989)	(0.0120)	(0.0108)	(0.0104)	(0.0101)	(0.0173)	(0.0158)
Urban	−0.00222	−0.0301	−0.0994**	0.0593	−0.00924	0.219***	−0.204**	0.105
	(0.0324)	(0.0369)	(0.0341)	(0.0383)	(0.0418)	(0.0477)	(0.0724)	(0.0710)
Age	−0.040***	−0.00645	−0.0277**	−0.0195^{+}	−0.0325**	−0.0238*	−0.0100	−0.0805***
	(0.0089)	(0.00993)	(0.00981)	(0.0108)	(0.0101)	(0.0111)	(0.0141)	(0.0149)
Age squared	0.0003***	−0.000105	0.000267*	0.000204	0.000318**	0.000206	0.0000750	0.00102***
	(0.0001)	(0.000116)	(0.000116)	(0.000128)	(0.000120)	(0.000132)	(0.000172)	(0.000183)
Married	0.108***	0.737***	0.129***	0.360***	0.102**	0.540***	0.0958^{+}	0.468***
	(0.0296)	(0.0346)	(0.0362)	(0.0407)	(0.0373)	(0.0425)	(0.0557)	(0.0596)
Gender	−0.122***	−0.182***	−0.0113	0.0361	−0.0342	−0.0425	0.0364	−0.0464
(Female = 1)	(0.0297)	(0.0338)	(0.0339)	(0.0377)	(0.0369)	(0.0416)	(0.0513)	(0.0536)
Higher education	0.112***	0.194***	0.102***	0.188***	0.0332*	0.143***	0.102***	0.145***
	(0.0108)	(0.0127)	(0.0122)	(0.0136)	(0.0131)	(0.0146)	(0.0191)	(0.0200)
Internet access	0.295***	0.745***	0.300***	0.649***	0.199***	0.589***	0.454***	0.528***
	(0.0507)	(0.0564)	(0.0456)	(0.0505)	(0.0431)	(0.0478)	(0.0568)	(0.0584)
Empl_status1	−0.764***	−0.988***	−0.466***	−0.669***	−0.455***	−0.732***	−0.342**	−0.461***
(unemployed)	(0.0895)	(0.0962)	(0.0688)	(0.0781)	(0.0736)	(0.0821)	(0.113)	(0.122)
Empl_status1#	0.316**	0.00354	0.0781	0.0187	0.259*	0.156	0.396*	−0.0253
Female	(0.116)	(0.126)	(0.0979)	(0.109)	(0.104)	(0.114)	(0.174)	(0.185)
Empl_status3	0.0990	0.0402	−0.0557	−0.0682	−0.0925	0.0838	−0.0557	−0.0682
(self-employed)	(0.0828)	(0.0993)	(0.0800)	(0.0922)	(0.105)	(0.121)	(0.0800)	(0.0922)
Empl_status3#	0.0167	0.00352	0.0926	0.0646	0.0559	−0.284	0.0926	0.0646
Female	(0.125)	(0.152)	(0.132)	(0.148)	(0.155)	(0.181)	(0.132)	(0.148)
Empl_status4	0.280**	0.499***	0.359**	0.740***	0.289^{+}	0.425*	0.359**	0.740***
(business owner)	(0.101)	(0.128)	(0.110)	(0.133)	(0.164)	(0.206)	(0.110)	(0.133)
Empl_status4#	0.191	0.357	−0.0404	0.0570	0.242	0.324	−0.0404	0.0570
Female	(0.173)	(0.237)	(0.197)	(0.248)	(0.296)	(0.352)	(0.197)	(0.248)
Phys_infrast_satisf	0.0819***	0.122***	0.124***	0.0249	0.121***	0.0427^{+}	0.0636*	0.0356
	(0.0220)	(0.0252)	(0.0186)	(0.0206)	(0.0229)	(0.0253)	(0.0280)	(0.0291)
Phys_infrast_satisf (NUTS3-country)	0.132^{+}	0.0657	0.0493	−0.00436	−0.0222	0.0835	0.00937	0.0446
	(0.0705)	(0.0914)	(0.0473)	(0.0662)	(0.0604)	(0.0628)	(0.0391)	(0.0358)
Inst_Trust	0.255***	0.0975***	0.197***	0.0715**	0.131***	−0.00700	0.124**	−0.0202
	(0.0239)	(0.0271)	(0.0220)	(0.0247)	(0.0249)	(0.0280)	(0.0394)	(0.0423)
Inst_Trust	0.108	0.210^{+}	0.0137	0.0103	0.0344	−0.0609	−0.0710	−0.115^{+}
(NUTS3-country)	(0.0898)	(0.123)	(0.0609)	(0.0806)	(0.0631)	(0.0670)	(0.0692)	(0.0614)
Family_Trust	0.0875	0.301**	0.0750	0.249*	−0.0945	0.216*	0.187	0.427*

(Continued)

Table 5. (Continued).

	CEB		SEE		EEC		CA	
Variables/Model specification	Model 5 Subjective	Model 6 Objective	Model 7 Subjective	Model 8 Objective	Model 9 Subjective	Model 10 Objective	Model 11 Subjective	Model 12 Objective
	(0.0803)	(0.0930)	(0.0898)	(0.101)	(0.0740)	(0.0865)	(0.150)	(0.166)
Neighbourhood_Trust	0.0369	0.0221	0.0491	0.0332	0.0366	−0.0130	0.141*	0.0643
	(0.0321)	(0.0366)	(0.0348)	(0.0391)	(0.0360)	(0.0410)	(0.0604)	(0.0642)
Family_Trust	0.0995	1.769*	−1.103	1.245	−0.329	−0.623	2.400^{+}	−1.395
(NUTS3-country)	(0.594)	(0.837)	(0.730)	(0.977)	(0.507)	(0.521)	(1.284)	(1.125)
Neighbourhood_Trust	−0.189	−0.846^{+}	−0.127	−0.0785	−0.286	−0.115	−0.484	0.141
(NUTS3-country)	(0.289)	(0.434)	(0.261)	(0.369)	(0.296)	(0.316)	(0.357)	(0.327)
Informal_contract	−0.626	−0.162	−0.500^{+}	−0.144	−0.272	−0.631**	−0.625**	−0.155
(NUTS3-country)	(0.524)	(0.718)	(0.295)	(0.406)	(0.226)	(0.235)	(0.203)	(0.182)
Institutional_quality	−0.0611	−0.0770	−0.331	−0.381	−0.0372	0.332*	−0.588	−0.821
(country-level)	(0.249)	(0.247)	(0.319)	(0.359)	(0.154)	(0.158)	(0.777)	(0.688)
GDP growth	0.102^{+}	−0.0544	0.0622	−0.0474	0.0297*	−0.0112	0.0356	0.0116
(country-level)	(0.0529)	(0.0512)	(0.0646)	(0.0692)	(0.0147)	(0.0153)	(0.0563)	(0.0494)
GDPpc (iq2)	0	0	−0.0392	0.243	−0.336^{+}	−0.288	0	0
	(.)	(.)	(0.203)	(0.233)	(0.178)	(0.184)	(.)	(.)
GDPpc (iq3)	0	0	−0.122	0.583	−0.147	−0.281*	−0.0172	0.416
	(.)	(.)	(0.312)	(0.365)	(0.120)	(0.125)	(0.609)	(0.539)
GDPpc (iq4)	0.00864	−0.353*	0	0	0	0	0	0
	(0.148)	(0.144)	(.)	(.)	(.)	(.)	(.)	(.)
GDPpc (iq5)	0	0	0	0	0	0	0	0
	(.)	(.)	(.)	(.)	(.)	(.)	(.)	(.)
var(CountryTE)	0.0167	0.00795	0.00738	3.93e-34	2.82e-32	4.20e-37	4.01e-37	9.33e-39
_cont	(0.0107)	(0.0128)	(0.00733)	(4.53e-18)	(1.02e-17)	(1.43e-20)	(8.38e-21)	(5.13e-22)
var(NUTS3_CountryTE)	0.0573***	0.120***	0.0645***	0.160***	0.141***	0.141***	0.211***	0.128***
_cont	(0.0143)	(0.0245)	(0.0151)	(0.0286)	(0.0222)	(0.0237)	(0.0364)	(0.0269)
N	6066	4595	5063	3958	4458	3496	2396	2054

Standard errors in parentheses; $^{+}p < 0.10$, $^{*}p < 0.05$, $^{**}p < 0.01$, $^{***}p < 0.001$.
Note: CEB- Central Europe and Baltic states; SEE – South East Europe; ECC – Eastern Europe; CA – Central Asia.

Table 6. Subjective and objective poverty occurrence: Regional differences & gender-employment status interaction effects (poverty measures reflect the bottom quintile of the self-perceived and reported poverty income ladder distribution).

	CEB		SEE		EEC		CA	
	Model 13	Model 14	Model 15	Model 16	Model 17	Model 18	Model 19	Model 20
Variables/model specification	Subjective Poverty20th centile	Objective Poverty20th centile	Subjective Poverty20th centile	Objective Poverty20th centile	Subjective Poverty20th centile	Objective Poverty20th centile	Subjective Poverty20th centile	Objective Poverty20th centile
Subjective poverty20th centile (t-4)	2.077***	0.385***	2.146***	0.487***	1.783***	0.377***	1.846***	0.340**
	(0.0826)	(0.108)	(0.0919)	(0.104)	(0.0786)	(0.0952)	(0.135)	(0.107)
Urban	0.0384	−0.0519	0.137	0.0697	−0.0755	−0.150$^+$	0.304$^+$	−0.151
	(0.0756)	(0.0784)	(0.0858)	(0.0724)	(0.0731)	(0.0800)	(0.161)	(0.102)
Age	0.0750**	0.0101	0.0283	−0.0215	0.0502*	0.0426*	0.0279	0.100***
	(0.0238)	(0.0219)	(0.0239)	(0.0197)	(0.0201)	(0.0212)	(0.0378)	(0.0249)
Age squared	−0.000762**	0.0000434	−0.000266	0.000265	−0.000489*	−0.000400	−0.000126	−0.00125***
	(0.000273)	(0.000253)	(0.000280)	(0.000233)	(0.000234)	(0.000248)	(0.000452)	(0.000307)
Married	−0.127$^+$	−0.799***	−0.166$^+$	−0.240**	−0.285***	−0.517***	−0.205	−0.440***
	(0.0734)	(0.0852)	(0.0893)	(0.0780)	(0.0689)	(0.0786)	(0.135)	(0.0947)
Gender	−0.0494	0.204*	−0.0167	0.0897	0.107	0.0436	−0.0355	−0.0170
	(0.0798)	(0.0869)	(0.0925)	(0.0783)	(0.0735)	(0.0866)	(0.133)	(0.0888)
Higher education	−0.137***	−0.184***	−0.133***	−0.150***	−0.0745**	−0.118***	−0.165**	−0.200***
	(0.0294)	(0.0328)	(0.0324)	(0.0266)	(0.0247)	(0.0276)	(0.0514)	(0.0331)
Internet access	−0.403***	−0.693***	−0.606***	−0.559***	−0.331***	−0.498***	−0.646***	−0.588***
	(0.0991)	(0.0901)	(0.0911)	(0.0787)	(0.0727)	(0.0783)	(0.147)	(0.0937)
Empl_status1	0.903***	1.266***	0.348**	0.856***	0.604***	0.708***	0.453$^+$	0.682***
(unemployed)	(0.142)	(0.144)	(0.133)	(0.110)	(0.116)	(0.127)	(0.246)	(0.163)
Empl_status1#	−0.0862	−0.214	−0.122	−0.219	−0.186	−0.161	−0.665	−0.00991
Female	(0.190)	(0.188)	(0.199)	(0.161)	(0.164)	(0.178)	(0.430)	(0.247)
Empl_status3	−0.803*	0.0452	−0.0486	0.213	0.270	0.245	−0.0873	0.0199
(self-employed)	(0.363)	(0.259)	(0.204)	(0.168)	(0.188)	(0.221)	(0.294)	(0.181)
Empl_status3#	1.132**	−0.141	0.252	−0.227	−0.351	0.462	−0.0581	−0.694$^+$
Female	(0.420)	(0.376)	(0.323)	(0.279)	(0.279)	(0.299)	(0.514)	(0.387)
Empl_status4	0.0305	−0.250	−0.294	0	−0.350	0.426	0.0104	−0.398
	(0.286)	(0.488)	(0.618)	(.)	(0.460)	(0.362)	(0.636)	(0.376)
Empl_status4#	0.174	0.403	0	0	0	0	0	−0.218
Female	(0.480)	(0.685)	(.)	(.)	(.)	(.)	(.)	(0.740)
Phys_infrast_satisf	−0.108*	−0.0959$^+$	−0.145***	−0.0167	−0.156***	−0.103*	−0.0882	−0.0131
	(0.0518)	(0.0550)	(0.0416)	(0.0383)	(0.0384)	(0.0445)	(0.0700)	(0.0455)
Phys_infrast_satisf (NUTS3-country)	−0.174	0.0657	0.0228	0.0404	−0.107	−0.0865	0.0608	−0.0362
	(0.119)	(0.114)	(0.0677)	(0.0895)	(0.0906)	(0.0930)	(0.0825)	(0.0467)
Inst_Trust	−0.267***	−0.0458	−0.286***	−0.124**	−0.153**	0.00215	−0.216*	−0.0317

(Continued)

Table 6. (Continued).

	CEB		SEE		EEC		CA	
	Model 13	Model 14	Model 15	Model 16	Model 17	Model 18	Model 19	Model 20
Variables/model specification	Subjective Poverty20th centile	Objective Poverty20th centile	Subjective Poverty20th centile	Objective Poverty20th centile	Subjective Poverty20th centile	Objective Poverty20th centile	Subjective Poverty20th centile	Objective Poverty20th centile
	(0.0568)	(0.0632)	(0.0584)	(0.0465)	(0.0476)	(0.0525)	(0.0954)	(0.0704)
Inst_Trust	−0.145	−0.132	−0.0616	0.0770	0.0889	0.0492	−0.0996	0.141^{+}
(NUTS3-country)	(0.150)	(0.145)	(0.0911)	(0.115)	(0.0924)	(0.0963)	(0.136)	(0.0818)
Family_Trust	−0.0166	−0.382*	0.103	−0.363*	0.180	−0.207	−0.569^{+}	−0.592*
	(0.179)	(0.163)	(0.227)	(0.174)	(0.146)	(0.152)	(0.295)	(0.249)
Neighbourhood_Trust	0.0177	0.0320	−0.144^{+}	−0.0581	−0.110	0.0486	−0.190	0.0523
	(0.0774)	(0.0834)	(0.0869)	(0.0742)	(0.0691)	(0.0800)	(0.145)	(0.107)
Family_Trust	−0.569	−0.624	1.117	−2.917*	−0.375	0.407	−6.319**	1.193
(NUTS3-country)	(1.127)	(1.146)	(1.332)	(1.349)	(0.821)	(0.865)	(2.109)	(1.461)
Neighbourhood_Trust	0.528	0.857	0.249	0.311	0.646	0.467	1.974**	−0.417
(NUTS3-country)	(0.549)	(0.601)	(0.444)	(0.573)	(0.447)	(0.494)	(0.743)	(0.425)
Informal_contract	−0.296	1.320	1.065*	−0.163	−0.211	1.116***	1.158**	0.125
(NUTS3-country)	(0.871)	(0.830)	(0.426)	(0.548)	(0.324)	(0.320)	(0.368)	(0.235)
Institutional_quality	0.186	−0.118	0.172	0.204	−0.192	−0.353^{+}	4.676*	1.075
(country-level)	(0.238)	(0.242)	(0.392)	(0.483)	(0.189)	(0.193)	(1.898)	(0.927)
GDP growth	−0.0652	0.0908^{+}	−0.105	0.163^{+}	−0.00140	0.0425*	0.394**	0.0865
(country-level)	(0.0472)	(0.0484)	(0.0743)	(0.0934)	(0.0190)	(0.0208)	(0.130)	(0.0625)
GDPpc (iq2)	0	0	0.00323	−0.0637	0.212	0.334	0	0
	(.)	(.)	(0.238)	(0.299)	(0.229)	(0.229)	(.)	(.)
GDPpc (iq3)	0	0	0.409	−0.565	0.0450	0.179	−1.785	−0.169
	(.)	(.)	(0.361)	(0.470)	(0.166)	(0.169)	(1.348)	(0.739)
GDPpc (iq4)	0.132	0.0586	0	0	0	0	0	0
	(0.138)	(0.139)	(.)	(.)	(.)	(.)	(.)	(.)
GDPpc (iq5)	0	0	0	0	0	0	0	0
	(.)	(.)	(.)	(.)	(.)	(.)	(.)	(.)
_cons	−2.669*	−0.691	−3.077*	2.632^{+}	−2.469**	−2.401**	8.144*	−0.813
	(1.192)	(1.212)	(1.401)	(1.368)	(0.891)	(0.920)	(3.288)	(1.932)
Var(countryTE)	4.48e-35	4.40e-38	3.52e-35	1.16e-32	4.91e-35	3.64e-36	1.16e-34	2.10e-35
_cons	(4.39e-19)	(9.64e-21)	(3.93e-19)	(1.43e-17)	(3.35e-19)	(1.30e-19)	(2.49e-17)	(3.42e-19)
Var(NUTS3_CountryTE)	0.0451^{+}	0.0334	0.0398	0.191***	0.142***	0.123**	0.253*	0.116**
_cons	(0.0270)	(0.0282)	(0.0296)	(0.0461)	(0.0376)	(0.0435)	(0.120)	(0.0414)
N	6066	4595	4965	3861	4440	3481	2358	2054

Standard errors in parentheses; $^{+}p < 0.10$, $^{*}p < 0.05$, $^{**}p < 0.01$, $^{***}p < 0.001$

Note: CEB- Central Europe and Baltic states; SEE – South East Europe; ECC – Eastern Europe; CA – Central Asia.

only observe the positive effect of a better quality of institutional environment on poverty reduction in the context of EEA region (based on using objective measure of poverty). Interestingly enough, while GDPpc economic growth is important for the overall sample of transition economies for climbing the poverty ladder, its effect is only significant in CEB and EEA regions, using subjective measures of poverty.

Discussion

Using the recent wave of the EBRD Life in Transition Survey III (2016) data, this study explored empirically the relationship between poverty alleviation, entrepreneurship and gender. While entrepreneurship has been increasingly recognized as an important channel for combating poverty, an empirical evidence to support this claim, and also to shed more light on gender differences in shaping this relationship remains scarce. Our findings can be summarized as follows.

First of all, we found strong support for business ownership leading to reduction in poverty, though the benefits seem to accrue primarily to individuals at a higher level than bottom quantile of poverty ladder of income distribution. This may be attributed to the important role the accumulation of the financial, human and social resources plays in facilitating high-growth potential new venture creation. The phenomenon of business ownership with job creation among the lowest quintile of income-based poverty ladder distribution is still fairly rare, that leads to insignificant results. However, as evidenced by the main results based on the full poverty ladder distribution, business ownership comes across consistently positive and significant for transition economies, suggesting that high-potential entrepreneurship with ambitions to create jobs appears to be an effective instrument for policy-makers for improving individual's welfare.

Second, we do not find any significant association between self-employment and poverty reduction, emphasizing the overall greater importance of higher-potential entrepreneurship as opposed to subsistence entrepreneurship in combating poverty.

Third, our findings provide some evidence for reduction of gender poverty gap. The poverty gap to a disadvantage of females appears to be minimal, manifesting only in the CEB region, but not elsewhere across transition region. Interestingly, when we narrow our focus down to poverty occurrence defined based on the 20th centile of subjective and objective income distribution, we find some contrasting regional differences. More specifically, in the context of Central Europe and the Baltic States (CCB), we find that females engaged in self-employment are more likely to be associated with the lower 20th centile of income ladder distribution, whereas the opposite holds for the region of Central Asia, although the latter results are only marginally significant. This implies that self-employment in the context of the CA region may provide some opportunities to females to climb the poverty ladder, but in the context of the CEB, it is likely to be viewed as subsistence entrepreneurship where females resort to it because there are no alternative labour market opportunities available.

Based on this discussion, our findings make important contributions to the literature of entrepreneurship, poverty and gender studies. First of all, we develop a theoretical argument claiming a differential effect played by different types of entrepreneurial activity on poverty alleviation, and further test this empirically, utilizing the unique cross-individual, cross-region and cross-country EBRD Life in Transition Survey data for 2016. Second, this study also provides fairly novel and rich evidence on gender differences in the setting of transition economies, and illustrates to what extent engaging in entrepreneurial activity may economically empower women to climb up the poverty ladder in this region. Therefore, this paper fills some important gaps in the poverty and gender studies literature, offering new insights on gender–entrepreneurship–poverty relationship in the context of emerging economies of Central and Eastern Europe, and Central Asia.

Conclusions

Poverty reduction remains a critical agenda for policy-makers worldwide, urging academic scholars to search for new evidence on effective measures for fighting poverty. This study extends the understanding of the mechanism via which entrepreneurial process is likely to contribute to poverty reduction in transition region, distinguishing between subsistence and Schumpeterian entrepreneurship. It also provides some interesting findings on gender differences in entrepreneurship-poverty relationship, suggesting that increasing female participation in entrepreneurship can be one of the effective measures to increase females' welfare in the region. Overall, our study has important ramifications for researchers and policy makers. For researchers, it suggests that it is important to distinguish between different types of entrepreneurial activity in studying the poverty agenda, specifically across different regions. For policy-makers, it offers new insights on the greater importance of higher-potential entrepreneurship as opposed to subsistence entrepreneurship in combating poverty, and the important role entrepreneurship plays in empowering females in climbing up the poverty ladder. Our study is an early effort in offering a comparative perspective on differences across various regions of transition economies, calling for further qualitative and quantitative research in studying regional differences in more detail.

Notes

1. These figures reflect a group average for transition economies and are calculated based on 2015/2016 report. In the year of survey used for drafting this report, among transition economies there were the following countries that took part in the survey: Bulgaria, Croatia, Estonia, Hungary, Kazakhstan, Latvia, Macedonia, Poland, Romania, Slovak Republic, and Slovenia.
2. Here is a full list of countries comprising each of these groups: CEB: Croatia, Estonia, Hungary, Latvia, Lithuania, Poland, Slovak Republic, Slovenia. SEE: Albania, Bosnia and Herzegovina, Bulgaria, FYR Macedonia, Kosovo, Montenegro, Romania, Serbia. EEC: Armenia, Azerbaijan, Belarus, Georgia, Moldova, Ukraine. CA: Kazakhstan, Kyrgyz Republic, Tajikistan, Turkmenistan, Uzbekistan, Russia.
3. We also merged the third wave of the LiTS survey with the second one (2010). However, unlike the 2016, which offers measures of both subjective and objective poverty, the 2010 has only a subjective measure of poverty that prevents scholars to undertake full-scale comparisons across the two waves.
4. EBRD (2016) Life in Transition report III, available from litsonline-EBRD.com.

Disclosure statement

No potential conflict of interest was reported by the authors.

ORCID

Julia Korosteleva http://orcid.org/0000-0003-4000-5992
Paulina Stępień-Baig http://orcid.org/0000-0002-5664-7458

References

Ahlstrom, D., G. D. Bruton, and L. Zhao. 2013. "Turning Good Research into Good Publications." *Nankai Business Review International* 4 (2): 92–106. doi:10.1108/20408741311323317.

Ahlstrom, D., and Z. Ding. 2014. "Entrepreneurship in China: An Overview." *International Small Business Journal* 32 (6): 610–618. doi:10.1177/0266242613517913.

Aidis, R., F. Welter, D. Smallbone, and N. Isakova. 2007. "Female Entrepreneurship in Transition Economies: The case Of Lithuania and Ukraine." *Feminist Economics* 13 (2): 157–183. doi:10.1080/13545700601184831.

Aidis, R., S. Estrin, and T. Mickiewicz. 2008. "Institutions and Entrepreneurship Development in Russia: A Comparative Perspective." *Journal of Business Venturing* 23 (6): 656–672. doi:10.1016/j.jbusvent.2008.01.005.

Alam, A., M. Murthi, R. Yemtsov, E. Murrugarra, N. Dudwick, E. Hamilton., and E. Tiongson. 2005. *Growth, Poverty, and Inequality: Eastern Europe and the Former Soviet Union*. Washington, D.C: World Bank. http://documents.worldbank.

org/curated/en/750511468295836867/Growth-poverty-and-inequality-Eastern-Europe-and-the-Former-Soviet-Union
Alkire, S., and M. E. Santos. 2014. "Measuring Acute Poverty in The Developing World: Robustness and Scope Of The Multidimensional Poverty Index." *World Development* 59: 251–274. doi:10.1016/j.worlddev.2014.01.026.
Ashwin, S. 2010. "Understanding the Gender Dynamics of Russia's Economic Transformation: Women's and Men's Experiences of Employment, Domestic Labour and Poverty." In *The International Handbook of Gender and Poverty: Concepts, Research, Policy*, edited by S. Chant, 178–183. Northampton, Mass.: Edward Elgar Publishing.
Banerjee, A.V., S. Cole, E. Duflo, and L. Linden. "Remedying education: Evidence from two randomized experiments in India". *The Quarterly Journal of Economics* 122 (3): 1235–1264. doi:10.1162/qjec.122.3.1235.
Baumol, W. 1990. "Entrepreneurship: Productive, Unproductive, and Destructive." *Journal of Political Economy* 98 (5, Part I): 893–921. doi:10.1016/0883-9026(94)00014-X.
Berkowitz, D., and J. E. Jackson. 2006. "Entrepreneurship and the Evolution of Income Distributions in Poland and Russia." *Journal of Comparative Economics* 34 (2): 338–356. doi:10.1016/j.jce.2006.02.003.
Blackburn, R., and M. Ram. 2006. "Fix or Fixation? the Contributions and Limitations of Entrepreneurship and Small Firms to Combating Social Exclusion." *Entrepreneurship and Regional Development* 18 (1): 73–89. doi:10.1016/j.jce.2006.02.003.
Bruton, G. D., D. Ahlstrom, and S. Si. 2015. "Entrepreneurship, Poverty, and Asia: Moving beyond Subsistence Entrepreneurship." *Asia Pacific Journal of Management* 32 (1): 1–22. doi:10.1007/s10490-014-9404-x.
Bruton, G. D., D. J. Ketchen, and R. D. Ireland. 2013. "Entrepreneurship as A Solution to Poverty." *Journal of Business Venturing* 28 (6): 683–689. doi:10.1016/j.jbusvent.2013.05.002.
Bruton, G. D., S. Khavul, and H. Chavez. 2011. "Microlending in Emerging Economies: Building a New Line of Inquiry from the Ground Up." *Journal of International Business Studies* 42 (5): 718–739. doi:10.1057/jibs.2010.58.
Chasco, C., and J. L. Gallo. 2013. "The Impact of Objective and Subjective Measures of Air Quality and Noise on House Prices: A Multilevel Approach for Downtown Madrid." *Economic Geography* 89 (2): 127–148. doi:10.1111/ecge.2013.89.issue-2.
Chong, A., and C. Calderon. 2000. "Institutional Quality and Distribution of Income." *Economic Development and Cultural Change* 48 (4): 761–786. doi:10.1086/452476.
Dollar, D., and A. Kraay, 2013. "Growth Still Is Good for the Poor." World Bank Policy Research Working Paper. doi:10.1596/1813-9450-6568.
Duflo, E. 2012. "Women Empowerment and Economic Development." *Journal of Economic Literature* 50 (4): 1051–1079. doi:10.1257/jel.50.4.1051.
Efendic, A., T. Mickiewicz, and A. Rebmann. 2015. "Growth Aspirations and Social Capital: Young Firms in A Post-Conflict Environment." *International Small Business Journal* 33 (5): 537–561. doi:10.1177/0266242613516987.
Estrin, S., J. Korosteleva, and T. Mickiewicz. 2013. "Which Institutions Encourage Entrepreneurial Growth Aspirations?" *Journal of Business Venturing* 28 (4): 564–580. doi:10.1016/j.jbusvent.2012.05.001.
Estrin, S., and T. Mickiewicz. 2011a. "Institutions and Female Entrepreneurship." *Small Business Economics* 37 (4): 397. doi:10.1007/s11187-011-9373-0.
Estrin, S., and T. Mickiewicz. 2011b. "Entrepreneurship in Transition Economies: The Role of Institutions and Generational Change." In *The Dynamics of Entrepreneurship*, edited by M. Minniti, 293–338. Oxford: Oxford University Press.
Falkingham, J., and A. Baschieri. 2010. "Gender, Poverty and Transition in Central Asia." In *The International Handbook of Gender and Poverty: Concepts, Research, Policy*, edited by S. Chant, 184–189. Northampton, Mass.: Edward Elgar Publishing.
Frankish, J. S., R. G. Roberts, A. Coad, and D. J. Storey. 2014. "Is Entrepreneurship A Route Out of Deprivation?" *Regional Studies* 48 (6): 1090–1107. doi:10.1080/00343404.2013.871384.
GEM. 2015/2016. Global Entrepreneurship Monitor Report, Accessed. http://www.gemconsortium.org/report
Greene, F., J., . K. M. Mole, and D. J. Storey. 2008. *Three Decades of Enterprise Culture: Economic Regeneration and Public Policy*. London: Macmillan.
Harris, C. 2004. *Control and Subversion: Gender Relations in Tajikistan*. London: Pluto Press.
Henrekson, M., and T. Sanandaji. 2014. "Small Business Activity Does Not Measure Entrepreneurship." In *Proceedings of the National Academy of Sciences of the USA*. http://www.pnas.org/content/early/2014/01/15/1307204111.abstract
Jackson, J. E., J. Klich, and K. Poznanska. 1999. "Firm Creation and Economic Transitions." *Journal of Business Venturing* 14 (5-6): 427–450. doi:10.1016/S0883-9026(98)00029-9.
Jukkala, T., I. H. Mäkinen, O. Kislllitsyna, S. Ferlander, and D. Vägero. 2008. "Economic Strain, Social Relations, Gender and Binge Drinking in Moscow." *Social Science and Medicine* 66 (3): 663–674. doi:10.1016/j.socscimed.2007.10.017.
Khavul, S., H. Chavez, and G. D. Bruton. 2013. "When Institutional Change Outruns the Change Agent: The Contested Terrain of Entrepreneurial Microfinance for Those in Poverty." *Journal of Business Venturing* 28 (1): 30–50. doi:10.1016/j.jbusvent.2012.02.005.
Korosteleva, J., and M. Belitski. 2017. "Entrepreneurial Dynamics and Higher Education Institutions in the Post-Communist World." *Regional Studies* 51 (3): 439–453. doi:10.1080/00343404.2015.1103370.

Manolova, T., R. Eunni, and B. Gyoshev. 2008. "Institutional Environments for Entrepreneurship: Evidence from Emerging Economies in Eastern Europe." *Entrepreneurship Theory and Practice* 32 (1): 203–218. doi:10.1111/j.1540-6520.2007.00222.x.

McCloskey, D. N. 2010. *Bourgeois Dignity: Why Economics Can't Explain the Modern World*. Chicago, IL; London: University of Chicago Press.

McMullen, J. S. 2010. "Delineating the Domain of Development Entrepreneurship: A Market-Based Approach to Facilitating Inclusive Economic Growth." *Entrepreneurship Theory and Practice* 35 (1): 185–215. doi:10.1111/j.1540-6520.2010.00428.x.

Mickiewicz, T. 2010. *Economics of Institutional Change: Central and Eastern Europe Revisited*. 2nd ed. Basingstoke: Palgrave Macmillan.

Milanovic, B. 1998. *Income, Inequality, and Poverty during the Transition from Planned to Market Economy*. Washington, DC: World Bank.

Misturelli, F., and C. Heffernan."What is poverty? A diachronic exploration of the discourse on poverty from the 1970s to the 2000s." *The European journal of development research* 20, no. 4 (2008): 666–684. doi:10.1080/09578810802464888.

Munoz-Boudet, A. M. M., P. Buitrago, B. L. de la Briere, D. Newhouse, E. R. Matulevich, K. Scott, and P. Suarez-Becerra. 2018. "Gender Differences in Poverty and Household Composition through the Life-Cycle." *World Bank* (WPS8360). doi:10.1596/1813-9450-8360.

Muravyev, A., D. Schäfer, and O. Talavera. 2007. "Entrepreneurs' gender and financial constraints: evidence from international data. Berlin." *German Institute for Economic Research*.

Parker, S. 2018. *The Economics of Entrepreneurship. Second Edition*. Cambridge: Cambridge University Press.

Pettigrew, T. F. 1998. "Intergroup Contact Theory." *Annual Review of Psychology* 49 (1): 65–85. doi:10.1146/annurev.psych.49.1.65.

Phelps, E. S. 2013. *Mass Flourishing: How Grassroots Innovation Created Jobs, Challenge and Change*. Princeton, NJ: Princeton University Press.

Prahalad, C. K. 2005. *Fortune at the Bottom of the Pyramid: Eradicating Poverty through Profits*. Upper Saddle River: Wharton School Publishing.

Rosser, J. B., Jr., M. V. Rosser, and E. Ahmed. 2000. "Income Inequality and the Informal Economy in Transition Economies." *Journal of Comparative Economics* 28 (1): 156–171. doi:10.1006/jcec.2000.1645.

Sabarwal, S., and K. Terrell. 2008. "Does Gender Matter for Firm Performance? Evidence from Eastern Europe and Central Asia." Policy Research working paper; no. WPS 4705. Washington, DC: World Bank.

Sabatini, F. 2008. "Social Capital and the Quality of Economic Development." *Kyklos* 61 (3): 466–499. doi:10.1111/j.1467-6435.2008.00413.x.

Sanchez, C. 2018. "No, 70% of the World's Poor Aren't Women, but that Does Not Mean Poverty Isn't Exist." Word Bank Development Blog. Accessed 12 September 2018. http://blogs.worldbank.org/developmenttalk/no-70-world-s-poor-aren-t-women-doesn-t-mean-poverty-isn-t-sexist

Sattar, S. 2011. "Opportunities for Men and Women: Emerging Europe and Central Asia." World Bank OKR. Accessed 12 September 2018. https://openknowledge.worldbank.org/handle/10986/2800

Schumpeter, J. [1934] 2008. *The Theory of Economic Development*. Brunswick, NJ: Transaction Publishers.

Scott, L., C. Dolan, M. Johnstone-Lois, K. Sugden, and M. Wu. 2012. "Enterprise and Inequality: A Study of Avon in South Africa." *Entrepreneurship Theory and Practice* 36: 544–568. doi:10.1111/j.1540-6520.2012.00507.x.

Si, S., X. Yu, A. Wu, S. Chen, S. Chen, and Y. Su. 2015. "Entrepreneurship and Poverty Reduction: A Case Study of Yiwu, China." *Asia Pacific Journal of Management* 32 (1): 119–143. doi:10.1007/s10490-014-9395-7.

Simai, M., 2006. "Poverty and Inequality in Eastern Europe and the CIS Transition Economies." UN Department of Economic and Social Affairs Working Papers. Accessed on 17 November 2018. http://www.un.org/esa/desa/papers/2006/wp17_2006.pdf

Smallbone, D., and F. Welter. 2001. "The Distinctiveness of Entrepreneurship in Transition Economies." *Small Business Economics* 16 (4): 249–262. doi:10.1023/A:1011159216578.

Tomizawa, A., L. Zhao, G. Bassellier, and D. Ahlstrom. 2019. "Economic Growth, Innovation, Institutions, and the Great Enrichment." *Asia Pacific Journal of Management* 36 (forthcoming). doi:10.1007/s10490-019-09648-2.

Valliere, D., and R. Peterson. 2009. "Entrepreneurship and Economic Growth: Evidence from Emerging and Developed Countries." *Entrepreneurship & Regional Development* 21 (5–6): 459–480. doi:10.1080/08985620802332723.

Welter, F., D. Smallbone, E. Aculai, N. Isakova, and N. Schakirova. 2003. "Female Entrepreneurship in Post-Soviet Countries." In *New Perspectives on Women Entrepreneurs*, edited by J. E. Butler, 243–269. Greenwich, CT: Information Age Publishing.

World Bank. 2017. "Monitoring Global Poverty." Report of the Commission on Global Poverty. Accessed 10 August 2017. https://openknowledge.worldbank.org/bitstream/handle/10986/25141/9781464809613.pdf

Wu, J., and S. Si. 2018. "Poverty Reduction through Entrepreneurship: Incentives, Social Networks, and Sustainability." *Asian Business & Management* 17 (4): 243–259. doi:10.1057/s41291-018-0039-5.

Trust, poverty, and subjective wellbeing among Chinese entrepreneurs

Yiyi Su, Shaker A. Zahra, Rui Li and Di Fan

ABSTRACT

Entrepreneurs' subjective wellbeing has become an important topic in research: entrepreneurs undertake risks and create their companies seeking personal satisfaction and fulfillment. As a result, researchers have given considerable attention to the antecedents and the conditions under which wellbeing materializes, especially in emerging economies where poverty may be acute. In this study, we propose that generalized trust serves as an informal institution that affects entrepreneurs' subjective wellbeing. Further, we propose that this relationship is subject to boundary conditions of economic and social poverty as well as context-specific formal institutional features. We test our predictions using a multi-sourced sample of 818 Chinese entrepreneurs. We find that trust is positively associated with entrepreneurs' subjective wellbeing. This association is moderated by both economic poverty and social poverty. When high or low institutional voids are evident across the different regions of China, the main and moderating effects are further differentiated. The study suggests that, as a mechanism to mitigate the negative effect of lacking formal institutions, the level of trust in different regions is more relevant in social poverty rather than in economic poverty.

Introduction

While some entrepreneurs are motivated by the desire to create wealth, many seek autonomy and the opportunity to use their creative skills and enjoy a high quality of life (Carter 2011; Diener et al. 1999; Diener 2000). Indeed, research suggests that achieving 'subjective wellbeing', the feeling of life satisfaction, is among the key factors that drive entrepreneurs and ignite their passion for their work (Stephan 2018; Williams and Shepherd 2016). Ironically, entrepreneurial careers can be challenging, as many new ventures fail. Entrepreneurs also frequently face serious environmental turbulence in their industries (Gill and Larson 2014), requiring them to be risk-taking, innovative and proactive (Hoskisson et al. 2011). Such turbulence can cause stress and anxiety among entrepreneurs, undermining their sense of wellbeing.

Entrepreneurs' vulnerability to stress and turbulence may be even greater in emerging economies such as China, where resources are limited, opportunities are scarce, competition is high and support systems are widely lacking (cf. Ahlstrom and Ding 2014; Bruton and Ahlstrom 2003). In these economies, moreover, entrepreneurs cannot rely on formal institutions to protect their property or even their profits. Although some scholars (Mathews and Stokes 2013; Möllering 2006) suggest that trust plays a role in achieving subjective wellbeing, trust is a broad and debated construct in the field of entrepreneurship research (Welter 2012; Welter and Smallbone 2006). This creates ambiguity about its consequences for subjective wellbeing. Further, the conditions under which trust works to affect subjective wellbeing when institutions are lacking is unclear from the literature. Emerging economies often suffer from outdated institutions and the prevalence of institutional voids, i.e. absence of effective formal institutions (Khanna and Palepu 1997, 2006).

To examine these effects, we focus on generalized trust, which we define as the global trust entrepreneurs have in most people in a region (e.g. Ding, Au, and Chiang 2015; Lins, Servaes, and Tamayo 2017; Kwon and Arenius 2010). Unlike situational trust, generalized trust is equally given to members of a region, irrespective of individual traits, relationship and social capital (Fukuyama 1995; Kwon and Arenius 2010; Hart et al. 1986). Such generalized trust is positively linked with entrepreneurial activities in at least two ways. First, trust is featured as an ingredient that is closely associated with the process of creating and developing new ventures (Zahra, Yavuz, and Ucbasaran 2006) or is regarded as the lubricant for boosting business creation (Kim and Li 2014). Second, trust is an important element of the culture that exists in a nation, region or community. Where there is high trust, there is collective attention to infrastructure, education and the arts (Fukuyama 1995); high trust also promotes communication and frequent knowledge sharing that facilitate recognition and pursuit of entrepreneurial opportunities (Kwon and Arenius 2010). Although trust facilitates entrepreneurial activities, its implications for subjective wellbeing are not well studied or documented. This raises two important questions: 1) *how does trust affect subjective wellbeing among entrepreneurs?* and 2) *what are the boundary conditions affecting this relationship, if it exists?*

To address the two questions, our study examines the relationship between trust and entrepreneurs' subjective wellbeing in the context of poverty, as depicted in Figure 1. Viewing poverty as a multifaceted concept, we explore two of its key facets: economic and social. Economic poverty refers to the economic inability of an individual to address basic human needs (e.g. London and Hart 2004). Social poverty has been less discussed but is mostly inferred from in economics and sociology research. Lewandowski (2008) places an emphasis on a person's place in the bottom of the social hierarchy and the accompanying dearth of social capital – a person with a lower social status can hardly gain social capital from connections, relationships and good will that develops among members of a group or a community. While economic poverty is widely discussed in the literature, the social facet of poverty of entrepreneurs deserves careful research attention. Many

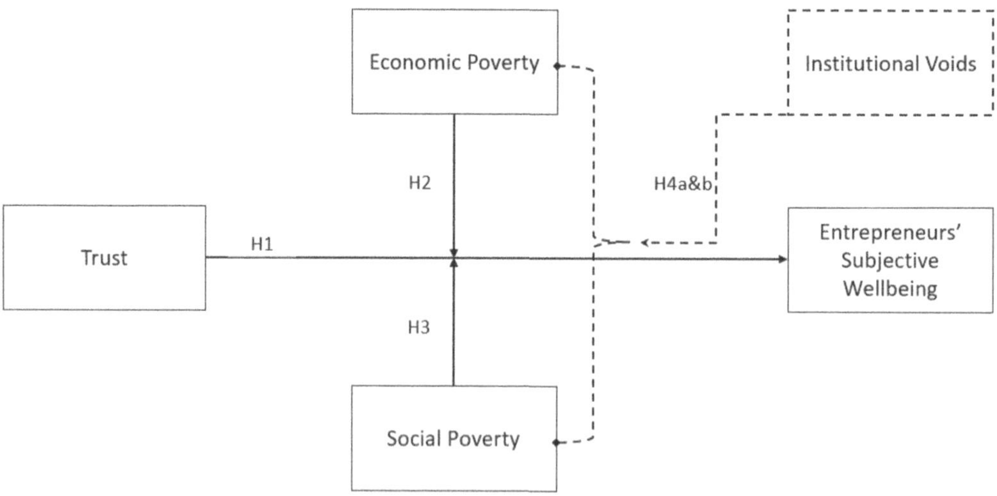

Figure 1. A conceptual framework.

entrepreneurs make less money from their jobs than do others in their community, affecting their social capital. Therefore, in this study, we propose that social and economic poverty could pose resource constraints on entrepreneurial activities and call for a high-trust regional environment that enables entrepreneurs to achieve subjective wellbeing. This proposition is consistent with the 'remediation perspective', where the focus is on facilitating entrepreneurship for poverty alleviation by addressing resource scarcity of the poor – as in Sutter, Bruton, and Chen (2018) recent review.

Moreover, as Figure 1 suggests, we link the interactive effects of trust and poverty to institutional voids (see the dotted lines and links in Figure 1), which is unique to emerging economies (Khanna and Palepu 1997). We propose that, in this setting, trust is an informal institution that works with formal institutions to enable entrepreneurs' subjective wellbeing. Figure 1 presents the study's key variables and related predictions. Building upon the national baseline survey – the Chinese General Social Survey (CGSS), together with National Economic Research Institute (NERI) Index of Marketization of China's Provinces – we constructed a multi-sourced database of 818 entrepreneurs in China and tested our hypotheses.

Theory and hypotheses

Trust and entrepreneurs' subjective wellbeing

Over the last several decades, researchers have studied entrepreneurship based on normative theories of opportunity. In these studies, the ultimate goal of any entrepreneurial process is viewed as maximizing profit and accumulating wealth (Shane and Venkataraman 2000). However, recent research shows that the entrepreneurial process cannot be understood solely as a profit-seeking activity. Van Praag and Versloot (2007) contend that the payoff structure for entrepreneurs should be properly re-examined. For example, some previous empirical research shows that many people turn to entrepreneurial activities or persist in their entrepreneurship without foreseeable profits (Reynolds 2001). In addition, recent evidence indicates that, in spite of availability of opportunities, many people never act on their intentions to create a business (Van Gelderen, Kautonen, and Fink 2015). Thus, entrepreneurs' payoff structure not only contains positive earnings, but also non-pecuniary returns from these activities. In particular, subjective wellbeing has been considered as an important consequence of entrepreneurs' engagement in business creation activities (Shir 2015).

According to Diener (2000, 34), subjective wellbeing refers to 'people's cognitive and affective evaluations of their lives'. As such, subjective wellbeing is an important topic in positive psychology, which asserts that 'happy people participate more in community organizations' and 'perform better at work' (Diener 2000, 41). Since subjective wellbeing is generally used by scholars as an umbrella term for how individuals feel about their lives (Diener et al. 1999; Fan et al. 2014), Shir (2015) calls for a closer understanding of entrepreneurs' subjective wellbeing. Such research is necessary, given the high vulnerability of entrepreneurial careers. Moreover, subjective wellbeing provides entrepreneurs with the motivational nourishment that allows them to persist, endure and succeed (Frey and Stutzer 2010).

Trust is an important source of social capital in a nation, region or community (Fukuyama 1995; Saxsinian 1994); it serves as the lubricant or safeguard for business transactions, benefiting entrepreneurs (Welter 2012). Some scholars (Brehm and Rahn 1997; Zolin, Kuckertz, and Kautonen 2011; Puffer, McCarthy, and Boisot 2010; Welter and Smallbone 2011) suggest that trust affects entrepreneurs and their entrepreneurial activities through several related mechanisms, such as transferring information, promoting cooperation and substituting formal institutions. Given their dependence on their immediate communities, especially regions, to acquire resources, test their ideas, and start their business, the culture of the region in which entrepreneurs operate can spell the difference between success and failure (Saxsinian 1994). This is why we emphasize trust levels in theorizing about the effect on entrepreneurs' wellbeing.

Table 1. Summary of different strands of the trust research.

	Situational Trust				
	Trait-based Trust	Relationship-based Trust	Interactionist Trust Model	Exchange-based Trust	Network-based Trust
Selected authors	Rotter (1967)	Mayer, Davis, and Schoorman (1995); Schoorman, Mayer, and Davis (2007)	Jones and George (1998)	Zaheer and Venkatraman (1995); Williamson (1993)	Glaeser et al. (2000); Carpenter, Daniere, and Takahashi (2004)
Trust defined as	A personal trait	Aspect of a relationship	A changing or evolving experience	Contracting behavior	Trusting attitudes and
	Propensity to trust	Willingness to be vulnerable	Distrust, conditional trust, and unconditional trust	A long-term hierarchy-like relationship	trusting behavior
Mechanisms	Developmental experiences, personality types, and cultural backgrounds	Ability, benevolence and integrity of the trustees	Values, attitudes, moods, and emotion	Transaction cost reasoning	Social capital (effectively functioning social network)
		Trustor's propensity, interdependence			Form and function
Analytical focus	Individual	Relationship	Process	Exchange	Individual/community

	Generalized Trust		
	Generalized Personal Trust	Generalized Collective Trust	Generalized Institutional Trust
Selected authors	Putnam (1993); Bjørnskov (2006); Ding, Au, and Chiang (2015); Lins, Servaes, and Tamayo (2017)	Hart et al. (1986);	Rothstein and Stolle (2008)
		Alesina and La Ferrara (2002)	
Trust defined as	Expectation toward each other and as members of their society	Perceptions about trust in the workplace and community	Judgement of the functioning of the overall political, legal or economic framework and its informal rules
Mechanisms	civic society, quality of institutions, culture and values, and ethnic heterogeneity	Organization: openness/congruity, shared values, and autonomy/feedback	Neutrality, fairness, and impartiality
	Social capital (enabler of collective action and cooperation)	Community: mixed	
Analytical focus	Region/country	Organization/Community	State

The definition of trust in bold is used in our study.

As shown in Table 1, we broadly divide trust into two categories: situational and generalized trust (Fukuyama 1995; Kwon and Arenius 2010; Hart et al. 1986). Situational trust is based on a relevant situation for determining a party's trust in specific others. A relevant situation can be a trustor's traits in trait-based trust (Rotter 1967), a relationship between a trustor and a trustee in relationship-based trust (e.g. Schoorman, Mayer, and Davis 2007), an evolving experience in the interactionist model of trust (e.g. Jones and George 1998), a contracting behaviour in exchange-based trust (Zaheer and Venkatraman 1995) and a trustor/trustee's social network in network-based trust (e.g. Carpenter, Daniere, and Takahashi 2004). Trait- and relationship-based trust are formed within a group of trustees on the basis of their ability and thus may be limited for poor entrepreneurs. Exchange-based trust is calculative and fostered by mutual hostages, whilst poor entrepreneurs do not have personal property as guaranty (Williamson 1993). Network-based trust is even more complex: both trusting and being trustworthy are dependent on and contribute to an individual's social capital (e.g. Glaeser et al. 2000). The poor may develop trust, reciprocity and even co-operation among their immediate community members, but still suffer from the scarcity of social capital.

But if we discuss generalized trust at the societal or regional levels, this issue seems more straightforward. Generalized trust is a global trust in generalized others, irrespective of all the situations cited above. Here, the 'generalized others' can be most people in a society, region or country (e.g. Kwon and Arenius 2010), collectives such as an organization or community (e.g. Hart et al. 1986), or an overall institutional framework (e.g. Rothstein and Stolle 2008). Consistent with prior studies (e.g. Ding, Au, and Chiang 2015; Lins, Servaes, and Tamayo 2017), we focus on trust that members of a region bestow on each other, irrespective of their traits, relationship, social network or capital. Regions characterized by high levels of trust offer safe environments that help entrepreneurs take the risks associated with new venture creation. These regions invest in 'common good' activities such as education, roads and infrastructure. Such investments create a setting that facilitates discovery and pursuit of entrepreneurial activities, using entrepreneurs' creativity and skills. As a result, they can enhance entrepreneurs' self-actualization and wellbeing. Further, trust may reduce transaction costs and facilitate the transfer of information (Brehm and Rahn 1997). Entrepreneurs who consider information from a variety of sources as credible have a greater chance of perceiving better opportunities. Lower transaction costs and better opportunities may increase entrepreneurs' sense of accomplishment, improving their subjective wellbeing. Moreover, trust often leads to cooperation (Fukuyama 1995). In a high-trust region, individuals are more likely to be inclined to organize and participate in entrepreneurial networks (Zolin, Kuckertz, and Kautonen 2011) and cooperate with others (Sarasvathy et al. 2003). Cooperation may improve entrepreneurial self-actualization (Chatman and Barsade 1995), which creates a sense of belonging. Further, feeling connected to others during cooperation may promote wellbeing in both physical and psychological dimensions (Lee and Robbins 1998). Last, trust can complement or substitute for formal institutions and legal frameworks (Bradach and Eccles 1989; Puffer, McCarthy, and Boisot 2010), reducing risks and safeguarding transactions when formal institutions are deficient or ineffective (Welter and Smallbone 2011), protecting entrepreneurs' gains, and improving their subjective wellbeing. Given these arguments, as indicated in Figure 1, we propose the following hypothesis:

Hypothesis 1: *The generalized trust in a region is positively related to entrepreneurs' subjective wellbeing.*

The moderating effect of economic poverty

Some earlier research suggested that income, self-reported happiness and life satisfaction are not correlated above income levels required to meet basic needs (Easterlin 1974). However, Haushofer and Fehr (2014) in a recent study finds that no such saturation point exists and that higher income is associated with more happiness and life satisfaction across and within 131 countries. Moreover, they point out, economic poverty leads to a psychological process that can lead to negative affection such as stress. People living in economic poverty usually struggle for their day-to-day necessities, experience pronounced deprivation and have few choices in terms of job opportunities (Houghton and Khandker 2009). Such a situation is even more severe in the context of developing countries (Khavul and Bruton 2013), where opportunities for jobs or social mobility are limited. These different challenges constrain the poor's cognitive capacity and further hurt their subjective wellbeing.

The negative psychological consequence of economic poverty can be observed also in the entrepreneurial context. Economically poor entrepreneurs may find it extremely difficult to discover and exploit opportunities because of their limited human, financial and social capital (e.g. Alvarez and Barney 2013). These people are more focused on meeting their immediate basic needs than on obtaining quality education or developing their human capital (Yunus 1999). Their inadequate education, skills and cognition create barriers to opportunity discovery and exploitation, further depressing their sense of wellbeing.

Further, securing a minimal amount of financial capital may place a burden on the subjective wellbeing of those living in poor economic conditions. Financial capital is usually absent for economically poor entrepreneurs, especially in developing countries (Ansari, Munir, and Gregg 2012; Banerjee and Duflo 2011). One reason is that, in an emerging economy such as China, poorly specified property rights or government regulations lock up the capital of the economically poor (Ahlstrom and Bruton 2001; Ahlstrom and Ding 2014; De Soto 2000). As a result, entrepreneurs operating under these conditions seldom own title to their property and thus lack the financial capital necessary for entrepreneurial investment. Those people are usually denied access to loans from the formal banking system. Their lack of acceptable collateral increases the screening, monitoring and enforcing costs of the banks in lending transactions. De Soto (2000) further points out that, because of the lack of formal property rights, the poor in developing countries are subject to expropriation, bureaucratic arbitrariness and political corruption.

Entrepreneurs experiencing economic poverty are also often short of the social capital necessary for business development. Their memberships in social groups are largely fixed by their economic status, making it difficult for them to develop effective networking for business advice, distribution channels and financial support (Hansen 1995). This isolation from the broader social community further negatively affects such entrepreneurs' subjective welling.

In this study, we propose that trust in a region works to address the psychological concerns of entrepreneurs living in economic poverty. By definition, this trust is a general perception of a region that others are trustworthy, irrespective of being economically poor or rich (De Rivera and Páez 2007). A region of low trust challenges entrepreneurs' access to opportunities, connections and resources, making their lives more difficult and dissatisfying. However, high levels of trust help to create an emotional environment of peace and patience, making it easier for entrepreneurs in regions of economic poverty to conquer the distress arising from limited human, finance and social capital. A region of high trust is more likely to incorporate the economically poor into a broader social community, provide them with more training and lending opportunities, and reduce discrimination against them as they undertake their entrepreneurial activities (e.g. Hart and Christensen 2002). As a result, those living in economic poverty can gradually accumulate their human capital, obtain small-size loans from various sources, and establish ties with different social groups: benefits that partially improve these entrepreneurs' subjective wellbeing. Given these arguments, as indicated in Figure 1, we propose the following hypothesis:

Hypothesis 2: *Economic poverty strengthens the positive relationship between trust and subjective wellbeing among entrepreneurs.*

The moderating effect of social poverty

Following Lewandowski (2008), the term social poverty refers to the absence or dearth of social resources (i.e. social networks and connections) that are accessible and appropriable between and among various socioeconomic strata. Social status is visible in the clothes people wear as well as in the nonverbal behaviors and physical characteristics of individuals (Anderson et al. 2012) or their schools and neighborhoods (Massey and Denton 1993). The lower the social hierarchy to which a person belongs, the less the social resources she/he is more likely to have. Social poverty, therefore, typically refers to those living at the bottom of social strata or hierarchies and having difficulty in building up a social network.

Prior studies show that 'entrepreneurship functions within a market as a social structure, system and formation or order rather than a strictly economic entity existing in a vacuum vis-à-vis society' (Zafirovski 1999, 363). Anderson et al. (2012) note that social status can generate feelings of power and social acceptance. Embracing this view, entrepreneurs experiencing high levels of social poverty (i.e. smaller social network and lower status in the social hierarchy) may develop perceptions of inferiority and feelings of shame (Chen and Williams 2016). Specifically, in China, status anxiety is prevalent among entrepreneurs (cf. Chen and Fan 2015) and this anxiety of being socially poorer has risen as inequality has grown over the last two decades (Chen and Williams 2016).

Although social poverty leads to status anxiety and distrust at the individual level, the generalized level of trust at the regional level matters more for socially poor entrepreneurs, leading them to struggle in garnering funding and accessing networks (Essers and Benschop 2009). Since their own friends and acquaintances can provide little or no help, they have to rely heavily on the trust of others they do not intimately know in order to acquire necessary resources for their entrepreneurial activities (Warnecke 2013). For instance, many Chinese entrepreneurs start as street vendors in lower socio-economic sectors. Though they may earn considerable money from their business, they operate in black markets and face harassment by city inspectors, distrust from customers and bullying by local gangs. As a result, a high-trust region is critical in this case because these entrepreneurs can survive only when they develop good interactions with external stakeholders.

Entrepreneurs who enjoy high status in the social hierarchy are more likely to be perceived as competent and independent (cf. Koski, Xie, and Olson 2015). Equipped with social acceptance and broader social networks, they can readily get access to kinds of resources and exploit the opportunities they have identified. Higher social status can even buffer these entrepreneurs from stress if they encounter severe challenges. Prior studies show that entrepreneurs with higher social status are more likely to make unethical decisions, break the law while driving, and even lie or cheat to get their way (cf. Piff et al. 2012). Clearly, they rely less on a high-trust regional environment to attain subjective wellbeing, given all these advantages from their higher social status. This means that generalized trust is equally given to each regional inhabitant but its effects differ for socially rich and socially poor entrepreneurs. These observations suggest that, while trust improves entrepreneurs' subjective wellbeing as we suggested in Hypothesis 1, this effect will get stronger if entrepreneurs cannot gain support from their social status or feel less accepted by their society because of the disadvantage arising from their social status. Thus, as indicated in Figure 1, we propose the following hypothesis:

Hypothesis 3: *Social poverty strengthens the positive relationship between trust and subjective wellbeing among entrepreneurs.*

Trust and poverty under institutional voids

Our study also explores the extent to which the relationships we outlined in Hypotheses 2 through 3 are strengthened or weakened under institutional voids. As regional or local phenomena, institutional voids feature prominently in emerging economies (Khanna and Palepu 1997). They refer to underdeveloped formal market-based institutions that have relatively weak specialized intermediaries, and less developed contract-enforcing mechanisms. These deficiencies inhibit firms from acquiring resources, knowledge and information through effective market transactions (Khanna, Palepu, and Sinha 2005). Thus, such voids do not emphasize whether formal market-based institutions exist or not but rather highlight features in higher enforcement and transaction costs and greater amounts of information asymmetry (Khanna and Palepu 1997; Kim and Song 2017). Gao et al. (2010) conceptualize emerging markets as falling along a continuum featuring different degrees of emergence: 'dysfunctional' markets that have an extreme degree of institutional voids at one end, and 'developed' markets that feature few institutional voids at the other end.

Unlike the supportive institutional environments in advanced economies (cf. Fan, Li, and Chen 2017), formal institutions are sorely inadequate in emerging markets such as China (Ahlstrom and Bruton 2001; Bruton and Ahlstrom 2003; Peng 2001, 2004; Puffer, McCarthy, and Boisot 2010) or less developed regions in China (Gao et al. 2010). Chinese entrepreneurs need to efficiently access resource-, technology- and management-*know-how* from related and supporting industries, which may be hindered by underdeveloped market intermediaries and legal protections (cf. Khanna and Palepu 2006). These intermediary services and a legal protective environment provide critical support to entrepreneurs who lack field-specific knowledge, experience and networks. Problems related to institutional voids in China also include banks that cannot always ensure access to credit, courts that cannot guarantee the enforcement of intellectual property rights or the security of private property rights, and auditors who cannot reliably certify a new venture's financial operations (Ahlstrom and Ding 2014; Gao et al. 2010). As a result, the demands, constraints and challenges facing entrepreneurs in emerging markets such as China are different from those in more mature markets. To address these extra burdens while operating in a commercial and competitive business environment that lacks clear 'rules of the game', Chinese entrepreneurs have to spend more time and energy avoiding extra agency costs. This may stress and frustrate them in a long run, depressing their subjective wellbeing. In the emerging economy context, generalized trust as an informal institution is found to either play a complementary or substitutive role with formal institution (e.g. Welter and Smallbone 2006; Zahra, Yavuz, and Ucbasaran 2006). On the one hand, trust works as a sanctioning mechanism by complementing the overall formal institutional framework, because trust is a reliable way to enforce contracting and transactional behaviors. On the other hand, trust can substitute for formal institutions when these do not work well, because trust, as a function of safeguarding transactions, offers more psychological safeguards to entrepreneurs undertaking new venture creation (Kim and Li 2014; Puffer, McCarthy, and Boisot 2010). In China, complete reliance on insufficient formal institutions can indeed be risky for entrepreneurs, especially in less protected economic sectors such as street vendors (Bruton and Ahlstrom 2003; Peng 2001, 2004). However, what remains unclear is which of the complementary or substitutive mechanisms, or both of them, take place in influencing entrepreneurial activities. Clearly, this is an empirical question that deserves a careful study.

Embracing the core principles of the institution-based view (cf. Bruton, Ahlstrom, and Li 2010; Peng 2001, 2004), we also propose that entrepreneurs rationally pursue their interests and make choices within the formal and informal constraints in a given institutional framework. While formal and informal constraints combine to influence entrepreneurs' behaviors, in situations where institutional voids are evident informal constraints (e.g. personal relationship or social norm) will play a larger role in reducing uncertainty for entrepreneurs. Individuals who encounter poor economic conditions and/or low social status are disadvantaged in their efforts to garner funding and gain access to networks (Essers and Benschop 2009). Thus, such entrepreneurs are more likely to engage in entrepreneurship out of necessity. Necessity entrepreneurs usually lack education, prior managerial experience and access to capital. They often operate in the informal sectors, where they are neither measured nor protected (or bound) by labor laws. In these cases, trust will help overcome these challenges and deficiencies in the institutional environment. It will function as an informal safeguard, protecting entrepreneurs' interests when formal institutions provide little or no protection (Bradach and Eccles 1989; Kim and Li 2014; Puffer, McCarthy, and Boisot 2010; Welter and Smallbone 2006). Given the current levels of unbalanced economic development across Chinese regions, entrepreneurs in less developed regions are likely to start as street vendors in lower socio-economic sectors with comparatively lesser formal institutional protection. In these cases, trust may matter more for these entrepreneurs because of their challenging institutional environments (Bruton and Ahlstrom 2003; Warnecke 2013). Thus, as indicated in Figure 1, we propose the following hypotheses:

Hypothesis 4a: *In the regions with a high level of institutional voids, the interaction effect between trust and economic poverty is stronger for entrepreneurs' subjective wellbeing.*

Hypothesis 4b: *In the regions with a high level of institutional voids, the interaction effect between trust and social poverty is stronger for entrepreneurs' subjective wellbeing.*

Methods

Data and sample

To test our hypotheses, our empirical setting is in China, which is a large emerging economy with substantial regional diversities in both economic and institutional development (Banalieva, Eddleston, and Zellweger 2015; Shi, Sun, and Peng 2012). The Chinese context is ideal to investigate how trust, as an informal institution, increases subjective wellbeing among economically or socially poor entrepreneurs by complementing or substituting for the lack of formal institutional development. We collected our data primarily from two sources. The first is the national baseline survey – the Chinese General Social Survey (CGSS). The CGSS project was launched in 2003 and is the newest member of the global General Social Survey family. The survey employs a multi-stage stratified random sampling approach to ensure the representativeness of the data. Face-to-face interviews are used in the CGSS to collect quantitative data, aiming to systematically monitor the changing relationship between social structure and the quality of life in both urban and rural China.

For this study, we selected data from the 2012 CGSS baseline survey, which includes the module of social network and social capital covering special topics on trust. We selected 965 entrepreneurs from 11,765 individuals in the 2012 CGSS. Consistent with an accepted definition of an entrepreneur (e.g. Bruton, Ahlstrom, and Si 2015), all sampled individuals were their own boss or self-employed (see the CGSS questionnaire in Appendix 1). In this way, the criteria of poverty do not exclude entrepreneurs in the sample.

The second source is the National Economic Research Institute (NERI) Index of Marketization of China's Provinces. China also has significant subnational diversity in economic and institutional environments, which is especially apparent across its provinces (Bruton and Ahlstrom 2003; Shi, Sun, and Peng 2012). We matched the institutional variables from NERI to the CGSS data in 2012 by province (Wang, Fan, and Yu 2017). Previous studies in economics, finance and international business have used the index extensively to measure institutional development in different regions in China (Banalieva, Eddleston, and Zellweger 2015; Shi, Sun, and Peng 2012; Zhou, Gao, and Zhao 2017). After data cleaning, we constructed a unique sample of 818 entrepreneurs from 27 provinces.

Measurements

The dependent variable is *entrepreneurs' subjective wellbeing*. It was measured by responses to the question in the 2012 CGSS, 'Generally speaking, how happy do you feel about your life?' with five possible ordered responses from 1 to 5 ('very unhappy', 'unhappy', 'neutral', 'happy', and 'very happy'). Our single-item measure of subjective wellbeing is consistent with Layard (2010) who validates this measurement by examining its reliability and correlations with other relevant factors.

The independent variable in our research, *trust*, is measured at the regional level. We followed previous studies by measuring trust as the general level of regional trust toward others (e.g. Ding, Au, and Chiang 2015; Uslaner 2002). Much of the generalized trust research relies upon individual-level attitudinal survey questions from the World Values Surveys or General Social Survey. In the 2012 CGSS, respondents are asked to evaluate their trust in others (i.e. to what extent they agree that most people in the society can be trusted) and provide ratings from 1 (completely disagree) to 5 (completely agree). We followed Ding, Au, and Chiang (2015) and calculated trust by averaging the individual trust scores in a specific region based on 11,765 respondents in our database. Here, a region refers to a county or district of a specific city (specified as city + county/district in the CGSS questionnaire: see Appendix 1). In China, 'city' is a very broad concept: it can be provincial, prefectural, county-level or township level. In other words, a region is an administrative unit, which consists of urban or rural areas and sometimes both. To distinguish a county from its actual urban area (the traditional meaning of the word 'city'), the term 'district' *(shìqū)* is used. For example, a region in our research can be Shunyi County, Beijing, or Xihu District, Hangzhou, although the two regions may belong to two different levels of the Chinese city tier system.[1]

The first moderator in our study is *economic poverty*. We identified the cut-offs for relative poverty line by using the definition proposed by the World Bank (below 60% of the median income) and median income based on the National Bureau of Statistics of China (NBSC). That is, our cut-offs for the relative poverty line are 1728.953 USD for urban areas and 560.251 USD for rural areas. We then used these cut-offs to measure economic poverty of each entrepreneur of our sample based on the data of individual income from the 2012 CGSS. Economic poverty was coded as 1 if an entrepreneur's income is below 60% of the median income of people in China, and 0 otherwise.

The second moderator, *social poverty*, was measured according to the question 'Which social hierarchy do you think you belong to?', with ten possible ordered responses from 1 (the lowest social status) to 10 (the highest social status). Hence, social poverty was captured by 11 minus social status). The other component of social poverty is smaller and low-quality social network, namely, the level of lacking the possibility to meet people and build a network (Nahapiet and Ghoshal 1998). We used a network-based indicator as an alternative measure of social poverty. It is measured by asking entrepreneurs to evaluate their frequency of social interaction ('How often do you socially interact with others?'), with five possible ordered responses from 1 (very frequently) to 5 (never) from the 2012 CGSS.

Institutional voids were measured using the index of 'development of market intermediaries and the legal environment' from the NERI Indices (Fan, Wang, and Zhu 2007), which aggregate the two sub-indices of development of market intermediaries and protection of property rights. More specifically, the two sub-indices refer to four aspects of assessment of market intermediaries and the legal enforcement environment, namely, 'development of intermediary in markets', 'protection of legal rights of producers', 'protection of intellectual rights', and 'protection of consumer rights'. Consistent with prior research, regions ranking in the first and the last 50% were classified into high- and low-institutional voids groups, respectively (cf. Fernández-Serrano, Martínez-Román, and Romero 2018). As a proxy measure, a lower score means the region with higher institutional voids, and *vice versa*. We have summarized the measures and data sources of the key constructs in Table 2.

Table 2. Key constructs, measures and data sources.

Construct	Measures	Source
Trust	Averaged individual trust scores in a region	CGSS
Subjective wellbeing	Generally speaking, how happy do you feel about your life?	CGSS
Economic poverty	Below 60% of the median income of people in China	CGSS/NBSC
Social poverty	*Social status*: Which social hierarchy do you think you belong to?	CGSS
	Social network: How often do you socially interact with others?	CGSS
Institutional voids	Development of market intermediaries and the legal environment	NERI

To avoid misestimating the effects of the key variables because of 'omitted variable' bias, our model specifications include a range of control variables. Following prior studies (Chen and Williams 2016; Luttmer 2005), we controlled for several demographic variables: an entrepreneur's *gender* (female = 1 and male = 0), *age*, *marital status* (married = 1 and single or divorced = 0), *annual income* (log-transformed individual income per year), *health level* (ordinal variables ranging from 1 to 5), *work hours* (the hours of working per week), *ethnicity* (Han Chinese = 1 and others = 0), *residential status* (rural = 1 and urban = 0), *Chinese Communist Party membership* (CCP member = 1 and others = 0), and *education dummies* (illiterate, primary school, middle school, high school, college, bachelor and above). Moreover, as some scholars suggest there is a U-shaped curve between *age* and subjective wellbeing (Ferrer-i-Carbonell and Gowdy 2007), we added the *age squared* term in our model to better interpret the relationship. In addition, except for the individual characteristics controls, *GDP per capita* at provincial level was included to control for regional economic heterogeneity.

Table 3 presents the variables and their descriptive statistics. The average trust score is 3.49 and the mean of entrepreneurs' subjective wellbeing is 3.85. Female entrepreneurs account for 36% of our sample. The average age of entrepreneurs is around 42 years old and most entrepreneurs only had middle school education. Variance inflation factors are all within acceptable ranges (i.e. none is larger than the critical value 10).

Next, we employed the CGSS data, including both entrepreneurs and non-entrepreneurs, in order to compare the levels of trust, income and social poverty between urban and rural areas.[2] On average, the trust level for urban areas is 3.413 and for rural areas is 3.549, indicating that trust in a rural area is significantly higher than that in an urban area, as would be expected. To better display the income distribution of the sample, we graphed the Probability Density Functions (PDFs) of incomes among overall urban and rural samples using Kernel density estimation in Figure 2 (Jenkins and Van Kerm 2005). Kernel density estimation is a non-parametric way to estimate the probability density function of a random variable. PDFs provide more information than histograms, because it is endowed with properties of smoothness and continuity. As Figure 2 indicates, the shapes of income distributions are similar across the three samples, while the income distribution of the urban sample is more right-sided than that of the rural sample, which indicates a higher income in rural areas. From these PDFs, the income of highest probability in the urban sample is around 2800 USD and in the rural sample is about 1500 USD. We also found that the average social poverty among entrepreneurs in urban areas is 6.731 and that in rural areas is 6.949, showing that rural entrepreneurs significantly feel socially poorer than their urban counterparts.

Analytical procedure

In order to examine the effect of trust on subjective wellbeing among entrepreneurs, we estimate the following equation:

$$SWB_i = \alpha + \beta Trust_i + \sum_m \gamma_m X_{m,i} + \varepsilon_i \qquad (1)$$

where i denotes individual observations, *SWB* is the measure of entrepreneurs' subjective well-being, *Trust* is our main explanatory variable, X_m is a set of control variables explained earlier, β and γ_m are the parameters to be estimated and ε is the random error term.

As discussed previously, economic poverty and social poverty are expected to play a role in the relationship between trust and their subjective wellbeing. Thus, to understand these moderating effects, we estimate the following models:

$$SWB_i = \alpha + \beta Trust_i + \theta Econpov_i + \rho Trust_i \times Econpov_i + \sum_m \gamma_m X_{m,i} + \varepsilon_i \qquad (2)$$

Table 3. Descriptive statistics and correlations.

	Mean	S.D.	1	2	3	4	5	6	7	8	9	10	11	12	13	14	15	16	17	18
1. Subjective wellbeing	3.85	0.84																		
2. Trust	3.49	0.23	0.12																	
3. Economic poverty	0.19	0.40	−0.15	0.06																
4. Social poverty	6.58	1.68	−0.24	−0.04	0.17															
5. Female	0.36	0.48	−0.07	−0.06	0.22	0.04														
6. Age	41.72	10.86	−0.07	0.02	0.18	−0.01	−0.11													
7. Married	0.90	0.29	0.10	0.06	−0.01	−0.12	0.02	0.11												
8. Log annual income	9.96	1.42	0.12	−0.08	−0.57	−0.19	−0.22	−0.11	0.01											
9. Health level	3.90	0.94	0.20	0.04	−0.18	−0.20	−0.07	−0.25	0.00	0.13										
10. Work hour	60.44	22.30	−0.08	−0.03	0.09	0.12	0.05	−0.00	−0.01	−0.04	−0.06									
11. Han (ethnicity)	0.92	0.27	−0.02	−0.13	−0.06	0.01	−0.02	−0.00	−0.02	0.07	0.02	−0.01								
12. Rural resident	0.57	0.49	−0.05	0.01	−0.05	0.08	−0.05	−0.10	0.01	−0.05	0.02	0.05	−0.06							
13. CCP member	0.08	0.27	0.05	0.03	−0.02	−0.06	−0.15	0.07	0.07	0.06	0.02	−0.06	−0.01	−0.04						
14. Primary school	0.19	0.40	−0.12	0.02	0.21	0.17	0.10	0.16	−0.03	−0.16	−0.10	0.10	−0.06	0.18	−0.11					
15. Middle school	0.44	0.50	0.04	0.03	−0.06	−0.03	−0.08	−0.01	0.10	−0.01	−0.03	0.02	0.01	0.10	−0.02	−0.43				
16. High school	0.24	0.43	0.04	−0.01	−0.10	−0.06	−0.05	−0.07	−0.01	0.05	0.11	−0.07	0.02	−0.15	0.05	−0.28	−0.50			
17. College	0.06	0.23	0.07	−0.02	−0.07	−0.09	0.05	−0.16	−0.06	0.15	0.05	−0.06	0.04	−0.13	0.04	−0.12	−0.22	−0.14		
18. Bachelor and above	0.03	0.18	0.07	−0.04	−0.07	−0.08	−0.05	−0.06	−0.08	0.15	0.01	−0.05	0.05	−0.20	0.18	−0.09	−0.16	−0.10	−0.04	
19. Provincial GDP per capital	10.63	0.37	0.12	−0.06	−0.14	−0.11	−0.01	−0.01	−0.04	0.19	0.08	−0.07	0.09	−0.07	−0.04	−0.09	−0.10	0.08	0.15	0.10

N = 818. Significant at the 0.05 level when Pearson correlations > 0.07 or < −0.07.

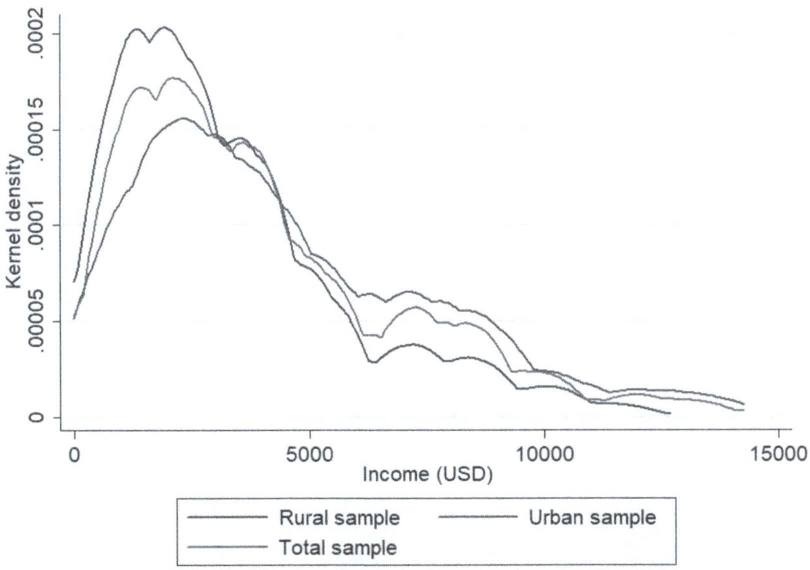

Figure 2. Income distribution across the overall, rural and urban samples.

$$SWB_i = \alpha + \beta Trust_i + \lambda Socpov_i + \delta Trust_i \times Socpov_i + \sum_m \gamma_m X_{m,i} + \varepsilon_i \quad (3)$$

where *Econpov* and *Socpov* denote economic poverty and social poverty respectively, ρ and δ are the moderating parameters.

To better interpret the interaction terms, hierarchical OLS regressions were used to test the multilevel effects. Given that our dependent variable, entrepreneurs' subjective wellbeing, is a five-point Likert scale with natural ordering, we also performed Ordered Probit (OProbit) regressions as robustness checks for our basic linear specifications.

Results

Table 4 presents the regression results for Hypotheses 1, 2 and 3. Model 1 is the baseline model that only includes the study's control variables; the independent variable, moderators and interaction terms are added sequentially in Models 2 to 5, respectively; Model 6 is the full model. Hypothesis 1 predicts that the trust level that exists in a region is positively related to entrepreneurs' subjective wellbeing. The coefficient of trust in Model 2 is positive and significant ($\beta = 0.393$, $p < 0.01$). This implies a 0.393 higher subjective wellbeing among entrepreneurs on a five-point Likert scale if the score of regional trust increases by 1. Therefore, Hypothesis 1 was supported.

The results related to the study's control variables are informative. Age is negatively associated with wellbeing, while its quadratic term is positively related to wellbeing. These results support the U-shape curve between age and wellbeing proposed by Ferrer-i-Carbonell and Gowdy (2007). The annual individual income and the provincial economic level both significantly enhance entrepreneurs' subjective wellbeing, which is consistent with prior research (e.g. Easterlin 1995). Consistent with previous findings by Baker et al. (2005) and Shields and Wheatley (2005), there is a strong linkage between physical health and subjective wellbeing in our tests. As shown in Table 4, married entrepreneurs tend to have a higher level of wellbeing compared with those who are single or divorced. Entrepreneurs with a higher education degree are more likely to have a higher level of subjective wellbeing. The remaining control variables are not statistically significant in our main empirical models.

Table 4. Models of entrepreneurs' subjective wellbeing.

Model	(1)	(2)	(3)	(4)	(5)	(6)
Controls						
Female	−0.049	−0.036	−0.035	−0.034	−0.031	−0.031
	(0.063)	(0.063)	(0.062)	(0.062)	(0.062)	(0.062)
Age	−0.040**	−0.039**	−0.036**	−0.035**	−0.033**	−0.033**
	(0.016)	(0.016)	(0.016)	(0.016)	(0.016)	(0.016)
Age squared	0.044**	0.042**	0.038**	0.037**	0.035**	0.034*
	(0.018)	(0.018)	(0.018)	(0.018)	(0.018)	(0.018)
Married	0.349***	0.331***	0.275***	0.277***	0.255**	0.259***
	(0.101)	(0.101)	(0.101)	(0.100)	(0.100)	(0.100)
Log annual income	0.034	0.040*	0.007	0.010	−0.002	0.001
	(0.022)	(0.022)	(0.025)	(0.025)	(0.025)	(0.025)
Health level	0.149***	0.144***	0.114***	0.116***	0.111***	0.113***
	(0.032)	(0.032)	(0.032)	(0.032)	(0.032)	(0.032)
Work hour	−0.002	−0.001	−0.001	−0.001	−0.001	−0.001
	(0.001)	(0.001)	(0.001)	(0.001)	(0.001)	(0.001)
Han (ethnicity)	−0.141	−0.102	−0.085	−0.095	−0.088	−0.095
	(0.104)	(0.104)	(0.103)	(0.103)	(0.102)	(0.102)
Rural resident	−0.046	−0.044	−0.048	−0.058	−0.048	−0.055
	(0.063)	(0.062)	(0.062)	(0.062)	(0.061)	(0.061)
CCP member	0.022	0.015	0.023	0.022	0.028	0.027
	(0.109)	(0.108)	(0.107)	(0.107)	(0.107)	(0.106)
Primary school	0.258	0.227	0.233	0.215	0.209	0.198
	(0.167)	(0.167)	(0.165)	(0.164)	(0.164)	(0.164)
Middle school	0.420**	0.390**	0.338**	0.321**	0.316**	0.305*
	(0.163)	(0.163)	(0.161)	(0.161)	(0.160)	(0.160)
High school	0.377**	0.351**	0.295*	0.271	0.277*	0.260
	(0.170)	(0.169)	(0.168)	(0.168)	(0.167)	(0.167)
College	0.497**	0.467**	0.393*	0.366*	0.385*	0.364*
	(0.205)	(0.204)	(0.202)	(0.202)	(0.201)	(0.201)
Bachelor and above	0.642***	0.625***	0.534**	0.503**	0.510**	0.489**
	(0.238)	(0.236)	(0.234)	(0.234)	(0.233)	(0.233)
Provincial GDP per capital	0.190**	0.199**	0.177**	0.171**	0.179**	0.174**
	(0.080)	(0.079)	(0.078)	(0.078)	(0.078)	(0.078)
Independent						
Trust		**0.393*****	**0.378*** **	**0.213**	**−1.017****	**−0.981****
		(0.127)	**(0.125)**	**(0.141)**	**(0.459)**	**(0.458)**
Moderators						
Economic poverty			−0.144	−2.705***	−0.163*	−2.169**
			(0.089)	(1.038)	(0.089)	(1.052)
Social poverty			−0.078***	−0.078***	−0.830***	−0.741***
			(0.018)	(0.018)	(0.239)	(0.243)
Interaction terms						
Economic poverty × Trust				**0.732****		**0.574***
				(0.295)		**(0.300)**
Social poverty × Trust					**0.215*****	**0.190*****
					(0.068)	**(0.069)**
Observations	818	818	818	818	818	818
R-squared	0.095	0.106	0.131	0.137	0.142	0.145

Standard errors in parentheses; *** $p < .01$, ** $p < .05$, * $p < .1$.

To assess Hypothesis 2, we added economic poverty and the interaction term, Economic poverty×Trust, in our regressions of Model 4. The interaction term is significant and positive ($\beta = 0.732$, $p < 0.05$), showing that economic poverty strengthens the positive relationship between trust and subjective wellbeing among entrepreneurs. Therefore, Hypothesis 2 was also supported. Next, we test the moderating effect of social poverty on the relationship between trust and subjective wellbeing among entrepreneurs. Social poverty and its interaction term with trust were included in our model specifications. Model 5 displays the results, showing that the interaction term is significant and positive ($\beta = 0.215$, $p < 0.01$). This indicates that social poverty strengthens the positive relationship between trust and entrepreneurs' subjective wellbeing.

Table 5. Models of entrepreneurs' subjective wellbeing under institutional voids.

	High Institutional Voids				Low Institutional Voids			
Model	(7)	(8)	(9)	(10)	(11)	(12)	(13)	(14)
Controls								
Female	0.048	0.047	0.063	0.062	−0.092	−0.087	−0.093	−0.088
	(0.099)	(0.098)	(0.097)	(0.097)	(0.081)	(0.081)	(0.081)	(0.081)
Age	−0.032	−0.032	−0.031	−0.031	−0.037*	−0.036*	−0.036*	−0.035*
	(0.026)	(0.026)	(0.026)	(0.026)	(0.021)	(0.020)	(0.021)	(0.021)
Age squared	0.035	0.035	0.033	0.033	0.040*	0.038*	0.038*	0.036
	(0.029)	(0.029)	(0.029)	(0.029)	(0.022)	(0.022)	(0.022)	(0.022)
Married	0.245	0.233	0.195	0.188	0.198	0.212*	0.195	0.209
	(0.164)	(0.163)	(0.162)	(0.162)	(0.128)	(0.128)	(0.128)	(0.128)
Log annual income	0.074	0.080*	0.061	0.066	−0.021	−0.019	−0.025	−0.021
	(0.045)	(0.045)	(0.045)	(0.045)	(0.030)	(0.030)	(0.030)	(0.030)
Health level	0.141***	0.145***	0.139***	0.143***	0.099**	0.099**	0.098**	0.098**
	(0.050)	(0.050)	(0.049)	(0.049)	(0.041)	(0.041)	(0.041)	(0.041)
Work hour	−0.004*	−0.003*	−0.003	−0.003	0.001	0.001	0.001	0.001
	(0.002)	(0.002)	(0.002)	(0.002)	(0.002)	(0.002)	(0.002)	(0.002)
Han (ethnicity)	−0.052	−0.031	−0.028	−0.013	−0.122	−0.159	−0.135	−0.164
	(0.137)	(0.137)	(0.136)	(0.136)	(0.165)	(0.166)	(0.165)	(0.166)
Rural resident	−0.044	−0.045	−0.034	−0.035	−0.052	−0.064	−0.054	−0.065
	(0.098)	(0.098)	(0.097)	(0.097)	(0.079)	(0.080)	(0.079)	(0.080)
CCP member	0.174	0.170	0.214	0.208	−0.030	−0.019	−0.034	−0.022
	(0.170)	(0.170)	(0.168)	(0.168)	(0.138)	(0.137)	(0.138)	(0.138)
Primary school	0.454*	0.435*	0.439*	0.425*	0.000	−0.016	−0.017	−0.025
	(0.256)	(0.256)	(0.253)	(0.253)	(0.215)	(0.215)	(0.216)	(0.216)
Middle school	0.567**	0.554**	0.555**	0.545**	0.070	0.056	0.055	0.048
	(0.254)	(0.253)	(0.250)	(0.250)	(0.209)	(0.209)	(0.210)	(0.210)
High school	0.372	0.356	0.357	0.345	0.162	0.136	0.152	0.132
	(0.267)	(0.266)	(0.263)	(0.263)	(0.215)	(0.216)	(0.216)	(0.216)
College	0.672**	0.642*	0.666**	0.643*	0.173	0.139	0.164	0.137
	(0.332)	(0.332)	(0.328)	(0.328)	(0.258)	(0.258)	(0.258)	(0.258)
Bachelor and above	0.832**	0.785**	0.772**	0.738*	0.327	0.301	0.318	0.298
	(0.380)	(0.379)	(0.375)	(0.375)	(0.296)	(0.296)	(0.296)	(0.296)
Provincial GDP per capital	0.717***	0.667***	0.702***	0.663***	0.071	0.094	0.078	0.097
	(0.189)	(0.190)	(0.186)	(0.188)	(0.123)	(0.123)	(0.123)	(0.124)
Independent								
Trust	**0.708*** **	**0.556*** **	**−1.181***	**−1.202***	**0.060**	**−0.112**	**−0.579**	**−0.483**
	(0.183)	**(0.202)**	**(0.616)**	**(0.616)**	**(0.176)**	**(0.202)**	**(0.700)**	**(0.702)**
Moderators								
Economic poverty	−0.034	−2.799*	−0.045	−2.246	−0.159	−2.609*	−0.170	−2.421
	(0.135)	(1.578)	(0.134)	(1.570)	(0.121)	(1.434)	(0.121)	(1.475)
Social poverty	−0.047*	−0.045*	−1.063***	−1.008***	−0.112***	−0.113***	−0.460	−0.322
	(0.026)	(0.026)	(0.318)	(0.320)	(0.024)	(0.024)	(0.369)	(0.380)
Interaction terms								
Economic poverty × Trust		**0.800***		**0.637**		**0.696***		**0.640**
		(0.455)		**(0.452)**		**(0.406)**		**(0.418)**
Social poverty × Trust			**0.291*** **	**0.276*** **			**0.100**	**0.060**
			(0.091)	**(0.091)**			**(0.106)**	**(0.109)**
Observations	361	361	361	361	457	457	457	457
R-squared	0.208	0.215	0.231	0.236	0.132	0.138	0.134	0.139

Standard errors in parentheses; *** $p < .01$, ** $p < .05$, * $p < .1$.

Thus, Hypothesis 3 is supported. The results from the fully specified Model 6 are also consistent with Hypotheses 2 and 3.

To explore the extent to which the moderating effects of economic and social poverty are strengthened or weakened by institutional voids, regressions were separately conducted for regions with high- and low-institutional voids groups. The econometric results of the separated regressions appear in Table 5. As Models 8 and 12 show, the interaction terms of trust and economic poverty are statistically positive under both high institutional voids ($\beta = 0.800$, $p < 0.1$) and low institutional voids ($\beta = 0.696$, $p < 0.1$). The magnitude and significance level of the coefficients is similar. Thus, Hypothesis 4a was not supported. However, in Models 9 and 13, the interaction term of trust and social poverty is statistically positive and significant in high institutional voids subsamples ($\beta = 0.291$, $p < 0.01$), but not significant in the low institutional voids subsamples ($\beta = 0.100$, $p > 0.1$). The interaction effect of trust and social poverty is significantly larger under high institutional voids than that under low institutional voids. Thus, Hypothesis 4b was supported.

Robustness checks

We also carried out several robustness checks to further validate the results we have just presented. First, research on the determinants of subjective wellbeing employs either ordinary least square or ordered outcome models (Churchill and Mishra 2017). Given that our dependent variable, entrepreneurs' subjective wellbeing, is a five-point Likert scale with natural ordering, we also performed Ordered Probit (OProbit) regressions to establish the robustness of our results to both empirical specifications. The results show that the estimated relationships largely remain the same, providing additional support for our theoretical framework.

Second, allowing for the multicollinearity of the variables annual income and economic poverty status, we performed regressions without controlling for annual income. The overall results are consistent with the findings we reported earlier, ruling out potential multicollinearity.

Third, as mentioned earlier, we employed limited social network as an alternative measure for social poverty and re-performed regressions. The overall results are consistent with those in our main analyses. Specifically, two types of social poverty both positively moderate the relationship between trust and entrepreneurs' subjective wellbeing.

Fourth, as variables at different levels were included in our analysis, we used hierarchical linear modeling (HLM) to check the robustness of our multilevel hypotheses. The HLM results show that the coefficient of trust is still significantly positive and the magnitude of the effect is similar to that in our baseline regression models. The interaction term between trust and economic poverty is significantly positive, as is the interaction term between trust and social poverty, indicating that economic and social poverty both strengthen the positive relationship between trust and subjective wellbeing among entrepreneurs.

Finally, to investigate the heterogeneity between the urban and the rural areas, we re-ran regressions using the rural and urban subsamples. Trust has a significant positive effect on entrepreneurs' subjective wellbeing both in rural and urban areas, although the effect is larger in the urban subsample than in the rural subsample. As for the moderating effect, social poverty plays a positive moderating role between trust and rural entrepreneurs' subjective wellbeing, while economic poverty positively moderates the relationship between trust and urban entrepreneurs' subjective wellbeing.

Discussion

Using a multi-sourced database of 818 Chinese entrepreneurs, this study has investigated entrepreneurs' benefits in terms of subjective wellbeing from trust in their region, whether those benefits are subject to entrepreneurs' economic and social poverty, and whether these relationships are still valid in the context of high institutional voids (see Figure 1). In general, the study finds support for the notion that entrepreneurs benefit from the prevalence of higher levels of trust in their region in terms of their subjective wellbeing. Further, this relationship is moderated by economic poverty and social poverty. Specifically, achieving a higher level of trust is more positively linked to subjective wellbeing for economic and social status disadvantaged entrepreneurs. In addition, we explore whether the effects of economic and social poverty are strengthened or weakened under institutional voids. The results show that the moderating effect of social poverty becomes stronger on the relationship between trust and entrepreneurs' subjective wellbeing in those regions where institutional voids exist. Yet the difference between regions with high and low institutional voids does not vary significantly for the moderating effect of economic poverty. This indicates that the interaction between informal and formal institutional environment is more complex than the literature suggests.

Our results reveal intriguing patterns of urban-rural differences in China. Rural entrepreneurs are more economically and socially poorer than their urban counterparts, which may result from China's uneven regional development to date. Moreover, rural entrepreneurs are more likely to enjoy a high-trust environment. The possible explanation is that the rural areas in China are more structurally stable, with less social mobility, and where people gradually develop generalized trust toward each other. Despite the varying levels of poverty and trust between rural and urban areas, trust plays a non-trivial role in maintaining entrepreneurs' subjective wellbeing. However, the working mechanism is subtly different for rural and urban entrepreneurs. While socially poor entrepreneurs in rural areas need trust more for their subjective wellbeing, the economically poor in urban areas are more reliant on trust. We speculate that the socioeconomic structure may account for such a discrepancy. Since the rural economy in China is self-supporting and self-sufficient, rural entrepreneurs tend to find ways to feed themselves and suffer less from economic poverty. However, products and services are primarily commercialized in the urban areas and entrepreneurs have to pay for everything they need in business creation. Although our study does not focus on an urban-rural divide, the findings lead us to reflect on the regional background of trust, poverty and entrepreneurs' subjective wellbeing.

Theoretical implications

Our study makes three contributions to the literature. First, we contribute to the literature by exploring unique antecedents of entrepreneurs' subjective wellbeing. Our study investigates the relationship between trust and entrepreneurs' wellbeing in the largest emerging economy context – China. As noted earlier, entrepreneurs' subjective wellbeing has attracted increasing scholarly attention (Chay 1993; Hahn et al. 2012; Stephan 2018; Williams and Shepherd 2016), because it is not only evident in its roles in entrepreneurs' decision-making, motivation and activities (Stephan 2018), but also provides context-specific feedback on preferences, progress and expectations in entrepreneurship (Shir 2015). Entrepreneurs' subjective wellbeing is an important dependent variable in 'its own right' (Uy, Foo, and Song 2012, 583; Williams and Shepherd 2016). Prior studies in this regard mainly cover the antecedents of entrepreneurs' subjective wellbeing in six aspects, namely, work characteristics, personality traits, values and other personal resources, firm and financial characteristics, social resources and stressors, and physical environment (see also Bjørnskov 2003; Bjørnskov, Dreher, and Fischer 2010; Helliwell 2006; Stephan 2018; Uy, Foo, and Song 2012). While Stephan (2018) calls for future research that identifies more unique antecedents of entrepreneurs' work that have impact on their wellbeing, we provide an institution-based antecedent to this field. We argue that generalized trust is not only an important individual phenomenon but also an indication of informal institutions in order to explain subjective wellbeing.

Second, our study contributes to the entrepreneurs' subjective wellbeing literature by examining situational effects of the two distinct types of poverty. The main stream entrepreneurship literature treats poverty reduction as one of the important consequences of entrepreneurial activities (e.g. Bruton, Ahlstrom, and Si 2015) or one of the significant indicators of entrepreneurs' objective wellbeing (e.g. Van Praag and Versloot 2007). However, in our study poverty is regarded as a moderating factor; that is, we argue the process of generalized trust in a region affecting entrepreneurs' subjective wellbeing is subject to these entrepreneurs' poverty levels. For example, our findings show that generalized trust plays a more significant role in low-income entrepreneurs' subjective wellbeing than in high-income ones. This finding pertains to the need to better understand the nature of entrepreneurs' subjective wellbeing as well as its boundary conditions, and pave the way to instigate the building blocks of future theory development on entrepreneurs' subjective wellbeing. Moreover, in line with Waglé (2008), we emphasize the multidimensional nature of poverty, conceptually distinguishing economic from social poverty (see Figure 1). Apart from the significant moderating effect of economic poverty, our analyses highlight the role of social poverty as an important consideration for poverty reduction. This moderating effect of social poverty also functions in the context of high institutional voids, but this is not true for economic poverty. Different from conventional research on poverty where self-reinforcing mechanisms cause poverty to persist (Azariadis and Stachurski 2005), our findings highlight a more socialized view of entrepreneurs in their work-life contexts (cf., Stephan 2018).

Third, this study contributes to entrepreneurship research by providing contextualized findings and robust evidence on entrepreneurs' subjective wellbeing. In so doing, the study not only addresses the field's call for future research to explore context sensitive findings (Stephan 2018), it also embraces the insights of identifying the heterogeneous nature of entrepreneurs (Davidsson 2016; Zahra and Wright 2011). For example, emerging markets are characterized by underdeveloped institutions and frequent environmental shifts (Khanna and Palepu 1997). As a large emerging economy with substantial regional diversities in both economic and institutional development (Banalieva, Eddleston, and Zellweger 2015; Shi, Sun, and Peng 2012), the Chinese empirical context provides an ideal opportunity to investigate how trust as an informal institution increases subjective wellbeing among poor entrepreneurs by complementing or substituting for the lack of formal institutional development – hence our empirical endeavors to generate some interesting findings that are worth reflecting on the theoretical underpinnings.

Moreover, this study contributes to the literature by positioning and explaining trust as an informal institution that can substitute for the absence of formal institutions, filling existing institutional voids, thereby safeguarding transactions and protecting entrepreneurs (Bradach and Eccles 1989; Puffer, McCarthy, and Boisot 2010). While there is no agreement in the literature as to whether the interactions between formal and informal institutions are complementary or substitutive, our findings indicate that generalized trust as an informal institutional mechanism plays a substitutive role for Chinese entrepreneurs who experience social, but not economic, poverty; they tend to report greater subjective wellbeing in regions with high institutional voids. Likewise, although our results do not show statistically significant differences with regard to economic poverty and may require further study, it is worth noting that economically poor Chinese entrepreneurs can benefit more from the informal institution – trust – in regions with higher institutional voids (the coefficient increases slightly from 0.696 to 0.800: see Table 5). This indicates a weak complementary role between informal and formal institutions. However, the value of trust and informal institutions cannot be overstated. For entrepreneurs, not all business relationships have to be regulated under formal institutions (e.g. via contracts), which would reduce their transaction costs (Das and Teng 1998). Entrepreneurs with lower occupational status are more likely to be in informal sectors, often operating with less protection from formal institutions (Webb et al. 2009). Previous empirical studies suggest that contract drafting is commonly used to represent the essence of formal institutional controls (Cannon and Perreault 1999). Today, China's evolving legal institutions are particularly inefficient in regulating entrepreneurial activities and this might lead to a remarkably low rate of drafting formal contracts (Yang, Zhou, and Jiang 2011). Informal institutions, embedded in a society or community, act as alternatives to facilitate entrepreneurial processes and protect entrepreneurs' ownership and other interests. Entrepreneurial activities are a stimulus for economic growth in developing and emerging economies; understanding the role of informal institutions in entrepreneurship therefore clearly has academic and practical relevance.

Practical and policy implications

Our findings also have implications for practitioners. First, since generalized trust in a region can positively affect entrepreneurs' subjective wellbeing, promoting a harmonized society and building local trustworthy communities are key policy implications proposed by this study. Uy, Foo, and Song (2012, 584) conclude that entrepreneurs should develop active and/or avoidance coping strategies effectively, which is critical to entrepreneurs' subjective wellbeing because of 'the stressful nature of the entrepreneurial environment'. While their 2012 study focuses on self-actions of entrepreneurs, our study argues that governments or local communities can attempt to make entrepreneurial environment more trustworthy and less stressful, such as by protecting fair transactions, fostering positive values, encouraging social commitment and responsible behaviours, promoting mutual respect and tolerance, completing the social credit system, and so on. In fact, these actions have been evident in China in the last two decades. Chinese government leaders, such as Hu Jintao and Xi Jinping, have endeavoured to promote a harmonized society. In so doing, these procedures can be deemed as a useful environmental rehabilitation approach towards improving entrepreneurs' subjective wellbeing.

Second, in relation to economic poverty, Haushofer and Fehr (2014) observe that poverty causes negative affective states which lead to risk aversion, probably at expense of future poverty reduction. To break this loop, our study places an emphasis on building up a trustworthy business environment that promotes entrepreneurs' subjective wellbeing. This approach complements the economic approaches for poverty reduction dominating in the literature, such as providing financial aid, microfinance, social entrepreneurship, and a base of pyramid initiatives (Alvarez, Barney, and Newman 2015). Our contention is that while these economic approaches can alleviate poverty quickly, the positive effects deriving from the high-trust region may be long-lasting. Low-income entrepreneurs probably face more psychological challenges in becoming entrepreneurs because of their disadvantaged economic or social status. From a remediation perspective (Sutter, Bruton, and Chen 2018), trust provides the most precious psychological resources – confidence, determination, persistence, etc. – that have to the potential to unleash the entrepreneurial spirit among low-income entrepreneurs. Our study calls for attention to building this trust by the government, public institutions and public policy makers in order to support the entrepreneurial activities of low-income entrepreneurs, because trust provides a possible solution to breaking down the institutionalized poverty in modern society (Suddaby, Bruton, and Walsh 2018).

Third, bringing social poverty back into the analytical framework can have profound practical and policy implications. The policy and academic arenas have witnessed an on-going debate about the definition of poverty, seeking a better understanding its levels (e.g. Tasavori, Zaefarian, and Ghauri 2015). The common practice is to resort to economic indicators by determining the absolute income level or percentile-based benchmarks (World Bank 2012). Our study suggests that such a practice is incomplete and may be harmful. Socially poor entrepreneurs can have necessities to live a humble life, but may suffer from psychological problems, hesitating to start their own businesses or operate them effectively. Even in a worse situation, millions of those low-social-status entrepreneurs are excluded from the current anti-poverty policies and programs in many countries, including China, because of their sufficient economic condition. The public does not hear the voices of these disadvantaged people, although they are denied access to entrepreneurial opportunities. Including them in public policy discussions can help reduce social inequality and enhance the vigour of would-be entrepreneurs operating at the bottom of the social hierarchy.

Limitations and future research

Even though the present study provides several interesting findings, it also has limitations that should be acknowledged. First, as the study used data that are cross-sectional in nature (although we aggregated the measurement of trust to a higher level), inferences regarding the direction of the relationship between trust and entrepreneurs' subjective wellbeing should be carefully drawn. Future researchers need to use longitudinal and experiment designs to analyze the dynamic relationship between trust and entrepreneurs' subjective wellbeing. Future investigations with more objective and sophisticated measures of trust and subjective wellbeing would also assist in validating our findings.

Second, we conducted our analysis in a single emerging economy: China. Although our results from the Chinese sample are robust across various model specifications with different sets of control variables, questions about generalizability cannot be ignored. Linking trust and entrepreneurs' subjective wellbeing may have been affected by cultures in nations or regions (Cruz, Justo, and De Castro 2012). Confucianism has dominated Chinese society for a long period, which means that Confucianism has become ingrained in Chinese mindsets. Confucian philosophy values the importance of trust in other people (Tan and Tambyah 2011). Therefore, results from China may differ from findings from other emerging countries where trust may not be a dominant value. Future researchers should seek to replicate our study in other countries and regions, aiming to ensure generalizability.

Third, our results show the different moderating effects for social and economic poverty – the substitutive relationship between trust and formal institutions for subjective wellbeing is only valid for social poverty. We believe that those living in social poverty are more eager to use trust to pursue happiness under institutional voids. However, we need more research that can further explore the differences between economic and social poverty.

Fourth, our results show varying levels of trust, individual income and social poverty, as well as the differing role of trust between rural and urban areas. Although we attribute the urban-rural differences to the socioeconomic structure, we do not provide in-depth and robust empirical analysis to identify the contributing factors. Future research needs to probe the reasons behind these rural and urban differences.

Finally, we used some single-item and self-reported measures such as trust and subjective wellbeing, because we were limited by the national baseline survey design. For example, in regard of subjective wellbeing, Diener (2000) argues that a single-item measure has some merits (e.g. it is less contaminated by biases), but he does encourage future measures to combine other methods, such as the experience-sampling method. Likewise, the self-reported measurement approach on subjective wellbeing can manifest 'subjective experience' in physiology, which has been often used by other scientific studies (e.g. Deaton and Stone 2013; Fan et al. 2014). Future research can develop measures that enable careful assessment of multiple aspects of these concepts. For instance, subjective wellbeing can be captured by reflecting multiple items of both life satisfaction and affect balance (cf. Fan et al. 2014). Furthermore, future research can include entrepreneurs' objective wellbeing as a complementary outcome.

Conclusion

This study reveals that a higher level of trust in a region that acts as an informal institution is positively associated with entrepreneurs' subjective wellbeing. It also finds that this trust is more positively linked to subjective wellbeing for those entrepreneurs who operate under poorer economic or social conditions. In addition, given the existence of institutional voids in mainland China, we have also explored these relationships in the context of high institutional voids, showing that economic poverty does not play a significant moderating role, while social poverty can strengthen the positive relationship between trust and entrepreneurs' subjective wellbeing. Our study offers insights into the importance of informal institutions in contributing to entrepreneurs' subjective wellbeing. We hope that these findings inspire future scholars to study entrepreneurs' wellbeing during the value creation and poverty reduction processes.

Notes

1. We cannot determine the specific region and its size in the CGSS dataset, because the detailed information of city, county and district is fuzzified to ensure confidentiality. What we can know is whether the respondents belong to a same region.
2. Thanks to one of the reviewers, we compared the urban and rural differences for trust, individual income and social poverty.

Acknowledgments

We would like to thank editor, Professors Steven Si, John Cullen, David Ahlstrom and Jiang Wei, and two anonymous reviewers for their insightful suggestions in the PDW and revision process.

Disclosure statement

No potential conflict of interest was reported by the authors.

Funding

This research was supported, in part, by the National Natural Science Foundation of China (Project No.71872043), the MOE (Ministry of Education in China) Project of Humanities and Social Sciences (Project No. 18YJA630097) and the Fundamental Research Funds for the Central Universities.

ORCID

Di Fan http://orcid.org/0000-0003-2737-4136

References

Ahlstrom, D., and G. D. Bruton. 2001. "Learning from Successful Local Private Firms in China: Establishing Legitimacy." *Academy of Management Perspectives* 15 (4): 72–83. doi:10.5465/ame.2001.5897661.

Ahlstrom, D., and Z. Ding. 2014. "Entrepreneurship in China: An Overview." *International Small Business Journal* 32 (6): 610–618. doi:10.1177/0266242613517913.

Alesina, A., and E. La Ferrara. 2002. "Who Trusts Others?" *Journal of Public Economics* 85: 207–234. doi:10.1016/S0047-2727(01)00084-6.

Alvarez, S. A., and J. B. Barney. 2013. "Epistemology, Opportunities, and Entrepreneurship: Comments on Venkataraman Et Al. (2012) and Shane (2012)." *Academy of Management Review* 38 (1): 154–157. doi:10.5465/amr.2012.0069.

Alvarez, S. A., J. B. Barney, and A. M. Newman. 2015. "The Poverty Problem and the Industrialization Solution." *Asia Pacific Journal of Management* 32 (1): 23–37. doi:10.1007/s10490-014-9397-5.

Anderson, C., M. W. Kraus, A. D. Galinsky, and D. Keltner. 2012. "The Local-Ladder Effect: Social Status and Subjective Well-being." *Psychological Science* 23 (7): 764–771. doi:10.1177/0956797611434537.

Ansari, S., K. Munir, and T. Gregg. 2012. "Impact at the "bottom of the Pyramid": The Role of Social Capital in Capability Development and Community Empowerment." *Journal of Management Studies* 49: 813–842. doi:10.1111/joms.2012.49.issue-4.

Azariadis, C., and J. Stachurski. 2005. "Poverty Traps." *Handbook of Economic Growth* 1: 295–384.

Baker, L. A., L. P. Cahalin, K. Gerst, and J. A. Burr. 2005. "Productive Activities and Subjective Well-being among Older Adults: The Influence of Number of Activities and Time Commitment." *Social Indicators Research* 73: 431–458. doi:10.1007/s11205-005-0805-6.

Banalieva, E. R., K. A. Eddleston, and T. M. Zellweger. 2015. "When Do Family Firms Have an Advantage in Transitioning Economies? toward a Dynamic Institution-based View." *Strategic Management Journal* 36 (9): 1358–1377. doi:10.1002/smj.2288.

Banerjee, A. V., and E. Duflo. 2011. *Poor Economics: A Radical Rethinking of the Way to Fight Global Poverty*. New York: Public Affairs.

Bank, W. 2012. "World Bank Sees Progress against Extreme Poverty, but Flags Vulnerabilities." *Press Release*, February 29. doi:10.1094/PDIS-11-11-0999-PDN

Bjørnskov, C. 2003. "The Happy Few: Cross-country Evidence on Social Capital and Life Satisfaction." *Kyklos* 56 (1): 3–16. doi:10.1111/kykl.2003.56.issue-1.

Bjørnskov, C. 2006. "The Multiple Facets of Social Capital." *European Journal of Political Economy* 22 (1): 22–40. doi:10.1016/j.ejpoleco.2005.05.006.

Bjørnskov, C., A. Dreher, and J. A. Fischer. 2010. "Formal Institutions and Subjective Well-being: Revisiting the Cross-country Evidence." *European Journal of Political Economy* 26 (4): 419–430. doi:10.1016/j.ejpoleco.2010.03.001.

Bradach, J. L., and R. G. Eccles. 1989. "Price, Authority, and Trust: From Ideal Types to Plural Forms." *Annual Review of Sociology* 15 (1): 97–118. doi:10.1146/annurev.so.15.080189.000525.

Brehm, J., and W. Rahn. 1997. "Individual-level Evidence for the Causes and Consequences of Social Capital." *American Journal of Political Science* 41: 999–1023. doi:10.2307/2111684.

Bruton, G. D., and D. Ahlstrom. 2003. "An Institutional View of China's Venture Capital Industry: Explaining the Differences between China and the West." *Journal of Business Venturing* 18 (2): 233–259. doi:10.1016/S0883-9026(02)00079-4.

Bruton, G. D., D. Ahlstrom, and H. L. Li. 2010. "Institutional Theory and Entrepreneurship: Where are We Now and Where Do We Need to Move in the Future?" *Entrepreneurship Theory and Practice* 34 (3): 421–440. doi:10.1111/j.1540-6520.2010.00390.x.

Bruton, G. D., D. Ahlstrom, and S. Si. 2015. "Entrepreneurship, Poverty, and Asia: Moving beyond Subsistence Entrepreneurship." *Asia Pacific Journal of Management* 32 (1): 1–22. doi:10.1007/s10490-014-9404-x.

Cannon, J. P., and W. D. Perreault. 1999. "Buyer-seller Relationships in Business Markets." *Journal of Marketing Research* 36 (4): 439–460.

Carpenter, J. P., A. G. Daniere, and L. M. Takahashi. 2004. "Social Capital and Trust in South-east Asian Cities." *Urban Studies* 41 (4): 853–874. doi:10.1080/0042098042000194142.

Carter, S. 2011. "The Rewards of Entrepreneurship: Exploring the Incomes, Wealth, and Economic Well-Being of Entrepreneurial Households." *Entrepreneurship Theory and Practice* 35 (1): 39–55. doi:10.1111/etap.2011.35.issue-1.

Chatman, J. A., and S. G. Barsade. 1995. "Personality, Organizational Culture, and Cooperation: Evidence from a Business Simulation." *Administrative Science Quarterly* 40: 423–443. doi:10.2307/2393792.

Chay, Y. W. 1993. "Social Support, Individual Differences and Well-being: A Study of Small Business Entrepreneurs and Employees." *Journal of Occupational and Organizational Psychology* 66 (4): 285–302. doi:10.1111/joop.1993.66.issue-4.

Chen, Y., and X. Fan. 2015. "Discordance between Subjective and Objective Social Status in Contemporary China." *Journal of Chinese Sociology* 2 (14): 1–13. doi:10.1186/s40711-015-0017-7.

Chen, Y., and M. Williams. 2016. "Subjective Well-being in the New China: Religion, Social Capital, and Social Status." *British Journal of Sociology* 67 (4): 719–746. doi:10.1111/1468-4446.12232.

Churchill, S. A., and V. Mishra. 2017. "Trust, Social Networks and Subjective Wellbeing in China." *Social Indicators Research* 132 (1): 313–339. doi:10.1007/s11205-015-1220-2.

Cruz, C., R. Justo, and J. O. De Castro. 2012. "Does Family Employment Enhance MSEs Performance? Integrating Socioemotional Wealth and Family Embeddedness Perspectives." *Journal of Business Venturing* 27: 62–76. doi:10.1016/j.jbusvent.2010.07.002.

Das, T. K., and B. S. Teng. 1998. "Between Trust and Control: Developing Confidence in Partner Cooperation in Alliances." *Academy of Management Review* 23 (3): 491–512. doi:10.5465/amr.1998.926623.

Davidsson, P. 2016. "A 'business Researcher' View on Opportunities for Psychology in Entrepreneurship Research." *Applied Psychology* 65 (3): 628–636. doi:10.1111/apps.12071.

De Rivera, J., and D. Páez. 2007. "Emotional Climate, Human Security, and Cultures of Peace." *Journal of Social Issues* 63 (2): 233–253. doi:10.1111/josi.2007.63.issue-2.

De Soto, H. 2000. *The Mystery of Capital: Why Capitalism Triumphs in the West and Fails Everywhere Else*. New York: Basic Civitas Books.

Deaton, A., and A. A. Stone. 2013. "Two Happiness Puzzles." *American Economic Review* 103 (3): 591–597. doi:10.1257/aer.103.3.591.

Diener, E. 2000. "Subjective Well-being: The Science of Happiness and a Proposal for a National Index." *American Psychologist* 55 (1): 34–43. doi:10.1037/0003-066X.55.1.34.

Diener, E., E. M. Suh, R. E. Lucas, and H. L. Smith. 1999. "Subjective Well-being: Three Decades of Progress." *Psychological Bulletin* 125 (2): 276–302. doi:10.1037/0033-2909.125.2.276.

Ding, Z., K. Au, and F. Chiang. 2015. "Social Trust and Angel Investors' Decisions: A Multilevel Analysis across Nations." *Journal of Business Venturing* 30 (2): 307–321. doi:10.1016/j.jbusvent.2014.08.003.

Easterlin, R. 1974. "Does Economic Growth Improve the Human Lot? Some Empirical Evidence." In *Nations and Households in Economic Growth: Essays in Honour of Moses Abramowitz.*, edited by P. A. David and M. W. Reder:, 89–125. New York: Academic Press.

Easterlin, R. A. 1995. "Will Raising the Incomes of All Increase the Happiness of All?" *Journal of Economic Behavior & Organization* 27 (1): 35–47. doi:10.1016/0167-2681(95)00003-B.

Essers, C., and Y. Benschop. 2009. "Muslim Business Women Doing Boundary Work: The Negotiation of Islam, Gender and Ethnicity within Entrepreneurial Context." *Human Relations* 62 (3): 403–423. doi:10.1177/0018726708101042.

Fan, D., L. Cui, M. M. Zhang, C. J. Zhu, C. E. Härtel, and C. Nyland. 2014. "Influence of High Performance Work Systems on Employee Subjective Well-being and Job Burnout: Empirical Evidence from the Chinese Healthcare Sector." *International Journal of Human Resource Management* 25 (7): 931–950. doi:10.1080/09585192.2014.876740.

Fan, D., Y. Li, and L. Chen. 2017. "Configuring Innovative Societies: The Crossvergent Role of Cultural and Institutional Varieties." *Technovation* 66: 43–56. doi:10.1016/j.technovation.2017.05.003.

Fan, G., X. L. Wang, and H. P. Zhu. 2007. *Marketization Index for China's Provinces. The Marketization Index in China.* Beijing: Economic Science Press.

Fernández-Serrano, J., J. A. Martínez-Román, and I. Romero. 2018. "The Entrepreneur in the Regional Innovation System. A Comparative Study for High-and Low-income Regions." *Entrepreneurship & Regional Development* (Advance online publication). doi:10.1080/08985626.2018.1513079.

Ferrer-i-Carbonell, A., and J. M. Gowdy. 2007. "Environmental Degradation and Happiness." *Ecological Economics* 60 (3): 509–516. doi:10.1016/j.ecolecon.2005.12.005.

Frey, B. S., and A. Stutzer. 2010. *Happiness and Economics: How the Economy and Institutions Affect Human Well-being*. New Jersey: Princeton University Press.

Fukuyama, F. 1995. *Trust: The Social Virtues and the Creation of Prosperity* (No. D10 301 c. 1/c. 2). New York: Free Press Paperbacks.

Gao, G. Y., J. Y. Murray, M. Kotabe, and J. Lu. 2010. "A "strategy Tripod" Perspective on Export Behaviors: Evidence from Domestic and Foreign Firms Based in an Emerging Economy." *Journal of International Business Studies* 41 (3): 377–396. doi:10.1057/jibs.2009.27.

Gill, R., and G. Larson. 2014. "Making the Ideal (local) Entrepreneur: Enterprise Discourse, Place, and the Construction of Entrepreneurial Identity." *Human Relations* 67 (5): 519–542. doi:10.1177/0018726713496829.

Glaeser, E. L., D. I. Laibson, J. A. Scheinkman., and C. L. Soutter. 2000. "Measuring Trust." *Quarterly Journal of Economics* 115 (3): 811–846. doi:10.1162/qjec.2000.115.issue-3.

Hahn, V. C., M. Frese, C. Binnewies, and A. Schmitt. 2012. "Happy and Proactive? the Role of Hedonic and Eudaimonic Well-Being in Business Owners' Personal Initiative." *Entrepreneurship Theory and Practice* 36 (1): 97–114. doi:10.1111/etap.2012.36.issue-1.

Hansen, E. L. 1995. "Entrepreneurial Networks and New Organization Growth." *Entrepreneurship Theory and Practice* 19 (4): 7–19. doi:10.1177/104225879501900402.

Hart, K. M., H. R. Capps, J. P. Cangemi, and L. M. Caillouet. 1986. "Exploring Organizational Trust and Its Multiple Dimensions: A Case Study of General Motors." *Organization Development Journal* 4 (2): 31–39.

Hart, S. L., and C. M. Christensen. 2002. "The Great Leap: Driving Innovation from the Base of the Pyramid." *MIT Sloan Management Review* 44 (1): 51.

Haushofer, J., and E. Fehr. 2014. "On the Psychology of Poverty." *Science* 344 (6186): 862–867. doi:10.1126/science.1232491.

Helliwell, J. F. 2006. "Well-Being, Social Capital and Public Policy: What's New?" *The Economic Journal* 116 (510): 34–45. doi:10.1111/j.1468-0297.2006.01074.x.

Hoskisson, R. E., J. Covin, H. W. Volberda, and R. A. Johnson. 2011. "Revitalizing Entrepreneurship: The Search for New Research Opportunities." *Journal of Management Studies* 48 (6): 1141–1168. doi:10.1111/j.1467-6486.2010.00997.x.

Houghton, J., and S. R. Khandker. 2009. *Handbook on Poverty and Inequality*. Washington, DC: World Bank.

Jenkins, S. P., and P. Van Kerm. 2005. "Accounting for Income Distribution Trends: A Density Function Decomposition Approach." *Journal of Economic Inequality* 3 (1): 43–61. doi:10.1007/s10888-004-8309-1.

Jones, G. R., and J. M. George. 1998. "The Experience and Evolution of Trust: Implications for Cooperation and Teamwork." *Academy of Management Review* 23 (3): 531–546. doi:10.5465/amr.1998.926625.

Khanna, T., and K. Palepu. 1997. "Why Focused Strategies May Be Wrong for Emerging Markets." *Harvard Business Review* 75 (4): 41–48.

Khanna, T., and K. G. Palepu. 2006. "Emerging Giants: Building World-class Companies in Developing Countries." *Harvard Business Review* 84 (10): 133–134.

Khanna, T., K. G. Palepu, and J. Sinha. 2005. "Strategies that Fit Emerging Markets." *Harvard Business Review* 83 (6): 63–76.

Khavul, S., and G. D. Bruton. 2013. "Harnessing Innovation for Change: Sustainability and Poverty in Developing Countries." *Journal of Management Studies* 50 (2): 285–306. doi:10.1111/joms.2013.50.issue-2.

Kim, H., and J. Song. 2017. "Filling Institutional Voids in Emerging Economies: The Impact of Capital Market Development and Business Groups on M&A Deal Abandonment." *Journal of International Business Studies* 48 (3): 308–323. doi:10.1057/s41267-016-0025-0.

Kim, P. H., and M. Li. 2014. "Seeking Assurances When Taking Action: Legal Systems, Social Trust, and Starting Businesses in Emerging Economies." *Organization Studies* 35 (3): 359–391. doi:10.1177/0170840613499566.

Koski, J. E., H. Xie, and I. R. Olson. 2015. "Understanding Social Hierarchies: The Neural and Psychological Foundations of Status Perception." *Social Neuroscience* 10 (5): 527–550. doi:10.1080/17470919.2015.1013223.

Kwon, S. W., and P. Arenius. 2010. "Nations of Entrepreneurs: A Social Capital Perspective." *Journal of Business Venturing* 25 (3): 315–330. doi:10.1016/j.jbusvent.2008.10.008.

Layard, R. 2010. "Measuring Subjective Well-being." *Science* 327 (5965): 534–535. doi:10.1126/science.1186315.

Lee, R. M., and S. B. Robbins. 1998. "The Relationship between Social Connectedness and Anxiety, Self-esteem, and Social Identity." *Journal of Counseling Psychology* 5: 338–345. doi:10.1037/0022-0167.45.3.338.

Lewandowski, J. D. 2008. "On Social Poverty: Human Development and the Distribution of Social Capital." *Journal of Poverty* 12 (1): 27–48. doi:10.1080/10875540801967908.

Lins, K. V., H. Servaes, and A. Tamayo. 2017. "Social Capital, Trust, and Firm Performance: The Value of Corporate Social Responsibility during the Financial Crisis." *Journal of Finance* 72 (4): 1785–1824. doi:10.1111/jofi.12505.

London, T., and S. L. Hart. 2004. "Reinventing Strategies for Emerging Markets: Beyond the Transnational Model." *Journal of International Business Studies* 35 (5): 350–370. doi:10.1057/palgrave.jibs.8400099.

Luttmer, E. F. 2005. "Neighbors as Negatives: Relative Earnings and Well-being." *Quarterly Journal of Economics* 120 (3): 963–1002.

Massey, D. S., and N. A. Denton. 1993. *American Apartheid: Segregation and the Making of the Underclass*. Boston: Harvard University Press.

Mathews, M., and P. Stokes. 2013. "The Creation of Trust: The Interplay of Rationality, Institutions and Exchange." *Entrepreneurship & Regional Development* 25 (9–10): 845–866. doi:10.1080/08985626.2013.845695.

Mayer, R. C., J. H. Davis., and F. D. Schoorman. 1995. "An Itegrative Model of Organizational Trust." *Academy of Management Review* 20 (3): 709–734. doi:10.5465/amr.1995.9508080335.

Möllering, G. 2006. *Trust: Reason, Routine, Reflexivity*. Amsterdam: Elsevier.

Nahapiet, J., and S. Ghoshal. 1998. "Social Capital, Intellectual Capital, and the Organizational Advantage." *Academy of Management Review* 23 (2): 242–266. doi:10.5465/amr.1998.533225.

Peng, M. W. 2001. "How Entrepreneurs Create Wealth in Transition Economies." *Academy of Management Executive* 15 (1): 95–108.

Peng, M. W. 2004. "Kinship Networks and Entrepreneurs in China's Transitional Economy." *American Journal of Sociology* 109 (5): 1045–1074. doi:10.1086/382347.

Piff, P. K., D. M. Stancato, S. Côté, R. Mendoza-denton, and D. Keltner. 2012. "Higher Social Class Predicts Increased Unethical Behavior." *PNAS* 109 (11): 4086–4091. doi:10.1073/pnas.1118373109.

Puffer, S. M., D. J. McCarthy, and M. Boisot. 2010. "Entrepreneurship in Russia and China: The Impact of Formal Institutional Voids." *Entrepreneurship Theory and Practice* 34 (3): 441–467. doi:10.1111/etap.2010.34.issue-3.

Putnam, R. 1993. "The Prosperous Community: Social Capital and Public Life." *The American Prospect* 4 (13) (Spring). Accessed7 April 2003. http://www.prospect.org/print/vol/13

Reynolds, P. D. 2001. "National Panel Study of US Business Startups: Background and Methodology." In *Databases for the Study of Entrepreneurship*, 153–227. West Yorkshire: Emerald Group Publishing Limited.

Rothstein, B., and D. Stolle. 2008. "The State and Social Capital: An Institutional Theory of Generalized Trust." *Comparative Politics* 40 (4): 441–459. doi:10.5129/001041508X12911362383354.

Rotter, J. B. 1967. "A New Scale for the Measurement of Interpersonal Trust." *Journal of Personality* 35: 651–665. doi:10.1111/jopy.1967.35.issue-4.

Sarasvathy, S., S. Venkataraman, N. Dew, and R. Velamuri. 2003. "Three Views of Entrepreneurial Opportunity." In *Handbook of Entrepreneurship Research*, edited by Z. J. Acs and D. B. Audretsch:, 141–160. Boston, MA: Springer.

Saxsinian, A. 1994. *Regional Advantage: Culture and Competition in Silicon Valley and Route 128*. Boston, MA: Harvard Business School Press.

Schoorman, F. D., R. C. Mayer, and J. H. Davis. 2007. "An Integrative Model of Organizational Trust: Past, Present, and Future." *Academy of Management Review* 32 (2): 344–354. doi:10.5465/amr.2007.24348410.

Shane, S., and S. Venkataraman. 2000. "The Promise of Entrepreneurship as a Field of Research." *Academy of Management Review* 25 (1): 217–226.

Shi, W. S., S. L. Sun, and M. W. Peng. 2012. "Sub-national Institutional Contingencies, Network Positions, and IJV Partner Selection." *Journal of Management Studies* 49 (7): 1221–1245. doi:10.1111/joms.2012.49.issue-7.

Shields, M., and P. S. Wheatley. 2005. "Exploring the Economic and Social Determinants of Psychological Wellbeing and Perceived Social Support in England." *Journal Royal Statistical Society* 168 (3): 513–537. doi:10.1111/j.1467-985X.2005.00361.x.

Shir, N. 2015. *Entrepreneurial Well-Being: The Payoff Structure of Business Creation*. Stockholm, Sweden: Stockholm School of Economics.

Stephan, U. 2018. "Entrepreneurs' Mental Health and Well-Being: A Review and Research Agenda." *Academy of Management Perspectives* 32 (3): 290–322. doi:10.5465/amp.2017.0001.

Suddaby, R., G. D. Bruton, and J. P. Walsh. 2018. "What We Talk about When We Talk about Inequality: An Introduction to the Journal of Management Studies Special Issue." *Journal of Management Studies* 55 (3): 381–393. doi:10.1111/joms.2018.55.issue-3.

Sutter, C., G. D. Bruton, and J. Chen. 2018. "Entrepreneurship as A Solution to Extreme Poverty: A Review and Future Research Directions." *Journal of Business Venturing* (Advance online publication). doi:10.1016/j.jbusvent.2018.06.003.

Tan, S. J., and S. K. Tambyah. 2011. "Generalized Trust and Trust in Institutions in Confucian Asia." *Social Indicators Research* 103 (3): 357–377. doi:10.1007/s11205-010-9703-7.

Tasavori, M., R. Zaefarian, and P. N. Ghauri. 2015. "The Creation View of Opportunities at the Base of the Pyramid." *Entrepreneurship & Regional Development* 27 (1–2): 106–126. doi:10.1080/08985626.2014.1002538.

Uslaner, E. M. 2002. *The Moral Foundations of Trust*. Cambridge, UK: Cambridge University Press.

Uy, M. A., M.-D. Foo, and Z. Song. 2012. "Joint Effects of Prior Start-up Experience and Coping Strategies on Entrepreneurs' Psychological Well-being." *Journal of Business Venturing* 28 (5): 583–597. doi:10.1016/j.jbusvent.2012.04.003.

Van Gelderen, M., T. Kautonen, and M. Fink. 2015. "From Entrepreneurial Intentions to Actions: Self-control and Action-related Doubt, Fear, and Aversion." *Journal of Business Venturing* 30 (5): 655–673. doi:10.1016/j.jbusvent.2015.01.003.

Van Praag, C. M., and P. H. Versloot. 2007. "What Is the Value of Entrepreneurship? A Review of Recent Research." *Small Business Economics* 29 (4): 351–382. doi:10.1007/s11187-007-9074-x.

Waglé, U. R. 2008. "Multidimensional Poverty: An Alternative Measurement Approach for the United States?" *Social Science Research* 37 (2): 559–580. doi:10.1016/j.ssresearch.2007.06.013.

Wang, X., G. Fan, and J. Yu 2017. *Marketization Index of China's Provinces: NERI Report 2016*. Beijing: Social Sciences Academic Press (China).

Warnecke, T. 2013. "Entrepreneurship and Gender: An Institutional Perspective." *Journal of Economic Issues* 47 (2): 455–464. doi:10.2753/JEI0021-3624470219.

Webb, J. W., L. Tihanyi, R. D. Ireland, and D. G. Sirmon. 2009. "You Say Illegal, I Say Legitimate: Entrepreneurship in the Informal Economy." *Academy of Management Review* 34 (3): 492–510. doi:10.5465/amr.2009.40632826.

Welter, F. 2012. "All You Need Is Trust? A Critical Review of the Trust and Entrepreneurship Literature." *International Small Business Journal* 30 (3): 193–212. doi:10.1177/0266242612439588.

Welter, F., and D. Smallbone. 2006. "Exploring the Role of Trust in Entrepreneurial Activity." *Entrepreneurship Theory and Practice* 30 (4): 465–475. doi:10.1111/etap.2006.30.issue-4.

Welter, F., and D. Smallbone. 2011. "Institutional Perspectives on Entrepreneurial Behavior in Challenging Environments." *Journal of Small Business Management* 49 (1): 107–125. doi:10.1111/jsbm.2011.49.issue-1.

Williams, T. A., and D. A. Shepherd. 2016. "Victim Entrepreneurs Doing Well by Doing Good: Venture Creation and Well-being in the Aftermath of a Resource Shock." *Journal of Business Venturing* 31 (4): 365–387. doi:10.1016/j.jbusvent.2016.04.002.

Williamson, O. E. 1993. "Calculativeness, Trust, and Economic Organization." *Journal of Law and Economics* 36 (1): 453–486. doi:10.1086/467284.

Yang, Z., C. Zhou, and L. Jiang. 2011. "When Do Formal Control and Trust Matter? A Context-based Analysis of the Effects on Marketing Channel Relationships in China." *Industrial Marketing Management* 40 (1): 86–96. doi:10.1016/j.indmarman.2010.09.013.

Yunus, M. 1999. "The Grameen Bank." *Scientific American* 281 (5): 114–119. doi:10.1038/scientificamerican1199-114.

Zafirovski, M. 1999. "Probing into the Social Layers of Entrepreneurship: Outlines of the Sociology of Enterprise." *Entrepreneurship & Regional Development* 11 (4): 351–371. doi:10.1080/089856299283155.

Zaheer, A., and N. Venkatraman. 1995. "Relational Governance as an Interorganizational Strategy: An Empirical Test of the Role of Trust in Economic Exchange." *Strategic Management Journal* 16 (5): 373–392. doi:10.1002/(ISSN)1097-0266.

Zahra, S. A., and M. Wright. 2011. "Entrepreneurship's Next Act." *Academy of Management Perspectives* 25 (4): 67–83. doi:10.5465/amp.2010.0149.

Zahra, S. A., R. I. Yavuz, and D. Ucbasaran. 2006. "How Much Do You Trust Me? the Dark Side of Relational Trust in New Business Creation in Established Companies." *Entrepreneurship Theory and Practice* 30 (4): 541–559. doi:10.1111/etap.2006.30.issue-4.

Zhou, K. Z., G. Y. Gao, and H. Zhao. 2017. "State Ownership and Firm Innovation in China: An Integrated View of Institutional and Efficiency Logics." *Administrative Science Quarterly* 62 (2): 375–404. doi:10.1177/0001839216674457.

Zolin, R., A. Kuckertz, and T. Kautonen. 2011. "Human Resource Flexibility and Strong Ties in Entrepreneurial Teams." *Journal of Business Research* 64 (10): 1097–1103. doi:10.1016/j.jbusres.2010.11.026.

Appendix 1. The CGSS questionnaire for identifying a region and an entrepreneur

4. Places for Interview:

Province/Autonomous Region/Municipality: (____________)
City + County/District: (____________)
Village/Town/Executive village committee: (____________)
Community No: |_|_|_|_|_|_|

5a. Supervisor's Record: Type of region where respondents live: []

1. living in the central district of a city or county
2. living in the peripheral district of a city or county
3. living in the urban-rural fringe of a city or county
4. living in the towns outside of a city or county
5. living in the countryside
6. Others (Please specify____________)

A59a. Which of the following situations is more suitable for your current working situation?

1. Being my own boss (or a partner)
2. Self-employed
3. Employed by others (with a fixed employer)
4. Laborer/labor dispatching
5. Part-time worker (without a fixed employer)
6. Working or helping in own family business (with wages)
7. Working or helping in own family business (without wages)
8. Freelancer
9. Others (Please specify____________)

Index

Notes: This has the reference of tables as "Bold".